Guide to Analyzing Primary and Secondary Sources

To understand the past, historians look at a variety of evidence — written sources, visual sources, and material artifacts. When they encounter any of these primary sources, historians ask questions. Sometimes historians don't know the answers, but they always ask the questions. As a student, you should ask these questions, too. Asking questions is the first step in writing history. Facts alone do not create history — it is the historian who organizes and interprets the facts in a reasoned and verifiable manner. The books and articles that historians publish after the events or conditions they are studying have occurred are secondary sources. Secondary sources become the basis for teaching and for other historians to use in researching and writing their own studies. Because they are interpretative and open for debate, secondary sources allow historians to move forward by modifying explanations of the past. Historical interpretations are constantly being revised, and *Exploring American Histories*, Fourth Edition, offers you an opportunity to explore this dynamic quality.

Analyzing a Written Primary Source

- What kind of source is this? For example, is it a diary, letter, speech, sermon, court opinion, newspaper article, witness testimony, poem, memoir, or advertisement?
- Who wrote the source? How can you identify the author? Was the source translated by someone other than the author or speaker (for example, Native American speeches translated by whites)?
- When and where was it written?
- Why was the source written? Is there a clear purpose?

- Who was, or who might have been, its intended audience?
- What point of view does it reflect?
- What can the source tell us about the individual(s) who produced it and the society from which he, she, or they came?
- How might individuals' race, ethnicity, class, gender, age, and region have affected the viewpoints in the sources?
- In what ways does the larger historical context help you evaluate individual sources?

Analyzing a Visual or Material Primary Source

- What kind of visual or material source is this? For example, is it a map, drawing, or engraving, a physical object, painting, photograph, census record, or political cartoon?
- Who made the image or artifact, and how was it made?
- When and where was the image or artifact made?
- Can you determine if someone paid for or commissioned it? If so, how can you tell that it was paid for or commissioned?
- Who might have been the intended audience or user? Where might it have originally been displayed or used?

- What message or messages is it trying to convey?
- How might it be interpreted differently depending on who viewed or used it?
- What can the visual or material source tell us about the individual who produced it and the society from which he or she came?
- In what ways does the larger historical context help you evaluate individual sources?

Comparing Multiple Primary Sources

- In what ways are the sources similar in purpose and content? In what ways are they different?
- How much weight should one give to who wrote or produced the source?
- Were the sources written or produced at the same time or at different times? If they were produced at different times, does this account for any of the differences between or among the sources?
- What difference does it make that some sources (such as diaries and letters) were intended to be private and some sources (such

as political cartoons and court opinions) were meant to be public?
- How do you account for different perspectives and conclusions? How might these be affected by the author's relative socioeconomic position or political power in the larger society?
- Is it possible to separate fact from personal opinion in the sources?
- Can the information in the sources under review be corroborated by other evidence? What other sources would you want to consult to confirm your conclusions?

Cautionary Advice for Interpreting Primary Sources

- A single source does not tell the whole story, and even multiple sources may not provide a complete account. Historians realize that not all evidence is recoverable.
- Sources have biases, whether they appear in personal or official accounts. Think of biases as particular points of view, and try to figure out how they influence the historical event and the accounts of that event.
- Sources reflect the period in which they were written or produced and must be evaluated within the historical time frame from which they came. Explain how people understood the world in which they lived, and be careful to avoid imposing contemporary standards on the past. Nevertheless, remember that even in a particular time period people disagreed over significant principles and practices such as slavery, imperialism, and immigration.
- Sources often conflict or contradict each other. Take into account all sides. Do not dismiss an account that does not fit into your interpretation; rather, explain why you are giving it less weight or how you are modifying your interpretation to conform to all the evidence.

Analyzing Secondary Sources

- Secondary sources are written or produced by people who did not participate in or experience first-hand the events that they are analyzing. Secondary sources in history usually appear as scholarly books and articles. Secondary sources underscore that history is an ever-changing enterprise.
- Identify the author's main interpretations.
- Describe the evidence the author uses to make that interpretation.
- Evaluate how well the evidence supports the author's interpretation.
- Describe whether the author considers alternative explanations and points of view.
- Compare the author's account with any other sources you have read.
- Assess whether the author has the credentials for making reliable historical judgments.
- Evaluate whether there is anything in the author's background or experience that might have influenced the author's point of view and interpretation.
- Identify the main audience that the author is addressing.

Comparing Secondary Sources

- Explain how two sources differ in interpretation. To what extent, if any, do they agree?
- Historians are products of their own times. Identify the date of publication for each of the sources and explain how the particular time periods might have shaped the authors' arguments.
- Compare the approaches each author takes to reach an interpretation. Describe whether they are looking at the events mainly from a political, social, cultural, or economic perspective.
- Compare the secondary sources with other secondary sources on the same subject, such as the historical narrative in this textbook.
- Taking these considerations into account, explain which secondary source you find more convincing or how the two interpretations might be combined.

Cautionary Advice for Analyzing Secondary Sources

- The secondary sources in this book are excerpts from longer books or articles. The selections are meant to provide a representative view of the authors' main interpretations and perspectives on the subject. Nevertheless, these excerpts do not show the broad sweep of evidence from which the authors draw their conclusions.
- No excerpt can provide a full appreciation of how historians gather evidence and present and defend their interpretations in a reliable manner. Only a more extensive reading of the secondary source can provide sufficient evidence for judging whether the author has presented a convincing account.
- As with primary sources, secondary sources have biases. Think of biases as particular points of view, and try to figure out how they influence the historical interpretation and the accounts of an event or development.
- Secondary sources often conflict with or contradict each other. Do not dismiss an account that does not fit with your perspective; rather, explain why you are giving it more or less weight or how you are modifying your interpretation to conform to all the arguments made by the authors of the secondary sources.
- Secondary sources reflect the period in which they are written or produced and must be evaluated within the historical time frame from which they originate. This doesn't mean that a newer book or article is more accurate than an older one. Interpretations may differ because new facts have been uncovered, but they are just as likely to change according to the contemporary concerns and perspectives of the authors. Moreover, even when analyzing the same time period, historians often disagree over controversial subjects due to different viewpoints on politics, religion, race, ethnicity, region, class, and gender.

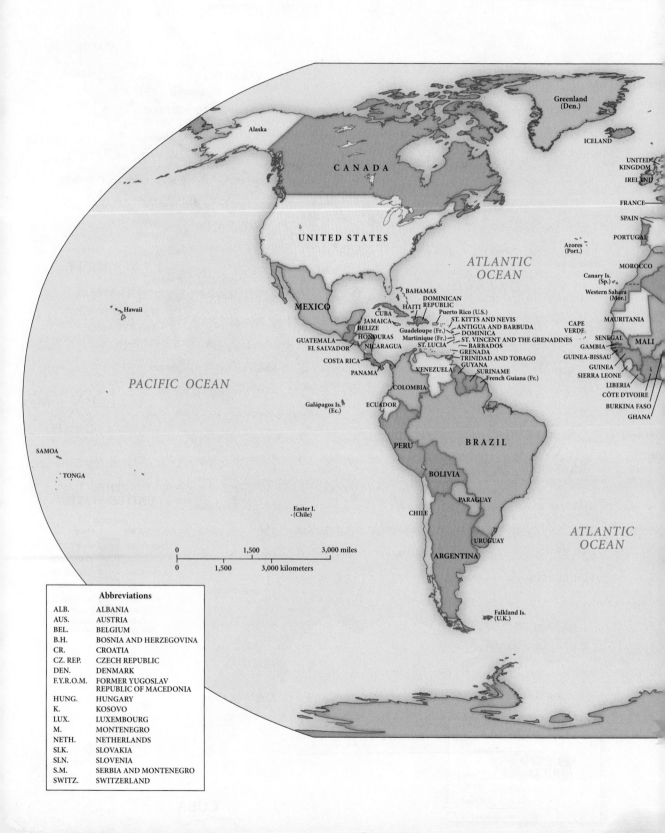

Greenland
(Den.)

ICELAND

UNITED
KINGDOM

IRELAND

FRANCE

SPAIN

PORTUGAL

Azores
(Port.)

MOROCCO

Canary Is.
(Sp.)

Western Sahara
(Mor.)

MAURITANIA

Alaska

CANADA

UNITED STATES

ATLANTIC
OCEAN

CAPE
VERDE

SENEGAL

MALI

GAMBIA

GUINEA-BISSAU

GUINEA

SIERRA LEONE

LIBERIA

CÔTE D'IVOIRE

BURKINA FASO

GHANA

MEXICO

BAHAMAS

DOMINICAN
REPUBLIC

HAITI

CUBA

JAMAICA

BELIZE

HONDURAS

GUATEMALA

EL SALVADOR

NICARAGUA

COSTA RICA

PANAMA

Puerto Rico (U.S.)

ST. KITTS AND NEVIS

ANTIGUA AND BARBUDA

DOMINICA

Guadeloupe (Fr.)

Martinique (Fr.)

ST. VINCENT AND THE GRENADINES

ST. LUCIA

BARBADOS

GRENADA

TRINIDAD AND TOBAGO

GUYANA

VENEZUELA

SURINAME

French Guiana (Fr.)

COLOMBIA

Galápagos Is.
(Ec.)

ECUADOR

Hawaii

PACIFIC OCEAN

PERU

BRAZIL

BOLIVIA

PARAGUAY

SAMOA

TONGA

CHILE

Easter I.
(Chile)

ATLANTIC
OCEAN

URUGUAY

ARGENTINA

Falkland Is.
(U.K.)

0		1,500		3,000 miles

0	1,500		3,000 kilometers	

Abbreviations	
ALB.	ALBANIA
AUS.	AUSTRIA
BEL.	BELGIUM
B.H.	BOSNIA AND HERZEGOVINA
CR.	CROATIA
CZ. REP.	CZECH REPUBLIC
DEN.	DENMARK
F.Y.R.O.M.	FORMER YUGOSLAV REPUBLIC OF MACEDONIA
HUNG.	HUNGARY
K.	KOSOVO
LUX.	LUXEMBOURG
M.	MONTENEGRO
NETH.	NETHERLANDS
SLK.	SLOVAKIA
SLN.	SLOVENIA
S.M.	SERBIA AND MONTENEGRO
SWITZ.	SWITZERLAND

ARCTIC OCEAN

RUSSIAN FEDERATION

NORWAY
SWEDEN
FINLAND
ESTONIA
LATVIA
LITHUANIA
DEN.
NETH.
POLAND BELARUS
GERMANY
BEL. LUX. CZ. REP.
AUS. SLK.
SWITZ. HUNG.
SLN. CR. ROMANIA
ITALY B.H. S.
M.FYR.O.M. BULGARIA
ALB. GREECE

KAZAKHSTAN

MONGOLIA

UKRAINE
MOLDOVA

GEORGIA
ARMENIA
TURKEY
MALTA
AZERBAIJAN
TUNISIA
CYPRUS LEBANON
ISRAEL SYRIA
Gaza Strip IRAQ
West Bank JORDAN

UZBEKISTAN
TURKMENISTAN
KYRGYZSTAN
TAJIKISTAN

CHINA

N. KOREA
S. KOREA
JAPAN

PACIFIC OCEAN

ALGERIA
LIBYA
EGYPT

AFGHANISTAN

IRAN
PAKISTAN

KUWAIT
BAHRAIN
SAUDI ARABIA
QATAR
UNITED ARAB
EMIRATES
OMAN
YEMEN

BHUTAN
NEPAL
BANGLADESH

INDIA

MYANMAR
(BURMA)

TAIWAN

LAOS
VIETNAM
THAILAND
CAMBODIA

Mariana Is.
(U.S.)

Guam
(U.S.)

MARSHALL
IS.

NIGER
CHAD
SUDAN
ERITREA
DJIBOUTI

NIGERIA
BENIN
TOGO
CAMEROON
CENTRAL
AFRICAN REP.
SOUTH
SUDAN
ETHIOPIA
SOMALIA

EQ.
GUINEA
GABON
CONGO
RWANDA
DEM. REP. OF
THE CONGO
UGANDA
KENYA

SÃO
TOMÉ
& PRÍNCIPE
BURUNDI
TANZANIA
COMOROS
SEYCHELLES

MALDIVES

SRI
LANKA

INDIAN OCEAN

PHILIPPINES

BRUNEI

MALAYSIA

SINGAPORE

INDONESIA

PALAU

FEDERATED STATES
OF MICRONESIA

NAURU

KIRIBATI

TUVALU

PAPUA
NEW
GUINEA

SOLOMON
IS.

ANGOLA
ZAMBIA
MALAWI

NAMIBIA
ZIMBABWE
BOTSWANA
MOZAMBIQUE
SWAZILAND
SOUTH
AFRICA
LESOTHO

MADAGASCAR

MAURITIUS

EAST
TIMOR

VANUATU

FIJI

New Caledonia
(Fr.)

AUSTRALIA

NEW
ZEALAND

Tasmania
(Aust.)

ANTARCTICA

Exploring American Histories

A SURVEY WITH SOURCES

FOURTH EDITION

VOLUME 2 Since 1865

Exploring American Histories

A SURVEY WITH SOURCES

FOURTH EDITION

VOLUME 2 Since 1865

Nancy A. Hewitt
Rutgers University

Steven F. Lawson
Rutgers University

bedford/st.martin's
Macmillan Learning

Boston | New York

To Mary and Charles Takacs, Florence and Hiram Hewitt,
Sarah and Abraham Parker, Lena and Ben Lawson,
Irene and Robert Hewitt, and Ceil and Murray Lawson
who made our American Histories possible.

Vice President: Leasa Burton
Program Director: Erika Gutierrez
Senior Program Manager: William J. Lombardo;
Director of Content Development: Jane Knetzger
Senior Development Editor: Leah R. Strauss
Assistant Editor: Julia Bell
Director of Media Editorial: Adam Whitehurst
Media Editor: Mollie Chandler
Marketing Manager: Melissa Rodriguez
Senior Director, Content Management Enhancement: Tracey Kuehn
Senior Managing Editor: Michael Granger
Executive Content Project Manager: Gregory Erb
Workflow Project Manager: Lisa McDowell
Production Supervisors: Robin Besofsky, Robert Cherry
Director of Design, Content Management: Diana Blume
Interior Design: Jerilyn DiCarlo
Cover Design: William Boardman

Cartographer: Mapping Specialists, Ltd.
Text Permissions Editor: Michael McCarty
Text Permissions Researcher: Elaine Kosta, Lumina Datamatics
Photo Permissions Editor: Christine Buese
Photo Researcher: Naomi Kornhauser, Cheryl DuBois, Lumina Datamatics
Director of Digital Production: Keri deManigold
Media Project Manager: Michelle Camisa
Editorial Services: Lumina Datamatics, Inc.
Copyeditor: Harold Johnson
Indexer: Michael Ferreira
Composition: Lumina Datamatics, Inc.
Cover Art: Traveling Carnival, Santa Fe, by John Sloan, 1924. Image: © Smithsonian American Art Museum, Washington, D.C./Art Resource, NY. Artwork: © 2021 Delaware Art Museum/Artists Rights Society (ARS), New York
Printing and Binding: LSC Communications

Library of Congress Control Number: 2021930838
ISBN: 978-1-319-24449-1 (Combined Edition)
ISBN: 978-1-319-33116-0 (Volume 1)
ISBN: 978-1-319-33126-9 (Volume 2)

Printed in the United States of America.
1   2   3   4   5   6   26   25   24   23   22   21

Acknowledgments
Text acknowledgments and copyrights appear at the back of the book on pages C-1–C-2, which constitute an extension of the copyright page. Art acknowledgments and copyrights appear on the same page as the art selections they cover.

For information, write: Bedford/St. Martin's, 75 Arlington Street, Boston, MA 02116

We are delighted to publish the fourth edition of *Exploring American Histories: A Survey with Sources.* We have sought to provide **a U.S. history survey text that makes a broad and diverse American history accessible** to a new generation of students and instructors. With each edition, our central focus has been to weave written and visual primary sources that represent a rich assortment of American perspectives throughout the book. Users of the previous editions have told us our book gives them and their students opportunities to actively engage with both the narrative of American history and primary sources from that history in a way previously not possible. The new edition's combination of narrative and diverse primary sources is available now for the first time in **Achieve**, Macmillan Learning's innovative new learning platform.

Engage Your Students with Achieve

Exploring American Histories, Fourth Edition, is available in a variety of print and digital formats, with Achieve offering the greatest value. Built with instructors and students in mind, Achieve includes the full-color e-book, gradebook, LearningCurve adaptive quizzing, assessment tools, insights and reporting, and integration options. Whenever an instructor assigns **Achieve** (with the option of bundling the print book at a low cost), students have access to all the resources of *Exploring American Histories*, including its unique collection of source features that appear in every chapter.

The Right Balance between Narrative and Primary Sources. Inspired by our own teaching, we wanted to create a textbook that would provide everything we would want to use in class, in one place. Many texts include some primary sources, but we found the balance between narrative (too much) and primary sources (too few) didn't suit our courses. We crafted the narrative to make room to include more primary sources and integrate them to

help students make the necessary connections that spur them to think critically. *Exploring American Histories* is comprehensive in the essentials of American history, but with a carefully selected amount of detail that is more in tune with what instructors can realistically expect their students to comprehend. *Exploring American Histories* offers a format which provides just the right balance between narrative and primary sources, along with consistent pedagogy that helps students analyze primary-source material.

Building-Blocks Approach to Analyzing Sources. We know that students in the introductory survey course often need help in developing the ability to think critically about primary sources. In the fourth edition, we continue to promote historical thinking skills by providing a consistent pedagogical framework for analyzing sources. In each chapter, our building-blocks approach ensures that students can progress from working with a single source (Guided Primary Source Analysis), to comparing paired sources (Comparative Primary Source Analysis), to tackling a set of sources from varied perspectives (Primary Source Project). In this way, students can increase their confidence and skills in analyzing primary sources. Students also have the chance to evaluate how historians use primary sources to construct their own interpretations (Comparative Secondary Source Analysis). In Achieve, each one of these features includes a short quiz as part of this wrap-around pedagogy.

Progression in Primary Source Work. Each chapter contains seven to eight substantial, featured primary sources — both written and visual — with unique pedagogy aimed at helping students make connections between the sources and the text's major themes. Each source is clearly cross-referenced within the text so that students can connect the source to the narrative text. We also underscore the importance of primary sources by opening each chapter with a **Window to the Past** — a facsimile of some portion of a primary source that appears in the chapter. To help students make connections between the narrative and sources, we embed

Explore prompts at key junctures in the narrative that describe what the sources illuminate. Such integration is designed to help students make a firm connection between the narrative of history and the evidence upon which it is built.

- Each chapter begins with a **Guided Primary Source Analysis** of a textual or visual source, with a headnote offering historical context and questions in the margins to help students consider a specific phrase or feature and analyze the source as a whole. These targeted questions are intended to guide students in reading and understanding a primary source. A **Put It in Context** question prompts students to consider the source in terms of the broad themes of the chapter. A multiple-choice quiz in Achieve for this and the following source features gauges students' understanding of the assignment.

- Next, each chapter contains a **Comparative Primary Source Analysis**, a paired set of primary sources that show contrasting or complementary perspectives on a particular issue. This feature marks a step up in difficulty from the previous Guided Primary Source Analysis by asking students to analyze sources through their similarities and differences. These primary sources are introduced by a single headnote and are followed by **Interpret the Evidence** and **Put It in Context** questions that prompt students to analyze and compare the items and place them in a larger historical framework.

- At the end of every chapter, a **Primary Source Project** provides the capstone of our integrated primary-sources approach. Each Primary Source Project brings together four or five sources focused on a critical issue central to that chapter. It is introduced by a brief overview and ends with **Interpret the Evidence** and **Put It in Context** questions that ask students to draw conclusions based on what they have learned in the chapter and read or seen in the sources.

An Introduction to Secondary Sources. In addition to the primary source features in each chapter, we extend the building-block approach by offering two scholars' perspectives on a significant topic related to the chapter. The **Comparative Secondary Source Analysis** feature includes a brief introduction and **Examine the Sources** and **Put It in Context** questions, which ask students to compare two secondary sources and identify how they reflect the primary sources and narrative of the textbook. For example, for the early republic, chapter 7 provides selections on partisanship in the 1800 election by Eric Burns and John Ferling. Chapter 11, on the expansion of slavery, contrasts a view of enslaved family life offered by Robert Fogelman and Stanley Engerman with one by Deborah Gray White. With respect to the Progressive Era, chapter 19 offers divergent excerpts on reform in the South by C. Vann Woodward and Glenda Elizabeth Gilmore. Chapter 23 on World War II compares a selection on FDR and the Holocaust by David Wyman with that of Richard Breitman and Allan J. Lichtman. These selections demonstrate how historical scholarship, built upon the analysis of primary sources, can generate different interpretations of the same topic. They reinforce the idea that history changes over time, and help students to get a glimpse into the debates among historians.

Variety of Perspectives. We have selected sources that provide multiple perspectives on important issues, including both well-known sources and those that are less familiar. In all time periods, some groups of Americans are far better represented in primary sources than others. Those who were wealthy, well educated, and politically powerful, produced and preserved many primary sources about their lives, and their voices are well represented in this textbook. We have provided sources by Native Americans, enslaved Africans, free blacks, racial and ethnic minorities, immigrants, rural residents, working people, women, and young people. The lives of those who left few primary sources of their own can often be illuminated by carefully reading sources written by elites to see what information they yield about less well-documented groups. The questions that we ask about these sources are intended to help students read between the lines or see beyond the main image to uncover new meanings. Firsthand accounts include paintings, illustrations, sermons, speeches, letters, diaries, newspaper articles, political cartoons, advertisements, and photographs.

We challenge students to consider diverse viewpoints. For example, in chapter 5, students read contradictory testimony and examine an engraving to analyze the events that became known as the Boston Massacre. In chapter 12, they compare the views on the Fugitive Slave Law of a black abolitionist and the president of the United States. In chapter 18, students have to reconcile two very different views by a Chinese immigrant and a Supreme Court justice concerning the status of Chinese Americans in the late nineteenth century. In chapter 28, we ask readers to reconsider the depiction of the 1980s as a conservative decade in light of widespread protests challenging President Reagan's military build-up against the Soviet Union.

Comparing Biographies

We believe that the most appealing entry to the past starts with individuals and how people in their daily lives connect to larger political, economic, cultural, and international developments. Each chapter opens with **Comparing American Histories**, a pair of biographies that showcase individuals who experienced and influenced events in a particular period, and then returns to them throughout the chapter to strengthen the connections and highlight their place in the larger picture. These biographies cover both well-known Americans — such as Daniel Shays, Frederick Douglass, Andrew Carnegie, and Eleanor Roosevelt — and those who never gained fame or fortune — such as the Cherokee chief John Ross, activist Amy Post, labor organizer Luisa Moreno, and World War II internee Fred Korematsu. Introducing such a broad range of biographical subjects illuminates the many ways that individuals shaped and were shaped by historical events. This strategy also makes visible throughout the text the intersections where history from the top down meets history from the bottom up, and the relationships between social and political histories and economic, cultural, and diplomatic developments.

New Content and Updates to the Narrative

We have engaged the most recent scholarship to ensure the most useful and accurate textbook. In addition to more expansive attention to regional, racial, and ethnic diversity, we have updated our approach to a number of other historical developments, such as systemic racism, pandemics, and the development of capitalist systems in various periods. We continue to pay significant attention to African Americans and women and to expand coverage on the histories of Native Americans, Mexican Americans, Latino Americans, and Asian Americans throughout the book in the narrative and sources.

Expanded Coverage of Diversity. We have made updates in each chapter, many of them focused on providing even greater representation of diverse peoples. In chapter 3, for example, the coverage of Native Americans has been amplified and more names of specific tribes are included to highlight the variety and number of Native American nations. Chapter 6 has been reorganized in order to expand coverage of multi-ethnic, multiracial forces fighting on both sides in the Revolution and to highlight the role and fate of various Native American nations. In chapter 9, there is a fuller discussion of Denmark Vesey and his planned rebellion, and more on anti-black violence in the North. Chapter 10 has been revised to highlight more black people as pioneers of the Antislavery Movement and the section on women's roles has been reorganized to emphasize black women and interracial efforts. Chapter 13 includes new material on Mexican Americans and Tejanos; enslaved blacks as contraband/refugees; and women as nurses, doctors, and soldiers. Chapter 21 includes new coverage of the Tulsa Race Massacre of 1921; the Osage Indians in Oklahoma and the murders to steal their oil rights; and the League of United Latin American Citizens (LULAC), which formed in 1929. Chapter 25 includes coverage of an important case affecting Mexican Americans, *Hernandez v. Texas (1954)*; and also new coverage on systemic racism in the North. Chapter 26 includes coverage of Mexican American activist, Rejes Tijerna, and also the 1968 Bilingual Education Act.

New Biographies. We have continued to diversify the biographies offered in the chapter-opening **Comparing American Histories**. Accordingly, in Volume 1 we introduce 4 new individuals. These include Powhatan, leader of the largest native confederacy in the mid-Atlantic region (chapter 2);

Pontiac, head of a pan-tribal alliance to force the British out of their territory (chapter 5); Elizabeth

(Mum Bett) Freeman, whose freedom suit contributed to Massachusetts ending slavery during the American Revolution (chapter 6); and José Antonio Menchaca, a Tejano military leader who fought for Texas independence (chapter 11). In Volume 2 we now include Pauli Murray, the African American civil rights activist and feminist (chapter 27); Demetria Martinez, the Mexican American writer and immigrant advocate (chapter 28); and Alicia Garza, the African American community organizer and co-founder of Black Lives Matter (chapter 29).

New Primary Source Projects. Volume 1 and Volume 2 each contain two new primary source projects. Chapter 9 offers a project on Cherokee engagement with white society and the chapter 12 project now focuses on the debates over secession. Chapter 19 provides a project on women's suffrage and the ratification of the nineteenth amendment, and chapter 20 includes a project on the 1918 influenza pandemic

Adjustments to Chapter Organization. The major organizational change in Volume 1 is the movement of the secession debates and the beginning of the Civil War from chapter 13 to chapter 12. This allows for extended discussions in chapter 13 of American Indians, Mexican Americans, African Americans, and women during the Civil War, and of black refugees who used the chaos of war to claim their independence.

In Volume 2, we have added material on the extremely divisive 2020 presidential election and Joseph Biden's victory over Donald Trump in the final chapter. Chapter 29 covers the COVID-19 pandemic; the police killings of George Floyd and Breonna Taylor and the nationwide protests they inspired; the collapse of the U.S. economy caused by the pandemic; the January 6, 2021 insurrection at the Capitol; and the subsequent second impeachment of Trump. These events are still unfolding and we intend to provide a framework to help students understand these controversial issues as they evolve.

New Maps and Figures. In Volume 1, we added maps on tribal locations of native peoples at the time of European contact (chapter 1) and revised maps to clarify the role of Native Americans in the American Revolution (chapter 6). We also added a table on migration to the Americas that illustrates the movement of Europeans as well as the forced migration of Africans (chapter 4). In Volume 2, we have added a table on World War I casualties by country (chapter 20); a table on nuclear warheads in the United States, Soviet Union, and United Kingdom, 1945–1960 (chapter 24); a revised table on immigrant growth by home region, 1981–2010 (chapter 28); and a new map on U.S. intervention in Central America and the Caribbean, 1954–1989 (chapter 28). In Achieve, every chapter includes a Map Quiz related to one of the chapter maps that helps students build their geographic literacy skills. We have also changed about one-quarter of the illustrations from the previous edition.

Achieve: Helping Instructors Teach with Digital Resources

Exploring American Histories is now available for the first time in **Achieve**, Macmillan Learning's new complete course platform, which provides access to the narrative as well as a wealth of primary sources and other features, along with assessments and robust insights and reports at the ready, all in one accessible and affordably priced product. Achieve also includes a downloadable e-book for reading offline. Whenever an instructor assigns **Achieve**, students have access to all the resources of the print text (*Exploring American Histories: A Survey with Sources*), including its special features and its primary and secondary sources.

Helping Students Understand the Narrative. Like the print book, each chapter in the **Achieve e-book** includes the following elements to help students make sense of their reading: **Learning Objectives** in the chapter openers prepare students to read the chapter with clear goals in mind; **chapter conclusions** summarize the chapters to help students identify main developments; **Review & Relate** questions help students focus on main themes and concepts presented in each major section of the chapter; **key terms** in boldface highlight important content. All terms are explained in the narrative as well as defined in a glossary at the end of the book; and the **Chapter Review** lets students review key terms, important concepts, and notable events.

Adaptive Learning with LearningCurve. Achieve offers access to **LearningCurve**, an online adaptive learning tool that helps students actively rehearse what they have read and foster a deeper understanding and retention of the material. With this adaptive quizzing, students accumulate points toward a target score as they go, giving the interaction a game-like feel. Feedback for incorrect responses explains why the answer is incorrect and directs students back to the text to review before they attempt to answer the question again. The end result is a better understanding of the key elements of the text. Instructors who actively assign LearningCurve report that their students come to class prepared for discussion and their students enjoy using it. In addition, Learning-Curve's reporting feature allows instructors to quickly diagnose which concepts students are struggling with so they can adjust lectures and activities accordingly.

Nurturing Skill Development. Further opportunities for skill development are available through the special activities provided in **Achieve**, many of which are available for the first time with the fourth edition of *Exploring American Histories*. These easy-to-use assignments include new **chronology exercises**, new **reflection activities** that invite students to reflect on what they have read in each chapter, **instructor activity guides** that instructors can use for either remote or in-person collaborative learning, **source and feature quizzes, research and writing tutorials with quizzes**, and more. Achieve is a rich asset for instructors who want to support students however they encounter them, whether teaching in a face-to-face, hybrid, or fully remote setting. *Exploring American Histories* combines an engaging narrative with a rich set of digital and print features that promote the comprehension of content, active learning, and skill development. (To learn more about the benefits of LearningCurve, Achieve, and the different versions to package with these digital tools, see the Versions and Supplements section on page xxv.)

Companion Primary Source Reader. For instructors who value even more options, a **companion primary source reader** is available in Achieve and as a printed text. ***Thinking through Sources for Exploring American Histories*** in **Achieve** provides an additional primary source project for each chapter along with activities. These activities supply self-graded exercises that help students not only understand the sources but also think critically about them. First, a short **quiz after each source** offers students the opportunity to check their understanding of materials that often derive from quite distant times and places. Some questions focus on audience, purpose, point of view, limitations, or context, while others challenge students to draw conclusions about the source or to compare one source with another. And a **Draw Conclusions from the Evidence activity** challenges students to assess whether a specific piece of evidence drawn from the sources supports or challenges a stated conclusion. Collectively these assignments create an active learning environment where reading with a purpose is reinforced by immediate feedback and support. This feedback for each rejoinder creates an active learning environment where students are rewarded for reaching the correct answer through their own process of investigation. **Achieve** is thus a rich asset for instructors who want to support students in all settings, from traditional lectures to "flipped" classrooms. *Exploring American Histories* seeks to promote active learning in various ways.

Teaching with Primary Sources. We understand that the instructor's role is crucial in teaching students how to analyze primary-source materials and develop interpretations. Instructors can use the primary sources in many different ways — as in-class discussion prompts, for take-home writing assignments, and as the basis for exam questions — and also in different combinations with primary sources throughout or across chapters being compared and contrasted with one another.

- **The Instructor's Manual.** The Instructor's Manual for *Exploring American Histories* (available in Achieve) provides a wealth of creative suggestions for using the primary source program effectively. We have written a section, entitled **"Teaching American Histories with Primary Sources,"** which provides ideas and resources for both new and experienced faculty. It offers basic guidelines for teaching students how to analyze sources critically and suggests ways to integrate selected primary sources into lectures, discussions, small group projects, and writing assignments. We also suggest ideas for linking in-text primary sources with the opening biographies, maps, and illustrations in a particular chapter and for using the **Primary Source Projects** to help students understand the entangled histories of the diverse groups that comprise North America and the United States. (See the Versions and Supplements section on page xxiii for more information on all the available instructor resources.)

- **Guide to Analyzing Primary and Secondary Sources.** This checklist at the start of the Achieve e-book gives students a quick and efficient lesson on how to read and analyze sources and what kinds of questions to ask in understanding them. We know that many students find primary sources intimidating. Eighteenth and nineteenth century sources contain spellings and language often difficult for modern students to comprehend. Yet, students also have difficulty with contemporary primary sources because in the digital age of Facebook and Twitter they are exposed to information in tiny fragments and without proper verification. Thus, the checklist will guide students in how to approach sources from any era and what to look for in exploring them.

Acknowledgments

We wish to thank the talented scholars and teachers who were kind enough to give their time and knowledge to help us with our revision, as well as those who provided advice in preparation for previous editions. Historians who provided special insight for the fourth edition include the following:

Jonathan Atkins, *Berry College;*
Joseph Cullon, *Worcester State University;*
Nancy Duke, *Daytona State College;*
Jared Eberle, *Oklahoma State University-Stillwater;*
Gary Edwards, *Arkansas State University-Main Campus;*
Keona Ervin, *University of Missouri-Columbia;*
Gabrielle Everett, *Jefferson College;*
Roger Flynn, *Anderson University;*
Melissa Franson, *SUNY College at New Paltz;*
Portia Hopkins, *Lee College;*
Richard Hughes, *Illinois State University;*

Tracy K'Meyer, *University of Louisville;*
Daniel Kotzin, *Medaille College;*
Stephanie Laffer, *University of West Georgia;*
Florence Lemoine, *Cosumnes River College;*
Alexander Marriott, *Alvin Community College;*
Jim McIntyre, *Moraine Valley Community College;*
Robert Parkinson, *Binghamton University-SUNY;*
Donald Seals, *Kilgore College;*
Sean Trundle, *University of Nebraska-Lincoln;*
Trey Welborn, *Georgia College & State University; and*
Adrienne Winans, *Utah Valley University.*

We are also grateful to those who provided ideas and suggestions for previous editions:

Rob Alderson, *Perimeter College at Georgia State University;*
Benjamin Allen, *South Texas College;*
Daniel Allen, *Trinity Valley Community College;*
Leann Almquist, *Middle Georgia State University;*
Christine Anderson, *Xavier University;*
Uzoamaka Melissa C. Anyiwo, *Curry College;*
Rebecca Arnfeld, *California State University, Sacramento;*
David Arnold, *Columbia Basin College;*
Brian Alnutt, *Northampton Community College;*
Anthony A. Ball, *Housatonic Community College;*
Terry A. Barnhart, *Eastern Illinois University;*
John Belohlavek, *University of South Florida;*
Edwin Benson, *North Harford High School;*
Paul Berk, *Christian Brothers University;*
Deborah L. Blackwell, *Texas A&M International University;*
Jeff Bloodworth, *Gannon University;*
Carl Bon Tempo, *University at Albany–SUNY;*
Thomas Born, *Blinn College;*
Margaret Bramlett, *St. Andrews Episcopal High School;*
Martha Jane Brazy, *University of South Alabama;*
Lauren K. Bristow, *Collin College;*
Tsekani Browne, *Duquesne University;*
Jon L. Brudvig, *Dickinson State University;*
Richard Buckelew, *Bethune-Cookman University;*
Timothy Buckner, *Troy University;*
Dave Bush, *Shasta College;*
Monica Butler, *Seminole State College of Florida;*
Barbara Calluori, *Montclair State University;*

Julia Schiavone Camacho, *The University of Texas at El Paso;*

Jacqueline Campbell, *Francis Marion University;*

Amy Canfield, *Lewis-Clark State College;*

Michael Cangemi, *Binghamton University;*

Roger Carpenter, *University of Louisiana, Monroe;*

Dominic Carrillo, *Grossmont College;*

Mark R. Cheathem, *Cumberland University;*

Keith Chu, *Bergen Community College;*

Laurel A. Clark, *University of Hartford;*

Myles L. Clowers, *San Diego City College;*

Remalian Cocar, *Georgia Gwinnett College;*

Lori Coleman, *Tunxis Community College;*

Wilbert E. Corprew, *SUNY Broome;*

Hamilton Cravens, *Iowa State University;*

Audrey Crawford, *Houston Community College;*

Vanessa Crispin-Peralta, *Moorpark College;*

John Crum, *University of Delaware;*

David Cullen, *Collin College;*

Gregory K. Culver, *Austin Peay State University;*

Alex G. Cummins, *St. Johns River State College;*

Robert Chris Davis, *Lone Star College–Kingwood;*

Susanne Deberry-Cole, *Morgan State University;*

Julian J. DelGaudio, *Long Beach City College;*

Patricia Norred Derr, *Kutztown University;*

Thomas Devine, *California State University, Northridge;*

Tom Dicke, *Missouri State University;*

Andy Digh, *Mercer University;*

Gary Donato, *Massachusetts Bay Community College;*

John Donoghue, *Loyola University Chicago;*

Timothy Draper, *Waubonsee Community College;*

David Dzurec, *University of Scranton;*

Susan Eckelmann, *University of Tennessee, Chattanooga;*

George Edgar, *Modesto Junior College;*

Keith Edgerton, *Montana State University Billings;*

Taulby Edmondson, *Virginia Tech;*

Ashton Ellett, *University of Georgia;*

Blake Ellis, *Lone Star College;*

Christine Erickson, *Indiana University–Purdue University Fort Wayne;*

Keona K. Ervin, *University of Missouri;*

Todd Estes, *Oakland University;*

Gabrielle Everett, *Jefferson College;*

Julie Fairchild, *Sinclair Community College;*

Robert Glen Findley, *Odessa College;*

Randy Finley, *Georgia Perimeter College;*

Tiffany Fink, *Hardin-Simmons University;*

Kirsten Fischer, *University of Minnesota;*

Michelle Fishman-Cross, *College of Staten Island;*

Roger Flynn, *TriCounty Technical College;*

Jeffrey Forret, *Lamar University;*

Jonathan Foster, *Great Basin College;*

Kristen Foster, *Marquette University;*

Sarah Franklin, *University of North Alabama;*

Michael Frawley, *University of Texas of the Permian Basin;*

Susan Freeman, *Western Michigan University;*

Nancy Gabin, *Purdue University;*

Kevin Gannon, *Grand View University;*

Benton Gates, *Indiana University–Purdue University Fort Wayne;*

Bruce Geelhoed, *Ball State University;*

Mark Gelfand, *Boston College;*

Robert Genter, *Nassau Community College;*

Jason George, *The Bryn Mawr School;*

Judith A. Giesberg, *Villanova University;*

Dana Goodrich, *Northwest Vista College;*

Sherry Ann Gray, *Mid-South Community College;*

Chad Gregory, *Tri-County Technical College;*

Patrick Griffin, *University of Notre Dame;*

Audrey Grounds, *University of South Florida;*

Abbie Grubb, *San Jacinto College–South;*

Kenneth Grubb, *Wharton County Junior College;*

Larry Grubbs, *Georgia State University;*

Aaron Gulyas, *Mott Community College;*

Scott Gurman, *Northern Illinois University;*

Melanie Gustafson, *University of Vermont;*

Ashley Haines, *Mt. San Antonio College;*

Dennis Halpin, *Virginia Tech;*

Hunter Hampton, *University of Missouri;*

Tona Hangen, *Worcester State University;*

Brian Hart, *Del Mar College;*

Paul Hart, *Texas State University;*

Paul Harvey, *University of Colorado Colorado Springs;*

Stephen Henderson, *William Penn University;*

Kimberly Hernandez, *University of Wisconsin-Milwaukee;*

Lacey A. Holley-McCann, *Columbia State Community College;*

Woody Holton, *University of Richmond;*

Vilja Hulden, *University of Arizona;*

Creed Hyatt, *Lehigh Carbon Community College;*

Colette A. Hyman, *Winona State University;*

Brenda Jackson-Abernathy, *Belmont University;*

Joe Jaynes, *Collin College;*

Troy R. Johnson, *California State University, Long Beach;*

Shelli Jordan-Zirkle, *Shoreline Community College;*

Stephen Katz, *Community College of Philadelphia;*

Lesley Kauffman, *San Jacinto College-Central;*

Jennifer Kelly, *The University of Texas at Austin;*

Kelly Kennington, *Auburn University;*

Andrew E. Kersten, *University of Wisconsin–Green Bay;*

Tina M. Kibbe, *Lamar University;*

Melanie Kiechle, *Virginia Tech;*

Janilyn M. Kocher, *Richland Community College;*

Don Knox, *Wayland Baptist University;*

Max Krochmal, *Duke University;*

Peggy Lambert, *Lone Star College;*

Stephanie Lamphere, *Sierra College;*

Jennifer R. Lang, *Delgado Community College;*

Todd Laugen, *Metropolitan State University of Denver;*

Carolyn J. Lawes, *Old Dominion University;*

John Leazer, *Carthage College;*

Marianne Leeper, *Trinity Valley Community College;*

Alan Lehmann, *Blinn College–Brenham;*

John S. Leiby, *Paradise Valley Community College;*

Leslie Leighton, *Georgia State University;*

Mitchell Lerner, *The Ohio State University;*

Carole N. Lester, *University of Texas at Dallas;*

Amanda Littauer, *Northern Illinois University;*

Matthew Loayza, *Minnesota State University, Mankato;*

Gabriel J. Loiacono, *University of Wisconsin Oshkosh;*

Carmen Lopez, *Miami Dade College;*

Robert Lyle, *University of North Georgia;*

John F. Lyons, *Joliet Junior College;*

Lorie Maltby, *Henderson Community College;*

Christopher Manning, *Loyola University Chicago;*

Amani Marshall, *Georgia State University;*

Phil Martin, *San Jacinto College–South;*

David Mason, *Georgia Gwinnett College;*

Marty D. Matthews, *North Carolina State University;*

Eric Mayer, *Victor Valley College;*

Suzanne K. McCormack, *Community College of Rhode Island;*

David McDaniel, *Marquette University;*

J. Kent McGaughy, *Houston Community College, Northwest;*

Alan McPherson, *Howard University;*

Sarah Hand Meacham, *Virginia Commonwealth University;*

Jason Mead, *Johnson University;*

Brian Craig Miller, *Emporia State University;*

Robert Miller, *California State University, San Marcos;*

Brett Mizelle, *California State University, Long Beach;*

Mark Moser, *The University of North Carolina at Greensboro;*

Ricky Moser, *Kilgore College;*

Jennifer Murray, *Coastal Carolina University;*

Peter C. Murray, *Methodist University;*

Steven E. Nash, *East Tennessee State University;*

Chris Newman, *Elgin Community College;*

David Noon, *University of Alaska Southeast;*

Richard H. Owens, *West Liberty University;*

Alison Parker, *College at Brockport, SUNY;*

Craig Pascoe, *Georgia College;*

David J. Peavler, *Towson University;*

Linda Pelon, *McLennan Community College;*

Laura A. Perry, *University of Memphis;*

Wesley Phelps, *University of St. Thomas;*

Jamie Pietruska, *Rutgers University;*

Sandra Piseno, *Clayton State University;*

Merline Pitre, *Texas Southern University;*

Eunice G. Pollack, *University of North Texas;*

Kimberly Porter, *University of North Dakota;*

Cynthia Prescott, *University of North Dakota;*

Gene Preuss, *University of Houston;*

Sandra Pryor, *Old Dominion University;*

Rhonda Ragsdale, *Lone Star College;*

Ray Rast, *Gonzaga University;*

Michaela Reaves, *California Lutheran University;*

Peggy Renner, *Glendale Community College;*

Steven D. Reschly, *Truman State University;*

Barney J. Rickman, *Valdosta State University;*

Pamela Riney-Kehrberg, *Iowa State University;*

Paul Ringel, *High Point University;*

Jason Ripper, *Everett Community College;*

Timothy Roberts, *Western Illinois University;*

Glenn Robins, *Georgia Southwestern State University;*

Alicia E. Rodriquez, *California State University, Bakersfield;*

Mark Roehrs, *Lincoln Land Community College;*

Patricia Roessner, *Marple Newtown High School;*
John G. Roush, *St. Petersburg College;*
James Russell, *St. Thomas Aquinas College;*
Eric Schlereth, *The University of Texas at Dallas;*
Gregory L. Schneider, *Emporia State University;*
Debra Schultz, *Kingsborough Community College, CUNY;*
Ronald Schultz, *University of Wyoming;*
Stanley K. Schultz, *University of Wisconsin–Madison;*
Scott Seagle, *University of Tennessee at Chattanooga;*
Donald Seals, *Kilgore College;*
Sharon Shackelford, *Erie Community College;*
Donald R. Shaffer, *American Public University System;*
Gregory Shealy, *Saint John's River State College;*
Cathy Hoult Shewring, *Montgomery County Community College;*
Jill Silos-Rooney, *Massachusetts Bay Community College;*
David J. Silverman, *The George Washington University;*
Beth Slutsky, *California State University, Sacramento;*
Andrea Smalley, *Northern Illinois University;*
Karen Smith, *Emporia State University;*
Molly Smith, *Friends School of Baltimore;*
Suzie Smith, *Trinity Valley Community College;*
Troy Smith, *Tennessee Tech University;*
David L. Snead, *Liberty University;*
David Snyder, *Delaware Valley College;*
David Soll, *University of Wisconsin-Eau Claire;*
Gary Sprayberry, *Columbus State University;*
Jodie Steeley, *Merced College;*
Bethany Stollar, *Tennessee State University;*
Bryan E. Stone, *Del Mar College;*
Jason Stratton, *Bakersfield College;*
Emily Straus, *SUNY Fredonia;*
Kristen Streater, *Collin College;*
Joseph Stromberg, *San Jacinto College–Central;*
Jean Stuntz, *West Texas A&M University;*
Sarah Swedberg, *Colorado Mesa University;*
Nikki M. Taylor, *University of Cincinnati;*
Heather Ann Thompson, *Temple University;*
Timothy Thurber, *Virginia Commonwealth University;*
Christopher Thrasher, *Calhoun Community College;*
T. J. Tomlin, *University of Northern Colorado;*
Jeffrey Trask, *Georgia State University;*
Laura Trauth, *Community College of Baltimore County–Essex;*
Russell M. Tremayne, *College of Southern Idaho;*

Laura Tuennerman-Kaplan, *California University of Pennsylvania;*
Linda Upham-Bornstein, *Plymouth State University;*
Mark VanDriel, *University of South Carolina;*
Kevin Vanzant, *Tennessee State University;*
Ramon C. Veloso, *Palomar College;*
Morgan Veraluz, *Tennessee State University;*
Vincent Vinikas, *The University of Arkansas at Little Rock;*
David Voelker, *University of Wisconsin–Green Bay;*
Melissa Walker, *Converse College;*
William Wantland, *Mount Vernon Nazarene University;*
Ed Wehrle, *Eastern Illinois University;*
David Weiland, *Collin College;*
Eddie Weller, *San Jacinto College-South;*
Shane West, *Lone Star College-Greenspoint Center;*
Geoffrey West, *San Diego Mesa College;*
Kenneth B. White, *Modesto Junior College;*
Matt White, *Paris Junior College;*
Anne Will, *Skagit Valley College;*
John P. Williams, *Collin College;*
Zachery R. Williams, *University of Akron;*
Gregory Wilson, *University of Akron;*
Kurt Windisch, *University of Georgia;*
Jonathan Wlasiuk, *The Ohio State University;*
Timothy Wright *Shoreline Community College;*
Timothy L. Wood, *Southwest Baptist University;*
Nancy Beck Young, *University of Houston;*
Maria Cristina Zaccarini, *Adelphi University;*
Nancy Zens, *Central Oregon Community College; and*
Jean Hansen Zuckweiler, *University of Northern Colorado*

We want to thank Bob and Sharon Constantine and Richard and Bobbie Sirmons for their good company and sustenance during the pandemic and other critical events of 2020. In addition a number of scholars generously answered our questions for this fourth edition and provided research critical to our latest revisions: Catherine Brekus, Lisa Brooks, Ellen Hartigan-O'Connor, April Haynes, Maeve Kane, William Link, Tiya Miles, Theda Perdue, Manisha Sinha, Amy Murrell Taylor, Kevin Vrevich, and Brenda Withington. We also appreciate the help the following scholars, archivists, and students gave us in providing the information we needed at critical points in the writing of earlier editions of this text: Lori Birrell, Julia Bowes, Leslie Brown, Andrew Buchanan, Gillian Carroll, Susan J. Carroll, Jacqueline Castledine, Derek Chang, Paul Clemens, Dorothy Sue Cobble, Jane Coleman-Harbison, Alison Cronk, Kayo Denda, Elisabeth Eittreim, David Foglesong, Phyllis Hunter, Tera Hunter, Molly Inabinett, Kenneth Kvamme, William Link, James Livingston, Julia Livingston, Justin Lorts, Melissa Mead, Gilda Morales, Andrew Preston, Vicki L. Ruiz, Julia Sandy-Bailey, Susan Schrepfer, Bonnie Smith, Melissa Stein, Margaret Sumner, Camilla Townsend, Jessica Unger, Anne Valk, and Melinda Wallington. We also want to thank Rob Heinrich and Julia Sandy for their work in compiling the primary source projects for the first edition of the companion source reader, *Thinking through Sources: Exploring American Histories.*

We would particularly like to applaud the many hardworking and creative people at Bedford/St. Martin's (Macmillan Learning) who guided us through the labyrinthine process of writing this fourth edition. No one was more important to us than Leah Strauss, our editor with a keen eye and a light touch, and William Lombardo, senior executive program manager, who has seen us through all four editions. They were joined by an excellent team at Macmillan, including Erika Gutierrez, senior program director; Gregory Erb, executive content project manager; Julia Bell, assistant editor; Mollie Chandler, media editor; Stephanie Sosa, associate editor; and Melissa Rodriguez, senior marketing manager. We thank cover designer, William Boardman, and Naomi Kornhauser for image research for which we are grateful. We will always remain thankful to Sara Wise and Patricia Rossi for their advice about and enthusiasm for a primary source-based American History textbook and to Joan Feinberg, who had the vision that guided us through every page of this book. Thanks as well to Michael Rosenberg whose enthusiasm inspired us to keep thinking anew about the past. Finally, we would like to express our gratitude to our friends and family who have encouraged us through every edition and have even read the book without it being assigned.

Nancy A. Hewitt and Steven F. Lawson

Adopters of *Exploring American Histories* and their students have access to abundant digital and print resources and tools, including documents, assessment and presentation materials, the acclaimed *Bedford Series in History and Culture* volumes, and much more. *Exploring American Histories* is now available for the first time in Achieve, Macmillan Learning's new complete course platform, which provides access to the narrative as well as a wealth of primary sources and other features, along with assessments and robust insights and reports at the ready, all in one affordably priced product. Achieve also includes a downloadable e-book for reading offline. See the following text for more information, visit the book's catalog site at **macmillanlearning.com**, or contact your local Macmillan Learning sales representative.

Get the Right Version and Volume for Your Class — Digital, Print, and Value Options.

Whether it's a digital course platform, e-book, print book, a value option, or a package combining digital and print products, *Exploring American Histories* is available in a variety of volumes and formats so you can choose what works best for your course. The **comprehensive *Exploring American Histories*** includes a full-color art and map program and a rich set of features and primary and secondary sources. Digital options for the comprehensive version include the full course platform of Achieve for *Exploring American Histories* (see below for the description of Achieve's benefits), as well as e-books. The comprehensive version is also available in print in three volume options. For great value in a stream-lined product, ***Exploring American Histories*, Value Edition**, offers the unabridged narrative and selected two-color art and maps — without special features or primary or secondary sources — at a steep discount. The Value Edition is available in e-book format, as

well as print, in three volume options, with loose-leaf format available for the least expensive price option. For the best value, purchase Achieve on its own or package it with the print version of your choice for a small add-on cost. *Exploring American Histories* is available in the following volume configurations:

- **Combined Volume** (Chapters 1–29). Available in Achieve (1- and 2-term subscriptions), e-books, and print volumes for the comprehensive and Value editions.
- **Volume 1: To 1877** (Chapters 1–14). Available in Achieve (1- and 2-term subscriptions), e-books, and print volumes for the comprehensive and Value editions, including loose-leaf format for the Value editions.
- **Volume 2: Since 1865** (Chapters 14–29). Available in Achieve (1- and 2-term subscriptions), e-books, and print volumes for the comprehensive and Value editions, including loose-leaf format for the Value editions.

As noted below, any of these volumes can be packaged with additional titles for a discount. To get ISBNs for discount packages, visit **macmillanlearning .com** or contact your Macmillan Learning sales representative.

Achieve READ & PRACTICE   Assign Achieve — A Comprehensive Course Platform with E-book, Skill-Building Assessments, and Analytics for Instructors

Affordably priced, intuitive and easy to use, Achieve is a breakthrough solution for building students' skills and confidence in history courses. Achieve for *Exploring American Histories* includes the rich resources and skill-building content of the e-books for the complete comprehensive text and companion reader, *Thinking through Sources for Exploring American Histories* alongside a robust set of summative and formative assessments — many autograded — that help students build confidence in their mastery of the material, reflect on their learning, and build critical, higher-level thinking skills. Achieve for *Exploring American Histories* includes LearningCurve adaptive quizzing that — when assigned — helps ensure students do the reading before class; autograded exercises that teach students how to build a thesis and support an argument; quizzes that check student comprehension of primary sources and boxed features; chapter summative quizzes that test student knowledge after they've completed the reading; tutorials with quizzing that build skills such as working with primary sources and avoiding plagiarism; assignable chapter reflection questions that encourage students to engage with their learning; active reading activities that help students read actively for key concepts; class activity guides that can be used in synchronous and asynchronous courses; and iClicker polling questions that engage students during class. These features, plus additional primary source documents, map quizzes, customizable test banks, and detailed reports on student progress make Achieve an invaluable asset for any instructor.

Achieve easily integrates with course management systems, and with fast ways to build assignments and organize content, it lets teachers build the courses they want to teach while holding students accountable. For more information, or to arrange a demo or class test, contact us at **historymktg@macmillan.com**.

LearningCurve Assign LearningCurve So Your Students Come to Class Prepared

Students using Achieve receive access to LearningCurve for *Exploring American Histories*. Assigning LearningCurve in place of reading quizzes is easy for instructors, and the reporting features help instructors track overall class trends and spot topics that are giving students trouble so they can adjust their lectures and class activities. This online learning tool is popular with students because it was designed to help them rehearse content at their own pace in a nonthreatening, game-like environment. The feedback for wrong answers provides instructional coaching and sends students back to the book for review. Students answer as many questions as necessary to reach a target score, with repeated chances to revisit material they haven't mastered. When LearningCurve is assigned, students come to class better prepared.

▷ iClicker iClicker Student App, Active Learning Simplified

The iClicker student app offers simple, flexible tools to help you give students a voice and facilitate active learning in the classroom. Students can participate with the devices they already bring to class using our iClicker student mobile app (which works with smart phones, tablets, or laptops). We've now integrated iClicker with Macmillan's Achieve to make it easier than ever to synchronize grades and promote engagement — both in and out of class. iClicker can be used synchronously through its polling feature, or asynchronously for assignments. To learn more, talk to your Macmillan Learning sales representative or visit us at **www.iclicker.com**.

Take Advantage of Instructor Resources

Bedford/St. Martin's has developed a rich array of teaching resources for this book and for this course. They range from lecture and presentation materials and assessment tools to course management options. Most can be found in Achieve or can be downloaded or ordered at **macmillanlearning.com**.

Instructor's Resource Manual. The Instructor's Resource Manual offers both experienced and first-time instructors tools for presenting textbook material in engaging ways. It includes content learning objectives, annotated chapter outlines, and strategies for teaching with the textbook, plus suggestions on how to get the most out of LearningCurve, and a survival guide for first-time teaching assistants.

Guide to Changing Editions. Designed to facilitate an instructor's transition from the previous edition of *Exploring American Histories* to the new edition, this guide presents an overview of major changes as well as of changes in each chapter.

Online Test Bank. The test bank includes a mix of fresh, carefully crafted multiple-choice, short-answer, and essay questions for each chapter. Some of the multiple-choice questions feature a map as the prompt. All questions appear in easy-to-use test bank software that allows instructors to add, edit, re-sequence, filter by question type, and print questions and answers. Instructors can also export questions into a variety of course management systems.

The Bedford Lecture Kit: *Lecture Outlines, Maps, and Images.* Look good and save time with *The Bedford Lecture Kit*. This resource includes fully customizable multimedia presentations built around chapter outlines that are embedded with maps, figures, and images from the textbook and are supplemented by more detailed instructor notes on key points and concepts.

Print, Digital, and Custom Options for More Choice and Value

For information on packages and discounts up to 50%, visit **macmillanlearning.com**, or contact your local Macmillan Learning sales representative.

Thinking through Sources for Exploring American Histories, **Third Edition.** This companion reader provides an additional primary source project with four to five written and visual sources focused on a central topic to accompany each chapter of *Exploring American Histories*. To aid students in approaching and interpreting the sources, the project for each chapter contains an introduction, document headnotes, and questions for discussion. This companion reader is an exceptional value for students and offers plenty of assignment options for instructors, and is included in Achieve with autograded quizzes for each source. *Thinking through Sources for Exploring American*

Histories is also available on its own as a downloadable e-book.

Bedford Document Collections. These affordable, brief document projects provide five to seven primary sources, an introduction, historical background, and other pedagogical features. Each curated project — designed for use in a single class period and written by a historian about a favorite topic — poses a historical question and guides students through analysis of the sources. Examples include "What Caused the Civil War?"; "The California Gold Rush: A Trans-Pacific Phenomenon"; and "War Stories: Black Soldiers and the Long Civil Rights Movement." These primary source projects are available in a low-cost, easy-to-use digital format or can be combined with other course materials in Bedford Select to create an affordable, personalized print product. For more information on using Bedford Select to customize your course materials with these and other resources, visit **macmillanlearning.com/bedfordselect.**

Bedford Tutorials for History. Designed to provide resources relevant to individual courses, this collection of over a dozen brief units, each 16 pages long and loaded with examples, guides students through basic skills such as using historical evidence effectively, working with primary sources, taking effective notes, avoiding plagiarism and citing sources, and more. For more information, visit **macmillanlearning .com/historytutorials.**

The Bedford Series in History and Culture. Now available in low-cost e-books as well as print volumes, the more than 100 titles in this highly praised series combine first-rate scholarship, historical narrative, and important primary documents for undergraduate courses. Each title is brief, inexpensive, and focused on a specific topic or period. Recent titles in the series include: *The Chinese Exclusion Act and Angel Island: A Brief History with Documents*, by Judy Yung; *The Life of P.T. Barnum, Written by Himself, with Related Documents*, edited with an introduction by Stephen Mihm; and *The California Gold Rush: A Brief History with Documents*, by Andrew C. Isenberg. For a complete list of titles, visit **macmillanlearning.com**. Package discounts are available.

Trade Books. History titles published by sister companies Hill and Wang; Farrar, Straus and Giroux; Henry Holt and Company; St. Martin's Press; Picador; and Palgrave Macmillan are available at a 50% discount when packaged with Bedford/St. Martin's textbooks. For more information, visit **macmillanlearning.com/tradeup**.

A Pocket Guide to Writing in History. Available in a low-cost e-book as well as in print and updated to reflect changes made in the 2017 Chicago Manual of Style revision, this portable and affordable reference tool by Mary Lynn Rampolla provides reading, writing, and research advice useful to students in all history courses. Concise yet comprehensive advice on approaching typical history assignments, developing critical reading skills, writing effective history papers, conducting research, using and documenting sources,

and avoiding plagiarism — enhanced with practical tips and examples throughout — has made this slim reference a best-seller. Deep discounts are available when bundled with a survey textbook.

A Student's Guide to History. Available in a low-cost e-book as well as in print and updated to reflect changes made in the 2017 Chicago Manual of Style revision, this complete guide to success in any history course provides the practical help students need to be successful. In addition to introducing students to the nature of the discipline, author Jules Benjamin teaches a wide range of skills from preparing for exams to approaching common writing assignments, and explains the research and documentation process with plentiful examples. Deep discounts are available when bundled with a survey textbook.

Brief Contents

Contents

chapter 17

Workers and Farmers in the Age of Organization 1877–1900   *567*

chapter 18

Cities, Immigrants, and the Nation 1880–1914   *601*

chapter 20

Empire, Wars, and Pandemic 1898–1919 *671*

chapter 21

The Twenties 1919–1929   707

chapter 26

Liberalism and Its Challengers 1960–1973 *891*

chapter 28

The Triumph of Conservatism, the End of the Cold War, and the Rise of the New World Order 1980–1992 *967*

chapter 29

The Challenges of a Globalized World 1993 to the present 1005

APPENDIX

Maps, Figures, and Tables

Maps

Figures and Tables

How to Use This Book

Use the chapter tools to focus on what's important as you read.

Learning Objectives preview what you will learn in the chapter.

Comparing American Histories biographies at the start of each chapter personalize the history of the period by describing the life of two individuals.

Review & Relate questions review key concepts at the end of each major section and repeat in the chapter review.

Learning Objectives

After reading this chapter you will be able to:

- Explain the relationship between the beginning of armed conflict and patriots' decision to declare independence.
- Understand the choices of colonists, American Indians, and African Americans to support or oppose independence.
- Analyze the military strategies of the British and the Americans in 1776–1777, the roles that various allies played, the importance of women and other groups on the home front, and the significance of smallpox among colonial soldiers
- Explain the major accomplishments of and conflicts within the new state and federal governments during the Revolution.
- Analyze the shift of warfare to the South and West from 1778 to 1781; the importance of American Indians, foreign allies, and colonial soldiers in patriot victories there; and the challenges Americans faced once they defeated the British.

Comparing American Histories

One of the foremost pamphleteers of the patriot cause, **Thomas Paine** was born in 1737 in England, where his parents trained him as a corset maker. Eventually he left home and found work as a seaman, a teacher, and a tax collector. He drank heavily and beat both his wives. Yet he also taught working-class

(left) **Thomas Paine** Library of Congress, Prints and Photographs Division, Washington, D.C. [LC-DIG-pga-12728]
(right) **Elizabeth Freeman (Mum Bett)** Bridgeman Images

178

children to read and pushed the British government to improve the working conditions and pay of tax collectors. In 1772 Paine was fired from his government job, but a pamphlet he wrote had caught the eye of Benjamin Franklin, who persuaded him to try his luck in the colonies.

Arriving in Philadelphia in November 1774 at age thirty-seven, Paine secured a job on the *Pennsylvania Magazine*. The newcomer quickly gained in-depth political knowledge of the intensifying conflicts between the colonies and Great Britain. He also gained patrons for his political tracts among Philadelphia's economic and political elite. When armed conflict with British troops erupted in April 1775, colonial debates over whether to declare independence intensified. Pamphlets were a popular means of influencing these debates, and Paine wrote one entitled *Common Sense* to tip the balance in favor of independence.

Published in January 1776, *Common Sense* proved an instant success. It provided a rationale for independence and an emotional plea for creating a new democratic republic. Paine urged colonists to separate from England and establish a political structure that would ensure liberty and equality for all Americans. "A government of our own is our natural right," he concluded. "'Tis time to part."

When *Common Sense* was published, an enslaved woman known as Bett was working for the Ashleys in Sheffield, Massachusetts. She was born to enslaved parents around 1742 in Claverack, New York, on the estate of Peiter Hogeboom. When Hogeboom's daughter Hannah married John Ashley, around 1750, the young Bett was given to them as a wedding present. Bett worked for the Ashleys for the next thirty years. Sometime in the late 1760s or early 1770s, the Ashleys allowed Bett to marry, and she gave birth to a daughter, Little Bett. By the 1770s, "Mum" Bett had gained skills as a nurse and midwife.

John Ashley, a wealthy lawyer and landowner, had fought in the French and Indian War. As conflicts between Britain and the colonies escalated, he joined the patriot cause. In January 1773, eleven patriots, including lawyer Theodore Sedgwick, met at his home. They drew up a series of resolutions known as the Sheffield Resolves that decried British tyranny and demanded individual rights. They were printed in the

delegates from twelve colonies approved the Declaration, with only New York abstaining. Independence was publicly proclaimed on July 4 when the Declaration was published as a broadside to be circulated throughout the colonies.

Review & Relate

What challenges did Washington face after accepting command of the Continental Army?

How and why did proponents of independence prevail in the debates that led to the Declaration of Independence?

Use the building blocks approach to primary sources to strengthen your interpretive skills.

STEP 1   Guided Primary Source Analysis

Near the start of each chapter, a **Guided Analysis** of a textual or visual source with annotated questions in the margins models how to analyze a specific phrase or detail of the source as well as the source as a whole.

⟫⟫

Guided Primary Source Analysis

Thomas Paine | *Common Sense*, January 1776

Thomas Paine's *Common Sense* was the most widely read pamphlet supporting American independence. Paine's plain style and use of biblical allusions appealed to ordinary people and ignited the Revolutionary movement. As a government employee in England, Paine had been hired, transferred, dismissed, rehired, and dismissed again, which likely influenced his critique of the monarchy. But he offered a broader vision as well, providing colonists with a new understanding of the relationship between a government and its citizens.

Source 6.1

How does Paine characterize the role of the King in England?

In England a King hath little more to do than to make war and give away places; which, in plain terms, is to impoverish the nation, and set it together by the ears. A pretty business, indeed, for a man to be allowed eight hundred thousand sterling a year for, and worshipped into the bargain! Of more worth is one honest man to society, and in the sight of God, than all the crowned ruffians that ever lived. . . .

But where, say some, is the King of America? I will tell you, friend, he reigns above, and does not make havock of mankind like the royal brute of Great Britain. Yet that we may not appear to be defective even in earthly honors, let a day be solemnly set apart for proclaiming the charter; let it be brought forth, placed on the divine law, the word of God: let a crown be placed thereon, by which the world may know that so far

What does Paine consider the proper relationship between the law and political authority?

we approve of monarchy, that in America, THE LAW IS KING. For as in absolute governments the King is law, so in free countries the Law *ought* to be King; and there ought to be no other. But lest any ill use should afterwards arise, let the crown, at the conclusion of the ceremony, be demolished, and scattered among the people whose right it is.

A government of our own is our natural right; and when a man seriously reflects on the precariousness of his human affairs, he will become convinced, that it is infinitely wiser and safer, to form a constitution of our own in a cool deliberate manner, while we have it in

What system of government does Paine advocate for the American colonies?

our power, than to trust such an interesting event to time and chance.

Source: Thomas Paine, *Common Sense; Addressed to the Inhabitants of America* (London: H. D. Symonds, 1792), 11, 20.

Put It in Context

To whom was this 1776 pamphlet addressed, and how did it influence colonial support for independence from Britain?

Explore ▸

Read some of Paine's arguments in Source 6.1.

Explore callouts help you make connections between the narrative and the sources.

See also the **Guide to Analyzing Primary Sources** at the front of the book for additional help with sources.

Next, each chapter progresses to the **Comparative Primary Source Analysis**, a paired set of documents that reveal contrasting or complementary perspectives on a particular issue or event.

Comparative Primary Source Analysis

Women and Free Blacks Claim Rights in the Nation

Limited in their civil and political rights and educational and economic opportunities, some women and African Americans demanded change. Many white women focused on gaining greater access to education. In the first selection, Judith Sargent Murray, a well-educated Massachusetts writer, insists that women are rational creatures who can make important contributions to society. Blacks had far fewer opportunities since the vast majority were enslaved, and even free blacks faced numerous restrictions. In the second selection, three free black men in Charleston, South Carolina petition the state legislature for increased judicial rights.

Source 7.2

Judith Sargent Murray | On the Equality of the Sexes, 1790

Are we [women] deficient in reason? . . . [I]f an opportunity of acquiring knowledge hath been denied us, the inferiority of our sex cannot fairly be deduced from thence. . . . May we not trace its source in the difference of education, and continued advantages? Will it be said that the judgment of a male of two years old, is more sage than that of a female's of the same age? . . . But from that period what partiality! . . . As their years increase, the sister must be wholly domesticated, while the brother is led by the hand through all the flowery paths of science. . . . Now, was she permitted the same instructors as her brother, . . . for the employment of a rational mind an ample field would be opened. In astronomy she might catch a glimpse of the immensity of the Deity, and thence she would form amazing conceptions of the august and supreme Intelligence. In geography she would admire Jehovah in the midst of his benevolence; thus adapting this globe to the various wants and amusements of its

inhabitants. In natural philosophy she would adore the infinite majesty of heaven, clothed in condescension; and as she traversed the reptile world, she would hail the goodness of a creating God. . . . Will it be urged that those acquirements

Source 7.3

Petition from Free Blacks of Charleston, 1791

That in the enumeration of free citizens by the Constitution of the United States for the purpose of representation of the Southern states in Congress your memorialists [petitioners] have been considered under that description as part of the citizens of this state.

Although by the fourteenth and twenty-ninth clauses in an Act of Assembly made in the year 1740 . . . commonly called the Negro Act, now in force, your memorialists are deprived of the rights and privileges of citizens by not having it in their power to give testimony on oath in prosecutions on behalf of the state; from which cause many culprits have escaped the punishment due to their atrocious crimes, nor can they give their testimony in recovering debts due to them, or in establishing agreements made by them within the meaning of the Statutes of Frauds and Perjuries in force in this state except in cases where persons of color

are concerned, whereby they are subject to great losses and repeated injuries without any means of redress.

That by the said clauses in the said Act, they are debarred of the rights of free citizens by being subject to a trial without the benefit of a jury and subject to prosecution by testimony of slaves without oath by which they are placed on the same footing.

Your memorialists show that they have at all times since the independence of the United States contributed and do now contribute to the support of the government by cheerfully paying their taxes proportionable to their property with others who have been during such period, and now are, in full enjoyment of the rights and immunities of citizens, inhabitants of a free independent state.

Source: Petition of Thomas Cole, Peter Bassnett Matthewes, and Matthew Webb to the South Carolina Senate, January 1, 1791, Records of the General Assembly, no. 181.

Interpret the Evidence

1. What kind of rights do Judith Sargent Murray and the free blacks in Charleston claim for women and free African Americans, respectively?
2. What explains the differences in the rights demanded by Murray and the black petitioners and the ways they justify those claims?

Put It in Context

What do these documents reveal about the positions of white women and free black men during the formation of the United States?

Next, the **Comparative Secondary Source Analysis**, presents two secondary sources by historians that offer differing perspectives on an important historical issue or event.

Comparative Secondary Source Analysis

Partisan Campaigning in the Election of 1800

While the election of 1796 was the first to involve candidates chosen by opposing parties, it was decidedly civil compared to that of 1800. Partisan differences intensified as divisions over domestic and foreign policies led each side to view the other as a threat to fundamental American values. Historians agree that the election of 1800 — between Federalist John Adams and Democratic-Republican Thomas Jefferson — marks a critical moment in U.S. history because it necessitated the peaceful transfer of power from one political party to another. Yet it was also marked by vitriol spewed by partisan newspapers. Eric Burns suggests that Federalists attacked Jefferson because they could not imagine a peaceful transfer of power to their opponents, while John Ferling focuses on the growing strength and reach of Democratic-Republican newspapers.

Source 7.4

Eric Burns | Federalists Attack Thomas Jefferson, 2006

[W]ould Federalists willingly and peacefully hand power over to their political enemies . . . , men whom they not only loathed but also considered dangerous to the rep[ublic's?] economic growth and to everything they ch[. . .]

The answer, at l[. . .] newspapers were co[. . .] to make sure that the[. . .] on the transfer of po[wer?] despised, they began[. . .] most dire of predicti[ons?] Jefferson be elected [. . .] *Hudson Bee* . . . , "th[. . .] set on our holy religi[on?] prostrated, and some[. . .]

the title the Goddess of Reason, will preside in the Sanctuaries now devoted to the Most High." . . .

The [Democratic-]Republican counterattack[. . .]

Source 7.5

John Ferling | Democratic-Republicans Attack John Adams, 2013

While most of the candidates avoided the hustings [public platforms], party activists were busy. For the most part, both sides spread their messages through pamphlets, broadsides, and newspapers. The Federalists had a decided edge in the press, but [Democratic-]Republican newspapers had climbed up from 15 percent of the total in 1796 to nearly one-third by 1800. The [Democratic-] Republicans were better organized for disseminating information, as they established committees of correspondence to funnel publications to the hinterland. . . .

Some [Democratic-]Republican penmen limned [depicted] Adams as a monarchist . . . , but their essayists focused mostly on the Federalist program. One writer after another attacked the

Alien and Sedition Acts, the taxes levied to pay for the debt . . . , and the very existence of a standing army. Much of their ink was [also] spilled on Hamilton's economic program. . . .

The abuse . . . directed against Hamilton paled in comparison to the calumny heaped on Jefferson. . . . Federalists charged that Jefferson's residence in France had transformed him into a dangerous radical. . . . A Federalist newspaper in Virginia alleged that Jefferson had a slave mistress. . . . [And] Federalists twisted Jefferson's advocacy of religious freedom in *Notes on the State of Virginia* to brand him an atheist.

Source: John Ferling, *Jefferson and Hamilton: The Rivalry That Forged a Nation* (New York: Bloomsbury Press, 2014), 320–321.

Examine the Sources

1. How do Ferling and Burns differ in their assessments of Federalist and Democratic-Republican attacks on each other's presidential candidates?
2. How effective are Ferling and Burns in using primary sources to make their argument? Do you find one argument more compelling than the other, and if so, why?

Put It in Context

Given the fierce attacks on Jefferson, what explains his victory in the 1800 election?

Examine the Sources questions help you evaluate and compare the historians' interpretations.

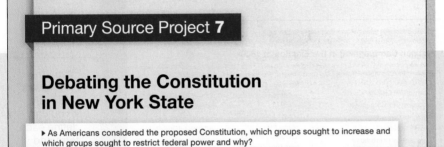

STEP 4 Primary Source Project

Finally, the **Primary Source Project** includes four or five sources that focus on a central topic and provide the opportunity to draw deeper conclusions.

Primary Source Project 7

Debating the Constitution in New York State

▶ As Americans considered the proposed Constitution, which groups sought to increase and which groups sought to restrict federal power and why?

Although the Constitution was eventually approved by all thirteen states, the battle over its ratification revealed a deeply divided nation. Antifederalist delegates dominated conventions in Massachusetts, Virginia, and New York; and when Massachusetts and Virginia finally ratified the Constitution by close votes, the New York convention was still in session.

As elsewhere, New York delegates debated questions of representation, the increased powers of the federal government, and a bill of rights. Before the convention opened, James Madison, Alexander Hamilton, and John Jay offered fellow New Yorkers pro-Constitution arguments in *The Federalist Papers* (Source 7.6). At the convention, Hamilton emphasized the need for a strong central government in which checks and balances limited the power of any single branch and insisted on accommodating the views of diverse groups, including southern slaveowners (Source 7.8).

A secretary recorded the speeches of Hamilton and other delegates. Melancton Smith was a large landowner and a New York City merchant, but he led the state's Antifederalists and questioned the expansion of federal power and the limits on representation (Source 7.7). John Williams, a farmer from rural Washington County and thus a more typical Antifederalist, criticized the Constitution more adamantly. He distrusted federal power, disliked the system of representation, and worried about America's moral decline (Source 7.9). However, the

Federalists eventually prevailed, w[...] Smith, and twenty-eight other delega[...] and Williams one of the twenty-seven [...] slim victory elated the Federalist ne[...] *Massachusetts Centinel*, which track[...] that ratified the Constitution (Source 7.[...]

The intensity of these debates [...] competing ideas and interests among [...] also shows the willingness of Federalis[...] mise on issues like a bill of rights whi[...] creating a new political structure.

Source 7.6

James Madison | *Federalis[...]* The Union as a Safeguard A[...] Domestic Faction and Insur[...] November 1787

James Madison wrote the most signific[...] pro-Constitution essays known collect[...] *Federalist Papers*. In this essay, Madis[...] the widely held belief that republican g[...] were most likely to succeed when they[...] and compact. He argued instead that a[...] diverse population in which various factions competed for support would keep any one faction from subverting the freedom of other groups.

To the People of the State of New York:

AMONG the numerous advantages promised by a well-constructed Union, none deserves to be more accurately developed than its tendency to break and control the violence of faction. The friend of popular

Source 7.7

Melancton Smith | Antifederalist Argument at the New York State Convention, June 1788

Melancton Smith was unusually wealthy for an Antifederalist delegate. Smith worked alongside Alexander Hamilton in the New York Manumission Society, which encouraged the gradual abolition of slavery. But while Hamilton accepted the three-fifths compromise as necessary, Smith found it odious. He also embraced the traditional view that republics were best governed by smaller governmental bodies.

In the discussion of this question, he [Smith] was disposed to make every reasonable concession, and, indeed, to sacrifice every thing for a union, except the liberties of his country. . . .

The defects of the Old Confederation needed as little proof as the necessity of an Union. But there was no proof in all this that the proposed Constitution was a good one. Defective as the Old Confederation is, . . . no one could deny but it was possible we might have a worse government. . . .

Use the Chapter Review to identify significant historical events and how they fit together over time.

Review the **Timeline of Events**, which shows the relationship among chapter events.

Timeline of Events

1783	Continental Army officers threaten to mutiny
1784	Treaty of Fort Stanwix
1785	Northwest Ordinance passed
	Annapolis Convention
1786–1787	Shays's Rebellion
1787	Constitutional Convention in Philadelphia
	Northwest Ordinance revised
1788	U.S. Constitution ratified
1789	Alexander Hamilton named secretary of the treasury
	Judiciary Act of 1789 passed
1789–1799	French Revolution
1790–1794	Little Turtle leads pan-Indian alliance in the Ohio valley
1791	Bill of Rights ratified
1793	Neutrality Proclamation
	Yellow fever epidemic paralyzes Philadelphia
1794	Whiskey Rebellion
	African Methodist Episcopal Church founded
1796	Jay Treaty and Pinckney Treaty ratified
	Democratic-Republican Party established
1798	Alien and Sedition Acts passed
1800	Election of Thomas Jefferson as president

Key Terms

Treaty of Fort Stanwix, *214*
Northwest Ordinance, *217*
republican motherhood, *220*
Shays's Rebellion, *222*
Virginia Plan, *225*
New Jersey Plan, *225*
three-fifths compromise, *225*
Federalists, *226*
Antifederalists, *227*

Bill of Rights, *228*
Jay Treaty, *232*
Whiskey Rebellion, *233*
Treaty of Greenville, *234*
Pinckney Treaty, *234*
Democratic-Republicans, *236*
XYZ affair, *236*
Alien and Sedition Acts, *237*
Virginia and Kentucky Resolutions, *237*

Study the **Key Terms** list to see if you can define each term and describe its significance.

Review & Relate

1. What challenges did the new nation face in the immediate aftermath of the Revolutionary War?
2. How did farmers, financial leaders, foreign nations, and Indians react to government efforts to address challenges after the Revolution?
3. How did America's experience of the Revolutionary War change the lives of African Americans and women?
4. What do uprisings by farmers and debtors tell us about social and economic divisions in the early Republic?
5. What issues attracted the most intense debate during the drafting and ratification of the Constitution? Why?
6. How did Hamilton's policies stabilize the national economy, and why did they nonetheless arouse opposition?
7. How did events overseas shape domestic American politics and frontier policy in the 1790s?
8. What common concerns underlay the Whiskey Rebellion and Shays's Rebellion? How did the U.S. government deal differently with each?
9. What were the main issues dividing the Federalists and the Democratic-Republicans?
10. What do the Alien and Sedition Acts and the election of 1800 tell us about political partisanship in late-eighteenth-century America?

Answer the **Review & Relate questions**, which prompt you to recall major concepts in each section.

241

Exploring American Histories

A SURVEY WITH SOURCES

FOURTH EDITION

VOLUME 2 Since 1865

Emancipation and Reconstruction

1863–1877

Window to the Past

Sharecropping Agreement, 1870

After the end of slavery, plantation owners needed to find new ways to work their land and formerly enslaved people needed to find employment. As a result, freedpeople sought to enter into sharecropping agreements, such as the one shown here, to farm on behalf of landowners because they lacked money and tools and wanted to farm their own land. However, despite their best efforts, they usually found themselves in debt to the white planter-merchants who controlled the accounts and sold them supplies. ▶ To learn more about this primary source, see Source 14.8 on page 492.

Alabama Department of Archives and History, Montgomery, Alabama

After reading this chapter you will be able to:

- Describe the challenges newly freed African Americans faced and how they responded to them.

- Analyze the influence of the president and Congress on Reconstruction policy and evaluate the successes and shortcomings of the policies they enacted.

- Evaluate the changes that took place in the society and economy of the South during Reconstruction.

- Explain how and why Reconstruction came to an end by the mid-1870s.

Comparing American Histories

Jefferson Franklin Long spent his life improving himself and the lives of others of his race. Born enslaved in Alabama in 1836, Long showed great resourcefulness in profiting from the limited opportunities available to him. His master, a tailor who moved his family to Georgia, taught him the trade, but Long taught himself to read and write. When the Civil War ended, he opened a tailor shop in Macon, Georgia. His business success allowed him to venture into Republican Party politics. Elected as Georgia's first black congressman in 1870, Long fought for the political rights of freed slaves. In his first appearance on the House floor, he opposed a bill that would allow former Confederate officials to return to Congress, noting that many belonged to secret societies, such as the Ku Klux Klan, that

(*left*) **Jefferson Franklin Long** Library of Congress, Prints and Photographs Division, Washington, D.C. [LC-DIG-cwpbh-00556]

(*right*) **Andrew Johnson** Library of Congress, Prints and Photographs Division, Washington, D.C. [LC-USZ62-13017]

intimidated black citizens. Despite his pleas, the measure passed, and Long decided not to run for reelection.

By the mid-1880s, Long had become disillusioned with the ability of black Georgians to achieve their objectives via electoral politics. Instead, he counseled African Americans to turn to institution building as the best hope for social and economic advancement. Long helped found the Union Brotherhood Lodge, a black mutual aid society with branches throughout central Georgia, which provided social and economic services for its members. He died in 1901, as political disfranchisement and racial segregation swept through Georgia and the rest of the South.

Jefferson Long and **Andrew Johnson** shared many characteristics, but their views on race could not have been more different. Whereas Long fought for the right of self-determination for African Americans, Johnson believed that whites alone should govern. Born in 1808 in Raleigh, North Carolina, Johnson grew up in poverty. At the age of thirteen or fourteen, he became a tailor's apprentice and, after moving to Tennessee in 1826, like Long, opened a tailor shop. The following year, Johnson married and began to prosper, purchasing a farm and a small number of enslaved workers.

As he made his mark in Greenville, Tennessee, Johnson became active in Democratic Party politics. A social and political outsider, Johnson gained support by championing the rights of workers and small farmers against the power of the southern aristocracy. Political success followed, and by the time the Civil War broke out, he was a U.S. senator.

When the Civil War erupted, Johnson remained loyal to the Union even after Tennessee seceded in 1861. President Abraham Lincoln rewarded Johnson by appointing him as military governor of Tennessee. In 1864 the Republican Lincoln chose the Democrat Johnson to run with him as vice president. Less than six weeks after their inauguration in March 1865, Johnson became president upon Lincoln's assassination.

Fate placed Reconstruction in the hands of Andrew Johnson. The brutal Civil War had come to a close, but the hard work of reunion remained. Toward this end, President Johnson oversaw the reestablishment of state governments in the former Confederate states. Even as southern states passed measures that restricted black civil and political rights, President Johnson declared them fit for rejoining the Union. Most Northerners reached a different conclusion. Having won the bloody war, they feared losing the peace to Johnson and the defeated South. ■

Comparing the American histories of Andrew Johnson and Jefferson Long highlights hard-fought battles to determine the fate of the postwar South and the meaning of freedom for newly emancipated African Americans. Former enslaved people sought to reunite their families, obtain land, and gain an education. President Johnson rejected their pleas for assistance to fulfill these aims. However, Congress passed laws to ensure civil rights and extend the vote to African American men, although African American women, like white women, remained disfranchised. In the South, whites attempted to restore their economic and political power over African Americans by resorting to intimidation and violence. By 1877, they succeeded in bringing Reconstruction to an end with the consent of the federal government.

Emancipation

Even before the war came to a close, Reconstruction had begun on a small scale. During the Civil War, blacks remaining in Union-occupied areas, such as the South Carolina Sea Islands, gained some experience with freedom. When Union troops arrived, most southern whites fled, but enslaved workers chose to stay on the land. Some farmed for themselves, but most worked for northern whites who moved south to demonstrate the profitability of free black labor. After the war, however, former plantation owners returned. Rather than work for these whites, freedpeople preferred to establish their own farms. If forced to hire themselves out, they insisted on negotiating the terms of their employment. Wives and mothers often refused to labor for whites at all in favor of caring for their own families. These conflicts reflected the priorities that would shape the actions of freedpeople across the South in the immediate aftermath of the war. For freedom to be meaningful, it had to include economic independence, the power to make family decisions, and the right to control some community decisions.

African Americans Embrace Freedom.
When U.S. troops arrived in Richmond, Virginia in April 1865, the city's enslaved population knew that freedom was, finally, theirs. Four days after Union troops arrived, 1,500 African Americans, including a large number of soldiers, packed First African Baptist, the largest of the city's black churches. During the singing of the hymn "Jesus My All to Heaven Is Gone," they raised their voices at the line "This is the way I long have sought." As news of the Confederacy's defeat spread, newly freed African Americans across the South experienced similar emotions. Many years later, Houston H. Holloway, an enslaved Georgian who had been sold three times before he was twenty years old, recalled the day of emancipation: "I felt like a bird out a cage. Amen. Amen, Amen. I could hardly ask to feel any better than I did that day."

For southern whites, however, the end of the war brought fear, humiliation, and uncertainty. From their perspective, the jubilation of former slaves poured salt in their wounds. In many areas, blacks celebrated their freedom under the protection of Union soldiers.

When the army moved out, freedpeople suffered deeply for their enthusiasm. Whites beat, whipped, raped, and shot blacks who they felt had been too joyous in their celebration or too helpful to the Yankee invaders. As one North Carolina freedman testified, the Yankees "tol' us we were free," but once the army left, the planters "would get cruel to the slaves if they acted like they were free."

Newly freed blacks also faced less visible dangers. During the 1860s, disease swept through the South and through the contraband camps that housed many former slaves; widespread malnutrition and poor housing heightened the problem. A smallpox epidemic that spread south from Washington, D.C. killed more than sixty thousand freedpeople.

Despite the dangers, southern blacks eagerly pursued emancipation. They moved; they married; they attended school; they demanded wages; they refused to work for whites; they gathered together their families; they created black churches and civic associations; they held political meetings. Sometimes, black women and men acted on their own, pooling their resources to advance their freedom. At other times, they received help from private organizations — particularly northern missionary and educational associations — staffed mostly by former abolitionists, free blacks, and evangelical Christians.

Emancipated slaves also called on federal agencies for assistance and support. The most important of these agencies was the newly formed Bureau of Refugees, Freedmen, and Abandoned Lands, popularly known as the **Freedmen's Bureau**. Created by Congress in 1865 and signed into law by President Lincoln, the bureau provided ex-slaves with economic and legal resources. The Freedmen's Bureau also aided many freedpeople in achieving one of their primary goals: obtaining land. A South Carolina freedman summed up the feeling of the newly emancipated. "Give us our own land and we take care of ourselves," he remarked. "But without land, the old masters can hire or starve us, as they

Explore ▶

See Source 14.1 for freedpeople's views about ownership of land.

please." During the last years of the war, the federal government had distributed to freedpeople around 400,000 acres of abandoned land from the South Carolina Sea Islands to Florida. Immediately after hostilities ceased, the Freedmen's Bureau made available hundreds of thousands of additional acres to recently emancipated slaves.

Reuniting Families Torn Apart by Slavery. The first priority for many newly freed blacks was to reunite families torn apart by slavery. Men and women traveled across the South to find family members. Well into the 1870s and 1880s, parents ran advertisements in newly established black newspapers, providing what information they knew about their children's whereabouts and asking for assistance in finding them. Milly Johnson wrote to the Freedmen's Bureau in March 1867, after failing to locate the five children she had lost under slavery. She finally located three of them, but any chance of discovering the whereabouts of the other two disappeared because the records of the slave trader who purchased them burned during the war. Despite such obstacles, thousands of formerly enslaved children were reunited with their parents in the 1870s.

Husbands and wives, or those who considered themselves as such despite the absence of legal marriage under slavery, also searched for each other. Those who lived on nearby plantations could live together for the first time. Those whose spouse had been sold to distant plantations had a more difficult time. They wrote (or had letters written on their behalf) to relatives and friends who had been sold with their mate; sought assistance from

Guided Primary Source Analysis

Freedpeople Petition for Land, 1865

A committee of the formerly enslaved in Edisto Island, South Carolina wrote President Johnson requesting that they be allowed to purchase land promised them by the government during the Civil War. The president intended to restore the properties to the former rebel landholders and did not respond to the black petitioners.

Source 14.1

Edisto Island S.C. Oct 28th 1865.

. . . Here is where secession was born and Nurtured Here is were we have toiled nearly all Our lives as slaves and were treated like dumb Driven cattle, This is our home, we have made These lands what they are. we were the only true and Loyal people that were found in posession of these Lands. we have been always ready to strike for Liberty and humanity yea to fight if needs be To preserve this glorious union. Shall not we who Are freedman and have been always true to this Union have the same rights as are enjoyed by Others? Have we broken any Law of these United States? Have we forfieted our rights of property In Land?—If not then! are not our rights as A free people and good citizens of these United States To be considered before the rights of those who were Found in rebellion against this good and just Government.

We have been encouraged by government to take up these lands in small tracts, receiving Certificates of the same—we have thus far Taken Sixteen thousand (16000) acres of Land here on This Island. We are ready to pay for this land When Government calls for it and now after What has been done will the good and just government take from us all this right and make us Subject to the will of those who have cheated and Oppressed us for many years God Forbid! We the freedmen of this Island and of the State of South Carolina–Do therefore petition to you as the President of these United States, that some provisions be made by which Every colored man can purchase land. and Hold it as his own. . . .

In behalf of the Freedmen Committee
Henry Bram. Ishmael. Moultrie. yates. Sampson.

Source: Henry Bram et al. to the President of these United States, 28 Oct. 1865, filed as P-27 1865, Letters Received, series 15, Washington Headquarters, Bureau of Refugees, Freedmen, & Abandoned Lands, Record Group 105, National Archives.

Why do the freedpeople believe their request justified?

Why do they think the former landowners do not deserve the land?

How does this show the importance of landownership to them?

Put It in Context

Why was landownership so important to newly freed blacks?

Winslow Homer, *A Visit from the Old Mistress*, 1876   Civil War correspondent and artist Winslow Homer visited Virginia in the mid-1870s and visually captured the tensions existing between freedpeople and former owners. Here, a former mistress visits the home of three black women. Although the house is humble, one woman refuses to stand for the "old mistress" and the other two, one holding a freeborn child, eye her warily. Smithsonian American Art Museum, Washington, D.C./Art Resource, NY

government officials, churches, and even their former masters; and traveled to areas where they thought their spouse might reside.

These searches were complicated by long years of separation and the lack of any legal standing for slave marriages. In 1866 Philip Grey, a Virginia freedman, located his wife, Willie Ann, and their daughter Maria, who had been sold away to Kentucky years before. Willie Ann was eager to reunite with her husband, but in the years since being sold, she had remarried and borne three children. Her second husband had joined the Union army and was killed in battle. When Willie Ann wrote to Philip in April 1866, she explained her new circumstances, concluding: "If you love me you will love my children and you will have to promise me that you will provide for them all as well as if they were your own. . . . I know that I have lived with you and loved you then and love you still."

Most black spouses who found each other sought to legalize their relationship. A superintendent for marriages for the Freedmen's Bureau in northern Virginia reported that he gave out seventy-nine marriage certificates on a single day in May 1866. In another case, four couples went right from the fields to a local schoolhouse, still dressed in their work clothes, where a parson married them.

Of course, some of the formerly enslaved hoped that freedom would allow them to leave unhappy relationships. Having never been married under the law, couples could simply separate and move on. Complications arose, however, if they had children. In Lake City, Florida in 1866, a Freedmen's Bureau agent asked his superiors for advice on how to deal with Madison Day and Maria Richards. They refused to legalize the relationship forced on them under slavery, but both sought custody of their three children. As with white couples in the mid-nineteenth century, the father was granted custody on the assumption that he had the best chance of providing for the children financially.

As was the custom and law of that time, wives were subordinate to their husbands. One North Carolina freedman said of his wife, "I consider her my property." This rankled Frances Gage, an antislavery and women's rights activist, who declared, "You give us a nominal freedom, but you leave us under the heel of our husbands." Yet there was an important trade-off that black women hoped to receive from this patriarchal arrangement: protection for themselves and their children.

Freedom to Learn.
Seeking land and reuniting families were only two of the many ways that southern blacks proclaimed their freedom. Learning to read and write was another. The desire to learn was all but universal. Enslaved persons had been forbidden to read and write. With emancipation they pursued what had been denied them. A newly liberated father in Mississippi proclaimed, "If I nebber does nothing more while I live, I shall give my children a chance to go to school, for I considers education [the] next best ting to liberty."

A variety of organizations opened schools for formerly enslaved persons during the 1860s and 1870s. By 1870 nearly a quarter million blacks were attending one of the 4,300 schools established by the Freedmen's Bureau. Black and white churches and missionary societies sent hundreds of teachers, black and white, into the South to establish schools in former plantation areas. Their attitudes were often paternalistic and the schools were segregated, but the institutions they founded offered important educational resources for African Americans.

Parents worked hard to keep their children in school during the day. As children gained the rudiments of education, they passed on their knowledge to parents and older siblings whose jobs prevented them from attending school. Still, many adult freedpeople insisted on getting a bit of education for themselves. In New Bern, North Carolina, where many blacks labored until eight o'clock at night, a teacher reported that they then spent at least an hour "in earnest application to study."

Freedpeople sought education for a variety of reasons. Some viewed it as a sign of liberation. Others knew the importance of reading the labor contracts they signed if they were ever to challenge exploitation by whites. Some freedpeople were eager to correspond with relatives, others to read the Bible. Growing numbers hoped to participate in politics, particularly the public meetings organized by blacks in cities across the South. When such gatherings set priorities for the future, the establishment of public schools was high on the list.

Despite the enthusiasm of blacks and the efforts of the federal government and private agencies, schooling remained severely limited throughout the South. A shortage of teachers and of funding kept enrollments low among blacks and whites alike. The isolation of black farm families and the difficulties in eking out a living limited the resources available for education. By 1880, only about a quarter of African Americans were literate.

Freedmen's Bureau School This photograph of a one-room Freedmen's Bureau school in North Carolina in the late 1860s shows the large number and diverse ages of students who sought to obtain an education following emancipation. The teachers included white and black northern women sent by missionary and reform organizations as well as southern black women who had already received some education. Granger

Freedom to Worship and the Leadership Role of Black Churches.

One of the constant concerns freedpeople expressed was the desire to read the Bible and interpret it for themselves. A few black congregations had existed under slavery, but most slaves were forced to listen to white preachers who claimed that God created slavery.

From the moment of emancipation, freedpeople gathered at churches to celebrate community events. Black Methodist and Baptist congregations spread rapidly across the South following the Civil War. In these churches, African Americans were no longer forced to sit in the back benches or punished for moral infractions defined by white masters. Now blacks invested community resources in their own religious institutions where they filled the pews, hired the preachers, and selected boards of deacons and elders. Churches were the largest structures available to freedpeople in many communities and thus were used by a variety of community organizations. They often served as schools and hosted picnics, dances, weddings, funerals, festivals, and other events that brought blacks together. Church leaders also often served as arbiters of community standards of morality.

In the early years of emancipation black churches also served as important sites for political organizing. Some black ministers worried that political concerns would overwhelm spiritual devotions. Others agreed with the Reverend Charles H. Pearce of Florida, who declared, "A man in this State cannot do his whole duty as a minister except he looks out for the political interests of his people." Whatever the views of ministers, black churches were among the few places where African Americans could express their political views free from white interference.

Review & Relate

▪ What were freedpeople's highest priorities in the years immediately following the Civil War? Why?

▪ How did freedpeople define freedom? What steps did they take to make freedom real for themselves and their children?

National Reconstruction

Presidents Abraham Lincoln and Andrew Johnson viewed Reconstruction as a process of national reconciliation. They sketched out terms by which the former Confederate states could reclaim their political representation in the nation without serious penalties. Congressional Republicans, however, had a more thoroughgoing reconstruction in mind. Like many African Americans, Republican congressional leaders expected the South to extend constitutional rights to the freedmen and to provide them with the political and economic resources to sustain their freedom. Over the next decade, these competing visions of Reconstruction played out in hard-fought and tumultuous battles over the meaning of the South's defeat and the emancipation of blacks.

Abraham Lincoln Plans for Reunification.

In December 1863, even as battles continued, President Lincoln issued a **Proclamation of Amnesty and Reconstruction**, outlining his vision of the postwar world. Lincoln declared that defeated states would have to accept the abolition of slavery, but then new governments could be formed when 10 percent of those eligible to vote in 1860 (which in practice meant white southern men but not blacks) swore an oath of allegiance to the United States. Lincoln's plan granted amnesty to all but the highest-ranking Confederate officials, and the restored voters in each state would elect members to a constitutional convention and representatives to take their seats in Congress. In the next year and a half, Arkansas, Louisiana, and Tennessee — which were already under Union control — reestablished their governments under Lincoln's conciliatory "Ten Percent Plan."

Republicans in Congress had other ideas. Radical Republicans argued that the Confederate states should be treated as "conquered provinces" subject to congressional supervision. In 1864 Congress passed the Wade-Davis bill, which established much higher barriers for readmission to the Union than did Lincoln's plan. For instance, the Wade-Davis bill substituted 50 percent of voters for the president's 10 percent requirement. Lincoln put a stop to this harsher proposal by using a pocket veto — refusing to sign it within ten days of Congress's adjournment.

Although Lincoln and congressional Republicans disagreed about many aspects of postwar policy, Lincoln was flexible, and his actions mirrored his desire both to heal the Union and to help southern blacks. For example, the president supported the **Thirteenth Amendment**, abolishing slavery, which passed Congress in January 1865 and was sent to the states for ratification. In March 1865, Lincoln signed the law to create the Freedmen's Bureau. That same month, the president expressed his sincere wish for reconciliation between the North and the South. "With malice toward none, with charity for all," Lincoln declared in his second inaugural address, "let us strive on to finish the work . . . to bind up the nation's wounds." Lincoln would not, however, have the opportunity to implement his approach to Reconstruction. When he was assassinated in April 1865, it fell to Andrew Johnson, a very different sort of politician, to lead the country through the process of reintegration.

Andrew Johnson and Presidential Reconstruction.
The nation needed a president who could transmit northern desires to the South with clarity and conviction and ensure that they were carried out. Instead, the nation got a president who substituted his own aims for those of the North, refused to engage in meaningful compromise, and misled the South into believing that he could achieve restoration quickly. In the 1864 election, Lincoln chose Johnson, a southern Democrat, as his running mate in a thinly veiled effort to attract border-state voters. The vice presidency was normally an inconsequential role, so it mattered little to Lincoln that Johnson was out of step with many Republican Party positions.

As president, however, Johnson's views took on profound importance. Born into rural poverty, Johnson had no sympathy for the southern aristocracy. Yet he had been a slave owner, so his political opposition to slavery was not rooted in moral convictions. Instead, it sprang from the belief that slavery gave plantation owners inordinate power and wealth, which came at the expense of the majority of white Southerners, who owned no slaves. Johnson saw emancipation as a means to "break down an odious and dangerous [planter] aristocracy," not to empower blacks. Consequently, he was unconcerned with the fate of African Americans in the postwar South. Six months after taking office, President Johnson rescinded the wartime order to distribute confiscated land to freedpeople in the Sea Islands. He saw no reason to punish the Confederacy's leaders, because he believed that the end of slavery would doom the southern aristocracy. He hoped to bring the South back into the Union as quickly as possible and then let Southerners take care of their own affairs.

Johnson's views, combined with a lack of political savvy and skill, ensured his inability to work constructively with congressional Republicans, even the moderates who constituted the majority. Moderate Republicans shared the prevalent belief of their time that blacks were inferior to whites, but they argued that the federal government needed to protect the enslaved people who were newly emancipated. Senator Lyman Trumbull of Illinois, for example, warned that without national legislation, ex-slaves would "be tyrannized over, abused, and virtually reenslaved." The moderates expected southern states, where 90 percent of African Americans lived, to extend basic civil rights to the freedpeople, including equal protection, due process of law, and the right to work and hold property.

Nearly all Republicans shared these positions, but the Radical wing of the party wanted to go further. Led by Senator Charles Sumner of Massachusetts and Congressman Thaddeus Stevens of Pennsylvania, this small but influential group advocated suffrage, that is voting rights, for African American men as well as the redistribution of southern plantation lands to the formerly enslaved. Stevens called on the federal government to provide freedpeople "a homestead of forty acres of land," which would give them some measure of autonomy. These efforts failed, and the Republican Party proved unable to pass a comprehensive land distribution program that enabled freed blacks to gain economic independence. Nonetheless, whatever disagreements between Radicals and moderates, all Republicans believed that Congress should have a strong voice in determining the fate of the former

Mourning at Stonewall Jackson's Gravesite, 1866
Many Northerners were concerned that the defeat of the Confederacy did not lessen white Southerners' devotion to the "Lost Cause" or the heroism of soldiers who fought to maintain a society based on the domination of African Americans. Women, who led the efforts to memorialize Confederate soldiers, are shown at the gravesite of General Stonewall Jackson in Lexington, Virginia. Virginia Military Institute Archives

Confederate states. From May to December 1865, with Congress out of session, they waited to see what Johnson's restoration plan would produce, ready to assert themselves if his policies deviated too much from their own.

At first, it seemed as if Johnson would proceed as they hoped. He appointed provisional governors to convene new state constitutional conventions and urged these conventions to ratify the Thirteenth Amendment, abolishing slavery, and revoke the states' ordinances of secession. He also allowed the majority of white Southerners to obtain amnesty and a pardon by swearing their loyalty to the U.S. Constitution, but he required those who had held more than $20,000 of taxable property — the members of the southern aristocracy — to petition him for a special pardon to restore their rights. Republicans expected him to be harsh in dealing with his former political foes. Instead, Johnson relished the reversal of roles that put members of the southern elite at his mercy. As the once prominent petitioners paraded before him, the president granted almost all of their requests for pardons.

By the time Congress convened in December 1865, Johnson was satisfied that the southern states had fulfilled his requirements for restoration. Moderate and Radical Republicans disagreed, seeing few signs of change or contrition in the South. Mississippi, for example, rejected ratification of the Thirteenth Amendment. As a result of Johnson's liberal pardon policy, many former leaders of the Confederacy won election to state constitutional conventions and to Congress. Indeed, Georgians elected Confederate vice president Alexander H. Stephens to the U.S. Senate. As one white Mississippian candidly forecast, "Our negroes . . . will learn that freedom and independence are different things."

Indeed they did. Far from providing freedpeople with basic civil rights, the southern states passed a variety of **black codes** intended to reduce African Americans to a condition as close to slavery as possible. Some laws prohibited blacks from bearing arms; others outlawed intermarriage and excluded blacks from serving on juries. The codes also made it difficult for blacks to leave plantations unless they proved they could support themselves. Other provisions sought to reduce the independence of black families. They empowered southern courts to assign black children to white employers without parental consent. Echoing the slave past, laws like these were designed to ensure that white landowners had a supply of cheap black labor despite the Thirteenth Amendment abolishing slavery.

Northerners viewed this situation with alarm. In their eyes, the postwar South looked very similar to the Old South, with a few cosmetic adjustments. If the black codes prevailed, one Republican proclaimed, "then I demand to know of what practical value is the amendment abolishing slavery?" Others wondered what their wartime sacrifices meant if the South admitted no mistakes, was led by the same people, and continued to oppress its black inhabitants. **See Primary Source Project 14: Testing and Contesting Freedom, page 490.**

Johnson and Congressional Resistance.

Faced with growing opposition in the North, Johnson stubbornly held his ground. He insisted that the southern states had followed his plan and were entitled to resume their representation in Congress. Republicans objected, and in December 1865 they barred the admission of southern lawmakers. But Johnson refused to compromise. In January 1866, the president rejected a bill passed by Congress to extend the life of the Freedmen's Bureau for two years. A few months later, he vetoed the Civil Rights Act, which Congress had passed to protect freedpeople from the restrictions placed on them by the black codes. These bills represented a consensus among moderate and Radical Republicans on the federal government's responsibility toward the formerly enslaved.

Johnson justified his vetoes on both constitutional and personal grounds. He and other Democrats contended that so long as Congress refused to admit southern representatives, it could not legally pass laws affecting the South. The president also condemned the Freedmen's Bureau bill because it infringed on the right of states to handle internal affairs such as education and economic policies. Johnson's vetoes exposed his racism and his lifelong belief that the evil of slavery lay in the harm it did to poor whites, not to enslaved blacks. Johnson argued that the bills he vetoed discriminated against whites, who would receive no benefits under them, and thus put whites at a disadvantage with blacks receiving government assistance. Johnson's private secretary reported in his diary, "The president has at times exhibited a morbid distress and feeling against the Negroes."

Johnson's actions united moderates and Radicals against him. In April 1866, Congress repassed both the Freedmen's Bureau extension and Civil Rights Act over the president's vetoes. In June, lawmakers adopted the **Fourteenth Amendment**, which incorporated many of the provisions of the Civil Rights Act, and submitted it to the states for ratification (see Appendix). Reflecting its confrontational dealings with the president, Congress wanted to ensure more permanent protection for African Americans than simple legislation could provide. Lawmakers also wanted to act quickly, as the situation in the South seemed to be deteriorating rapidly. In May 1866, a race riot had broken out in Memphis, Tennessee. For a day and a half, white mobs, egged on by local police, went on a rampage, during which they terrorized blacks and burned their homes and churches. "The late riots in our city," the white editor of a Memphis newspaper asserted, "have satisfied all of one thing, that the *southern man* will not be ruled

Explore ▶

See Sources 14.2 and 14.3 for two perspectives on the Freedmen's Bureau.

Memphis Race Riot A skirmish between white policemen and black Union veterans on May 1, 1866 resulted in three days of rioting by white mobs that attacked the black community of Memphis, Tennessee. Before federal troops restored peace, numerous women had been raped, and forty-six African Americans and two whites had been killed. This illustration from *Harper's Weekly* depicts the carnage. Sarin Images/Granger

by the *negro.*" A few months later, the New Orleans police, dominated by ex-Confederates, led a mob against black and white Republicans, killing thirty-four African Americans and three whites.

The Fourteenth Amendment defined citizenship to include African Americans, thereby nullifying the ruling in the *Dred Scott* case of 1857, which declared that blacks were not citizens. It extended equal protection and due process of law to all persons, not only citizens. The amendment repudiated Confederate debts, which some state governments had refused to do, and it barred Confederate officeholders from holding elective office unless Congress removed this provision by a two-thirds vote. Although most Republicans were upset with Johnson's behavior, at this point they were not willing to embrace the Radical position entirely. Rather than granting the right to vote to black males at least twenty-one years of age, the Fourteenth Amendment gave the states the option of excluding blacks and accepting a reduction in congressional representation if they did so.

Johnson remained inflexible. Instead of counseling the southern states to accept the Fourteenth Amendment, which would have sped up their readmission to the Union, he encouraged them to reject it. In the fall of 1866, Johnson decided to take his case directly to northern voters before the midterm congressional elections. Campaigning for candidates who shared his views, he embarked on a swing through the Midwest. Out of touch with northern opinion, Johnson attacked Republican lawmakers and engaged in shouting matches with audiences. On election day, Republicans increased their majorities in

Comparative Primary Source Analysis

Debating the Freedmen's Bureau

From the start, the Freedmen's Bureau generated controversy. To its Republican supporters, it helped southern blacks make the transition from slavery to freedom. For most white Southerners and many northern Democrats, however, the bureau was little more than an expensive social welfare program that rewarded idleness in blacks. Both points of view are represented in the following documents. In a report written to the Congressional Joint Committee on Reconstruction, Colonel Eliphalet Whittlesey, the assistant head of the Freedmen's Bureau in North Carolina, outlined the bureau's initial accomplishments. The anti-bureau cartoon reprinted here was created during the height of the conflict over Reconstruction between the Republican Congress and President Andrew Johnson and depicts the pervasive racism of the era; it was intended to support the election of a Democratic candidate for governor of Pennsylvania, an ally of Johnson.

Source 14.2

Colonel Eliphalet Whittlesey | Report on the Freedmen's Bureau, 1865

All officers of the bureau are instructed—

To aid the destitute, yet in such a way as not to encourage dependence.

To protect freedmen from injustice.

To assist freedmen in obtaining employment and fair wages for their labor.

To encourage education, intellectual and moral. . . .

. . . [W]e have in our camps at Roanoke Island and Newbern, many women and children, families of soldiers who have died in the service, and refugees from the interior during the war, for whom permanent provision must be made. . . . The reports prepared by Surgeon Hogan will show the condition of freedmen hospitals. In the early part of the summer much suffering and mortality occurred for want of medical attendance and supplies. This evil is now being remedied by the employment of surgeons by contract. . . .

Contrary to the fears and predictions of many, the great mass of colored people have remained quietly at work upon the plantations of their former masters during the entire summer. The crowds seen about the towns in the early part of the season had followed in the wake of the Union army, to escape from slavery. After hostilities ceased these refugees returned to their homes, so that but few vagrants can now be found. In truth, a much larger amount of vagrancy exists among the whites than among the blacks. It is the almost uniform report of officers of the bureau that freedmen are industrious.

The report is confirmed by the fact that out of a colored population of nearly 350,000 in the State, only about 5,000 are now receiving support from the government. Probably some others are receiving aid from kind-hearted men who have enjoyed the benefit of their services from childhood. To the general quiet and industry of this people there can be no doubt that the efforts of the bureau have contributed greatly.

Source: *The Reports of the Committees of the House of Representatives Made during the First Session, Thirty-Ninth Congress, 1865–1866* (Washington, DC: Government Printing Office, 1866), 186–87, 189.

Source 14.3

Democratic Flier Opposing the Freedmen's Bureau Bill, 1866

Interpret the Evidence

1. According to Colonel Whittlesey, what needs does the Freedmen's Bureau address? How does he measure the bureau's success?

2. Why might this portrayal of the Freedmen's Bureau have appealed to some whites, north and south? How would Whittlesey and other bureau supporters have responded?

Put It in Context

How did racism and prevailing racial assumptions shape both the cartoon and the report?

Congress and now controlled two-thirds of the seats, providing them with greater power to override presidential vetoes.

Congressional Reconstruction.

When the Fortieth Congress convened in 1867, Republican lawmakers charted a new course for Reconstruction. With moderates and Radicals united against the president, Congress intended to force the former Confederate states not only to protect the basic civil rights of African Americans but also to grant them the vote. Moderates now agreed with Radicals that unless blacks had access to the ballot, they would not be able to sustain their freedom. Extending the suffrage to African Americans also aided the fortunes of the Republican Party in the South by adding significant numbers of new voters. By the end of March, Congress enacted three Military Reconstruction Acts. Together they divided ten southern states into five military districts, each under the supervision of a Union general (Map 14.1). The male voters of each state, regardless of race, were to elect delegates to a constitutional convention; only former Confederate officials were disfranchised. The conventions were required to draft constitutions that guaranteed black suffrage and ratified the Fourteenth Amendment. Within a year, North Carolina, South Carolina, Florida, Alabama, Louisiana, and Arkansas had fulfilled these obligations and reentered the Union. In December 1866, only 0.5 percent of adult black males could vote in the United States; a year later the figure soared to 80.5 percent, with all of the gains made in the states subject to the military Reconstruction Acts.

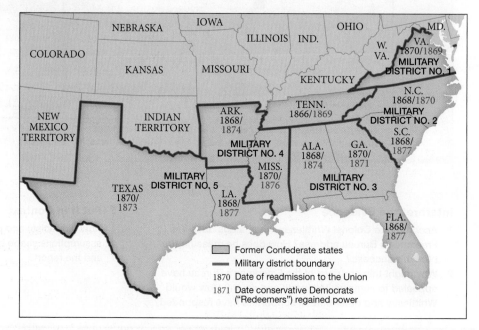

MAP 14.1   Reconstruction in the South

In 1867 Congress enacted legislation dividing the former Confederate states into five military districts. All the states were readmitted to the Union by 1870, and white conservative Democrats (Redeemers) had replaced Republicans in most states by 1875. Only in Florida, Louisiana, and South Carolina did federal troops remain until 1877.

Having ensured congressional Reconstruction in the South, Republican lawmakers turned their attention to disciplining the president. Johnson continued to resist their policies and used his power as commander in chief to order generals in the military districts to soften the intent of congressional Reconstruction. In response, Congress passed the Command of the Army Act in 1867, which required the president to issue all orders to army commanders in the field through the General of the Army in Washington, D.C., Ulysses S. Grant. The Radicals knew they could count on Grant to carry out their policies. Even more threatening to presidential power, Congress passed the **Tenure of Office Act**, which prevented Johnson from firing cabinet officers sympathetic to congressional Reconstruction. This measure barred the chief executive from removing from office any appointee that the Senate had ratified previously without returning to the Senate for approval.

Convinced that the new law was unconstitutional and outraged at this effort to limit his power, the quick-tempered Johnson chose to confront the Radical Republicans directly rather than seek a way around a congressional showdown. In February 1868, Johnson fired Secretary of War Edwin Stanton, a Lincoln appointee and a Radical sympathizer, without Senate approval. In response, congressional Radicals prepared articles of impeachment.

In late February, the House voted 126 to 47 to impeach Johnson, the first president ever to be impeached, or charged with unlawful activity. The case then went to trial in the Senate, where the chief justice of the United States presided and a two-thirds vote was necessary for conviction and removal from office. After a six-week hearing, the Senate fell one vote short of convicting Johnson. Most crucial for Johnson's fate were the votes of seven moderate Republicans who refused to find the president guilty of violating his oath to uphold the Constitution. They were convinced that Johnson's actions were insufficient to merit the enormous step of removing a president from office. Although Johnson remained in office, Congress effectively ended his power to shape Reconstruction policy.

The Republicans had restrained Johnson, and in 1868 they won back the presidency. Ulysses S. Grant, the popular Civil War general, ran against Horatio Seymour, the Democratic governor of New York. Although an ally of the Radical Republicans, Grant called for reconciliation with the South. He easily defeated Seymour, winning nearly 53 percent of the popular vote and 73 percent of the electoral vote.

The Struggle for Universal Suffrage.

In February 1869, Congress passed the **Fifteenth Amendment** to protect black male suffrage, which had initially been guaranteed by the Military Reconstruction Acts. A compromise between moderate and Radical Republicans, the amendment prohibited voting discrimination based on race, but it did not deny states the power to impose qualifications based on literacy, payment of taxes, moral character, or any other standard that did not directly relate to race. Subsequently, the wording of the amendment provided loopholes for white leaders to disfranchise large numbers of African Americans. The amendment did, however, cover the entire nation, including the North, where states like Connecticut, Kansas, Michigan, New York, Ohio, and Wisconsin still excluded blacks from voting.

The Fifteenth Amendment sparked serious conflicts not only within the South but also among old abolitionist allies. The American Anti-Slavery Society had disbanded with emancipation. Immediately following the war, the many members who believed that important work remained to be done to guarantee the rights of freedpeople formed the **American Equal Rights Association**. However, its members divided over the Fifteenth Amendment.

Frances Ellen Watkins Harper Born a free person of color in Baltimore, Frances Ellen Watkins Harper distinguished herself as a poet, a teacher, and an abolitionist. After the Civil War, she became a staunch advocate of women's suffrage and a supporter of the Fifteenth Amendment, which set her at odds with the suffragists Susan B. Anthony and Elizabeth Cady Stanton. Documenting the American South, University Library, The University of North Carolina at Chapel Hill, http://docsouth.unc.edu/neh/brownhal/ill22.html

Some women's rights advocates, including Elizabeth Cady Stanton and Susan B. Anthony, had earlier objected to the Fourteenth Amendment because it inserted the word *male* into the Constitution for the first time when describing citizens. Although they had supported abolition before the war, Stanton and Anthony worried that postwar policies intended to enhance the rights of southern black men would further limit the rights of women. While most African American activists embraced the Fifteenth Amendment, a few voiced concern. At a meeting of the Equal Rights Association in 1867, Sojourner Truth noted, "There is quite a stir about colored men getting their rights, but not a word about colored women."

At the 1869 meeting of the Equal Rights Association, differences over the measure erupted into open conflict. Stanton and Anthony denounced suffrage for black men only, and Stanton now supported her position on racial grounds. She claimed that the "dregs of China, Germany, England, Ireland, and Africa" were degrading the U.S. polity and argued that white, educated women should certainly have the same rights as immigrant and African American men. Black and white supporters of the Fifteenth Amendment, including Frances Ellen Watkins Harper, Wendell Phillips, Abby Kelley, and Frederick Douglass, denounced Stanton's bigotry. Believing that southern black men urgently needed suffrage to protect their newly won freedom, they argued that ratification of the Fifteenth Amendment would speed progress toward the enfranchisement of women, black and white.

This conflict led to the formation of competing organizations committed to women's suffrage. The National Woman Suffrage Association, established by Stanton and Anthony, allowed only women as members and opposed ratification of the Fifteenth Amendment. The American Woman Suffrage Association, which attracted the support of women and men, white and black, supported ratification. Less than a year later, in the spring of 1870, the Fifteenth Amendment was ratified and went into effect.

Since the amendment did not grant the vote to either white or black women, women suffragists attempted to use the Fourteenth Amendment to achieve their goal. In 1875 Virginia Minor, who had been denied the ballot in Missouri, argued that the right to vote was one of the "privileges and immunities" granted to all citizens under the Fourteenth Amendment. In *Minor v. Happersett*, the Supreme Court ruled against her, and most women were denied national suffrage for decades thereafter.

Review & Relate

■ What was President Johnson's plan for reconstruction? How were his views out of step with those of most Republicans?

■ What characterized congressional Reconstruction? What priorities were reflected in congressional Reconstruction legislation?

Remaking the South

With President Johnson's power effectively curtailed, reconstruction of the South moved quickly. New state legislatures, ruled by a coalition of southern whites and blacks and white northern migrants, enacted political, economic, and social reforms that improved the overall quality of life in the South. Despite these changes, many black and white Southerners barely eked out a living under the planter-dominated sharecropping system. Moreover, the biracial Reconstruction governments lasted a relatively short time, as conservative whites used a variety of tactics, including terror and race baiting, to defeat their opponents at the polls.

Whites Reconstruct the South. During the first years of congressional Reconstruction, two groups of whites occupied the majority of elective offices in the South. A significant number of native-born Southerners joined Republicans in forging postwar constitutions and governments. Before the war, some had belonged to the Whig Party and opposed secession from the Union. Western sections of Alabama, Georgia, North Carolina, and Tennessee had demonstrated a fiercely independent strain, and many residents had remained loyal to the Union. Small merchants and farmers who detested large plantation owners also threw in their lot with the Republicans. Even a few ex-Confederates, such as General James A. Longstreet, decided that the South must change and allied with the Republicans. The majority of whites who continued to support the Democratic Party viewed these whites as traitors. They showed their distaste by calling them **scalawags**, an unflattering term meaning "scoundrels."

At the same time, Northerners came south to support Republican Reconstruction. They had varied reasons for making the journey, but most considered the South a new frontier to be conquered culturally, politically, and economically. Some — white and black — had served in the Union army during the war, liked what they saw of the region, and decided to settle there. Some of both races came to provide education and assist the freedpeople in adjusting to their new lives. As a relatively underdeveloped area, the South also beckoned fortune seekers and adventurers who saw opportunities to get rich. Southern Democrats denounced such northern interlopers, particularly whites, as **carpetbaggers**, suggesting that they invaded the region with all their possessions in a satchel, seeking to plunder it and then leave. While Northerners did seek economic opportunity, they were acting as Americans always had in settling new frontiers and pursuing dreams of success. In fact, much of the animosity directed toward them resulted primarily not from their mere presence, but from their efforts to ally with African Americans in reshaping the South.

Black Political Participation and Economic Opportunities.
Still, the primary targets of southern white hostility were African Americans who attempted to exercise their hard-won freedom. Blacks constituted a majority of voters in five states — Alabama, Florida, South Carolina, Mississippi, and Louisiana — while in Georgia, North Carolina, Texas, and Virginia they fell short of a majority. They did not use their ballots to impose black rule on the South, as many white Southerners feared. Only in South Carolina did African Americans control the state legislature, and in no state did they manage to elect a governor. Nevertheless, for the first time in American history, blacks won a wide variety of elected positions. More than six hundred blacks served in state legislatures; another sixteen, including Jefferson Long, held seats in the U.S. House of Representatives; and two from Mississippi were chosen to serve in the U.S. Senate.

> **Explore ▶**
>
> Compare two opposing views of southern blacks in Reconstruction-era governments in Sources 14.4 and 14.5.

Former slaves showed enthusiasm for politics in other ways, too. African Americans considered politics a community responsibility, and in addition to casting ballots, they held rallies and mass meetings to discuss issues and choose candidates. Although they could not vote, women attended these gatherings and helped influence their outcome. Covering a Republican convention in Richmond in October 1867, held in the First African Baptist Church, the *New York Times* reported that "the entire colored population of Richmond" attended. In addition, freedpeople formed mutual aid associations to promote education, economic advancement, and social welfare programs, all of which they saw as deeply intertwined with politics.

Southern blacks also bolstered their freedom by building alliances with sympathetic whites. These interracial political coalitions produced considerable reform in the South. They created the first public school systems; provided funds for social services, such as poor relief and state hospitals; upgraded prisons; and rebuilt the South's transportation system. Moreover, the state constitutions that the Republicans wrote brought a greater measure of political democracy and equality to the South by extending suffrage to poor white men as well as black men. Some states allowed married women greater control over their property and liberalized the criminal justice system. In effect, these Reconstruction governments brought the South into the nineteenth century.

Obtaining political representation was one way in which African Americans defined freedom. Economic independence constituted a second. Without government-sponsored land redistribution, however, the options for southern blacks remained limited. Lacking capital to purchase farms, most entered into various forms of tenant contracts with large landowners. **Sharecropping** proved the most common arrangement. Blacks and poor whites became sharecroppers for much the same reasons. They received tools and supplies from landowners and farmed their own plots of land on the plantation. In exchange, sharecroppers turned over a portion of their harvest to the owner and kept the rest for themselves.

The benefits of sharecropping proved less valuable to black farmers in practice than in theory. To tide them over during the growing season, croppers had to purchase household provisions on credit from a local merchant, who was often also their landlord. At the mercy of store owners who kept the books and charged high interest rates, tenants usually found themselves in considerable debt at the end of the year. To satisfy the debt, merchants devised a crop lien system in which tenants pledged a portion of their yearly crop to satisfy what they owed. Falling prices for agricultural crops in this period ensured that most indebted tenants did not receive sufficient return on their produce to get out of debt and thus remained bound to their landlords. For many African Americans, sharecropping turned into a form of virtual slavery.

The picture for black farmers was not all bleak, however. About 20 percent of black farmers managed to buy their own land. Through careful management and extremely hard work, black families planted gardens for household consumption and raised chickens for eggs and meat. Despite its pitfalls, even sharecropping provided a limited measure of independence and allowed some blacks to accumulate small amounts of cash.

Following the war's devastation, many of the South's white small farmers, known as yeomen, also fell into sharecropping. Meanwhile, many planters' sons abandoned farming and became lawyers, bankers, and merchants. Despite these changes, one thing remained the same: White elites ruled over blacks and poor whites, and they kept these two economically exploited groups from uniting by fanning the flames of racial prejudice.

Economic hardship and racial bigotry drove many blacks to leave the South. In 1879 former slaves, known as **Exodusters**, pooled their resources to create land companies and purchase property in Kansas on which to settle. They encouraged an exodus of some 25,000 African Americans from the South. Kansas was ruled by the Republican Party and had been home to the great antislavery martyr John Brown. As one hopeful freedman from

Exodusters   This photograph of two black couples standing on their homestead was taken around 1880 in Nicodemus, Kansas. These settlers, known as Exodusters, had migrated to northwest Kansas following the end of Reconstruction. They sought economic opportunity free from the racial repression sweeping the South. Library of Congress, Prints and Photographs Division [HABS KANS, 33-NICO, 1-6]

Race and Reconstruction

Although the Civil War ended slavery, it left deep and unresolved racial tensions that continued to incite conflict. In the years immediately following the war, freedmen were allowed to vote for representatives and to serve in newly formed southern state governments. These developments outraged many white Confederates who insisted that these governments were corrupt and that blacks were especially vulnerable to graft and manipulation. Many prominent historians accepted such views of postwar southern politics until the 1960s, when a younger generation of scholars argued for a reconsideration of race and Reconstruction. William A. Dunning, a white southern historian, wrote about Reconstruction in 1907, at the height of rigid racial segregation and extreme white supremacy. Fifty-three years later, the African American historian John Hope Franklin writing during the civil rights movement in 1961, reached a very different conclusion about the participation of blacks during Reconstruction. (Until the 1970s, the term *negro* or *Negro* was used by most scholars to denote African American or black.)

Source 14.4

William A. Dunning | Radical Reconstruction, 1907

. . . [T]he southerners felt that the policy of Congress had no real cause save the purpose of radical politicians to prolong and extend their party power by means of negro suffrage. . . . It was as inconceivable to the southerners that rational men of the North should seriously approve of negro suffrage *per se* as it had been in 1860 to the northerners that rational men of the South should approve of secession *per se*.

. . . . The registration of voters was so directed as to insure . . . the fullest enrollment of the blacks and the completest exclusion of disfranchised whites. . . . The result of the elections was a group of constituent assemblies whose unfitness for their task was pitiful. . . . [T]he mass of the delegates consisted of whites and blacks whose ignorance and inexperience in respect to political methods were equaled only by the crudeness and distortion of their ideas as to political and social ends.

. . . . But a solitary chance presented itself of escape from the disasters of negro political supremacy: if the freedmen could be won to look for guidance in their new duties to their old masters, all might yet be well. . . . [However], to the emancipated race all the astounding changes of the recent wonder years had come through other sources, and the vague but intoxicating delights of political privilege must, they felt, be enjoyed under the same auspices that had brought them freedom, schools, and the unlimited indulgence of those weird emotions which they called religion.

Source: William Archibald Dunning, *Reconstruction Political and Economic, 1865–1877* (New York: Harper and Brothers Publishers, 1907), pp. 110–11, 112, 114–15.

Louisiana wrote to the Kansas governor in 1879, "I am anxious to reach your state . . . because of the sacredness of her soil washed in the blood of humanitarians for the cause of black freedom." Yet poor-quality land and unpredictable weather often made farming on the Great Plains hard and unrewarding. Nevertheless, for many black migrants, the chance to own their own land and escape the oppression of the South was worth the hardships. In 1880 the census counted 40,000 blacks living in Kansas.

Source 14.5

John Hope Franklin | The South's New Leaders, 1961

The entrance of Negroes into the political arena was the most revolutionary aspect of the Reconstruction program. Out of a population of approximately four million, some 700,000 qualified as voters, but the most of them were without the qualifications to participate effectively in a democracy. In this they were not unlike the large number of Americans who were enfranchised during the Age of Jackson. . . . None of this is surprising. It had been only two years since emancipation from a system that for more than two centuries had denied slaves most rights as human beings. And it must be remembered that in these two years the former Confederates, in power all over the South, did nothing to promote the social and political education of the former slaves. What is surprising is that there were some—and no paltry number—who in 1867 were able to assume the responsibilities of citizens and leaders.

. . . . One of the really remarkable features of the Negro leadership was the small amount of vindictiveness in their words and their actions. There was no bully, no swagger, as they took their places in the state and federal governments traditionally occupied by the white planters of the South. . . . Negroes generally wished to see political disabilities removed from the whites. . . . Negroes attempted no revolution in the social relations of the races in the South. . . . Nor did any considerable number of Negroes seek to effect an economic revolution in the South.

Source: John Hope Franklin, *Reconstruction After the Civil War* (Chicago: University of Chicago Press, 1961), pp. 86–87, 88, 89–90, 91.

Examine the Sources

1. How do Dunning and Franklin differ in their interpretations of the role played by African Americans during Reconstruction?
2. Drawing on evidence from this chapter, including the Primary Source Project, how would you evaluate the strengths and weaknesses of Dunning's and Franklin's interpretations?

Put It in Context

How might the fact that these interpretations were written fifty-four years apart (1907/1961) influence their conclusions?

White Resistance to Congressional Reconstruction. Despite the Republican record of accomplishment during Reconstruction, white Southerners did not accept its legitimacy. They accused interracial governments of conducting a spending spree that raised taxes and encouraged corruption. Indeed, taxes did rise significantly, but mainly because legislatures funded much-needed educational and social services. Corruption on building projects and railroad construction was common during this time. Still, it is unfair to single out Reconstruction governments and especially black legislators as inherently depraved since their Democratic opponents acted the same way when given the opportunity. Economic scandals were part of American life after the Civil War. As enormous business opportunities arose in the postwar years, many economic and political leaders made unlawful deals to enrich themselves. Furthermore, southern opponents of Reconstruction exaggerated its harshness. In contrast to revolutions and civil wars in other countries, only one rebel was executed for war crimes (the commandant of Andersonville Prison in Georgia); only one high-ranking official went to prison (Jefferson Davis); no official was forced into exile, though some fled voluntarily; and most rebels regained voting rights and the ability to hold office within seven years after the end of the rebellion.

Most important, these Reconstruction governments had only limited opportunities to transform the South. By the end of 1870, civilian rule had returned to all of the former Confederate states, and they had reentered the Union. Republican rule did not continue past 1870 in Virginia, North Carolina, and Tennessee and did not extend beyond 1871 in Georgia and 1873 in Texas. In 1874 Democrats deposed Republicans in Arkansas and Alabama; two years later, Democrats triumphed in Mississippi. In only three states — Louisiana, Florida, and South Carolina — did Reconstruction last until 1877.

The Democrats who replaced Republicans trumpeted their victories as bringing "redemption" to the South. Of course, these so-called **Redeemers** were referring to the white South. For black Republicans and their white allies, redemption meant defeat. Democratic victories came at the ballot boxes, but violence, intimidation, and fraud paved the way. In 1865 in Pulaski, Tennessee General Nathan Bedford Forrest organized Confederate veterans into a social club called the **Knights of the Ku Klux Klan (KKK)**. Spreading throughout the South, its followers donned robes and masks to hide their identities and terrify their victims. Gun-wielding Ku Kluxers rode on horseback to the homes and churches of black and white Republicans to keep them from voting. When threats did not work, they beat and murdered their victims. In 1871, for example, 150 African Americans were killed in Jackson County in the Florida Panhandle. A black clergyman lamented, "That is where Satan has his seat." There and elsewhere, many of the individuals targeted had managed to buy property, gain political leadership, or in other ways defy white stereotypes of African American inferiority. Other white supremacist organizations joined the Klan in waging a reign of terror. During the 1875 election in Mississippi, which toppled the Republican government, armed terrorists killed hundreds of Republicans and scared many more away from the polls.

To combat the terror unleashed by the Klan and its allies, Congress passed three **Force Acts** in 1870 and 1871. These measures empowered the president to dispatch officials into the South to supervise elections and prevent voting interference. Directed specifically at the KKK, one

Ku Klux Klansmen   Photographed wearing their robes and hoods, these Klansmen usually came out under cover of evening darkness to terrorize the freedpeople and keep them politically and economically subservient. The Klan also attacked northern whites (carpetbaggers) and southern white unionists (scalawags) who participated in Reconstruction. Bridgeman Images law barred secret organizations from using force to violate equal protection of the laws. In 1872 Congress established a joint committee to probe Klan tactics, and its investigations produced thirteen volumes of gripping testimony about the horrors perpetrated by the Klan. Elias Hill, a freedman from South Carolina who had become a Baptist preacher and teacher, was one of those who appeared before Congress. He and his brother lived next door to each other. The Klansmen went first to his brother's house, where, as Hill testified, they "broke open the door and attacked his wife, and I heard her screaming and mourning [moaning]. . . . At last I heard them have [rape] her in the yard." When the Klansmen discovered Elias Hill, they dragged him out of his house and beat, whipped, and threatened to kill him. On the basis of such testimony, the federal government prosecuted some 3,000 Klansmen. Only 600 were convicted, however. As the Klan disbanded in the wake of federal prosecutions, other vigilante organizations arose to take its place.

Review & Relate

▌ What role did black people play in remaking southern society during Reconstruction?

▌ How did southern whites fight back against Reconstruction? What role did terrorism and political violence play in this effort?

The **Unraveling** of **Reconstruction**

The violence, intimidation, and fraud perpetrated by white Redeemers does not fully explain the unraveling of Reconstruction. By the early 1870s most white Northerners had come to believe that they had done more than enough for black Southerners, and it was time to focus on other issues. Growing economic problems intensified this feeling. Still reeling from the amount of blood shed during the war, white Americans, north and south, turned their attention toward burying and memorializing the Civil War dead. White America was once again united, if only in the shared belief that it was time to move on, consigning the issues of slavery and civil rights to history.

The Republican Retreat. Most northern whites shared the racial prejudices of their counterparts in the South. Although they had supported protection of black civil rights and suffrage, they still believed that African Americans were inferior to whites and were horrified by the idea of social integration. They began to sympathize with Southern whites' racist complaints that blacks were not capable of governing honestly and effectively.

In 1872 a group calling themselves Liberal Republicans challenged the reelection of President Grant. Financial scandals had racked the Grant administration. This high-level corruption reflected other get-rich-quick schemes connected to economic speculation and development following the Civil War. Outraged by the rising level of immoral behavior in government and business, Liberal Republicans nominated Horace Greeley, editor of the *New York Tribune*, to run against Grant. They linked government corruption to the expansion of federal power that accompanied Reconstruction and called for the removal of troops from the South and amnesty for all former Confederates. They also campaigned for civil service reform, which would base government employment on a merit system and abolish the "spoils system" — in which the party in power rewarded loyal supporters with political appointments — that had been introduced by Andrew Jackson in the 1820s.

The Democratic Party believed that Liberal Republicans offered the best chance to defeat Grant, and it endorsed Greeley. Despite the scandals that surrounded him, Grant remained popular. Moreover, the main body of Republicans "waved the bloody shirt," reminding northern voters that a ballot cast for the opposition tarnished the memory of brave Union soldiers killed during the war. The president won reelection with an even greater margin than he had four years earlier. Nevertheless, the attacks against Grant foreshadowed the Republican retreat on Reconstruction. Among the Democrats sniping at Grant was Andrew Johnson. Johnson had returned to Tennessee, and in 1874 the state legislature chose the former president to serve in the U.S. Senate. He continued to speak out against the presence of federal troops in the South until his death in 1875.

Congressional and Judicial Retreat. By the time Grant began his second term, Congress was already considering bills to restore officeholding rights to former Confederates who had not yet sworn allegiance to the Union. Black representatives, including Georgia congressman Jefferson Long, as well as some white lawmakers, remained opposed to such measures, but in 1872 Congress removed the penalties placed on former Confederates by the Fourteenth Amendment and permitted nearly all rebel leaders the right to vote and hold office. Two years later, for the first time since the start of the Civil War, the Democrats gained a majority in the House of Representatives and prepared to remove the remaining troops from the South.

Republican leaders also rethought their top priority with economic concerns increasingly replacing racial considerations. In 1873 a financial panic resulting from the collapse of the Northern Pacific Railroad triggered a severe economic depression lasting late into the decade. Tens of thousands of unemployed workers across the country worried more about finding jobs than they did about black civil rights. Businessmen, too, were plagued with widespread bankruptcies. When strikes erupted across the country in 1877, most notably the Great Railway Strike, in which more than half a million workers walked off the job, employers asked the U.S. government to remove troops from the South and dispatch them against strikers in the North and West.

While white Northerners sought ways to extricate themselves from Reconstruction, the Supreme Court weakened enforcement of the civil rights acts. In 1873 the *Slaughterhouse* cases defined the rights that African Americans were entitled to under the Fourteenth Amendment very narrowly. Reflecting the shift from moral to economic concerns, the justices interpreted the amendment as extending greater protection to corporations in conducting business than to blacks. As a result, blacks had to depend on southern state governments to protect their civil rights, the same state authorities that had deprived them of their rights in the first place. In *United States v. Cruikshank* (1876), the high court narrowed the Fourteenth Amendment further, ruling that it protected blacks against abuses only by state officials and agencies, not by private groups such as the Ku Klux Klan. Seven years later, the Court struck down the Civil Rights Act of 1875, which had extended "full and equal treatment" in public accommodations for persons of all races.

The Presidential Compromise of 1876. The presidential election of 1876 set in motion events that officially brought Reconstruction to an end. The Republicans nominated the governor of Ohio, Rutherford B. Hayes, who was chosen partly because he was untainted by the corruption that plagued the Grant administration. The Democrats selected their own anticorruption crusader, Governor Samuel J. Tilden of New York.

The outcome of the election depended on twenty disputed electoral votes, nineteen from the South and one from Oregon. Tilden won 51 percent of the popular vote, but Reconstruction political battles in Florida, Louisiana, and South Carolina put the election up for grabs. In each of these states, the outgoing Republican administration certified Hayes as the winner, while the incoming Democratic regime declared for Tilden.

The Constitution assigns Congress the task of counting and certifying the electoral votes submitted by the states. Normally, this is a mere formality, but 1876 was different. Democrats controlled the House, Republicans controlled the Senate, and neither branch would budge on which votes to count. Hayes needed all twenty for victory; Tilden needed only one. To break the logjam, Congress created a fifteen-member Joint Electoral Commission, composed of seven Democrats, seven Republicans, and one independent. Ultimately, a majority voted to count all twenty votes for the Republican Hayes, making him president (Map 14.2).

Still, Congress had to ratify this count, and disgruntled southern Democrats in the Senate threatened a filibuster — unlimited debate — to block certification of Hayes. With the March 4, 1877 date for the presidential inauguration creeping perilously close and no winner officially declared, behind-the-scenes negotiations finally settled the controversy. A series of meetings between Hayes supporters and southern Democrats led to a bargain. According to the agreement, Democrats would support Hayes in exchange for the president appointing a Southerner to his cabinet, withdrawing the last federal troops from the South, and endorsing construction of a transcontinental railroad through the South. This **compromise of 1877** averted a crisis over presidential succession, underscored increased southern Democratic influence within Congress, and marked the end of strong federal protections for African Americans in the South.

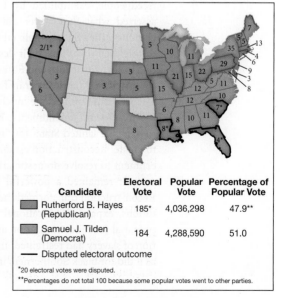

MAP 14.2   The Election of 1876

The presidential election of 1876 got swept up in Reconstruction politics. Democrats defeated Republicans in Florida, Louisiana, and South Carolina, but both parties claimed the electoral votes for their candidates. A federal electoral commission set up to investigate the twenty disputed votes, including one from Oregon, awarded the votes and the election to the Republican, Rutherford B. Hayes.

Candidate	Electoral Vote	Popular Vote	Percentage of Popular Vote
Rutherford B. Hayes (Republican)	185*	4,036,298	47.9**
Samuel J. Tilden (Democrat)	184	4,288,590	51.0

— Disputed electoral outcome

*20 electoral votes were disputed.
**Percentages do not total 100 because some popular votes went to other parties.

Review & Relate

- Why did northern interest in Reconstruction wane in the 1870s?

- What common values and beliefs among white Americans were reflected in the compromise of 1877?

Conclusion: The Legacies of Reconstruction

Reconstruction was, in many ways, profoundly limited. Notwithstanding the efforts of the Freedmen's Bureau, African Americans did not receive the landownership that would have provided them with economic independence and bolstered their freedom from the racist assaults of white Southerners. The civil and political rights that the federal government conferred did not withstand the efforts of former Confederates to disfranchise and deprive the freedpeople of equal rights. The Republican Party shifted its priorities, and Democrats gained enough political power nationally to short-circuit federal intervention, even as numerous problems remained unresolved in the South. Northern support for racial equality did not run very deep, so white Northerners, who shared many of the prejudices of white Southerners, were happy to extricate themselves from further intervention in southern racial matters. Nor was there sufficient support to give women, white or black, the right to vote. Finally, federal courts, with growing concerns over economic rather than social issues, sanctioned Northerners' retreat by providing constitutional legitimacy for abandoning black Southerners and rejecting women's suffrage in court decisions that narrowed the interpretation of the Fourteenth and Fifteenth Amendments.

Despite all of this, Reconstruction did transform the country. As a result of Reconstruction, slavery was abolished and the legal basis for freedom was enshrined in the Constitution. Indeed, blacks exercised a measure of political and economic freedom during Reconstruction that never entirely disappeared over the decades to come. In many areas, freedpeople, exemplified by Congressman Jefferson Franklin Long and many others, asserted what they never could have during slavery—control over their lives, their churches, their labor, their education, and their families. What they could not practice during their own time, their descendants would one day revive through the promises codified in the Fourteenth and Fifteenth Amendments.

African Americans transformed not only themselves; they transformed the nation. The Constitution became much more democratic and egalitarian through inclusion of the Reconstruction amendments. Reconstruction lawmakers took an important step toward making the United States the "more perfect union" that the nation's Founders had pledged to create. Reconstruction established a model for expanding the power of the federal government to resolve domestic crises that lay beyond the abilities of states and ordinary citizens. It remained a powerful legacy for elected officials who dared to invoke it. And Reconstruction transformed the South to its everlasting benefit. It modernized state constitutions, expanded educational and social welfare systems, and unleashed the repressed potential for industrialization and new forms of economic development that the preservation of slavery had restrained. Ironically, Reconstruction did as much for white Southerners as it did for black Southerners in liberating them from the past.

Timeline of Events

1863	Lincoln issues Proclamation of Amnesty and Reconstruction
1865	Ku Klux Klan formed
	Freedmen's Bureau established
	Thirteenth Amendment passed
	Lincoln assassinated; Andrew Johnson becomes president
1866	Freedmen's Bureau and Civil Rights Act extended over Johnson's presidential veto
	Fourteenth Amendment passed
1867	Military Reconstruction Acts
	Command of the Army and Tenure of Office Acts passed
1868	Andrew Johnson impeached
1869	Fifteenth Amendment passed
	Women's suffrage movement splits over support of Fifteenth Amendment
1870	250,000 blacks attend schools established by the Freedmen's Bureau
	Civilian rule returns to the South
1870–1872	Congress takes steps to curb Ku Klux Klan violence in the South
1873	Financial panic sparks depression
1873–1883	Supreme Court limits rights of African Americans
1875	Civil Rights Act passed
1877	Rutherford B. Hayes becomes president
	Reconstruction ends
1879	Black Exodusters migrate from South to Kansas

Key Terms

Freedmen's Bureau, *464*

Proclamation of Amnesty and Reconstruction, *469*

Thirteenth Amendment, *469*

black codes, *471*

Fourteenth Amendment, *472*

Tenure of Office Act, *477*

Fifteenth Amendment, *477*

American Equal Rights Association, *477*

scalawags, *479*

carpetbaggers, *479*

sharecropping, *480*

Exodusters, *481*

Redeemers, *484*

Knights of the Ku Klux Klan (KKK), *484*

Force Acts, *484*

compromise of 1877, *487*

Review & Relate

1. What were freedpeople's highest priorities in the years immediately following the Civil War? Why?

2. How did freedpeople define freedom? What steps did they take to make freedom real for themselves and their children?

3. What was President Johnson's plan for reconstruction? How were his views out of step with those of most Republicans?

4. What characterized congressional Reconstruction? What priorities were reflected in congressional Reconstruction legislation?

5. What role did black people play in remaking southern society during Reconstruction?

6. How did southern whites fight back against Reconstruction? What role did terrorism and political violence play in this effort?

7. Why did northern interest in Reconstruction wane in the 1870s?

8. What common values and beliefs among white Americans were reflected in the compromise of 1877?

Testing and Contesting Freedom

▶ How did blacks and whites view emancipation and what role did the federal government play in overseeing the transition from slavery to freedom?

Nine months after the Civil War ended in April 1865, twenty-seven states ratified the Thirteenth Amendment, abolishing slavery throughout the United States. Freedom, however, did not guarantee equal rights or the absence of racial discrimination. Immediately following the North's victory, white southern leaders enacted black codes, which aimed to prevent freedpeople from improving their social and economic status (Source 14.6). Although Lincoln's successor, Andrew Johnson, did not support the codes, he did nothing to overturn them. A southern advocate of limited government, Johnson clashed repeatedly with Congress over Reconstruction. In 1867 the Republican majority in Congress took control and passed the Military Reconstruction Acts, placing the South under military rule and forcing whites to extend equal political and civil rights to African Americans.

Then in 1870, ratification of the Fifteenth Amendment extended suffrage to black men. In alliance with white Republicans, blacks won election to a variety of public offices, including seats in local and state governments. These interracial legislatures improved conditions for blacks and whites, providing funds for public education, hospitals, and other social services. But their opponents succeeded in tarring them with claims of fraud, corruption, wasteful spending, and "Black Rule" (Sources 14.7 and 14.10). Most newly freed blacks were eager to acquire land so they could support themselves, but many were forced to sign sharecropping agreements with white landowners. Although sharecropping provided some benefits to freed people as well as white landowners, blacks' limited economic and political leverage ensured that these agreements gave more authority to landowners than laborers (Sources 14.7 and 14.8).

By the mid-1870s, many white Northerners sought reconciliation rather than continued conflict while southern whites created vigilante groups like the Ku Klux Klan that used violence to intimidate black and white Republicans. By the mid-1870s, northern magazines as well as southern newspapers began challenging black political rule, further isolating blacks from popular and government support (Sources 14.9 and 14.10). Ultimately, the withdrawal of federal oversight crushed southern Republicanism, leaving African Americans struggling to retain the freedoms they had supposedly gained.

Source 14.6

Mississippi Black Code, 1865

Southern legislatures created black codes primarily to limit the rights of free blacks after emancipation and return them to a condition as close as possible to slavery. Mississippi was one of the first states to enact a black code. Although its laws did legalize marriage for blacks and allowed them to own property and testify in court, its primary intent was to limit freedpeople's mobility and economic opportunities.

An Act to Confer Civil Rights on Freedmen, and for other Purposes . . .

Section 2. All freedmen, free negroes and mulattoes may intermarry with each other, in the same manner and under the same regulations that are provided by law for white persons: Provided, that the clerk of probate shall keep separate records of the same.

Section 3. All freedmen, free negroes or mulattoes who do now and have herebefore lived and cohabited together as husband and wife shall be taken and held in law as legally married, and the issue shall be taken and held as legitimate for all purposes; and it shall not be lawful for any freedman, free negro or mulatto to intermarry with any white person; nor for any person to intermarry with any freedman, free negro or mulatto; and any person who shall so intermarry shall be deemed guilty of felony, and on conviction thereof shall be confined in the State penitentiary for life; and those shall be deemed freedmen, free negroes and mulattoes who are of pure negro blood, and those descended from a negro to the third generation, inclusive, though one ancestor in each generation may have been a white person.

Section 4. In addition to cases in which freedmen, free negroes and mulattoes are now by law competent witnesses, freedmen, free negroes or mulattoes shall be competent in civil cases, when a party or parties to the suit, either plaintiff or plaintiffs, defendant or defendants; also in cases where freedmen, free negroes and mulattoes is or are either plaintiff or plaintiffs, defendant or defendants. They shall also be competent witnesses in all criminal prosecutions where the crime charged is alleged to have been committed by a white person upon or against the person or property of a freedman, free negro or mulatto. . . .

An Act to Amend the Vagrant Laws of the State . . .

Section 2. All freedmen, free negroes and mulattoes in this State, over the age of eighteen years, found on the second Monday in January, 1866, or thereafter, with no lawful employment or business, or found unlawful[ly] assembling themselves together, either in the day or night time, and all white persons assembling themselves with freedmen, free negroes or mulattoes, or usually associating with freedmen, free negroes or mulattoes, on terms of equality, or living in adultery or fornication with a freed woman, freed negro or mulatto, shall be deemed vagrants, and on conviction thereof shall be fined in a sum not exceeding, in the case of a freedman, free negro or mulatto, fifty dollars, and a white man two hundred dollars, and imprisonment at the discretion of the court, the free negro not exceeding ten days, and the white man not exceeding six months. . . .

Section 6. The same duties and liabilities existing among white persons of this State shall attach to freedmen, free negroes or mulattoes, to support their indigent families and all colored paupers; and that in order to secure a support for such indigent freedmen, free negroes, or mulattoes, it shall be lawful, and is hereby made the duty of the county police of each county in this State, to levy a poll or capitation tax on each and every freedman, free negro, or mulatto, between the ages of eighteen and sixty years, not to exceed the sum of one dollar annually to each person so taxed, which tax, when collected, shall be paid into the county treasurer's hands, and constitute a fund to be called the Freedman's Pauper Fund, . . . for the maintenance of the poor of the freedmen, free negroes and mulattoes of this State.

Source: *Laws of the State of Mississippi, Passed at a Regular Session of the Mississippi Legislature, Held in the City of Jackson, October, November, and December, 1865* (Jackson, MS, 1866), 82–86, 165–67.

Source 14.7

Richard H. Cain | Federal Aid for Land Purchase, 1868

Richard H. Cain, a free black minister raised in Ohio, went to South Carolina after the war and served as a Republican member of the U.S. House of Representatives for two terms in the 1870s. The following excerpt comes from a speech Cain made in 1868 as a representative to the South Carolina constitutional convention. Cain proposed that the convention petition Congress for a $1 million loan to purchase land that could be resold to freedmen at a reasonable price.

believe the best measure to be adopted is to bring capital to the State, and instead of causing revenge and unpleasantness, I am for even-handed justice. I am for allowing the parties who own lands to bring them into the market and sell them upon such terms as will be satisfactory to both sides. I believe a measure of this kind has a double effect: first, it brings capital, what the people want; second, it puts the people to work; it gives homesteads, what we need; it relieves the Government and takes away its responsibility of feeding the people; it inspires every man with a noble manfulness, and by the thought that he is the possessor of something in the State; it adds also to the revenue of the country. By these means men become interested in the country as they never were before. . . . I will also guarantee that after one year's time, the Freedman's Bureau will not have to give any man having one acre of land anything to eat.

Source: *Proceedings of the South Carolina Constitutional Convention of 1868* (Charleston, SC, 1868), 420–21.

Source 14.8

Willis B. Bocock and Black Laborers | Sharecropping Agreement, 1870

Because Congress did not generally provide freedpeople with land, African Americans lacked the means to start their own farms. At the same time, plantation owners needed labor now that slavery was abolished. Out of mutual necessity, white plantation owners such as Willis B. Bocock entered into sharecropping agreements with blacks to work their farms in exchange for a portion of the crop. Several of the blacks who signed this agreement had previously been enslaved to Bocock.

Contract made the 3rd day of January in the year 1870 between us the free people who have signed this paper of one part, and our employer, Willis P. Bocock, of the other part. . . . We are to furnish the necessary labor . . . and are to have all proper work done, ditching, fencing, repairing, etc., as well as cultivating and saving the crops of all

kinds, so as to put and keep the land we occupy and tend in good order for cropping, and to make a good crop ourselves; and to do our fair share of job work about the place. . . . We are to be responsible for the good conduct of ourselves, our hands, and families, and agree that all shall be respectful to employer, owners, and manager, honest, industrious, and careful about every thing . . . and then our employer agrees that he and his manager shall treat us kindly, and help us to study our interest and do our duty. If any hand or family proves to be of bad character, or dishonest, or lazy, or disobedient, or any way unsuitable our employer or manager has the right, and we have the right, to have such turned off. . . .

For the labor and services of ourselves and hands rendered as above stated, we are to have one third part of all the crops, or their net-proceeds, made and secured, or prepared for market by our force. . . .

We are to be furnished by our employer through his manager with provisions if we call for them . . . to be charged to us at fair market prices.

And whatever may be due by us, or our hands to our employer for provisions or any thing else, during the year, is to be a lien on our share of the crops, and is to be retained by him out of the same before we receive our part.

Source: Waldwick Plantation Records, 1834–1971, LPR174, box 1, folder 9, Alabama Department of Archives and History.

Source 14.9

Ellen Parton | Testimony on Klan Violence, 1871

In March 1871, white mobs killed some thirty African Americans in Meridian, Mississippi. Later that month, a joint committee of the United States Congress held hearings on the violence, which included the following testimony by Ellen Parton of Mississippi, a former slave and domestic worker. The Klan suspected that Parton's husband was involved in the Union League, a southern affiliate of the Republican Party. Congress also conducted hearings on the vigilante violence against blacks throughout the South.

Ellen Parton, being sworn, states:

I reside in Meridian; have resided here nine years; occupation, washing and ironing and scouring; Wednesday night was the last night they came to my house; by "they" I mean bodies or companies of men; they came on Monday, Tuesday, and Wednesday. On Monday night they said that they came to do us no harm. On Tuesday night they said they came for the arms; I told them there was none, and they said they would take my word for it. On Wednesday night they came and broke open the wardrobe and trunks, and committed rape upon me; there were eight of them in the house; I do not know how many there were outside; they were white men; there was a light in the house; I was living in Marshal Ware's house; there were three lights burning. Mr. Ware has been one of the policemen of this town. He was concealed at the time they came; they took the claw hammer and broke open the pantry where he was lying; he was concealed in the pantry under some plunder, covered up well; I guess he covered himself up. A man said "here is Marshal's hat, where is Marshal?" I told him "I did not know"; they went then into everything in the house, and broke open the wardrobe; I called upon Mr. Mike Slamon, who was one of the crowd, for protection; I said to him "please protect me tonight, you have known me for a long time." This man covered up his head then; he had a hold of me at this time; Mr. Slamon had an oil-cloth and put it before his face, trying to conceal himself, and the man that had hold of me told me not to call Mr. Slamon's name any more. He then took me in the dining room, and told me that I had to do just what he said: I told him I could do nothing of that sort; that was not my way, and he replied "by God, you have got to," and then threw me down. This man had a black eye, where some one had beaten him; he had a black velvet cap on. After he got through with me he came through the house, and said that he was after the Union Leagues; I yielded to him because he had a pistol drawn; when he took me down he hurt me of course; I yielded to him on that account.

Source: *Report of the Joint Select Committee [of Congress] to Inquire into the Condition of Affairs in the Late Insurrectionary States, Mississippi* (Washington, DC: Government Printing Office, 1872), 1:38–39.

Source 14.10

Thomas Nast | *Colored Rule in a Reconstructed (?) State*, 1874

Thomas Nast began drawing for the popular magazine *Harper's Weekly* in 1859. Nast initially used his illustrations to rouse northern public sentiment for the plight of blacks in the South after the Civil War. By 1874, however, many Northerners had become disillusioned with federal efforts to enforce Reconstruction. Like them, Nast accepted the white southern point of view that "Black Reconstruction" was a recipe for corruption and immorality. The figure of Columbia (at the top right) represents the nation, and the caption captures the view of many Northerners by 1874: "You are Aping the lowest Whites. If you disgrace your Race in this way you had better take Back Seats."

COLORED RULE IN A RECONSTRUCTED (?) STATE.—[See Page 244.]
[THE NEGROES CALL EACH OTHER THIEVES, LIARS, RASCALS AND COWARDS.]
COLUMBIA. "You are Aping the lowest Whites. If you disgrace your Race in this way you had better take Back Seats."

Library of Congress, Prints and Photographs Division, Washington, D.C. [LC-USZ62-102256]

Interpret the Evidence

1. How did black codes and sharecropping agreements (Sources 14.6 and 14.8) attempt to reimpose bondage on the formerly enslaved? How did they differ from pre-Civil War slave laws?

2. Why did freedpeople consider property holding a fundamental right and to what extent did sharecropping agreements allow them to gain some economic benefits from their labor (Sources 14.7 and 14.8)?

3. Contrast the image of South Carolina's black politicians presented in Richard Cain's speech (Source 14.7) and Thomas Nast's cartoon (Source 14.10). What does Nast's cartoon suggest about white northern attitudes toward freedpeople in the South by 1874?

4. Despite the fear and physical danger caused by the Ku Klux Klan, what does the testimony of Ellen Parton (Source 14.9) reveal about black attempts to resist it?

Put It in Context

How much did Reconstruction transform the South and the nation?

What were the greatest limitations of federal Reconstruction policies and the greatest challenges to implementing them?

The West

1865–1896

Window to the Past

Buffalo Hunting, c. 1875

This image of a buffalo (bison) hunt was rendered on a buffalo hide. Buffalo were an important resource for Native Americans on the Great Plains, and the decline of this resource at the hands of white settlers not only changed the landscape of the West but also irreparably changed the lives of the Indians who lived there. ▶ **To learn more about this primary source, see Source 15.1 on page 504.**

Werner Forman/TopFoto

After reading this chapter you will be able to:

- Analyze the motives and incentives that led to settling of the trans-Mississippi West and the technological developments that encouraged it.

- Evaluate the strategies used by the U.S. government to control the lives of Native Americans in the West and Indians' reactions to these efforts.

- Compare the roles of the mining and lumber industries in the economic and social development of the West.

- Summarize the factors that led to the rise of commercial ranching and contrast the image of life in the West for ranchers and farmers with the reality.

- Analyze the cultural diversity of the far West and the ethnic tensions that followed from this diversity.

Comparing American Histories

Born in 1860, Phoebe Ann Moses grew up east of the Mississippi, seventy miles north of Cincinnati, Ohio. One of seven surviving children, she was sent to an orphanage at the age of nine, after her father died and her mother could not care for all her children. After working for a farm family, she ran away at the age of twelve and found a new home with a recently remarried widow. There, Phoebe Ann learned to ride and hunt and became an expert shot with a rifle. At fifteen, she entered a shooting contest and defeated a professional marksman, Frank Butler. The two married in 1876. Phoebe Ann changed her

(*left*) **Annie Oakley** Yale Collection of Western Americana, Beinecke Rare Book and Manuscript Library, Yale University

(*right*) **Geronimo** Library of Congress, Prints and Photographs Division [LC-USZ62-124560]

professional name to "**Annie Oakley**," and she and Butler toured the Midwest in an act that featured precision shooting.

In 1884 Oakley and Butler met William F. "Buffalo Bill" Cody in New Orleans. In 1883, as the western frontier began to recede and the U.S. government relocated Native Americans who lived there, Cody attempted to recapture and reinvent the frontier experience by staging "Wild West" shows. A year later, he hired Oakley, with Butler serving as her manager. For the next fifteen years, Oakley was the star of the show. Wearing a fringed skirt, an embroidered blouse, and a broad felt hat, she stood atop her horse and performed amazing feats of marksmanship. Oakley toured Europe and fascinated heads of state and audiences alike with her version of "western authenticity." Fans at home and overseas displayed great nostalgia for a fast-diminishing era. When the census of 1890 reported that no open land was left to settle and thus no western frontier was left to conquer, Oakley's popularity soared. She continued performing in Wild West shows until her death in 1926.

While Annie Oakley portrayed the Wild West, **Geronimo** had lived it. Born to a Chiricahua Apache family in what was then northern Mexico (present-day Arizona and New Mexico), Geronimo led Apaches in a constant struggle against Spain, Mexico, and the United States. In 1851 a band of Mexicans raided an Apache camp, murdering Geronimo's mother, wife, and three children. After fighting Mexicans, Geronimo clashed with U.S. troops and evaded capture until 1877, when an Indian agent arrested him in New Mexico. Sent to a reservation, Geronimo escaped and for eight years engaged in daring raids against his foes. In 1886 two Chiricahua scouts led the U.S. military to Geronimo. Against an army of five thousand soldiers, the Apache warrior, with a band of eighteen fighters and some women and children, finally surrendered and was eventually relocated by the U.S. government to Fort Sill, Oklahoma.

The once-elusive warrior decided to take advantage of his legendary reputation and America's growing fascination with the mythic West. He sold photos of himself and pieces of his clothing; he appeared at the 1904 World's Fair in St. Louis, selling bows and arrows and autographs; and in 1905 he rode in President Theodore Roosevelt's inaugural parade as an example of a "tamed" Indian. Despite all of this, Geronimo never gave up the idea of returning to his birthplace. As long as the U.S. government prohibited him from going back to his ancestral lands in the Southwest, he considered himself a "prisoner of war." And so he remained until his death in 1909. ■

The American histories of Annie Oakley and Geronimo were profoundly different, yet they both contributed to the creation of a shared story, the myth of the American West. The West has great fascination in American culture. Stories about the frontier have romanticized both cowboys and Indians. These stories have also glorified individualism, self-help, and American ingenuity and minimized cooperation, organization, and the role of foreign influence in developing the West. As the American histories of Annie Oakley and Geronimo make clear, reality presents a more complicated picture of a diverse region initially inhabited by native peoples who were pushed aside by the arrival of white settlers and immigrants. In the areas known as the Great Plains and the far West, women took on new roles, and new cities emerged to accommodate the influx of miners, ranchers, and farmers.

Opening the West

The area west of the Mississippi was not hospitable to farmers and other adventurers lured by the appeal of cheap land and a fresh start. These pioneers demonstrated rugged determination; however, they could not have settled the West on their own. Federal policy and foreign investment played a large role in encouraging and financing the development of the West. Railroads were essential in transforming the region (Map 15.1).

The Great Plains. In the mid-nineteenth century, the western frontier lay in the **Great Plains**. Lying on both sides of the Rocky Mountains, the Great Plains plateau was a semiarid territory with an average yearly rainfall sufficient to sustain short grasslands but not many trees. Prospects for sedentary farmers in this dry region did not appear promising. In 1878 geologist John Wesley Powell issued a report that questioned whether the land beyond the easternmost portion of the Great Plains could support small farming. Lack of rainfall, he argued, would make it difficult or even impossible for homesteaders to support themselves on family farms of 160 acres. Instead, he recommended that for the plains to prove economically sustainable, settlers would have to work much larger stretches of land, around 2,560 acres (4 square miles). This would provide ample room to raise livestock under dry conditions.

Powell's words of caution did little to dissuade Americans who intended to pursue Thomas Jefferson's vision of small farmers who would populate U.S. territories and demonstrate democratic values. Rejecting the idea that the Great Plains should remain a "perpetual desert," Charles Dana Wilber, a land speculator and journalist, asserted that "in reality there is no desert anywhere except by man's permission or neglect." Along with millions of others, he had great faith in Americans' ability to turn the Great Plains into a place where Jefferson's republican vision could take root and prosper.

MAP 15.1 The American West, 1860–1900

Railroads played a key role in the expansion and settlement of the American West. The network of railroads running throughout the West opened the way for extensive migration from the East and for the development of a national market. None of this would have been possible without the land grants provided to the railroads by the U.S. government.

Federal Policy and Foreign Investment.

Despite the popular association of the West with individual initiative and self-sufficiency, the federal government played a huge role in facilitating the settlement of the West. National lawmakers enacted legislation offering free or cheap land to settlers and to mining, lumber, and railroad companies. The U.S. government also provided subsidies for transporting mail and military supplies, recruited soldiers to subdue Indian people who stood in the way of expansion, and appointed officials to govern the territories. Through these efforts, the government provided a necessary measure of safety and stability for new businesses to start up and grow as well as interconnected transportation and communication systems to supply workers and promote opportunities to develop new markets across North America.

Along with federal policy, foreign investment helped fuel development of the West. Lacking sufficient funds of its own, the United States turned to Europe to finance the sale of public bonds and private securities. European firms also invested in American mines, with the British leading the way. The development of the western cattle range — the symbol of

[handwritten margin notes: "Federal support" with arrow pointing down; "International investment"]

FIGURE 15.1 British Foreign Investment in the United States, 1876

British investment was an important source of funding for westward expansion following the Civil War. Nearly half of all British loans went toward financing railroad construction, which required large capital expenditures. The British also invested heavily in government bonds and to a lesser extent in cattle ranching and mining enterprises. Why did American railroads attract so much British investment?

Source: Data from Mina Wilkins, *The History of Foreign Investment in the United States to 1914* (Cambridge, MA: Harvard University Press, 1989), 164.

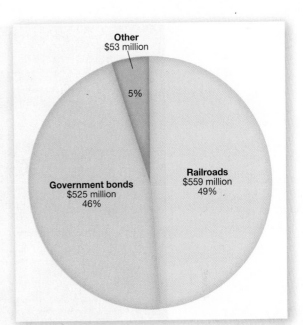

the American frontier and the heroic cowboy — was also funded by overseas financiers. At the height of the cattle boom in the 1880s, British firms supplied some $45 million to underwrite ranch operations. The largest share of money, however, that flowed from Europe to the United States came with the expansion of the railroads, the most important ingredient in opening the West (Figure 15.1).   ↳ *communication and transport*

The **transcontinental railroad** became the gateway to the West. In 1862 the Republican-led Congress appropriated vast areas of land that railroad companies could use to lay their tracks or sell to raise funds for construction. The Central Pacific Company built from west to east, starting in Sacramento, California. The construction project attracted thousands of Chinese railroad workers. From the opposite direction, the Union Pacific Company began laying track in Council Bluffs, Iowa, and hired primarily Irish workers. In May 1869, the Central Pacific and Union Pacific crews met at Promontory Point, Utah. Workmen from the two companies drove a golden spike to complete the connection. For many Americans recovering from four years of civil war and still embroiled in southern reconstruction, the completion of the transcontinental railroad renewed their faith in the nation's ingenuity and destiny. A wagon train had once taken six to eight weeks to travel across the West. That trip could now be completed by rail in seven days. The railroad allowed both people and goods to move faster and in greater numbers than before. The West was now open not just to rugged pioneers but to anyone who could afford a railroad ticket.

The building of the railroads also provided new business opportunities, albeit more questionable. For example, Union Pacific promoters created a fake construction company called the Crédit Mobilier, which they used to funnel government bond and contract money into their own pockets. They also bribed congressmen to avoid investigation into their sordid dealings. Despite these efforts, in 1872 Congress exposed this corruption.

John Gast's "American Progress," 1872 This is a lithograph of an 1872 oil painting by John Gast. Published in 1873, this print depicts a female figure, representing America, leading pioneers westward, as they travel on foot, in a stagecoach, conestoga wagon, and by railroad, where they encounter Native Americans and herds of bison. This mythical version of westward expansion leaves out the role played by the government, corporations, and the military in paving the way for settlers to follow. Library of Congress, 09855

Review & Relate

- What role did the federal government play in opening the West to settlement and economic exploitation?

- Explain the determination of Americans to settle in land west of the Mississippi River despite the challenges the region presented.

Indians and Resistance to Expansion

American pioneers may have thought they were moving into a wilderness, but the West was home to large numbers of American Indians. Before pioneers and entrepreneurs could go west to pursue their economic dreams, the U.S. government would decide to remove this obstacle to American expansion. Through treaties — most of which Americans broke — and war, white Americans conquered the Indian tribes inhabiting the Great Plains during the nineteenth century. After the native population was largely subdued, those who wanted to reform Indian policy focused on carving up tribal lands and forcing Indians to assimilate into American society.

Indian Civilizations.

Indian Civilizations. Long before white settlers appeared, the frontier was already home to diverse peoples. The many native groups who inhabited the West spoke distinct languages, engaged in different economic activities, and competed with one another for power and resources. The descendants of Spanish conquistadors had also lived in the Southwest and California since the late sixteenth century, pushing the boundaries of the Spanish empire northward from Mexico. Indeed, Spaniards established the city of Santa Fe as the territorial capital of New Mexico years before the English landed at Jamestown, Virginia in 1607.

By the end of the Civil War, around 350,000 Indians were living west of the Mississippi. They constituted the surviving remnants of the 1 million people who had occupied the land for thousands of years before Europeans set foot in America. Nez Percé, Ute, and Shoshone Indians lived in the Northwest and the Rocky Mountain region; Lakota, Cheyenne, Blackfoot, Crow, and Arapaho tribes occupied the vast expanse of the central and northern plains; and Apaches, Comanches, Kiowas, Navajos, and Pueblos made up the bulk of the population in the Southwest. Some of the tribes, such as the Cherokee, Creek, and Shawnee, had been forcibly removed from the East during Andrew Jackson's presidency in the 1830s.

Indian tribes each adapted in unique ways to the geography and climate of their home territories, spoke their own language, and had their own history and traditions. Some were hunters, others farmers; some nomadic, others sedentary. In New Mexico, for example, Apaches were expert horsemen and fierce warriors, while the Pueblo Indians built homes out of adobe and developed a flourishing system of agriculture. Also, they cultivated the land through methods of irrigation that foreshadowed modern practices. The Pawnees in the Great Plains periodically set fire to the land to improve game hunting and the growth of vegetation. Indians on the southern plains gradually became enmeshed in the market economy for bison robes, which they sold to American traders (Map 15.2).

The lives of all Indian peoples were affected by the arrival of Europeans, but the consequences of cross-cultural contact varied considerably depending on the circumstances of each tribe. Whites trampled on Indian hunting grounds, polluted streams with acid run-off from mines, and introduced Indians to liquor. They inflicted the greatest damage through diseases for which Indians lacked the immunity that Europeans and white Americans had acquired. By 1870, smallpox had wiped out half the population of Plains Indians, and cholera, diphtheria, and measles caused serious but lesser harm. Nomadic tribes such as the Lakota Sioux were able to flee the contagion, while agrarian tribes such as the Mandan suffered extreme losses. As a result, the balance of power among Plains tribes shifted to the more mobile Sioux. Indians engaged in warfare with their enemies in disputes over hunting grounds, horses, and honor. However, the introduction of guns by European and American traders transformed Indian warfare into a much more deadly affair than had existed previously. And by the mid-nineteenth century, some tribes had become so deeply engaged in the commercial fur trade with whites that they had depleted their own hunting grounds.

Indian peoples taught their customs, which they considered divinely inspired, to their children in systematic fashion. Ancestral worship played a large part in this education. Mothers recounted to their children tales of heroic ancestors they wished them to emulate. The young learned their lessons through an array of songs, ceremonies, myths, and true stories.

Native Americans had their own approach toward nature and the land they inhabited. Most tribes did not accept private ownership of land, as whites did. Indians recognized the

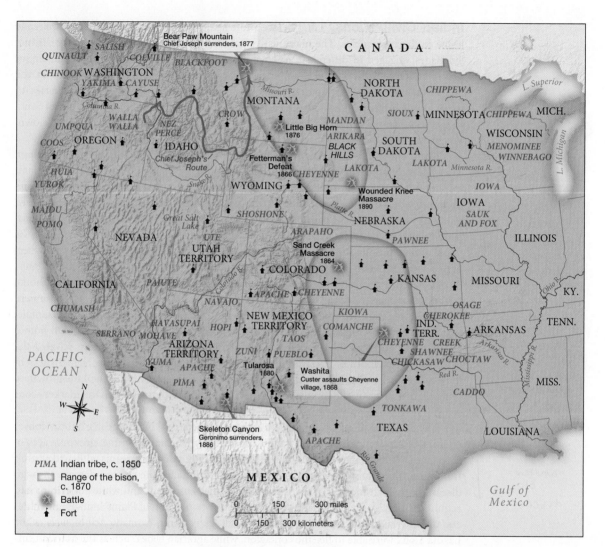

MAP 15.2 The Indian Frontier, 1870

Western migration posed a threat to the dozens of Indian tribes and the immense herds of bison in the region. The tribes had signed treaties with the U.S. government recognizing the right to live on their lands. The presence of U.S. forts did not protect the Indians from settlers who invaded their territories.

relationship w/ environment

concept of private property in ownership of their horses, weapons, tools, and shelters, but they viewed the land as the common domain of their tribe, for use by all members. "The White man knows how to make everything," the Hunkpapa Lakota chieftain Sitting Bull remarked, "but he does not know how to distribute it." This communitarian outlook also reflected native attitudes toward the environment. Indians considered human beings not as superior to the rest of nature's creations, but rather as part of an interconnected world of animals, plants, and natural elements.

assimilation into american culture

Bison (commonly known as buffalo) played a central role in the religion and society of many Indian tribes. By the mid-nineteenth century, approximately thirty million bison grazed on the Great Plains. Before acquiring guns, Indians used a variety of means to hunt their prey, including bows and arrows and spears. Some rode their horses to chase bison and stampede them over cliffs. The meat from the buffalo provided food; its hide provided material to construct tepees and make blankets and clothes; bones were crafted into tools, knives, and weapons; dried bison dung served as an excellent source of fuel. The Plains Indians dressed up in colorful outfits, painted their bodies, and danced to the almighty power of the buffalo and the spiritual presence within it. → *connection w/ nature*

> **Explore ▶**
>
> See Source 15.1 for a depiction of buffalo hunting.

Indian hunting societies, such as the Lakota Sioux and Apache, contained gender distinctions. The task of riding horses to hunt bison became men's work; women then prepared the buffalo hides when the hunters returned. Women saw themselves as an integral part of providing food, shelter, and clothing for the members of their tribe. Similarly, the religious belief that the spiritual world touched every aspect of the material world gave women an opportunity to experience this transcendent power without the mediation of male leaders.

Federal Policy toward Indians before 1870.

Initially, the U.S. government treated western Indians as autonomous nations and recognized their stewardship over the land they occupied. In 1851 the **Treaty of Fort Laramie** confined tribes on the northern plains to designated areas in an attempt to keep white settlers from encroaching on their land. A treaty two years later applied these terms to tribes on the southern plains. Indians kept their part of the agreement, but white miners did not. They roamed through Indian hunting grounds in search of ore and faced little government enforcement of the existing treaties. In fact, the U.S. military made matters considerably worse. On November 29, 1864, a peaceful band of 700 Cheyennes and Arapahos under the leadership of Chief Black Kettle gathered at Sand Creek, Colorado, supposedly under guarantees of U.S. protection. Instead, Colonel John M. Chivington and his troops launched an attack, despite a white flag of surrender hoisted by the Indians, and brutally killed some 270 Indians, mainly women and children. A congressional investigation later determined that the victims "were mutilated in the most horrible manner." Although there was considerable public outcry over the incident, the government did nothing to increase enforcement of its treaty obligations. In almost all disputes between white settlers and Indians, the government sided with the whites, regardless of the Indians' legal rights. In 1867, the government signed the **Treaty of Medicine Lodge**, which provided reservation lands for the Comanche, Kiowa-Apache, and Southern Arapaho to settle. Despite this agreement, white hunters soon invaded this territory and decimated the buffalo herds.

bad faith treaties

terrorizing Indian tribes

The duplicity of the U.S. government had consequences for tribes' relationships among each other. The Sand Creek massacre unleashed Indian wars throughout the central plains, where the Lakota Sioux led the resistance from 1865 to 1868. After two years of fierce fighting, both sides signed a second Treaty of Fort Laramie, which gave northern tribes control over the "Great Reservation" set aside in parts of present-day Montana, Wyoming, North Dakota, and South Dakota. Another treaty placed the southern tribes in a reservation carved out of western Oklahoma. Meanwhile, the government recognized no differences among the tribes. In issuing his annual report in 1868, the Commissioner of Indian Affairs recommended that the Indians' "barbaric dialects should be blotted out and the English language substituted" in order to "fuse" different tribes "into one homogeneous mass."

Source 15.1

Buffalo Hunting, c. 1875

This pictograph from around 1875 portrays a Shoshone man on a buffalo hunt. This drawing was made on a buffalo skin robe quilled by a tribal woman and worn by a hunter.

Why do you think the person who made this drawing placed such a design on the robe?

What evidence appears to show this Indian has made use of some items from the culture of white settlers?

Why is the buffalo drawn so much larger than the Indian on his horse?

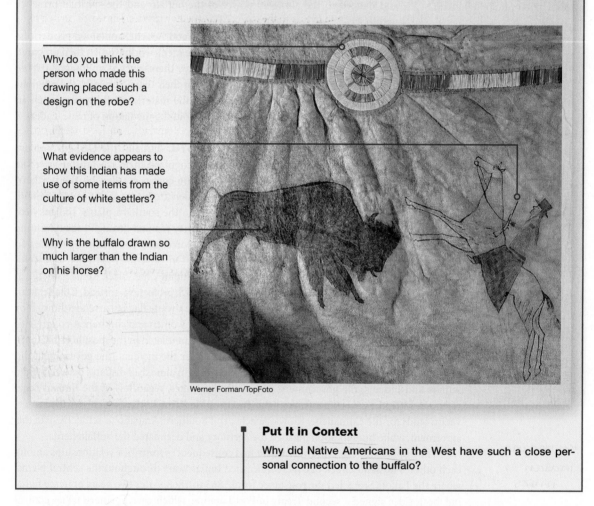

Werner Forman/TopFoto

▌ **Put It in Context**

Why did Native Americans in the West have such a close personal connection to the buffalo?

Reconstruction and Indians   Much of federal policy toward Indians was shaped during the period of Reconstruction (see Chapter 14). When Ulysses S. Grant became president in 1869, he endorsed the passage of the Fifteenth Amendment and pledged to support the goals of the Military Reconstruction Act in the South. His next priority, he declared in his inaugural address, was "the proper treatment of the original occupants of this land — the Indians." He went on to affirm, "I will favor any course toward them which tends to their civilization and ultimate citizenship." However, Indians in the West did not receive any of

gives Americans agency

the benefits granted by the post–Civil War Thirteenth, Fourteenth, and Fifteenth Amendments. In fact, the Fourteenth Amendment excluded from citizenship tribal Indians.

Despite President Grant's hopeful message, Indian Reconstruction sought to destroy and subjugate native tribes. The Nez Perce tribe was coerced to sign a treaty ceding most of its land to the United States. Intending to flee to Canada, Chief Joseph led the Nez Percé out of the Pacific Northwest in 1877 in a daring march of 1,400 miles as federal troops pursued them. The Nez Percé were finally intercepted in the mountains of northern Montana, just thirty miles from the border. Subsequently, the government relocated them to the southwestern territory of Oklahoma. In 1879 Chief Joseph pleaded with lawmakers in Congress to return his people to their home and urged the U.S. government to live up to the original intent of the treaties. His words carried some weight, and the Nez Percé returned under armed escort to a reservation in Washington.

The treaties did not produce a lasting peace. Though most of the tribes relocated onto reservations, some refused. The Apache chief Victorio explained why he would not resettle his people on a reservation. "We prefer to die in our own land under the tall cool pines," he declared. "We will leave our bones with those of our people. It is better to die fighting than to starve." General William Tecumseh Sherman, commander of the military forces against the Indians, ordered the army to wage a merciless war of annihilation "against all hostile Indians till they are obliterated or beg for mercy." In November 1868, Lieutenant Colonel George Armstrong Custer took Sherman at his word and assaulted a Cheyenne village, killing more than one hundred Indians. Nearly a decade later, in 1876, the Indians, this time Lakota Sioux, exacted revenge by killing Custer and his troops at the **Battle of the Little Big Horn** in Montana. Yet this proved to be the final victory for the Lakota nation, as the army mounted an extensive and fierce offensive against them that shattered their resistance.

Indian Drawing of Battle of Little Big Horn   This ink-on-paper drawing by Amos Bad Heart Buffalo (1869–1913) depicts the June 1876 Battle of Little Big Horn, also known as Custer's Last Stand. It portrays the retreat of Major Marcus Reno's forces. The painted warrior on the white horse who is shooting a soldier from his saddle is Crazy Horse, the Sioux chieftain. The Stapleton Collection/Bridgeman Images

Among the troops that battled the Indians were African Americans. Known as **buffalo soldiers**, they represented a cross section of the postwar black population looking for new opportunities that were now available after their emancipation. Some blacks enlisted to learn how to read and write; others sought to avoid unpleasant situations back home. In 1875, the army had around 25,500 men, and African Americans comprised about 10 percent of the regular army and about 20 percent of the cavalry. As was the practice during the Civil War, black soldiers served in segregated units under white commanders. A few gained more glory than money. In May 1880, Sergeant George Jordan of the Ninth Cavalry led troops under his command to fend off Apache raids in Tularosa, New Mexico, for which he was awarded the Congressional Medal of Honor.

opportunity

Indian Defeat.

By the late 1870s, Indians had largely succumbed to U.S. military supremacy. The tribes contained agile horsemen and skilled warriors, but the U.S. army was backed by the power of an increasingly industrial economy. Telegraph lines and railroads provided logistical advantages in the swift deployment of U.S. troops and the ability of the central command to communicate with field officers. Although Indians had acquired firearms, the army boasted an essentially unlimited supply of superior weapons. The diversity of Indians and historic rivalries among tribes also made it difficult for them to unite against their common enemy. The federal government exploited these divisions by hiring Indians to serve as army scouts against their traditional tribal foes. **See Primary Source Project 15: American Indians and Whites in the West, page 526.**

US → industrial military

The wholesale destruction of the bison was the final blow to Indian independence. As railroads pushed their tracks beyond the Mississippi, they cleared bison from their path by sending in professional hunters with high-powered rifles to shoot the animals. At the same time, buffalo products such as shoes, coats, and hats became fashionable in the East. By the mid-1880s, hunters had killed more than thirteen million bison. As a result of the relentless move of white Americans westward and conspicuous consumption back east, bison herds were almost annihilated.

Faced with decimation of the bison, broken treaties, and their opponents' superior military technology, Native Americans' capacity to wage war collapsed. Indians had little choice but to settle on shrinking reservations that the government established for them. The absence of war, however, did not bring them security. In the late 1870s, gold discoveries in the Black Hills of North Dakota ignited another furious rush by miners onto lands supposedly guaranteed to the Lakota people. Rather than honoring its treaties, the U.S. government forced the tribes to relinquish still more land. General Custer's Seventh Cavalry was part of the military force trying to push Indians out of this mining region, when it was annihilated at the Little Big Horn in 1876. Elsewhere, Congress opened up a portion of western Oklahoma to white homesteaders in 1889. Although this land had not been assigned to specific tribes relocated in Indian Territory, more than eighty thousand Indians from various tribes lived there. This government-sanctioned land rush opened the door for whites to acquire more land at the expense of the Indians. A decade later, Congress officially ended Indian control of Indian Territory.

loss of power

To add to the humiliation of Native Americans, the U.S. Supreme Court ruled in *Elk v. Wilkins* (1884) that although Indians were born in the United States, they were not entitled to citizenship under the Fourteenth Amendment. A Winnebago Indian born on a reservation, John Elk moved to Omaha, Nebraska. He lived among whites and renounced his allegiance to his tribe. When he tried to register to vote, he was turned down. After Elk filed litigation to obtain the right to vote, the high court turned him down. In a 7-2 opinion, the justices decided that Elk was born a Winnebago and owed his allegiance to the tribe in perpetuity. Thus, no Indian had birthright citizenship.

↪ *despite being Americans*

Reforming Indian Policy. As reservations continued to shrink under expansionist assault and government acquiescence, a movement arose to reform Indian policy. Largely centered in the East, where few Indians lived, reformers came to believe that the future welfare of Indians lay not in sovereignty but in assimilation. In 1881 Helen Hunt Jackson published *A Century of Dishonor*, her exposé of the unjust treatment the Indians had received. Roused by this depiction of the Indians' plight, groups such as the Women's National Indian Association joined with ministers and philanthropists to advocate the transformation of native peoples into full-fledged Americans.

Judged by the standards of their own time, these well-intentioned reformers wanted to save the Indians from the brutality and corrupt behavior they had endured, and they believed they were acting in the Indians' best interests. The most advanced thinking among anthropologists at the time offered an approach that supported assimilation as the only alternative to extinction. The influential Lewis Morgan, author of *Ancient Society* (1877), concluded that all cultures evolved through three stages: savagery, barbarism, and civilization. Indians occupied the lower rungs, but reformers argued that by adopting white values they could become civilized.   *assimilation or extinction*

old argument

Reformers faced opposition from white Americans who doubted that Indian assimilation was possible. For many Americans, secure in their sense of their own superiority, the decline and eventual extinction of the Indian peoples was an inevitable consequence of what they saw as Indians' innate inferiority. For example, a Wyoming newspaper predicted: "The same inscrutable Arbiter that decreed the downfall of Rome has pronounced the doom of extinction upon the red men of America." *INEVITABLE*

Reformers found their legislative spokesman in long-time Republican Senator Henry Dawes of Massachusetts. As legislative director of the Boston Indian Citizenship Association, Dawes shared Christian reformers' belief that becoming a true American would save both the Indians and the soul of the nation. Dawes had the same paternalistic attitude toward Indians as he had toward freed slaves. He believed that if both degraded groups worked hard and practiced thrift and individual initiative in the spirit of Dawes's New England Puritan forebears, they would succeed. The key for Dawes was private ownership of land.

full control of FEDS

Passed in 1887, the **Dawes Act** ended tribal rule and divided Indian lands into 160-acre parcels. The act allocated one parcel to each family head. The government held the lands in trust for the Indians for twenty-five years; at the end of this period, the Indians would receive American citizenship. In return, the Indians had to abandon their religious and cultural rites and practices, including storytelling and the use of medicine men. Whatever lands remained after this reallocation — and the amount was considerable — would be sold on the open market, and the profits from the sales would be placed in an educational fund for Indians.

Unfortunately, like most of the policies it replaced, the Dawes Act proved detrimental to Native Americans. Indian families received inferior farmlands and inadequate tools to cultivate them, while speculators reaped profits from the sale of the "excess" Indian lands. A little more than a decade after the Dawes Act went into effect, Indians controlled 77 million acres of land, down sharply from the 155 million acres they held in 1881. Additional legislation in *forced assimilation*

1891 forced Indian parents to send their children to boarding schools or else face arrest. At these educational institutions, Indian children were given "American" names, had their long hair cut, and wore uniforms in place of their native dress. The program for boys provided manual and vocational training and that for girls taught domestic skills, so that they could emulate the gender roles in middle-class American families. However, this schooling offered few skills of use in an economic world undergoing industrial transformation.

Indian Assimilation and Resistance. Not all Indians conformed to the government's attempt at forced acculturation. Some refused to abandon their traditional social practices, and others rejected the white man's version of private property and civilization. Even on reservations, Indians found ways to preserve aspects of their native traditions. Through close family ties, they communicated to sons and daughters their languages, histories, and cultural practices. Parents refused to grant full control of their children to white educators and often made sure that schools were located on or near reservations where they fit into the pattern of their lives. Yet, many others displayed more complicated approaches to survival in a world that continued to view Indians with prejudice. Geronimo and Sitting Bull participated in pageants and Wild West shows but refused to disavow their heritage. Ohiyesa, a Lakota also known as Charles Eastman, went to boarding school, graduated from Dartmouth College, and earned a medical degree from Boston University. He supported passage of the Dawes Act, believed in the virtues of an American education, and worked for the Bureau of Indian Affairs. At the same time, he spoke out against government corruption and fraud perpetrated against Indians. Reviewing his life in his later years, Eastman/Ohiyesa reflected: "I am an Indian and while I have learned much from civilization . . . I have never lost my Indian sense of right and justice."

Disaster loomed for those who resisted assimilation and held on too tightly to the old ways. In 1888 the prophet Wovoka, a member of the Paiute tribe in western Nevada, had a vision that Indians would one day regain control of the world and that whites would disappear. He believed that the Creator had provided him with a **Ghost Dance** that would make this happen. The dance spread to thousands of Lakota Sioux in the northern plains. Seeing the Ghost Dance as a sign of renewed Indian resistance, the army attempted to put a stop to the revival. On December 29, 1890, the Seventh Cavalry chased three hundred ghost dancers to Wounded Knee Creek on the Pine Ridge Reservation in present-day South Dakota. In a confrontation with the Lakota leader Big Foot, a gunshot accidentally rang out during a struggle with one of his followers. The cavalry then turned the full force of their weaponry on the Indians, killing 250 Native Americans, many of them women and children.

putting down resistance ↓

The message of the massacre at Wounded Knee was clear for those who raised their voices against Americanization. As Black Elk, a spiritual leader of the Oglala Lakota tribe, asserted: "A people's dream died there. . . . There is no center any longer, and the sacred tree is dead." It may not have been the policy of the U.S. government to exterminate the Indians as a people, but it was certainly U.S. policy to destroy Indian culture and society once and for all.

Review & Relate

▪ How and why did federal Indian policy change during the nineteenth century?

▪ Describe some of the ways that Indian peoples responded to federal policies. Which response do you think offered their greatest chance for survival?

The **Mining** and **Lumber Industries**

disillusion ment

spurred by discovery of gold

expensive business

much like the North

Among the settlers pouring into Indian Territory in the Rocky Mountains were miners in search of gold and silver. These prospectors envisioned instant riches that would come from a lucky strike. The vast majority found only backbreaking work, danger, and frustration. Miners continued to face hardship and danger as industrial mining operations took over from individual prospectors, despite the efforts of some miners to fight for better wages and working conditions. By 1900 the mining rush had peaked, and many of the boomtowns that had cropped up around the mining industry had emptied out. Still, mining companies and the workers they attracted forged big cities of diverse peoples and commerce. Closely related to mining, the lumber industry was less demographically diverse but also followed the pattern of domination by big business.

capitalized on the American Dream

The Business of Mining. The discovery of gold in California in 1848 had set this mining frenzy in motion. Over the next thirty years, successive waves of gold and silver strikes in Colorado, Nevada, Washington, Idaho, Montana, and the Dakotas lured individual prospectors with shovels and wash pans. One of the biggest finds came with the **Comstock Lode** in the Sierra Nevada, where miners extracted around $350 million worth of silver (in nineteenth century dollars). One of those who came to try to share in the wealth was Samuel Clemens. Like most of his fellow miners, Clemens did not find his fortune in Nevada and soon turned his attention to writing, finally achieving success as the author called Mark Twain.

immigrants

Like Twain, many of those who flocked to the Comstock Lode and other mining frontiers were men. Nearly half were foreign-born, many of them coming from Mexico or China. Using pans and shovels, prospectors could find only the ore that lay near the surface of the earth and water and could not afford to buy the equipment needed to dig out the vast deposits of gold and silver buried deep in the earth. As a result, western mining became a business run by men with the financial resources necessary to purchase industrial mining equipment.

When mining became an industry, prospectors became wageworkers. In Virginia City, Nevada miners labored for $4 a day, an amount that barely covered the expenses of life in a mining boomtown. Moreover, the work was extremely dangerous. Mine shafts extended down more than a thousand feet, and working temperatures regularly exceeded 100 degrees Fahrenheit. Noxious fumes, fires, and floods of scalding water flowed through the shafts, and other threats killed or disabled thousands each year.

Struggling with low pay and dangerous work, western miners sought to organize. In the mid-1860s, unions formed in the Comstock Lode areas of Virginia City and Gold Hill, Nevada. Although these unions had some success, they also provoked a violent backlash from mining companies determined to resist union demands. Companies hired private police forces to help break strikes. Such forces were often assisted by state militias deployed by elected officials with close ties to the companies. For example, in 1892 the governor of Idaho crushed an unruly strike by calling up the National Guard, a confrontation that resulted in the deaths of seven strikers. A year later, in 1893, mine workers formed one of the most militant labor organizations in the nation, the Western Federation of Miners. Within a decade, it had attracted fifty thousand members, though membership excluded Chinese, Mexican, and Indian workers.

Life in the Mining Towns. Men worked the mines, but women arrived as well in search of economic opportunity. In Storey County, Nevada, the heart of the Comstock Lode, the 1875 census showed that women made up about half the population. Most employed women worked long hours as domestics in boardinghouses, hotels, and private homes. Prostitution, which was legal, accounted for the single-largest segment of the female workforce. Most prostitutes were between the ages of nineteen and twenty-four, and they entered this occupation because few other well-paying jobs were available to them. Prostitutes faced constant danger, and many were victims of physical abuse, robbery, and murder.

men and women alike

As early as the 1880s, gold and silver discoveries had played out in the Comstock Lode. Boomtowns, which had sprung up almost overnight, became ghost towns as gold and silver deposits dwindled. Even more substantial places like Virginia City, Nevada experienced a severe decline as the veins of ore ran out. One revealing sign of the city's plummeting fortunes was the drop in the number of prostitutes, which declined by more than half by 1880. The mining business then shifted from gold and silver to copper, lead, and zinc, centered in Montana and Idaho. As with the early prospectors in California and Nevada, these miners eventually became wageworkers for giant consolidated mining companies. By the end of the nineteenth century, the Amalgamated Copper Company and the American Smelting and Refining Company dominated the industry.

big businesses ↓

Mining towns that survived settled into a more complex pattern of urban living. At its height in the 1870s, Virginia City contained 25,000 residents and was among the largest cities west of the Mississippi River. It provided schools and churches and featured such cultural amenities as theaters and opera houses. Though the population in mining towns remained predominantly young and male, the young men were increasingly likely to get married and raise families. Residents lived in neighborhoods divided by class and ethnicity. For example, in Butte, Montana the west side of town became home to the middle and upper classes. Mine workers lived on the east side in homes subdivided into apartments and in boardinghouses. The Irish lived in one section; Finns, Swedes, Serbs, Croatians, and Slovenes in other sections. Each group formed its own social, fraternal, and religious organizations to relieve the harsh conditions of overcrowding, poor sanitation, and discrimination. Residents of the east side relied on one another for support and frowned on those who deviated from their code of solidarity. "They didn't try to outdo the other one," one neighborhood woman remarked. "If you did, you got into trouble. . . . If they thought you were a little richer than they were, they wouldn't associate with you." Although western mining towns retained distinctive qualities, in their social and ethnic divisions they came to resemble older cities east of the Mississippi River.

ethnic and class division within mining cities

The Lumber Boom. The mining industry created a huge demand for timber, as did the railroad lines that operated in the West. Initially small logging firms moved into the Northwest and California, cut down all the trees they could, sent them to nearby sawmills for processing, and moved on. By 1900, a few large firms came to dominate the industry and acquired vast tracts of forests. Frederick Weyerhaeuser purchased 900,000 acres of prime timberland in the Western Cascades of Oregon, largely bringing an end to the often chaotic competition of small firms that had characterized the industry in its early days. Increasingly, the western lumber industry became part of a global market that shipped products to Hawaii, South America, and Asia.

drove demand

Loggers and sawmill workers did not benefit from these changes. Exclusively male, large numbers of workers came from Scandinavia, and only a few were Asian or African American. Men died or lost limbs in cutting down the trees, transporting them in the rivers, or processing the wood in sawmills. As lumber camps and mill villages became urbanized, those who gained the most were the merchants and bankers who supplied the goods and capital.

dangerous

Review & Relate

- How and why did the nature of mining in the West change during the second half of the nineteenth century?

- How did the mining and lumber industries reshape the frontier landscape?

The **Cattle Industry** and **Commercial Farming**

Like mining and lumber, cattle ranching and farming in the West increasingly became dominated by big business. Foreign investors from England, Scotland, Wales, and South America poured in money to fund the cattle industry and placed day-to-day control of their ranches in the hands of experienced corporate managers. Cowboys functioned as industrial laborers. They worked long hours in tough but boring conditions on the open range. Similarly, commercial farmers who headed west endured great hardships in trying to raise crops in an often inhospitable climate. Extreme weather and falling crop prices, however, forced many ranchers and farmers out of business, and their lands and businesses were snatched up by larger, more consolidated commercial ranching and agricultural enterprises. Despite difficult physical and economic conditions, many of the women and men who ranched and farmed in the West showed grit and determination not only in surviving but in improving their lives as well. → *determination*

The Life of the Cowboy. There is no greater symbol of the frontier West than the cowboy. As portrayed in novels and film, the cowboy hero was the essence of manhood, an independent figure who fought for justice and defended the honor and virtue of women. Never the aggressor, he fought to protect law-abiding residents of frontier communities.

This romantic image excited generations of American readers and later movie and television audiences. In reality, cowboys' lives were much more mundane. Rather than working as independent adventurers, they increasingly operated in an industrial setting dominated by large cattle companies. Cowpunchers worked for paltry monthly wages, put in long days herding cattle, and spent part of the night guarding them on the open range. Their major task was to make the 1,500-mile **Long Drive** along the Chisholm Trail. Beginning in the late 1860s, cowboys moved cattle from ranches in Texas through Oklahoma to rail depots in Kansas towns such as Abilene and Dodge City; from there, cattle were shipped by train eastward to slaughterhouses in Chicago. Life along the trail was monotonous, and riders had to contend with bad weather, dangerous work, and disease.

Numbering around forty thousand and averaging twenty-four years of age, the cowboys who rode through the Great Plains from Texas to Kansas came from diverse backgrounds. The majority, about 66 percent, were white, predominantly Southerners who had fought for the South during the Civil War. Most of the rest were divided evenly

Explore ▶

See Sources 15.2 and 15.3 for two depictions of cowboy life.

between Mexicans and African Americans, some of whom were former slaves and others Union veterans of the Civil War.

Besides experiencing rugged life on the range, black and Mexican cowboys faced racial discrimination. Jim Perry, an African American who rode for the three-million-acre XIT Ranch in Texas for more than twenty years, complained: "If it weren't for my damned old black face I'd have been boss of one of these divisions long ago." Mexican *vaqueros*, or cowboys, earned one-third to one-half the wages of whites, whereas blacks were usually paid on a par with whites. Because the cattle kingdoms first flourished during Reconstruction, racial discrimination and segregation carried over into the Southwest. On one drive along the route to Kansas, a white boss insisted that a black cowboy eat and sleep separately from whites and shot at him when he refused to heed this order. Nevertheless, the proximity in which cowboys worked and the need for cooperation to overcome the pitfalls of the long drive made it difficult to enforce rigid racial divisions on the open range.

The Rise of Commercial Ranching.
Commercial ranches absorbed cowboys into their expanding operations. Spaniards had originally imported cattle into the Southwest, and by the late nineteenth century some five million Texas longhorn steers grazed in the area. The extension of railroads across the West opened up a quickly growing market for beef in the East. The development of refrigerated railroad cars guaranteed that meat from slaughtered cattle could reach eastern consumers without spoiling. With money to be made, the cattle industry rose to meet the demand. Fewer than 40 ranchers owned more than 20 million acres of land. Easterners and Europeans joined the boom and invested money in giant ranches. By the mid-1880s, approximately 7.5 million head of cattle roamed the western ranges, and large cattle ranchers became rich. Cattle ranching had become fully integrated into the national commercial economy.

Then the bubble burst. Ranchers, who were already raising more cattle than the market could handle, increasingly faced competition from cattle producers in Canada and Argentina. Prices spiraled downward. Another source of competition came from homesteaders who moved into the plains and fenced in their farms with barbed wire, thereby reducing the size of the open range. Yet the greatest disaster occurred from 1885 to 1887. Two frigid winters, together with a torrid summer drought, destroyed 90 percent of the cattle on the northern plains of the Dakotas, Montana, Colorado, and Wyoming. Under these conditions, outside capital to support ranching diminished, and many of the great cattle barons went into bankruptcy. This economic collapse consolidated the remaining cattle industry into even fewer hands. The cowboy, never more than a hired hand, became a laborer for large corporations.

Commercial Farming.
Like cowboys, farm families endured hardships to make their living in the West. They struggled to raise crops in an often inhospitable climate in hopes that their yields would be sold for a profit. Falling crop prices, however, led to soaring debt and forced many farmers into bankruptcy and off their land, while others were fortunate enough to survive and make a living.

The federal government played a major role in opening up the Great Plains to farmers, who eventually clashed with cattlemen. The Republican Party of Abraham Lincoln had opposed the expansion of slavery in order to promote the virtues of free soil and free labor for white men and their families. In 1862, during the Civil War, preoccupation with battlefield losses did not stop the Republican-controlled Congress from passing the **Homestead Act**.

"Vaqueros in a Horse Corral," 1877   In this lithograph, James Walker captures vaqueros (cowboys) on a Texas ranch corralling horses. "Vaquero" is derived from the Spanish word for "cow," and "corral" comes from Spanish for "enclosure" or "pen." Originating in Spain and brought to Mexico, vaquero culture influenced the development of the southwestern United States and California. Peter Newark Pictures/Bridgeman Images

Homestead Act

As an incentive for western migration, the act established procedures for distributing 160-acre lots to western settlers, on condition that they develop and farm their land. What most would-be settlers did not know, however, was that lots of 160 acres were not viable in the harsh, dry climate of the Great Plains.

Reality did not deter pioneers and adventurers. In fact, weather conditions in the region temporarily fooled them. The decade after 1878 witnessed an exceptional amount of rainfall west of the Mississippi. Though not precisely predictable, this cycle of abundance and drought had been going on for millennia. In addition, innovation and technology bolstered dreams of success. Farmers planted hardy strains of wheat imported from Russia that survived the fluctuations of dry and wet and hot and cold weather. Machines produced by industrial laborers in northern factories to the east allowed farmers to plow tough land and harvest its yield. Steel-tipped plows, threshers, combines, and harvesters expanded production greatly, and windmills and pumping equipment provided sources of power and access to scarce water. These improvements in mechanization led to a significant expansion in agricultural production, which helped to lower food prices for consumers.

The people who accepted the challenge of carving out a new life were a diverse lot. The Great Plains attracted a large number of immigrants from Europe, some two million by 1900. Minnesota and the Dakotas welcomed communities of settlers from Sweden and Norway. Nebraska housed a considerable population of Germans, Swedes, Danes, and Czechs. About one-third of the people who migrated to the northern plains came directly from a foreign country.

immigrants

Railroads and land companies lured settlers to the plains with tales of the fabulous possibilities that awaited their arrival. The federal government had given railroads generous

Cowboy Myths and Realities

William F. Cody, known as "Buffalo Bill," had been a real-life bison hunter in the American West and an army scout in the Indian wars of the 1860s and 1870s. Drawing on his authentic adventures and his heroism, Cody helped romanticize the figures that populated the American frontier, especially the cowboys, through his Wild West shows, a poster from which is shown here. The diary entries of George C. Duffield present a more mundane description of cowboy life. Duffield drove cattle on the open range in 1866 from Texas, where they were bred, to Iowa, where they went to market.

Source 15.2

Poster Advertising Buffalo Bill's Wild West Show, 1893

Bridgeman Images

Source 15.3

George C. Duffield | Diary of a Real Cowboy, 1866

12th

Hard Rain & Wind. Big stampede & here we are among the Indians with 150 head of Cattle gone. Hunted all day & the Rain pouring down with but poor success. Dark days are these to me. Nothing but Bread & Coffee. Hands all Growling & Swearing — everything wet & cold. Beeves [steers] gone. Rode all day & gathered all but 35 mixed with 8 other Herds. Last Night 5000 Beeves stampeded at this place & a general mix up was the result. . . .

14th

Last night there was a terrible storm. Rain poured in torrents *all* night & up to 12 AM today. Our Beeves left us in the night but for *once* on the whole trip we found them *all* together near camp at day break. *All*

the other droves as far as I can hear are scattered to the four winds. Our Other Herd was all gone. We are now 25 Miles from Ark River & it is Very High. We are water bound by two creeks & but Beef & Flour to eat, am not Homesick but Heart sick. . . .

16th

Last night was a dark Gloomey night but we made it all right. Today it is raining & we have crossed Honey creek & am informed that there is another creek 6 miles ahead swimming. Twelve o clock today it rained one Hour so hard that a creek close by rose 20 ft in the afternoon. All wet.

Source: George C. Duffield, "Driving Cattle from Texas to Iowa, 1866," *Annals of Iowa* 14, no. 4 (1924): 253–54.

Interpret the Evidence

1. What does the placement of Cody's portrait in the poster suggest about the role of white men in the West?
2. How does Duffield's experience of the West differ from that conveyed in the poster?

Put It in Context

Why do you think Americans remember Buffalo Bill's version of the West rather than Duffield's?

massive federal interference ↓

grants of public land on which to build their tracks as well as parcels surrounding the tracks that they could sell off to raise revenue for construction. Western railroads advertised in both the United States and Europe, proclaiming that migrants to the plains would find "the garden spot of the world."

Having enticed prospective settlers with exaggerated claims, railroads offered bargain rates to transport them to their new homes. Families and friends often journeyed together and rented an entire car on the train, known as "the immigrant car," in which they loaded their possessions, supplies, and even livestock. Often migrants came to the end of the rail line before reaching their destination. They completed the trip by wagon or stagecoach.

Commercial advertising alone did not account for the desire to journey westward. Settlers who had made the trip successfully wrote to relatives and neighbors back east and in the old country about the chance to start fresh. Linda Slaughter, the wife of an army doctor in the Dakotas, gushed: "The farms which have been opened in the vicinity of Bismarck

possibility {

have proven highly productive, the soil being kept moist by frequent rains. Vegetables of all kinds are grown with but little trouble."

Those who took the chance shared a faith in the future and a willingness to work hard and endure misfortune. They found their optimism and spirits sorely tested. Despite the company of family members and friends, settlers faced a lonely existence on the vast expanse of the plains. Homesteads were spread out, and a feeling of isolation became a routine part of daily life.

With few trees around, early settlers constructed sod houses. These structures let in little light but a good deal of moisture, keeping them gloomy and damp. A Nebraskan who lived in this type of house jokingly remarked: "There was running water in our sod house. It ran through the roof." Bugs, insects, and rodents, like the rain, often found their way inside to make living in such shelters even more uncomfortable.

If these dwellings were bleak, the climate posed even greater challenges. After the unusually plentiful rainfall in the late 1870s and early 1880s, severe drought followed. Before that, a plague of grasshoppers ravaged the northern plains in the late 1870s, destroying fruit trees and plants. Intense heat in the summer alternated with frigid temperatures in

Harsh weather conditions

the winter. The Norwegian American writer O. E. Rolvaag, in *Giants in the Earth* (1927), described the extreme hardships that accompanied the fierce weather: "Blizzards from out of the northwest raged, swooped down and stirred up a greyish-white fury, impenetrable to human eyes. As soon as these monsters tired, storms from the northeast were sure to come, bringing more snow."

Women Homesteaders.
The women of the family were responsible for making homesteads more bearable. Mothers and daughters were in charge of household duties, cooking the meals, canning fruits and vegetables, and washing and ironing clothing. Women contributed significantly to the economic well-being of the family by occasionally
→ taking in boarders and selling milk, butter, and eggs.

In addition, a surprisingly large number of single women staked out homestead claims by themselves. Some were young, unmarried women seeking, like their male counterparts, economic opportunity. Others were widows attempting to take care of their children after their husband's death. One such widow, Anne Furnberg, settled a homestead in the Dakota Territory in 1871. Born in Norway, she had lived with her husband and son in Minnesota. After her husband's death, the thirty-four-year-old Furnberg moved with her son near Fargo and eventually settled on eighty acres of land. She farmed, raised chickens and a cow, and sold butter and eggs in town. The majority of women who settled in the Dakotas were between the ages of twenty-one and twenty-five, had never been married, and were native-born children of immigrant parents. A sample of nine counties in the Dakotas shows that more than 4,400 women became landowners. Nora Pfundheler, a single woman, explained her motivation: "Well I was 21 and had no prospects of doing anything. The land was there, so I took it."

Once families settled in and towns began to develop, women, married and single, directed some of their energies to moral reform and extending democracy on the frontier. Because of loneliness and grueling work, some men turned to alcohol for relief. Law enforcement in newly established communities was often no match for the saloons that catered to a raucous and drunken crowd. In their roles as wives, mothers, and sisters, many women tried to remove the source of alcohol-induced violence that disrupted both family relationships and public decorum. In Kansas in the late 1870s, women flocked to the state's Woman's Christian Temperance Union, founded by Amanda M. Way. Although they did not yet have the vote, in 1880 these women vigorously campaigned for a constitutional amendment that banned the sale of liquor. *prohibition*

Temperance women also threw their weight behind the issue of women's suffrage. In 1884 Kansas women established the statewide Equal Suffrage Association, which delivered to the state legislature a petition with seven thousand signatures in support of women's suffrage. Their attempt failed, but in 1887 women won the right to vote and run for office in all Kansas municipal elections. Julia Robinson, who campaigned for women's suffrage in Kansas, recalled the positive role that some men played: "My father had always said his family of girls had just as much right to help the government as if we were boys, and mother and he had always taught us to expect Woman Suffrage in our day." Kansas did not grant equal *suffrage*

Women at Work in Kansas   Women pioneers in the West worked in a variety of jobs besides homemakers and farmers. In the 1880s, these two women worked as typesetters for the *Kansas Workman*, a weekly newspaper that supported equal rights for workers. Women were often chosen for this job of arranging tiny pieces of lead, inky type because it required sure fingers and sober attention to detail. Kansas State Historical Association voting rights in state and national elections until 1912, but women obtained full suffrage before then in many western states.

Farming on the Great Plains.
Surviving loneliness, drudgery, and bad weather still did not guarantee financial success for homesteaders. In fact, the economic realities of farming on the plains proved formidable. Despite the image of yeomen farmers — individuals engaged in subsistence farming with the aid of wives and children — most agriculture was geared to commercial transactions. Few farmers were independent or self-reliant. Farmers depended on barter and short-term credit. They borrowed from banks to purchase the additional land necessary to make agriculture economically feasible in the semiarid climate. They also needed loans to buy machinery to help increase production and to sustain their families while they waited for the harvest.

Instead of raising crops solely for their own use, farmers concentrated on the cash crops of corn and wheat. The price of these commodities depended on the vagaries of an international market that connected American farmers to growers and consumers throughout the world. When supply expanded and demand remained relatively stable during the 1880s and 1890s, prices fell. This deflation made it more difficult for farmers to pay back their loans, and banks moved to foreclose.

Under these challenging circumstances, almost half of the homesteaders in the Great Plains picked up and moved either to another farm or to a nearby city. Large operators bought up the farms they left behind and ran them like big businesses. As had been the case in mining, logging, and ranching, western agriculture was increasingly commercialized and consolidated over the course of the second half of the nineteenth century.

The federal government unwittingly aided this process of commercialization and consolidation, to the benefit of large companies. The government sought to make bigger plots of land available in regions where small farming had proved impractical. The Desert Land Act (1877) offered 640 acres to settlers who would irrigate the land, but it brought small relief for farmers because the land was too dry. These properties soon fell out of the hands of homesteaders and into those of cattle ranchers. The Timber and Stone Act (1878) allowed homesteaders to buy 160 acres of forestland at $2.50 an acre. Lumber companies hired "dummy entrymen" to file claims and then quickly transferred the titles and added the parcels to their growing tracts of woodland.

Review & Relate

■ How did market forces contribute to the boom and bust of the cattle ranching industry and commercial farming?

■ How did women homesteaders on the Great Plains in the late nineteenth century respond to frontier challenges?

Diversity in the Far West

Some pioneers settled on the Great Plains or moved west for reasons beyond purely economic motives. The Mormons, for example, settled in Utah to find a religious home. The West Coast states of Washington, Oregon, and especially California, with their abundant resources and favorable climates, beckoned adventurers to travel beyond the Rockies and settle along the Pacific Ocean. The far West attracted many white settlers and foreign immigrants — especially Chinese — who

[margin handwritten notes:] Farmers need financial credit

not independent or untouched →

companies > settlers

clash

Explore ▶

See Sources 15.4 and 15.5 for
two different interpretations of
the significance of the frontier.

encountered Spaniards and Mexicans already inhabiting the region. This interweaving among diverse cultural groups sparked clashes that produced more oppression than opportunity for nonwhites.

Mormons. Unlike miners, cowboys, and farmers, **Mormons** sought refuge in the West for religious reasons. By 1870 the migration of Mormons (members of the Church of Jesus Christ of Latter-Day Saints) into the Utah Territory had attracted more than 85,000 settlers, most notably in Salt Lake City. Originally traveling to Utah under the leadership of Brigham Young in the late 1840s, Mormons had come under attack from opponents of their religion and the federal government for several reasons. Most important, Mormons believed in polygamy, the practice of having more than one wife at a time. Far from seeing the practice as immoral, Mormon doctrine held polygamy as a blessing that would guarantee both husbands and wives an exalted place in the afterlife. Non-Mormons denounced polygamy as a form of involuntary servitude. In reality, only a small minority of Mormon men had multiple wives, and most of these polygamists had only two wives.

seeking refuge

?

Mormons also departed from the mainstream American belief in private property. The church considered farming a communal enterprise. To this end, church elders divided land among their followers, so that, as Brigham Young explained, "each person perform[ed] his several duties for the good of the whole more than for individual aggrandizement."

Kind of like socialism

In the 1870s, the federal government took increased measures to control Mormon practices. In *Reynolds v. United States* (1879), the Supreme Court upheld the criminal conviction of a polygamist Mormon man. Previously in 1862 and 1874, Congress had banned plural marriages in the Utah Territory. Congress went further in 1882 by passing the Edmunds Act, which disfranchised men engaging in polygamy. In 1887 Congress aimed to slash the economic power of the church by limiting Mormon assets to $50,000 and seizing the rest for the federal Treasury. A few years later, under this considerable pressure, the Mormons officially abandoned polygamy.

federal attempt for control

Related to the attack on polygamy was the question of women's suffrage. In 1870 voters in Utah endorsed a referendum granting women the right to vote, which enfranchised more than seventeen thousand women. Emmeline B. Wells, a Mormon woman who defended both women's rights and polygamy, argued that women "should be recognized as . . . responsible being[s]," capable of choosing plural marriage of their own free will. Opponents of enfranchisement contended that as long as polygamy existed, extending the vote to "enslaved" Mormon women would only perpetuate the practice because they would vote the way their husbands did. This point of view prevailed, and the Edmunds-Tucker Act (1887) rescinded the right to vote for women in the territory. Only with the rejection of polygamy did Congress accept statehood for Utah in 1896. The following year, the state extended the ballot to women.

Californios and Mexican Americans. As with the nation's other frontiers, migrants to the West Coast did not find uninhabited territory. Besides Indians, the largest group that lived in California consisted of Spaniards and Mexicans. Since the eighteenth century, these **Californios** had established themselves as farmers and ranchers. The 1848 Treaty of Guadalupe Hidalgo, which ended the Mexican-American War, supposedly guaranteed the property rights of Californios and granted them U.S. citizenship, but reality proved different. Mexican American miners had to pay a "foreign miners tax," and Californio

landowners lost their holdings to squatters, settlers, and local officials. By the end of the nineteenth century, about two-thirds of all land originally owned by Spanish-speaking residents had fallen into the hands of Euro-American settlers. By this time, many of these once wealthy Californios had been forced into poverty and the low-wage labor force. The loss of land was matched by a diminished role in the region's government, as economic decline, ethnic bias, and the continuing influx of white migrants combined to greatly reduce the political influence of the Californio population.

Spaniards and Mexicans living in the Southwest met the same fate as the Californios. When Anglo cattle ranchers began forcing Mexican Americans off their land near Las Vegas, New Mexico, a rancher named Juan Jose Herrera assembled a band of masked night riders known as Las Gorras Blancas (The White Caps). According to fliers that they distributed promoting their grievances, the group sought "to protect the rights and interests of the people in general and especially those of the helpless classes." Enemies of "tyrants," they desired a "free ballot and fair court." In 1889 and 1890, as many as seven hundred White Caps burned Anglo fences, haystacks, barns, and homes. In the end, however, Spanish-speaking inhabitants could not prevent the growing number of whites from pouring onto their lands and isolating them politically, economically, and culturally. The most notorious of these Anglo-American landgrabbers was the Santa Fe Ring. Consisting of lawyers, politicians, and speculators, they convinced the federal government to grant them millions of acres of public land on which thousands of Mexican American farmers had lived and worked. Despite these incursions, Mexican Americans remained a majority of the territorial population throughout the late nineteenth century. With this ethnic majority in mind, Congress twice refused New Mexico's application for statehood in the 1870s and 1880s. Not until 1912 did New Mexico become a state, no longer with Mexican Americans in the majority.

The impact on Mexican Americans in California, New Mexico, and Texas was devastating. By seizing their land and erecting legal barriers to keep them from retrieving it, Anglos damaged the economic prospects of a majority of Mexicans. Once property owners, many Mexican Americans became landless tenant farmers or low-paid wage laborers in mines and ranches. Also, they remained vulnerable to extra-legal, vigilante violence by Anglos if they stepped out of their subordinate place. Between 1861 and 1900, an estimated 287 Mexican Americans were lynched. As might be expected given the history of the region, disputes over property and economic resources triggered a large number of these brutal killings.

The Chinese.
California and the far West also attracted a large number of Chinese immigrants. Migration to California and the West Coast was part of a larger movement in the nineteenth century out of Asia that brought impoverished Chinese to Australia, Hawaii, Latin America, and the United States. The Chinese migrated for several reasons in the decades after 1840. Economic dislocation related to the British Opium Wars (1839–1842 and 1856–1860), along with bloody family feuds and a decade of peasant rebellion from 1854 to 1864, propelled migration. Faced with unemployment and starvation, the Chinese sought economic opportunity overseas.

Chinese immigrants were attracted first by the 1848 gold rush and then by jobs building the transcontinental railroad. By 1880 the Chinese population had grown to 200,000, most of whom lived in the West. San Francisco became the center of the transplanted

Chinese population, which congregated in the city's Chinatown. Under the leadership of a handful of businessmen, Chinese residents found jobs, lodging, and meals, along with social, cultural, and recreational outlets. Most of those who came were young, unmarried men who intended to earn enough money to return to China and start anew. The relatively few women who immigrated came as servants or prostitutes.

For many Chinese, the West proved unwelcoming. When California's economy slumped in the mid-1870s, many whites looked to the Chinese as scapegoats. White workingmen believed that Chinese laborers in the mines and railroads undercut their demands for higher wages. They contended that Chinese would work for less because they were racially inferior people who lived degraded lives. Anti-Chinese clubs mushroomed in California during the 1870s, and they soon became a substantial political force in the state. The Workingmen's Party advocated laws that restricted Chinese labor, and it initiated boycotts of goods made by Chinese people. Vigilantes attacked Chinese in the streets and set fire to factories that employed Asians. The Workingmen's Party and the Democratic Party joined forces in 1879 to craft a new state constitution that blatantly discriminated against Chinese residents. In many ways, these laws resembled the Jim Crow laws passed in the South that deprived African Americans of their freedom following Reconstruction (discussed in chapter 16).

vigilantism

Pressured by anti-Chinese sentiment on the West Coast, the U.S. government enacted drastic legislation to prevent any further influx of Chinese. The **Chinese Exclusion Act** of 1882 banned Chinese immigration into the United States and prohibited those Chinese

Rock Springs Massacre   This engraving depicts the Rock Springs massacre in Wyoming. On September 3, 1885, a mob of white coal miners killed at least 28 Chinese miners, injured 15, and burned 75 homes of Chinese residents. The violence came after years of anti-Chinese sentiment in the western United States. White miners blamed the Chinese for working for lower wages and taking their jobs. Granger

Comparative Secondary Source Analysis

The Significance of the Frontier

The expansion of the American West beyond the Mississippi River to the West Coast has become a symbol of freedom, democracy, and national renewal. Popular novels, films, and television shows have depicted adventurous pioneers rebuilding their lives economically, politically, and spiritually by moving to the vastness of the Great Plains and Far West. In something of a morality play, righteous cowboys spread civilization and maintain law and order so that others might settle peacefully. American Indians, who already inhabited these supposed open lands, were considered enemies of American progress and collateral damage as the government reneged on its treaty obligations and the military defeated them. The historian Frederick Jackson Turner wrote about the significance of the West in 1893, just three years after the Census Bureau reported that the frontier was closed and amid concerns for its disappearance. In 1987, the historian Patricia Limerick, influenced by new research on and changing attitudes towards Native Americans and Latino Americans, reconceived how scholars view the significance of the West.

Source 15.4

Frederick Jackson Turner | The Significance of the Frontier in American History, 1893

"[W]e have . . . a recurrence of the process of evolution in each western area reached in the process of expansion. Thus American development has exhibited not merely advance along a single line, but a return to primitive conditions on a continually advancing frontier line, and a new development for that area. American social development has been continually beginning over again on the frontier. This perennial rebirth, this fluidity of American life, this expansion westward with its new opportunities, its continuous touch with the simplicity of primitive society, furnish the forces dominating American character. . . . The frontier is the line of most rapid and effective Americanization. The wilderness masters the colonist. It finds him a European in dress, industries, tools, models of travel, and thought. It takes him from the railroad car and puts him in the birch canoe. It strips off the garments of civilization and arrays him in the hunting shirt and moccasin. . . . In short, at the frontier the environment is at first too strong for the man. . . . Little by little he transforms the wilderness, but the outcome is not the old Europe. . . . The fact is that here is a new product that is American. . . . Thus the advance of the frontier has meant a steady movement away from the influence of Europe, a steady growth of independence on American lines."

Source: Frederick Jackson Turner, *The Frontier in American History.* New York: Henry Holt and Company, 1920, 2–3, 4.

already in the country from becoming naturalized American citizens. The exclusion act, however, did not stop anti-Chinese assaults. In the mid-1880s, white mobs drove Chinese out of Eureka, California; Seattle and Tacoma, Washington; and Rock Springs, Wyoming. These attacks were often organized. In 1885, the Tacoma mayor and police led a mob that rounded up 700 Chinese residents and forced them to leave the city on a train bound for Portland.

Source 15.5

Patricia Nelson Limerick | Deemphasizing the Concept of the Frontier, 1987

"Turner's frontier was a process, <u>not</u> a place. When 'civilization' had conquered 'savagery' at any one location, the process—and the historian's attention—moved on. In rethinking Western history, we gain the freedom to think of the West as a place—as many complicated environments occupied by natives who considered their homelands to be the center, not the edge. . . . Deemphasize the frontier and its supposed end, conceive of the West as a place and not a process, and Western American history has a new look. First, the American West was an important meeting ground, the point where Indian America, Latin America, Anglo-America, Afro-America, and Asia America intersected. . . . Second, the working of conquest tied these diverse groups into the same story. Happily or not, minorities and majorities occupied a common ground. Conquest basically involved the drawing of lines on a map, the definition and allocation of ownership (personal, tribal, corporate, state, federal, and international), and the evolution of land from matter to property."

Source: Patricia Nelson Limerick, *The Legacy of Conquest: The Unbroken Path of the American West*. New York: W.W. Norton & Company (1987), 26, 27, 31.

Examine the Sources

1. How do Turner and Limerick differ in their understanding of the frontier and the West?
2. Based on evidence in this chapter, evaluate the main arguments of Turner and Limerick.

Put It in Context

On another page of her book, Limerick writes, "Just as Turner, I take my cues from the present." How does each author's main thesis reflect their "present"?

Review & Relate

■ What migrant groups were attracted to the far West? What drew them there?

■ Explain the rising hostility to the Chinese and other minority groups in the late-nineteenth-century far West.

Conclusion: The **Ambiguous Legacy** of the **West**

The legacy of the pioneering generation of Americans has proven mixed. Men and women pioneers encountered numerous obstacles posed by difficult terrain, forbidding climate, and unfamiliar inhabitants of the land they sought to harness. They built their homes, tilled the soil to raise crops, and mined the earth to remove the metals it contained. They developed cities that would one day rival those back east: San Francisco, Los Angeles, Seattle, and Denver. These pioneers served as the advance guard of America's expanding national and international industrial and commercial markets. As producers of staple crops and livestock and consumers of manufactured goods, they contributed to the expansion of America's factories, railroads, and telegraph communication system. The nation would memorialize their spirit as a model of individualism and self-reliance.

In fact, settlement of the West required more than individual initiative and self-determination. Without the direct involvement of the federal government, settlers would not have received free or inexpensive homesteads and military protection to clear native inhabitants out of their way. Without territorial governors and judges appointed by Washington to preside over new settlements, there would have been even less law, order, and justice than appeared in the rough-and-tumble environment of the West. Railroads, mining, and cattle ventures all relied heavily on foreign investors. Moreover, all the individualism and self-reliance that pioneers brought would not have saved them from the harsh conditions and disasters they faced without banding together as a community and pitching in to create institutions that helped them collectively. Despite their desire to achieve success, various pioneers — farmers, prospectors, cowboys — mostly found it difficult to make it on their own and began working for larger farming, mining, and ranching enterprises, with many of them becoming wageworkers. And for an experience that has been portrayed as a predominantly male phenomenon, settlement of the West depended largely on women.

Pioneers did not fully understand the land and people they encountered. More from ignorance than design, settlers engaged in agricultural, mining, and ranching practices that damaged fragile ecosystems. The settlement of the West nearly wiped out the bison and left Native Americans psychologically demoralized, culturally endangered, and economically impoverished. Some Indians willingly adopted white ways, but most of them fiercely resisted acculturation. Other minorities in the West, such as Mexicans and Chinese, also experienced harsh treatment at the hands of whites and suffered greatly.

Timeline of Events

1848	Gold discovered in California
1851	First Treaty of Fort Laramie
1862	Homestead Act
1864	Sand Creek massacre
1865–1868	Lakota Sioux lead Indian resistance
Late 1860s	Large-scale cattle drives begin
1868	Second Treaty of Fort Laramie
1869	Transcontinental railroad completed
1870s	Gold discovered in Black Hills of North Dakota
1876	Battle of the Little Big Horn
1877	Desert Land Act
	Timber and Stone Act
1881	Helen Hunt Jackson publishes *A Century of Dishonor*
1882	Edmunds Act
	Chinese Exclusion Act
1884	Annie Oakley joins William Cody's Wild West show
1885–1887	Cattle industry collapses
1886	Geronimo captured
1887	Dawes Act
	Kansas women win right to vote in municipal elections
1889–1890	Mexican American White Caps attack Anglo property
1890	Massacre at Wounded Knee
1893	Western Federation of Miners formed

Key Terms

Great Plains, *497*
transcontinental railroad, *499*
Treaty of Fort Laramie, *503*
Treaty of Medicine Lodge, *503*
Battle of the Little Big Horn, *505*
buffalo soldiers, *506*
Dawes Act, *507*
Ghost Dance, *508*
Comstock Lode, *509*
Long Drive, *511*
Homestead Act, *512*
Mormons, *519*
Californios, *519*
Chinese Exclusion Act, *521*

Review & Relate

1. What role did the federal government play in opening the West to settlement and economic exploitation?

2. Explain the determination of Americans to settle in land west of the Mississippi River despite the challenges the region presented.

3. How and why did federal Indian policy change during the nineteenth century?

4. Describe some of the ways that Indian peoples responded to federal policies. Which response do you think offered their greatest chance for survival?

5. How and why did the nature of mining in the West change during the second half of the nineteenth century?

6. How did the mining and lumber industries reshape the frontier landscape?

7. How did market forces contribute to the boom and bust of the cattle ranching industry and commercial farming?

8. How did women homesteaders on the Great Plains in the late nineteenth century respond to frontier challenges?

9. What migrant groups were attracted to the far West? What drew them there?

10. Explain the rising hostility to the Chinese and other minority groups in the late-nineteenth-century far West.

American Indians and Whites in the West

▶ Evaluate the extent to which the U.S. government from 1865 to 1890 balanced its commitment to both continental expansion and equal justice under the law and explain how Native Americans forged strategies in response to U.S. policy.

Views on the relationship between whites and American Indians varied widely in the late-nineteenth-century West, though most shared a basic premise — that Indian cultures and tribal identities did not deserve to be preserved and defended. Some white Americans advocated exterminating the Indians, whereas others sought to assimilate them (Sources 15.6 and 15.7). These attitudes differed significantly by region. Whites who were most likely to encounter Indians were generally the least sympathetic (Source 15.8). Government officials were also divided. The most notable differences were between civilians in the Interior Department who favored peaceful solutions and those in the War Department who were inclined to use military force to resolve conflicts. However, even reform-minded whites often failed to understand or pay heed to actual Indian culture, and they developed many policies that led to the decline of Indian tribal societies. Facing a dominant white American society that could see only two options — eliminating Indian culture outright, or fundamentally changing its core — Indian attitudes ranged from fierce resistance, to accommodation to, in rare cases, assimilation (Sources 15.9 and 15.10).

Source 15.6

James Michael Cavanaugh | Support for Indian Extermination, 1868

James Michael Cavanaugh was originally from Springfield, Massachusetts, but moved to Minnesota in 1854, where he served in Congress for one term. He subsequently moved to Colorado and then Montana and served in the House of Representatives as a Democrat from 1867 to 1871. In the following congressional speech, Cavanaugh explains his attitude toward Indians in a discussion about Indian appropriations with Republican representative Benjamin Butler of Massachusetts.

→ going westward

will say that I like an Indian better dead than living. I have never in my life seen a good Indian (and I have seen thousands) except when I have seen a dead Indian. I believe in the Indian policy pursued by New England in years long gone. I believe in the Indian policy which was taught by the great chieftain of Massachusetts, Miles Standish. I believe in the policy that exterminates the Indians, drives them outside the boundaries of civilization, because you cannot civilize them. Gentlemen may call this very harsh language; but perhaps they would not think so if they had had my experience in Minnesota and Colorado. In Minnesota the almost living babe has been torn from its mother's womb; and I have seen the child, with its young heart palpitating, nailed to the window-sill. I have seen women who were scalped, disfigured, outraged. In Denver, Colorado Territory, I have seen women and children brought in scalped. Scalped why? Simply because the Indian was "upon the war-path," to satisfy his devilish and barbarous propensities. You have made your treaties with the Indians, but they have not been observed. . . . The Indian will make a treaty in the fall, and in the spring he is again "upon the war-path." The torch, the scalping-knife, plunder, and desolation follow wherever the Indian goes.

But, Mr. Chairman, I will answer the gentleman's question more directly. My friend from Massachusetts [Mr. Butler] has never passed the barrier of the frontier. All he knows about Indians (the gentleman will pardon me for saying it) may have been gathered, I presume, from the brilliant pages of the author of "The Last of the Mohicans," or from the lines of the poet Longfellow in "Hiawatha." The gentleman has never yet seen the Indian upon the war-path. He has never been chased, as I have been, by these red devils—who seem to be the pets of the eastern philanthropists.

Source: U.S. Congress, *The Congressional Globe: Containing the Debates and Proceedings of the Second Session of the Fortieth Congress*, May 28, 1868, 2638.

Source 15.7

Helen Hunt Jackson | Challenges to Indian Policy, 1881

Helen Hunt Jackson's book *A Century of Dishonor* severely criticized U.S. policy toward Indians. Jackson sent a copy of her book to every member of Congress. Despite her attack on the government's treatment of Indians and her advocacy of reform, Jackson believed that American Indians could not become citizens until they received proper training from enlightened white teachers.

There is not among these three hundred bands of Indians one which has not suffered cruelly at the hands either of the Government or of white settlers. The poorer, the more insignificant, the more helpless the band, the more certain the cruelty and outrage to which they have been subjected. This is especially true of the bands on the Pacific slope. These Indians found themselves of a sudden surrounded by and caught up in the great influx of gold-seeking settlers, as helpless creatures on a shore are caught up in a tidal wave. There was not time for the Government to make treaties; not even time for communities to make laws. The tale of the wrongs, the oppressions, the murders of the Pacific-slope Indians in the last thirty years would be a volume by itself, and is too monstrous to be believed. . . .

To assume that it would be easy, or by any one sudden stroke of legislative policy possible, to undo the mischief and hurt of the long past, set the Indian policy of the country right for the future, and make the Indians at once safe and happy, is the blunder of a hasty and uninformed judgment. The notion which seems to be growing more prevalent, that simply to make all Indians at once citizens of the United States would be a sovereign and instantaneous panacea for all their ills and all the Government's perplexities, is a very inconsiderate one. To administer complete citizenship of a sudden, all round, to all Indians, barbarous and civilized alike, would be as grotesque a blunder as to dose them all round with any one medicine, irrespective of the symptoms and needs of their diseases. It would kill more than it would cure. . . . All judicious plans and measures for their safety and salvation must embody provisions for their becoming citizens as fast as they are fit, and must protect them till then in every right and particular in which our laws protect other "persons" who are not citizens. . . .

Cheating, robbing, breaking promises—these three are clearly things which must cease to be done. One more thing, also, and that is the refusal of the protection of the law to the Indian's rights of property, "of life, liberty, and the pursuit of happiness."

When these four things have ceased to be done, time, statesmanship, philanthropy, and Christianity can slowly and surely do the rest. Till these four things have ceased to be done, statesmanship and philanthropy alike must work in vain, and even Christianity can reap but small harvest.

Source: Helen Hunt Jackson, *A Century of Dishonor: A Sketch of the United States Government's Dealings with Some of the Indian Tribes* (New York: Harper and Brothers, 1881), 337–38, 340–42.

Source 15.8

Thomas Nast | "Patience until the Indian Is Civilized — So to Speak," 1878

Through his cartoons, artist Thomas Nast crusaded against political corruption and mistreatment of freedpeople in the South. Although generally sympathetic to the rights of American Indians, in this illustration he raises questions about what the federal government should do regarding conflicts between white settlers and Indians in the West. Nast depicts Secretary of the Interior Carl Schurz (left), an Indian reformer, counseling patience to western settlers.

Library of Congress, Prints and Photographs Division [LC-DIG-ds-01283]

Source 15.9

Zitkala-Ša | Life at an Indian Boarding School, 1921

Gertrude Simmons Bonnin, who later took the Indian name Zitkala-Ša, lived on the Yankton Reservation in South Dakota, with her mother and brother until 1884, when missionaries recruited her to attend school so that she would become assimilated into Anglo-American culture. After attending a Quaker school in Wabash, Indiana, Zitkala-Ša briefly attended Earlham College and then taught at the Carlisle Indian Industrial School in Pennsylvania for two years. During that time, she experienced a reawakening of her American Indian heritage and consciousness and began publishing autobiographical accounts criticizing the educational practices of the schools she attended and at which she taught. In 1921 she recounted her own experiences in these Indian schools, including the incident she describes in the following selection.

The first day in the land of apples was a bitter-cold one; for the snow still covered the ground, and the trees were bare. A large bell rang for breakfast, its loud metallic voice crashing through the belfry overhead and into our sensitive ears. The annoying clatter of shoes on bare floors gave us no peace. The constant clash of harsh noises, with an undercurrent of many voices murmuring an unknown tongue, made a bedlam within which I was securely tied. And though my spirit tore itself in struggling for its lost freedom, all was useless.

A paleface woman, with white hair, came up after us. We were placed in a line of girls who were marching into the dining room. These were Indian girls, in stiff shoes and closely clinging dresses. The small girls wore sleeved aprons and shingled hair [haircut with the hair cut short from the back of the head to the nape of the neck]. As I walked noiselessly in my soft moccasins, I felt like sinking to the floor, for my blanket had been stripped from my shoulders. I looked hard at the Indian girls, who seemed not to care that they were even more immodestly dressed than I, in their tightly fitting clothes. . . .

A small bell was tapped, and each of the pupils drew a chair from under the table. Supposing this act meant they were to be seated, I pulled out mine and at once slipped into it from one side. But when I turned my head, I saw that I was the only one seated, and all the rest at our table remained standing. Just as I began to rise, looking shyly around to see how chairs were to be used, a second bell was sounded. All were seated at last, and I had to crawl back into my chair again. I heard a man's voice at one end of the hall, and I looked around to see him. But all the others hung their heads over their plates. As I glanced at the long chain of tables, I caught the eyes of a paleface woman upon me. Immediately I dropped my eyes, wondering why I was so keenly watched by the strange woman. The man ceased his mutterings, and then a third bell was tapped. Every one picked up his knife and fork and began eating. I began crying instead, for by this time I was afraid to venture anything more.

But this eating by formula was not the hardest trial in that first day. Late in the morning, my friend Judéwin gave me a terrible warning. Judéwin knew a few words of English; and she had overheard the paleface woman talk about cutting our long, heavy hair. Our mothers had taught us that only unskilled warriors who were captured had their hair shingled by the enemy. Among our people, short hair was worn by mourners, and shingled hair by cowards!

We discussed our fate some moments, and when Judéwin said, "We have to submit, because they are strong," I rebelled.

"No, I will not submit! I will struggle first!" I answered.

I watched my chance, and when no one noticed I disappeared. I crept up the stairs as quietly as I could in my squeaking shoes—my moccasins had been exchanged for shoes. Along the hall I passed, without knowing whither I was going. Turning aside to an open door, I found a large room with three white beds in it. The windows were covered with dark green curtains, which made the room very dim. Thankful that no one was there, I directed my steps toward the corner farthest from the door. On my hands and knees I crawled under the bed, and cuddled myself in the dark corner.

From my hiding place I peered out, shuddering with fear whenever I heard footsteps near by. Though in the hall loud voices were calling my name, and I knew that even Judéwin was searching for me, I did not open my mouth to answer. Then the steps were quickened and the voices became excited. The sounds came nearer and nearer. Women and girls entered the room. I held my breath and watched them open closet doors and peep behind large trunks. Some one threw up the curtains, and the room was filled with sudden light. What caused them to stoop and look under the bed I do not know. I remember being dragged out, though I resisted by kicking and scratching wildly. In spite of myself, I was carried downstairs and tied fast in a chair.

I cried aloud, shaking my head all the while until I felt the cold blades of the scissors against my neck, and heard them gnaw off one of my thick braids. Then I lost my spirit. Since the day I was taken from my mother I had suffered extreme indignities. People had stared at me. I had been tossed about in the air like a wooden puppet. And now my long hair was shingled like a coward's! In my anguish I moaned for my mother, but no one came to comfort me. Not a soul reasoned quietly with me, as my own mother used to do; for now I was only one of many little animals driven by a herder.

Source: Zitkala-Ša (Gertrude Bonnin), *American Indian Stories* (Washington, DC: Hayworth, 1921), 52–56.

Source 15.10

Chief Joseph | Views on Indian Affairs, 1879

In 1877, following a string of treaties broken by the U.S. government, Chief Joseph led the Nez Percé on a 1,300-mile march from their tribal land in Oregon to Canada, in search of a home. Thirty miles from the Canadian border, they were surrounded by U.S. troops. After his capture, Chief Joseph was taken to Washington, D.C., where he addressed a gathering of cabinet members and congressmen and tried to convince them to return tribal lands to the Nez Percé.

At last I was granted permission to come to Washington and bring my friend Yellow Bull and our interpreter with me. I am glad we came. I have shaken hands with a great many friends, but there are some things I want to know which no one seems able to explain. I can not understand how the Government sends a man out to fight us, as it did General [Nelson A.] Miles, and then breaks his word. Such a government has something wrong about it. I can not understand why so many chiefs are allowed to talk so many different ways, and promise so many different things. . . . I do not understand why nothing is done for my people. I have heard talk and talk, but nothing is done. Good words do not last long unless they amount to something. Words do not pay for my dead people. They do not pay for my country, now overrun by white men. They do not protect my father's grave. They do not pay for all my horses and cattle. Good words will not give me back my children. . . . Good words will not give my people good health and stop them from dying. Good words will not get my people a home where they can live in peace and take care of themselves. I am tired of talk that comes to nothing. It makes my heart sick when I remember all the good words and all the broken promises. . . . Too many misrepresentations have been made, too many misunderstandings have come up between the white men about the Indians. If the white man wants to live in peace with the Indian he can live in peace. There need be no trouble. Treat all men alike. Give them all the same law. Give them all an even chance to live and grow. All men were made by the same Great Spirit Chief. They are all brothers. The earth is the mother of all people, and all people should have equal rights upon it. You might as well expect the rivers to run backward as that any man who was born a free man should be contented when penned up and denied liberty to go where he pleases. If you tie a horse to a stake, do you expect he will grow fat? If you pen an Indian up on a small spot of earth, and compel him to stay there, he will not be contented, nor will he grow and prosper. . . .

I know that my race must change. We can not hold our own with the white men as we are. We only ask an even chance to live as other men live. We ask to be recognized as men. We ask that the same law shall work alike on all men. If the Indian breaks the law, punish him by the law. If the white man breaks the law, punish him also.

Whenever the white man treats the Indian as they treat each other, then we shall have no more wars. . . . For this time the Indian race are waiting and praying. I hope that no more groans of wounded men and women will ever go to the ear of the Great Spirit Chief above, and that all people may be one people.

Source: "An Indian's View of Indian Affairs," *North American Review*, April 1879, 431–33.

Interpret the Evidence

1. Explain why James Michael Cavanaugh (Source 15.6) and Helen Hunt Jackson (Source 15.7) reach different conclusions concerning Indian policy.

2. How does Thomas Nast's illustration (Source 15.8) reflect the historical situation in 1878?

3. What options did Indians have when confronted with white determination to eradicate their culture? What choice does Zitkala-Ša (Source 15.9) make? Why?

4. How does Chief Joseph's experience (Source 15.10) reflect the fundamental contradiction of federal policy toward Indians?

5. Explain which audience would have been most likely to respond positively to each document's argument.

Put It in Context

Imagine that you are an American president in the second half of the nineteenth century and can design Indian policy. Based on what you have read, what would you do, and why? What challenges might you face as you attempted to implement your policy?

Industrial America

1877–1900

Window to the Past

Alice Austen and Trude Eccleston, 1891

This photograph taken in 1891 of Alice Austen and her friend Trude Eccleston provides some insight into images of women near the turn of the twentieth century. Eccleston's father was a minister, but this photograph suggests both the intimate and rebellious nature of the young women. ▸ **To learn more about this primary source, see Source 16.3 on page 549.**

Collection of Historic Richmond Town. Staten Island Historical Society

After reading this chapter you will be able to:

- Summarize the causes of American industrialization and evaluate the impact of industrialization on business and the economy.

- Analyze popular doctrines guiding social and economic policy during the industrial age and evaluate prominent critiques of these ideas.

- Describe new lifestyles that emerged from industrialization and explain how Americans reacted to anxieties about changing gender and racial roles that resulted.

- Describe the forces that constrained and influenced national politics in the late 1800s.

Comparing American Histories

In 1848 Will and Margaret Carnegie left Scotland and sailed to America, hoping to find a better life for themselves and their children. Once settled in Pittsburgh, Pennsylvania, the family went to work, including thirteen-year-old Andrew, who found a job in a textile mill. For $1.25 per week, he dipped spools into an oil bath and fired the factory furnace — tasks that left him nauseated by the smell of oil and frightened by the boiler. Nevertheless, like the hero of the rags-to-riches stories that were so popular in his era, **Andrew Carnegie** persevered, rising from poverty to great wealth through a series of jobs and clever investments. As a teenager, he worked in a telegraph

the American story
rags-to-riches

(*left*) **Andrew Carnegie** Library of Congress, Prints and Photographs Division [LC-USZ62-88699]

(*right*) **John Sherman** Library of Congress, Prints and Photographs Division [LC-DIG-cwpbh-05141]

office. A superintendent of the Pennsylvania Railroad Company noticed Andrew's aptitude and made him his personal assistant and telegrapher. While in this position, Carnegie learned about the railroad industry and purchased stock in a sleeping car company; the returns from that investment tripled his annual salary. Carnegie then became a railroad superintendent in western Pennsylvania, and by the time he was thirty-five, he had grown wealthy from his investments in a wide variety of industries.

Andrew Carnegie eventually founded the greatest steel company in the world and became one of the wealthiest men of his time. He also became one of the era's greatest philanthropists, fulfilling his sense of community obligation by giving away a great deal of his fortune.

John Sherman also believed in public service, but for him it would come through politics. Born in Lancaster, Ohio in 1823, Sherman became a lawyer like his father, an Ohio Supreme Court judge. Like Carnegie, Sherman made shrewd investments that brought him wealth, although not on the same scale as Carnegie.

Sherman decided to enter politics and in 1854 won election from Ohio to the House of Representatives as a member of the newly created Republican Party. He rose up the leadership ranks as Republicans came to national power with the election of Abraham Lincoln to the presidency in 1860. From 1861 to 1896, Sherman held a variety of major political positions, including U.S. senator from Ohio and secretary of the treasury under President Rutherford B. Hayes. After his term as treasury secretary ended, he returned to the Senate and wielded power as one of the top Republican Party leaders. With his background as chair of the Senate Finance Committee and as secretary of the treasury, Sherman was the most respected Republican of his time in dealing with monetary and financial affairs. Sherman believed that government should encourage business. His most famous accomplishment, the Sherman Antitrust Act, which authorized the government to break up organizations that restrained competition, embodied this belief. It enacted limited reforms without harming powerful business interests. ∎

promoted competition

The American histories of Andrew Carnegie and John Sherman began very differently. Both men played a prominent role in developing the government-business partnership that was crucial to the rapid industrialization of the United States. Carnegie's organization and management skills helped shape the formation of large-scale business. At the same time, Sherman and his fellow lawmakers provided support for that enterprise, using the power of government to reduce risks for businessmen and to increase incentives for economic expansion. They often did so in ways that made politics more corrupt and made politicians less respected. Nevertheless, the public took politics seriously and turned out at the polls in great numbers. Corporate leaders joined with the clergy and writers to defend the established hierarchy of wealth and power. These businessmen used the doctrines of laissez-faire and Social Darwinism to justify their ruthless practices in the name of progress.

Industrialization and big business reshaped the nation. Railroads expanded national and international markets for American factory goods. Innovations and new inventions promoted business consolidation. Industrialization even brought changes to the agricultural South, all within the framework of racial segregation. Great fortunes were made, and the rich showcased their lavish lifestyles. Corporate consolidation also created a new middle class. The men of this group used their leisure to create new social and professional organizations while the women devoted more time to clubs and charitable associations.

America Industrializes

Between 1870 and 1900, the United States grew into a global industrial power. Transcontinental railroads spurred this breathtaking transformation, linking regional markets into a national market; at the same time, railroads themselves served as a massive new market for raw materials and new technologies. Building on advantages developed over the course of the nineteenth century, the Northeast, Midwest, and West led the way in the new economy, while efforts to industrialize the South met with uneven success. Men like Andrew Carnegie became both the heroes and the villains of their age. They engaged in ruthless practices that would lead some to label the new industrialists "robber barons," but they also created systems of industrial organization and corporate management that altered the economic landscape of the country and changed the place of the United States in the world.

The New Industrial Economy. The industrial revolution of the late nineteenth century originated in Europe. Great Britain was the world's first industrial power, but by the 1870s Germany had emerged as a major challenger for industrial dominance, increasing its steel production at a rapid rate and leading the way in the chemical and electrical industries. The dynamic economic growth and innovation stimulated by industrial competition quickly crossed the Atlantic.

Industrialization transformed the American economy. As industrialization took hold, the U.S. gross domestic product, the output of all goods and services produced annually, quadrupled—from $9 billion in 1860 to $37 billion in 1890. During this same period, the number of Americans employed by industry doubled. Moreover, the nature of industry itself changed, as small factories catering to local markets were displaced by large-scale firms producing for national and international markets. The midwestern cities of Chicago, Cincinnati, and St. Louis joined Boston, New York, and Philadelphia as centers of factory

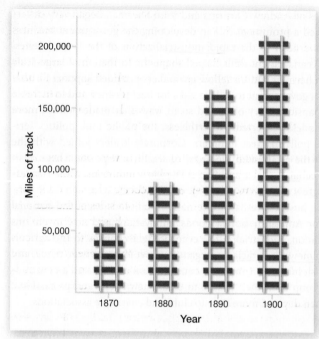

FIGURE 16.1 Expansion of the Railroad System, 1870–1900

The great expansion of the railroads in the late nineteenth century fueled the industrial revolution and the growth of big business. Connecting the nation from East Coast to West Coast, transcontinental railroads created a national market for natural resources and manufactured goods. The biggest surge in railroad construction occurred west of the Mississippi River and in the South. Describe the political and technological forces that promoted enormous railroad expansion from 1870–1900.

railroad is central

production, while the exploitation of the natural resources in the West took on an increasingly industrial character. Trains, telegraphs, and telephones connected the country in ways never before possible.

From 1870 to 1913, the United States experienced an extraordinary rate of growth in industrial output: In 1870 American industries turned out 23.3 percent of the world's manufacturing production; by 1913 this figure had jumped to 35.8 percent. In fact, U.S. output in 1913 almost equaled the combined total for Europe's three leading industrial powers: Germany, the United Kingdom, and France. By the end of the nineteenth century, the United States was surging ahead of northern Europe as the manufacturing center of the world.

At the heart of the American industrial transformation was the railroad. Large-scale business enterprises would not have developed without a national market for raw materials and finished products. A consolidated system of railroads crisscrossing the nation facilitated the creation of such a market (Figure 16.1). In addition, railroads were direct consumers of industrial products, stimulating the growth of a number of industries through their consumption of steel, wood, coal, glass, rubber, brass, and iron. Finally, railroads contributed to economic growth by increasing the speed and efficiency with which products and materials were transported.

Before railroads could create a national market, they had to overcome several critical problems. In 1877 railroad lines dotted the country in haphazard fashion. They primarily served local markets and remained unconnected at key points. This lack of coordination stemmed mainly from the fact that each railroad had its own track gauge (the width between the tracks), making shared track use impossible and long-distance travel extremely difficult.

The consolidation of railroads solved many of these problems. In 1886 railroad companies finally agreed to adopt a standard gauge. Railroads also standardized time zones, thus eliminating confusion in train schedules. During the 1870s, towns and cities each set their own time zone, a practice that created discrepancies among them. In 1882 the time in New York City and in Boston varied by 11 minutes and 45 seconds. The following year, railroads agreed to coordinate times and divided the country into four standard time zones. Most cities soon cooperated with the new system, but not until 1918 did the federal government legislate the standard time zones that the railroads had first adopted.

Innovation and Inventions.

In addition to railroads, there were other engines of industrialization. American technological innovation created new industries, while expanding the efficiency and productivity of old ones. In 1866 a transatlantic telegraph cable connected the United States and Europe, allowing businessmen on both sides of the ocean to pursue profitable commercial ventures. New inventions also allowed business offices to run more smoothly: Typewriters were invented in 1868, carbon paper in 1872, adding machines in 1891, and mimeograph machines in 1892. As businesses grew, they needed more space for their operations. The construction of towering skyscrapers in the 1880s in cities such as Chicago and New York was made possible by two innovations: structural steel, which had the strength to support tall buildings, and elevators.

Alexander Graham Bell's telephone revolutionized communications. By 1880 fifty-five cities offered local service and catered to a total of 50,000 subscribers, most of them business customers. In 1885, Bell established the American Telephone and Telegraph Company (AT&T), and long-distance service connected New York, Boston, and Chicago. By 1900 around 1.5 million telephones were in operation.

Perhaps the greatest technological innovations that advanced industrial development came in steel manufacturing. In 1859 Henry Bessemer, a British inventor, designed a furnace that burned the impurities out of melted iron and converted it into steel. The open-hearth process, devised by another Englishman, William Siemens, further improved the quality of steel by removing additional impurities from the iron. Railroads replaced iron rails with steel because it was lighter, stronger, and more durable than iron. Steel became the major building block of industry, furnishing girders and cables to construct manufacturing plants and office structures. As production became cheaper and more efficient, steel output soared from 13,000 tons in 1860 to 28 million tons in the first decade of the twentieth century.

Factory machinery needed constant lubrication, and the growing petroleum industry made this possible. A new drilling technique devised in 1859 tapped into pools of petroleum located deep below the earth's surface. In the post–Civil War era, new distilling techniques transformed petroleum into lubricating oil for factory machinery. This process of "cracking" crude oil also generated lucrative by-products for the home, such as kerosene and paraffin for heating and lighting and salve to soothe cuts and burns. After 1900, the development of the gasoline-powered, internal combustion engine for automobiles opened up an even richer market for the oil industry.

Locomotives also benefited from innovations in technology. Improvements included air brakes and automatic coupling devices to attach train cars to each other. Elijah McCoy, a trained engineer and the son of former slaves, was forced because of racial discrimination to work at menial railroad jobs shoveling coal and lubricating train parts every few miles to

The Thomas Edison Team at Menlo Park
Thomas A. Edison relied on cooperation to produce the inventions pouring out of his Menlo Park, New Jersey laboratory. In this photograph, Edison is seated in the center surrounded by members of his team. Fred Ott sits on the left and George Gouraud on the right. Standing (left to right) are W. K. L. Dickson, Charles Batchelor, A. Theodore Wangemann, John Ott, and Charles Brown. Edison and his associates first invented the phonograph in 1877, and they are gathered around their "perfected" wax-recording phonograph, completed in 1888. Library of Congress, 3a15704

keep the gears from overheating. This experience encouraged him to invent and patent an automatic lubricating device to improve efficiency.

By the late nineteenth century technological progress was increasingly an organized, collaborative effort. Thomas Alva Edison and his team served as the model. In 1876 Edison set up a research laboratory in Menlo Park, New Jersey. Housed in a two-story, white frame building, Edison's "invention factory" was staffed by a team of inventors and craftsmen. In 1887 Edison opened another laboratory, ten times bigger than the one at Menlo Park, in nearby Orange, New Jersey. These facilities pioneered the research laboratories that would become a standard feature of American industrial development in the twentieth century.

Edison's laboratories produced inventions that revolutionized American business and culture. The phonograph and motion pictures changed the way people spent their leisure time. The electric light bulb illuminated people's homes and made them safer by eliminating the need for candles and gas lamps, which were fire hazards. It also brightened city streets, making them available for outdoor evening activities, and lit up factories so that they could operate all night long.

Like his contemporaries who were building America's huge industrial empires, Edison cashed in on his workers' inventions. He joined forces with the Wall Street banker J. P. Morgan to finance the Edison Electric Illuminating Company, which in 1882 provided lighting to customers in New York City. Goods produced by electric equipment jumped in value from $1.9 million in 1879 to $21.8 million in 1890. In 1892, Morgan helped Edison merge his companies with several competitors and reorganized them as the General Electric Corporation, which became the industry leader.

Building a New South.

Although the largely rural South lagged behind the North and the Midwest in manufacturing, industrial expansion did not bypass the region. Well aware of global economic trends and eager for the South to achieve its economic potential, southern business leaders and newspaper editors saw industrial development as the key to the creation of a **New South**. Attributing the Confederate defeat in the Civil War to the North's superior manufacturing output and railroad supply lines, New South proponents hoped to modernize their economy in a similar fashion. One of those boosters was

Richard H. Edmonds, editor of the *Manufacturers' Record*. He extolled the virtues of the "real South" of the 1880s, characterized by "the music of progress — the whirr of the spindle, the buzz of the saw, the roar of the furnace, the throb of the locomotive." Edmonds envisioned a South that would move beyond regional separatism and become fully integrated into the national economy. → a rebirth

Railroads were the key to achieving such economic integration, so after the Civil War new railroad tracks were laid throughout the South. This expanded railroad system created direct connections between the North and the South, and it facilitated the growth of the southern textile industry. Seeking to take advantage of plentiful cotton, cheap labor, and the improved transportation system, investors built textile mills throughout the South. Victims of falling prices and saddled with debt, sharecroppers and tenant farmers moved into mill towns in search of better employment. Mill owners preferred to hire girls and young women, who worked for low wages, to spin cotton and weave it on the looms. To do so, however, owners had to employ their entire family, for mothers and fathers would not let their daughters relocate without their supervision. Whatever attraction the mills offered applied only to whites. The pattern of white supremacy in the post-Reconstruction South kept blacks out of all but the most menial jobs.

Impact on African Americans

Blacks contributed greatly to the construction of railroads in the New South, but they did not do so as free men. Convicts, most of whom were African American, performed the exhausting work of laying tracks through hills and swamps. Southern states used the **convict lease** system, in which blacks, usually imprisoned for minor offenses, were hired out to private companies to serve their time or pay off their fine. The convict lease system brought additional income to the state and supplied cheap labor to the railroads and planters, but it left convict laborers impoverished and virtually enslaved.

exception to 13th amendment

money?

The South attracted a number of industries besides textile manufacturing. In the 1880s, James B. Duke established a cigarette manufacturing empire in Durham, North Carolina. Nearby tobacco fields provided the raw material that black workers prepared for white workers, who then rolled the cigarettes by machine. Acres of timber pines in the Carolinas, Florida, and Alabama sustained a lucrative lumber industry. Rich supplies of coal and iron in Alabama fostered the growth of the steel industry in Birmingham (Map 16.1).

Despite this frenzy of industrial activity, the New South in many ways resembled the Old South. Southern entrepreneurs still depended on northern investors to supply much of the capital for investment. Investors were attracted by the low wages that prevailed in the South, but low wages also meant that southern workers remained poor and, in many cases, unable to buy the manufactured goods produced by industry. Efforts to diversify agriculture beyond tobacco and cotton were constrained by a sharecropping system based on small, inefficient plots. In fact, even though industrialization did make considerable headway in the South, the economy remained overwhelmingly agricultural. This suited many white southerners who wanted to hold on to the individualistic, agrarian values they associated with the Old South. Tied to old ideologies and a system of forced labor, modernization in the South could go only so far.

Industrial Consolidation. In the North, South, and West, nineteenth-century industrialists strove to minimize or eliminate competition. To gain competitive advantages and increase profits, industrial entrepreneurs concentrated on reducing production costs, charging lower prices, and outselling the competition. Successful firms could then

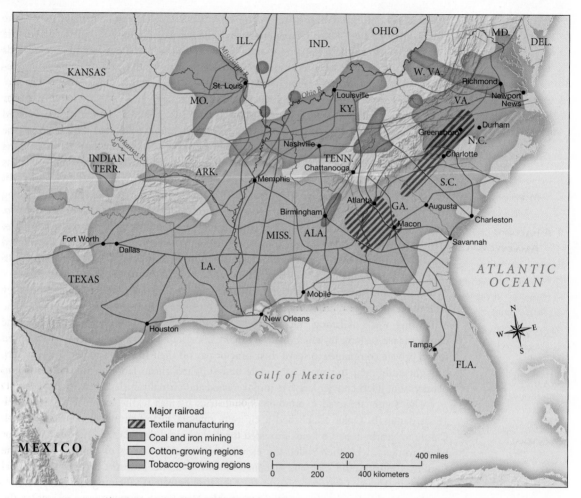

MAP 16.1   The New South, 1900

Although the South remained largely agricultural by 1900, it had made great strides toward building industries in the region. This so-called New South boasted an extensive railway network that provided a national market for its raw materials and manufactured goods, including coal, iron, steel, and textiles. Still, the southern economy in 1900 depended primarily on raising cotton and tobacco.

acquire rival companies that could no longer afford to compete, creating an industrial empire in the process.

Building such industrial empires was not easy, however, and posed creative challenges for business ventures. Heavy investment in machinery resulted in very high fixed costs (or overhead) that did not change much over time. Because overhead costs remained stable, manufacturers could reduce the per-unit cost of production by increasing the output of a product — what economists call "economy of scale." Manufacturers aimed to raise the volume of production and find ways to cut variable costs — for labor and materials, for example.

Through such savings, a factory owner could sell his product more cheaply than his competitors and gain a larger share of the market.

A major organizational technique for reducing costs and underselling the competition was **vertical integration**. "Captains of industry," as their admirers called them, did not just build a business; they created a system — a network of firms, each contributing to the final product. Men like Andrew Carnegie controlled the various phases of production from top to bottom (vertical), extracting the raw materials, transporting them to the factories, manufacturing the finished products, and shipping them to market. By using vertical integration, Carnegie eliminated middlemen and guaranteed regular and cheap access to supplies. He also lowered inventories and gained increased flexibility by shifting segments of the labor force to areas where they were most needed. His credo became "Watch the costs and the profits will take care of themselves."

Businessmen also employed another type of integration — **horizontal integration**. This approach focused on gaining greater control over the market by acquiring firms that sold the same products. John D. Rockefeller, the founder of the mammoth Standard Oil Company, specialized in this technique. In the mid-1870s, he brought a number of key oil refiners into an alliance with Standard Oil to control four-fifths of the industry. At the same time, the oil baron ruthlessly drove out of business or bought up marginal firms that could not afford to compete with him.

Horizontal integration was also a major feature in the telegraph industry. By 1861 Western Union had strung 76,000 miles of telegraph line throughout the nation. Founded in 1851, the company had thrived during the Civil War by obtaining most of the federal government's telegraph business. The firm had 12,600 offices housed in railroad depots throughout the country and strung its lines adjacent to the railroads. Seeing an opportunity to make money, Wall Street tycoon Jay Gould set out to acquire Western Union. In the mid-1870s, Gould, who had obtained control over the Union Pacific Railway, financed companies to compete with the giant telegraph outfit. Gould finally succeeded in 1881, when he engineered a takeover of Western Union by combining it with his American Union Telegraph Company. Gould made a profit of $30 million on the deal. On February 15, the day after the agreement, the *New York Herald Tribune* reported: "The country finds itself this morning at the feet of a telegraphic monopoly," a business that controlled the market and destroyed competition.

Bankers played a huge role in industrial consolidation. No one did it more skillfully than John Pierpont Morgan. In the 1850s, Morgan started his career working for a prominent American-owned banking firm in London, and in 1861 he created his own investment company in New York City. Morgan played the central role in channeling funds from Britain to support the construction of major American railroads. During the 1880s and 1890s, Morgan orchestrated the refinancing of several ailing railroads. To maintain control over these enterprises, the Wall Street financier placed his allies on their boards of directors and selected the companies' chief operating officers. Morgan then turned his talents for organization to the steel industry. In 1901 he was instrumental in merging Carnegie's company with several competitors in which he had a financial interest. United States Steel, Morgan's creation, became the world's largest industrial corporation, worth $1.4 billion. By the end of the first decade of the twentieth century, Morgan's investment house held more than 340 directorships in 112 corporations, amounting to more than $22 billion in assets, all at a time when there was no income tax.

The Growth of Corporations.

With economic consolidation came the expansion of corporations. Before the age of large-scale enterprise, the predominant form of business ownership was the partnership. Unlike a partnership, a **corporation** provided investors with "limited liability." This meant that if the corporation went bankrupt, shareholders could not lose more than they had invested. Limited liability encouraged investment by keeping the shareholders' investment in the corporation separate from their other assets. In addition, corporations provided "perpetual life." Partnerships dissolved on the death of a partner, whereas corporations continued to function despite the death of any single owner. This form of ownership brought stability and order to financing, building, and perpetuating complex business endeavors.

[margin handwritten notes: joint + share company; bring stability]

Capitalists devised new corporate structures to gain greater control over their industries. Rockefeller's Standard Oil Company led the way by creating the **trust**, a monopoly formed by a small group of leading stockholders from several firms who manage the consolidated enterprise. To evade state laws against monopolies, Rockefeller created a petroleum trust. He combined other oil firms across the country with Standard Oil and placed their owners on a nine-member board of trustees that ran the company. Subsequently, Rockefeller created another method of bringing rival businesses together. Through a holding company, he obtained stock in a number of other oil companies and held them under his control. *horizantal integration*

[margin handwritten notes: monopolized the market]

Explore ▶

See Source 16.1 for one cartoonist's interpretation of Rockefeller's power.

Between 1880 and 1905, more than three hundred mergers occurred in 80 percent of the nation's manufacturing firms. Great wealth became heavily concentrated in the hands of a relatively small number of businessmen. Around two thousand businesses, a tiny fraction of the total number, dominated 40 percent of the nation's economy.

In their drive to consolidate economic power and shield themselves from risk, corporate titans generally had the courts on their side. In *Santa Clara County v. Southern Pacific Railroad Company* (1886), the Supreme Court decided that under the Fourteenth Amendment, which originally dealt with the issue of federal protection of African Americans' civil rights, a corporation was considered a "person." In effect, this ruling gave corporations the same right of due process that the framers of the amendment had meant to give to former slaves. In the 1890s, a majority of the Supreme Court embraced this interpretation. The right of due process shielded corporations from government regulation of the workplace, including the passage of legislation reducing the number of hours in the workday.

[margin handwritten notes: shielded by government]

Yet trusts did not go unopposed. In 1890 Congress passed the **Sherman Antitrust Act**, which outlawed monopolies that prevented free competition in interstate commerce. The bill passed easily with bipartisan support because it merely codified legal principles that already existed. Senator Sherman and his colleagues intended to limit underhanded actions that destroyed competition. However, the judicial system shielded large corporations. In *United States v. E.C. Knight Company* (1895), a case against the "sugar trust," the Supreme Court rendered the Sherman Act virtually toothless by ruling that manufacturing was a local activity within a state and that, even if it was a monopoly, it was not subject to congressional regulation. This ruling left most trusts in the manufacturing sector beyond the jurisdiction of the Sherman Antitrust Act.

[margin handwritten notes: what capitalism is built on]

As the expanding labor force worked to produce a rapidly rising volume of goods, efficiency experts sought to cut labor costs and make the production process operate more smoothly. Frederick W. Taylor, a Philadelphia engineer and businessman, developed the

Guided Primary Source Analysis

Horace Taylor | What a Funny Little Government, 1900

As large firms merged with competitors to form giant companies that dominated the marketplace, opponents of such trusts decried the power that these enterprises wielded over the economy and the political system. Responding to such concerns, Congress passed the Sherman Antitrust Act in 1890, but the law proved weak and was loosely enforced. In the following illustration, cartoonist Horace Taylor, a Democrat, sought to make trusts an issue in the 1900 election by attacking John D. Rockefeller, whose Standard Oil Company embodied the evils of trusts for many critics.

Source 16.1

New York Historical Society/Bridgeman Images

How are the Capitol and Treasury depicted?

What is Rockefeller holding in his hand?

How does this illustration of Rockefeller emphasize the cartoonist's antitrust position?

▮ Put It in Context

What does this cartoon suggest about the relationship between big business and the federal government at the start of the twentieth century?

principles of scientific management. Based on his concept of reducing manual labor to its simplest components and eliminating independent action on the part of workers, managers introduced time-and-motion studies. Using a stopwatch, they calculated how to break down a job into simple tasks that could be performed in the least amount of time. From this perspective, workers were no different from the machines they operated. With production soaring, marketing and advertising managers were called upon to devise new techniques to gauge consumer interests and stimulate their demands.

mundane repetitive jobs

Another vital factor in creating large-scale industry was the establishment of retail outlets that could sell the enormous volume of goods pouring out of factories. As consumer goods became less expensive, retail outlets sprang up to serve the growing market for household items. Customers could shop at department stores — such as Macy's in New York City, Filene's in Boston, Marshall Field's in Chicago, May's in Denver, Nordstrom's in Seattle, and Jacome's in Tucson — where they were waited on by an army of salesclerks. Or they could buy the cheaper items in Frank W. Woolworth's five and ten cent stores, which opened in towns and cities nationwide. Chain supermarkets — such as the Great Atlantic and Pacific Tea Company (A&P), founded in 1869 — sold fruits and vegetables packed in tin cans. They also sold foods from the meatpacking firms of Gustavus Swift and Philip Armour, which shipped them on refrigerated railroad cars. Mail-order catalogs allowed Americans in all parts of the country to buy consumer goods without leaving their home. The catalogs of Montgomery Ward (established in 1872) and Sears, Roebuck (founded in 1886) offered tens of thousands of items. Rural free delivery (RFD), instituted by the U.S. Post Office in 1891, made it easier for farmers and others living in the countryside to obtain these catalogs and buy their merchandise without having to travel miles to the nearest post office. By the end of the nineteenth century, the industrial economy had left its mark on almost all aspects of life in almost every corner of America.

increased demand

consumerism

Review & Relate

- What were the key factors behind the acceleration of industrial development in late-nineteenth-century America?

- How did industrialization change the way American businessmen thought about their companies and the people who worked for them?

Laissez-Faire, Social Darwinism, and Their Critics

American industrialization developed as rapidly as it did in large part because it was reinforced by traditional ideas and values. The notion that hard work and diligence would result in success meant that individuals felt justified, even duty-bound, to strive to achieve upward mobility and accumulate wealth. Those who succeeded believed that they had done so because they were more talented, industrious, and resourceful than others. Prosperous businessmen regarded competition and the free market as essential to the health of an economic world they saw based on merit. Yet these same businessmen also created trusts that destroyed competition, and they depended on the government for resources and protection. This contradiction, along with the profoundly unequal distribution of wealth that characterized the late-nineteenth-century economy, generated a good deal of criticism of business tycoons and their beliefs.

The Doctrines of Success. Those at the top of the new industrial order justified their great wealth in a manner that most Americans could understand. The ideas of the Scottish economist Adam Smith, in *The Wealth of Nations* (1776), had gained popularity during the American Revolution. Advocating **laissez-faire** ("let things alone"), Smith contended that an "Invisible Hand," guided by natural law, guaranteed the greatest economic success if the government let individuals pursue their own self-interest unhindered by outside and artificial influences. In the late nineteenth century, businessmen and their conservative allies on the Supreme Court used Smith's doctrines to argue against restrictive government regulation. They equated their right to own and manage property with the personal liberty protected by the Fourteenth Amendment. Thus the Declaration of Independence, with its defense of "life, liberty, and the pursuit of happiness," and the Constitution, which enshrined citizens' political freedom, became instruments to guarantee unfettered economic opportunity and safeguard private property.

The view that success depended on individual initiative was reinforced in schools and churches. The McGuffey Readers, widely used to educate children, taught moral lessons of hard work, individual initiative, reliability, and thrift. The popular dime novels of Horatio Alger portrayed the story of young men who rose from "rags to riches." Americans could also hear success stories in houses of worship. Russell Conwell, pastor of the Grace Baptist Church in Philadelphia, delivered a widely printed sermon entitled "Acres of Diamonds," which equated godliness with riches and argued that ordinary people had an obligation to strive for material wealth. "I say that you ought to get rich, and it is your duty to get rich," Conwell declared, "because to make money honestly is to preach the gospel."

A concern for the welfare of children expressed in the McGuffey Readers and the pulp fiction of Horatio Alger reflected a larger societal problem. Thirteen percent of white children and thirty percent of black children lived with a single parent, most likely a woman. By 1900, 20 to 30 percent of all children under sixteen had lost one parent. Thus, the orphans that Horatio Alger wrote about were not a far-fetched idea.

If economic success was a matter of personal merit, it followed that economic failure was as well. The British philosopher Herbert Spencer proposed a theory of social evolution based on this premise in his book *Social Statics* (1851). Imagining a future utopia, Spencer wrote, "Man was not created with an instinct for his own degradation, but from the lower he has risen to the higher forms. Nor is there any conceivable end to his march to perfection." In his view, those at the top of the economic ladder were closer to perfection than were those at the bottom. Any effort to aid the unfortunate would only slow the march of progress for society as a whole. Spencer's book proved extremely popular, selling nearly 400,000 copies in the United States by 1900. Publication of Charles Darwin's landmark *On the Origin of Species* (1859) appeared to provide some scientific legitimacy for Spencer's view. The British naturalist argued that plants, animals, and humans progressed or declined because of their ability or inability to adapt favorably to the environment and transmit these characteristics to future generations. The connection between the two men's ideas led some people decades later to label Spencer's theory **"Social Darwinism."**

Doctrines of success, such as Social Darwinism, gained favor because they helped Americans explain the rapid economic changes that were disrupting their lives. Although most ordinary people would not climb out of poverty to middle-class respectability, let alone affluence, they clung to ideas that promised hope. Theories such as Spencer's that linked success with progress provided a way for those who did not do well to understand

[handwritten: not the system]

their failure and blame themselves for their own inadequacies. At the same time, the notion that economic success derived from personal merit legitimized the fabulous wealth of those who did rise to the top.

Capitalists such as Carnegie found a way to soften both the message of extreme competition and its impact on the American public. Denying that the government should help the poor, they proclaimed that men of wealth had a duty to furnish some assistance. In his famous essay **"The Gospel of Wealth"** (1889), Carnegie argued that the rich should act as stewards of the wealth they earned. As trustees, they should administer their surplus income for the benefit of the community. Carnegie distinguished between charity (direct handouts to individuals), which he deplored, and philanthropy (building institutions that would raise educational and cultural standards), which he advocated. Carnegie was particularly generous in funding libraries (he provided the buildings but not the books) because they allowed people to gain knowledge through their own efforts.

[handwritten margin: Philanthropists]

Capitalists may have sung the praises of individualism and laissez-faire but this approach did not extend to industrial competition. Successful industrialists in the late nineteenth century sought to destroy competition. Their efforts over the course of several decades produced giant corporations that measured the worth of individuals by calculating their value to the organization. As John D. Rockefeller, the master of consolidation, proclaimed, "The day of individual competition in large affairs is past and gone." **See Primary Source Project 16: Debates about Laissez-Faire, page 562.**

[handwritten margin: contradictory]

Capitalists also sought government involvement that would favor business. Industrialists did not want the federal government to take any action that *retarded* their economic efforts, but they favored the use of the government's power to *promote* their enterprises and to stimulate entrepreneurial energies. Manufacturers pushed for congressional passage of high tariffs to protect goods from foreign competition and to foster development of the national marketplace. Industrialists demanded that federal and state governments dispatch troops when labor strikes threatened their businesses. They persuaded Washington to provide land grants for railroad construction and to send the army to clear Native Americans and bison from their tracks. They argued for state and federal courts to interpret constitutional and statutory law in a way that shielded property rights against attacks from workers. In large measure, capitalists succeeded not in spite of governmental support but because of it.

[handwritten margin: wanted intervention that promoted business]

Challenges to Laissez-Faire.
Proponents of government restraint and unbridled individualism did not go unchallenged. Critics of laissez-faire created an alternative ideology for those who sought to organize workers and expand the role of government as ways of restricting capitalists' power over labor and ordinary citizens.

Lester Frank Ward attacked laissez-faire in his book *Dynamic Sociology* (1883). Ward did not disparage individualism but viewed the main function of society as "the organization of happiness." Contradicting Herbert Spencer, Ward maintained that societies progressed when government directly intervened to help citizens—even the unfortunate. Rejecting laissez-faire, he argued that what people "really need is more government in its primary sense, greater protection from the rapacity of the favored few."

Some academics supported Ward's ideas. Most notably, economist Richard T. Ely applied Christian ethics to his scholarly assessment of capital and labor. He condemned the railroads for dragging "their slimy length over our country, and every turn in their progress is marked by a progeny of evils." In his book *The Labor Movement* (1886), Ely suggested that the ultimate solution for social ills resulting from industrialization lay in "the union of capital and labor in the same hands, in grand, wide-reaching, co-operative enterprises."

Two popular writers, Henry George and Edward Bellamy, added to the critique of materialism and greed. In *Progress and Poverty* (1879), George lamented: "Amid the greatest accumulations of wealth, men die of starvation." He blamed the problem on rent, which he viewed as an unjustifiable payment on the increase in the value of land. His remedy was to have government confiscate rent earned on land by levying a single tax on landownership. Though he advocated government intervention, he did not envision an enduring role for the state once it had imposed the single tax. By contrast, Bellamy imagined a powerful central government. In his novel *Looking Backward, 2000–1887* (1888), Bellamy attacked industrialists who "maim and slaughter workers by thousands." In his view, the federal government should take over large-scale firms, administer them as workers' collectives, and redistribute wealth equally among all citizens.

Neither Bellamy, George, Ward, nor Ely endorsed the militant socialism of Karl Marx. The German philosopher predicted that capitalism would be overthrown and replaced by a revolutionary movement of industrial workers that would control the means of economic production and establish an egalitarian society. Although his ideas gained popularity among European labor leaders, they were not widely accepted in the United States during this period. Most critics believed that the American political system could be reformed without resorting to the extreme solution of a socialist revolution. They favored a cooperative commonwealth of capital and labor, with the government acting as an umpire between the two.

[margin notes: various views; Marxism]

Review & Relate

■ In the late nineteenth century, how did many Americans explain individual economic success and failure?

■ How did the business community view the role of government in the economy at the end of the nineteenth century?

Society and Culture in the Gilded Age

[margin notes: as a disguise; social change]

Wealthy people in the late nineteenth century used their fortunes to support lavish lifestyles. For many of them, especially those with recent wealth, opulence rather than good taste was the standard of adornment. This tendency inspired writer Mark Twain and his collaborator Charles Dudley Warner to describe this era of wealth creation as the **Gilded Age**. Glittering on the outside, the enormous riches covered up the unbridled materialism and political rottenness that lay below the surface.

Twain and Warner had the very wealthy in mind when they coined the phrase, but others further down the social ladder found ways to participate in the culture of consumption. The rapidly expanding middle class enjoyed modest homes furnished with mass-produced consumer goods. Women played the central role in running the household, as most wives remained at home to raise children. Women and men often spent their free time attending meetings and other events sponsored by social, cultural, and political organizations. Such prosperity was, however, largely limited to whites. For the majority of African Americans

The Breakers, Newport, Rhode Island   Newport, Rhode Island was the summer home for many of the wealthy in the Gilded Age. There was no mansion more spectacular than Cornelius Vanderbilt's "The Breakers," completed in 1895 with seventy rooms spread out over five floors. This photograph of the Main Hall illustrates the expanse and opulence of the residence. © Look and Learn/ Bridgeman Images

still living in the South, life proved much harder. In response to black aspirations for social and economic advancement, white politicians imposed a rigid system of racial segregation on the South. Although whites championed the cause of individual upward mobility, they restricted opportunities to achieve success to whites only.

Wealthy and Middle-Class Leisure-Time Pursuits. Industrialization and the rise of corporate capitalism led to the expansion of the wealthy upper class as well as the expansion of the middle class, and new lifestyles emerged. Urban elites lived lives of incredible material opulence. J. P. Morgan, William Vanderbilt, and John D. Rockefeller built lavish homes in New York City. High-rise apartment buildings also catered to the wealthy. Overlooking Central Park, the nine-story Dakota Apartments boasted fifty-eight suites, a banquet hall, and a wine cellar. Millionaire residents furnished their stately homes with an eclectic mix of priceless art objects and furniture in a jumble of diverse styles. The rich and famous established private social clubs, sent their children to exclusive prep schools and colleges, and worshiped in the most fashionable churches.

Second homes, usually for use in the summer, were no less expensively constructed and decorated. Besides residences in Manhattan and Newport, Rhode Island, the Vanderbilts constructed a "home away from home" in the mountains of Asheville, North Carolina. The Biltmore, as they named it, contained 250 rooms, 40 master bedrooms, and an indoor swimming pool.

The wealthy also built and frequented opera houses, concert halls, museums, and historical societies as testimonies to their taste and sophistication. For example, the Vanderbilts, Rockefellers, Goulds, and Morgans financed the completion of the Metropolitan Opera House in New York City in 1883. When the facility opened, a local newspaper commented about the well-heeled audience: "The Goulds and the Vanderbilts and people of that ilk perfumed the air with the odor of crisp greenbacks." Upper-class women often traveled abroad to visit the great European cities and ancient Mediterranean sites.

Industrialization and the rise of corporate capitalism also brought an array of white-collar workers in managerial, clerical, and technical positions. These workers formed a new, expanded middle class and joined the businesspeople, doctors, lawyers, teachers, and clergy who constituted the old middle class. More than three million white-collar workers were employed in 1910, nearly three times as many as in 1870.

Middle-class families decorated their residences with mass-produced furniture, musical instruments, family photographs, books, periodicals, and a variety of memorabilia collected in their leisure time. They could relax in their parlors and browse through mass-circulation magazines and popular newspapers. Or they could read some of the era's outpouring of fiction, including romances, dime novels, westerns, humor, and social realism, an art form that depicted working-class life.

Explore ▸

See Sources 16.2 and 16.3 for two images of women.

With more money and time on their hands, middle-class women and men were able to devote their efforts to charity. They joined a variety of social and professional organizations that were arising to deal with the problems accompanying industrialization (Table 16.1). During the 1880s, charitable organizations such as the American Red Cross were established to provide disaster relief. In 1892 the General Federation of Women's Clubs was founded to improve women's educational and cultural lives. Four years later, the National Association of Colored Women organized to help relieve suffering among the black poor, defend black women, and promote the interests of the black race.

During these swiftly changing times, adults became increasingly concerned about the nation's youth and sought to create organizations that catered to young people. Formed before the Civil War in England and expanded to the United States, the Young Men's Christian Association (YMCA) grew briskly during the 1880s as it erected buildings where young men could socialize, build moral character, and engage in healthy physical exercise. The Young Women's Christian Association (YWCA) provided similar opportunities for women. African Americans also participated in "Y" activities through the creation of racially separate branches.

↳ organizations for youth

TABLE 16.1   An Age of Organizations, 1876–1896

Category	Year of Founding	Organization
Charitable	1881	American Red Cross
	1887	Charity Organization Society
	1889	Educational Alliance
	1893	National Council of Jewish Women
Sports/Fraternal	1876	National League of Baseball
	1882	Knights of Columbus
	1888	National Council of Women
	1892	General Federation of Women's Clubs
	1896	National Association of Colored Women
Professional	1883	Modern Language Association
	1884	American Historical Association
	1885	American Economic Association
	1888	American Mathematical Society

Comparative Primary Source Analysis

Leisure-Class Women

The spectacular economic growth in the second half of the nineteenth century spawned a rise in leisure activities. In wealthy and middle-class families, women were central in shaping household consumption. Expected to conform to public standards of female decorum, some young leisure-class women challenged established gender roles in private. Contrast the cover of *The Delineator* (1900), one of America's foremost women's magazines, with the photograph taken by Alice Austen in 1891. In this photograph Austen and her friend, Trude Eccleston, whose father was an Episcopalian minister, are pictured in Eccleston's bedroom.

Source 16.2

The Delineator, 1900

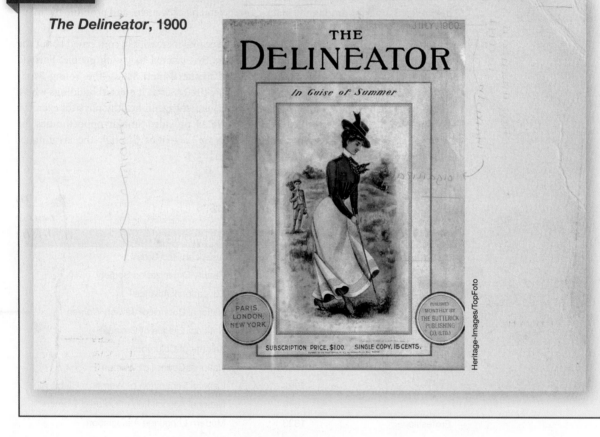

Heritage-Images/TopFoto

Changing Gender Roles. Economic changes led to adjustments in lifestyles and gender roles during the industrial era. Middle-class women generally remained at home, caring for the house and children, often with the aid of a servant. Whereas in the past farmers and artisans had worked from the home, now most men and women accepted as natural

Source 16.3

Alice Austen and Trude Eccleston, 1891

Collection of Historic Richmond Town. Staten Island Historical Society

Interpret the Evidence

1. What do the clothing and activity of the woman on the cover of *The Delineator* suggest about her background?

2. Compare the image of Austen and her friend with the magazine's cover woman. What norms of female behavior are they contesting?

Put It in Context

What social and political trends during the late nineteenth century gave middle-class women increased opportunities to express themselves?

→ still domestic

the separation of the workplace and the home caused by industrialization and urbanization. Although the birthrate and marriage rates among the middle class dropped during the late nineteenth century, wives were still expected to care for their husbands and family first to fulfill their feminine duties. Even though daughters increasingly attended colleges reserved

→ social change

same goal ↓

for women, their families viewed education as a means of providing refinement rather than a career. One physician summed up the prevailing view that women could only use their brains "but little and in trivial matters" and should concentrate on serving as "the companion or ornamental appendage to man."

the housewife →

Middle-class women were part of a new consumer culture. Department stores, chain stores, ready-made clothes, and packaged goods, from Jell-O and Kellogg's Corn Flakes to cake mixes, competed for the money and loyalty of female consumers. Hairdressers, cosmetic companies, and department stores offered a growing and ever-changing assortment of styles. The expanding array of consumer goods did not, however, decrease women's domestic workload. They had more furniture to dust, fancier meals to prepare, changing fashions to keep up with, higher standards of cleanliness to maintain, and more time to devote to entertaining. The availability of mass-produced goods to assist the housewife in her chores made her role as consumer highly visible, while making her role as worker nearly invisible.

more opportunities {

For the more socially and economically independent young women — those who attended college or beauty and secretarial schools — new worlds of leisure opened up. Bicycling, tennis, and croquet became popular sports for women in the late nineteenth century. So, too, did playing basketball, both in colleges and through industrial leagues. Indeed, women's colleges made sports a requirement, to offset the stress of intellectual life and produce a more well-rounded woman.

Middle-class men enjoyed new leisure pursuits, too. During the late nineteenth century 5.5 million men (of some 19 million adult men in the United States) joined fraternal orders, such as the Odd Fellows, Masons, Knights of Pythias, and Elks. These fraternities were divided along class lines with the Masons attracting the wealthiest, the Odd Fellows those in the middle, and the Knights of Pythias bringing in those lower down on the economic ladder. The fraternal orders offered middle-class men a network of business contacts and a communal, masculine social environment otherwise lacking in their lives. This notion of fraternity, however, did not apply to all. These organizations were racially exclusive, and African American men had to form their own lodges.

Women Bicyclists   In the 1890s, with improvements in technology, middle-class women had both more leisure time and access to easy-to-ride bicycles. This photograph shows women at an early stage of the bicycle craze before changes in fashion allowed women to wear less-restrictive clothing that permitted exposed ankles and visible bloomers. In 1895, a Nebraska newspaper commented on the larger social implications of women bicyclists: The bicycle took "old-fashioned, slow-going notions of the gentler sex," and replaced them with "some new woman, mounted on her steed of steel." Robert Alexander/Getty Images

In fact, historians have referred to a "crisis of masculinity" afflicting a segment of middle- and upper-class men in the late nineteenth and early twentieth centuries. Middle-class occupations whittled away the sense of autonomy that men had experienced in an earlier era when they worked for themselves. The emergence of corporate capitalism had swelled the ranks of the middle class who held salaried jobs in managerial departments. At the same time, the expansion of corporations and big business stimulated a demand for clerical workers, female as well as male. This offered women many new opportunities to enter the job market. Along with this development, the push for women's rights, especially the right to vote, and women's increasing involvement in civic associations threatened to reduce absolute male control over the public sphere. *loss of control*

Responding to this gender crisis, middle-class men sought ways to exert their masculinity. Psychologists like G. Stanley Hall warned that unless men returned to a primitive state of manhood, they risked becoming spiritually paralyzed. To avoid this, went their advice, men should build up their bodies and engage in strenuous activities to improve their physical fitness.

Men turned to sports to cultivate their masculinity. Besides playing baseball and football, they could attend various sporting events. Baseball became the national pastime, and men could root for their home team and establish a community with the thousands of male spectators who filled up newly constructed ballparks. Baseball, a game played by elites in New York City in the 1840s, soon became a commercially popular sport. It spread across the country as baseball clubs in different cities competed with each other. The sport came into its own with the creation of the professional National League in 1876, and the introduction of the World Series in 1903 between the winners of the National League and the American League pennant races.

Boxing also became a popular spectator sport in the late nineteenth century. Bare-knuckle fighting — without the protection of gloves — epitomized the craze to display pure masculinity. A boxing match lasted until one of the fighters was knocked out, leaving both fighters bloody and battered.

During the late nineteenth century, middle-class women and men also had increased opportunities to engage in different forms of sociability and sexuality. Gay men and lesbians could find safe havens in New York City's Greenwich Village and Chicago's North Side for their own entertainment. Although treated by medical experts as sexual "inverts" who might be cured by an infusion of "normal" heterosocial contact, gay men and lesbians began to emerge from the shadows of Victorian-era sexual constraints around the turn of the twentieth century. "Boston marriages" constituted another form of relationship between women. The term apparently came from Henry James's book *The Bostonians* (1886), which described a female couple living together in a monogamous, long-term relationship. This type of relationship appealed to financially independent women who did not want to get married. Many of these relationships were sexual, but some were not. In either case, they offered women of a certain class an alternative to traditional, heterosexual marriage.

Black America and Jim Crow.
While wealthy and middle-class whites experimented with new forms of social behavior, African Americans faced greater challenges to preserving their freedom and dignity. In the South, where the overwhelming majority of blacks lived, post-Reconstruction governments adopted various techniques to keep blacks from voting. To circumvent the Fifteenth Amendment, southern states devised suffrage

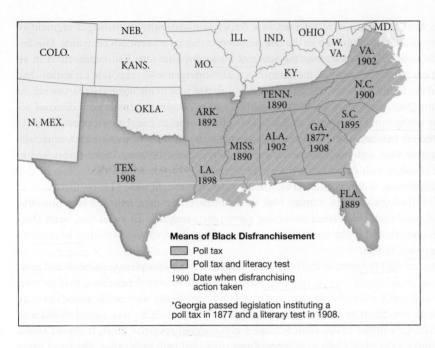

MAP 16.2   Black Disfranchisement in the South, 1889–1908

After Reconstruction, black voters posed a threat to the ruling Democrats by occasionally joining with third-party insurgents. To repel these challenges, Democratic Party leaders made racial appeals to divide poor whites and blacks. Chiefly in the 1890s and early twentieth century, white leaders succeeded in disfranchising black voters (and some poor whites), mainly by adopting poll taxes and literacy requirements.

Means of Black Disfranchisement

- [ ] Poll tax
- [ ] Poll tax and literacy test
- 1900 Date when disfranchising action taken

*Georgia passed legislation instituting a poll tax in 1877 and a literary test in 1908.

[margin note: shift of national attention]

qualifications that they claimed were racially neutral, and the Supreme Court ruled in their favor. They instituted the poll tax, a tax that each person had to pay in order to cast a ballot. Poll taxes fell hardest on the poor, a disproportionate number of whom were African American. Disfranchisement reached its peak in the 1890s, as white southern governments managed to deny the vote to most of the black electorate (Map 16.2). Literacy tests officially barred the uneducated of both races, but they were administered in a manner that discriminated against blacks while allowing illiterate whites to satisfy the requirement. Many literacy tests contained a loophole called a "grandfather clause." Under this exception, men whose father or grandfather had voted in 1860 — a time when white men but not black men, most of whom were slaves, could vote in the South — were excused from taking the test.

[margin note: segregation]

In the 1890s, white southerners also imposed legally sanctioned racial segregation on the region's black citizens. Commonly known as **Jim Crow** laws (named for a character in a minstrel show, where whites performed in blackface), these new statutes denied African Americans equal access to public facilities and ensured that blacks lived apart from whites. In 1883, when the Supreme Court struck down the 1875 Civil Rights Act, it gave southern states the freedom to adopt measures confining blacks to separate schools, public accommodations, seats on transportation, beds in hospitals, and sections of graveyards. In 1896 the Supreme Court sanctioned Jim Crow, constructing the constitutional rationale for legally keeping the races apart. In *Plessy v. Ferguson*, the high court ruled that a Louisiana law providing for "equal but separate" accommodations for "whites" and "coloreds" on railroad cars did not violate the equal protection clause of the Fourteenth Amendment. In its decision, the Court concluded that civil rights laws could not change racial destiny. "If one race be inferior to the other socially," the justices explained, "the Constitution of the United

States cannot put them on the same plane." In practice, however, white southerners obeyed the "separate" part of the ruling but never provided equal services. If blacks tried to over-step the bounds of Jim Crow in any way that whites found unacceptable, they risked their lives. Between 1884 and 1900, nearly 1,700 blacks were lynched in the South. Victims were often subjected to brutal forms of torture before they were hanged or shot.

Along with Jim Crow and disfranchisement laws, southerners buttressed white supremacy by erecting monuments to the political and military leaders of their Lost Cause Confederacy. Immediately following the Civil War, white southerners remembered their dead soldiers through memorials and grave markers. In the 1890s and for decades follow-ing, they erected public monuments in town squares to communicate their message that although the Confederacy had lost the Civil War, it had won the peace. By 1899, the state of Virginia, for example, had erected over 40 Confederate monuments. These monuments were vivid symbols of a system that sought to perpetuate white domination and black subservience.

In everyday life, African Americans carried on as best they could. Segregation pro-vided many African Americans with opportunities to build their own businesses; control their own churches; develop their own schools, staffed by black teachers; and form their own civic associations and fraternal organizations. Segregation, though harsh and unequal, did foster a sense of black community, promote a rising middle class, and create social networks that enhanced racial pride. Founded in 1898, the North Carolina Life Insurance Company, one of the leading black-owned and black-operated businesses, employed many African Americans in managerial and sales positions. Burial societies ensured that their members received a proper funeral when they died. As with whites, black men joined lodges such as the Colored Masons and the Colored Odd Fellows, while women partici-pated in the YWCA and the National Association of Colored Women. A small percentage of southern blacks resisted Jim Crow by migrating to the North, where blacks still exer-cised the right to vote, more jobs were open to them, and segregation was less strictly enforced.

Review & Relate

■ What role did consumption play in the society and culture of the Gilded Age?

■ How did industrialization contribute to heightened anxieties about gender roles and race?

National Politics in the Era of Industrialization

Politicians played an important role in the expand-ing industrial economy that provided new oppor-tunities for the wealthy and the expanding middle class. For growing companies and corpo-rations to succeed, they needed a favorable political climate that would support their inter-ests. Businessmen frequently looked to Washington for assistance. Marcus Alonzo Hanna, a wealthy industrialist, considered Ohio senator John Sherman "our main dependence in the Senate for the protection of our business interests." During this era, the office of the president was a weak and largely administrative post and legislators and judges were highly influenced and sometimes directly controlled by business leaders. For much of this period, the two national political parties battled to a standoff, which resulted in congressional gridlock with little accomplished. Yet spurred by fierce partisan competition, political participation grew among the electorate.

The Weak Presidency.

James Bryce, a British observer of American politics, devoted a chapter of his book *The American Commonwealth* (1888) to "why great men are not chosen presidents." He believed that the White House attracted mediocre occupants because the president functioned mainly as an executor. The stature of the office had shrunk following the impeachment of Andrew Johnson and the reassertion of congressional power during Reconstruction. Presidents considered themselves mainly as the nation's top administrator. They did not see their roles as formulating policy or intervening on behalf of legislative objectives. With the office held in such low regard, great men became corporate leaders, not presidents.

Perhaps aware that they could expect little in the way of assistance or imagination from national leaders, voters refused to give either Democrats or Republicans solid support. No president between Ulysses S. Grant and William McKinley won back-to-back elections or received a majority of the popular vote. The only two-time winner, the Democrat Grover Cleveland, lost his bid for reelection in 1888 before triumphing again in 1892.

Nevertheless, the presidency attracted accomplished individuals. Rutherford B. Hayes (1877–1881), James A. Garfield (1881), and Benjamin Harrison (1889–1893) all had served ably in the Union army as commanding officers during the Civil War and had prior political experience. The nation greatly mourned Garfield following his assassination in 1881 by Charles Guiteau, a disgruntled applicant for federal patronage. Upon Garfield's death, Chester A. Arthur (1881–1885) became president. He had served as a quartermaster general during the Civil War, had a reputation as being sympathetic to African American civil rights, and had run the New York City Customs House effectively. Grover Cleveland (1885–1889, 1893–1897) first served as mayor of Buffalo and then as governor of New York. All of these men, as even Bryce admitted, worked hard, possessed common sense, and were honest. However, they were uninspiring individuals who lacked qualities of leadership that would arouse others to action.

Congressional Inefficiency.

The most important factor in the weakened presidency was the structure of Congress, which prevented the president from providing vigorous leadership. Throughout most of this period, Congress remained narrowly divided. Majorities continually shifted from one party to the other. For all but two terms, Democrats controlled the House of Representatives, while Republicans held the majority in the Senate. Divided government meant that during his term in office no late-nineteenth-century president had a majority of his party in both houses of Congress. Turnover among congressmen in the House of Representatives, who were elected every two years, was quite high, and there was little power of incumbency. The Senate, however, provided more continuity and allowed senators, with six-year terms of office, to amass greater power than congressmen could.

For all the power that Congress wielded, it failed to govern effectively or efficiently. In the House, measures did not receive adequate attention on the floor because the Speaker did not have the power to control the flow of systematic debate. Committee chairmen held a tight rein over the introduction and consideration of legislation and competed with one another for influence in the chamber. Congressmen showed little decorum as they conducted business on the House floor and often chatted with each other or read the newspaper rather than listen to the speakers at the podium.

The Senate, though more manageable in size and more stable in membership (only one-third of its membership stood for reelection every two years), did not function much more smoothly. Senators valued their own judgments and business interests more than party unity. The position of majority leader, someone who could impose discipline on his colleagues and design a coherent legislative agenda, had not yet been created. Woodrow Wilson, the author of *Congressional Government* (1885) and a future president, concluded: "Our government is defective as it parcels out power and confuses responsibility." Under these circumstances, neither the president nor Congress governed efficiently.

corruption

The Business of Politics. Many lawmakers viewed politics as a business enterprise that would line their pockets with money. One cabinet officer grumbled, "A Congressman is a hog! You must take a stick and hit him on the snout!" Senators were elected by state legislatures, and these bodies were often controlled by well-funded corporations that generously spread their money around to gain influence. In both branches of Congress, party leaders handed out patronage to supporters regardless of their qualifications for the jobs (a practice known as the spoils system). Modern-day standards of ethical conduct did not exist; nor did politicians see a conflict of interest in working closely with corporations. Indeed, there were no rules to prevent lawmakers from accepting payments from big business. Most congressmen received free passes from railroads and in turn voted on the companies' behalf. To be fair, most politicians such as Senator Sherman did not see a difference between furthering the legislative agenda of big corporations and promoting the nation's economic interests. Nevertheless, the public held politicians in very low esteem because they resented the influence of corporate money in politics. *lack of public confidence*

normal

Explore ▶

Compare two opposing views of John D. Rockefeller in Sources 16.4 and 16.5.

The 1890 Congress stands out as an example of fiscal irresponsibility. Known as the **Billion Dollar Congress**, the same Republican legislative majority that passed the Sherman Anti-Trust Act adopted the highest tariff in U.S. history. Sponsored by Ohio congressman William McKinley, a close associate of the industrialist Marcus Hanna, it lavishly protected manufacturing interests. Congress also spent enormous sums on special projects to enrich their constituents and themselves. Republicans spent so much money on extravagant enterprises that they wiped out the federal budget surplus.

Increasingly throughout the 1890s, corporate leaders and their political allies joined together in favor of extending American influence and control over foreign markets and natural resources abroad, especially in Central America and the Pacific regions. They agreed that cyclical fluctuations in the domestic economy required overseas markets to assure high profits. To accomplish this would necessitate building up American military and commercial power. *→ imperialist aspirations*

An Energized and Entertained Electorate. Despite all the difficulties of the legislative process, political candidates eagerly pursued office and conducted extremely heated campaigns. The electorate considered politics a form of entertainment. Political parties did not stand for clearly stated issues or offer innovative solutions; instead, campaigns

Comparative Secondary Source Analysis

Robber Baron or Captain of Industry?

Matthew Josephson did not coin the phrase *Robber Barons*; the term first appeared in the 1880s in an anti-railroad pamphlet circulated by agrarian reformers in Kansas. The publication of his book of the same name in 1934, nevertheless, provided a vivid description of the greed, ruthlessness, and corruption that characterized the late nineteenth century industrialists and capitalists. Josephson wrote during the Great Depression, with tens of millions of Americans out of work and many questioning the legitimacy of the capitalist system. Yet the notion of avaricious Robber Barons did not go unchallenged. Writing in the late 1990s in the midst of economic prosperity and new technological innovation, writers such as Ron Chernow recognized the dark sides of development of industrialization and big business, but emphasized the qualities of risk taking, creativity, hard work, and leadership.

Source 16.4

Matthew Josephson | *The Robber Barons*, 1934

"But for the very reason that forces leading to combination were at work in the society, the general effect of the period [1877–1900] was one of strenuous contest for the market, of anarchic, individual appetite and money-lust, of ruinous competition conducted with more terrible instruments than before, out of which a few giant industrialists arose. . . .

With his measured spirit, with his organized might, [John D. Rockefeller] tested men and things. There were men and women of all sorts who passed under his implacable rod, and their tale . . . has contributed to the legend of the 'white devil' who came to rule over American industry.

A certain widow, a Mrs. [Fred M.] Backus of Cleveland, who had inherited an oil-refinery, had appealed to Mr. Rockefeller to preserve her, 'the mother of fatherless children." And he had promised 'with tears in his eyes that he would stand by her.' But in the end he offered her only $79,000 for a property which had cost $200,000. The whole story of the defenseless widow and her orphans, the stern command, the confiscation of two-thirds of her property, when it came out made a deep stir and moved many hearts."

Source: Matthew Josephson, *The Robber Barons*. New York: Harcourt, Brace & World, Inc., 1962, 254, 267.

increased voter partisanship + participation

took on the qualities of carefully staged performances. Candidates crafted their oratory to arouse the passions and prejudices of their audiences, and their managers handed out buttons, badges, and ceramic and glass plates stamped with the candidates' faces and slogans.

Partisanship helped fuel high political participation. During this period, voter turnout in presidential elections was much higher than at any time in the twentieth century. Region, as well as historical and cultural allegiances, replaced ideology as the key to party affiliation. The wrenching experience of the Civil War had cemented voting loyalties for many Americans. After Reconstruction, white southerners tended to vote Democratic;

Source 16.5

Ron Chernow, John D. Rockefeller | Industrial Statesman, 1998

"'If it were true [the Widow Backus story],' Rockefeller later conceded, it 'would represent a shocking instance of cruelty in crushing a defenceless [sic] woman. It is probable that its wide circulation and its acceptance as true by those who know nothing of the facts has awakened more hostility against the Standard Oil Company and against me personally than any charge which has been made.'

. . . While Backus wanted Rockefeller to conduct the negotiations for her plant, he knew nothing about lubricants [lubricating oils and grease] and sent his associates instead. According to Backus, Rockefeller's hirelings bilked her unmercifully. . . . Backus's negotiator. . . later swore that his client, in an estimated inventory of her assets, had written down $71,000

for plant and goodwill—not much more than Rockefeller finally paid her. Yet she grew incensed over the purchase price and drafted a savage latter to Rockefeller accusing him of double-dealing . . . [Rockefeller] then pointed out that the $60,000 paid for the property was two to three times the cost of constructing equal or better facilities. . . . In investing her proceeds in Cleveland real estate . . . Backus far from being reduced to filth and misery, became an extremely rich woman. . . . The notion of Rockefeller gleefully ruining a poor widow was such a good story, with so fine a Dickensian ring, that gullible reporters gave it fresh circulation for many years."

Source: Ron Chernow, *Titan: The Life of John D. Rockefeller, Sr.* New York: Random House, 1998, 445–447.

Examine the Sources

1. How do Josephson and Chernow differ in their interpretations of Rockefeller's business practices?
2. Drawing upon evidence in this chapter, evaluate the main arguments of Josephson and Chernow.

▮ Put it in Context

How might the fact that these interpretations were written sixty-four years apart (1934/1998) influence their conclusions?

northerners and newly enfranchised southern blacks generally voted Republican. However, geography alone did not shape political loyalties; a sizable contingent of Democratic voters remained in the North, and southern whites and blacks periodically abandoned both the Democratic and Republican parties to vote for third parties.

Religion played an important role in shaping party loyalties during this period of intense partisanship. The Democratic Party tended to attract Protestants of certain sects, such as German Lutherans and Episcopalians, as well as Catholics. These faiths emphasized religious ritual and the acceptance of personal sin. They believed that the government

1892 Presidential Campaign Plate
Before radio, television, and the Internet, political parties advertised candidates in a variety of colorful ways, including banners, buttons, ribbons, and ceramic and glass plates. Voters, who turned out in record numbers during the late nineteenth century, coveted these items. This plate shows the 1892 Democratic presidential ticket of Grover Cleveland and Adlai Stevenson, who won the election. Collection of Steven F. Lawson

should not interfere in matters of morality, which should remain the province of Christian supervision on earth and divine judgment in the hereafter. By contrast, other Protestant denominations, such as Baptists, Congregationalists, Methodists, and Presbyterians, highlighted the importance of individual will and believed that the law could be shaped to eradicate ignorance and vice. These Protestants were more likely to cast their ballots for Republicans, except in the South, where regional loyalty to the Democratic Party trumped religious affiliation.

Some people went to the polls because they fiercely disliked members of the opposition party. Northern white workers in New York City or Cincinnati, Ohio, for example, might vote against the Republican Party because they viewed it as the party of African Americans. Other voters cast their ballots against Democrats because they identified them as the party of Irish Catholics, intemperance, and secession.

Although political parties commanded fierce loyalties, the parties remained divided internally. For example, the Republicans pitted "Stalwarts" against "Half Breeds." The Stalwarts presented themselves as the "Old Guard" of the Republican Party, what they called the "Grand Old Party" (GOP). The Half Breeds, a snide name given to them by the Stalwarts, claimed to be more open to new ideas and less wedded to the old causes that the Republican Party promoted, such as racial equality. In the end, however, the differences between the two groups had less to do with ideas than with which faction would have greater power within the Republican Party.

Overall, the continuing strength of party loyalties produced equilibrium as voters cast their ballots primarily along strict party lines. The outcome of presidential elections depended on key "undecided" districts in several states in the Midwest and in New York and nearby states, which swung the balance of power in the electoral college. Indeed, from 1876 to 1896 all winning candidates for president and vice president came from Ohio, Indiana, Illinois, New York, and New Jersey.

Review & Relate

| What accounted for the inefficiency and ineffectiveness of the federal government in the late nineteenth century?

| How would you explain the high rates of voter turnout and political participation in an era of uninspiring politicians and governmental inaction?

Conclusion: Industrial America

From 1877 to 1900, American businessmen demonstrated a zeal for organization. Prompted by new technology that opened up national markets of commerce and communication, business entrepreneurs created large-scale corporations that promoted industrial expansion. Borrowing from European investors and importing and improving on European technology, by 1900 U.S. industrialists had surpassed their overseas counterparts. *growth of American enterprise*

Capitalists made great fortunes and lived luxurious lifestyles, emulating the fashions of European elites. Most corporate leaders did not rise from poverty but instead came from the upper middle class and had access to education and connections. Those like Andrew Carnegie, who rose from rags to riches, were the exceptions. The wealthy explained their success as the result of individual effort and hard work. This idea was reinforced in schoolbooks such as the McGuffey Readers, the novels of Horatio Alger, and religious sermons like those of Russell Conwell.

Although most working Americans did not achieve much wealth during this era of industrialization, they had faith in the possibility of improving their economic positions. Members of the middle class lived less extravagantly than did the wealthy; nonetheless, they enjoyed the comforts of the growing consumer economy. Although Jim Crow restricted the black middle class and a heightened sense of masculinity inhibited opportunities available to white women, both groups managed to carve out ways to lift themselves economically and socially. → *American dream*

In gaining success, the wealthy exchanged individualism for organization, competition for consolidation, and laissez-faire for government support. Without pro-business policies from Washington lawmakers and favorable decisions from the Supreme Court, big business would not have developed as rapidly as it did in this era. To prosper, corporations needed sympathetic politicians — whether to furnish free land for railroad expansion, enact tariffs to protect manufacturers, or protect private property. Even when a public outcry led to the regulation of trusts, the pro-business senator John Sherman and his colleagues shaped the legislation so as to minimize damage to corporate interests. In general, national politicians

federal intervention

avoided engaging in fierce ideological conflicts, but they, too, organized. The political parties they fashioned encouraged a high level of political participation among voters.

It remained for those who did not share in the glittering wealth of the Gilded Age to find ways to resist corporate domination. While corporate leaders and the expanding middle class enjoyed the fruits of industrial capitalism, workers, farmers, and reformers sought to remedy the economic, social, and political ills that accompanied industrialization.

Timeline of Events

1859	Charles Darwin publishes *On the Origin of Species*
	Henry Bessemer improves steel production process
1860–1890	U.S. gross domestic product quadruples
1866	Transatlantic telegraph cable completed
1868	Typewriter invented
1870–1900	U.S. becomes a global industrial power
1870–1910	Number of U.S. white-collar workers triples
1870s	John D. Rockefeller takes control of oil refining business
1872	Montgomery Ward established
1876	Thomas Edison establishes research laboratory
1881	James Garfield assassinated
1884–1900	1,700 blacks lynched in the South
1885	Alexander Graham Bell founds American Telephone and Telegraph
1886	U.S. railroads adopt standard gauge
	Santa Clara County v. Southern Pacific Railroad Company
1889	Andrew Carnegie publishes "The Gospel of Wealth"
1890	Sherman Antitrust Act
1890s	African Americans disfranchised in the South
1895	*United States v. E.C. Knight Company*
1896	*Plessy v. Ferguson*
1901	United States Steel established

Key Terms

New South, *536*

convict lease, *537*

vertical integration, *539*

horizontal integration, *539*

corporation, *540*

trust, *540*

Sherman Antitrust Act, *540*

laissez-faire, *543*

Social Darwinism, *543*

"The Gospel of Wealth," *544*

Gilded Age, *545*

Jim Crow, *552*

Plessy v. Ferguson, *552*

Billion Dollar Congress, *555*

Review & Relate

1. What were the key factors behind the acceleration of industrial development in late-nineteenth-century America?

2. How did industrialization change the way American businessmen thought about their companies and the people who worked for them?

3. In the late nineteenth century, how did many Americans explain individual economic success and failure?

4. How did the business community view the role of government in the economy at the end of the nineteenth century?

5. What role did consumption play in the society and culture of the Gilded Age?

6. How did industrialization contribute to heightened anxieties about gender roles and race?

7. What accounted for the inefficiency and ineffectiveness of the federal government in the late nineteenth century?

8. How would you explain the high rates of voter turnout and political participation in an era of uninspiring politicians and governmental inaction?

Debates about Laissez-Faire

▶ Evaluate the extent to which differing ideas of competition and cooperation influenced views about obtaining wealth in late-nineteenth-century America.

From the nation's founding, the pursuit of individual opportunity has held a central place among American values. In the late nineteenth century, as big business consolidated and giant trusts came to dominate whole industries, defenders of unfettered big business argued that individual effort and initiative were still the central engine of the American economy. Championing Adam Smith's notion of laissez-faire — the idea that the marketplace should be left to regulate itself — they argued that government should do nothing to constrain the development of industry (Source 16.6). Yet as poverty expanded while a small number of industrialists and financiers accumulated great wealth, reformers questioned whether individualism undermined community, and contended that the government should regulate the free market to promote the greater public welfare (Sources 16.7 and 16.9). With the gap between rich and poor growing, even industrialists realized that if they did not help the poor in some way, the working classes would rise up against them (Source 16.8). Nevertheless, they continued to resist government interference.

Defenders of the status quo argued that individualism must be preserved as the natural order of society. Critics countered that cooperation rather than individual competition made social progress possible and that the government should protect ordinary people from the harm done by greedy capitalists.

Source 16.6

William Graham Sumner | A Defense of Laissez-Faire, 1883

Yale professor William Graham Sumner believed that millionaires deserved their wealth, a notion that appealed to successful industrialists. Men like Andrew Carnegie, he declared, "may fairly be regarded as the naturally selected agents of society." The poor, he argued, also justly deserved their fate. Sumner and other defenders of economic inequality maintained that if the government tried to help these unfortunate losers in the competitive struggle, progress would be halted and civilization would decay.

[It] may be said that those whom humanitarians and philanthropists call the weak are the ones through whom the productive and conservative forces of society are wasted. They constantly neutralize and destroy the finest efforts of the wise and industrious, and are a dead-weight on the society in all its struggles to realize any better things. Whether the people who mean no harm, but are weak in the essential powers necessary to the performance of one's duties in life, or those who are malicious and vicious, do the more mischief, is a question not easy to answer. . . .

The humanitarians, philanthropists, and reformers, looking at the facts of life as they present themselves, find enough which is sad and unpromising in the condition of many members of society. They see wealth and poverty side by side.

They note great inequality of social position and social chances. They eagerly set about the attempt to account for what they see, and to devise schemes for remedying what they do not like. In their eagerness to recommend the less fortunate classes to pity and consideration they forget all about the rights of other classes; they gloss over all the faults of the classes in question, and they exaggerate their misfortunes and their virtues. They invent new theories of property, distorting rights and perpetrating injustice, as any one is sure to do who sets about the re-adjustment of social relations with the interests of one group distinctly before his mind, and the interests of all other groups thrown into the background. When I have read certain of these discussions I have thought that it must be quite disreputable to be respectable, quite dishonest to own property, quite unjust to go one's own way and earn one's own living, and that the only really admirable person was the good-for-nothing. The man who by his own effort raises himself above poverty appears, in these discussions, to be of no account. The man who has done nothing to raise himself above poverty finds that the social doctors flock about him, bringing the capital which they have collected from the other class, and promising him the aid of the State to give him what the other had to work for. In all these schemes and projects the organized intervention of society through the State is either planned or hoped for, and the State is thus made to become the protector and guardian of certain classes. The agents who are to direct the State action are, of course, the reformers and philanthropists. . . . Here it may suffice to observe that, on the theories of the social philosophers to whom I have referred, we should get a new maxim of judicious living: Poverty is the best policy. If you get wealth, you will have to support other people; if you do not get wealth, it will be the duty of other people to support you.

Source: William Graham Sumner, *What the Social Classes Owe Each Other* (New York: Harper and Brothers, 1883), 19–24.

Source 16.7

Edward Bellamy | *Looking Backward, 2000–1887*, 1888

Edward Bellamy's best-selling novel *Looking Backward, 2000–1887*, offered utopian socialist solutions to the problems facing the rapidly industrializing United States. After falling into a medically induced sleep, Bellamy's narrator, Julian West, awakens in the year 2000 to find that many of the social inequities of the late nineteenth century have been resolved.

The records of the period show that the outcry against the concentration of capital was furious. Men believed that it threatened society with a form of tyranny more abhorrent than it had ever endured. They believed that the great corporations were preparing for them the yoke of a baser servitude than had ever been imposed on the race, servitude not to men but to soulless machines incapable of any motive but insatiable greed. Looking back, we cannot wonder at their desperation, for certainly humanity was never confronted with a fate more sordid and hideous than would have been the era of corporate tyranny which they anticipated.

Meanwhile, without being in the smallest degree checked by the clamor against it, the absorption of business by ever larger monopolies continued. In the United States, where this tendency was later in developing than in Europe, there was not, after the beginning of the last quarter of the century, any opportunity whatever for individual enterprise in any important field of industry, unless backed by a great capital. During the last decade of the century, such small businesses as still remained were fast failing survivals of a past epoch, or mere parasites on the great corporations, or else existed in fields too small to attract the great capitalists. Small businesses, as far as they still remained, were reduced to the condition of rats and mice, living in holes and corners, and counting on evading notice for the enjoyment of existence. The railroads had gone on combining till a few great syndicates controlled every rail in the land. In manufactories, every important staple was controlled by a syndicate. These syndicates, pools, trusts, or whatever their name, fixed prices and crushed all competition except when combinations as vast as themselves arose. Then a struggle, resulting in a still greater consolidation, ensued. The great city bazar crushed its country rivals with branch stores, and in the city itself absorbed its smaller rivals till the business of a whole quarter was concentrated under one roof with a hundred former proprietors of shops serving as clerks. Having no business of his own to put his money in, the small capitalist, at the same time that he took service under the corporation, found no other investment for his money but its stocks and bonds, thus becoming doubly dependent upon it.

The fact that the desperate popular opposition to the consolidation of business in a few powerful hands had no effect to check it, proves that there must have been a strong economical reason for it. The small capitalists, with their innumerable petty concerns, had, in fact, yielded the field to the great aggregations of capital, because they belonged to a day of small things and were totally incompetent to the demands of an age of steam and telegraphs and the gigantic scale of its enterprises. To restore the former order of things, even if possible, would have involved returning to the day of stage-coaches. Oppressive and intolerable as was the regime of the great consolidations of capital, even its victims, while they cursed it, were forced to admit the prodigious increase of efficiency which had been imparted to the national industries, the vast economies effected by concentration of management and unity of organization, and to confess that since the new system had taken the place of the old, the wealth of the world had increased at a rate before undreamed of. To be sure this vast increase had gone chiefly to make the rich richer, increasing the gap between them and the poor; but the fact remained that, as a means merely of producing wealth, capital had been proved efficient in proportion to its consolidation. The restoration of the old system with the subdivision of capital, if it were possible, might

indeed bring back a greater equality of conditions with more individual dignity and freedom, but it would be at the price of general poverty and the arrest of material progress. . . .

Early in the last century the evolution was completed by the final consolidation of the entire capital of the nation. The industry and commerce of the country, ceasing to be conducted by a set of irresponsible corporations and syndicates of private persons at their caprice and for their profit, were intrusted to a single syndicate representing the people, to be conducted in the common interest for the common profit. The nation, that is to say, organized as the one great business corporation in which all other corporations were absorbed; it became the one capitalist in the place of all other capitalists, the sole employer, the final monopoly in which all previous and lesser monopolies were swallowed up, a monopoly in the profits and economies of which all citizens shared.

Source: Edward Bellamy, *Looking Backward, 2000–1887* (Boston: Ticknor, 1888), 71–78.

Andrew Carnegie | The Gospel of Wealth, 1889

Andrew Carnegie, who immigrated to the United States and experienced poverty as a young boy, made his fortune in the steel industry and became one of the richest men in the United States. Recognizing the dangers of widespread poverty among the mass of American workers, Carnegie sought to use philanthropy to provide opportunities for individuals to help themselves, as he explains in the following essay, which is usually referred to as "The Gospel of Wealth."

The best uses to which surplus wealth can be put have already been indicated. Those who would administer wisely must, indeed, be wise; for one of the serious obstacles to the improvement of our race is indiscriminate charity. It were better for mankind that the millions of the rich were thrown into the sea than so spent as to encourage the slothful, the drunken, the unworthy. Of every thousand dollars spent in so-called charity today, it is probable that nine hundred and fifty dollars is unwisely spent—so spent, indeed, as to produce the very evils which it hopes to mitigate or cure. . . .

In bestowing charity, the main consideration should be to help those who will help themselves; to provide part of the means by which those who desire to improve may do so; to give those who desire to rise the aids by which they may rise; to assist, but rarely or never to do all. Neither the individual nor the race is improved by almsgiving. Those worthy of assistance, except in rare cases, seldom require assistance. The really valuable men of the race never do, except in case of accident or sudden change. Every one has, of course, cases of individuals brought to his own knowledge where temporary assistance can do genuine good, and these he will not overlook. But the amount which can be wisely given by the individual for individuals is necessarily limited by his lack of knowledge of the circumstances connected with each. He is the only true reformer who is as careful and as anxious not to aid the unworthy as he is to aid the worthy, and, perhaps, even more so, for in almsgiving more injury is probably done by rewarding vice than by relieving virtue.

[T]he best means of benefiting the community is to place within its reach the ladders upon which the aspiring can rise—free libraries, parks, and means of recreation, by which men are helped in body and mind; works of art, certain to give pleasure and improve the public taste; and public institutions of various kinds, which will improve the general condition of the people; in this manner returning their surplus wealth to the mass of their fellows in the forms best calculated to do them lasting good.

Thus is the problem of rich and poor to be solved. The laws of accumulation will be left free, the laws of distribution free. Individualism will continue, but the millionaire will be but a trustee for the poor, intrusted for a season with a great part of the increased wealth of the community, but administering it for the community far better than it could or would have done for itself. The best minds will thus have reached a stage in the development of the race in which it is clearly seen that there is no mode of disposing of surplus wealth creditable to thoughtful and earnest men into whose hands it flows, save by using it year by year for the general good. . . . [T]he day is not far distant when the man who dies leaving behind him millions of available wealth, which was free for him to administer during life, will pass away "unwept, unhonored, and unsung," no matter to what uses he leaves the dross which he cannot take with him. Of such as these the public verdict will then be: "The man who dies thus rich dies disgraced."

Such, in my opinion, is the true gospel concerning wealth, obedience to which is destined some day to solve the problem of the rich and the poor, and to bring "Peace on earth, among men good will."

Source: Andrew Carnegie, *The Gospel of Wealth and Other Timely Essays* (New York: Century, 1901), 16–19.

Source 16.9

Henry Demarest Lloyd | Critique of Wealth, 1894

Many academics and writers attacked industrial capitalists, claiming that their excessive wealth came at the expense of workers and the general public. Lawyer and journalist Henry Demarest Lloyd wrote numerous articles for the *Chicago Tribune* exposing corruption in business and politics. A reformer influenced by British socialists, Lloyd supported legislation to ban child labor and to allow women to vote. In his 1894 book *Wealth against Commonwealth*, he denounced ruthless and unsavory competitive practices by industrialists who created monopolies that exploited working people. In the following excerpt, Lloyd raises questions about the fundamental value of industrial capitalism and its threat to social progress.

If our civilization is destroyed, . . . it will not be by . . . barbarians from below. Our barbarians come from above. Our great money-makers have sprung in one generation into seats of power kings do not know. The forces and the wealth are new, and have been the opportunity of new men. Without restraints of culture, experience, the pride, or even the inherited caution of class or rank, these men, intoxicated, think they are the wave instead of the float, and that they have created the business which has created them. To them science is but a never-ending repertoire of investments stored up by nature for the syndicates, government but a fountain of franchises, the nations but customers in squads, and a million the unit of a new arithmetic of wealth written for them. They claim a power without control, exercised through forms which make it secret, anonymous, and perpetual. . . .

. . . In casting about for the cause of our industrial evils, public opinion has successively found it in "competition," "combination," the "corporations," "conspiracies," "trusts." But competition has ended in combination, and our new wealth takes as it chooses the form of corporation or trust, or corporation again, and with every change grows greater and worse. Under these kaleidoscopic masks we begin at last to see progressing to its terminus a steady consolidation, the end of which is one-man power. The conspiracy ends in one, and one cannot conspire with himself. When this solidification of many into one has been reached, we shall be at last face to face with the naked truth that it is not only the form but the fact of arbitrary power, of control without consent, of rule without representation that concerns us.

Business motivated by the self-interest of the individual runs into monopoly at every point it touches the social life—land monopoly, transportation monopoly, trade monopoly, political monopoly in all its forms, from contraction of the currency to corruption in office. The society in which in half a lifetime a man without a penny can become a hundred times a millionaire is as over-ripe, industrially, as was, politically, the Rome in which the most popular bully could lift himself from the ranks of the legion on to the throne of the Caesars. Our rising issue is with business. Monopoly is business at the end of its journey. It has got there. The irrepressible conflict is now as distinctly with business as the issue so lately met was with slavery. Slavery went first only because it was the cruder form of business. . . .

Our system, so fair in its theory and so fertile in its happiness and prosperity in its first century, is now, following the fate of systems, becoming artificial, technical, corrupt; and, as always happens in human institutions, after noon, power is stealing from the many to the few. Believing wealth to be good, the people believed the wealthy to be good. But, again in history, power has intoxicated and hardened its possessors, and Pharaohs are bred in counting-rooms as they were in palaces. Their furniture must be banished to the world-garret [attic], where lie the out-worn trappings of the guilds and slavery and other old lumber of human institutions.

Source: Henry Demarest Lloyd, *Wealth against Commonwealth* (New York: Harper and Brothers, 1902), 510–12, 515.

Interpret the Evidence

1. Compare the attitudes of William Graham Sumner (Source 16.6) and Andrew Carnegie (Source 16.8) toward whether the wealthy have a responsibility to help the poor.
2. What historical evidence would support or refute the argument for federal intervention against big business found in Edward Bellamy's novel, Looking Backward (Source 16.7)?
3. How do wealthy Americans maintain their power at the expense of everyone else, according to Henry Demarest Lloyd (Source 16.9)?
4. What changes in U.S. society and government might Sumner, Carnegie, Bellamy, and Lloyd recommend for individuals to achieve success?

Put It in Context

Despite their different philosophies, what do these men think about the growth of organizations during the late nineteenth century?

Workers and Farmers in the Age of Organization

1877–1900

Detail from Walter Huston, "Here Lies Prosperity," 1895

As this cartoon shows, the depression of 1893 had a devastating impact on American workers and farmers. According to critics, the economic policies of President Grover Cleveland and Congress increased the debt of working people and made it more difficult to repay. This situation led to protests and the formation of a new third party — the Populists. ▶ To learn more about this primary source, see Source 17.2 on page 586.

"The Situation: The Result of Interest Bearing Bonds and Sherman." *Sound Money* (Massillon, OH), August 22, 1895. Reproduced from Worth Robert Miller, *Populist Cartoons: An Illustrated History of the Third Party Movement in the 1890s* (Truman State University Press, 2011).

Learning Objectives

After reading this chapter you will be able to:

- Explain how industrialization spurred the formation of labor organizations and how the government, in turn, responded to unionization.

- Analyze how industrialization affected rural life and how farmers responded to these changes.

- Compare the responses of industrial workers and farmers to the rise of big business.

- Explain the causes of the depression of 1893 and its consequences for workers, farmers, and politics.

Comparing American Histories

John McLuckie worked at Andrew Carnegie's steel works in Homestead, Pennsylvania. In this town of some eleven thousand residents, where nearly everyone worked for Carnegie, the popular McLuckie was twice elected mayor and headed the Amalgamated Association of Iron and Steel Workers, one of the largest unions in the country. Although McLuckie earned a relatively decent income for that time, steelworkers and other industrial laborers had little power over the terms and conditions under which they worked. Visiting fraternal lodges and saloons, where steelworkers congregated, he spread the message of standing up to corporate leaders. "The constitution of this country," McLuckie declared, "guarantees all men the right to live, but in order to live we must keep up a continuous struggle."

(*left*) **John McLuckie**
(*right*) **Mary Elizabeth Lease** Kansas State Historical Society

In 1892 McLuckie faced the fight of his life when he battled with Carnegie and his plant manager, Henry Clay Frick, over wages and working conditions at the Homestead plant. Like Carnegie, the owners of a host of industries had created giant organizations that produced great wealth but also reshaped the working conditions of ordinary Americans. Toward the end of the nineteenth century, workers who labored for these industrial giants sought greater control over their employment by organizing unions to increase their power to negotiate with their employers. The events that unfolded in Homestead in 1892 revealed that workers were vastly outmatched in their struggle with management.

Mary Elizabeth Clyens was the daughter of Irish Catholic parents who came to the United States as part of the great wave of Irish immigration that began in the 1840s. Mary was raised in western Pennsylvania but moved to Kansas in 1870 to teach at a Catholic girls' school. There she met and married Charles L. Lease, a pharmacist turned farmer. The couple, however, could not support themselves and their children through farming, and in 1883 the Leases moved to Wichita. In Wichita, Mary found a much wider scope to express her interests and beliefs than she had on the farm. She joined a variety of organizations and worked in support of Irish independence, women's suffrage, and movements to advance the cause of industrial workers and farmers exploited by big business, railroads, and banks.

Mary Elizabeth Lease entered state and national politics through the Populist Party, which formed in 1890 to challenge the power of large corporations and their political allies, promote the interests of small farmers, and create an alliance between farmers and industrial workers. A mesmerizing speaker, she urged her audiences, according to reporters, to "raise less corn and more hell." Lease offered a variety of remedies for late-nineteenth-century America's economic and political ills, including nationalizing railroad and telegraph lines, increasing the currency supply, and expanding popular democracy. She also agitated for women's rights and voiced her determination "to place the mothers of this nation on an equality with the fathers." Following the collapse of the Populist Party in 1896, Lease and her family moved to New York City. She worked as a journalist, divorced her husband, and remained active as a speaker for educational reform and birth control until her death in 1931. ∎

The American histories of John McLuckie and Mary Elizabeth Lease were linked by the economic and political forces that shaped the lives of both factory workers and farmers in industrialized America. Even though the culture of rural America was quite different from that of the nation's industrial towns and cities, farmers and workers faced many of the same problems. Over the course of the late nineteenth century, both groups had seen control over the nature and terms of their work pass from the individual worker or farmer to large corporations and financial institutions. McLuckie and Lease were part of a larger effort by laborers and farmers to fight for their own interests against the concentrated economic and political power of big business and to regain control of their lives and their work. In the 1890s, a severe economic depression made the situation even worse for farmers and industrial workers. Many of them joined the newly formed Populist Party to challenge the two major political parties for failing to represent their concerns.

no longer controlled by them

rise of sentiment against big business

Working People Organize

not a formidable source

Industrialists were not the only ones who built organizations to promote their economic interests. Like their employers, working men and women also saw the benefits of organizing to increase their political and economic leverage. Determined to secure decent wages and working conditions, workers joined labor unions, formed political parties, and engaged in a variety of collective actions, including strikes. However, workers' organizations were beset by internal conflicts over occupational status, race, ethnicity, and gender. They proved no match for the powerful alliance between corporations and the federal government that stood against them, and they failed to become a lasting national political force. Workers fared better in their own communities, where family, neighbors, and local businesses were more likely to come to their aid.

The Industrialization of Labor. The industrialization of the United States transformed the workplace, bringing together large numbers of laborers under difficult conditions. In 1870 few factories employed 500 or more workers. Thirty years later, more than 1,500 companies had workforces of this size. Just after the Civil War, manufacturing employed 5.3 million workers; thirty years later, the figure soared to more than 15.1 million. Most of these new industrial workers came from two main sources. First, farmers like the Leases who could not make a decent living from the soil moved to nearby cities in search of factory jobs. Although mostly white, this group also included blacks who sought to escape the oppressive conditions of sharecropping. Between 1870 and 1890, some 80,000 African Americans journeyed from the rural South to cities in the South and the North to search for employment. Second, the economic opportunities in America drew millions of immigrants from Europe over the course of the nineteenth century. Immigrant workers initially came from northern Europe. However, by the end of the nineteenth century, the number of

many looking for factory jobs

immigrants from southern and eastern European countries had surpassed those coming from northern Europe.

Inside factories, **unskilled workers**, those with no particular skill or expertise, encountered a system undergoing critical changes, as small-scale manufacturing gave way to larger and more mechanized operations. Immigrants, who made up the bulk of unskilled laborers, had to adjust both to a new country and to unfamiliar, unpleasant, and often dangerous industrial work. A traveler from Hungary who visited a steel mill in Pittsburgh that employed many Hungarian immigrants compared the factories to prisons where "the heat is most insupportable, the flames most choking." Nor were any government benefits — such as workers' compensation or unemployment insurance — available to industrial laborers who were hurt in accidents or laid off from their jobs.

Skilled workers, who had particular training or abilities and were more difficult to replace, were not immune to the changes brought about by industrialization and the rise of large-scale businesses. In the early days of manufacturing, skilled laborers operated as independent craftsmen. They provided their own tools, worked at their own pace, and controlled their production output. This approach to work enhanced their sense of personal dignity, reflected their notion of themselves as free citizens, and distinguished them from the mass of unskilled laborers. Mechanization, however, undercut their autonomy by dictating both the nature and the speed of production through practices of scientific management. Instead of producing goods, skilled workers increasingly applied their craft to servicing machinery and keeping it running smoothly. While owners reaped the benefits of the mechanization and regimentation of the industrial workplace, many skilled workers saw such "improvements" as a threat to their freedom.

Explore ▶

See Source 17.1 for one worker's opinion on mechanization.

Still, most workers did not oppose the technology that increased their productivity and resulted in higher wages. Compared to their mid-nineteenth-century counterparts, industrial laborers now made up a larger share of the general population, earned more money, and worked fewer hours. During the 1870s and 1880s, the average industrial worker's real wages (actual buying power) increased by 20 percent. At the same time, the average workday declined from ten and a half hours to ten hours. From 1870 to 1890, the general price index dropped 30 percent, allowing consumers to benefit from lower prices.

The lives of industrial workers remained extremely difficult. Although workers as a group saw improvements in wages and hours, they did not earn enough income to support their families adequately. Also, there were widespread disparities based on job status, race, ethnicity, sex, and region. Skilled workers earned more than unskilled workers. Whites were paid more than blacks, who were mainly shut out of better jobs. Immigrants from northern Europe, who had settled in the United States before southern Europeans, tended to hold higher-paying skilled positions. Southern factory workers, whether in textiles, steel, or armaments, earned less than their northern counterparts. Women, an increasingly important component of the industrial workforce, earned, on average, only 25 percent of what men did.

Between 1870 and 1900, the number of female wageworkers grew by 66 percent, accounting for about one-quarter of all nonfarm laborers. The majority of employed women, including those working in factories, were single and between the ages of sixteen and twenty-four. Overall, only 5 percent of married women worked outside the home, although 30 percent of African American wives were employed. Women workers were

Guided Primary Source Analysis

John Morrison | Testimony on the Impact of Mechanization, 1883

Like other skilled laborers, New York City machinist John Morrison saw the introduction of machinery that accompanied industrialization as a threat to his identity as a craftsman. In the following excerpt from his testimony before a U.S. Senate committee investigating conflicts between capital and labor, Morrison discusses the source of many skilled workingmen's discontent.

Source 17.1

Question: Is there any difference between the conditions under which machinery is made now and those which existed ten years ago?

Answer: A great deal of difference.

Question: State the differences as well as you can.

What are the problems with subdividing the machinist trade?

Answer: Well, the trade has been subdivided and those subdivisions have been again subdivided, so that a man never learns the machinist's trade now. Ten years ago he learned, not the whole of the trade, but a fair portion of it. Also, there is more machinery used in the business, which again makes machinery. The different branches of the trade are divided and subdivided so that one man may make just a particular part of a machine and may not know anything whatever about another part of the same machine. In that way machinery is produced a great deal cheaper than it used to be formerly, and in fact, through this system of work, 100 men are able to do now what it took 300 or 400 men to do fifteen years ago. By the use of machinery and the subdivision of the trade they so simplify the work that it is made a great deal easier and put together a great deal faster. There is no system of apprenticeship, I may say, in the

Why do manufacturers favor subdivision of labor?

business. You simply go in and learn whatever branch you are put at, and you stay at that unless you are changed to another. . . .

Question: Are the machinists here generally contented, or are they in a state of discontent and unrest?

Which of these tactics do you think might have benefited skilled workers the most?

Answer: There is mostly a general feeling of discontent, and you will find among the machinists the most radical workingmen, with the most revolutionary ideas. You will find that they don't so much give their thoughts simply to trade unions and other efforts of that kind, but they go far beyond that; they only look for relief through the ballot or through a revolution, a forcible revolution.

Source: *Report of the Committee of the Senate upon the Relations between Labor and Capital*, 48th Cong. (1885), 755–59.

▌ Put It in Context

How did the introduction of machinery affect skilled workers?

concentrated in several areas. White and black women continued to serve as maids and domestics. Others took over jobs that were once occupied by men. They became teachers, nurses, clerical workers, telephone operators, and department store salesclerks. Other women toiled in manufacturing jobs requiring fine eye-hand coordination, such as cigar rolling and work in the needle trades and textile industry.

Women also turned their homes into workplaces. In crowded apartments, they sewed furs onto garments, made straw hats, prepared artificial flowers, and fashioned jewelry. Earnings from piecework (work that pays at a set rate per unit) were even lower than factory wages, but they allowed married women with young children to contribute to the family income. When sufficient space was available, families rented rooms to boarders, and women provided meals and housekeeping for the lodgers. Some female workers found other ways to balance work with the needs and constraints of family life. To gain greater autonomy in their work, black laundresses began cleaning clothes in their own homes rather than their white employers' homes, so that they could control their own work hours. In 1881 black washerwomen in Atlanta conducted a two-week strike to secure higher fees from white customers.

Manufacturing also employed many child workers. By 1900 about 10 percent of girls and 20 percent of boys between the ages of ten and fifteen worked, and at least 1.7 million children under the age of sixteen held jobs. Employers often exposed children to dangerous and unsanitary conditions. Most child workers toiled long, hard hours breathing in dust and fumes as they labored in textile mills, tobacco plants, print shops, and coal mines. In Indiana, young boys worked the night shift in dark, windowless glass factories. Children under the age of ten, known as "breaker boys," climbed onto filthy coal heaps and picked out unprocessed material. Working up to twelve-hour days, these children received less than a dollar a day.

The burden of child labor fell more heavily on some groups than others. Among children between the ages of ten and nineteen, black males (66 percent) and black females (44 percent) were more likely to work than white males (43 percent) and white females (13.1 percent). Immigrant boys and girls were also more likely to be employed than their American-born counterparts. Thus, these disparities in child labor indicated the relatively higher earnings of white and native-born families.

Women and children worked because the average male head of household could not support his family on his own pay, despite the increase in real wages. As Carroll D. Wright, director of the Massachusetts Bureau of the Statistics of Labor, reported in 1882, "A family of workers can always live well, but the man with a family of small children to support, unless his wife works also, has a small chance of living properly." For example, in 1883 in Joliet, Illinois, a railroad brakeman tried to support his wife and eight children on $360 a year. A state investigator described the way they lived: "Clothes ragged, children half dressed and dirty. They all sleep in one room regardless of sex. The house is devoid of furniture, and the entire concern is as wretched as could be imagined." Not all laborers lived in such squalor, but many wageworkers barely lived at subsistence level.

Although the average number of working hours dropped during this era, many laborers put in more than 10 hours a day on the job. In the steel industry, blast-furnace operators toiled 12 hours a day, 7 days a week. They received a day off every 2 weeks, but only if they worked a 24-hour shift. Given the long hours and backbreaking work, it is not surprising that accidents were a regular feature of industrial life. Each year tens of thousands were injured on

Chinese American Telephone Operator   The invention of the telephone brought jobs to many Americans, especially women. Yet not all operators were women, as this photograph shows. San Francisco's Chinatown employed workers from its own community, and in this photo a Chinese man works as a telephone operator while a child in a school uniform and another man stand by him.   Library of Congress, Prints and Photographs Division [LC-USZ62-37204]

the job, and thousands died as a result of mine cave-ins, train wrecks, explosions in industrial plants, and fires at textile mills and garment factories. Railroad employment was especially unsafe — accidents ended the careers of one in six workers.

Agricultural refugees who flocked to cotton mills in the South also faced dangerous working conditions. Working twelve-hour days breathing the lint-filled air from the processed cotton posed health hazards. Textile workers also had to place their hands into heavy machinery to disentangle threads, making them extremely vulnerable to serious injury. Wages scarcely covered necessities, and on many occasions families did not know where their next meal was coming from. North Carolina textile worker J. W. Mehaffry complained that the mill owners "were slave drivers" who "work their employees, women, and children from 6 a.m. to 7 p.m. with a half hour for lunch." Mill workers' meals usually consisted of potatoes, cornbread, and dried beans cooked in fat. This diet, without dairy products and fresh meat, led to outbreaks of pellagra, a debilitating disease caused by niacin (vitamin B3) deficiency.

Although wages and working hours improved slightly for some workers, employers kept the largest share of the increased profits that resulted from industrialization. In 1877 John D. Rockefeller collected dividends at the rate of at least $720 an hour, roughly double what his average employee earned in a year. Despite some success stories, prospects for upward mobility for most American workers remained limited. A manual worker might rise into the ranks of the semiskilled but would not make it into the middle class. And to achieve even this small upward mobility required putting the entire family to work and engaging in rigorous economizing, what one historian called "ruthless underconsumption." Despite their best efforts, most Americans remained part of the working class.

Organizing Unions.   Faced with improving but inadequate wages and with hazardous working conditions, industrial laborers sought to counter the concentrated power of corporate capitalists by joining forces. They attempted to organize **unions** — groups of workers seeking rights and benefits from their employers through their collective efforts. Union organizing was prompted by attitudes that were common among employers. Most employers were convinced that they and their employees shared identical interests, and they believed that they were morally and financially entitled to establish policies on their workers' behalf. They refused to engage in negotiations with labor unions (a process known as **collective bargaining**). Although owners appreciated the advantages of companies banding together to eliminate competition or to lobby for favorable regulations, similar collective efforts by workers struck them as unfair, even immoral. It was up to the men who supplied the money and the machines — rather than the workers — to determine what was a fair wage and what were satisfactory working conditions. In 1877 William H. Vanderbilt, the son of transportation tycoon Cornelius Vanderbilt, explained this way of thinking: "Our men feel that although I . . . may have my millions and they the rewards of their daily toil, still we are about equal in the end. If they suffer, I suffer, and if I suffer they cannot escape." Needless to say, many workers disagreed.

Industrialists expected their paternalistic values to reduce grievances among their workforce. They sponsored sports teams, set up social clubs, and offered cultural activities. The railroad magnate George Pullman built a model village to house his workers. In return, capitalists demanded unquestioned loyalty from their employees.

Yet a growing number of working people failed to see the relationship between employer and employee as mutually beneficial. Increasingly, they considered labor unions to be the best vehicle for communication and negotiation between workers and owners. Though not the first national workers' organization, the **Noble Order of the Knights of Labor**, founded by Uriah Stephens in 1869, initiated the most extensive and successful campaign after the Civil War to unite workers and challenge the power of corporate capitalists. "There is no mutuality of interests . . . [between] capital and labor," the Massachusetts chapter of the Knights proclaimed. "It is the iron heel of a soulless monopoly, crushing the manhood out of sovereign citizens." In fact, the essential premise of the Knights was that all workers shared common interests that were very different from those of owners.

The Knights did not really begin to flourish until Terence V. Powderly became Grand Master of the organization in 1879. Powderly advocated the eight-hour workday, the abolition of child labor, and equal pay for women. Under his leadership, the Knights accepted African Americans, immigrants, and women as members, though they excluded Chinese immigrant workers, as did other labor unions. As a result, the Knights experienced a surge in membership from 9,000 in 1879 to nearly a million in 1885, about 10 percent of the industrial workforce.

Rapid growth proved to be a mixed blessing. As membership grew, Powderly and the national organization exercised less and less control over local chapters. In fact, local chapters often defied the central organization by engaging in strikes, a tactic Powderly had officially disavowed. Nonetheless, members of the Knights struck successfully against the Union Pacific Railroad and the Missouri Pacific Railroad in 1885. The following year, on May 1, 1886, local assemblies of the Knights joined a nationwide strike to press for an eight-hour workday. However, this strike was soon overshadowed by events in Chicago that would prove to be the undoing of the Knights (Figure 17.1).

For months before the general strike, the McCormick Harvester plant in Chicago had been at the center of an often violent conflict over wages and work conditions. On May 3, 1886, police killed two strikers in a clash between union members and strikebreakers who tried to cross the picket lines. In response, a group of anarchists led by the German-born activist August Spies called for a rally in **Haymarket Square** to protest police violence. Consisting mainly of foreign-born radicals, such anarchists believed that government represented the interests of capitalists and stifled freedom for workers. Anarchists differed among themselves, but they generally advocated tearing down government authority,

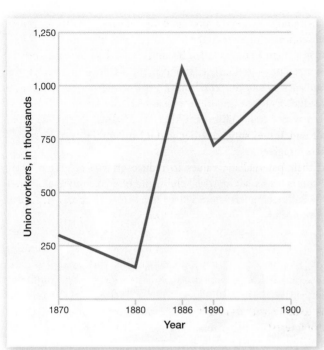

FIGURE 17.1 Union Membership, 1870–1900

Union membership fluctuated widely in the late nineteenth century. After reaching a low point in 1880, the number of union members rebounded. However, membership plummeted after 1886 only to soar again in the 1890s. Explain the rise and fall of union membership from 1880 through 1900.

Source: Data from Richard B. Freeman, "Spurts in Union Growth: Defining Moments and Social Processes," working paper 6012, National Bureau of Economic Research, Cambridge, MA, 1997.

restoring personal freedom, and forming worker communes to replace capitalism. To achieve their goals, anarchists like Spies advocated the violent overthrow of government.

The Haymarket rally began at 8:30 in the evening of May 4 and attracted no more than 1,500 people, who listened to a series of speeches as rain fell. By 10:30 p.m., when the crowd had dwindled to some 300 people, 180 policemen decided to break it up. As police moved into the square, someone set off a bomb. The police fired back, and when the smoke cleared, seven policemen and four protesters lay dead. Most of the fatalities and injuries resulted from the police crossfire. A subsequent trial convicted eight anarchists of murder, though there was no evidence that any of them had planted the bomb or used weapons. Four of them, including Spies, were executed. Although Powderly and other union leaders denounced the anarchists and the bombing, the incident greatly tarnished the labor movement. Capitalists and their allies in the press attacked labor unionists as radicals prone to violence and denounced strikes as un-American. Following the Haymarket incident, the membership rolls of the Knights plunged to below 500,000. By the mid-1890s, the Knights had fewer than 20,000 members.

As the Knights of Labor faded, the **American Federation of Labor (AFL)** grew in prominence, offering an alternative vision of unionization. Instead of one giant industrial union that included all workers, skilled and unskilled, the AFL organized only skilled craftsmen — the labor elite — into trade unions. In 1886 Samuel Gompers became president of the AFL. Gompers considered trade unions "the business organizations of the wage earners to attend to the business of the wage earners" and favored the use of strikes. No social reformer, the AFL president concentrated on obtaining better wages and hours for workers so that they could share in the prosperity generated by industrial capitalism. By 1900 the AFL had around a million members. It achieved these numbers by recruiting the most

Women in the Labor Movement, 1884   This wood engraving shows the wives of striking coal miners jeering at Pinkerton detectives as they escort strikebreakers into the mines in Buchtel, Ohio, in 1884. It was common for the family and friends of strikers in local communities to rally support on their behalf. Granger

independent, highest-paid, and least replaceable segment of the labor force — white male skilled workers. Unlike the Knights, the AFL had little or no place for women and African Americans in its ranks.

As impressive as the AFL's achievement was, the union movement as a whole experienced only limited success in the late nineteenth century. Only about one in fifteen industrial workers belonged to a union in 1900. Union membership was low for a variety of reasons. First, the political and economic power of corporations and the prospects of retaliation made the decision to sign up for union membership a risky venture. Second, the diversity of workers made organizing a difficult task. Foreign-born laborers came from many countries and were divided by language, religion, ethnicity, and history. Moreover, European immigrants quickly adopted native-born whites' racial prejudices against African Americans. Third, despite severe limitations in social mobility, American workers generally retained their faith in the benefits of the capitalist system. Finally, the government used its legal and military authority to side with employers and suppress militant workers.

Southern workers were the most resistant to union organizing. The agricultural background of mill workers left them with a heightened sense of individualism and isolation. In addition, their continued connection to family and friends in the countryside offered a potential escape route from industrial labor. Employers' willingness to use racial tensions to divide working-class blacks and whites prevented them from joining together to further their common economic interests.

Clashes between Workers and Owners. Despite the difficulties of organizing workers, labor challenged some of the nation's largest industries in the late nineteenth century. Faced with owners' refusal to recognize or negotiate with unions, workers marshaled their greatest source of power: <u>withholding</u> their labor and <u>going</u> on strike. Employers in turn had powerful weapons at their command to break strikes. They could recruit strikebreakers and mobilize private and public security forces to protect their businesses. That workers went on strike against such odds testified to their desperation and courage (Map 17.1).

Workers in the United States were not alone in their efforts to combat industrial exploitation. In England, laborers organized for better wages and working conditions. In 1888 in London, young women who worked at a match factory staged a walkout to protest the exorbitant fines that employers imposed on them for arriving even one minute late to work. With community support, they won their demands. From 1888 to 1890, the number of strikes throughout Europe grew from 188 to 289. In 1890 thousands of workers in Budapest, Hungary rose up to protest unsafe working conditions. European workers also campaigned for the right to vote, which unlike white male American workers, they were denied on economic grounds.

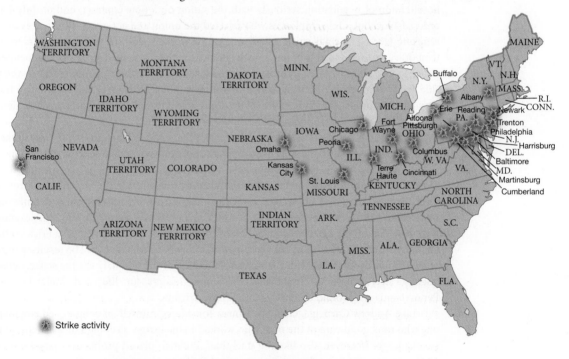

※ Strike activity

MAP 17.1   The Great Railroad Strike

This nationwide strike, precipitated by falling wages during the Depression of 1873, started in West Virginia and Pennsylvania and spread to Chicago, St. Louis, and San Francisco. The strike brought a halt to rail traffic as over 100,000 workers and another half a million sympathizers walked off their jobs. Violence broke out in Pittsburgh, resulting in more than twenty deaths. Federal troops were eventually dispatched to end the strike. Many workers quickly recognized the need to form unions to gain power to stand up against employers and the government.

In the United States in the 1890s, labor mounted several highly publicized strikes. Perhaps the most famous was the 1892 **Homestead strike**. Steelworkers at Carnegie's Homestead, Pennsylvania factory near Pittsburgh played an active role in local politics and civic affairs. Residents generally believed that Andrew Carnegie's corporation paid decent wages that allowed them to support their families and buy their own homes. In 1892 craftsmen earned $180 a month, and they appeared to have Carnegie's respect. Others, like John McLuckie, earned less than half that amount, and unskilled workers made even less.

In 1892, with steel prices falling, Carnegie decided to replace some of his skilled craftsmen with machinery, cut wages, save on labor costs, and bust McLuckie's union, the Amalgamated Association of Iron and Steel Workers. Knowing that his actions would provoke a strike and seeking to avoid the negative publicity that would result, Carnegie left the country and went to Scotland, leaving his plant manager, Henry Clay Frick, in charge.

Fiercely anti-union, Frick prepared for the strike by building a three-mile, fifteen-foot-high fence, capped with barbed wire and equipped with searchlights, around three sides of the Homestead factory. A hated symbol of the manager's hostility, the fence became known as "Fort Frick." Along the fourth side of the factory flowed the Monongahela River. Frick had no intention of negotiating seriously with the union on a new contract, and on July 1 he ordered a lockout. Only employees who rejected the union and accepted lower wages could return to work. The small town rallied around the workers, and the union members won a temporary victory. On July 6, barge-loads of armed Pinkerton detectives (an independent police force), hired by Frick to protect the plant, set sail toward the factory entrance alongside the Monongahela. From the shore, union men shot at the barges and set fire to a boat they pushed toward the Pinkertons. When the smoke cleared, the Pinkertons surrendered and hastily retreated onshore as women and men chased after them.

This triumph proved costly for the union. The battle left nine strikers and three Pinkerton detectives dead. Frick convinced the governor of Pennsylvania to send in state troops to protect the factory and the strikebreakers. Frick's efforts to end the strike spurred some radicals to action. Emma Goldman, an anarchist who advocated the violent overthrow of capitalism, declared that a blow against Frick would "strike terror in the enemy's ranks and make them realize that the proletariat of America had its avengers." On July 23, Alexander Berkman, Goldman's partner, who had no connection with the union, entered Frick's office and shot the steel executive in the neck, leaving him wounded but alive. The resulting unfavorable publicity, together with the state's prosecution of the union, broke the strike. Subsequently, steel companies blacklisted the union leaders for life, and McLuckie fled Pennsylvania and wound up nearly penniless in Arizona.

Like Andrew Carnegie, George Pullman considered himself an enlightened employer, one who took good care of the men who worked in his luxury sleeping railcar factory outside Chicago. However, also like the steel titan, Pullman placed profits over personnel. In 1893 a severe economic depression prompted Pullman to cut wages without correspondingly reducing the rents that his employees paid for living in company houses. This dual blow to worker income and purchasing power led to a fierce strike the following year. The Pullman workers belonged to the American Railway Union, headed by Eugene V. Debs. After George Pullman refused to negotiate, the union voted to go on strike.

In the end, the **Pullman strike** was broken by the federal government. President Grover Cleveland ordered federal troops to get the railroads operating, but the workers still refused to capitulate. Richard Olney, Cleveland's attorney general, then obtained an order from the federal courts to restrain Debs and other union leaders from continuing the strike. The government used the Sherman Antitrust Act to punish unions for conspiring to restrain trade, something it had rarely done with respect to large corporations. Refusing to comply, Debs and other union officials were charged with contempt, convicted under the Sherman Antitrust Act, and sent to jail. The strike collapsed. **See Primary Source Project 17: The Pullman Strike of 1894, page 596.**

Debs remained unrepentant. After serving his jail sentence, he became even more radical. In 1901 he helped establish the Socialist Party of America. German exiles who came to the United States following revolutions in Europe in 1848 had brought with them the revolutionary ideas of the German philosopher Karl Marx. Marx argued that capital and labor were engaged in a class struggle that would end with the violent overthrow of capitalist government and its replacement by communism. Marxist ideas attracted a small following in the United States, mainly among the foreign-born population. By contrast, other types of European socialists, including the German Social Democratic Party, appealed for working-class support by advocating the creation of a more just and humane economic system through the ballot box, not by violent revolution. Debs favored this nonviolent, democratic brand of socialism and managed to attract a broader base of supporters by articulating socialist doctrines in the language of cooperation and citizenship that many Americans shared. Debsian socialism appealed not only to industrial workers but also to dispossessed farmers and miners in the Southwest and Midwest.

Western miners had a history of labor activism, and by the 1890s they were ready to listen to radical ideas. Shortly after the Homestead strike ended in 1892, silver miners in Coeur d'Alene, Idaho walked out after owners slashed their wages. Employers refused to recognize any union, obtained an injunction against the strike, imported strikebreakers to run the mines, and persuaded Idaho's governor to impose martial law, in which the military took over the normal operation of civilian affairs. The work stoppage lasted four months, resulting in the arrest of six hundred strikers. Although the workers lost, the following year they succeeded in forming the Western Federation of Miners, which continued their fight.

The **Industrial Workers of the World (IWW)**, which emerged largely through the efforts of the Western Federation of Miners, sought to raise wages, improve working conditions, and gain union recognition for the most exploited segments of American labor. The IWW, or "Wobblies" as they were popularly known, sought to unite all skilled and unskilled workers in an effort to overthrow capitalism. The Wobblies favored strikes and direct-action protests rather than collective bargaining or mediation. At their rallies and strikes, they often encountered government force and corporation-inspired mob violence. Nevertheless, the IWW had substantial appeal among lumberjacks in the Northwest, dockworkers in port cities, miners in the West, farmers in the Great Plains, and textile workers in the Northeast.

Even though industrialists usually had state and federal governments as well as the media on their side, workers continued to press for their rights. Workers used strikes as a last resort when business owners refused to negotiate or recognize their demands to organize themselves into unions. Although most late-nineteenth-century strikes failed, striking unionists nonetheless called for collective bargaining, higher wages, shorter hours, and improved working conditions — an agenda that unions and their political allies would build on in the future.

Working-Class Leisure in Industrial America. Despite the hardships industrial laborers faced in the late nineteenth century, workers carved out recreational spaces that they could control and that offered relief from their backbreaking toil. For many, Sunday became a day of rest that took on a secular flavor.

Working-class leisure patterns varied by gender, race, and region. Women did not generally attend spectator sporting events, such as baseball and boxing matches, which catered to men. Nor did they find themselves comfortable in union halls and saloons, where men found solace in drink. Working-class wives preferred to gather to prepare for births, weddings, and funerals or to assist neighbors who had suffered some misfortune.

Once employed, working-class daughters found a greater measure of independence and free time by living in rooming houses on their own. Women's wages were only a small fraction of men's earnings, so workingwomen rarely made enough money to support a regular social life. Still, they found ways to enjoy their free time. Some single women went out in groups, hoping to meet men who would pay for drinks, food, or a vaudeville show. Others dated so that they knew they would be taken care of for the evening. Some of the men who "treated" on a date assumed a right to sexual favors in return, and some of these women then expected men to provide them with housing and gifts in exchange for an ongoing sexual relationship. Thus emotional and economic relationships became intertwined.

Fun at Coney Island, c.1898 Circuses and amusement parks were two forms of entertainment that attracted working-class and middle-class audiences. This poster announces the performance of Barnum and Bailey's "Greatest Show on Earth" at the water carnival in Coney Island. Clowns, boxers, divers, and log rollers would be among the variety of performers at the beach. Library of Congress, LC-DIG-ppmsca-54817

Around the turn of the twentieth century, dance halls flourished as one of the mainstays of working-class communities. Huge dance palaces were built in the entertainment districts of most large cities. They made their money by offering music with lengthy intermissions for the sale of drinks and refreshments. Women and men also attended nightclubs, some of which were racially integrated. In so-called red-light districts of the city, prostitutes earned money entertaining their clients with a variety of sexual pleasures.

Not all forms of leisure were strictly segregated along class lines. A number of forms of cheap entertainment appealed not only to working-class women and men but also to their middle-class counterparts. By the turn of the twentieth century, most large American cities featured amusement parks. Brooklyn's Coney Island stood out as the most spectacular of these sprawling playgrounds. In 1884, the world's first roller coaster was built at Coney Island, providing thrills to those brave enough to ride it. In Chicago at the 1893 World's Columbian Exposition, residents enjoyed the new Ferris wheel, which soared 250 feet in the air. Vaudeville houses — with their minstrel shows (whites in blackface) and comedians, singers, and dancers — brought howls of laughter to working-class audiences. Nickelodeons charged five cents to watch short films. Live theater generally attracted more wealthy patrons; however, the Yiddish theater, which flourished on New York's Lower East Side, and other immigrant-oriented stage productions appealed mainly to working-class audiences.

Itinerant musicians entertained audiences throughout the South. Lumber camps, which employed mainly African American men, offered a popular destination for these musicians. Each camp contained a "barrelhouse," also called a honky tonk or a juke joint. Besides showcasing music, the barrelhouse also gave workers the opportunity to "shoot craps, dice, drink whiskey, dance, every modern devilment you can do," as one musician who played there recalled. From the Mississippi delta emerged a new form of music — the blues. W. C. Handy, "the father of the blues," discovered this music in his travels through the delta, where he observed southern blacks performing songs of woe, accompanying themselves with anything that would make a "musical sound or rhythmical effect, anything from a harmonica to a washboard." Meanwhile in New Orleans, an amalgam of black musical forms evolved into jazz. Musicians such as "Jelly Roll" Morton experimented with a variety of sounds, putting together African and Caribbean rhythms with European music, mixing pianos with clarinets, trumpets, and drums. Blues and jazz spread throughout the South.

In mountain valley mill towns, southern whites preferred "old-time" music, but with a twist: they modified the lyrics of traditional ballads and folk songs, originally enjoyed by British settlers, to extol the exploits of outlaws and adventurers. Country music, which combined romantic ballads and folk tunes to the accompaniment of guitars, banjos, autoharps, dulcimers, and organs, emerged as a distinct brand of music by the twentieth century. As with African Americans, in the late nineteenth century working-class and rural whites found new and exciting types of music to entertain them in their leisure. Religious music also appealed to both white and black audiences and drew crowds to evangelical revivals.

Mill workers also amused themselves by engaging in social, recreational, and religious activities. Women visited each other and exchanged confidences, gossip, advice on child rearing, and folk remedies. Men from various factories organized baseball teams that competed in leagues. Managers of a mill in Charlotte, North Carolina, admitted that they "frequently hired men better known for their batting averages than their work records."

Review & Relate

▪ How did industrialization change the American workplace? What challenges did it create for American workers?

▪ How did workers resist the concentrated power of industrial capitalists in the late nineteenth century, and why did such efforts have only limited success?

Farmers Organize

Like industrial workers, farmers experienced severe economic hardships and a loss of political power in the face of rapid industrialization. The introduction of new machinery such as the combine harvester, introduced in 1878, led to substantial increases in the productivity of American farms. Soaring production, however, led to a decline in agricultural prices in the late nineteenth century, a trend that was accelerated by increased agricultural production around the world. In addition, the role of agriculture in the economy was steadily declining and taking second place to commerce and industry. Agriculture had slipped from a majority of economic production in 1860 to 40 percent in 1890, behind manufacturing and mining. Faced with an economic crisis caused by falling prices and escalating debt, farmers fought back, creating new organizations to champion their collective economic and political interests.

Farmers Unite. From the end of the Civil War to the mid-1890s, increased production of wheat and cotton, two of the most important American crops, led to a precipitous drop in the price for these crops. Falling prices created a debt crisis for many farmers. Most American farmers were independent businessmen who borrowed money to pay for land, seed, and equipment. When their crops were harvested and sold, they repaid their debts with the proceeds. As prices fell, farmers increased production in an effort to cover their debts. This tactic led to a greater supply of farm produce in the marketplace and even lower prices. Unable to pay back loans, many farmers lost their property in foreclosures to the banks that held their mortgages and furnished them credit.

To make matters worse, farmers lived isolated lives. Spread out across vast acres of rural territory, farmers had few social and cultural diversions. Even more than the families of industrial workers, farmers put their children to work; rural youngsters were 8 percent more likely to work than their urban counterparts. As the farm economy declined, more and more of their children left the monotony of rural America behind and headed for cities in search of new opportunities and a better life. Early efforts to organize farmers were motivated by a desire to counteract the isolation of rural life by creating new forms of social interaction and cultural engagement. In 1867, Oliver H. Kelly founded the Patrons of Husbandry to brighten the lonely existence of rural Americans through educational and social activities. Known as **Grangers** (from the French word for "granary"), the association grew rapidly in the early 1870s, especially in the Midwest and the South. Between 1872 and 1874, approximately fourteen thousand new Grange chapters were established.

Granger Movement, 1876   As the farmer's central placement in this lithograph implies, farmers were the heart of the Granger movement. The title is a variation on the movement's motto, "I Pay for All." A farmer with a plough and two horses stands at the center of the scene providing food for all, while other occupational types positioned around him echo a similar refrain based on their profession. Note the attitude toward the broker implied by the label "I Fleece You All." Library of Congress, Prints and Photographs Division [LC-DIG-pga-00025]

Grangers also formed farm cooperatives to sell their crops at higher prices and pool their purchasing power to buy finished goods at wholesale prices. The Grangers' interest in promoting the collective economic interests of farmers led to their increasing involvement in politics. Grangers endorsed candidates who favored their cause, and perhaps their most important objective was the regulation of shipping and grain storage prices. In many areas, individual railroads had monopolies on both of these services, and were able to charge farmers higher-than-usual rates to store and ship their crops. By electing sympathetic state legislators, Grangers managed to obtain regulations that placed a ceiling on the prices railroads and grain elevators could charge. The Supreme Court temporarily upheld these victories in *Munn v. Illinois* (1877). In 1886, however, in *Wabash v. Illinois* the Supreme Court reversed itself and struck down these state regulatory laws as hindering the free flow of interstate commerce.

Another apparent victory for regulation came in 1887 when Congress passed the Interstate Commerce Act, establishing the **Interstate Commerce Commission (ICC)** to regulate railroads. Although big businessmen could not prevent occasional government regulation, they managed to render it largely ineffective. In time, railroad advocates came to dominate the ICC and enforced the law in favor of the railway lines rather than the shippers. Implementation of the Sherman Antitrust Act also favored big business. From the standpoint of most late-nineteenth-century capitalists, national regulations often turned out to be more of a help than a hindrance.

By the late 1880s, the Grangers had abandoned electoral politics and once again devoted themselves strictly to social and cultural activities. A number of factors explain the Grangers' return to their original mission. First, prices began to rise for some crops, particularly corn, relieving the economic pressure on midwestern farmers. Second, the passage of regulatory legislation in a number of states convinced some Grangers that their political goals had been achieved. Finally, a lack of marketing and business experience led to the collapse of many agricultural collectives.

The withdrawal of the Grangers from politics did not, however, signal the end of efforts by farmers to form organizations to advance their economic interests. While farmers in the midwestern corn belt experienced some political success and an economic upturn, farmers farther west in the Great Plains and in the Lower South fell more deeply into debt, as the price of wheat and cotton on the international market continued to drop. In both of these regions, farmers organized **Farmers' Alliances**. In the 1880s, Milton George formed the Northwestern Farmers' Alliance. At the same time, Dr. Charles W. Macune organized the much larger Southern Farmers' Alliance. Southern black farmers, excluded from the Southern Farmers' Alliance, created a parallel Colored Farmers' Alliance. The Alliances formed a network of recruiters to sign up new members. No recruiter was more effective than Mary Elizabeth Lease, who excited farm audiences with her forceful and colorful rhetoric, delivering 160 speeches in the summer of 1890 alone. The Southern Farmers' Alliance advocated a sophisticated plan to solve the farmers' problem of mounting debt. Macune devised a proposal for a **subtreasury system**. Under this plan, the federal government would locate offices near warehouses in which farmers could store nonperishable commodities. In return, farmers would receive federal loans for 80 percent of the current market value of their produce. In theory, temporarily taking crops off the market would decrease supply and, assuming demand remained stable, lead to increased prices. Once prices rose, farmers would return to the warehouses, redeem their crops, sell them at the higher price, repay the government loan, and leave with a profit.

The first step toward creating a nationwide farmers' organization came in 1889, when the Northwestern and Southern Farmers' Alliances agreed to merge. Alliance leaders, including Lease, saw workers as fellow victims of industrialization, and they invited the Knights of Labor to join them. They also attempted to lower prevailing racial barriers by bringing the Colored Farmers' Alliance into the coalition. The following year, the National Farmers' Alliance and Industrial Union held its convention in Ocala, Florida. The group adopted resolutions endorsing the subtreasury system, as well as recommendations that would promote the economic welfare of farmers and extend political democracy to "the plain people." These proposals included tariff reduction, government ownership of banks and railroads, and political reforms to extend democracy, such as direct election of U.S. senators.

Finally, the Alliance pressed the government to increase the money supply by expanding the amount of silver coinage in circulation. In the Alliance's view, such a move would have two positive, and related, consequences. First, the resulting inflation would lead to higher prices for agricultural commodities, putting more money in farmers' pockets. Second, the real value of farmers' debts would decrease, since the debts were contracted in pre-inflation dollars and would be paid back with inflated currency. Naturally, the eastern bankers who supplied farmers with credit opposed such a policy. In fact, in 1873 Congress, under the leadership of Senator John Sherman, had halted the purchase of silver by the Treasury Department, a measure that helped reduce the money supply. Later, however, under the Sherman Silver Purchase Act (1890), the government resumed buying silver, but the act placed limits on its purchase and did not guarantee the creation of silver coinage by the Treasury. In the past, some members of the Alliance had favored expanding the money supply with greenbacks (paper money). However, to attract support from western silver miners, Alliance delegates emphasized the free and unlimited coinage of silver. Alliance supporters met with bitter disappointment, though, as neither the Republican nor the Democratic Party embraced their demands. Rebuffed, farmers took an independent path and became more directly involved in national politics through the formation of the Populist Party.

Populists Rise Up. In 1892 the National Farmers' Alliance moved into the electoral arena as a third political party. The People's Party of America, known as the **Populists**, held its first nominating convention in Omaha, Nebraska, in 1892. In addition to incorporating the Alliance's Ocala planks into their platform, they adopted recommendations to broaden the party's appeal to industrial workers. Populists endorsed a graduated income tax, which would impose higher tax rates on higher income levels, the eight-hour workday, and immigration restriction, which stemmed from the unions' desire to keep unskilled workers from glutting the market and depressing wages. Reflecting the influence of women such as Mary Lease, the party endorsed women's suffrage. The party did not, however, offer specific proposals to prohibit racial discrimination or segregation. Rather, the party focused on remedies to relieve the economic plight of impoverished white and black farmers in general.

Explore ▶

See Sources 17.2 and 17.3 to compare views of the Populists.

In 1892 the Populists nominated for president former Union Civil War general James B. Weaver. Although Weaver came in third behind the Democratic victor, Grover Cleveland, and the Republican incumbent, Benjamin Harrison, he managed to win more than 1 million popular votes and 22 electoral votes.

At the state level, Populists performed even better. They elected 10 congressional representatives, 5 U.S. senators, 3 governors, and 1,500 state legislators. Two years later, the party made even greater strides by increasing its total vote by 42 percent and achieving its greatest strength in the South. This electoral momentum positioned the Populists to make an even stronger run in the next presidential election. The economic depression that began in 1893 and the political discontent it generated enhanced Populist chances for success.

Review & Relate

▌ Why was life so difficult for American farmers in the late nineteenth century?

▌ What were the similarities and differences between farmers' and industrial workers' efforts to organize in the late nineteenth century?

Comparative Primary Source Analysis

Farmers and Workers Organize: Two Views

Farmers in the Midwest and the South organized to address the problems they faced as a result of industrialization and the growth of big business. The Populists in the 1880s and 1890s tried to deal with various social and economic issues. Compare the following excerpt from the Populist Party platform, adopted on July 4, 1892, in Omaha, Nebraska, with the pro-Populist cartoon that focuses on one source of its grievance.

Source 17.2

Walter Huston | Here Lies Prosperity, 1895

The "money question" became a focus of American politics in the first half of the 1890s and was exacerbated by the depression of 1893. Those who supported the gold standard believed that it provided the basis for a sound and stable economy. Proponents of the unlimited coinage of silver, especially Populists and Democrats such as William Jennings Bryan, asserted that expansion of the money supply would liberate farmers and workers from debt and bring prosperity to more Americans. This cartoon illustrates the "free silver" point of view.

"The Situation: The Result of Interest Bearing Bonds and Sherman," *Sound Money* (Massillon, OH), August 22, 1895. Reproduced from Worth Robert Miller, *Populist Cartoons: An Illustrated History of the Third Party Movement in the 1890s* (Truman State University Press, 2011).

Source 17.3

Populist Party Platform, 1892

[handwritten: economically radical, socially and racially conservative]

FINANCE—We demand a national currency, safe, sound, and flexible issued by the general government. . . .

1. We demand free and unlimited coinage of silver and gold at the present legal ratio of 16 to 1. . . .
3. We demand a graduated income tax.
4. We believe that the money of the country should be kept as much as possible in the hands of the people, and hence we demand that all State and national revenues shall be limited to the necessary expenses of the government, economically and honestly administered. . . .

TRANSPORTATION—Transportation being a means of exchange and a public necessity, the government should own and operate the railroads in the interest of the people. The telegraph and telephone . . . should be owned and operated by the government in the interest of the people.

[handwritten: nationalization regulated by government]

LAND—The land, including all the natural sources of wealth, is the heritage of the people, and should not be monopolized for speculative purposes, and alien ownership of land should be prohibited. All land now held by railroads and other corporations in excess of their actual needs, and all lands now owned by aliens should be reclaimed by the government and held for actual settlers only.

[handwritten: "real americans"]

EXPRESSION OF SENTIMENTS

1. Resolved, That we demand a free ballot, and a fair count in all elections . . . without Federal intervention, through the adoption by the States of the . . . secret ballot system.
2. Resolved, That the revenue derived from a graduated income tax should be applied to the reduction of the burden of taxation now levied upon the domestic industries of this country. . . .
4. Resolved, That we condemn the fallacy of protecting American labor under the present system, which opens our ports to [immigrants including] the pauper and the criminal classes of the world and crowds out our [American] wage-earners; and we . . . demand the further restriction of undesirable immigration. *[handwritten: xenophobia]*
5. Resolved, That we cordially sympathize with the efforts of organized workingmen to shorten the hours of labor. . . . *[handwritten: unions! strikers]*
6. Resolved, That we regard the maintenance of a large standing army of mercenaries, known as the Pinkerton system, as a menace to our liberties, and we demand its abolition.

Source: "People's Party Platform," *Omaha Morning World-Herald*, July 5, 1892.

[handwritten: private detectives hired to keep workers in factories]

Interpret the Evidence

1. Explain how these two sources emphasize different aspects of Populist grievances.
2. How do these two sources appeal to the same audience in different ways?

Put It in Context

How did the Populists respond to the shifts in economic and political power that occurred at the end of the nineteenth century?

The **Depression** of the **1890s**

When the Philadelphia and Reading Railroad went bankrupt in early 1893, it set off a chain reaction that pushed one-quarter of American railroads into insolvency. As a result, on May 5, 1893, "Black Friday," the stock market collapsed in a panic, triggering the **depression of 1893**. Making this situation worse, England and the rest of industrial Europe had experienced an economic downturn several years earlier. In the early 1890s foreign investors began selling off their American stocks, leading to a flow of gold coin out of the country and further damage to the banking system. Hundreds of banks failed, which hurt the businesspeople and farmers who relied on a steady flow of bank credit. By the end of 1894, nearly 12 percent of the American workforce remained unemployed. The depression became the chief political issue of the mid-1890s and resulted in a realignment of power between the two major parties. Unable to capitalize on depression discontent, however, the Populist Party split apart and collapsed.

Depression Politics. President Grover Cleveland's handling of the depression, accompanied by protest marches and labor strife, only made a bad situation worse. In the spring of 1894, Jacob Coxey, a Populist reformer from Ohio, led a march on Washington, D.C., demanding that Cleveland and Congress initiate a federal public works program to provide jobs for the unemployed. Though highly critical of the favored few who dominated the federal government, Coxey had faith that if "the people . . . come in a body like this, peaceably to discuss their grievances and demanding immediate relief, Congress . . . will heed them and do it quickly." After traveling for a month from Ohio, Coxey led a parade of some five hundred unemployed people into the nation's capital. Attracting thousands of spectators, **Coxey's army** attempted to mount their protest on the grounds of the Capitol building. In response, police broke up the demonstration and arrested Coxey for trespassing. Cleveland turned a deaf ear to Coxey's demands for federal relief and also disregarded protesters participating in nearly twenty other marches on Washington.

Explore ▶

Compare Sources 17.4 and 17.5 to evaluate different interpretations of the Populists.

In the coming months, Cleveland's political stock plummeted further. He responded to the Pullman strike in the summer of 1894 by obtaining a federal injunction against the strikers and dispatching federal troops to Illinois to enforce it. The president's action won him high praise from the railroads and conservative business interests, but it showed millions of American workers that the Cleveland administration did not have a solution for ending the suffering caused by the depression. "While the people should patriotically and cheerfully support their Government," the president declared, "its functions do not include the support of the people."

Making matters worse, Cleveland convinced Congress to repeal the Sherman Silver Purchase Act. This angered western miners, who relied on strong silver prices, along with farmers in the South and Great Plains who were swamped by mounting debt. At the same time, the removal of silver as a backing for currency caused private investors to withdraw their gold deposits from the U.S. Treasury. To keep the government financially solvent, Cleveland worked out an agreement with a syndicate led by J. P. Morgan to help sell government bonds, a deal that netted the banker a huge profit. In the midst of economic suffering, this deal looked like a corrupt bargain between the government and the rich.

In 1894 Congress also passed the Wilson-Gorman Act, which raised tariffs on imported goods. Intended to protect American businesses by keeping the price of imported

Coxey's Army, 1894   Some 400 members of Jacob Coxey's Commonwealth Army break camp at Brightwood Park in Washington, D.C., on horseback, carriage, bicycle, and on foot heading toward the Capitol. Coxey led a group of the unemployed to demand that the Cleveland administration create public works jobs during the economic depression. They did not succeed, and Coxey and his followers were arrested on the grounds of the Capitol. Library of Congress, 3b42632

goods high, it also deprived foreigners of the necessary income with which to buy American exports. This drop in exports did not help economic recovery. The Wilson-Gorman Act did include a provision that the Populists and other reformers endorsed: a progressive income tax of 2 percent on all annual earnings over $4,000. No federal income tax existed at this time, so even this mild levy elicited cries of "socialism" from conservative critics, who challenged the tax in the courts. In *Pollack v. Farmers Loan and Trust* (1895), the Supreme Court declared the income tax unconstitutional and denounced it as the opening wedge in "a war of the poor against the rich; a war constantly growing in intensity and bitterness."

With Cleveland's legislative program in shambles and his inability to solve the depression abundantly clear, the Democrats suffered a crushing blow at the polls. In the congressional elections of 1894, the party lost an astonishing 120 seats in the House. This defeat offered a preview of the political shakeup that loomed ahead.

Political Realignment in the Election of 1896.

The presidential election of 1896 marked a turning point in the political history of the nation. Democrats nominated William Jennings Bryan of Nebraska, a farmers' advocate. He embodied the belief that farmers still formed the backbone of the republic despite the fact they no longer dominated the nation economically. "Burn down your cities," Bryan declared, "and leave our farms, and your cities will spring up again as if by magic; but destroy our farms and the grass will grow in the streets of every city in the country." Bryan also favored silver coinage and when he vowed that he would not see Republicans "crucify mankind on a cross of gold," the Populists endorsed him as well."

Republicans nominated William McKinley, the governor of Ohio and a supporter of the gold standard and high tariffs on manufactured and other goods. McKinley's campaign manager, Marcus Alonzo Hanna, an ally of Ohio senator John Sherman, raised an unprecedented amount of money, about $16 million, mainly from wealthy industrialists who feared that the free and unlimited coinage of silver would debase the U.S. currency. Hanna saturated the country with pamphlets, leaflets, and posters, many of them written in the native languages of immigrant groups. He also hired a platoon of speakers to fan out across the country denouncing Bryan's free silver cause as financial madness. By contrast, Bryan raised about $1 million.

Comparative Secondary Source Analysis

The Agrarian Myth and Populism

The Merriam-Webster dictionary defines populism as a belief in the "rights, wisdom, or virtues of the common people," and those who identify with this label share a common belief in challenging the established political and economic order. In contemporary times the word is associated with politicians across a broad scale of the political spectrum, both on the left and the right. The Populist (or Peoples) Party of the 1890s was a movement that challenged the two major political parties before its demise at the turn of the twentieth century. The selections below show how historians, writing in different time periods and with different assumptions, can reach contrasting conclusions. When Richard Hofstadter wrote in 1955, the nation was gripped by fears of alleged conspiracies threatening the "American Way of Life." In 2007, when Charles Postel analyzed Populism, many Americans had turned their attention to the inequality of wealth and the role played by corporations in perpetuating it.

Source 17.4

Richard Hofstadter | The Agrarian Myth, 1955

"As a businessman, the farmer was appropriately hardheaded; he tried to act upon a cold and realistic strategy of self-interest. As the head of the family, however, the farmer felt that . . . when he risked the farm he risked his home – that he was, in short, a single man running a personal enterprise in a world of impersonal forces. It was from this aspect of his situation – seen in the hazy glow of the agrarian myth – that his political leaders in the 1890s developed their rhetoric and some of their concepts of political action.

The utopia of the Populists was in the past, not the future. According to the agrarian myth, the health of the state was proportionate to the degree to which it was dominated by the agricultural class, and this assumption pointed to the superiority of an earlier age. The Populists looked backward with longing to the lost agrarian Eden, to the Republican America of the early years of the nineteenth century in which there

were few millionaires, and as they saw it, no beggars when the laborer had excellent prospects and the farmer had abundance, when the statesman still responded to the mood of the people and there was no such thing as money power. What they meant – though they did not express themselves in such terms – was that they would like to restore the conditions prevailing before the development of industrialism and the commercialization of agriculture. . . . There was in fact a widespread Populist idea that all American history since the Civil War could be understood as a sustained conspiracy of the international money power. . . . In Populist thought the farmer is not a speculating businessman, victimized by the risk economy of which he is a part, but rather a wounded yeoman preyed upon by those who are alien to the life of folkish virtue."

Source: Richard Hofstadter, *The Age of Reform: From Bryan to F.D.R.* New York: Vintage Books, 1955, 46, 62.

Source 17.5

Charles Postel | The Populist Vision, 2007

"The Populist world was too commercially and intellectually dynamic to resemble a traditional society in any meaningful sense of the term. This tells us something important about the nature of late nineteenth-century: the men and women of the Populist movement were modern people. The term *modern* does not mean "good.' Nor is it a value judgment across the political spectrum from right to left. Moreover, to say that the Populists were modern does not imply that they were more modern than, say, their Republican or Democratic opponents. Nor does it imply that all rural people shared the Populists' modern sensibility. On the contrary, the Populists understood that the transformations they sought required the uprooting of ignorance, inertia, and force of habit. Populism formed a unique social movement that represented a distinctly modernizing impulse. . . .

Modernity also implied a particular kind of people with particular types of strivings . . . Modern men and women . . . 'look forward to future developments in their conditions of life and their relations with their fellow men.' The Populists were just this kind of people. They sought to improve their domestic economy and their national government. They sought renewal in local schoolhouses and federal credit systems. They sought to refashion associational ties with neighbors and commercial relations with the world. They sought new techniques, new acreage, and new avenues of spiritual expression."

Source: Charles Postel, *The Populist Vision*. New York: Oxford University Press, 2007, 9, 10.

Examine the Sources

1. How do Hofstadter and Postel differ in their assessments of Populism?
2. Drawing upon evidence in this chapter, how would you evaluate the strengths and weaknesses of Hofstadter and Postel's presentations?

Put It in Context

Evaluate the historical legacy of the Populist Party.

The outcome of the election transformed the Republicans into the majority party in the United States. McKinley won 51 percent of the popular vote and 61 percent of the electoral vote. More important than this specific contest, however, was that the election proved critical in realigning the two parties. Voting patterns shifted with the 1896 election, giving Republicans the edge in party affiliation among the electorate not only in this contest but also in presidential elections over the next three decades (Map 17.2).

What happened to produce this critical realignment in electoral power? The main ingredient was Republicans' success in forming a coalition that included both corporate capitalists and their workers. Many urban dwellers and industrial workers took out their anger on Cleveland's Democratic Party and Bryan as its standard-bearer for failing to end the depression. In addition, Bryan, who hailed from Nebraska and reflected small-town agricultural America and its values, could not win over the swelling numbers of urban immigrants who considered Bryan's world alien to their experience.

The election of 1896 broke the political stalemate in this age of organization. The core of Republican backing came from industrial cities of the Northeast and Midwest. Republicans won support from their traditional constituencies of Union veterans, business people, and African Americans and added to it the votes of a large number of urban wageworkers. The campaign persuaded voters that the Democratic Party represented the party of depression and that Republicans stood for prosperity and progress. They were soon able to take credit for ending the depression when, in 1897, gold discoveries in Alaska helped increase the money supply and foreign crop failures raised American farm prices. Democrats managed to hold on to the South as their solitary political base.

The Decline of the Populists.   The year 1896 also marked the end of the Populists as a national force, as the party was torn apart by internal divisions over policy and strategy. Populist leaders such as Tom Watson of Georgia did not want the Populist Party to emphasize free silver above the rest of its reform program. Northern Populists, who either had fought on the Union side during the Civil War or had close relatives who did, such as Mary Lease whose father and brother died on the Union side, could not bring themselves to join the Democrats, the party of the old Confederacy. Nevertheless, the Populist Party officially backed Bryan, but to retain its identity, the party nominated Watson for vice president on its own ticket. After McKinley's victory, the Populist Party collapsed.

In addition to losing the presidential election, several other problems plagued the third party. The nation's recovery from the depression removed one of the Populists' prime sources of electoral attraction. Despite appealing to

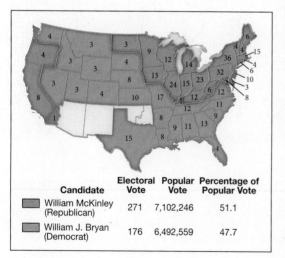

Candidate	Electoral Vote	Popular Vote	Percentage of Popular Vote
William McKinley (Republican)	271	7,102,246	51.1
William J. Bryan (Democrat)	176	6,492,559	47.7

MAP 17.2   The Election of 1896

William McKinley's election in 1896 resulted in a realignment of political power in the United States that lasted until 1932. Republicans became the nation's majority party by forging a coalition of big business and urban industrial workers from the Northeast and Midwest. Democratic strength was confined to the South and to small towns and rural areas of the Great Plains and Rocky Mountain states.

industrial workers, the Populists were unable to capture their support. The free silver plank attracted silver miners in Idaho and Colorado, but the majority of workers failed to identify with a party composed mainly of farmers. As consumers of agricultural products, industrial laborers did not see any benefit in raising farm prices. Populists also failed to create a stable, biracial coalition of farmers. Most southern white Populists did not truly accept African Americans as equal partners, even though these groups had mutual economic interests.

To eliminate Populism's insurgent political threat, southern opponents found ways to disfranchise black and poor white voters. During the 1890s, southern states inserted into their constitutions voting requirements that virtually eliminated the black electorate and greatly diminished the white electorate. Seeking to circumvent the Fifteenth Amendment's prohibition against racial discrimination in the right to vote, conservative white lawmakers adopted regulations based on wealth and education because blacks were disproportionately poor and had lower literacy rates. They instituted poll taxes, which imposed a fee for voting, and literacy tests, which asked questions designed to trip up black would-be voters. In 1898 the Supreme Court upheld the constitutionality of these voter qualifications in *Williams v. Mississippi.* Recognizing the power of white supremacy, the Populists surrendered to its appeals.

Tom Watson provides a case in point. He started out by encouraging racial unity but then switched to divisive politics. In 1896 the Populist vice presidential candidate called on citizens of both races to vote against the crushing power of corporations and railroads. By whipping up antagonism against blacks, his Democratic opponents appealed to the racial

Wilmington, North Carolina Massacre, 1898   In 1898, Populists in alliance with the Republican Party in Wilmington, N.C. elected a white mayor and a biracial city council. Two days after the election, on November 10, armed members of the defeated Democratic Party, the party of white supremacy, overthrew the new city government. A mob of around 2000 white men, some of whom are pictured above, set fire to the city's black newspaper building. White terrorists killed at least fifteen people and forced more than 2000 blacks to flee the city permanently. The success of this *coup d'état* dealt Populism a mortal blow. Library of Congress, Prints and Photographs Division [LC-USZ62-51942]

pride of poor whites to keep them from defecting to the Populists. Chastened by the outcome of the 1896 election and learning from the tactics of his political foes, Watson embarked on a vicious campaign to exclude blacks from voting. "What does civilization owe the Negro?" he bitterly asked. "Nothing! Nothing! NOTHING!!!" Only by disfranchising African Americans and maintaining white supremacy, Watson and other white reformers reasoned, would poor whites have the courage to vote against rich whites.

Nevertheless, even in defeat the Populists left an enduring legacy. Many of their political and economic reforms—direct election of senators, the graduated income tax, government regulation of business and banking, and a version of the subtreasury system (called the Commodity Credit Corporation, created in the 1930s)—became features of reform in the twentieth century. Perhaps their greatest contribution, however, came in showing farmers that their old individualist ways would not succeed in the modern industrial era. Rather than re-creating an independent political party, most farmers looked to organized interest groups, such as the Farm Bureau, to lobby on behalf of their interests.

Review & Relate

� How did the federal government respond to the depression of 1893?

▐ What were the long-term political consequences of the depression of 1893?

Conclusion: A Passion for Organization

From 1877 to 1900, industrial workers and farmers joined the march toward organization led by the likes of Carnegie, Rockefeller, and Morgan. These wealthy titans of industry and finance had created the large corporations that transformed the rhythms and meanings of life in workplaces, farms, and leisure activities. Working people such as John McLuckie met the challenges of the new industrial order by organizing unions. Lacking the power of giant companies and confronted by the federal government's use of force to break up strikes, labor unions nevertheless carved out sufficient space for workers to join together in their own defense to resist absolute corporate rule. At the same time, farmers, perhaps the most individualistic workers, and their advocates, such as Mary Elizabeth Lease, created organizations that proposed some of the most forward-looking solutions to remedy the ills accompanying industrialization. Though the political fortunes of the Grangers and Populists declined, their message persisted: Resourceful and determined workers and farmers could, and should, join together to ensure survival not just of the fittest but of the neediest as well.

Under the pressure of increased turmoil surrounding industrialization and a brutal economic depression, the political system reached a crisis in the 1890s. Despite the historic shift in party loyalties brought about by the election of William McKinley, it remained to be seen whether political party realignment could furnish the necessary leadership to address the problems of workers and farmers. The events of the 1890s convinced many Americans, including many in the middle class, that the hands-off approach to social and economic problems that had prevailed in the past was no longer acceptable. In cities and states across the country, men and women took up the cause of reform. They had to wait for national leaders to catch up to them.

Timeline of Events

1865–1895	U.S. manufacturing jobs jump from 5.3 million to 15.1 million
1867	Grange founded
1869	Knights of Labor founded
1870–1900	Number of female wageworkers increases by 66 percent
1877	Great Railroad Strike
1879	Terence Powderly becomes leader of Knights of Labor
1880s	Northwestern, Southern, and Colored Farmers' Alliances formed
1886	Haymarket Square violence
	American Federation of Labor founded
1887	Interstate Commerce Act
1889	Northwestern and Southern Farmers' Alliances merge
1890	Sherman Silver Purchase Act
1890s	Southern states restrict blacks' right to vote
1892	Homestead steelworkers' strike
	Populist Party established
1893	Depression triggered by stock market collapse
1894	Pullman strike
	Coxey's army marches to Washington
	Sherman Silver Purchase Act repealed
1896	Populist William Jennings Bryan runs for president
1897	Populist Party declines
1901	Eugene Debs establishes Socialist Party of America

Key Terms

unskilled workers, *570*
skilled workers, *570*
unions, *573*
collective bargaining, *574*
Noble Order of the Knights of Labor, *574*
Haymarket Square, *574*
American Federation of Labor (AFL), *575*
Homestead strike, *578*
Pullman strike, *578*
Industrial Workers of the World (IWW), *579*
Grangers, *582*
Interstate Commerce Commission (ICC), *584*
Farmers' Alliances, *584*
subtreasury system, *584*
Populists, *585*
depression of 1893, *588*
Coxey's army, *588*

Review & Relate

1. How did industrialization change the American workplace? What challenges did it create for American workers?

2. How did workers resist the concentrated power of industrial capitalists in the late nineteenth century, and why did such efforts have only limited success?

3. Why was life so difficult for American farmers in the late nineteenth century?

4. What were the similarities and differences between farmers' and industrial workers' efforts to organize in the late nineteenth century?

5. How did the federal government respond to the depression of 1893?

6. What were the long-term political consequences of the depression of 1893?

The Pullman Strike of 1894

▶ Explain the reasons industrial workers sought to organize against their employers and evaluate why they were not more successful in gaining a larger share of economic and political power in the late nineteenth century.

Late-nineteenth-century industrialists exercised massive power over workers and the conditions of labor. Workers organized into unions to secure higher wages, shorter hours, improved safety, and a fairer measure of control of the labor process. Even those corporate owners who were considered sympathetic to the needs of laborers and their families, such as railcar magnate George Pullman, assumed the right to manage their businesses as they saw fit (Source 17.6). Though Pullman had constructed a model town with clean housing and parks for his employees, he refused to heed workers' economic complaints after the depression of 1893 began (Source 17.8).

Yet this power did not go unchallenged. When the American Railway Union (ARU), headed by Eugene V. Debs (Source 17.7), launched a nation-wide strike against the Pullman company in May 1894 to improve economic conditions and gain recognition for the union, Pullman refused to negotiate. Rebuffed by Pullman, the union coordinated strike activities across the country from its headquarters in Chicago. Workers refused to operate trains with Pullman cars attached, and when the railroads hired strikebreakers, some 260,000 strikers brought rail traffic to a halt. In response, U.S. attorney general Richard Olney, a member of many railroad boards, obtained a federal injunction ordering strikers back to work, but without success. At Olney's recommendation, President Grover Cleveland ordered federal troops into Chicago to enforce the injunction. Their clash with strikers resulted in thirteen deaths, more than fifty injuries, hundreds of thousands of dollars in property damages, and the spread of violence to twenty-six states (Source 17.9). After the government arrested union leaders, including Debs, for disobeying the injunction, the strike collapsed in July 1894, and the Supreme Court upheld Debs's imprisonment.

The following sources reveal the points of view from four major combatants in the labor struggle. Explain the reasons industrial workers sought to organize against their employers, and evaluate why they were not more successful in gaining a larger share of economic and political power in the late nineteenth century.

Source 17.6

George Pullman | Testimony before the U.S. Strike Commission, 1894

In July 1894, President Grover Cleveland appointed a commission to investigate the Chicago (Pullman) strike. Although the Cleveland administration played a major role in ending the strike to the detriment of the American Railway Union, the president selected Carroll D. Wright, the U.S. commissioner of labor, to chair the commission. Wright had significant experience investigating labor conditions and collecting statistical data, and he was sympathetic to the plight of workers. George Pullman appeared before the commission to explain his position on the strike.

COMMISSIONER WRIGHT . . . State generally what the idea was of establishing the town [of Pullman] in connection with your manufacturing plant. . . .

PULLMAN [reading from a statement] The object in building Pullman was the establishment of a great manufacturing business on the most substantial basis possible, recognizing, as we did, and do now, that the working people are the most important element which enters into the successful operation of any manufacturing enterprise. We decided to build, in close proximity to the shops, homes for workingmen of such character and surroundings as would prove so attractive as to cause the best class of mechanics to seek that place for employment in preference to others. We also desired to establish the place on such a basis as would exclude all baneful [harmful] influences, believing that such a policy would result in the greatest measure of success, both from a commercial point of view, and also, what was equally important, or perhaps of greater importance, in a tendency toward continued elevation and improvement of the conditions not only of the working people themselves, but of their children growing up about them. . . .

If any lots had been sold in Pullman it would have permitted the introduction of the baneful elements which it was the chief purpose to exclude from the immediate neighborhood of the shops, and from the homes to be erected about them. The plan was to provide homes in the first place for all people who should desire to work in the shops, at reasonable rentals, with the expectation that as they became able and should desire to do so, they would purchase lots and erect homes for themselves within convenient distances, or avail themselves of the opportunity to rent homes from other people who should build in that vicinity. As a matter of fact, at the time of the strike 563 of the shop employees owned their homes, and 461 of that number are now employed in the shops; 560 others at the time of the strike lived outside; and, in addition, an estimated number from 200 to 300 others employed at Pullman were owners of their homes. . . .

Due attention was paid to the convenience and general well-being of the residents by the erection of stores and markets, a church, public schools, a library, and public halls for lectures and amusements; also a hotel and boarding houses. The basis on which rents were fixed was to make a return of 6 percent on the actual investment, which at that time, 1881, was a reasonable return to be expected from such an investment; and in calculating what, for such a purpose, was the actual investment in the dwellings on the one hand and the other buildings on the other, an allowance was made for the cost of the streets and other public improvements, just as it has to be considered in the valuation of any property for renting anywhere, all public improvements having to be paid for by the owner of a lot, either directly or by special assessment, and by him considered in the valuation. The actual operations have never shown a net return of 6 percent, the amount originally contemplated. The investment for several years returned a net revenue of about 4½ percent, but during the last two years additional taxes and heavier repairs have brought the net revenue down to 3.82 percent. . . .

COMMISSIONER NICOLAS WORTHINGTON I wanted to know what you had in mind at the time you made the statement that "it was very clear that no prudent man could submit to arbitration in this matter" when you were referring to your daily losses as a reason why any prudent man could not submit to arbitration?

PULLMAN The amount of the losses would not cut any figure; it was the principle involved, not the amount that would affect my views as to arbitration.

WORTHINGTON Then it was not the amount of losses that the company was then sustaining, but it was the fact that a continuance of the business at the rates that had been paid would entail loss upon the company?

PULLMAN It was the principle that that should not be submitted to a third party. That was a matter that the company should decide for itself. . . .

WORTHINGTON Now, let me ask you if, taking all the revenues of the Pullman company for the last year, so far as you are advised, if the company has lost money or made money during the last year?

PULLMAN The company has made money during the last year.

Source: *Executive Documents of the Senate of the United States*, 53rd Cong. (1894–1895), 529–30, 553.

Eugene V. Debs | On Radicalism, 1902

American Railway Union leader Eugene Debs served six months in jail after leading the Pullman strike. This experience moved him in more radical directions politically, and he established the Socialist Party. He ran as the party's presidential candidate five times, and in 1905 Debs helped form the Industrial Workers of the World, an organization interested in uniting all workers and challenging the capitalist system. In 1902 he described to the readers of the *Comrade*, a New York socialist newspaper, his thoughts on the Pullman strike and how he became a socialist.

n 1894 the American Railway Union was organized and a braver body of men never fought the battle of the working class.

Up to this time I had heard but little of Socialism, knew practically nothing about the movement, and what little I did know was not calculated to impress me in its favor. I was bent on thorough and complete organization of the railroad men and ultimately the whole working class, and all my time and energy were given to that end. My supreme conviction was that if they were only organized in every branch of the service and all acted together in concert they could redress their wrongs and regulate the conditions of their employment. The stockholders of the corporation acted as one, why not the men? It was such a plain proposition — simply to follow the example set before their eyes by their masters — surely they could not fail to see it, act as one, and solve the problem. . . .

Next followed the final shock — the Pullman strike — and the American Railway Union again won, clear and complete. The combined corporations were paralyzed and helpless. At this juncture there [was] delivered, from wholly unexpected quarters, a swift succession of blows that blinded me for an instant and then opened wide my eyes — and in the gleam of every bayonet and the flash of every rifle *the class struggle was revealed.* This was my first practical lesson in Socialism, though wholly un-aware that it was called by that name.

An army of detectives, thugs, and murderers [was] equipped with badge and beer and bludgeon and turned loose; old hulks of cars were fired; the alarm bells tolled; the people were terrified; the most startling rumors were set afloat; the press volleyed and thundered, and over all the wires sped the news that Chicago's white throat was in the clutch of a red mob; injunctions flew thick and fast, arrests followed, and our office and headquarters, the heart of the strike, was sacked, torn out, and nailed up by the "lawful" authorities of the federal government; and when in company with my loyal comrades I found myself in Cook county jail at Chicago, with the whole press screaming conspiracy, treason, and murder. . . .

. . . But the tempest gradually subsided and with it the bloodthirstiness of the press and "public sentiment." We were not sentenced to the gallows, nor even to the penitentiary — though put on trial for conspiracy — for reasons that will make another story.

The Chicago jail sentences were followed by six months at Woodstock [the Illinois jail where Debs was imprisoned] and it was here that Socialism gradually laid hold of me in its own irresistible fashion. Books and pamphlets and letters from socialists came by every mail and I began to read and think and dissect the anatomy of the system in which workingmen, however organized, could be shattered and battered and splintered at a single stroke. . . .

The American Railway Union was defeated but not conquered — overwhelmed but not destroyed. It lives and pulsates in the Socialist movement, and its defeat but blazed the way to economic freedom and hastened the dawn of human brotherhood.

Source: Eugene V. Debs, *Debs: His Life, Writings, and Speeches* (Chicago: Charles Kerr, 1908), 81–84.

Jennie Curtis | Testimony before the U.S. Strike Commission, 1894

During the Pullman strike, seamstress Jennie Curtis was president of the American Railway Union Local 269, known as the "girls' union." Following a stirring speech by Curtis at an ARU convention, the union agreed to support workers striking against Pullman. In the following excerpt, Curtis explains to Carroll D. Wright, chairman of the congressional commission that later investigated the strike, the dire economic situation employees faced as the company cut back wages and raised rents.

COMMISSIONER WRIGHT State your name, residence, and occupation.

CURTIS Jennie Curtis; reside at Pullman; have been a seamstress for the Pullman company in the repair shops sewing room; worked for them five years.

WRIGHT Are you a member of any labor organization?

CURTIS Yes, sir; I am a member of the American Railway Union.

WRIGHT How long have you been a member of that union?

CURTIS Since about the 8th day of last May.

WRIGHT Do you hold any position in the union?

CURTIS I am president of the girls' union, local, No. 269, at Pullman.

WRIGHT Did you have anything to do with the strike at Pullman, which occurred on the 11th of May, 1894?

CURTIS No, sir.

WRIGHT Had you anything to do with any of the efforts to avoid the strike, or to settle the difficulties?

CURTIS I had not, further than being on a committee which called to see Mr. Pullman and Mr. Wickes, the general manager of the company, to ask for more wages, asking to arbitrate, and such as that.

WRIGHT Were you on those committees, or some of them?

CURTIS Yes, sir; I was.

WRIGHT State briefly what you did as a member serving upon those committees.

CURTIS I was on a committee that went from Pullman to speak for the girls in May before the strike, to ask for more wages. . . .

WRIGHT State what took place at the first interview.

CURTIS We went there and asked, as the men did, for more wages; we were cut lower than any of the men's departments throughout the works; in 1893 we were able to make 22 cents per hour, or $2.25 per day, in my department, and on the day of the strike we could only earn, on an average, working as hard as we possibly could, from 70 to 80 cents a day.

COMMISSIONER JOHN D. KERNAN Can you give us how the wages changed from month to month?

CURTIS Whenever the men were cut in their wages the girls also received a cut. We were cut twice inside of a week in November, 1893, and in January our wages were cut again; that was the last cut we received, and we worked as hard as we possibly could and doing all we could, too. The most experienced of us could only make 80 cents per day, and a great many of the girls could only average 40 to 50 cents per day. . . .

WRIGHT Do you pay rent in Pullman?

CURTIS No, sir; not now.

WRIGHT You pay board?

CURTIS Yes, sir. My father worked for the Pullman company for thirteen years. He died last September, and I paid the rent to the Pullman company up to the time he died; I was boarding at the time of my father's death. He being laid off and sick for three months, owed the Pullman company $60 at the time of his death for back rent, and the company made me, out of my small earnings, pay that rent due from my father.

KERNAN How did they make you do it?

CURTIS The contract was that I should pay $3 on the back rent every pay day; out of my small earnings I could not give them $3 every pay day, and when I did not do so I was insulted and almost put out of the bank by the clerk for not being able to pay it to them. My wages were cut so low that I could not pay my board and give them $3 on the back rent, but if I had $2 or so over my board I would leave it at the bank on the rent. On the day of the strike I still owed them $15, which I am afraid they never will give me a chance to pay back.

Source: *Executive Documents of the Senate of the United States*, 53rd Cong. (1894–1895).

Report from the Commission to Investigate the Chicago Strike, 1895

The commission appointed by President Grover Cleveland to investigate the Pullman strike concluded that strikes were wasteful, disruptive, and unlawful. Blaming both capital and labor for the strike, the commission believed that the Pullman trouble originated because neither the public nor the government had taken adequate measures to control monopolies and corporations and had failed "to reasonably protect the rights of labor and redress its wrongs."

Committee Recommendations Following Investigation of the Chicago Strike

I.

(1) That there be a permanent United States strike commission of three members, with duties and powers of investigation and recommendation as to disputes between railroads and their employees similar to those vested in the Interstate Commerce Commission as to rates, etc. . . . .

II.

(1) The commission would suggest the consideration by the States of the adoption of some system of conciliation and arbitration like that, for instance, in use in the Commonwealth of Massachusetts. That system might be reenforced by additional provisions giving the board of arbitration more power to investigate all strikes, whether requested so to do or not, and the question might be considered as to giving labor organizations a standing before the law, as heretofore suggested for national trade unions.

(2) Contracts requiring men to agree not to join labor organizations or to leave them, as conditions of employment, should be made illegal, as is already done in some of our States.

III.

(1) The commission urges employers to recognize labor organizations; that such organizations be dealt with through representatives, with special reference to conciliation and arbitration when difficulties are threatened or arise. It is satisfied that employers should come in closer touch with labor and should recognize that, while the interests of labor and capital are not identical, they are reciprocal.

(2) The commission is satisfied that if employers everywhere will endeavor to act in concert with labor; that if when wages can be raised under economic conditions they be raised voluntarily, and that if when there are reductions reasons be given for the reduction, much friction can be avoided. It is also satisfied that if employers will consider employees as thoroughly essential to industrial success as capital, and thus take labor into consultation at proper times, much of the severity of strikes can be tempered and their number reduced.

Source: *Report on the Chicago Strike of June–July, 1894 by the United States Strike Commission* (Washington, DC: Government Printing Office, 1895), LII–LIV.

Interpret the Evidence

1. Compare the views of George Pullman (Source 17.6) with those of Jennie Curtis (Source 17.8) concerning whether Pullman treated his workers fairly.

2. How does being a woman affect Jennie Curtis's experiences as a Pullman worker (Source 17.8)?

3. According to Eugene V. Debs (Source 17.7), what is the purpose of labor activism? How does the Pullman strike teach Debs about socialism?

4. By comparison, how do you think Pullman and Debs would have responded to the report on the Pullman strike issued by the commission to investigate the Chicago strike (Source 17.9)?

Put It in Context

Using these sources, evaluate the complex relationship among labor, management, and government at the close of the nineteenth century.

Cities, Immigrants, and the Nation

1880–1914

Window to the Past

"The Mortar of Assimilation — and the One Element That Won't Mix," 1889

This image from the magazine *Puck* portrays the United States as a melting pot. Yet not all ethnic groups were considered suitable for becoming citizens. In this instance, the cartoon casts doubt about the worthiness of the Irish for citizenship. ▶ **To learn more about this primary source, see Source 18.7 on page 630.**

Bridgeman Images

After reading this chapter you will be able to:

- Explain the reasons late nineteenth- and early twentieth-century immigrants came to the United States and evaluate how they were received by native-born Americans.

- Explain why farmers, small-town residents, and African Americans from the South migrated to cities, and summarize the challenges and technological changes they encountered.

- Assess the benefits and liabilities of urban political machines and compare those who supported and opposed them.

Comparing American Histories

In the fall of 1905, **Beryl Lassin** faced a difficult choice. Living in a *shtetl* (a Jewish town) in western Russia, Lassin had few if any opportunities as a young blacksmith. Beryl and his wife, Lena, lived at a dangerous time in Russia. Jews were subject to periodic pogroms, state-sanctioned outbreaks of anti-Jewish violence carried out by local Christians. Beryl also faced a discriminatory military draft that required conscripted Jews to serve twenty-year terms in the army, far longer than Christians. Beryl decided he should quickly follow his wife's brother to the United States. With the understanding that his wife would follow as soon as possible, Beryl set sail for America on October 7, 1905. He was crammed into the steerage belowdecks with hundreds of other passengers. Ten days later he disembarked in New York harbor at Ellis Island, the processing center for immigrants, where he stood in long lines and underwent a strenuous medical examination to ensure that he was fit to enter the country. Once he proved he had someplace to go, Beryl boarded a ferry across the Hudson that took him to a new life in the United States.

Less than a year later, Lena joined her husband. Over the next decade, the couple had five children. Shortly after the youngest girl was born, Lena died and Beryl, now called Ben, was forced to place his children in a group home and foster care. The children were reunited with their father when Ben remarried, but life was still difficult. To make ends meet, his three eldest boys left school and went to work. Still, Ben's family managed to leave the crowded Lower East Side for Harlem and then the Bronx. Ben preferred to speak in Yiddish and never learned to read English. Nor did he become an American citizen. His children, however, were all citizens because they had been born in the United States.

On June 8, 1912, another immigrant followed a similar route but ended up taking a different path. Seventeen years old and unmarried, **Maria Vik Takacs** decided to leave her home in rural Hungary. As a Catholic, Maria did not experience the religious persecution that Beryl did. Like many other Hungarians, Maria left to help support her family back in the old country. She had an aunt living in the United States, and she came across with a Hungarian couple who escorted young women for domestic service in America.

Maria, too, landed at Ellis Island and passed the rigorous entry exams. Soon she boarded a train for Rochester in western New York. There she worked as a cook for a German physician, learned English, and led an active social life within the local Hungarian community. She married Karoly (Charles) Takacs, a cabinetmaker from Hungary, who had come to avoid the military draft. Charles became a U.S. citizen in May 1916. By marrying him, Mary, as she was now called, became a citizen as well.

The couple purchased a farm in Middleport, New York. Because so many Hungarians lived in the area, Mary only began to speak more English when the oldest of her four children entered kindergarten.

(left) **Beryl Lassin** Steven F. Lawson
(right) **Maria Vik Takacs** Courtesy of Irene Hewitt

The American histories of Beryl and Maria took one to the urban bustle of New York City, the other to a quiet rural village in western New York State. However, as different as their lives in America were, neither regretted their choice to immigrate. Like millions of others, they had come to America to build better lives for themselves and their families, and both saw their children and grandchildren succeed in ways that they could have only dreamed of in their native countries. Indeed, two grandchildren of Beryl and Maria, Steven Lawson and Nancy Hewitt, respectively — became historians, got married, and wrote this textbook. The experiences of these families, like countless others, reflect the complicated ways that immigrants' lives were transformed at the same time the nation itself was being transformed. ∎

Lassin and Vik were part of a flood of immigrants who entered the United States from 1880 to the outbreak of World War I in 1914. Unlike the majority of earlier immigrants, who had come from northern Europe, most of the more than 20 million people who arrived during this period came from southern and eastern Europe. A smaller number of immigrants came from Asia and Mexico. Most remained in cities, which grew as a result. Urban immigrants were welcomed by political bosses, who saw in them a chance to gain the allegiance of millions of new voters. At the same time, their coming upset many middle- and upper-class city dwellers who blamed these new arrivals for lowering the quality of urban life.

A New Wave of Immigrants

For more than three hundred years following the settlement of the North American colonies, the majority of immigrants to America were white northern European Protestants. During this same time, blacks had been brought forcibly from Africa and enslaved, mainly by way of the West Indies and the Caribbean. By the end of the nineteenth century, a new pattern of immigration emerged, one that included greater ethnic and religious diversity. These new immigrants often encountered hostility from those whose ancestors had arrived generations earlier, and faced the difficult challenge of retaining their cultural identities while becoming assimilated as Americans.

→ met w/hostility

Immigrants Arrive from Many Lands. Immigration to the United States was part of a worldwide phenomenon. In addition to the United States, European immigrants also journeyed to other countries in the Western Hemisphere, especially Canada, Argentina, Brazil, and Cuba. Others left China, Japan, and India and migrated to Southeast Asia and Hawaii. From England and Ireland, migrants ventured to other parts of the British empire. As with those who came to the United States, these immigrants left their homelands to find new job opportunities or to obtain land to start their own farms. In countries like Australia, New Zealand, and South Africa, white settlers often pushed aside native peoples to make communities for themselves. Whereas most immigrants chose to relocate voluntarily, some made the move bound by labor contracts that limited their movement during the terms of the agreement. Chinese, Mexican, and Italian workers made up a large portion of this group.

native displacement

The late nineteenth century saw a shift in the country of origin of immigrants to the United States: Instead of coming from northern and western Europe, many now came from

on average poor

southern and eastern European countries, most notably Italy, Greece, Austria-Hungary, Poland, and Russia. Most of those settling on American shores after 1880 were Catholic or Jewish and hardly knew a word of English. They tended to be even poorer than immigrants who had arrived before them, coming mainly from rural areas and lacking suitable skills for a rapidly expanding industrial society. Even after relocating to a new land and a new society, such immigrants struggled to break patterns of poverty that were, in many cases, centuries in the making.

Immigrants came from other parts of the world as well. From 1860 to 1924, some 450,000 Mexicans migrated to the U.S. Southwest. Many traveled to El Paso, Texas, near the Mexican border, and from there hopped aboard one of three railroad lines to jobs on farms and in mines, mills, and construction. Cubans, Spaniards, and Bahamians traveled to the Florida cities of Key West and Tampa, where they established and worked in cigar factories. Although Congress excluded Chinese immigration after 1882, it did not close the door to migrants from Japan. Unlike the Chinese, the Japanese had not competed with white workers for jobs on railroad and other construction projects. Moreover, Japan was a major world power in the late nineteenth century and held American respect by defeating Russia in the Russo-Japanese War of 1904–1905. Some 260,000 Japanese arrived in the United States during the first two decades of the twentieth century. Many of them settled on the West Coast, where they worked as farm laborers and gardeners and established businesses catering to a Japanese clientele. Nevertheless, Japanese immigrants were considered part of an inferior "yellow race" and encountered discrimination in their West Coast settlements.

Angel Island Physical Exam Beginning in 1910, tens of thousands of Chinese tried to immigrate to the United States through Angel Island in San Francisco Bay. Thousands were detained for long periods until they could prove their identities and demonstrate they had relatives in the country. One of the hurdles they had to overcome was the medical examination. In this photo taken in 1923, a group of Chinese boys waits to see the doctor while a military official inspects one of them. National Archives

Despite the 1882 **Chinese Exclusion Act**, tens of thousands of Chinese attempted to immigrate, many claiming to be family members of those already in the country. Some first went to Canada or Mexico, but few managed to cross the border illegally. In 1910 the government established an immigration station at Angel Island in San Francisco Bay. In contrast to Ellis Island, Angel Island served mainly as a detention center where Chinese immigrants were imprisoned for months, even years, while they sought to prove their eligibility to enter the United States. Nevertheless, over the next thirty years, some 50,000 Chinese successfully passed through Angel Island.

This wave of immigration changed the composition of the American population. By 1910 one-third of the population was foreign-born or had at least one parent who came from abroad. Foreigners and their children made up more than three-quarters of the population of New York City, Detroit, Chicago, Milwaukee, Cleveland, Minneapolis, and San Francisco. Immigration, though not as extensive in the South as in the North, also altered the character of southern cities. About one-third of the population of Tampa, Miami, and New Orleans consisted of foreigners and their descendants. The borderland states of Texas, New Mexico, Arizona, and southern California contained similar percentages of immigrants, most of whom came from Mexico (Map 18.1).

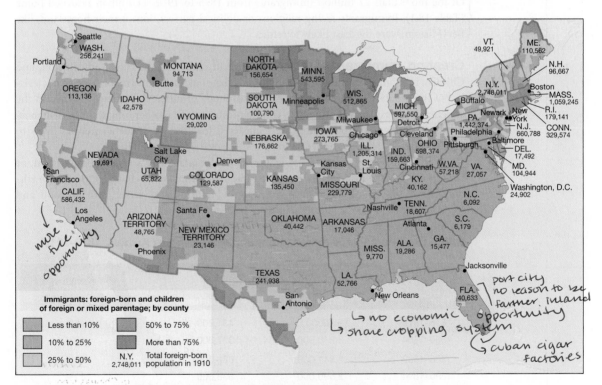

MAP 18.1 Immigrants in the U.S., 1910

By 1910, immigrants had come to the United States from primarily Europe, Asia, Mexico, and Latin America. They tended to settle near their ports of entry in cities, where they usually joined people from their own country who had settled previously. The pattern of settlement varied widely among regions of the country, as the map shows.

Mexican immigration began to increase significantly after the Chinese Exclusion Act shut off Chinese immigration, thereby creating a demand for cheap labor in mining and agriculture in the Southwest. American companies and commercial farmers were eager to hire Mexican immigrants because they considered them docile and physically strong enough to handle unhealthy working and living conditions. More important, they saw Mexicans as temporary residents who would return to their nearby homeland upon completing their jobs. The number of Mexican nationals living in the United States doubled from 100,000 in 1890 to 200,000 in 1910. It would increase even further with the outbreak of the Mexican Revolution in 1910.

These immigrants came to the United States largely for economic, political, and religious reasons. Nearly all were poor and expected to find ways to make money in America. U.S. railroads and steamship companies advertised in Europe and recruited passengers by emphasizing economic opportunities in the United States. Early immigrants wrote to relatives back home extolling the virtues of what they had found, perhaps exaggerating their success.

The importance of economic incentives in luring immigrants is underscored by the fact that millions returned to their home countries after they had earned sufficient money. Of the more than 27 million immigrants from 1875 to 1919, 11 million returned home (Table 18.1). Immigrants facing religious or political persecution in their homeland, like Beryl Lassin, were the least likely to return.

Migration for opportunity [handwritten margin note]

Creating Immigrant Communities.
In cities such as New York, Boston, and Chicago, immigrants occupied neighborhoods that took on the distinct ethnic characteristics of the groups that inhabited them. A cacophony of different languages echoed in the streets as new residents continued to communicate in their mother tongues. The neighborhoods of immigrant groups often were clustered together, so residents were as likely to learn phrases in their neighbors' languages as they were to learn English.

The formation of **ghettos** — neighborhoods dominated by a single ethnic, racial, or class group — eased immigrants' transition into American society. Living within these ethnic enclaves made it easier for immigrants to find housing, hear about jobs, buy food, and

TABLE 18.1   Percentage of Immigrant Departures versus Arrivals, 1875–1914

Year	Arrivals	Departures	Percentage of Departures to Arrivals
1875–1879	956,000	431,000	45%
1880–1884	3,210,000	327,000	10%
1885–1889	2,341,000	638,000	27%
1890–1894	2,590,000	838,000	32%
1895–1899	1,493,000	766,000	51%
1900–1904	3,575,000	1,454,000	41%
1905–1909	5,533,000	2,653,000	48%
1910–1914	6,075,000	2,759,000	45%

seek help from those with whom they felt most comfortable. **Mutual aid societies** sprang up to provide social welfare benefits, including insurance payments and funeral rites. Group members established social centers where immigrants could play cards or dominoes, chat and gossip over tea or coffee, host dances and benefits, or just relax among people who shared a common heritage. In San Francisco's Chinatown, the largest Chinese community in California, such organizations usually consisted of people who had come from the same towns in China. These groups performed a variety of services, including finding jobs for their members, resolving disputes, campaigning against anti-Chinese discrimination, and sponsoring parades and other cultural activities. One society member explained: "We are strangers in a strange country. We must have an organization to control our country fellows and develop our friendship."

The same impulse to band together occurred in immigrant communities throughout the nation. On the West Coast, Japanese farmers joined *kenjinkai*, which not only provided social activities but also helped first-generation immigrants locate jobs and find housing. In Ybor City, Tampa's cigar-making section, mutual aid organizations rose to meet the needs of Spaniards, Cubans, Afro-Cubans, and Italians. El Centro Asturiano constructed a building that contained a 1,200-seat theater, "$4,000 worth of modern lighting fixtures, a cantina, and a well stocked *biblioteca* (library)." Cubans constructed their own palatial clubhouse, El Circulo Cubano, with stained-glass windows, a pharmacy, a theater, and a ballroom. The modest La Union Martí-Maceo catered to Tampa's Afro-Cubans and sponsored its own baseball team. The establishment of such clubs and cultural centers speaks to the commitment of immigrant groups there and elsewhere to enhance their communities.

Besides family and civic associations, churches and synagogues provided religious and social activities for urban immigrants. Between 1865 and 1900, the number of Catholic churches nationwide more than tripled. Like mutual aid societies, churches offered food and clothing to those who were ill or unable to work and fielded sports teams to compete in recreational leagues. Immigrants altered the religious practices and rituals in their churches to meet their own needs and expectations, many times over the objections of their clergy. Various ethnic groups challenged the orthodox practices of the Catholic Church and insisted that their parishes adopt religious icons that they had worshipped in the old country. These included patron saints or protectresses from Old World towns, such as the Madonna del Carmine, whom Italian Catholics in New York's East Harlem celebrated with an annual festival that their priests considered a pagan ritual. Women played the predominant role in running these street festivities. German Catholics challenged Vatican policy by insisting that each ethnic group have its own priests and parishes. Some Catholics, like Mary Vik, who lived in rural areas that did not have a Catholic Church in the vicinity, attended services with local Christians from other denominations.

Religious worship also varied among Jews. German Jews had arrived in the United States in an earlier wave of immigration than eastern European Jews. By the early twentieth century, they had achieved some measure of economic success and founded Reform Judaism, with Cincinnati, Ohio as its center. This brand of Judaism relaxed strict standards of worship, including absolute fidelity to kosher dietary laws, and allowed prayers to be said in English. By contrast, eastern European Jews, like Beryl Lassin, observed the traditional faith, maintained a kosher diet, and prayed in Hebrew.

With few immigrants literate in English, foreign-language newspapers proliferated to inform their readers of local, national, and international events. Between the mid-1880s

Mexican American Immigrant, 1912   This photograph captures a Mexican man emigrating to the United States from Nuevo Laredo, Mexico. This man chose to travel on a cart drawn by a donkey. The unidentified man was part of a great wave of Mexicans in the early twentieth century seeking employment in the U.S. mainly as low-wage agricultural workers and miners in the Southwest. Library of Congress, 3b43585

and 1920, 3,500 new foreign-language newspapers came into existence. These newspapers helped sustain ethnic solidarity in the New World as well as maintain ties to the Old World. Newcomers could learn about social and cultural activities in their communities and keep abreast of news from their homeland.

Saloons were a central institution of immigrant culture, where men spent a good deal of leisure time. They read newspapers written in their native languages, swapped information about job opportunities, enjoyed time away from overcrowded tenements, discussed politics, and fostered bonds of masculinity exclusive of women. However, the excessive drinking associated with saloons put a severe strain on family health and finances, especially when inebriated husbands and fathers lost their tempers at home or squandered their wages on alcohol.

Like other communities with poor, unskilled populations, immigrant neighborhoods bred crime. Young men joined gangs based on ethnic heritage and battled with those of other immigrant groups to protect their turf. Adults formed underworld organizations — some of them tied to international criminal syndicates, such as the Mafia — that trafficked in prostitution, gambling, robbery, and murder. Tongs (secret organizations) in New York City's and San Francisco's Chinatowns controlled the opium trade, gambling, and prostitution in their communities. A survey of New York City police and municipal court records from 1898 concluded that some Jews "are prominent in their commission of forgery, violation of corporation ordinance, as disorderly persons (failure to support wife or family), both grades of larceny, and of the lighter grade of assault."

Crime was not the only social problem that plagued immigrant communities. Newspapers and court records reported husbands abandoning wives and children, engaging in drunken and disorderly conduct, or abusing their family. Boarders whom immigrant families took into their homes for economic reasons also posed problems. Cramped spaces created a lack of privacy, and male boarders sometimes attempted to assault the woman of the house while her husband and children were out to work or in school. Finally, generational conflicts within families began to develop as American-born children of immigrants questioned their parents' values. Thus the social organizations and mutual aid societies that immigrant groups established were more than a simple expression of ethnic solidarity and pride. They were also a response to the very real problems that challenged the health and stability of immigrant communities.

Explore ▶

See Source 18.1 for a depiction of one immigrant family's intergenerational conflict.

Hostility toward Recent Immigrants. On October 28, 1886, the United States held a gala celebration for the opening of the Statue of Liberty in New York harbor, a short distance from Ellis Island. French sculptors Frédéric-Auguste Bartholdi and Alexandre-Gustave Eiffel had designed the monument to appear at the Centennial Exposition in Philadelphia in 1876. Ten years overdue, the statue arrived in June 1885, but funds were still needed to finish construction of a base on which the sculpture would stand. Ordinary people dipped into their pockets for spare change, contributing to a campaign that raised $100,000 so that Lady Liberty could finally hold her uplifted torch for all to see. In 1903 the inspiring words of Emma Lazarus, a Jewish poet, were inscribed on the pedestal welcoming new generations of immigrants.

> Give me your tired, your poor,
> Your huddled masses yearning to breathe free,
> The wretched refuse of your teeming shore,
> Send these, the homeless, tempest-tossed to me,
> I lift my lamp beside the golden door!

Despite the welcoming inscription on the Statue of Liberty, many Americans whose families had arrived before the 1880s considered the influx of immigrants from southern and eastern Europe, Mexico, the Caribbean, and Asia at best a necessary evil and at worst a menace. Industrialists counted on immigrants to provide cheap labor. Existing industrial workers saw the newcomers as a threat to their economic livelihoods and believed that their arrival would result in greater competition for jobs and lower wages. And, while most immigrants came to America to find work and improve the lives of their families, a small portion antagonized and frightened capitalists and middle-class Americans with radical calls for the reorganization of society and the overthrow of the government. Of course, the vast majority of immigrants were not radicals, but many radicals were recent immigrants. During times of labor-management strife, this fact made it easier for businessmen and their spokesmen in the press to associate all immigrants with anti-American radicalism.

Anti-immigrant fears linked to ideas about race and ethnicity had a long history in the United States. In 1790 Congress passed a statute restricting citizenship to those deemed white. Among those excluded from citizenship were Native Americans, who were regarded as "savages," and African Americans, most of whom were slaves at the time. In 1857 the Supreme Court ruled that even free blacks were not citizens, while at the same time declaring that Native Americans could become citizens. From the very beginning of the United States, largely Protestant lawmakers debated whether Catholics and Jews qualified as whites.

Guided Primary Source Analysis

Anzia Yerzierska | Immigrant Fathers and Daughters, 1925

Anzia Yerzierska, a Jewish immigrant who came to the United States from Poland around 1890, wrote about the struggles of immigrant families in adjusting to their new world. Her novel *Bread Givers* focuses on the conflict of a Jewish daughter, Sara Smolinski, patterned after herself, and the girl's father, Reb Smolinski, a Talmudic scholar. Intent on taking advantage of new opportunities in America, Sara resists her father's attempts to impose his Old World beliefs about the traditional duties of a subservient female.

Source 18.1

As I came through the door with my bundle, Father caught sight of me. "What's this?" he asked. "Where are you going?"

"I'm going back to work, in New York."

"What? Wild-head! Without asking, without consulting your father, you get yourself ready to go? Do you yet know that I want you to work in New York? Let's first count out your carfare to come home every night. Maybe it will cost so much there wouldn't be anything left from your wages."

"But I'm not coming home!"

"What? A daughter of mine, only seventeen years old, not home at night?"

How does Sara's father view the father-daughter relationship?

"I'll go to Bessie or Mashah."

"Mashah is starving poor, and you know how crowded it is by Bessie."

"If there's no place for me by my sisters, I'll find a place by strangers."

"A young girl, alone, among strangers? Do you know what's going on in the world? No girl can live without a father or a husband to look out for her. It says in the Torah, only through a man has a woman an existence. Only through a man can a woman enter Heaven."

What role does religion play in shaping Sara's father's point of view?

"I'm smart enough to look out for myself. It's a new life now. In America, women don't need men to boss them."

"*Blut-und-Eisen!* [Blood and iron!] They ought to put you in a madhouse till you're cured of your crazy nonsense!" . . .

Wild with all that was choked in me since I was born, my eyes burned into my father's eyes. "My will is as strong as yours. I'm going to live my own life. Nobody can stop me. I'm not from the old country. I'm American!"

How does Sara view herself as different from her father?

"You blasphemer!" His hand flung out and struck my cheek. "Denier of God! I'll teach you respect for the law!"

I leaped back and dashed for the door. The Old World had struck its last on me.

Source: Anzia Yerzierska, *Bread Givers* (New York: Persea Books, 1975), 136–38.

▌ Put It in Context

What pressures did immigrants face in adjusting to their new home?

Although lawmakers ultimately included Catholics and Jews within their definition of "white," over the next two centuries Americans viewed racial categories as not simply matters of skin color. Ethnicity (country or culture of origin) and religion became absorbed into and intertwined with racial categories. A sociological study of Homestead, Pennsylvania published in 1910 broke down the community along the following constructed racial lines: "Slav, English-speaking European, native white, and colored." Russian Jewish immigrants such as Beryl Lassin were recorded as Hebrews rather than as Russians, suggesting that Jewishness was seen by Christian America as a racial identity.

Natural scientists and social scientists gave credence to the idea that some races and ethnic groups were superior and others were inferior. Referring to Darwin's theory of evolution, biologists and anthropologists constructed measures of racial hierarchies, placing descendants of northern Europeans with lighter complexions — Anglo-Saxons, Teutonics, and Nordics — at the top of the evolutionary scale. Those with darker skin were deemed inferior "races," with Native Americans, African Americans, and Chinese at the bottom. Scholars attempting to make disciplines such as history more "scientific" accepted these racial classifications. The prevailing sentiment of this era reflected demeaning images of many immigrant groups: Irish as drunkards, Mexicans and Cubans as lazy, Italians as criminals, Hungarians as ignorant peasants, Jews as cheap and greedy, and Chinese as drug addicts. These characteristics supposedly resulted from inherited biological traits, rather than from extreme poverty or other environmental conditions.

Newer immigrants, marked as racially inferior, became a convenient target of hostility. Skilled craftsmen born in the United States viewed unskilled workers from abroad who would work for low wages as a threat to their attempts to form unions and keep wages high. Middle-class city dwellers blamed urban problems on the rising tide of foreigners. In addition, Protestant purists felt threatened by Catholics and Jews and believed these "races" incapable or unworthy of assimilation into what they considered to be the superior white, Anglo-Saxon, and Protestant culture.

Nativism — the belief that foreigners pose a serious danger to one's native society and culture — arose as a reactionary response to immigration. In 1887 Henry F. Bowers of Clinton, Iowa founded the American Protective Association. The group proposed restricting Catholic immigration, making English a prerequisite to American citizenship, and prohibiting Catholics from teaching in public schools or holding public offices. New England elites, such as Massachusetts senator Henry Cabot Lodge and writer John Fiske, argued that southern European, Semitic, and Slavic races did not fit into the "community of race" that had founded the United States. In 1893 Lodge and fellow Harvard graduates established the Immigration Restriction League and lobbied for federal legislation that would exclude adult immigrants unable to read in their own language.

Explore ▶

See Sources 18.2 and 18.3 on different perspectives of Chinese immigration.

To preserve their status and power and increase the size of the native-born population, nativists embraced the idea of eugenics — a pseudoscience that advocated "biological engineering" — and supported the selective breeding of "desirable" races to counter the rapid population growth of "useless" races. Accordingly, eugenicists promoted the institutionalization of people deemed "unfit," sterilization of those considered mentally impaired, and the licensing and regulation of marriages to promote better breeding. In pushing for such measures, eugenicists believed that they were following the dictates of modern science and acting in a humane fashion to prevent those deemed unfit from causing further harm to themselves and to society.

Comparative Primary Source Analysis

The Chinese in America

The harshest response against immigration came against the Chinese. In the West, violence against the Chinese was commonplace. White workers feared that Chinese laborers would take jobs away from them and contaminate their cities with vice and drugs. Based on racist assumptions of uncivilized Chinese, the exclusion act of 1882 banned Chinese from entering the country. In 1885, not long after passage of this law, one Chinese resident of New York, Saum Song Bo, used the occasion of the celebration of the Statue of Liberty to express disappointment in his adopted country. Soon after, in its decision in *Yick Wo v. Hopkins*, the U.S. Supreme Court affirmed the right of Chinese to equal protection of the law.

Source 18.2

Saum Song Bo | "A Chinese View of the Statue of Liberty," 1885

SIR: A paper was presented to me yesterday for inspection, and I found it to be specially drawn up for subscription among my countrymen toward the Pedestal Fund of the . . . Statue of Liberty. Seeing that the heading is an appeal to American citizens, to their love of country and liberty. . . . But the word liberty makes me think of the fact that this country is the land of liberty for men of all nations except the Chinese. I consider it as an insult to us Chinese to call on us to contribute toward building in this land a pedestal for a statue of Liberty. That statue represents Liberty holding a torch which lights the passage of those of all nations who come into this country. But are the Chinese allowed to come? As for the Chinese who are here, are they allowed to enjoy liberty as men of all other nationalities enjoy it? Are they allowed to go about everywhere free from the insults, abuse, assaults, wrongs and injuries from which men of other nationalities are free?

. . . Whether this statute [Exclusion Act] against the Chinese or the statue to Liberty will be the more lasting monument to tell future ages of the liberty and greatness of this country, will be known only to future generations.

Liberty, we Chinese do love and adore thee; but let not those who deny thee to us, make of thee a graven image and invite us to bow down to it.

Source: Saum Song Bo, "A Chinese View of the Statue of Liberty," *American Missionary* 39, no. 10 (1885): 290.

Others took a less harsh approach. As had been the case with Native Americans, reformers stressed the need for immigrants to assimilate into the dominant culture, embrace the values of individualism and self-help, adopt American styles of dress and grooming, and exhibit loyalty to the U.S. government. They encouraged immigrant children to attend public schools, where they would learn to speak English and adopt American cultural rituals by celebrating holidays such as Thanksgiving and Columbus Day and reciting the pledge of allegiance, introduced in 1892. Educators encouraged adult immigrants to attend night classes to learn English.

Source 18.3

Yick Wo v. Hopkins, 1886

Mr. Justice [Stanley] Matthews delivered the opinion of the court

[I]n 1880, San Francisco passed a fire-safety ordinance that all laundries operating in wooden buildings be licensed or the owners would risk criminal penalties. After the city government refused to grant licenses to nearly all Chinese laundries while approving those run by whites, Yick Wo, the owner of one rejected establishment, refused to close his business and was prosecuted.

[P]etitioners have complied with every requisite, deemed by the law or by the public officers charged with its administration, necessary for the protection of neighboring property from fire, or as a precaution against injury to the public health. No reason whatever, except the will of the supervisors, is assigned why they should not be permitted to carry on, in the accustomed manner, their harmless and useful occupation, on which they depend for a livelihood. And while this consent of the supervisors is withheld from them and from two hundred others who have also petitioned, all of whom happen to be Chinese subjects, eighty others, not Chinese subjects, are permitted to carry on the same business under similar conditions. The fact of this discrimination is admitted. No reason for it is shown, and the conclusion cannot be resisted, that no reason for it exists except hostility to the race and nationality to which the petitioners belong, and which in the eye of the law is not justified. The discrimination is, therefore, illegal, and the public administration which enforces it is a denial of the equal protection of the laws and a violation of the Fourteenth Amendment of the Constitution. The imprisonment of the petitioners is, therefore, illegal, and they must be discharged.

Source: *Yick Wo v. Hopkins*, 118 U.S. 356, 374 (1886).

Interpret the Evidence

1. Why does Saum Song Bo believe the sentiments of the Statue of Liberty do not apply to the treatment of Chinese?
2. According to Justice Matthews, why does the treatment of Chinese laundrymen violate the Fourteenth Amendment?

Put It in Context

What were American attitudes toward Chinese immigrants in the nineteenth century? What pressures and changes influenced these views?

The Assimilation Dilemma. If immigrants were not completely assimilated, neither did they remain the same people who had lived on the farms and in the villages of Europe, Asia, Mexico, and the Caribbean. Some, like Mary Vik, sought to become full-fledged Americans or at least see that their children did so. Writer Israel Zangwill, an English American Jew, furnished the enduring image of assimilation in his 1908 play *The Melting-Pot.* Zangwill portrayed people from distinct backgrounds entering the cauldron of American life, mixing together, and emerging as citizens identical to their native-born counterparts.

hybrid life ✓

However, the image of America as a **melting pot** worked better as an ideal than as a mirror of reality. Immigrants during this period never fully lost the social, cultural, religious, and political identities they had brought with them. And, anti-immigrant sentiment of many native-born Americans perceived them as strangers and aliens. The same year that Zangwill's play was published, Alfred P. Schultz, a New York physician, provided a dim view of the prospects of assimilation in his book *Race or Mongrel*. Schultz dismissed the melting pot theory that public schools could convert the children of all races into Americans. **See Primary Source Project 18: "Melting Pot" or "Vegetable Soup"? page 629**.

While recent immigrants faced the dilemma of assimilating, sociologist W. E. B. Du Bois analyzed the predicament experienced by African Americans following Reconstruction. In *The Souls of Black Folk* (1903), Du Bois wrote that African Americans felt a "two-ness," an identity carved out of their African heritage together with their lives as slaves and free people in America. This "double-consciousness . . . two souls, two thoughts, two unreconciled strivings" describes the particular identity of African Americans at the turn of the century. While this echoes the experience of the diverse groups who arrived in the country after 1880, African Americans were faced with systemic racial segregation and oppression unlike any other group of people experienced.

Review & Relate

- What challenges did new immigrants to the United States face?

- What steps did immigrants take to meet these challenges?

Becoming an Urban Nation

urbanization

In the half century after the Civil War, the population of the United States quadrupled, but the urban population soared sevenfold. In 1870 one in five Americans lived in cities with a population of 8,000 or more. By 1900 one in three resided in cities of this size. In 1870 only Philadelphia and New York had populations over half a million. Twenty years later, in addition to these two cities, Chicago's population exceeded 1 million; St. Louis, Boston, and Baltimore had more than 500,000 residents; and Cleveland, Buffalo, San Francisco, and Cincinnati boasted populations over 250,000. Urbanization was not confined to the Northeast and Midwest. Denver's population jumped from 4,700 in 1870 to more than 107,000 in 1890. During that same period, Los Angeles grew nearly fivefold, from 11,000 to 50,000, and Birmingham leaped from 3,000 to 26,000. This phenomenal urban growth also brought remarkable physical changes to the cities, as tall buildings reached toward the skies, electric lights brightened the nighttime hours, and water and gas pipes, sewers, and subways snaked below the ground.

The New Industrial City. Although cities have long been a part of the landscape, Americans have felt ambivalent about their presence. Many Americans have shared Thomas Jefferson's idea that democratic values were rooted in the soil of small, independent farms. In contrast to the natural environment of rural life, cities have been perceived as artificial creations in which corruption and contagion flourish. In the 1890s, the very identity of Americans seemed threatened as the frontier came to an end. Some agreed with the historian Frederick Jackson Turner, who believed the closing of the western frontier endangered

threatened yeomen identity

the existence of democracy because it removed the opportunity for the pioneer spirit that built America to regenerate. Rural Americans were especially uncomfortable with the country's increasingly urban life. When the small-town lawyer Clarence Darrow moved to Chicago in the 1880s he was horrified by the "solid, surging sea of human units, each intent upon hurrying by." Still, like Darrow, millions of people were drawn to the new opportunities cities offered.

seasonal employment

Urban growth in America was part of a long-term worldwide phenomenon. Between 1820 and 1920, some 60 million people globally moved from rural to urban areas. Most of them migrated after the 1870s, and millions journeyed from towns and villages in Europe to American cities (Table 18.2). Yet the number of Europeans who migrated internally was greater than those who went overseas. As in the United States, Europeans moved from the countryside to urban areas in search of jobs. Many migrated to the city on a seasonal basis, seeking winter employment in cities and then returning to the countryside at harvest time.

Before the Civil War, commerce was the engine of growth for American cities. Ports like New York, Boston, New Orleans, and San Francisco became distribution centers for imported goods or items manufactured in small shops in the surrounding countryside. Cities in the interior of the country located on or near major bodies of water, such as Chicago, St. Louis, Cincinnati, and Detroit, served similar functions. As the extension of railroad transportation led to the development of large-scale industry, these cities and others became industrial centers as well.

boredom

Industrialization contributed to rapid urbanization in several ways. It drew those living on farms, who either could not earn a satisfactory living or were bored by the isolation of rural areas, into the city in search of better-paying jobs and excitement. One rural dweller in Massachusetts complained: "The lack of pleasant, public entertainments in this town has much to do with our young people feeling discontented with country life." In addition, while the mechanization of farming increased efficiency, it also reduced the demand for farm labor. In 1896 one person could plant, tend, and harvest as much wheat as it had taken eighteen farmworkers to do sixty years before.

Industrial technology and other advances also made cities more attractive and livable places. Electricity extended nighttime entertainment and powered streetcars to convey people around town. Improved water and sewage systems provided more sanitary conditions, especially given the demands of the rapidly expanding population. Structural steel and electric elevators made it possible to construct taller and taller buildings, which gave cities such as Chicago and New York their distinctive skylines. Scientists and physicians made

TABLE 18.2 Percentage of Rural and Urban Population in U.S., 1880–1910

Year	Rural	Urban
1880	71.8	28.2
1890	64.9	35.1
1900	60.4	39.5
1910	54.4	45.6

Source: U.S. Department of Commerce, Bureau of the Census, Table 4, https://www.census.gov/population/censusdata/table-4.pdf

significant progress in the fight against the spread of contagious diseases, which had become serious problems in crowded cities.

Many of the same causes of urbanization in the Northeast and Midwest applied to the far West. The development of the mining industry attracted business and labor to urban settlements. Cities grew up along railroad terminals, and railroads stimulated urban growth by bringing out settlers and creating markets. By 1900, the proportion of residents in western cities with a population of at least ten thousand was greater than in any other section of the country except the Northeast. More so than in the East, Asians and Hispanics inhabited western urban centers along with whites and African Americans. In 1899 Salt Lake City boasted the publication of two black newspapers as well as the president of the Western Negro Press Association. Western cities also took advantage of the latest technology, and in the 1880s and 1890s electric trolleys provided mass transit in Denver and San Francisco.

In addition to immigrants who populated the cities across the nation, before 1890 the rise in urban population came mainly from Americans on the move. Young men and young women left the farm to seek their fortune. The female protagonist of Theodore Dreiser's novel *Sister Carrie* (1900) abandons small-town Wisconsin for the lure of Chicago. In real life, mechanization on farms created many "Sister Carries" by making women less valuable in the fields. The possibility of purchasing mass-produced goods from mail-order houses such as Sears, Roebuck also left young women less essential as homemakers because they no longer had to sew their own clothes and could buy labor-saving appliances from catalogs.

Similar factors drove rural black women and men into cities. Plagued by the same poverty and debt that white sharecroppers and tenants in the South faced, blacks suffered from the added burden of racial oppression and violence in the post-Reconstruction period. From 1870 to 1890, the African American population of Nashville, Tennessee, soared from just over 16,000 to more than 29,000. In Atlanta, Georgia, the number of blacks jumped from slightly above 16,000 to around 28,000.

Economic opportunities were more limited for black migrants than for whites. African American migrants found work as cooks, janitors, and domestic servants. Many found employment as manual laborers in manufacturing companies—including tobacco factories, which employed women and men; tanneries; and cottonseed oil firms—and as dockworkers. Although the overwhelming majority of blacks worked as unskilled laborers for very low wages, others opened small businesses such as funeral parlors, barbershops, and construction companies or went into professions such as medicine, law, banking, and education that catered to residents of segregated black neighborhoods. Despite considerable individual accomplishments, by the turn of the twentieth century most blacks in the urban South had few prospects for upward economic mobility.

In 1890, although 90 percent of African Americans lived in the South, a growing number were moving to northern cities to seek employment and greater freedom. Boll weevil (beetle) infestations during the 1890s decimated cotton production and forced sharecroppers and tenants off farms. At the same time, blacks saw significant erosion of their political and civil rights in the last decade of the nineteenth century. Most black citizens in the South were denied the right to vote and experienced rigid, legally sanctioned racial segregation in all aspects of public life. Between 1890 and 1914 approximately 485,000 African Americans left the South. By 1914 New York, Chicago, and Philadelphia each counted more than 100,000 African Americans among their population. An African American woman

African American Family, 1900   Despite the rigid racial segregation and oppression that African Americans faced in the late nineteenth century, some black families found ways to achieve economic success and upward mobility. With its piano and fine furniture, the home of this African American family reflects middle-class conventions of the period. The father is a graduate of Hampton Institute, a historically black university founded after the Civil War to educate freedpeople. Library of Congress, Prints and Photographs Division [LC-USZ62-38150]

expressed her enthusiasm about the employment she found in Chicago, where she earned $3 a day working in a railroad yard. "The colored women like this work," she explained, because "we make more money . . . and we do not have to work as hard as at housework," which required working sixteen-hour days, six days a week.

Although many blacks found they preferred their new lives to the ones they had led in the South, the North did not turn out to be the promised land of freedom. Black newcomers encountered discrimination in housing and employment. Residential segregation confined African Americans to racial ghettos. Black workers found it difficult to obtain skilled employment despite their qualifications, and women and men most often toiled as domestics, janitors, and part-time laborers.

Nevertheless, African Americans in northern cities built communities that preserved and reshaped their southern culture and offered a degree of insulation against the harshness of racial discrimination. A small black middle class appeared consisting of teachers, attorneys, and small business owners. In 1888 African Americans organized the Capital Savings Bank of Washington, D.C. Ten years later, two black real estate agents in New York City were worth more than $150,000 each, and one agent in Cleveland owned $100,000 in property. The rising black middle class provided leadership in the formation of mutual aid societies, lodges, and women's clubs. Newspapers such as the *Chicago Defender* and *Pittsburgh Courier* furnished local news to their subscribers and reported national and international events affecting people of color. As was the case in the South, the church was at the center of black life in northern cities. More than just religious institutions, churches furnished space for social activities and the dissemination of political information. By the first decade of the twentieth century, more than two dozen churches had sprung up in Chicago alone. Whether housed in newly constructed buildings or in storefronts, black churches provided worshippers freedom from white control. They also allowed members of the northern black middle class to demonstrate what they considered to be respectability and refinement. This meant discouraging enthusiastic displays of "old-time religion," which celebrated more exuberant forms of worship. As the Reverend W. A. Blackwell of Chicago's AME Zion Church declared, "Singing, shouting, and talking [were] the most useless ways of proving Christianity." This conflict over modes of religious expression reflected a larger process that was under way in black communities at the turn of the twentieth century. As black urban communities in the North grew and developed, tensions and divisions emerged within the increasingly diverse black community, as a variety of groups competed to shape and define black culture and identity.

Expand Upward and Outward. As the urban population increased, cities expanded both up and out. Before 1860, the dominant form of brick and stone construction prevented buildings from rising more than four or five stories. However, as cities became much more populous, land values soared. Steep prices prompted architects to make the most of small, expensive plots of land by finding ways to build taller structures. Architects began using cast-iron columns instead of the thick, heavy walls of brick that limited floor space. The resulting "cloudscrapers" raised the urban skyline to ten stories. The development of structural steel, which was stronger and more durable than iron, turned cloudscrapers into **skyscrapers**, which stretched some thirty stories into the air. With the development of the electric elevator and the radiator, which replaced fireplaces with hot water circulated through pipes, even taller skyscrapers came to loom over downtown business districts in major cities.

Cities also expanded horizontally, as new transportation technology made it possible for residents to move around a much larger urban landscape. In the mid-nineteenth century in cities such as Boston and Philadelphia, pedestrians could still walk from one end of the city to the other within an hour. If residents preferred, they could pay a fare and hop on board a horse-drawn railcar. These vehicles moved slowly and left tons of horse manure in the streets. To avoid such problems, in 1873 San Francisco, followed by Seattle and Chicago, installed a system of cable-driven trolley cars. At first, these trolleys proved slow and unreliable. But by 1914, advances in transportation converted walking cities into riding cities.

Electricity provided the transportation breakthrough. In 1888 naval engineer Frank J. Sprague completed the first electric trolley line in Richmond, Virginia. Electric-powered streetcars traveled twice as fast as horse-drawn railcars and left little mess on the streets. Subways could run underground without asphyxiating passengers and workmen with a steam engine's smoke and soot. Boston opened the first subway in 1897, followed by New York City in 1904.

Bridges spanning large rivers and waterways also helped extend the boundaries of the inner city. In 1883 the Brooklyn Bridge opened, connecting Manhattan with the city of Brooklyn. Designed and engineered by John Augustus Roebling, and completed by his son Washington and Washington's wife Emily, the bridge had taken thirteen years to construct and cost twenty men their lives. It stretched more than a mile across the East River and was broad enough for a footpath, two double carriage lanes, and two railroad lines. During its first year in operation, more than 11 million people passed over the bridge; today, more than 51 million vehicles cross the bridge each year.

The electrification of public transportation and the construction of bridges made it feasible for some people to live considerable distances from their workplace. In the eighteenth and nineteenth centuries, middle- and upper-class merchants and professionals usually lived near their shops and offices in the heart of the city, surrounded by their employees. After 1880, the huge influx of immigration brought large numbers of impoverished workers to city centers. The resulting traffic congestion and overcrowded housing pushed wealthier residents to seek more open spaces in which to build houses. The new electric trolley lines allowed middle-class urbanites to move miles away from downtown areas. In 1850 the Boston metropolis spread in a radius of two to three miles around the city and had a population of 200,000. In 1900 suburban Boston ringed the city in a ten-mile radius, with a population of more than 1 million. Increasingly, cities divided into two parts: an inner commercial and industrial core housing the working class, and outer communities occupied by a wealthier class of white, older-stock Americans.

How the Other Half Lived.

As the middle and upper classes fled the industrial urban center for the suburbs, the working poor moved in to replace them. They lived in old factories and homes and in shanties and cellars. Because land values were higher in the city, rents were high and the poorest people could least afford them. To make ends meet, families crowded into existing apartments, sometimes taking in boarders to help pay the rent. This led to increased population density and overcrowding in the urban areas where immigrants lived. On New York's Lower East Side, the population density was the highest in the world. Such overcrowding fostered communicable diseases and frustration, giving the area the nicknames "typhus ward" and "suicide ward."

Overcrowding combined with extreme poverty turned immigrant neighborhoods into slums, which were characterized by substandard housing. Impoverished immigrants typically lived in multiple-family apartment buildings called **tenements** (legally defined as containing more than three families). First constructed in 1850, these early dwellings often featured windowless rooms and little or no plumbing and heating. In 1879 a New York law reformed the building codes to require minimal plumbing facilities and to stipulate that all bedrooms (but not all rooms) have a window. Constructed on narrow 25-by-100-foot lots, these five- and six-story buildings included four small apartments on a floor and had only two toilets off the hallway. Tenements stood right next to each other, with only an air shaft separating them. Although these dwellings marked some improvement in living conditions, they proved miserable places to live in — dark, damp, and foul smelling. In 1895 a federal government housing inspector observed that the air shafts provided "imperfect light and ventilation" and that "refuse matter or filth of one kind or another [was] very apt to accumulate at the bottom, giving rise to noxious odors." The air shafts also operated as a conduit for fires that moved swiftly from one tenement to another.

In fact, the density of late-nineteenth-century cities could turn individual fires into citywide disasters. The North Side of Chicago burned to the ground in 1871, and Boston and Baltimore suffered catastrophic fires as well. On April 18, 1906, an earthquake in San Francisco set the city ablaze, causing about 1,500 deaths. Such fires could, however, have long-term positive consequences. The great urban conflagrations encouraged construction of fireproof buildings made of brick and steel instead of wood. In addition, citizens organized fire watches and established municipal fire departments to replace volunteer companies. An unintended side effect, fires provided cities with a chance to rebuild. Chicago's skyscrapers and its system of urban parks were built on land cleared by fire.

In 1890 Jacob Riis, a Danish immigrant, newspaperman, and photographer, illustrated the brutal conditions endured by tenement families such as Beryl Lassin's on New York's Lower East Side. "In the stifling July nights," he wrote in *How the Other Half Lives*, "when the big barracks are like fiery furnaces, their very walls giving out absorbed heat, men and women lie in restless, sweltering rows, panting for air and sleep." Under these circumstances, Riis lamented, an epidemic "is excessively fatal among the children of the poor, by reason of the practical impossibility of isolating the patient in a tenement." Despite their obvious problems, tenements soon spread to other cities such as Cleveland, Cincinnati, and Boston, and one block might have ten of these buildings, housing as many as four thousand people.

With all the misery they spawned as places to live, tenements also functioned as workplaces. Czech immigrants made cigars in their apartments from six in the morning until nine at night, seven days a week, for about 6 cents an hour. By putting an entire family to work, they could make $15 a week and pay their rent of $12 a month. Clothing contractors in particular saw these tenement **sweatshops** as a cheap way to produce their products. By jamming two or three sewing machines into an apartment and paying workers a fixed amount for each item they produced, contractors kept their costs down and avoided factory regulations.

Even when immigrants left sweatshop apartments and went to work in factories, they continued to face exploitation. The 600 Jewish and Italian clothing workers, most of whom were women, who toiled in the **Triangle Shirtwaist Company**, located in New York City's Greenwich Village, worked long hours for little pay. On March 25, 1911, a fire broke out on the eighth story of the factory and quickly spread to the ninth and tenth floors. The fire engines' ladders could not reach that high, and one of the exits on the ninth floor was locked to keep workers from stealing material. One hundred forty-six people died in the blaze — some by jumping out the windows, but most by getting trapped behind the closed exit door. In the aftermath of the fire, Rose Schneiderman, a Polish Jewish immigrant who had led a strike at the Triangle Shirtwaist Company in 1909, addressed a memorial gathering at the Metropolitan Opera House. Following public outrage over the fire and through the efforts of reformers, New York City established a Bureau of Fire Protection, required safety devices in buildings, and prohibited smoking in factories. Furthermore, this tragedy spearheaded legislative efforts to improve working conditions in general, protect women workers, and abolish child labor.

Slums compounded the potential for disease, poor sanitation, fire, congestion, and crime. Living on poor diets, slum dwellers proved particularly vulnerable to epidemics. Cholera, yellow fever, and typhoid killed tens of thousands. Tuberculosis was even deadlier. An epidemic that began in a slum neighborhood could easily spread into more affluent areas of the city. Children suffered the most. Almost one-quarter of the children born in American cities in 1890 did not live to celebrate their first birthdays.

Women Sweatshop Workers, 1900   Taken around 1900, this photograph shows women working in a hat factory. The room has light coming in from the windows and is also illuminated by electric lamps. Nevertheless, such factories did not put safety at a premium and were susceptible to the kind of danger evidenced in the tragic Triangle Shirtwaist Company fire in 1911. The Granger Collection, NY

Contributing to the outbreak of disease was faulty sewage disposal, a problem that vexed city leaders. Until the invention of the modern indoor flush toilet in the late nineteenth century, people relied on outdoor toilets, with as many as eight hundred people using a single facility. All too often, cities dumped human waste into rivers that also supplied drinking water. In 1881 the exasperated mayor of Cleveland called the Cuyahoga River "an open sewer through the center of the city." At the same time, the great demand for water caused by the population explosion resulted in lower water pressure. Consequently, residents in the upper floors of tenements had to carry buckets of water from the lower floors. Until cities overcame their water and sanitation challenges, epidemics plagued urban dwellers.

Urban crowding created other problems as well. Traffic moved slowly through densely populated cities. Pedestrians and commuters had to navigate around throngs of people walking on sidewalks and streets, peddlers selling out of pushcarts, and piles of garbage cluttering the walkways. Streets remained in poor shape. In 1889 the majority of Cleveland's 440 miles of streets consisted of sand and gravel. Chicago did not fare much better. In 1890 most road surfaces were covered with wooden blocks, and three-quarters of the city's more than 2,000 miles of streets remained unpaved. Rainstorms quickly made matters worse by turning foul-smelling, manure-filled streets into mud.

Poverty and overcrowding contributed to increased crime. The U.S. murder rate quadrupled between 1880 and 1900, at a time when the murder rates in most European cities were declining. In New York City, crime thrived in slums with the apt names of "Bandit's Roost" and "Hell's Kitchen," and groups of young hoodlums preyed on unsuspecting citizens. Poverty forced some of the poor to turn to theft or prostitution. One twenty-year-old prostitute, who supported her sickly mother and four brothers and sisters, lamented: "Let God Almighty judge who's to blame most, I that was driven, or them that drove me to the pass I'm in." Rising criminality led to the formation of urban police departments, though many law officers supplemented their incomes by collecting graft (illegal payments) for ignoring criminal activities.

Review & Relate

- What factors contributed to rapid urban growth in the late nineteenth century?

- How did the American cities of 1850 differ from those of 1900? What factors account for these differences?

Urban Politics at the Turn of the Century

The problems that booming cities faced in trying to absorb millions of immigrants proved formidable and at times seemed insurmountable. From a governmental standpoint, cities had limited authority over their own affairs. They were controlled by state legislatures and needed state approval to raise revenues and pass regulations. For the most part, there were no zoning laws to regulate housing construction. Private companies owned public utilities, and competition among them produced unnecessary duplication and waste. The government services that did exist operated on a segmented basis, with the emphasis on serving wealthier neighborhoods at the expense of the city at large. Missing was a vision of the city as a whole, working as a single unit.

Political Machines and City Bosses.   City government in the late nineteenth century was fragmented. Mayors usually did not have much power, and decisions involving public policies such as housing, transportation, and municipal services often rested in the hands of private developers. Bringing some order out of this chaos, the **political machine** functioned to give cities the centralized authority and services that they otherwise lacked. At the head of the machine was the political **boss**. Although the boss himself (and they were all men) held some public office, his real authority came from leadership of the machine. These organizations maintained a tight network of loyalists throughout city wards (districts), each of which contained designated representatives responsible for catering to the needs of their constituents. Whether Democratic or Republican, political machines did not care about philosophical issues; they were concerned primarily with staying in power.

The strength of political machines rested in large measure on immigrants. The organization provided a kind of public welfare when private charity could not cope satisfactorily with the growing needs of the poor. Machines doled out turkeys on holidays, furnished a load of coal for the winter, provided jobs in public construction, arranged for shelter and meals if tenement houses burned down, and intervened with the police and the courts when a constituent got into trouble. Bosses sponsored baseball clubs, held barbecues and picnics, and attended christenings, bar mitzvahs, weddings, and funerals. For enterprising members of immigrant groups — and this proved especially true for the Irish during this period — the machine offered upward mobility out of poverty as they rose through its ranks. Not all immigrants benefited from political bosses equally, however. In San Francisco, Abe Ruef, whose parents were French Jews, became a political boss around the turn of the twentieth century. His sympathies for immigrants did not extend to the Chinese, however. Following the 1906 earthquake, he led an effort to expel residents of the city's Chinatown.

Explore ▶

Compare two historians' interpretations of nativism and who is classified as white in Sources 18.4 and 18.5.

The poor were not the only group that benefited from connections to political machines. The machine and its functionaries helped businessmen maneuver through the maze of contradictory and overlapping codes regulating building and licenses that impeded their routine course of activities. In addition to assisting legitimate businessmen, the machine facilitated the underworld commerce of vice, prostitution, and gambling by acting as an arbiter to keep this trade within established boundaries — all for a cut of the illegal profits.

In return for these services, the machine received the votes of immigrants and money from businessmen. When challenged by reformers or other political rivals, the machine readily engaged in corrupt election practices to maintain its power. Mobilizing the "graveyard vote," bosses took names from tombstones to pad lists of registered voters. They also hired "repeaters" to vote more than once under phony names and did not flinch from dumping whole ballot boxes into the river or using hired thugs to scare opponents from the polls.

Boss Abe Reuf   In 1908 Abe Ruef, the political boss of San Francisco, was tried and convicted on charges of bribery and influence peddling. Ruef served four and a half years of a fourteen-year sentence at San Quentin. This photo captures a worried-looking Ruef listening to his attorney, Henry Ach, outside the courthouse during his trial. Courtesy of the Bancroft Library, University of California, Berkeley, call no. BANC PIC 1905.02623-A

Immigration, Nativism, and Whiteness

Since its founding, the United States has been a nation of immigrants, a haven for people all over the world seeking a better life whether for political, economic, or religious reasons. At the same time, hostility toward foreigners — nativism — has moved in tandem with immigration as an expression of concern that the influx of new arrivals, especially from certain regions of the world, would threaten jobs and debase American culture. From the very beginning of the country, immigration and citizenship were tied to race, but the question remained of which nationalities were white, the predominant race of the Europeans who settled and conquered North America. Writing fifty-four years apart, John Higham and Katherine Benton-Cohen agree that race is socially constructed, but they approach the subject from different perspectives.

Source 18.4

John Higham | Nativism and Race, 1955

"What concerns us is the intersection of racial attitudes with nationalistic ones-in other words, the extension to European nationalities of that sense of absolute difference which already divided white Americans from people of other colors. When sentiments analogous to those already discharged against Negroes, Indians, and Orientals spilled over into anti-European channels, a force of tremendous intensity entered the stream of American nativism. The whole story of modern racial ferment, nativist and otherwise, has two levels, one involving popular emotions, the other concerning more or less systematic ideas. Most of the emotions flow from a reservoir of habitual suspicion and distrust accumulated over the span of American history toward human groups stamped by obvious differences of color. The ideas, on the other hand, depend on the speculations of intellectuals on the nature of races. . . .

However, the evolution of white supremacy into a comprehensive philosophy of life,

grounding human values in the innate constitution of nature, required a major theoretical effort. It was the task of the racethinkers to organize specific antipathies toward dark-hued peoples into a generalized, ideological structure. To the development of racial nativism, the thinkers have made a special contribution. Sharp physical differences between Native Americans and European immigrants were not readily apparent; to a large extent they had to be manufactured. A rather elaborate, well-entrenched set of racial ideas was essential before the newcomers from Europe could seem a fundamentally different order of men. Accordingly, a number of race-conscious intellectuals blazed the way for ordinary nativists, and it will be useful to tell their story before turning in later chapters to the popular emotions their ideas helped to orient."

Source: John Higham, *Strangers in the Land: Patterns of American Nativism, 1860–1925*. New Brunswick, New Jersey: Rutgers University Press, 1925, 132, 133.

Bosses enriched themselves through graft and corruption. They secured protection money from both legitimate and illegitimate business interests in return for their services. In the 1860s and 1870s, Boss William Marcy Tweed, the head of Tammany Hall, New York City's political machine, swindled the city out of a fortune while supervising the construction of a lavish three-story courthouse in lower Manhattan. The original budget for the building was $250,000, but the city spent more than $13 million on the structure.

Source 18.5

Katherine Benton-Cohen | Nativism, Mexicans, and Whiteness, 2009

"In the mid-nineteenth century, 'Mexican' and 'white' were overlapping categories, not opposite poles in a regional racial system. In this world, Apaches were not Americans, but Mexicans might be. These categories were, however, highly contingent on local conditions . . . Building national and racial boundaries required the removal and exclusion of some peoples, and the new inclusion of others. In small irrigated farm and ranch communities, the Apache Wars encouraged close settlement patterns and intermarriage among Mexican and European Americans. But race relations in place with different economic systems soon became more problematic. Where Mexicans owned ranches and farms, racial categories were blurry and unimportant. But in the industrial copper-mining town of Bisbee [Arizona], Mexican workers were segregated economically by their lower pay ('Mexican wage') and geographically by new town-planning experiments. To most non-Mexican residents of Bisbee, Mexicans were peon workers or potential public charges, not neighbors or business partners, not co-workers or co-worshippers and certainly not potential marriage partners.

In Cochise County [Arizona], corporations and governments exerted enormous influence over the creation of racial categories. Ideas about masculinity, femininity, nationhood and class colored ordinary people's judgements about race in tangible ways . . . Mexicans could be white, and Italians could fail to be. Rich and poor, immigrant and native, miner and farmer, manager and workers, man and woman: they all fought over how race would be defined and who would benefit from these definitions."

Source: Katherine Benton-Cohen, *Borderline Americans: Racial Division and Labor War in the Arizona Borderlands.* Cambridge, Massachusetts Harvard University Press, 2009, 7–8, 14.

Examine the Sources

1. How do Higham and Benton-Cohen agree and differ in their views of nativism and whiteness?

2. What evidence can you find in these sources that nativism did not simply fall on a black-white spectrum but that there were racial categories in between white and black, and they were fluid?

Put It in Context

Evaluate the reasons that nativism flourished in the late nineteenth and early twentieth centuries and discuss how it affected different immigrant groups.

The building remained unfinished in 1873, when Tweed was convicted on fraud charges and went to jail. In later years, Tammany Hall's George Washington Plunkitt distinguished this kind of "dishonest graft" from the kind of "honest graft" that he practiced. If he received inside information about a future sale of city property, Plunkitt reasoned, why shouldn't he get a head start, buy it at a low price, and then sell it at a higher figure? As he delighted in saying, "I seen my opportunities and I took 'em." Still, courts did not see such behavior so favorably. In 1908, San Francisco's Boss Ruef was convicted of bribery and imprisoned at San Quentin.

The services of political machines came at a high cost. Corruption and graft led to higher taxes on middle-class residents. Much of the proceeds of machine activities went into the private coffers of machine bosses and other functionaries. The romanticized image of the political boss as a modern-day Robin Hood who stole from the rich and gave to the poor is greatly exaggerated. Trafficking in vice might have run more smoothly under the coordination of the machine, but the safety and health of city residents hardly improved. Most important, although immigrants and the poor did benefit from an informal system of social welfare, the machine had no interest in resolving the underlying causes of their problems. As the dominant urban political party organization, the machine cared little about issues such as good housing, job safety, and sufficient wages. It remained for others to provide alternative approaches to relieving the plight of the urban poor.

Urban Reformers.

The men and women who criticized the political bosses and machines — and the corruption and vice they fostered — usually came from the ranks of the upper middle class and the wealthy. Their solutions to the urban crisis typically centered around toppling the political machine and replacing it with a civil service that would allow government to function on the basis of merit rather than influence peddling and cronyism. Both locally and nationally, they pushed for civil service reform. In 1883 Congress responded to this demand by passing the **Pendleton Civil Service Reform Act**, which required federal jobs to be awarded on the basis of merit, as determined by competitive examinations, rather than through political connections. As for the immigrants who supported machine politics, these reformers preferred to deal with them from afar and expected that through proper education they might change their lifestyles and adopt American ways.

Another group of Americans from upper- and middle-class backgrounds put aside whatever prejudices they might have held about working-class immigrants and dealt directly with newcomers to try to solve various social problems. These reformers — mostly young people, and many of them women and college graduates — took up residence in **settlement houses** located in urban slums. Settlement houses offered a variety of services to community residents, including day care for children; cooking, sewing, and secretarial classes; neighborhood playgrounds; counseling sessions; and meeting rooms for labor unions. Settlement house organizers understood that immigrants gravitated to the political machine or congregated in the local tavern not because they were inherently immoral but because these institutions helped mitigate their suffering and, in some cases, offered concrete paths to advancement. Although settlement house workers wanted to Americanize immigrants, they also understood immigrants' need to hold on to remnants of their original culture. By 1900 approximately one hundred settlement houses had been established in major American cities.

Religiously inspired reform provided similar support for slum dwellers. Some Protestant ministers began to argue that immigrants' problems resulted not from chronic racial or ethnic failings but from their difficult environment. Some of them preached Christianity as a "social gospel," which included support for civil service reform, antimonopoly regulation, income tax legislation, factory inspection laws, and workers' right to strike.

Despite the efforts of social gospel advocates and the charitable organizations that arose to help relieve human misery, private attempts to combat the various urban ills, however well-meaning, proved insufficient. The problems were structural, not personal, and one group or even several operating together did not have the resources or power to make urban institutions more efficient, equitable, and humane. If reformers were to succeed in tackling the most significant social problems and make lasting changes in American society and politics, they would have to enlist state and federal governments.

Review & Relate

▪ What role did political machines play in late-nineteenth-century cities?

▪ Who led the opposition to machine control of city politics, and what solutions and alternatives did they offer?

Conclusion: A **Nation** of **Cities**

Immigrants from southern and eastern Europe, as well as from Asia and points south, who came to the United States between the 1880s and 1914 survived numerous hardships as they strove to create better lives for their families. They persevered despite discrimination, overcrowding in slums, and dangerous working conditions, long hours, and low wages. Immigrants joined neighborhood groups—houses of worship, fraternal organizations, burial societies, political machines, and settlement houses—to promote their own welfare. Some achieved success and returned to their homelands. Most of those who remained in the United States, like Mary Vik and Ben Lassin, struggled to earn a living but managed to pave the way for their children and grandchildren to obtain better education and jobs. Mary's granddaughter, Nancy A. Hewitt, earned a Ph.D. in history from the University of Pennsylvania, and Ben's grandson, Steven F. Lawson, earned a doctorate in history from Columbia University. They became university professors and, through their teaching and writing, have tried to preserve their grandparents' legacy.

Immigrants were not the only group on the move in the late nineteenth century. Rural dwellers left their farms seeking new job opportunities as well as the excitement cities provided. Among them, African Americans migrated in search of political freedom and economic opportunity. They relocated from the rural South to the urban South and North, where they continued to encounter discrimination. Yet cities gave them more leeway to develop their own communities and institutions than they had before. And African Americans in the North were allowed to vote, a tool they would use to gain equality in the future. Nevertheless, because of long-standing patterns of racism, supported by law, African Americans would struggle much longer than did white immigrants to obtain equality and justice.

Few public institutions attempted to aid immigrants or racial minorities as they made the difficult transition to urban and industrial life. Yet immigrants did participate in urban politics through the efforts of political bosses and their machines who sought immigrant votes. In return, political machines provided immigrants with rudimentary social and political services. Political machines, however, bred corruption, along with higher taxes to fund their extravagances. Dishonest government prompted middle- and upper-class urban dwellers to take up reform in order to sweep the political bosses out of office and diminish the power of their immigrant supporters, as we will see in the next chapter.

chapter 18 review

Timeline of Events

1880–1914	Period of significant immigration to United States
1882	Chinese Exclusion Act
1883	Pendleton Civil Service Reform Act
	Brooklyn Bridge opens
1886	Statue of Liberty opens
1887	American Protective Association formed
1892	U.S. schools adopt pledge of allegiance
1893	Immigration Restriction League founded
1897	Boston opens first subway system in the United States
1903	W. E. B. Du Bois publishes *The Souls of Black Folk*
1906	San Francisco earthquake
1908	Israel Zangwill publishes *The Melting-Pot*
	San Francisco's Boss Ruef convicted of bribery
1911	Triangle Shirtwaist Company fire in New York City

Key Terms

Chinese Exclusion Act, *605*

ghettos, *606*

mutual aid societies, *607*

nativism, *611*

eugenics, *611*

melting pot, *614*

skyscrapers, *618*

tenements, *619*

sweatshops, *620*

Triangle Shirtwaist Company, *620*

political machine, *622*

boss, *622*

Pendleton Civil Service Reform Act, *626*

settlement houses, *626*

Review & Relate

1. What challenges did new immigrants to the United States face?

2. What steps did immigrants take to meet these challenges?

3. What factors contributed to rapid urban growth in the late nineteenth century?

4. How did the American cities of 1850 differ from those of 1900? What factors account for these differences?

5. What role did political machines play in late-nineteenth-century cities?

6. Who led the opposition to machine control of city politics, and what solutions and alternatives did they offer?

"Melting Pot" or "Vegetable Soup"?

▸ Describe and evaluate the competing ideas about race and ethnicity that shaped opinions about immigrants and their place in American society at the turn of the twentieth century.

In his play *The Melting-Pot* (1908), writer Israel Zangwill created what would become the dominant metaphor of immigrant assimilation (Source 18.6). Zangwill portrayed people from different backgrounds entering American society, undergoing a process of assimilation, and becoming citizens virtually indistinguishable from their native-born counterparts. When the play premiered at the Columbia Theater in Washington, D.C., President Theodore Roosevelt, to whom the play was dedicated, was in the audience and reportedly cheered the production. The play went on to become a hit on Broadway the following year.

The reality of immigrant assimilation was more complicated than Zangwill's "melting pot" metaphor suggested (Source 18.7). There is some truth in Zangwill's metaphor: In the days before radio and television, immigrants absorbed new values, language, style of dress, taste in foods, and sense of humor from schools, newspapers, magazines, and silent movies. However, many of them also valued aspects of their native cultural and social heritages and took pains to preserve cherished traditions and beliefs (Source 18.8). Although immigrants saw the necessity of some degree of assimilation, many were unwilling to become "fully American" if that meant completely abandoning their previous cultural identities. In this way, the immigrant experience resembled vegetable soup — a mixture of distinct pieces in the same broth — more complex than a melting pot. Assimilation also varied by generation, with the children of immigrants becoming more Americanized than their parents.

While many Americans saw assimilation as a requirement of true citizenship (Source 18.9), others rejected the very possibility of assimilation, arguing that immigrants were inherently inferior and could not be absorbed into American society (Sources 18.8 and 18.10).

Source 18.6

Israel Zangwill | *The Melting-Pot*, 1908

The Melting-Pot explores the experiences of David Quixano, a Jewish immigrant and musician, as he writes a symphony that puts to music the racial and ethnic harmony created by the assimilation of immigrant groups in America at the turn of the twentieth century. In the following scene, David explains the process of assimilation to his love interest, Vera, and his uncle Mendel.

VERA So your music finds inspiration in America?

DAVID Yes — in the seething of the Crucible.

VERA The Crucible? I don't understand!

DAVID Not understand! You, the Spirit of the Settlement! Not understand that America is God's Crucible, the great Melting-Pot where all the races of Europe are melting and re-forming! Here you stand, good folk, think I, when I see them at Ellis Island, here you stand in your fifty groups, with your fifty languages and histories, and your fifty blood hatreds and rivalries. But you won't be long like that, brothers, for these are the fires of God you've come to — these are the fires of God. A fig for your feuds and vendettas! Germans and Frenchmen, Irishmen and Englishmen, Jews and Russians—into the Crucible with you all! God is making the American.

MENDEL I should have thought the American was made already—eighty millions of him.

DAVID Eighty millions! Eighty millions! Over a continent! Why, that cockleshell of a Britain has forty millions! No, uncle, the real American has not yet arrived. He is only in the Crucible, I tell you—he will be the fusion of all races, the coming superman. Ah, what a glorious Finale for my symphony—if I can only write it.

Source: Israel Zangwill, *The Melting-Pot: Drama in Four Acts* (New York: Macmillan, 1909), 36–38.

Source 18.7

"The Mortar of Assimilation — and the One Element That Won't Mix," 1889

Before Zangwill's play appeared, the magazine *Puck* published a cartoon that contains the concept of the melting pot. In it Columbia, the female symbol of the United States, draped in an American flag, is stirring a pot labeled "Citizenship" with a spoon called "Equal Rights." Various nationalities can be seen in the pot, but only one group, the Irish, appears to resist assimilation.

THE MORTAR OF ASSIMILATION — AND THE ONE ELEMENT THAT WON'T MIX.

Bridgeman Images

"Be Just — Even to John Chinaman," 1893

The following cartoon appeared in the satirical magazine *Judge* the year after Congress renewed the Chinese Exclusion Act and added provisions requiring the Chinese already living in the United States to carry certificates of identity and residence. A caption beneath the cartoon states: "Judge (*to Miss Columbia*) — 'You allowed that boy to come into your school, it would be inhuman to throw him out now — it will be sufficient in the future to keep his brothers out!'" While the cartoon favors the Chinese Exclusion Act, it presents a more complex message. It accepts the presence of other immigrant groups and Native Americans, shown in stereotyped depictions, suggesting that schooling will turn them into true Americans. It also expresses some sympathy for the Chinese remaining in the country. The cartoon also proposes that some of these earlier immigrants harbored anti-Chinese feelings. Note the Irish American holding up a blackboard that says, "Kick Out the Heathen; He's Got No Vote."

BE JUST—EVEN TO JOHN CHINAMAN.

Judge (*to Miss Columbia*)—"You allowed that boy to come into your school, it would be inhuman to throw him out now—it will be sufficient in the future to keep his brothers out!"

William Birney | Deporting Mohammedans, 1897

Born in the South, William Birney was educated in the North, spent time in Europe, supported the abolition of slavery, and became a general in the Union Army during the Civil War. In civilian life he was a journalist, author, and attorney. In this letter to the editor of the *Washington Post* during the upsurge of immigration to the United States in the 1890s, Birney protested religious discrimination against Muslims from Turkey as well as that against Catholics, Jews, and those of any religion. It should be noted that the federal official who banned the "Mohammedans" was an Armenian, a group of people subjected to persecution by the Turks.

F ive Men and a lad of fifteen, immigrants from Turkey, passengers on the Caledonia, have been held in custody in New York since last Monday and are to be deported, by order of the United States Supervisors of Immigration. The cause of the imprisonment and banishment is that the newcomers, on being questioned by a subordinate official, admitted that they were Mohammedans. This official happened to be Armenian.

. . .Where is this sort of thing to end? If the Turks can be deported this year, they may have the upper hand next year, and deport the Armenians. And if the principle should be approved, it may be applied to any persons whom officials at the time may think dangerous, to Jews, Catholics, Mormons, Cubans, Spaniards. . . .

This deportation by order of a board, because of religion, is too absurd to be tolerated by the authorities. . . . It is the glory of our country that a man may believe in anything; but if he injures other people, the law takes hold of him. If anyone commits bigamy he is punishable.

There are Mohammedans in the United States. Some of them are missionaries sent to New York to convert the people.

If we do deport Mohammedans, the Sultan [of Turkey] may retort by deporting American missionaries—whom he regards as a demoralizing and dangerous class. If he should what can we say against it?

If we let Mohammedan immigrants alone, showing ourselves civilized and kind-hearted, they will soon become Americans in feeling and habits.

Source: William Birney, Deporting Mohammedans [Letter to the Editor], *Washington Post*, November 21, 1897, p. 13.

Alfred P. Schultz | The Mongrelization of America, 1908

Using the fall of Rome as his example, Alfred P. Schultz argued in *Race or Mongrel* that the mixing of races produced a mongrel civilization and inevitably led to the decay of a nation. As one reviewer noted at the time, the author's "apparent object is to check alien immigration into the United States." Like most opponents of the new immigrants, Schultz used arguments based on moral judgments and supposedly sound medical and scientific information.

T he influx of these races cannot be without consequences. The surgeons at the ports of immigration observe that the present immigrants have a much higher percent of loathsome diseases, and that, in general physique, it is very much inferior to the immigration of thirty years ago. The history of the races now coming proves beyond doubt their mental inferiority to the races that immigrated before the advent of Slavs and Latins. If immigration is still a blessing, then the sturdy Northern races are in every way preferable to the Southern and Southeastern debris of races that have been. The free admission of these latter prevents the coming of the former, for if content to compete with Slavs and Latins, the Northerners need not migrate as far as the United States. Much more important than the economic effects of immigration are the racial effects of immigration. . . .

Up to the middle of the last century a distinct national character was developing in the United States, and certain distinctive traits were forming. The addition of millions of other races has caused a decomposition which prevented the endurance of these characteristics, and caused this development to cease. . . .

One cause only is sufficiently powerful to cause the decay of a nation. This cause is promiscuousness. A nation is decayed that consists of degenerates, and it consists of degenerates when it no longer constitutes a distinct race. A degenerated race is one that has no longer the same internal worth which it had of old, for the reason that incessant infusions of foreign blood have diluted and weakened the old blood. In other words, a nation is deteriorated that consists of individuals not at all related or very distantly related to the founders of the nation. . . .

The principle that all men are created equal is still considered the chief pillar of strength of the United States. It is a little declamatory phrase, and only one objection can be raised against it, that it does not contain one iota of truth. Every man knows that the phrase is a falsehood. The truth is that all men are created unequal. Even the men of one and the same race are unequal; the inequalities, however, are not greater than the inequalities existing between the individual leaves of one tree, for they are variations of one and the same type. The differences between individuals of distinct races are essential, and, as they are differences that exist between one species and another, they are lasting. The attempts at creating perfect man, man pure and simple, or "The American," by a fusion of all human beings, is similar to the attempt of creating the perfect dog by a fusion of all canine races. Every animal breeder knows that it cannot be done. . . .

The United States is not much less cosmopolitan today than imperial Rome was. The friends of universal uniformity and of eternal peace will say: "Well, as soon as we are equally worthless, we will not know it, and happiness and peace will prevail." The conclusion is false. The mongrels are equally worthless, but there is no harmony in the depraved lot. The instincts of the different races do not entirely disappear, but they cannot develop. The result is internal unhappiness as far as the individual is concerned, and discord, chronic civil war, as far as the state is concerned. Anarchy within the individual, anarchy in the state.

And why should promiscuousness in the United States have a different effect than it had in Rome and elsewhere? The opinion is advanced that the public schools change the children of all races into Americans. Put a Scandinavian, a German, and a Magyar boy in at one end, and they will come out Americans at the other end. Which is like saying, let a pointer, a setter, and a pug enter one end of a tunnel and they will come out three greyhounds at the other end.

Public schools are in our time not educational institutions, but information bureaus, and the cultivation of the memory predominates. The children of every race can be trained to the cultivation of memory, but they cannot all be educated alike. The instincts of the different races are too much out of harmony. It is for this reason that the schools give information, with very little education. Schools cannot accomplish the impossible. To express the same opinion biologically, "All animals cannot be fed with the same fodder." . . .

This is the truth: schools, political institutions, and environment are utterly incapable to produce anything. No man can ever become anything else than he is already potentially and essentially. Education and schools are favourable or detrimental to development. They cannot create. To express it differently, no man can ever learn anything or know anything that he does not know already potentially and essentially. . . . Biologically expressed, this sentence reads as follows: A young pug develops into nothing but an old pug, a young greyhound into nothing but an old greyhound; and never, in all the ages between the creation of the world and doomsday, does a pug develop into a greyhound, no matter what the education, the training, the political institutions, and the environment.

Source: Alfred P. Schultz, *Race or Mongrel* (Boston: L. C. Page, 1908), 254–55, 257–61, 266.

Interpret the Evidence

1. Explain why Israel Zangwill thinks immigrants will become "real Americans" (Source 18.6).
2. Compare the two cartoons (Sources 18.7 and 18.8). What are their views of the melting pot?
3. Describe Alfred Schultz's view of the melting pot and the possibilities of assimilation (Source 18.10) and explain how he would evaluate the two cartoons.
4. How does William Birney's view of "Mohammedans" and other immigrants (Source 18.9) differ from that of Schultz (Source 18.10)?

Put It in Context

What are the limitations of the melting pot metaphor for immigrant assimilation?

What metaphor would you choose to describe the assimilation process? Explain your choice.

Progressivism and the Search for Order

1900–1917

America When Feminized, 1920

This cartoon illustrates the opposition to extending the ballot to women as a threat to long-established masculine and feminine roles. Such arguments slowed but could not stop ratification of the Nineteenth Amendment in 1920, which stated that women could not be denied the right to vote in all elections on the basis of sex. ▶ To learn more about this primary source, see Source 19.10 on page 670.

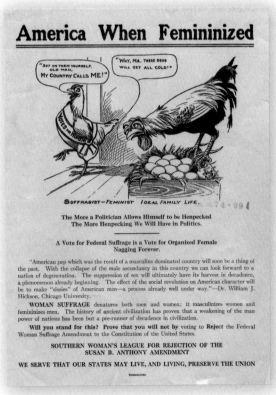

America When Femininized

"SET ON THEM YOURSELF, OLD MAN, MY COUNTRY CALLS ME!"

"WHY, MA, THESE EGGS WILL GET ALL COLD!"

SUFFRAGIST—FEMINIST IDEAL FAMILY LIFE.

The More a Politician Allows Himself to be Henpecked The More Henpecking We Will Have in Politics.

A Vote for Federal Suffrage is a Vote for Organized Female Nagging Forever.

"American pep which was the result of a masculine dominated country will soon be a thing of the past. With the collapse of the male ascendancy in this country we can look forward to a nation of degeneration. The suppression of sex will ultimately have its harvest in decadence, a phenomenon already beginning. The effect of the social revolution on American character will be to make "sissies" of American men—a process already well under way."—Dr. William J. Hickson, Chicago University.

WOMAN SUFFRAGE denatures both men and women; it masculinizes women and feminizes men. The history of ancient civilization has proven that a weakening of the man power of nations has been but a pre-runner of decadence in civilization.

Will you stand for this? Prove that you will not by voting to Reject the Federal Woman Suffrage Amendment to the Constitution of the United States.

SOUTHERN WOMAN'S LEAGUE FOR REJECTION OF THE SUSAN B. ANTHONY AMENDMENT

WE SERVE THAT OUR STATES MAY LIVE, AND LIVING, PRESERVE THE UNION

Courtesy of the Tennessee State Library and Archives, Josephine A. Pearson Papers, 1860–1943, Accession Number 74-099

After reading this chapter you should be able to:

- Compare progressivism with Populism.
- Describe the problems progressives tried to address.
- Explain the reasons progressives engaged in moral reform and evaluate how their views of immigrants shaped their efforts.
- Analyze how the notions of efficiency, openness, and accountability influenced the progressives' approach to political and environmental reform.
- Compare the ways in which the federal government handled progressive reform during the administrations of Presidents Theodore Roosevelt, William Howard Taft, and Woodrow Wilson.

Comparing American Histories

Gifford Pinchot grew up on a Connecticut estate where he learned to hunt, fish, and enjoy nature. Yet Pinchot rejected a life of leisure and instead sought to make his mark through public service by working to conserve and protect America's natural resources. After graduating from Yale in 1889, Pinchot had to study forestry abroad. No American university offered a forestry program, reflecting the predominant view that, for all practical purposes, the nation's natural resources were unlimited. As a consequence, Pinchot took courses at the French National School of Forestry, where the curriculum treated forests as crops that needed care and replenishing.

On his return in 1890, Pinchot began finding likeminded Americans who had begun to see the need to conserve the nation's natural resources and protect its wild spaces. Drawing on his scientific training and his experiences in Europe, Pinchot advocated the use of natural resources by sportsmen and businesses under carefully regulated governmental authority. Appointed to head the Federal Division of Forestry in 1898, Pinchot found a vigorous ally in the White House when Theodore Roosevelt took office in 1901. In 1907 Pinchot began to speak of the need for *conservation*, which he defined as the use of America's natural resources "for the benefit of the people who live here now." This use of resources included responsible business practices in industries such as logging and mining.

Not all environmentalists agreed. In contrast to Pinchot, author and nature photographer **Geneva (Gene) Stratton-Porter** focused her energies on *preservation*, the protection of public land from any private development. Born in 1863 in Wabash County, Indiana, Stratton-Porter grew up roaming through fields, watching birds, and observing "nature's rhythms." After marrying in 1886, Stratton-Porter took up photography and hiked into the wilderness of Indiana to take pictures of wild birds.

Stratton-Porter built a reputation as a nature photographer. She also published a series of widely read novels and children's books that revealed her vision of the harmony between human beings and nature. She urged readers to preserve the environment so that men and women could lead a truly fulfilling existence on earth and not destroy God's creation. One area on which she and Pinchot agreed was support for national parks. ■

(*left*) **Gifford Pinchot** Library of Congress, Prints and Photographs Division [LC-DIG-ggbain-04976]

(*right*) **Geneva Stratton-Porter** Indiana Historical Society, P0391 (detail)

The American histories of Gifford Pinchot and Gene Stratton-Porter reveal the efforts of two of the many individuals who searched for ways to limit the damaging impact of modernization on the United States. From roughly 1900 to 1917, many Americans sought to bring order out of the chaos accompanying rapid industrialization and urbanization. Despite the magnitude of the issues, those who believed in the need to combat the problems of industrial America possessed an optimistic faith — sometimes derived from religious principles, sometimes from a secular outlook — that they could relieve the stresses and strains of modern life. Such people were united by faith in the notion that if people joined together and applied human intelligence to the task of improving the nation, progress was inevitable. So widespread was this hopeful conviction that we call this period the Progressive Era.

In pursuit of progress and stability, some reformers tried to control the behavior of groups they considered a threat to the social order. Equating difference with disorder, many progressives tried to impose white middle-class standards of behavior on diverse immigrant populations. Some sought to eliminate the "problem" altogether by curtailing immigration from southern and eastern Europe. Others advocated birth control as a means to preserve the lives of childbearing women, but also to promote ethnic and racial engineering. In addition, progressives fought for women's suffrage, consumer protection, regulation of business, and good government reform. Many white progressives, particularly in the South, favored racial segregation and disfranchisement of African Americans. At the same time, however, black progressives and their white allies created organizations dedicated to securing racial equality. Despite their disparate and sometimes conflicting aims, progressives maintained a passion for change as a means of improving the nation.

The **Roots** of **Progressivism**

At the turn of the twentieth century, many Americans believed that the nation was in dire need of reform. Two decades of westward expansion, industrialization, urbanization, and skyrocketing immigration had transformed the country in unsettling ways. In the aftermath of the social and economic turmoil that accompanied the depression of the 1890s, many members of the middle and upper classes were convinced that unless they took remedial measures, the country would collapse under the weight of class conflict. Progressives advocated governmental intervention, yet they sought change without radically altering capitalism or the democratic political system. Not everyone endorsed progressives' goals, however. Conservatives continued to support individualism and the free market as the determinant of political and economic power, and radicals pressed for the socialist reorganization of the economy and the democratization of politics. Yet the public showed widespread support for progressivism by electing the reformers Theodore Roosevelt and Woodrow Wilson as presidents.

Progressive Origins. Progressives contended that old ways of governing and doing business did not address modern conditions. In one sense, they inherited the legacy of the Populist movement of the 1890s. Progressives attacked laissez-faire capitalism, and by regulating monopolies they aimed to limit the power of corporate trusts. Like the Populists, progressives advocated instituting an income tax as well as a variety of initiatives designed to give citizens a greater say in government. Progressives differed from Populists in fundamental ways. Perhaps most important, progressives were interested primarily in urban and industrial America, while the Populist movement had emerged in direct response to the problems that plagued rural America.

Progressives were heirs to the intellectual critics of the late nineteenth century who challenged laissez-faire and rejected Herbert Spencer's doctrine of the "survival of the fittest." **Pragmatism** greatly influenced progressives. Pragmatists contended that the meaning of truth could be discovered only through experience. Ideas had to be measured by their practical consequences. From pragmatists, progressive reformers derived a skepticism toward rigid dogma and instead relied on human experience to guide social action.

Progressive reformers also drew inspiration from the religious ideals of the **social gospel**. In *Christianity and the Social Crisis* (1907), Walter Rauschenbusch urged Christians to embrace the teachings of Jesus on the ethical obligations for social justice

Explore ▶

See Source 19.1 for Walter Rauschenbusch's views on the social responsibility of Christianity.

and to put these teachings into action by working among the urban poor. Washington Gladden argued that unregulated private enterprise was "inequitable" and compared financial speculators to vampires "sucking the life-blood of our commerce." Progressive leaders such as Theodore Roosevelt and Gifford Pinchot combined the moral fervor of the social gospel with the rationalism of scientific efficiency.

Pragmatism and the social gospel appealed to members of the new middle class. Before the Civil War, the middle class had consisted largely of ministers, lawyers, physicians, and small proprietors. The growth of large-scale businesses during the second half of the nineteenth century expanded the middle class, which now included men and women whose professions grew out of industrialization, such as engineering, corporate management, and social work. Progressivism drew many of its most devoted adherents from this new middle class.

Ida B. Wells   Born a slave in Holly Springs, Mississippi, Ida B. Wells rose to become a teacher, writer, editor, and civil rights activist. As an investigative journalist — muckrakers, as they were known at the time — she wrote about and campaigned against lynching. This photograph from 1910 shows Wells around the age of forty-eight. That same year she joined in the founding of the NAACP. Special Collections Research Center, University of Chicago Library

Guided Primary Source Analysis

Walter Rauschenbusch | Christianity and the Social Crisis, 1907

Walter Rauschenbusch was a Protestant theologian and Baptist minister from Rochester, New York, who preached the message of the social gospel in his writings and sermons. He believed that Christianity was revolutionary, that Jesus died to substitute love for selfishness, and that capitalism produced inequality. Establishing the Kingdom of God on earth would mean working to end income inequality, child labor, and other harmful results of industrialization.

Source 19.1

According to Rauschenbusch, what does Christianity demand?

What are the fictions of capitalism?

Why do industrialists deceive the public?

Social religion, too, demands repentance and faith; repentance for our social sins; faith in the possibility of a new social order. . . . In the same way we have to see through the fictions of capitalism. We are assured that the poor are poor through their own fault; that rent and profit are the just dues of foresight and ability; that the immigrants are the cause of corruption in our city politics; that we cannot compete with foreign countries unless our working class will descend to the wages paid abroad. These are all very plausible assertions, but they are lies dressed up in truth. . . . Industrialism as a whole sends out deceptive prospectuses just like single corporations within it. But in the main these misleading theories are the self-deception of those who profit by present conditions and are loath to believe that their life is working harm. It is very rare for a man to condemn the means by which he makes a living, and we must simply make allowance for the warping influence of self-interest when he justifies himself and not believe him entirely.

Source: Walter T. Rauschenbusch, *Christianity and the Social Crisis* (New York: Macmillan, 1907), 349, 350, 351.

Put It in Context

How did the social gospel provide a justification for progressive reform?

Muckrakers. The growing desire for reform at the turn of the century received a boost from investigative journalists known as **muckrakers**. Popular magazines such as *McClure's* and *Collier's* sought to increase their readership by publishing exposés of corruption in government and the shady operations of big business. Filled with details uncovered through intensive research, these articles had a sensationalist appeal that both informed and aroused their mainly middle-class readers. In 1902 journalist Ida Tarbell lambasted the ruthless and dishonest business practices of the Rockefeller family's Standard Oil Company, the model of corporate greed. Journalists Lincoln Steffens wrote about machine bosses' shameful rule in many American cities and Ida B. Wells wrote scathing articles and pamphlets condemning the lynching of African Americans. Other muckrakers exposed fraudulent practices in insurance companies, child labor, drug abuse, and prostitution.

Review & Relate

▪ What late-nineteenth-century trends and developments influenced the progressives?

▪ Why did the progressives focus on urban and industrial America?

Humanitarian and Social Justice Reform

Progressivism took different paths based on the interests and concerns of its participants. Although many of the reform efforts overlapped, it is useful to examine them in specific categories. Humanitarian reformers focused on the plight of urban immigrants, African Americans, and the underprivileged. They tried to improve housing and working conditions for impoverished city dwellers. Their motives were not always purely altruistic. Unless living standards improved, many reformers reasoned, immigrants and racial minorities would "contaminate" the cities' middle-class inhabitants with communicable diseases, escalating crime, and threats to traditional cultural norms. These reformers also supported suffrage for women, whose votes, they believed, would help purify electoral politics and elect candidates committed to social and moral reform.

Female Progressives and the Poor. Women played the leading role in efforts to improve the lives of the impoverished. Jane Addams had toured Europe after graduating from a women's college in Illinois. The Toynbee Hall settlement house (see "Urban Reformers," in chapter 18) in London impressed her for its work in helping poor residents of the area. After returning home to Chicago in 1889, Addams and her friend Ellen Starr established **Hull House** as a center for social reform. Hull House inspired a generation of young women to work directly in immigrant communities. Many were college-educated, professionally trained women who were shut out of jobs in male-dominated professions. Staffed mainly by women, settlement houses became all-purpose urban support centers providing recreational facilities, social activities, and educational classes for neighborhood residents. Calling on women to take up **civic housekeeping**, Addams maintained that women could protect their households from the chaos of industrialization and urbanization only by attacking the sources of that chaos in the community at large.

Settlement houses and social workers occupied the front lines of humanitarian reform, but they found considerable support from women's clubs. Formed after the Civil War, these local groups provided middle-class women places to meet, share ideas, and work on common projects. By 1900 these clubs counted 160,000 members. Initially devoted to discussions of religion, culture, and science, club women began to help the needy and lobby for social justice legislation. "Since men are more or less closely absorbed in business," one club woman remarked about this civic awakening, "it has come to pass that the initiative in civic matters has devolved largely upon women." Starting out in towns and cities, club women carried their message to state and federal governments and campaigned for legislation that would establish social welfare programs for working women and their children.

In an age of strict racial segregation, African American women formed their own clubs. They sponsored day care centers, kindergartens, and work and home training projects. The activities of black club women, like those of white club women, reflected a class bias, and they tried to lift up poorer blacks to ideals of middle-class womanhood. Yet in doing so, they challenged racist notions that black women and men were incapable of raising healthy and strong families. By 1916 the National Association of Colored Women (NACW), whose motto was "lifting as we climb," boasted 1,000 clubs and 50,000 members.

One organization that attracted both white and black women in the South was the Young Women's Christian Association (YWCA). College women created student chapters of the "Y," which they devoted to working with the poor in settlement houses, prisons, orphanages, and other areas of public service. Two white sisters in North Carolina, Grace and Katharine Lumpkin, tried to carry out the social gospel mission of Walter Rauschenbusch and pledged "to lend to those less fortunate a helping hand" without concern for "culture, wealth, or pedigree." Black women such as Juliette Derricotte, Juanita Saddler, and Frances Williams built up college YWCA chapters on black campuses, though operating mainly in a segregated environment.

White working-class women also organized, but because of employment discrimination there were few, if any, black female industrial workers to join them. Building on the settlement house movement and together with middle-class and wealthy women, working-class women founded the National Women's Trade Union League (WTUL) in 1903. Recognizing that many women needed to earn an income to help support their families, the WTUL was dedicated to securing higher wages, an eight-hour day, and improved working conditions. Believing women to be physically weaker than men, most female reformers advocated special legislation to protect women in the workplace. They campaigned for state laws prescribing the maximum number of hours women could work, and they succeeded in 1908 when they won a landmark victory in the Supreme Court in *Muller v. Oregon*, which upheld an Oregon law establishing a ten-hour workday for women. These reformers also convinced lawmakers in forty states to establish pensions for mothers and widows. In 1912 their focus shifted to the federal government with the founding of the Children's Bureau in the Department of Commerce and Labor. Headed by Julia Lathrop, the bureau collected sociological data and devised a variety of publicly funded social welfare measures. In 1916 Congress enacted a law banning child labor under the age of fourteen (it was declared unconstitutional in 1918). In 1921 Congress passed the Shepherd-Towner Act, which allowed nurses to offer maternal and infant health care information to mothers.

Not all women believed in the idea of protective legislation for women. In 1898 Charlotte Perkins Gilman published *Women and Economics*, in which she argued against the notion that women were ideally suited for domesticity. She contended that women's reliance on men was unnatural: "We are the only animal species in which the female depends on the male for food." Emphasizing the need for economic independence, Gilman advocated the establishment of communal kitchens that would free women from household chores and allow them to compete on equal terms with men in the workplace. Emma Goldman, an anarchist critic of capitalism and middle-class sexual morality, also spoke out against the kind of marriage that made women "keep their mouths shut and their wombs open." These women considered themselves as feminists—women who aspire to reach their full potential and gain access to the same opportunities as men. Even those less radical than Gilman and Goldman, such as Louisa Dana Haring of Chicago, argued that the 1908 *Muller* opinion would hinder sexual equality. "If men want to curtail the hours of work for women," Haring wrote, "let them see to it that the rates per hour are raised, so as to afford compensation for loss of time." She went on to point out the obvious: "Who ever heard of limiting a working woman in a home (where she often does the rudest, heaviest sort of work) to eight hours of toil a day?" **See Primary Source Project 19: Women's Suffrage and Passage of the Nineteenth Amendment, page 666.**

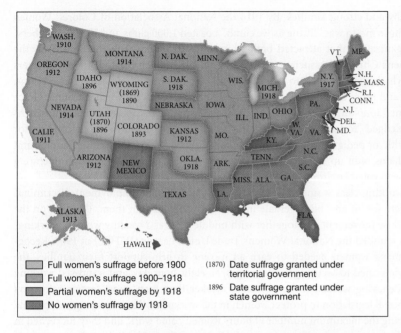

MAP 19.1 Women's Suffrage

Western states and territories were the first to approve women's suffrage. Yet even as western states enfranchised women, most placed restrictions on or excluded African American, American Indian, Mexican American, and Asian American women. States granting partial suffrage allowed women to vote only in certain contests, such as local, primary, or presidential elections.

Full women's suffrage before 1900
Full women's suffrage 1900–1918
Partial women's suffrage by 1918
No women's suffrage by 1918

(1870) Date suffrage granted under territorial government

1896 Date suffrage granted under state government

Fighting for Women's Suffrage. Before 1900 women did not have the full right to vote, except in a handful of western states. Although the Fourteenth and Fifteenth Amendments extended citizenship to African Americans and protected the voting rights of black men, they left women, both white and black, ineligible to vote. Following Reconstruction, the two major organizations campaigning for women's suffrage at the state and national levels — Susan B. Anthony and Elizabeth Cady Stanton's National Woman Suffrage Association and Lucy Stone and Julia Ward Howe's American Woman Suffrage Association — failed to achieve major victories. In 1890 the two groups combined to form the National American Woman Suffrage Association, and by 1918 women could vote fully in fifteen states and the territory of Alaska (Map 19.1).

Suffragists included a broad coalition of supporters and based their campaign on a variety of arguments. Reformers such as Jane Addams attributed corruption in politics to the absence of women's maternal influence. In this way, mainstream suffragists couched their arguments within traditional conceptions of women as family nurturers and claimed that men should see women's vote as an expansion of traditional household duties into the public sphere. By contrast, suffragists such as Alice Paul rejected such arguments, asserting that women deserved the vote on the basis of their equality with men as citizens. She founded the National Woman's Party and in 1923 proposed that Congress adopt an Equal Rights Amendment to provide full legal equality to women.

Both male and female opponents fought against women's suffrage. They believed that women were best suited by nature to devote themselves to their families and leave the world of politics to men. Suffrage critics insisted that extending the right to vote to women would destroy the home, lead to the moral degeneracy of children, and tear down the social fabric of the country.

Campaigns for women's suffrage did not apply to women of all races and classes. White suffragists in the South supported white female enfranchisement while maintaining racial

THE AWAKENING

The Awakening / Henry Mayer, 1915   This illustration depicts Lady Liberty with her torch raised high and her flowing cape inscribed with the words, "Votes for Women." She is striding from the West, where women first obtained the ballot, and heading toward the East and South, where by 1915 women could only vote partially or not at all. Henry Mayer drew this image, which appeared in the magazine *Puck*. Underneath it appeared a poem by Alice Duer Miller urging women to unite to extend suffrage. Library of Congress, 3b49106

prejudice against black men and women. Outspoken white suffragists such as Rebecca Latimer Felton from Georgia, Belle Kearney from Mississippi, and Kate Gordon from Louisiana contended that allowing southern white women to vote would preserve white supremacy by offsetting any black men's votes granted by the Fifteenth Amendment. Due to restrictive poll tax requirements, extending the vote to white women would benefit only those in the middle and upper-classes who had enough family income to pay in order to vote.

Many middle-class women outside the South used similar reasoning, but they targeted newly arrived immigrants instead of African Americans. Many Protestant women and men viewed Catholics and Jews from southern and eastern Europe as racially inferior and spiritually dangerous. They blamed such immigrants for the ills of the cities in which they congregated, and some suffragists believed that the vote of middle-class Protestant women would help clean up the mess the immigrants created.

African American women challenged these racist arguments and mounted their own drive for female suffrage. They had an additional incentive to press for enfranchisement. As the target of white sexual predators during slavery and its aftermath, some black women saw the vote as a way to address this problem. "The ballot," Nannie Helen Burroughs, the founder of the NACW remarked, is the black woman's "weapon of moral defense." Although they did not gain much support from white suffragists, by 1916 African American women worked through the NACW and formed suffrage clubs throughout the nation.

The women's suffrage campaign adopted a variety of tactics. Reformers launched orderly parades on foot and in automobiles through the streets of American cities and towns. Growing numbers of working-class and immigrant women joined these parades, which gained widespread publicity. In attempting to promote suffrage, advocates embraced consumer culture. Macy's and other department stores sold blouses, skirts, and pins in suffrage colors — gold, white, and purple. Suffragists decorated store windows and created posters and slogans to appeal to diverse voters. Radical activists such as Alice Paul conducted confrontational demonstrations in Washington, D.C., in front of the gates of the White House. As a result, they were arrested, sent to prison, and force-fed after embarking on a hunger strike. Although mainstream suffrage leaders denounced these new tactics, they gained much-needed publicity for the movement, which in turn aided the lobbying efforts of more moderate activists. In 1919 Congress passed the Nineteenth Amendment, granting women the vote. The following year, the amendment was ratified by the states.

The campaign for women's suffrage in the United States was part of an international movement. Victories in New Zealand (1893), Australia (1902), and Norway (1913) spurred on American suffragists. Indeed, Alice Paul and other radical American activists found inspiration in the militant tactics employed by some in the British suffrage movement.

Progressivism and African Americans. As with suffrage, social justice progressives faced huge barriers in the fight for racial equality. By 1900 white supremacists in the South had disfranchised most black voters and imposed a rigid system of segregation in education and all aspects of public life, which they enforced with violence. From 1884 to 1900, approximately 2,500 people were lynched, most of them southern blacks. Antiblack

Nannie Burroughs and the National Women's Baptist Convention, c.1905   Nine African American women stand with Nannie Burroughs holding a banner reading, "Banner State Woman's National Baptist Convention." This organization, which Burroughs co-founded, provided support for southern black women in their efforts to promote education, suffrage, and anti-lynching measures. Library of Congress, LC-DIG-ds-13272 violence also took the form of race riots that erupted in southern cities. Farther north, in Springfield, Illinois, a riot broke out in 1908 when the local sheriff tried to protect two black prisoners from a would-be lynch mob. This confrontation triggered two days of white violence against blacks, some of whom fought back, leaving twenty-four businesses and forty homes destroyed and seven people (two blacks and five whites) dead.

As the situation for African Americans deteriorated, black leaders responded in several ways. Booker T. Washington espoused an approach that his critics called accommodation but that he defended as practical. Born a slave and emancipated at age nine, Washington attended Hampton Institute, run by sympathetic whites in his home state of Virginia. School officials believed that African Americans would first have to build up their character and accept the virtues of abstinence, thrift, and industriousness before seeking a more intellectual education. In 1881 Washington founded **Tuskegee Institute** in Alabama, which he modeled on Hampton. In 1895, he received an enthusiastic reception from white business and civic leaders in Atlanta for his message urging African Americans to remain in the South, accept racial segregation, concentrate on moral and economic development, and avoid politics. At the same time, he called on white leaders to protect blacks from the growing violence directed at them.

White leaders in both the South and the North embraced Washington, and he became the most powerful African American of his generation. Although he discouraged public protests against segregation, he emphasized racial pride and solidarity among African Americans. Yet Washington was a complex figure who secretly financed and supported court challenges to electoral disfranchisement and other forms of racial discrimination.

Washington's enormous power did not discourage opposing views among African Americans. Ida B. Wells, like Washington, had been born a slave. In 1878 she took a job in Memphis as a teacher. Six years later, Wells sued the Chesapeake & Ohio Railroad for moving her from the first-class "Ladies Coach" to the segregated smoking car because she was black. She won her case in the lower court, but her victory was reversed by the Tennessee Supreme Court. Undeterred, she began writing for the newspaper *Free Speech*, and when her articles exposing injustices in the Memphis school system got her fired from teaching, she took up journalism full-time.

Unlike Washington, Wells believed that black leaders had to speak out vigorously against racial inequality and lynching. On March 9, 1892, three black men in Memphis were murdered by a white mob. The victims had operated a grocery store that became the target of hostility from white competitors. The black businessmen fought back and shot three armed attackers in self-defense. In support of their actions, Wells wrote, "When the white man . . . knows he runs as great a risk of biting the dust every time his Afro-American victim does, he will have greater respect for Afro-American life." Subsequently arrested for their armed resistance, the three men were snatched from jail and lynched.

In response to Wells's articles about the Memphis lynching, a white mob burned down her newspaper's building. She fled to Chicago, where she published a report refuting the myth that the rape of white women by black men was the leading cause of lynching. She concluded that racists used this brand of violence to ensure that African Americans would not challenge white supremacy. Wells waged her campaign throughout the North and in Europe. She also joined the drive for women's suffrage, which she hoped would give black women a chance to use their votes to help combat racial injustice.

Explore ▶

See Sources 19.2 and 19.3 for Washington's and Wells's responses to inequality.

Comparative Primary Source Analysis

Addressing Racial Inequality

By the end of the nineteenth century, the former Confederate states had stripped most blacks of the right to vote and instituted legal forms of segregation. In the face of violence, hostility, and widespread discrimination, African American leaders Booker T. Washington and Ida B. Wells developed alternative approaches to the problem of racial inequality. Washington emphasized accommodation within the existing social and political system, whereas Wells insisted that blacks must secure the right to vote.

Source 19.2

Booker T. Washington | The Atlanta Compromise, 1895

The wisest among my race understand that the agitation of questions of social equality is the extremest folly, and that progress in the enjoyment of all the privileges that will come to us must be the result of severe and constant struggle rather than of artificial forcing. No race that has anything to contribute to the markets of the world is long in any degree ostracized. It is important and right that all privileges of the law be ours, but it is vastly more important that we be prepared for the exercise of those privileges. The opportunity to earn a dollar in a factory just now is worth infinitely more than the opportunity to spend a dollar in an opera house.

. . . I pledge that in your [white race] effort to work out the great and intricate problem which

God has laid at the doors of the South, you shall have at all times the patient, sympathetic help of my race; only let this be constantly in mind that, while from representations in these buildings of the product of field, of forest, of mine, of factory, letters, and art, much good will come, yet far above and beyond material benefits will be that higher good, that, let us pray God, will come, in a blotting out of sectional differences and racial animosities and suspicions, in a determination to administer absolute justice, in a willing obedience among all classes to the mandates of law. This, coupled with our material prosperity, will bring into our beloved South a new heaven and a new earth.

Source: Booker T. Washington, *The Story of My Life and Work* (Cincinnati: W. W. Ferguson, 1900), 170–71.

W. E. B. Du Bois also rejected Washington's accommodationist stance and urged blacks to demand first-class citizenship. In contrast to Washington's and Wells's families, Du Bois's ancestors were free blacks, and he grew up in Great Barrington, Massachusetts. He earned a Ph.D. in history from Harvard. Du Bois agreed with Washington about advocating self-help as a means for advancement, but he did not believe this effort would succeed without a proper education and equal voting rights. In *The Souls of Black Folk* (1903), Du Bois argued that African Americans needed a liberal arts education. Du Bois contended that a classical, humanistic education would produce a cadre of leaders, the "Talented Tenth," who would guide African Americans to the next stage of their development. African American leaders should demand the universal right to vote, and only then, Du Bois contended, would African Americans gain equality, self-respect, and dignity as a race.

Source 19.3

Ida B. Wells | A Critique of Booker T. Washington, 1904

Industrial education for the Negro is Booker T. Washington's hobby. He believes that for the masses of the Negro race an elementary education of the brain and a continuation of the education of the hand is not only the best kind, but he knows it is the most popular with the white South. He knows also that the Negro is the butt of ridicule with the average white American, and that the aforesaid American enjoys nothing so much as a joke which portrays the Negro as illiterate and improvident [shortsighted]; a petty thief or a happy-go-lucky inferior. . . .

There are many who can never be made to feel that it was a mistake thirty years ago to give the unlettered freedman the franchise, their only weapon of defense, any more than it was a mistake to have fire for cooking and heating purposes in the home, because ignorant or careless servants sometimes burn themselves. . . .

Does this mean that the Negro objects to industrial education? By no means. It simply means that he knows by sad experience that industrial education will not stand him in place of political, civil and intellectual liberty, and he objects to being deprived of fundamental rights of American citizenship to the end that one school for industrial training shall flourish. To him it seems like selling a race's birthright for a mess of pottage.

Source: Ida B. Wells, "The Negro Problem from the Negro Point of View," *World Today*, April 1904, 518, 520, 521.

Interpret the Evidence

1. Why does Washington believe that economic development is the key to racial progress?
2. How does Wells challenge Washington's agenda? Why does she insist that industrial education is not enough and political and social reforms are essential to black economic progress?

Put It in Context

How do Washington and Wells reflect, in different ways, the status of African Americans in the United States at the turn of the twentieth century?

Du Bois was an intellectual who put his ideas into action. In 1905 he spearheaded the creation of the Niagara Movement, a group that first met on the Canadian side of Niagara Falls. The all-black organization demanded the vote and equal access to public facilities for African Americans. By 1909 internal squabbling and a shortage of funds had crippled the group. That same year, however, Du Bois became involved in the creation of an organization that would shape the fight for racial equality throughout the twentieth century: the **National Association for the Advancement of Colored People (NAACP)**. In addition to Du Bois, Ida B. Wells, and veterans of the Niagara Movement, white activists such as Jane Addams joined in forming the organization. Beginning in 1910, the NAACP initiated court cases challenging racially discriminatory voting practices and other forms of bias in housing and criminal justice. Its first victory came in 1915, when its lawyers convinced the

Supreme Court to strike down the grandfather clause that discriminated against black voters (*Guinn v. United States*).

African Americans also pursued social justice initiatives outside the realm of politics. Southern blacks remained committed to securing a quality education for their children after whites failed to live up to their responsibilities under *Plessy v. Ferguson*. Black schools remained inferior to white schools, and African Americans did not receive a fair return from their tax dollars; in fact, a large portion of their payments helped subsidize white schools.

Black women played a prominent role in promoting education. For example, in 1901 Charlotte Hawkins Brown set up the Palmer Memorial Institute outside of Greensboro, North Carolina. In these endeavors, black educators received financial assistance from northern philanthropists, white club women interested in moral uplift of the black race, and religious missionaries seeking converts in the South. By 1910 more than 1.5 million black children went to school in the South, most of them taught by the region's 28,560 black teachers. Thirty-four black colleges existed, and more than 2,000 African Americans held college degrees.

Progressivism and Indians.
Like African Americans, Native Americans struggled against injustice. Indian muckrakers criticized government policies and anti-Indian attitudes, but the magazines that exposed the evils of industrialization often ignored their plight. Instead, Indian reformers turned to the *Quarterly Journal*, published by the Society of American Indians, to air their grievances. Carlos Montezuma was the most outspoken critic of Indian policy. A Yavapai tribe member from Arizona, he called for the abolition of the Indian Office as an impediment to the welfare of Native Americans. Montezuma argued that Native Americans had to free themselves to gain their independence and advocated for extending full citizenship and equal rights to all Indians. Arthur C. Parker, an anthropologist from the eastern tribe of the Seneca, challenged the notion that Indians suffered mainly because of their own backwardness. In scathing articles, he condemned the United States for robbing American Indians of their cultural and economic independence. One Indian who wrote for non-Indian magazines such as *Harper's Weekly* was Zitkala-Ša. This Sioux woman published essays exposing the practices of boarding schools designed to assimilate Indians. Non-Indian anthropologists such as Franz Boas and Ruth Benedict added their voices to those of Indian journalists in attacking traditional views of Native Americans as inferior and uncivilized.

Dr. Carlos Montezuma at Carlisle Indian School, c. 1895   This photograph was taken of Carlos Montezuma, a member of the Yavapai tribe, who served as resident physician at the Carlisle Indian School from 1895–1897. Surrounding him are the trained nurses at the hospital. Although the Carlisle School was created to assimilate Indians, Dr. Montezuma spoke out for full citizenship and equal rights for all Native Americans. National Anthropological Archives, Smithsonian Institution [06912100]

Indian reformers did not succeed in convincing state and federal governments to pass legislation to address their concerns. Nevertheless, activists did succeed in filing thirty-one complaints with the U.S. Court of Claims for monetary compensation for federal payments to which they were entitled but had not received. Like other exploited groups during the Progressive Era, Indians created organizations, such as the Black Hills Treaty Council and others, to pressure the federal government and to publicize their demands.

Review & Relate

▪ What role did women play in the early-twentieth-century fight for social justice?

▪ How did social reformers challenge discrimination against women, racial and ethnic minorities, and Indians?

Morality and Social Control

In many cases, progressive initiatives crossed the line from social reform to social control. Convinced that the "immorality" of the poor was the cause of social disorder, some reformers sought to impose middle-class standards of behavior and morality on the lower economic classes. As with other forms of progressivism, reformers interested in social control were driven by a variety of motives. Regardless, efforts to prohibit alcohol, fight prostitution, and combat juvenile delinquency often involved attempts to repress the poor. So, too, did protective health measures such as birth control. Some social control progressives went even further in their efforts to impose their own morality, calling for restrictions on immigration, which they saw as a cultural threat.

Prohibition. Prohibition campaigns began long before the Civil War but scored few important successes until 1881, when Kansas became the first state whose constitution banned the consumption of alcohol. Women spearheaded the prohibition movement by forming the **Woman's Christian Temperance Union (WCTU)** in 1874 under the leadership of Frances Willard. Willard built the temperance movement around the need to protect the home. Husbands and fathers who drank excessively were also likely to abuse their wives and children and to drain the family finances. Prohibiting the consumption of alcohol would therefore help combat these evils. At the same time, the quality of family and public life would be improved if women received the right to vote and young children completed their education without having to go to work.

After Willard's death in 1898, the Anti-Saloon League (ASL) became the dominant force in the prohibition movement. Established in 1893, the league grew out of evangelical Protestantism. The group had particular appeal in the rural South, where Protestant fundamentalism flourished. Between 1906 and 1917, twenty-one states, mostly in the South and West, banned liquor sales. However, concern over alcohol was not confined to these regions. Middle-class progressives in northern cities, who identified much of urban decay with the influx of immigrants, saw the tavern as a breeding ground for immoral activities. In 1913 the ASL convinced Congress to pass the Webb-Kenyon Act, which banned the transportation of alcoholic beverages into dry states. After the United States entered World War I in 1917, reformers argued that prohibition would help win the war by conserving grain used to make liquor and by saving soldiers from intoxication. The Eighteenth Amendment, ratified in 1919, made prohibition the law of the land until it was repealed in 1933.

Prostitution, Narcotics, and Juvenile Delinquency. Alarmed by the increased number of brothels and "streetwalkers" that accompanied the growth of cities, progressives sought to eliminate prostitution. Some framed the issue in terms of public health, linking prostitution to the spread of sexually transmitted diseases. Others presented it as an effort to protect female virtue. Such reformers were generally interested only in white women, who, unlike African American and Asian women in similar circumstances, were considered sexual innocents coerced into prostitution. Still others claimed that prostitutes themselves were to blame, seeing women who sold their sexual favors as inherently immoral.

Reformers offered two different approaches to the problem. Taking the moralistic solution, Representative James R. Mann of Chicago steered through Congress the White Slave Trade Act (known as the Mann Act) in 1910, banning the transportation of women across state lines for immoral purposes. By contrast, the American Social Hygiene Association, founded in 1914, subsidized scientific research into sexually transmitted diseases, funded investigations to gather more information, and drafted model ordinances for cities to curb prostitution. By 1915 every state had laws making sexual solicitation a crime.

Prosecutors used the Mann Act to enforce codes of racial as well as sexual behavior. In 1910 Jack Johnson, an African American boxer, defeated the white heavyweight champion, Jim Jeffries. His victory upset some white men who were obsessed with preserving their racial dominance and masculine integrity. Johnson's relationships with white women further angered some whites, who eventually succeeded in bringing down the outspoken black champion by prosecuting him on morals charges in 1913.

Moral crusaders also sought to eliminate the use and sale of narcotics. By 1900 approximately 250,000 people in the United States were addicted to opium, morphine, or cocaine — far fewer, however, than those who abused alcohol. On the West Coast, immigration opponents associated opium smoking with the Chinese and tried to eliminate its use as part of their wider anti-Asian campaign. In alliance with the American Medical Association, reformers convinced Congress to pass the Harrison Narcotics Control Act of 1914, prohibiting the sale of narcotics except by a doctor's prescription.

Progressives also tried to combat juvenile delinquency, and this effort often involved attempts to control disadvantaged youth, especially immigrant children. Inspired by new ideas about children as a distinct category — not simply small adults — reformers succeeded in establishing a juvenile court system that focused on rehabilitation rather than punishment for youthful offenders. Juvenile courts conducted civil rather than criminal proceedings, thereby allowing local officials greater flexibility as they extended their supervision of boys and girls over such noncriminal behavior as smoking, truancy, and sexual activity. Rehabilitation of delinquent boys, regardless of their suspect behavior, often turned into punitive treatment. Fewer girls got caught up in the juvenile courts, but those who did appeared mainly on charges of "sexual precocity." In replacing criminal penalties with juvenile rehabilitation progressive reformers sought to impose middle-class norms on disadvantaged youth.

Birth Control. The health of women and families occupied reformers such as Margaret Sanger, the leading advocate of birth control. Working as a nurse mainly among poor immigrant women in New York City, she witnessed the damage that unrestrained childbearing produced on women's health. According to Sanger, contraception — the use of artificial

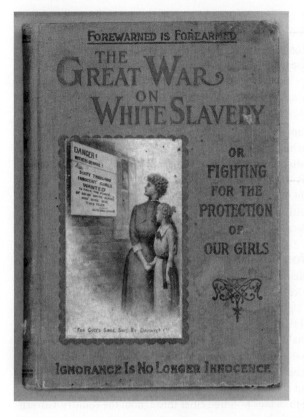

FOREWARNED IS FOREARMED

THE GREAT WAR ON WHITE SLAVERY

OR FIGHTING FOR THE PROTECTION OF OUR GIRLS

IGNORANCE IS NO LONGER INNOCENCE

The Crusade against White Slavery   Published by Clifford B. Roe and B. S. Steadwell in 1911, *The Great War on White Slavery* campaigned against prostitution and the criminals who lured impoverished young women into what they called "the human stockyards . . . for girls." As an assistant state's attorney in Chicago, Roe prosecuted more than 150 cases against sex traffickers. He exemplified progressivism's moral reform impulse. Chronicle/Alamy

means to prevent pregnancy — would save the lives of mothers by preventing unwanted childbearing and avoiding unsafe and illegal abortions, and would keep families from having large numbers of children they could not afford. Moreover, Sanger believed that if women were freed from the anxieties of becoming pregnant, they would experience more sexual enjoyment and make better companions for their spouses. Her arguments for birth control also had a connection to eugenics. Contraception, she believed, would "raise the quality" of the white race by reducing the chances of immigrants and women from ethnic and racial minorities reproducing so-called unfit children.

Sanger and her supporters encountered enormous opposition. It was illegal to sell contraceptive devices or furnish information about them. Nevertheless, in 1916 Sanger opened up the nation's first birth control clinic in an immigrant section of Brooklyn. The police quickly closed down the facility and arrested Sanger. Undeterred, she continued to agitate for her cause and push to change attitudes toward women's health and reproductive rights.

Immigration Restriction. Sanger wanted to lessen the problems faced by immigrant women. However, other moral reformers sought to restrict immigration itself. Anti-immigrant sentiment often reflected racial and religious bigotry, as reformers concentrated on preventing Catholics, Jews, and all non-Europeans from entering the United States. Social scientists validated these prejudices by categorizing darker-skinned immigrants as inferior races. The harshest treatment was reserved for Asians. In 1908 President Theodore Roosevelt entered into an executive agreement with Japan that reduced Japanese immigration to the United States. In 1913 the California legislature passed a statute barring Japanese immigrants from buying land, a law that twelve other states subsequently enacted.

In 1917 reformers succeeded in further restricting immigration. Congress passed legislation to ban people who could not read English or their native language from entering the country. The act also denied entry to other undesirables: "alcoholics," "feeble-minded persons," "epileptics," "people mentally or physically defective," "professional beggars," "anarchists," and "polygamists." In barring people considered unfit to enter the country, lawmakers intended to keep out those who could not support themselves and might become public wards of the state and, in the case of anarchists and polygamists, those who threatened the nation's political and religious values.

Review & Relate

- What practices and behaviors of the poor did social control progressives find most alarming? Why?

- What role did anti-immigrant sentiment play in motivating and shaping progressives' social control initiatives?

Good Government Progressivism

In an effort to diminish the power of corrupt urban political machines and unregulated corporations, progressives pushed for good government reforms, promoting initiatives they claimed would produce greater efficiency, openness, and accountability in government. Many of the progressives' proposed reforms appeared, at least on the surface, to give citizens more direct say in their government; however, a closer look reveals a more complicated picture.

Municipal and State Reform. Cities were at the forefront of government reform during the Progressive Era. Municipal governments failed to keep up with the problems of accelerated urban growth. Political machines distributed city services within a system bloated by corruption and graft. Upper-middle-class businessmen and professionals fed up with wasteful and inefficient political machines sought to institute new forms of government that functioned more rationally and cost less.

The adoption of the commission form of government was a hallmark of urban reform. Commission governments replaced the old form of a mayor and city council with elected commissioners, each of whom ran a municipal department as if it were a business. By 1917 commissions had spread to more than four hundred cities throughout the country. Governments with a mayor and city council also began to appoint city managers, who functioned as chief operating officers, to foster businesslike efficiency. The head of the National Cash Register Company, who helped bring the city manager system to Dayton, Ohio, praised it for resembling "a great business enterprise whose stockholders are the people."

Reformers also adopted direct primaries for voters to select candidates rather than allowing a handful of machine politicians to decide elections behind closed doors. To reverse the influence of immigrants who supported their own ethnic candidates and to topple the machines that catered to them, municipal reformers replaced district elections with citywide "at-large" elections. Ethnic enclaves lost not only their ward representatives but also a good deal of their influence because citywide election campaigns were expensive, shifting power to those who could afford to run. Working- and lower-class residents of cities still retained the right to vote, but their power was diluted.

Explore ▶

Read Sources 19.4 and 19.5 for two historians' perspectives on southern progressivism.

In the South, where fewer immigrants lived, white supremacists employed these tactics to further disfranchise African Americans. Southern lawmakers diminished whatever black political power remained by adopting at-large elections and commission governments. Throughout the South, direct primary contests (or "white primaries") were closed to blacks.

Urban progressivism did produce a number of mayors who carried out genuine reforms. Elected in 1901, Cleveland mayor Tom L. Johnson implemented measures to assess taxes more equitably, regulate utility companies, and reduce public transportation fares. Samuel "Golden Rule" Jones, who served as Toledo's mayor from 1897 to 1903, supported social justice measures by establishing an eight-hour workday for municipal employees, granting them paid vacations, and prohibiting child labor. Under Mayor Hazen Pingree, who served from 1889 to 1896, Detroit constructed additional schools and recreational facilities and put the unemployed to work on municipal projects during economic hard times.

Progressives also took action at the state level. Robert M. La Follette, Republican governor of Wisconsin from 1901 to 1906, led the way by initiating a range of reforms to improve the performance of state government and increase its accountability to constituents. During his tenure as governor, La Follette dismantled the statewide political machine by instituting direct party primaries, an expanded civil service, a law forbidding direct corporate contributions to political parties, a strengthened railroad regulatory commission, and a graduated income tax. In 1906 La Follette entered the U.S. Senate, where he battled for further reform.

Other states picked up and expanded La Follette's progressive agenda. In 1913 three-quarters of the states ratified the Seventeenth Amendment, which mandated that U.S. senators would be elected by popular vote instead of being chosen by state legislatures. This constituted another effort to remove the influence of money from politics.

Conservation and Preservation of the Environment.
The penchant for efficiency that characterized government progressivism also shaped progressive efforts to conserve natural resources. As chief forester in the Department of Agriculture, Gifford Pinchot emphasized the efficient use of resources and sought ways to reconcile the public interest with private profit motives. His approach often won support from large lumber companies, which had a long-term interest in sustainable forests. Large companies also saw conservation as a way to drive their smaller competitors out of business, as large companies could better afford the additional costs associated with managing healthy forests.

Theodore Roosevelt and John Muir, 1903
Taken in 1903, this photograph pictures President Theodore Roosevelt and his associates standing in front of the "Grizzly Giant," a towering sequoia tree over 200 feet in height in Yosemite National Park, California. Roosevelt is in the center, and standing to his front left is John Muir, the founder of the Sierra Club, who convinced Roosevelt to place Yosemite under federal control and establish it as a national park in 1906. Also shown in this photo from left to right are an unidentified secret serviceman; William H. Moody, secretary of the navy; George Pardee, governor of California; Presley Marion Rixey, White House physician; Nicholas Murray Butler, president of Columbia University; William Loeb, Roosevelt's personal secretary; and Benjamin Ide Wheeler, president of the University of California.

Comparative Secondary Source Analysis

Progressivism in White and Black

The Progressive Era produced an outpouring of reforms on the local, state, and national levels. Originally viewed as an attempt to spread political and economic democracy, historians have increasingly questioned the motives of progressives and the reforms they championed. Two historians of the South, a generation apart, analyzed the impact of progressivism in the region. Whereas C. Vann Woodward focuses on reform as primarily a white movement, Glenda Gilmore broadens her perspective to include black women.

Source 19.4

C. Vann Woodward | Progressivism for Whites Only, 1951

"Southern progressivism was essentially urban and middle class in nature, and the typical leader was a city professional man or businessman, rather than a farmer. Under the growing pressure of monopoly, the small businessmen and urban middle-class overcame their fear of reform and joined hands with the discontented farmers. They envisaged as a common enemy the plutocracy of the Northeast, together with its agents, banks, insurance companies, public utilities, oil companies, pipelines, and railroads.

. . . The direct primary system of nominating party candidates was not invented in Wisconsin in 1903 . . . for by that time a majority of the Southern states were already practicing the system. . . . The joker in the Southern primaries was the fact that they were *white* primaries. Southern progressivism generally was progressivism for white men only. . . . The paradoxical combination of white supremacy and progressivism was not new to the region, but it never ceased to be a cause of puzzlement and confusion above the Potomac—and not a little, below. The paradox nevertheless had its counterpart in the North, where it was not uncommon for one man to champion both progressivism and imperialism. In such instances it was a matter of white supremacy over browns instead of blacks."

Source: C. Vann Woodward, *Origins of the New South, 1877–1913* (Baton Rouge, Louisiana: Louisiana State University Press, 1971), 372, 373.

Source 19.5

Glenda Elizabeth Gilmore | Southern Black Women and Progressivism, 1996

"From the debris of disfranchisement, black women discovered fresh approaches to serving their communities and crafted new tactics to dull the blade of white supremacy. . . . After disfranchisement . . . the political culture black women had created through thirty years of work in temperance organizations, Republican Party aid societies, and churches furnished both an ideological basis and an organization structure from which black women could take on those tasks. After black men's banishment from politics, North Carolina's black women added a network of women's groups that crossed denominational and—later party lines—and took a multi-issue approach to civic action. In a nonpolitical guise, black women became the black community's diplomats to the white community. Black women might not be voters, but they could be clients, and in that role they could become spokespeople for and motivators of black citizens. They could claim a distinctly female moral authority and pretend to eschew any political motivation. The deep camouflage of their leadership style—their womanhood—helped them remain invisible as they worked toward political ends. At the same time, they could deliver not votes but hands and hearts through community organization: willing workers in city clean up campaigns, orderly children who complied with state educational requirements and hookworm-infested people eager for treatment at public health fairs.

. . . As much as southern whites plotted to reserve progressivism for themselves, and as much as they schemed to alter the ill-fitting northern version accordingly, they failed. African American women embraced southern white progressivism, reshaped it, and sent back a new model that included black power brokers and grass roots activists. . . . Southern black women initiated every progressive reform that southern white women initiated, a feat they accomplished without financial resources, without the civic protection of their husbands, and without publicity."

Source: Glenda Elizabeth Gilmore, *Gender and Jim Crow: Women and the Politics of White Supremacy in North Carolina: 1896–1920* (Chapel Hill: University of North Carolina Press, 1996), 147, 148, 174.

Examine the Sources

1. Describe one major difference between Woodward's and Gilmore's interpretations of progressivism.
2. Explain how evidence in this chapter can be used to support or refute either Woodward's or Gilmore's interpretation of progressivism.

Put It in Context

Compare northern and southern progressivism and consider how regional factors influenced the development of progressivism.

MAP 19.2 National Parks and Forests

In 1872, the federal government created the first national park at Yellowstone, which spread over portions of the future states of Wyoming, Montana, and Idaho. President Theodore Roosevelt added six sites — Crater Lake, Wind Cave, Petrified Forest, Lassen Volcanic, Mesa Verde, and Zion — to the park system. The construction of a dam and reservoir in Yosemite National Park's Hetch Hetchy Valley divided conservationists Gifford Pinchot and John Muir during the Roosevelt administration.

This gospel of efficiency faced a stiff test in California. After the devastating earthquake of 1906, San Francisco officials, coping with water and power shortages, asked the federal government to approve construction of a hydroelectric dam and reservoir in **Hetch Hetchy valley**, located in Yosemite National Park (Map 19.2). Pinchot supported the project because he saw it as the best use of the land for the greatest number of people. The famed naturalist John Muir strongly disagreed. He campaigned to save Hetch Hetchy from "ravaging commercialism" and warned against choosing economic gains over spiritual values. After a bruising seven-year battle, Pinchot (by this time a private citizen) triumphed. Still, this incursion into a national park helped spur the development of environmentalism as a political movement.

Besides the clash with preservationists, the Hetch Hetchy Dam project reveals progressive conservationists' racial bias. Conservationists such as Pinchot may have seen themselves as acting in the public interest, but their definition of "the public" did not include all Americans. In planning for the Hetch Hetchy Dam, progressives did not consult with the Mono Lake Paiutes who lived in Yosemite and who were most directly affected by the project. Conservation was meant to serve the interests of white San Franciscans and not those of the Indian inhabitants of Yosemite.

Review & Relate

■ Who gained and who lost political influence as a result of progressive reforms?

■ How did a commitment to greater efficiency shape progressives' political and environmental initiatives?

Presidential Progressivism

The problems created by industrialization and the growth of big business were national in scope. Recognizing this fact, prominent progressives sought national leadership positions, and two of them, Presidents Theodore Roosevelt and Woodrow Wilson, instituted progressive reforms during their terms. In the process, they reinvigorated the presidency, an office that had declined in power and importance during the late nineteenth century.

Theodore Roosevelt and the Square Deal.

Born into a moderately wealthy New York family, Theodore Roosevelt graduated from Harvard in 1880 and entered government service. Elected as governor of New York in 1898, two years later he became William McKinley's vice president. After McKinley's assassination in 1901, Roosevelt took over the presidency.

Roosevelt brought an activist style to the presidency. He considered his office a **bully pulpit** — a platform from which to promote his programs and from which he could rally public opinion. To this end, he used his energetic and extroverted personality to establish an unprecedented rapport with the American people.

For all his exuberance and energy, President Roosevelt pursued a moderate domestic course. Like his progressive colleagues, he opposed ideological extremism in any form. Roosevelt believed that as head of state he could serve as an impartial arbiter among competing factions and determine what was best for the public. To him, reform was the best defense against revolution.

As president, Roosevelt sought to provide economic and political stability, what he referred to as a "Square Deal." The coal strike that began in Pennsylvania in 1902 gave Roosevelt an opportunity to play the role of defender of the public good. Miners had gone on strike for an eight-hour workday, a pay increase of 20 percent, and recognition of their union. Union representatives agreed to have the president create a panel to settle the dispute, but George F. Baer, president of the Reading Railroad, which also owned the mines, pledged that he would never agree to the workers' demands. Disturbed by what he considered the owners' "arrogant stupidity," Roosevelt threatened to dispatch federal troops to take over and run the mines. When the owners backed down, the president established a commission that hammered out a compromise, which raised wages and reduced working hours but did not recognize the union.

At the same time, Roosevelt tackled the problems caused by giant business trusts. In February 1902, the president instructed the Justice Department to sue the Northern Securities Company under the Sherman Antitrust Act. Financed by J. P. Morgan, Northern Securities held monopoly control of the northernmost transcontinental railway lines. In 1904 the Supreme Court ordered that the Northern Securities Company be dissolved, ruling that the firm had restricted competition. With this victory, Roosevelt affirmed the federal government's power to regulate business trusts that violated the public interest. Overall,

Roosevelt initiated twenty-five suits under the Sherman Antitrust Act, including litigation against the tobacco and beef trusts and the Standard Oil Company, which earned him the title of "trustbuster."

Roosevelt distinguished between "good" trusts, which acted responsibly, and "bad" trusts, which abused their power. Railroads had earned an especially bad reputation with the public for charging higher rates to small shippers and those in remote regions while granting rebates to favored customers, such as Standard Oil. In 1903 Roosevelt helped persuade Congress to pass the Elkins Act, which outlawed railroad rebates. Three years later, the president increased the power of the Interstate Commerce Commission to set maximum railroad freight rates. Also in 1903 Roosevelt secured passage of legislation that established the Department of Commerce and Labor. Within this cabinet agency, the Bureau of Corporations gathered information about large companies in an effort to promote fair business practices.

Soaring in popularity, Roosevelt easily won reelection in 1904. During the next four years, the president applied antitrust laws even more vigorously than before. He steered through Congress various reforms concerning the railroads, such as the Hepburn Act (1906), which standardized shipping rates. Roosevelt charted a middle course between preservationists and conservationists. He reserved 150 million acres of timberland as part of the national forests, but he authorized the expenditure of more than $80 million in federal funds to construct dams, reservoirs, and canals largely in the West.

Not all reform came from Roosevelt's initiative. Congress passed two notable consumer laws in 1906 that reflected the multiple and sometimes contradictory forces that shaped progressivism. That year, Upton Sinclair published *The Jungle*, a muckraking novel that portrayed the impoverished lives of immigrant workers in Packingtown (Chicago) and the deplorable working conditions they endured. Outraged readers responded to the vivid description of the shoddy and filthy ways the meatpacking industry slaughtered animals and prepared beef for sale. The largest and most efficient meatpacking firms had financial reasons to support reform as well. They were losing money because European importers refused to purchase tainted meat. Congress responded by passing the Meat Inspection Act, which benefited consumers and provided a way for large corporations to eliminate competition from smaller, marginal firms that could not afford to raise standards to meet the new federal meat-processing requirements.

In 1906 Congress also passed the Pure Food and Drug Act, which prohibited the sale of adulterated and fraudulently labeled food and drugs. The impetus for this law came from consumer groups, medical professionals, and government scientists. Dr. Harvey Wiley, a chemist in the Department of Agriculture, drove efforts for reform from within the government. He considered it part of his professional duty to eliminate harmful products (Table 19.1).

Roosevelt initially gave African Americans reason to believe that they, too, would get a square deal. In October 1901, at the outset of his first term, Roosevelt invited Booker T. Washington to a dinner at the White House, outraging white supremacists in the South. Though Roosevelt dismissed this criticism, he never invited another black guest. Also in his first term, Roosevelt supported the appointment of a few black Republicans to federal posts in the South.

Nevertheless, Roosevelt lacked a commitment to black equality and espoused the racist ideas of eugenics then in fashion. He deplored the declining birthrate of native-born white

TABLE 19.1 National Progressive Legislation

1903	Department of Labor and Commerce established to promote fair business practices
	Elkins Act
1906	Pure Food and Drug Act
	Meat Inspection Act; Hepburn Act
1910	White Slave Trade Act
1913	Underwood Act reduces tariffs to benefit farmers
	Sixteenth Amendment (graduated income tax)
	Seventeenth Amendment (election of senators by popular vote)
	Federal Reserve System
1914	Harrison Narcotics Control Act
	Federal Trade Commission
	Clayton Antitrust Act
1916	Adamson Act provides eight-hour workday for railroad workers
	Keating-Owen Act outlaws child labor in firms engaged in interstate commerce
	Workmen's Compensation Act
1919	Eighteenth Amendment (prohibition)
1920	Nineteenth Amendment (women's suffrage)

Americans compared with that of eastern and southern European newcomers and African Americans, whom he considered inferior. He argued that unless Anglo-Saxon women produced more children, whites would end up committing "race suicide." "If the women flinch from breeding," Roosevelt worried, "the . . . death of the race takes place even quicker."

Once he won reelection in 1904, Roosevelt had less political incentive to defy the white South. He stopped cooperating with southern black officeholders and maneuvered to build the Republican Party in the region with all-white support. However, his most reprehensible action involved an incident that occurred in Brownsville, Texas, in 1906. White residents of the town charged that black soldiers stationed at Fort Brown shot and killed one man and wounded another. Roosevelt ordered that unless the alleged perpetrators stepped forward, the entire regiment would receive dishonorable discharges without a court-martial. Roosevelt never doubted the guilt of the black soldiers, and when no one admitted responsibility, he summarily dismissed 167 men from the military.

Roosevelt's racial attitudes also shaped his policies with respect to American Indians. Like nearly all Americans, Roosevelt believed that Native Americans were inferior to Anglo-Saxons. The president contended that enlightened white people had the duty to assimilate "primitive" Indians and make them more "civilized." Roosevelt was an enthusiastic supporter of the 1887 Dawes Act, which sold off Native lands and attempted to convert Indians into small farmers as a "vast pulverizing engine to break up the tribal mass." Within this paternalistic and racist framework, Roosevelt did act against corruption in the Bureau of Indian Affairs and initiated investigations into the treatment of Indians on reservations. The president thought that education for Indians should be "elementary and largely industrial," and their need of higher education was "very, very limited." In 1902, his administration issued an order requiring Indian men on reservations to cut their hair short, arguing that this "will be a great step in advance and will certainly hasten their progress towards civilization." Native Americans found it deeply offensive.

Taft Retreats from Progressivism.

When Roosevelt decided not to seek another term as president in 1908, choosing instead to back William Howard Taft as his successor, he thought he was leaving his reform legacy in capable hands. A Roosevelt loyalist, Taft easily defeated the Democratic candidate, William Jennings Bryan, who was running for the presidency for the third and final time.

Taft's presidency did not proceed as Roosevelt and his progressive followers had hoped. Taft proved a weak leader and frequently took stands opposite to Roosevelt and the progressives, such as in the field of conservation. When Pinchot criticized Taft's secretary of the interior, Richard Ballinger, for returning restricted Alaskan coal mines to private mining companies in 1910, Taft fired Pinchot. Taft did not oppose conservation — he transferred more land from private to public control than did Roosevelt — but his dismissal of Pinchot angered conservationists.

Subsequently, Roosevelt turned against his handpicked successor. After returning from overseas in 1910, Roosevelt became increasingly troubled by Taft's missteps. The loss of the House of Representatives to the Democrats in the 1910 elections raised alarms among Roosevelt Republicans. A year later, relations between the ex-president and the incumbent further deteriorated when Roosevelt attacked Taft for filing antitrust litigation against U.S. Steel for a deal that the Roosevelt administration had approved in 1907. Ironically, Roosevelt, known as a trustbuster, believed that filing more lawsuits under the Sherman Antitrust Act yielded diminishing returns, whereas Taft, the conservative, initiated more antitrust litigation than did Roosevelt.

The Election of 1912.

Convinced that only he could lead the party to victory, Roosevelt announced his candidacy for the 1912 Republican presidential nomination. Despite Roosevelt's popularity among rank-and-file Republicans, Taft still controlled the party machinery and the majority of convention delegates. Losing to Taft on the first ballot, an embittered Roosevelt formed a third party to sponsor his run for the presidency. Roosevelt excitedly told thousands of supporters gathered in Chicago that he felt "as strong as a BULL MOOSE," which became the nickname for Roosevelt's new **Progressive Party**.

In accepting the nomination, Roosevelt articulated the philosophy of **New Nationalism**. He argued that the federal government should use its power to fight against the forces of special privilege and for social justice for the majority of Americans. To this end, the Progressive Party platform advocated income and inheritance taxes, an eight-hour workday, the abolition of child labor, workers' compensation, fewer restrictions on labor unions, and women's suffrage.

The Democrats also nominated a progressive candidate, Woodrow Wilson, the reform governor of New Jersey. As an alternative to Roosevelt's New Nationalism, Wilson offered his **New Freedom**. As a Democrat and a southerner (he was born in Virginia), Wilson had a more limited view of government than did the Republican Roosevelt. Wilson envisioned a society of small businesses, with the government's role confined to ensuring open competition among businesses and freedom for individuals to make the best use of their opportunities. Wilson's New Freedom did not embrace social reform and rejected federal action in support of women's suffrage and the elimination of child labor.

Eugene V. Debs, the Socialist Party candidate who had been imprisoned for his leadership in the Pullman strike, was a fourth candidate in the race. He favored overthrowing capitalism through peaceful, democratic methods and replacing it with government ownership of business and industry for the benefit of the working class.

The Republican Party split decided the outcome of the election. The final results gave Roosevelt 27 percent of the popular vote and Taft 23 percent. Together they had a majority, but because they were divided, Wilson became president, with 42 percent of the popular vote and 435 electoral votes. Finishing fourth, Debs did not win any electoral votes, but he garnered around a million popular votes (6 percent).

Woodrow Wilson and the New Freedom Agenda.

Once in office, Wilson hurried to fulfill his New Freedom agenda. An admirer of the British parliamentary system, Wilson viewed the president as an active and strong leader whose job was to provide his party with a legislative program. The 1912 elections had given the Democrats control over Congress, and Wilson expected his party to support his New Freedom measures.

Tariff reduction came first. The Underwood Act of 1913 reduced import duties, a measure that appealed to southern and midwestern farmers who sought lower prices on the manufactured goods they bought that were subject to the tariff. The law also incorporated a

Woodrow Wilson's New Freedom　Before Woodrow Wilson was elected president in 1912 he had been a college professor of political science and president of Princeton University. Having stepped out of the university's ivory tower into the White House, Wilson was prepared to "educate" his opponents about their economic and civic duties to the nation. How does this political cartoon depict this? Sarin Images/Granger reform that progressives had adopted from the Populists: the graduated income tax (tax rates that increase at higher levels of income). The ratification of the Sixteenth Amendment in 1913 provided the legal basis for the income tax after the Supreme Court had previously declared such a levy unconstitutional. The graduated income tax was meant to advance the cause of social justice by moderating income inequality. The need to recover revenues lost from lower tariffs provided an additional practical impetus for imposing the tax. Because the law exempted people earning less than $4,000 a year from paying the income tax, more than 90 percent of Americans owed no tax. Those with incomes exceeding this amount paid rates ranging from 1 percent to 6 percent on $500,000 or more.

Also in 1913, Wilson pressed Congress to consider banking reform. Farmers favored a system supervised by the government that afforded them an ample supply of credit at low interest rates. Eastern bankers wanted reforms that would stabilize a system plagued by cyclical financial panics, the most recent in 1907, while keeping the banking system under the private control of bankers. The resulting compromise created the Federal Reserve System. The act established twelve regional banks. These banks lent cash reserves to member banks in their districts at a "rediscount rate," a rate that could be adjusted according to the fluctuating demand for credit. Federal Reserve notes became the foundation for a uniform currency. The Federal Reserve Board, appointed by the president and headquartered in Washington, D.C., supervised the system. Nevertheless, as with other progressive agencies, the experts selected to oversee the new banking system came from within the banking industry itself. Although farmers won a more rational and flexible credit supply, Wall Street bankers retained considerable power over the operation of the Federal Reserve System.

Next, President Wilson took two steps designed to help resolve the problem of economic concentration. First, in 1914 he persuaded Congress to create the Federal Trade Commission. The commission had the power to investigate corporate activities and prohibit "unfair" practices (which the law left undefined). Wilson's second measure directly attacked monopolies. Enacted in 1914, the Clayton Antitrust Act strengthened the Sherman Antitrust Act by banning certain corporate operations, such as price discrimination and overlapping membership on company boards, which undermined economic competition. The statute also exempted labor unions from prosecution under antitrust legislation, reversing the policy initiated by the federal government in the wake of the Pullman strike.

By the end of his second year in office, Wilson had achieved most of his New Freedom objectives. In response to political pressure and looking ahead to reelection, he was forced to widen his progressive agenda and support measures he had previously rejected. With the Republican Party once again united after the electoral fiasco of 1912, Wilson looked to gain support from Roosevelt's constituency by supporting New Nationalism social justice measures. In 1916 he signed into law the Adamson Act, which provided an eight-hour workday and overtime pay for railroad workers; the Keating-Owen Act, outlawing child labor in firms that engaged in interstate commerce; and the Workmen's Compensation Act, which provided insurance for federal employees in case of injury. In supporting programs that required greater intervention by the federal government, Wilson had placed political expediency ahead of his professed principles. He would later show a similar flexibility when he lent his support to a women's suffrage amendment, a cause he had long opposed.

Despite facing a challenge from a united Republican Party, Wilson won the 1916 election against former New York governor Charles Evans Hughes with slightly less than 50 percent of the vote. Wilson's reelection owed little to support from African Americans.

W. E. B. Du Bois, who backed Wilson in 1912 for pledging to "assist in advancing the interest of [the black] race," had become disillusioned with the president. The southern-born Wilson had surrounded himself with white appointees from the South. Despite black protests, Wilson held a screening in the White House of the film *Birth of a Nation*, which glorified the Ku Klux Klan and denigrated African Americans. Making the situation worse, Wilson introduced racial segregation into government offices and dining facilities in the nation's capital, and blacks lost jobs in post offices and other federal agencies throughout the South. In Wilson's view, segregation was in the "best interests" of African Americans.

Still, President Wilson achieved much of the progressive agenda — more, in fact, than he had intended to when he first came to office. By the beginning of his second term, the federal government had further extended regulation over the activities of corporations and banks. Big business and finance still wielded substantial power, but Wilson had steered the government on a course that also benefited ordinary citizens, including passage of social justice measures he had initially opposed.

Review & Relate

- How did the progressive agenda shape presidential politics in the first two decades of the twentieth century?

- How did the progressive policies of Presidents Roosevelt and Wilson apply to African Americans and Indians?

Conclusion: The Progressive Legacy

By the end of the Progressive Era, Americans had come to expect more from their government. They were more confident that their food and medicine were safe, that children would not have to sacrifice their health and education by going to work, that women laborers would not be exploited, and that political officials would be more responsive to their wishes. As a result of the efforts of environmentalists as different as Gifford Pinchot and Gene Stratton-Porter, the nation expanded its efforts both to conserve and to preserve its natural resources. These and other reforms accomplished what Theodore Roosevelt, Woodrow Wilson, and their fellow progressives wanted: to bring order out of chaos.

In challenging laissez-faire and championing governmental intervention, progressives sought to balance individualism with social justice and social control. Despite well-intentioned political reforms, middle- and upper-class progressives generally were more interested in augmenting their ability to advance their own agenda than in expanding opportunities for political participation for all Americans. Confident that they spoke for the "interests of the people," progressives believed that increasing their own political power would be good for the nation as a whole.

Progressivism was not for whites only, but racism constrained the progressive movement. Native Americans campaigned and organized to get the federal government to repair its broken promises of justice. Blacks were active participants in progressivism, whether through extending educational opportunities, working in settlement houses, campaigning for women's suffrage, or establishing the NAACP. Nevertheless, racism was also a characteristic of progressivism. White southern reformers generally favored disfranchisement and segregation. Northern whites did not prove much more sympathetic. Immigrants also found themselves unwelcome targets of moral outrage as progressives forced these new-comers to conform to middle-class standards of social behavior. Campaigns for temper-ance, moral reform, and birth control all shared a desire to mold people deemed inferior into proper citizens, uncontaminated by chronic vice and corruption.

Progressivism included a range of disparate and overlapping efforts to reorder politi-cal, social, moral, and physical environments. Except for the brief existence of the Progres-sive Party in 1912, reformers did not have a tightly knit organization or a fixed agenda. Leaders were more likely to come from the middle class, but support came from the rich as well as the poor, depending on the issue. Of course, many Americans did not embrace pro-gressive principles, as conservative opponents continued to hold power and to fight against reform. Nevertheless, by 1917 a combination of voluntary changes and government inter-vention had cleared the way to regulate corporations, increase governmental efficiency, and promote social justice. Progressives succeeded in ameliorating conditions that might have produced violent revolution and more disorder. In time, they would bring their ideas to reordering international affairs.

Timeline of Events

1874	Woman's Christian Temperance Union founded
1889	Jane Addams and Ellen Starr establish Hull House
1890	National American Woman Suffrage Association formed
1895	Booker T. Washington delivers Atlanta address
1900	First commission form of government established in Galveston, Texas
1902	President Roosevelt settles coal strike
1903	National Women's Trade Union League founded
	Roosevelt orders male Indians on reservations to cut hair
1906	Meat Inspection Act and Pure Food and Drug Act
1908	Race riot in Springfield, Illinois
1909	National Association for the Advancement of Colored People founded
1910	President Taft fires Gifford Pinchot
1912	Roosevelt forms Progressive Party
	Children's Bureau of the Department of Commerce and Labor established
1913	Sixteenth Amendment (graduated income tax) ratified
	Federal Reserve System created
1914	Harrison Narcotics Control Act
	Federal Trade Commission created Clayton Antitrust Act
1916	Keating-Owen Act
	Workmen's Compensation Act
1919	Eighteenth Amendment (prohibition) ratified
1920	Nineteenth Amendment (women's vote) ratified

Key Terms

pragmatism, *638*

social gospel, *638*

muckrakers, *639*

Hull House, *640*

civic housekeeping, *640*

suffragists, *642*

Tuskegee Institute, *645*

National Association for the Advancement of Colored People (NAACP), *647*

Woman's Christian Temperance Union (WCTU), *649*

Hetch Hetchy valley, *656*

bully pulpit, *657*

Progressive Party, *660*

New Nationalism, *660*

New Freedom, *660*

Review & Relate

1. What late-nineteenth-century trends and developments influenced the progressives?

2. Why did the progressives focus on urban and industrial America?

3. What role did women play in the early-twentieth-century fight for social justice?

4. How did social reformers challenge discrimination against women, racial and ethnic minorities, and Indians?

5. What practices and behaviors of the poor did social control progressives find most alarming? Why?

6. What role did anti-immigrant sentiment play in motivating and shaping progressives' social control initiatives?

7. Who gained and who lost political influence as a result of progressive reforms?

8. How did a commitment to greater efficiency shape progressives' political and environmental initiatives?

9. How did the progressive agenda shape presidential politics in the first two decades of the twentieth century?

10. How did the policies of Presidents Roosevelt and Wilson apply to African Americans and Indians?

Women's Suffrage and Passage of the Nineteenth Amendment

▶ Evaluate the arguments for and against women's suffrage and explain how women won the adoption of the Nineteenth Amendment.

In 1919, Congress approved the Nineteenth Amendment, which prohibited states from denying citizens voting rights on account of sex. The amendment was ratified by the necessary three-quarters of the states in August 1920 and became part of the U.S. Constitution.

Women's suffrage advocates, such as Jane Addams, argued that voting was a natural extension of household duties to the civic arena (Source 19.6), The National American Woman Suffrage Association (NAWSA) led the movement by staging massive parades in New York City, Washington, D.C., Chicago, Los Angeles, and elsewhere. In addition, a militant group of suffragists broke from NAWSA and established the National Women's Party in 1916. They staged protests outside the White House, demanding that President Woodrow Wilson make the United States "safe for democracy" (Source 19.10).

In contrast, women were also among the most prominent anti-suffragists. Many were well-to-do white women who believed they would lose their moral influence in the home and the community by entering a political arena rife with graft and corruption. They also insisted that the vote would create masculinized women and feminized men stuck at home with crying babies (Source 19.10). Many male anti-suffragists were focused on how the change would affect men's lives. If women gained the vote, they feared they would outlaw the manufacture and sale of alcohol, close houses of prostitution, and interfere in other ways with male rituals and habits.

Some white suffragists, like other white progressives, relied on racist and nativist prejudices. Many southern white suffragists claimed that the votes of white women would outnumber those of black women, thereby countering the arguments of anti-suffragists who insisted that enfranchising women would open the door to black voters and threaten white supremacy (Source 19.8).

At the same time, African American women demanded equal voting rights. Most worked through separate black women's organizations, for example, the National Association of Colored Women, or worked within mixed-sex, racial justice organizations, such as the NAACP, to advance their cause. African American women claimed they were in particular need of the ballot because their communities suffered the most from the racial biases built into the political and legal systems and were most vulnerable to the police, judges, and public officials who enforced white supremacy (Source 19.7). In fact, their fears were well-founded. Even after ratification of the Nineteenth Amendment, African American and other women of color were denied the right to vote through poll taxes, literacy tests, and other restrictions instituted earlier against adult black-male citizens.

Jane Addams | "Why Women Should Vote," 1910

Jane Addams was part of a large group of women who campaigned for progressive reforms. Best known for her work with immigrants at Hull House in Chicago, Addams combined her concern for humanitarian reforms with advocacy of women's suffrage. In this essay first published in *Ladies Home Journal* and reprinted as a pamphlet, she argues that women need the right to vote to fulfill their duties as caretakers of the home and family, an idea called civic housekeeping.

. . . Public-spirited women who wish to use the ballot, as I know them, do not wish to do the work of men nor to take over men's affairs. They simply want an opportunity to do their own work and to take care of those affairs which naturally and historically belong to women, but which are constantly being overlooked and slighted in our political institutions. In a complex community like the modern city all points of view need to be represented; the resultants of diverse experiences need to be pooled if the community would make for sane and balanced progress. If it would meet fairly each problem as it arises, whether it be connected with a freight tunnel having to do largely with business men, or with the increasing death rate among children under five years of age, a problem in which women are vitally concerned, or with the question of more adequate streetcar transfers, in which both men and women might be said to be equally interested, it must not ignore the judgments of its entire adult population. To turn the administration of our civic affairs wholly over to men may mean that the American city will continue to push forward in its commercial and industrial development, and continue to lag behind in those things which make a City healthful and beautiful. After all, woman's traditional function has been to make her dwelling-place both clean and fair. Is that dreariness in city life . . . due to a withdrawal of one of the naturally co-operating forces? If women have in any sense been responsible for the gentler side of life which softens and blurs some of its harsher conditions, may they not have a duty to

perform in our American cities? In closing, may I recapitulate that if woman would fulfill her traditional responsibility to her own children; if she would educate and protect from danger factory children who must find their recreation on the street; if she would bring the cultural forces to bear upon our materialistic civilization; and if she would do it all with the dignity and directness fitting one who carries on her immemorial duties, then she must bring herself to the use of the ballot - that latest implement for self-government. May we not fairly say that American women need this implement in order to preserve the home?

Source: Jane Addams, "Why Women Should Vote," *Ladies Home Journal*, 7, January 1910, 21–22.

Adella Hunt Logan | "Colored Women as Voters," 1912

Adella Hunt Logan was born in Georgia during the Civil War. Her mother was a free woman of color and her father was a white plantation owner. A member of the National American Woman Suffrage Association, she campaigned for the franchise making similar arguments to those offered by Jane Addams. The following excerpt is from an essay she contributed to the *Crisis*, the journal of the NAACP. She died three years later before she could see the passage of the Nineteenth Amendment.

More and more colored women are studying public questions and civics. As they gain information and have experience in their daily vocations and in their efforts for human betterment they are convinced as many other women have long ago been convinced, that their efforts would be more telling if women had the vote.

The fashion of saying "I do not care to meddle with politics" is disappearing among the colored woman faster than most people think, for this same woman has learned that politics meddle constantly with her and hers.

Good women try always to do good housekeeping. Building inspectors, sanitary inspectors and food inspectors owe their positions to politics. Who then is so well informed as to how well these inspectors perform their duties as the women who live in inspected districts and inspected houses, and who buy food from inspected markets?

Adequate school facilities in city, village and plantation districts greatly concern the black mother. But without a vote she has no voice in educational legislation, and no power to see that her children secure their share of public school funds.

Negro parents admit that their own children are not all angels, but they know that the environments which they are hopeless to regulate increase misdemeanor and crime. They know, too that officers, as a rule, recognize few obligations to voteless citizens.

When colored juvenile delinquents are arraigned, few judges or juries feel bound to give them the clemency due to a neglected class. When sentence is pronounced on these mischievous youngsters, too often they are imprisoned with adult criminals and come out hardened and not helped by their punishment. When colored mothers ask for reform school for a long time they receive no answer. They must wait while they besiege their legislature. Having no vote they need not be feared or heeded. The "right of petition" is good; but it is much better when well voted in.

. . . A number of colored women are active members of the National [American] Woman Suffrage Association. They are well informed and are diligent in the spread of propaganda. Women who see that they need the vote see also that the vote needs them. Colored women feel keenly that they may help in civic betterment, and that their broadened interests in matters of good government may arouse the colored brother, who for various reasons has become too indifferent to his duties of citizenship. . . .

This much, however, is true now: the colored American believes in equal justice to all, regardless of race, color, creed or sex, and longs for the day when the United States shall indeed have a government of the people, for the people and by the people-even including the colored people.

Source: Adella Hunt Logan, "Colored Women as Voters," *Crisis*, 4, September 1912, 242–43.

Source 19.8

Belle Kearney │ "The South and Women's Suffrage," 1903

Carrie Belle Kearney was born on her family's plantation in Mississippi during the Civil War. She became a teacher and a social reformer, joining the Women's Christian Temperance Union and the National American Woman Suffrage Association. An avid exponent of white supremacy, Kearney wrote the excerpt below at a time when most southern states were passing poll tax and educational qualifications to vote. She was the first woman elected to the Mississippi Senate in 1924.

. . .The enfranchisement of women would insure immediate and durable white supremacy, honestly attained; for, upon unquestionable authority, it is stated that "in every Southern State but one, there are more educated women than all the illiterate voters, white and black, native and foreign, combined." As you probably know, of all the women in the South who can read and write, ten out of every eleven are white. When it comes to the proportion of property between the races, that of the white outweighs that of the black immeasurably. The South is slow to grasp the great fact that the enfranchisement of women would settle the race question in politics.

The civilization of the North is threatened by the influx of foreigners with their imported customs; by the greed of monopolistic wealth, and the unrest among the working classes; by the strength of the liquor traffic, and by encroachments upon religious belief.

Some day the North will be compelled to look to the South for redemption from these evils, on account of the purity of its Anglo-Saxon blood, the simplicity of its social and economic structure, the great advance in prohibitory law, and the maintenance of the sanctity of its faith, which has been kept inviolate. Just as surely as the North will be forced to turn to the South for the nation's salvation, just so surely will the South be compelled to look to its Anglo-Saxon women as the medium through which to retain the supremacy of the white race over the African.

I have heard it said in the South, "Oh, well, suffrage may be a good thing for women in other sections of the United States, but not here. Our women are different." How are they unlike those of their own sex elsewhere? They are certainly as intelligent as any upon the face of the earth; they have the same deep love for the home, the same devotion to their country.

"Oh, yes; but, you see, if the white woman were allowed to vote, the [N]egro woman would have the same privilege, and that would mean the humiliation of having to meet them at the polls on a basis of equality."

That difficulty would be settled by having separate polling places. When the ballot is given to the women of the South, you will find that these distinct voting precincts for the two races will be quickly established.

. . . The South, which has wrought so splendidly in the past, surely will measure up to its responsibility of taking the forward step of women's enfranchisement in order to render justice to its own firesides and to fix the status of the white race for future years.

Source: Belle Kearney, "The South and Woman Suffrage," *Woman's Journal,* April 4, 1903, 106–07.

Source 19.9

Rose Winslow | Prison Notes, 1917

Rose Winslow, born Ruza Wenclawska, had immigrated from Poland and joined the National Woman's Party (NWP), founded by Alice Paul. She, Paul, and other NWP members picketed the White House, were arrested for obstructing traffic, and were imprisoned in Virginia. She and her companions conducted a hunger strike, prompting prison officials to initiate harsh force-feedings. The following excerpt from Winslow's secret prison diary describes the horror of that experience as well as the strength and camaraderie of the activists.

The women are all so magnificent, so beautiful. Alice Paul is as thin as ever, pale and large-eyed. We have been in solitary for five weeks. There is nothing to tell but that the days go by somehow. I have felt quite feeble the last few days—faint, so that I could hardly get my hair brushed, my arms ached so. But to-day I'm well again. Alice Paul and I talk back and forth though we are at opposite ends of the building and a hall door also shuts us apart. But occasionally—thrills—we escape from behind our iron-barred doors and visit. Great laughter and rejoicing!

. . . Alice Paul is in the psychopathic ward. She dreaded forcible feeding frightfully, and I hate to think how she must be feeling. I had a nervous time of it, gasping a long time afterward, and my stomach rejecting during the process. I spent a bad, restless night, but otherwise I am all right. The poor soul who fed me got liberally besprinkled during the process.

I heard myself making the most hideous sounds, like an animal in pain, and thought how dreadful of me to make such horrible sounds . . . One feels so forsaken when one lies prone and people shove a pipe down one's stomach.

This morning but for an astounding tiredness, I am all right. I am waiting to see what happens when the President realizes that brutal bullying isn't quite a statesmanlike method for settling a demand for justice at home. At least, if men are supine enough to endure it, women—to their eternal glory—are not . . . I am really all right. If this continues very long perhaps I won't be. I am interested to see how long our so-called "splendid American men" will stand for this form of discipline.

All the officers here know we are making this hunger strike that women fighting for liberty may be considered political prisoners; we have told them. God knows we don't want other women ever to have to do this over again.

Source: "Prison Notes Smuggled to Friends from the District Jail," *The Suffragist*, December 5, 1917, 6–7.

America When Feminized, c. 1919–1920

Tennessee was the final state to ratify the Nineteenth Amendment before it went into effect in 1920. Although Tennessee allowed women to vote in party primary and municipal elections, critics wanted to uphold state's rights against national interference in their political affairs. This cartoon and flyer, created by the Southern Woman's League for Rejection of the Susan B. Anthony Amendment, humorously represents the view of anti-suffragists that the amendment would turn men into "sissies."

Source: Courtesy of the Tennessee State Library & Archives, Josephine A. Pearson Papers, 1860–1943, Accession Number 74-099

Courtesy of the Tennessee State Library and Archives, Josephine A. Pearson Papers, 1860–1943, Accession Number 74-099

Interpret the Evidence

1. How did Jane Addams (Source 19.6) use the conception of women's traditional household role to argue for the extension of the suffrage?
2. With respect to black women, how does Adella Hunt Logan's case for women's suffrage (Source 19.7) compare to that of Jane Addams?
3. Contrast Belle Kearney's arguments for women's suffrage (Source 19.8) with those of Adella Hunt Logan's (Source 19.7).
4. What were the effects of imprisonment on Rose Winslow's resolve to fight for the suffrage (Source 19.9)? How did her tactics differ from those of Addams (Source 19.6), Logan (Source 19.7), and Kearney (Source 19.8)?
5. Why did Tennessee women oppose the Nineteenth Amendment (Source 19.10)? How might Jane Addams (Source 19.6) have responded to them?

Put It In Context

How did women's suffrage reform relate to other aspects of progressivism?

Empire, Wars, and Pandemic

1898–1919

Detail from Cartoon "A Bigger Job than He Thought For," 1899

This image portrays a cartoon from a newspaper in 1899 opposing the war in the Philippines. The annexation of the island after the War of 1898 led to a rebellion against U.S. military occupation by the Filipinos, a bloody insurrection that lasted for three years. ▶ To learn more about this primary source, see Source 20.3 on page 685.

Granger

After reading this chapter you will be able to:

- Analyze the reasons behind U.S. imperialism in the 1890s and early twentieth century.

- Compare the interventions in Cuba and the Philippines and their effects on U.S. attitudes toward nation building.

- Compare Roosevelt's "big stick" diplomacy, Taft's dollar diplomacy, and Wilson's moral diplomacy and identify their benefits and drawbacks.

- Summarize the reasons for U.S. intervention in World War I and evaluate their relative importance.

- Evaluate the domestic effects of World War I on U.S. economics, culture, politics, and public health.

Comparing American Histories

Alfred Thayer Mahan came from a military family. Born in 1840, he grew up in West Point, New York, where his father served as dean of the faculty at the U.S. Military Academy. Seeking to emerge from his father's shadow, Alfred attended the U.S. Naval Academy, receiving his commission in 1861, just as the Civil War was getting under way. His wartime experience convinced him that the navy needed a dramatic overhaul.

After the war, Captain Mahan built his reputation as a military historian and strategist at the U.S. Naval

(left) **Alfred Thayer Mahan** Library of Congress, Prints and Photographs Division [LC-DIG-ggbain-17956]

(right) **José Martí** Library of Congress, Prints and Photographs Division, photograph by Harris & Ewing [LC-DIG-hec-08533]

War College. In 1890 he published *The Influence of Sea Power upon History,* in which he argued that great imperial powers in modern history had succeeded because they possessed strong navies and merchant marines. In his view, sea power had allowed these nations to defeat their enemies, conquer territories, and establish colonies. Appearing at a time when European nations were embarking on a new round of empire building, this book had an enormous influence on U.S. imperialists, including Theodore Roosevelt. Mahan's work reinforced the belief of men like Roosevelt that the long-term prospects of the United States depended on the acquisition of strategic outposts in Asia and the Caribbean that could guarantee U.S. access to overseas markets.

As the economic and strategic importance of the Caribbean grew in the minds of imperial strategists such as Mahan and Roosevelt, the Cuban freedom fighter **José Martí** developed a very different vision of the region's future. Born in 1853, Martí got involved in the fight for Cuban independence from Spain as a teenager. In 1869, at age seventeen, he was arrested for protest activities during a revolutionary uprising against Spain. Sentenced to six years of hard labor, Martí was released after six months and was forced into exile. He returned to Cuba in 1878, only to be arrested and deported again the following year.

Martí settled in the United States, and with other Cuban exiles, he continued to promote Cuban independence and the establishment of a democratic republic under the banner of the Cuban Revolutionary Party. He conceived of the idea of Cuba Libre (Free Cuba) not just as a struggle for political independence but also as a social revolution that would erase unfair distinctions based on race and class.

When Cubans once again rebelled against Spain in 1895, Martí returned to Cuba to fight alongside his comrades. On May 19, only three months after he had returned to Cuba, Martí died in battle. Cuba ultimately won its independence from Spain, but Martí's vision of Cuba Libre was only partially realized. In 1898 the United States intervened on the side of the Cuban rebels, guaranteeing their victory but not their freedom. ■

By comparing the American histories of Alfred Thayer Mahan and José Martí, we see disparate understandings of the United States' relationship with the rest of the world. Up until the late nineteenth century, most Americans associated colonialism with the European powers and saw overseas expansion as incompatible with U.S. values. In this context, they shared Martí's point of view. The imperialism espoused by Mahan and others therefore represented a reversal of traditional U.S. attitudes. Supporters of U.S. imperialism saw the acquisition and control of overseas territories, by force if necessary, as essential to the protection of U.S. interests. This perspective would come to dominate U.S. foreign policy in the early twentieth century. Theodore Roosevelt and Woodrow Wilson, progressive presidents who sanctioned intervention in economic and moral issues at home, supported vigorous intervention in world affairs. Just as they used government power to institute economic, political, and social reforms at home, so too did many progressives advocate U.S. intervention to reshape world affairs. Although Roosevelt and Wilson differed in style and approach, in foreign affairs they asserted America's right to use its power to secure order and thwart revolution wherever U.S. interests were seen to be threatened. Having become a major power on the world stage in the early twentieth century, the United States chose to enter World War I, in which rival European alliances battled for imperial domination. The end of the war did not bring peace; indeed, the war helped spread a worldwide influenza pandemic.

The **Awakening** of **Imperialism**

In the decades following the Civil War, the U.S. government concentrated on settling the western territories, decimating Native Americans, and extracting the region's resources. In many ways, westward expansion and the conquest of Indians in the nineteenth century foreshadowed international expansion. Arguments based on racial superiority and the nation's duty to expand became justifications for expansion in North America and overseas. By the end of the nineteenth century sweeping economic, cultural, and social changes led many in the United States to conclude that the time had come for the country to assert its power beyond its borders. In 1893, the influential U.S. historian Frederick Jackson Turner argued that the ending of the frontier necessitated a "wider field" for the "exercise [of] American energy" and reinvigorating the nation's political, economic, and cultural strengths. Convinced of the argument for empire advanced by Mahan and other imperialists, U.S. officials led the nation in a burst of overseas expansion from 1898 to 1904, in which the United States acquired Guam, Hawaii, the Philippines, and Puerto Rico; established a protectorate in Cuba; and exercised force to build a canal through Panama. These gains paved the way for subsequent U.S. intervention in Haiti, the Dominican Republic, and Nicaragua.

The Economics of Expansion. The industrialization of the United States and the growth of corporate capitalism stimulated imperialist desires in the late nineteenth century. Throughout its early history, the United States had sought overseas markets for exports. However, the importance of exports to the U.S. economy increased dramatically in the second half of the nineteenth century, as industrialization gained momentum. In 1870 U.S. exports totaled $500 million. By 1910 the value of U.S. exports had increased threefold to $1.7 billion (Figure 20.1).

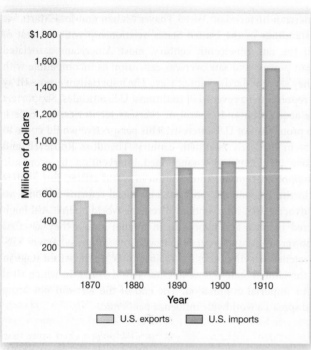

FIGURE 20.1   U.S. Exports and Imports, 1870–1910

As U.S. industrial power expanded at the end of the nineteenth century, exports increased dramatically. Between 1870 and 1910, U.S. exports more than tripled. Imports rose as well but were restrained by protective tariffs. How did the desire for overseas trade influence U.S. expansion overseas?

The bulk of U.S. exports went to the developed markets of Europe and Canada. Although the less economically advanced nations of Latin America and Asia did not have the same ability to buy U.S. products, businessmen still considered these regions — especially China, with its large population — as future markets for U.S. industries.

The desire to expand foreign markets remained a steady feature of U.S. business interests. The fear that the domestic market for manufactured goods was shrinking gave this expansionist hunger greater urgency. The fluctuating business cycle of boom and bust that characterized the economy in the 1870s and 1880s reached its peak in the depression of the 1890s. The social unrest that accompanied this depression worried business and political leaders about the stability of the country. The way to sustain prosperity and contain radicalism, many businessmen agreed, was to find foreign markets for U.S. goods. Senator William Frye of Maine argued, "We must have the market [of China] or we shall have revolution."

Similar commercial ambitions led many in the United States to covet Hawaii. U.S. missionaries first visited the Hawaiian Islands in 1820. As missionaries tried to convert native peoples to Christianity, U.S. businessmen sought to establish plantations on the islands, especially to grow sugarcane. In exchange for duty-free access to the U.S. sugar market, white Hawaiians signed an agreement in 1887 that granted the United States exclusive rights to a naval base at Pearl Harbor in Honolulu.

The growing influence of white sugar planters on the islands alarmed native Hawaiians. In 1891 Queen Liliuokalani, a strong nationalist leader who voiced the slogan "Hawaii for the Hawaiians," sought to increase the power of the indigenous peoples she governed, at the expense of the sugar growers. In 1893 white plantation owners, with the cooperation of the U.S. ambassador to Hawaii and 150 U.S. marines, overthrew the queen's government. Once in command of the government, they entered into a treaty of annexation with the

United States. However, President Grover Cleveland opposed annexation and withdrew the treaty. Nevertheless, planters remained in power and waited for a suitable opportunity to seek annexation.

Cultural Justifications for Imperialism.
Imperialists linked overseas expansion to economic considerations but race was also a key component in their arguments for empire. Many in the United States and western Europe deemed themselves superior to non-white peoples of Latin America, Asia, and Africa. Buttressing their arguments with racist studies claiming to demonstrate scientifically the "racial superiority" of white Protestants, imperialists asserted a "natural right" of conquest and world domination.

Imperialists added an ethical dimension to this ideology by contending that "higher civilizations" had a duty to uplift inferior nations. In *Our Country* (1885), the Congregationalist minister Josiah Strong proclaimed the superiority of the Anglo-Saxon, or white northern European, race and the responsibility of the United States to spread its Christian way of life throughout the world. Secular intellectuals, such as historian John Fiske, praised the English race for settling the United States and predicted that English society and culture would become "predominant" in the less civilized parts of the globe.

As in Hawaii, Christian missionaries served as foot soldiers for the advancing U.S. commercial empire. In fact, there was often a clear connection between religious and commercial interests. For example, in 1895 industrialists John D. Rockefeller Jr. and Cyrus McCormick created the World Student Christian Federation, which dispatched more than five thousand young missionaries throughout the world, many of them women. China became a magnet for U.S. missionary activity. Many Americans hoped that, under missionary supervision, the Chinese would become consumers of both U.S. ideas and U.S. products.

Gender and Empire.
Gender anxieties provided additional motivation for U.S. imperialism. In the late nineteenth century, with the Civil War long over, many in the United States worried that the rising generation of U.S. men lacked opportunities to test and strengthen their manhood. In 1897 Mississippi congressman John Sharp Williams lamented the waning of "the dominant spirit which controlled in this Republic [from 1776 to 1865] . . . one of honor, glory, chivalry, and patriotism." The depression of the 1890s hit working-class men hard, causing them to question their self-worth as they lost the ability to support their families. By embracing the imperialist project, they would regain their manly honor.

Explore ▶

See Source 20.1 for part of Kipling's poem in support of white men's imperial ambitions in the Philippines.

The growing presence of women as political activists in campaigns for suffrage and moral, humanitarian, and governmental reforms threatened male identity. Concerned over the feminization of politics, Alfred Thayer Mahan warned that women's suffrage would undermine the nation's military security because women lacked the will to use physical force. He asserted that giving women the vote would destroy the "constant practice of the past ages by which to men are assigned the outdoor rough action of life and to women that indoor sphere which we call the family."

Males in the United States could reassert their manhood by adopting a militant spirit. Known as **jingoists**, war enthusiasts such as Theodore Roosevelt and Alfred Thayer Mahan saw war as necessary to the development of a generation of men who could meet the challenges of the modern age. "No greater danger could befall civilization than the

Guided Primary Source Analysis

Rudyard Kipling | "The White Man's Burden," 1899

The English writer Rudyard Kipling was a leading exponent of British imperialism. His famous poem "The White Man's Burden" originally appeared in the popular U.S. magazine *McClure's* with the subtitle "The United States and the Philippine Islands." Given this subtitle, the poem can be seen as a direct appeal to U.S. men to join their British counterparts in the global imperial project.

Source 20.1

Take up the White Man's burden—
Send forth the best ye breed—
Go, bind your sons to exile
To serve your captives' need;
To wait, in heavy harness,
On fluttered folk and wild—   *→ passive*
Your new-caught sullen peoples,   *agressivness*
Half devil and half child. . . .

What does Kipling's characterization of the colonized people suggest about his point of view?

Take up the White Man's burden—
The savage wars of peace—
Fill full the mouth of Famine,   *arrogance*
And bid the sickness cease;
And when your goal is nearest   *heroism*
(The end for others sought)   *and*
Watch sloth and heathen folly   *duty*
Bring all your hope to nought. . . .

According to Kipling, why is it appropriate to describe imperialism as a "burden"?

What does the reward for colonizers suggest about his purpose in writing this poem?

Take up the White Man's burden!
Have done with childish days—
The lightly-proffered laurel,
The easy ungrudged praise:
Comes now, to search your manhood
Through all the thankless years,
Cold, edged with dear-bought wisdom,
The judgment of your peers.

Source: Rudyard Kipling, "The White Man's Burden," *McClure's Magazine*, February 1899, 290–91.

▌ **Put It in Context**

How was the notion of "the white man's burden" used to justify expansion and annexation?

disappearance of the warlike spirit (I dare say war) among civilized men," Mahan asserted. "There are too many barbarians still in the world." Mahan and Roosevelt promoted naval power, and by 1900 the U.S. fleet contained seventeen battleships and six armored cruisers, making it the third most powerful navy in the world, up from twelfth place in 1880. Having built a powerful navy, the United States would soon find opportunities to use it.

Review & Relate

∎ What role did economic developments play in prompting calls for a U.S. empire? What role did social and cultural developments play?

∎ Why did the United States embark on building an empire in the 1890s and not decades earlier?

The **War** with **Spain**

The United States went to war with Spain over Cuba in 1898 because U.S. policymakers decided that Cuban independence from Spain was in the United States' economic and strategic interests. Victory over Spain, however, brought the United States much more than control over Cuba. In the peace negotiations following the war, the United States acquired a significant portion of Spain's overseas empire, turning the United States into a major imperial power. To Americans, the war has traditionally been called the Spanish-American War, but this term fails to take into account the significant role played by the Cuban people and subsequently by the Filipino people who were also under Spanish rule.

Revolution in Cuba. The Cuban War for Independence began in 1895 around the concept of *Cubanidad*—pride of nation. José Martí envisioned that this war of national liberation from Spain would provide land to impoverished peasants and offer genuine racial equality for the large Afro-Cuban population that had been liberated from slavery less than a decade earlier, in 1886. "Our goal," the revolutionary leader declared in 1892, "is not so much a mere political change as a good, sound, and just and equitable system." Black Cubans, such as Antonio Maceo, flocked to the revolutionary cause and constituted a significant portion of the senior ranks in the rebel army.

The insurgents fought a brilliant guerrilla war. Facing some 200,000 Spanish troops, 50,000 rebels ground them down in a war of attrition. Within eighteen months, the rebellion had spread across the island and garnered the support of all segments of the Cuban population. By the end of 1897, the Spanish government offered the rebels a series of reforms that would give the island home rule within the empire but not independence. Sensing victory, the insurgents held out for total separation to realize their vision of **Cuba Libre**, an independent Cuba with social and racial equality.

The revolutionaries had every reason to feel confident as they wore down Spanish troops. First, they had help from the climate. One-quarter of Spanish soldiers had contracted yellow fever, malaria, and other tropical illnesses and remained confined to hospitals. Second, mounting a successful counterinsurgency would have required far more troops than Spain could spare. Its forces were spread too thin around the globe to keep the empire intact. Finally, antiwar sentiment was mounting in Spain, and on January 12, 1898 Spanish troops mutinied in Havana. Speaking for many, a former president of Spain

Cuban Revolutionary Soldiers   Under the command of General Maximo Gómez, these Cuban soldiers fought against Spain in 1898. Gómez waged guerrilla warfare for Cuban independence from Spain before the United States entered the war. His army consisted of numerous Afro-Cubans, whose race troubled white U.S. commanders when they occupied Cuba. Granger

asserted: "Spain is exhausted. She must withdraw her troops and recognize Cuban independence before it is too late."

The War of 1898. With the Cuban insurgents on the verge of victory, President William McKinley favored military intervention as a way to increase U.S. control of postwar Cuba. By intervening before the Cubans won on their own, the United States could determine the postwar relationship and protect its vital interests in the Caribbean, including the private property rights of U.S. landowners in Cuba.

The U.S. press helped build support for U.S. intervention by framing the war as a matter of U.S. honor. William Randolph Hearst's *New York Journal* competed with Joseph Pulitzer's *New York World* to see which could provide the most lurid coverage of Spanish atrocities. Known disparagingly as **yellow journalism**, these sensationalist newspaper accounts aroused jingoistic outrage against Spain.

On February 15, 1898, the battleship *Maine*, anchored in Havana harbor, exploded, killing 266 U.S. sailors. Newspapers in the United States blamed Spain. The *World* shouted the rallying cry "Remember the *Maine*! To hell with Spain!" Assistant Secretary of the Navy Theodore Roosevelt seconded this sentiment by denouncing the explosion as a Spanish "act of treachery." Why the Spaniards would choose to blow up the *Maine* and provoke war with the United States while already losing to Cuba remained unanswered, but the incident was enough to turn U.S. opinion toward war.

On April 11, 1898, McKinley asked Congress to declare war against Spain. The declaration included an amendment proposed by Senator Henry M. Teller of Colorado declaring that Cuba "ought to be free and independent." Yet in endorsing independence, the war proclamation asserted the right of the United States to remain involved in Cuban affairs until it had achieved "pacification." On April 21, the United States officially went to war with Spain. In going to war, McKinley embarked on an imperialistic course that had been building since the early 1890s. The president signaled the broader expansionist concerns behind the war when, shortly after it began, he successfully steered a Hawaiian annexation treaty through Congress.

It was fortunate for the United States that the Cuban insurgents had seriously weakened Spanish forces before the U.S. fighters arrived. The U.S. army lacked sufficient strength to conquer Cuba on its own, and McKinley had to mobilize some 200,000 National Guard troops and assorted volunteers. Theodore Roosevelt resigned from his post as assistant secretary of the navy and organized his own regiment, called "Rough Riders." U.S. forces lacked battle experience; supplies were inadequate; their uniforms were not suited for the hot, humid climate of a Cuban summer; and the soldiers did not have immunity from tropical diseases.

African American soldiers, who made up about one-quarter of the troops, encountered racial discrimination and violence. As more and more black troops arrived in southern U.S. ports for deployment to Cuba, they faced increasingly hostile crowds. In Tampa, Florida, where troops gathered from all over the country to be transported to Cuba, racial tensions exploded on June 8. Intoxicated white soldiers from Ohio grabbed a two-year-old black boy from his mother and used him for target practice, shooting a bullet through his shirtsleeve. In retaliation, African American soldiers stormed into the streets and exchanged gunfire with whites, leaving three whites and twenty-seven black soldiers wounded.

African American Soldiers and the War of 1898 This photograph shows a group portrait of African American soldiers in Company E, 9th United States Volunteer Infantry who were sent to Cuba in the war against Spain. Black soldiers were recruited because it was mistakenly believed that they were "immune" to tropical diseases such as yellow fever, which killed white soldiers in Cuba. Black soldiers were organized in segregated units under the command of white officers, such as the one on the left side of the photograph. Library of Congress, LC-DIG-ppmsca-54528

Despite military inexperience, logistical problems, and racial tensions, the United States quickly defeated the weakened Spanish military, and the war was over four months after it began. During this war, 460 U.S. soldiers died in combat, while more than 5,000 lost their lives to disease. The subsequent peace treaty ended Spanish rule in Cuba, ceded Puerto Rico and the Pacific island of Guam to the United States, and recognized U.S. occupation of the Philippines until the two countries could arrange a final settlement. U.S. foreign-policy strategists could now construct the empire that Mahan had envisioned.

The Pacification of Cuba. Although Congress had adopted the **Teller Amendment** in 1898 pledging Cuba's independence from Spain, President McKinley and his supporters insisted that Cuban self-rule would come only after pacification. Racial prejudice and cultural chauvinism blinded Americans to the contributions Cubans had made to defeat Spain. One U.S. officer reported to the *New York Times*: "The typical Cuban I encountered was a treacherous, lying, cowardly, thieving, worthless half-breed mongrel, born of a mongrel spawn of [Spain], crossed upon the fetches of darkest Africa and aboriginal America." José Martí may have been fighting for racial equality, but the U.S. government certainly was not.

U.S. officials presumed that Cuba was unfit to be independent and kept the island under U.S. military occupation until 1902. Cuba's transition to self-rule came with the adoption of a governing document based on the U.S. Constitution. However, the Cuban constitution came with strings attached. In March 1901, Congress passed the **Platt Amendment**, introduced by Senator Orville Platt of Connecticut, which limited Cuban sovereignty. The amendment prohibited the Cuban government from signing treaties with other nations without U.S. consent, permitted the United States to intervene in Cuba to preserve independence and remove threats to economic stability, and leased Guantánamo Bay to the United States as a naval base. U.S. officials pressured Cuban leaders to incorporate the Platt Amendment into their constitution. When U.S. occupation ended in 1902, Cuba was not fully independent.

The Philippine War. Before invading Cuba, the United States had won a significant battle against Spain on the other side of the world. At the outset of the war, the U.S. Pacific Fleet, under the command of Commodore George Dewey, attacked Spanish forces in their colony of the Philippines. Dewey defeated the Spanish flotilla in Manila Bay on May 1, 1898. Two and a half months later, U.S. troops followed up with an invasion of Manila, and Spanish forces promptly surrendered (Map 20.1).

While pacifying Cuba, the U.S. government had to decide what action to take in the Philippines. Imperialists viewed U.S. control of the islands as an important step forward in the quest for entry into the China market. The Philippines could serve as a naval station for the merchant marine and the navy to safeguard potential trade with the Asian mainland. Also, President McKinley believed that if the United States did not act, another European power would take Spain's place, something he thought would be "bad business and deplorable."

With this in mind, McKinley decided to annex the Philippines. As with Cuba, McKinley and most U.S. citizens believed that nonwhite Filipinos were not yet capable of self-government. Thus, McKinley set out "to educate the Filipinos, and uplift and Christianize them." As was often the case with imperialism, assumptions about racial superiority were used as justification for the pursuit of economic and strategic advantage.

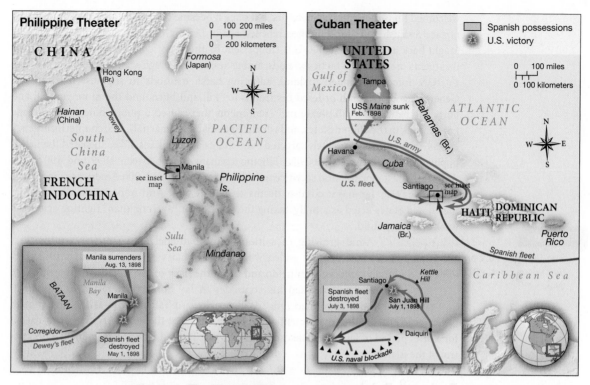

MAP 20.1 The War of 1898

The United States and Spain fought the War of 1898 (sometimes referred to as the Spanish-American War) on two fronts — the Philippines and Cuba. Naval forces led by Commodore George Dewey made the difference in the U.S. victory by defeating the Spaniards first in Manila Bay and then off the coast of Cuba. In Cuba, rebels had seriously weakened the Spanish military before U.S. ground troops secured victory.

The president's plan ran into vigorous opposition. Anti-imperialists in Congress took a strong stand against annexing the Philippines. Their cause drew support from such prominent Americans as industrialist Andrew Carnegie, social reformer Jane Addams, writer Mark Twain, and labor organizer Samuel Gompers, all of whom joined the **Anti-Imperialist League**, founded in November 1898. Progressives like Addams who were committed to humanitarian reforms at home questioned whether the United States should exploit colonial people overseas. Union leaders feared that annexation would prompt the migration of cheap laborers into the country and undercut wages. Others worried about the financial costs of supporting military forces across the Pacific. Most anti-imperialists had racial reasons for rejecting the treaty. Like imperialists, they considered Asians to be inferior to Europeans. In fact, many anti-imperialists held an even dimmer view of the capabilities of people of color than did their opponents, rejecting the notion that Filipinos could be "civilized" under U.S. tutelage.

Despite this opposition, McKinley and the imperialists won out. Approval of the treaty annexing the Philippines in 1898 marked the beginning of problems for the United States. As in Cuba, a popular revolt had preceded U.S. occupation. At first, Filipino people welcomed the Americans as liberators, but once it became clear that U.S. rule would simply replace Spanish rule, the Filipinos rebelled again. Led by Emilio Aguinaldo, rebel forces fought back against the 70,000 U.S. troops sent by this latest colonial power. The Filipino insurgents used guerilla tactics of raids, ambushes, and sabotage against the U.S. army.

U.S. forces responded in kind, adopting harsh methods to suppress the uprising. General Jacob H. Smith ordered his troops to "kill and burn, and the more you kill and burn, the better you will please me" (sentiments that caused a public outcry when made known back in the United States, and which led to his court-martial). U.S. counterinsurgency efforts, which indiscriminately targeted combatants and civilians alike, alienated the native population. An estimated 200,000 Filipino civilians died between 1899 and 1902. The Americans' taste for war and sacrifice quickly waned, as nearly 5,000 Americans died in the Philippine War, far more combat deaths than in Cuba. Anti-imperialists claimed that the United States acted as a bully, taking the position of "a strong man" fighting against "a weak and puny child."

Explore ▸

See Sources 20.2 and 20.3 for two views on the Philippine War.

Amid growing casualties on the battlefield and antiwar sentiment at home, the conflict ended with a U.S. military victory. In March 1901, U.S. forces captured Aguinaldo and broke the back of the rebellion. Exhausted, the Filipino leader asked his comrades to lay down their arms. In July 1901, McKinley appointed Judge William Howard Taft of Ohio as the first civilian governor to oversee the government of the Philippines. For the next forty-five years, except for a brief period of Japanese rule during World War II, the United States remained in control of the islands.

Review & Relate

▍ Why did the United States go to war with Spain in 1898?

▍ In what ways did the War of 1898 mark a turning point in the relationship between the United States and the rest of the world?

Extending U.S. Imperialism, 1899–1913

The War of 1898 turned the United States into an imperial nation. Once the war was over, and with its newly acquired empire in place, the United States sought to achieve even greater global power. President Theodore Roosevelt and his successors achieved Captain Mahan's dream of building a Central American canal and wielded U.S. military and financial might in the Caribbean with little restraint. At the same time, the United States took a more active role in Asian affairs.

Theodore Roosevelt and "Big Stick" Diplomacy.

After President McKinley was assassinated in 1901, Vice President Theodore Roosevelt succeeded him as president. A progressive reformer at home, Roosevelt advocated using military power to protect U.S. commercial and strategic interests as well as to preserve international order. "It is contemptible for a nation, as for an individual," Roosevelt instructed Congress, "[to] proclaim its purposes, or to take positions which are ridiculous if unsupported by potential force, and then to refuse to provide this force." This Progressive Era interventionist, inspired by Captain Mahan's writings, welcomed his nation's new role as an international policeman.

To fulfill his international agenda, Roosevelt sought to demonstrate U.S. might and preserve order in the Caribbean and Central and South America. The building of the Panama Canal provides a case in point. Mahan considered a canal across Central America as vital because it would provide faster access to Asian markets and improve the U.S. navy's ability to patrol two oceans effectively. The United States took a step toward realizing Mahan's goal in 1901, when it signed the Hay-Pauncefote Treaty with Britain, granting the United States the right to construct such a canal. A French company had already begun construction at a site in Panama and had completed two-fifths of the operation; when it ran out of money, it sold its holdings to the United States.

Before the United States could resume building the canal, it had to negotiate with the South American country of Colombia, which controlled Panama. Secretary of State John Hay and Colombian representatives reached an agreement highly favorable to the United States, which the Colombian government refused to ratify. When Colombia held out for a higher price, Roosevelt accused the Colombians of being "utterly incapable of keeping order" in Panama and declared that transit across Panama was vital to world commerce. In 1903 the president supported a pro-U.S. uprising by sending warships into the harbor of Panama City, an action that prevented the Colombians from quashing the insurrection. Roosevelt signed a treaty with the new government of Panama granting the United States the right to build the canal and exercise "power and authority" over it. In 1914, under U.S. control, the Panama Canal opened to sea traffic.

With the United States controlling Cuba, the Panama Canal, and Puerto Rico, President Roosevelt intended to deter any threats to U.S. power in the region. The economic instability of Central American and Caribbean nations gave Roosevelt the opportunity to brandish what he called a "big stick" to keep these countries in check and prevent intervention by European powers also interested in the area. In 1904, when the government of the Dominican Republic was teetering on the edge of bankruptcy and threatened to default on $22 million in European loans, Roosevelt sprang into action. He announced U.S. opposition to any foreign intervention to reclaim debts, a position that echoed the principles of the Monroe Doctrine, which in 1823 proclaimed that the United States would not tolerate outside intervention in the Western Hemisphere. Roosevelt added his own corollary to the Monroe Doctrine by affirming the right of the United States to intervene in the internal affairs of any country in Latin America or the Caribbean that displayed "chronic wrong-doing" and could not preserve order and manage its own affairs. The **Roosevelt Corollary** proclaimed that the countries of Central America and the Caribbean had to behave according to U.S. wishes or face American military invasion.

Opening the Door in China.

Roosevelt displayed U.S. power in other parts of the world. His major concern was protecting the **Open Door** policy in China that his predecessor McKinley had engineered to secure naval access to the Chinese market. By 1900 European powers had already dominated foreign access to Chinese markets, leaving scant room for newcomers. When the United States sent 2,500 troops to China in August 1900 to help quell a nationalist rebellion against foreign involvement known as the Boxer uprising, European competitors in return were compelled to allow the United States free trade access to China.

In 1904 the Russian invasion of the northern Chinese province of Manchuria prompted the Japanese to attack the Russian fleet. Roosevelt admired Japanese military prowess, but he worried that if Japan succeeded in driving the Russians out of the area, it would cause "a real

Comparative Primary Source Analysis

Fighting in the Philippines

After defeating Spain, the United States annexed the Philippines. Despite considerable U.S. opposition to annexation, President William McKinley declared it his duty to uplift an "uncivilized" people (Source 20.2). However, Filipino rebels rejected U.S. occupation and continued their struggle for independence. As the fighting wore on, many Americans turned against the war. In the cartoon, penned by William Carson of the *Saturday Globe* (Utica, New York), in Source 20.3, Uncle Sam is saying to a Filipino insurgent: "Behave, You Fool! Durn Me, If I Ain't Most Sorry I Undertook to Rescue You."

Source 20.2

President McKinley Defends His Decision, 1903

When I next realized that the Philippines had dropped into our laps I confess I did not know what to do with them. . . . And one night late it came to me this way . . . 1) That we could not give them back to Spain—that would be cowardly and dishonorable; 2) that we could not turn them over to France and Germany—our commercial rivals in the Orient—that would be bad business and discreditable; 3) that we [could] not leave them to themselves—they are unfit for self-government—and they would soon have anarchy and misrule over there worse than Spain's wars; and 4) that there was nothing left for us to do but to take them all, and to educate the Filipinos, and uplift and civilize and Christianize them, and by God's grace do the very best we could by them, as our fellow-men for whom Christ also died.

Source: General James Rusling, "Interview with President William McKinley," *Christian Advocate*, January 22, 1903, 17.

shifting of equilibrium as far as the white races are concerned." To prevent that from happening, Roosevelt convened a peace conference in Portsmouth, New Hampshire, in 1905. Under the agreement reached at the conference, Japan received control over Korea and parts of Manchuria but pledged to support the United States' Open Door policy. In 1906 the president sent sixteen U.S. battleships on a trip around the globe in a show of force meant to demonstrate that the United States was serious about taking its place as a premier world power.

When Roosevelt's secretary of war, William Howard Taft, became president (1909–1913), he continued his predecessor's foreign policy with slight modification. Proclaiming that he

Source 20.3

William Carson | "A Bigger Job Than He Thought For," 1899

A BIGGER JOB THAN HE THOUGHT FOR.
UNCLE SAM—Behave, You Fool! Durn Me, If I Ain't Most Sorry I Undertook to Rescue You.

Granger

Interpret the Evidence

1. As represented by this cartoon, why did Americans turn against the Philippines War?
2. Compare the views presented here about Filipinos. What other sources might you consult to understand American views about Filipinos in this period?

Put It in Context

What role did annexation of the Philippines play in U.S. imperialism?

would rather substitute "dollars for bullets," Taft encouraged private bankers to invest money in the Caribbean and Central America, a policy known as **dollar diplomacy**.

Yet Taft did not rely on financial influence alone. He dispatched more than 2,000 U.S. troops to the region to guarantee economic stability. In 1909 when rebels in Nicaragua threatened. U.S. fruit and mining companies in the nation, Taft sent in U.S. marines to police the country, deter further uprisings, and oversee the economy. They remained there for another twenty-five years, thereby placing Nicaragua under U.S. "protection."

Boxer Uprising　In 1900 the Society of Righteous and Harmonious Fists, a Chinese militaristic and secret society known as the Boxers, attacked foreign diplomatic offices in Beijing to expel outsiders. This illustration from Hunan province portrays the Boxers killing foreigners and burning Christian books. The Boxers viewed Christian missionaries as cultural enemies. A coalition of multinational forces crushed the uprising. Kharbine-Tapabor/Shutterstock

Review & Relate

- How did the United States assert its influence and control over Latin America in the early twentieth century?

- How did U.S. policies in Latin America mirror U.S. policies in Asia?

Wilson and American Foreign Policy, 1912–1917

When Woodrow Wilson became president in 1913, he pledged to open a new chapter in the United States' relations with Latin America and the rest of the world. Disdaining power politics and the use of force, Wilson vowed to place diplomacy and moral persuasion at the center of U.S. foreign policy. Despite Wilson's stated commitment to the peaceful resolution of international issues, during his presidency the U.S. military intervened repeatedly in Latin America, and U.S. troops fought on European soil in the global conflict that contemporaries called the Great War.

Diplomacy and War. Though he voiced a preference for moral diplomacy, Wilson preserved the U.S. sphere of influence in the Caribbean using much the same methods as had Roosevelt and Taft. To protect U.S. investments, the president sent marines to Haiti in 1915, to the Dominican Republic in 1916, and to Cuba in 1917.

The most serious challenge to Wilson's diplomacy came in Mexico. The **Mexican revolution** in 1911 spawned a civil war among various insurgent factions. The resulting instability threatened U.S. interests in Mexico, particularly oil. When Mexicans refused to accept Wilson's demands to install leaders he considered "good men," Wilson withdrew diplomatic recognition from Mexico. In a disastrous attempt to influence Mexican politics, Wilson sent the U.S. navy to the port of Veracruz on April 22, 1914, leading to a bloody clash that killed 19 Americans and 126 Mexicans. The situation worsened after Wilson first supported and then turned against one of the rebel competitors for power in Mexico, General Francisco "Pancho" Villa. In response to this betrayal, Villa and 1,500 troops rode across the border and attacked the town of Columbus, New Mexico. In July 1916, Wilson ordered General John Pershing to send 10,000 army troops into Mexico in an attempt to capture Villa. The operation was a complete failure that further angered Mexican leaders and confirmed their sense that Wilson had no respect for Mexican sovereignty.

At the same time as the situation in Mexico was deteriorating, a more serious problem was developing in Europe. On June 28, 1914, a Serbian nationalist, intending to strike a blow against Austria-Hungary, assassinated the Austrian archduke Franz Ferdinand in Sarajevo, the capital of the province of Bosnia. This terrorist attack plunged Europe into a world war. On August 4, 1914, the Central Powers—Germany, the Ottoman empire, and Austria-Hungary—officially declared war against the Allies—Great Britain, France, and Russia. (Italy joined the Allies in 1915.)

For the first three years of the Great War, Wilson kept the United States neutral. Though privately he supported the British, the president urged Americans to remain "impartial in thought as well as action." Peace activists sought to keep Wilson to his word. In 1915 women reformers and suffragists such as Jane Addams and Carrie Chapman Catt organized the Women's Peace Party to keep the United States out of the war.

Explore ▶

Read Sources 20.4 and 20.5 for two historians' arguments about Wilson's handling of neutrality in World War I.

Wilson faced two key problems in maintaining neutrality. First, the United States had closer and more important economic ties with the Allies than with the Central Powers, a disparity that would only grow as the war went on. The Allies purchased more than $750 million in U.S. goods in 1914, a figure that quadrupled over the next three years. By contrast, the Germans bought approximately $350 million worth of U.S. products in 1914; by 1917 the figure had shrunk to $30 million. When the Allies did not have the funds to pay for U.S. goods, they sought loans from private bankers. Initially, the Wilson administration resisted such requests. In 1915, however, Wilson reversed course. Concerned that failure to keep up the prewar level of commerce with the Allies would hurt the country economically, the president authorized private loans. The gap in financial transactions with the rival war powers grew even wider; by 1917 U.S. bankers had loaned the Allies $2.2 billion, compared with just $27 million to Germany.

The second problem facing Wilson arose from Great Britain's and Germany's differing war strategies. As the superior naval power, Britain established a blockade of the North Sea to quarantine Germany and starve it into submission. The British navy violated international law by mining the waters to bottle up the German fleet and keep foreign ships from

The U.S. Chooses to Enter World War I

The entry of the United States into World War I proved controversial. Wilson had pledged to remain neutral, as most Americans remained divided and reluctant to join the overseas fight. The causes of U.S. entry into the war are complicated and have been debated by historians, with the focus on Wilson's handling of neutrality and his desire to create a system of international relations based on morality. Arthur Link and John Chambers wrote the accounts excerpted below nearly forty years apart. They present different perspectives about the president's role in shaping foreign affairs, the first influenced by America's victory in World War II in the 1940s and the second by the nation's defeat in Vietnam in the 1960s and 1970s.

Source 20.4

Arthur S. Link | Woodrow Wilson and Neutrality, 1963

"In the final analysis, American policy was determined by the President and public opinion, which had a great, if unconscious, influence upon him. It was Wilson who decided to accept the British maritime system in the first instance, who set the American government against unrestricted use of the submarine, and who made the final decision for war instead of a continuance of armed neutrality.

. . . [I]f the German leaders had at any time desired a genuinely reasonable settlement and evidenced a willingness to help build a peaceful and orderly postwar world, they would have found a friend in the White House eager to join them in accomplishing these high goals.

The German decision to gamble on all-out victory or complete ruin . . . alone compelled Wilson to break diplomatic relations, to adopt a policy of armed neutrality, and finally to ask for a declaration of war—because American ships were being sunk and American citizens were being killed on the high seas, and because armed neutrality seemed no longer possible. Considerations of America's alleged economic stake in an Allied victory did not influence Wilson's thought during the critical weeks from February 1 to April 2, 1917. Nor did considerations of national interest, or of the great ideological issues at stake in the conflict."

Source: Arthur S. Link, *Woodrow Wilson and the Progressive Era, 1910–1917* (New York: Harper and Row), 1963, 280, 281.

supplying Germany with food and medicines. Although Wilson protested this treatment, he did so weakly. He believed that the British could pay compensation for such violations of international law after the war.

Confronting a strangling blockade, Germany depended on the newly developed U-boat (*Unterseeboot*, or submarine) to counter the British navy. In February 1915, Germany declared a blockade of the British Isles and warned citizens of neutral nations to stay off British ships in the area. U-boats, which were lighter and sleeker than British battleships, relied on surprise. This strategy violated the rules of engagement under international maritime law, which required belligerent ships to allow civilians to leave

Source 20.5

John Whiteclay Chambers II | Woodrow Wilson's Unneutral Neutrality, 2000

"Although the president emphasized German violation of neutral rights, neither American tradition nor law nor economic necessity required him to guarantee the right of Americans to travel on armed belligerent ships. Though he couched his policies in terms of international law and principle, Wilson was responsible for defining the growth of trade with Britain as a legitimate and profitable expression of neutral rights. He rejected definitions of other neutrals—Spain, the Netherlands, and the Scandinavian countries—that banned such passenger travel and embargoed guns and ammunition. In addition, he refused to consider the German and British blockades similarly or to hold Germany to a postwar accounting, as he did in the case of Britain. Thus by 1917 Wilson found himself constrained by the framework created by his earlier decisions about American rights.

. . . Wilson's policies reflected the traditional American belief that the ideals of America were the ideals of all humankind and that the other nations must conform to Americans prescriptions and ideals. . . . This global interventionism was new, but it drew on an attitude of superiority that had much earlier become a part of American culture. Germany had to be restrained because it had broken America's rules, disputed its ideals, threatened the rights and property of American citizens, and even challenged its security and hegemony through the proposed military alliance with Mexico."

Source: John Whiteclay Chambers II, *The Tyranny of Change: America in the Progressive Era, 1890–1920*. Second Edition (New Brunswick, New Jersey: Rutgers University Press, 2000), 229, 231.

Examine the Sources

1. Compare Link and Chambers's interpretations of Wilson's handling of neutrality and explain the basis of their disagreement.
2. Based on the evidence in this chapter, who do you think presents a stronger argument and why?

Put It in Context

What would it have cost the United States to refrain from entering World War I? Do you think the decision to go to war was worth the price?

passenger liners and cargo ships before firing. The British complicated the situation for the Germans by flying flags of neutral countries on merchant vessels and arming them with small "defensive" weapons. If U-boats played by the rules and surfaced before inspecting merchant ships, they risked being blown out of the water by disguised enemy guns.

Under these circumstances, U.S. neutrality could not last long. On May 15, 1915, catastrophe struck. Without surfacing and identifying itself, a German submarine off the Irish coast attacked the British luxury liner *Lusitania*, which had departed from New York City en route to England. Although the ship's stated objective was to provide passengers with transport, its cargo contained a large supply of ammunition for British weapons. The U-boat's torpedoes rapidly sank the ship, killing 1,198 people, including 128 Americans.

Outraged Americans called on the president to respond; some, including Theodore Roosevelt, advocated the immediate use of military force. Despite his pro-British sentiments, Wilson resisted going to war. Instead, he held the Germans in "strict accountability" for their action. Wilson demanded that Germany refrain from further attacks against passenger liners and offer a financial settlement to the *Lusitania*'s survivors. Unwilling to risk war with the United States, Germany consented.

Wilson had only delayed the United States' entry into the war. By pursuing a policy of neutrality that treated the combatants unequally and by insisting that Americans had a right to travel on the ships of belligerent nations, the president diminished the chance that the United States would stay out of the war.

Throughout 1916, Wilson pursued two separate but interrelated policies that embodied the ambivalence that he and the U.S. people shared about the war. On the one hand, with Germany alternating between continued U-boat attacks and apologies, the president sought to build the country's military preparedness in the event of war. He signed into law the National Defense Act, which increased the size of the army, navy, and National Guard. On the other hand, with U.S. public opinion divided on the Great War, Wilson chose to run for reelection as a peace candidate. The Democrats adopted the slogan "He kept us out of war" and also emphasized the president's substantial record of progressive reform. Wilson won a narrow victory against Charles Evans Hughes, the former governor of New York, who wavered between advocating peace and criticizing Wilson for not sufficiently supporting the Allies.

Making the World Safe for Democracy. As 1917 dawned, the bloody war dragged on. Neither side wanted a negotiated peace because each counted on victory to gain sufficient territory and financial compensation to justify the great sacrifices in human lives and materiel caused by the conflict. Nevertheless, Wilson tried to persuade the belligerents to abandon the battlefield for the bargaining table. On January 22, 1917, he declared that the world needed a "peace without victory," one based on self-determination, freedom of the seas, respect for international law, and the end of hostile alliances.

Germany quickly rejected Wilson's proposal. The United States had never been truly neutral, and Germany's leaders saw no reason to believe that the situation would change.

An American Nurse Comforts a Wounded Soldier, 1918   Women played important roles as nurses and ambulance drivers in combat areas during World War I. The nurse in this photograph, Ethel Goede, attends a wounded American soldier from the Choctaw Nation in Oklahoma. The nurse and Army surgeon, standing at the right, worked in the American Military Hospital No. 5 at Auteuil, France, a tent hospital put up and supported by the American Red Cross, which recruited women volunteer nurses. Library of Congress, LC-A6199-7529

In 1915 and again in 1916, to prevent the United States from entering the war, Germany had pledged to refrain from using its U-boats against passenger and merchant ships. However, on February 1, 1917 the Germans changed course and resumed unrestricted submarine warfare, calculating that they could defeat the Allies before the United States declared war. In response, Wilson used his executive power to arm merchant ships, bringing the United States one step closer to war.

The country moved even closer to war after the **Zimmermann telegram** became public. On February 24, the British turned over to Wilson an intercepted message from Arthur Zimmermann, the German foreign minister, to the Mexican government. The note revealed that Germany had offered Mexico an alliance in the event that the United States joined the Allies. If the Central Powers won, Mexico would receive the territory it had lost to the United States in the mid-nineteenth century—Texas, New Mexico, and Arizona. When U.S. newspapers broke the story several days later, it inflamed public opinion and provided the Wilson administration another reason to fear a German victory.

In late February and March, German U-boats sank several armed U.S. merchant ships, and on April 2, 1917 President Wilson asked Congress to declare war against Germany and the other Central Powers. After four days of vigorous debate led by opponents of the war—including Senator Robert M. La Follette of Wisconsin and the first female elected representative, Jeanette P. Rankin from Montana—Congress voted to approve the war resolution.

For three years, President Wilson had resisted calls for war. However, Wilson finally decided that only by going to war would he be able to ensure that the United States played a role in shaping the peace. "The world must be made safe for democracy," he informed Congress in his war message, and he had concluded that the only way to guarantee this outcome was by helping to defeat Germany. This need became even more urgent when in November 1917 the Russian Revolution installed a Bolshevik (Communist) regime that negotiated a separate peace with the Central Powers (Map 20.2).

It would take a while for Americans to make their presence felt in Europe. The United States needed a large army, which it created through the draft. The Selective Service Act of 1917 conscripted 3 million

MAP 20.2 European Alliances, 1914

Pre-war alliances helped precipitate World War I. The assassination of Archduke Ferdinand of Austria-Hungry by a Serbian revolutionary in Sarajevo set the countries in the Austro-Hungarian and German-led Central Alliance against the British-French-Russian Entente, as the map shows.

men by war's end. Mobilizing such a large force required substantial time, and the **American Expeditionary Forces (AEF)**, established in 1917 under General Pershing, did not make much of an impact until 1918. Before then, U.S. warships joined the British in escorting merchant vessels, combating German submarines, and laying mines in the North Sea. The United States also provided crucial funding and supplies to the Allies as their reserves became depleted.

The AEF finally began to make an impact in Europe in May 1918. From May through September, more than 1 million U.S. troops helped the Allies repel German offensives in northern France near the Belgian border. One momentous battle in the Argonne Forest lasted two months until the Allies broke through enemy lines and pushed toward Germany. Nearly 50,000 U.S. troops died in the fierce fighting, and another 230,000 were injured (Table 20.1). Like their European counterparts, who suffered a staggering 8 to 10 million casualties, Americans experienced the horrors of war magnified by new technology. Dug into filthy trenches, soldiers dodged rapid machine-gun fire, heavy artillery explosions, and poison gas shells. In the end, however, the AEF succeeded in tipping the balance in favor of the Allies. On November 11, 1918, an exhausted Germany surrendered.

Review & Relate

- In what ways, if any, did President Wilson's approach to Latin American affairs differ from that of his predecessors?

- Why did President Wilson find it so difficult to keep the United States out of World War I?

TABLE 20.1 World War I Casualties

Percentage of Deaths in Mobilized Forces in World War I by Country

Country	Total Mobilized Forces	Deaths	Percentage
Allied Powers			
Romania	750,000	335,706	45%
Russia	12,000,000	1,700,000	14%
Canada	424,000	56,694	14%
Italy	5,615,000	650,000	12%
British Empire	8,904,467	908,307	10%
Portugal	100,000	7,222	7%
Serbia	707,343	45,000	6%
Belgium	267,000	13,716	5%
United States	4,734,991	116,516	2%
Greece	230,000	5,000	2%
Japan	800,000	300	.03%
Central Powers			
Germany	11,000,000	1,773,700	16%
Austria-Hungary	7,800,000	1,200,000	15%
Turkey	2,850,000	325,000	11%
Bulgaria	1,200,000	87,500	7%

Fighting the War at Home

Modern global warfare required full mobilization at home. In preparing to support the war effort, the country drew on recent experience. The progressives' passion for organization, expertise, efficiency, and moralistic control was harnessed to the effort of placing the economy on a wartime footing and rallying the American people behind the war. In the process, the government gained unprecedented control over American life. The war effort also produced unforeseen economic and political opportunities.

Government by Commission. Progressives had relied on government commissions to regulate business practices as well as health and safety standards. In July 1917 the Wilson administration followed suit by establishing the **War Industries Board (WIB)** to supervise the purchase of military supplies and to gear up private enterprise to meet demand. The WIB was largely ineffective until the president found the right man to lead it. In March 1918, he chose Wall Street financier Bernard Baruch, who recruited staff from business enterprises that the board regulated. Baruch prodded businesses into compliance mainly by offering lucrative contracts rather than by coercion. Ultimately, the WIB created a government partnership with the corporate sector that would last beyond the war.

Labor also experienced significant gains through government regulation. Shortages of workers and an outbreak of strikes hampered the war effort. In April 1918, Wilson created the **National War Labor Board (NWLB)** to settle labor disputes. The agency consisted of representatives from unions, corporations, and the public. In exchange for obtaining a "no strike pledge" from organized labor, the NWLB supported an eight-hour workday with time-and-a-half pay for overtime, labor's right to collective bargaining, and equal pay for equal work by women.

While the NWLB fell short of reaching this last goal, the war employed more than a million women who had not held jobs before. As military and government services expanded, women found greater opportunities as telephone operators, nurses, and clerical workers. At the same time, the number of women employed as domestic servants declined. Women took over formerly male jobs driving streetcars, delivering ice, assembling airplane motors, operating drill presses, oiling railroad engines, and welding parts. Yet women's incomes continued to lag significantly behind those of men performing the same tasks.

Americans experienced the expanding scope of government intervention most directly through the efforts of three new agencies that regulated consumption and travel. Wilson appointed Herbert Hoover to head the Food Administration. Hoover sought to increase the military and civilian food supply mainly through voluntary conservation measures. He generated a massive publicity campaign urging Americans to adopt "wheatless Mondays," "meatless Tuesdays," and "porkless Thursdays and Saturdays." The government also mobilized schoolchildren to plant vegetable gardens to increase food production for the home front.

Consumers saved gas and oil under the prodding of the Fuel Administration. The agency encouraged fuel "holidays" along the line of Hoover's voluntary restrictions and created daylight savings time to conserve fuel by adding an extra hour of sunlight to the end of the workday. The Fuel Administration also offered higher prices to coal companies to increase productivity. The Railroad Administration acted more forcefully than most other agencies. Troop and supply shipments depended on the efficient operation of the railways. The

World War I Posters   Many of the wartime posters were aimed at rallying women to provide help on the home front and mobilizing men to defend women by joining the military. The poster on the left was put out by the Young Women's Christian Association (YWCA) and the one at the right, illustrated by Fred Spear for the Boston Committee of Public Safety, shows a mother and her infant drowning with the sinking of the *Lusitania* in 1915. Left: Marka/Universal Images Group via Getty Images; right: Gift of John T. Spaulding/Bridgeman Images

administration controlled the railroads during the war, coordinating train schedules, overseeing terminals and regulating ticket prices, upgrading tracks, and raising workers' wages.

Winning Hearts and Minds.
Faced with significant antiwar sentiment, Wilson waged a campaign to rally support for his aims and to stimulate patriotic fervor. To generate enthusiasm and ensure loyalty, the president appointed journalist George Creel to head the **Committee on Public Information (CPI)**, which focused on generating propaganda. Creel recruited a vast network of lecturers to speak throughout the country and spread patriotic messages. The committee coordinated rallies to sell bonds and raise money to fund the war. The CPI persuaded reporters to censor their war coverage, and most agreed in order to avoid government intervention. The agency helped produce films depicting the Allies as heroic saviors of humanity and the Central Powers as savage beasts. The CPI also distributed colorful and sometimes lurid posters emphasizing the depravity of the enemy and the nation's moral responsibility to defeat the Central Powers.

Propaganda did not prove sufficient, however, and Americans remained deeply divided about the war. To suppress dissent, Congress passed the Espionage Act in 1917 and the Sedition Act a year later. Both limited freedom of speech by criminalizing certain forms of expression. The **Espionage Act** prohibited antiwar activities, including interfering with the draft. It also banned the mailing of publications advocating forcible interference with any laws. The **Sedition Act** punished individuals who expressed beliefs disloyal or abusive to the U.S. government, flag, or military uniform. Of the slightly more than two thousand prosecutions under these laws, only a handful concerned charges of actual sabotage or espionage. Most defendants brought to trial were critics who merely spoke out against the war. In 1918, for telling a crowd that the military draft was a form of slavery, the Socialist Party's Eugene V. Debs was tried, convicted, and sentenced to ten years under the Espionage Act. (President Warren G. Harding pardoned Debs in 1921.) The Justice Department also went after the Industrial Workers of the World (IWW), which continued to initiate labor strikes during the war. The government broke into the offices of the IWW, ransacked the group's files for evidence of disloyalty, and arrested more than 130 members.

Government efforts to promote national unity and punish those who did not conform prompted local communities to enforce "one hundred percent Americanism." Civic groups banned the playing of German music and operas from concert halls, and schools prohibited teaching the German language. Foods with German origins were renamed — sauerkraut became "liberty cabbage," and hamburgers became "liberty sandwiches." Such sentiments were expressed in a more sinister fashion when mobs assaulted German Americans.

Prejudice toward German Americans was further inflamed by the formation of the **American Protective League (APL)**, a quasi-official association endorsed by the Justice Department. Consisting of 200,000 chapters throughout the country, the APL employed individuals to spy on German residents suspected of disloyal behavior. Most often, APL agents found little more than German immigrants who merely retained attachments to family and friends in their homeland.

Anti-immigrant bias, shared by many progressive reformers, flourished in other ways as well. The effort to conserve manpower and grain supplies bolstered the impulse to control standards of moral behavior, particularly those associated with immigrants, such as drinking. This anti-immigrant prejudice in part explains the ratification of the Eighteenth Amendment in 1919, prohibiting the sale of all alcoholic beverages. Yet not all the moral indignation unleashed by the war resulted in restriction of freedom. After considerable wartime protest and lobbying, women suffragists succeeded in securing the right to vote.

President Wilson's goal "to make the world safe for democracy" appealed to oppressed racial minorities. They hoped the war would push the United States to live up to its rhetoric and extend freedom at home. Nearly 400,000 African Americans served in the war and more than 40,000 saw combat, but most were assigned to service units and worked in menial jobs. The army remained segregated, and few black officers commanded troops. Despite this discrimination, W. E. B. Du Bois echoed African Americans' hope that their patriotism would be rewarded at the war's end: "We of the colored race have no ordinary interest in the outcome."

The same held true for American Indians. More than ten thousand Indians participated in the war. Recruited from Arizona, Montana, and New York, they fought in the major battles in France and Belgium. Unlike African Americans, they did not fight in segregated units and saw action as scouts and combat soldiers. They gained recognition by communicating messages in their native languages to confuse the Germans listening in. Aware of the contradiction between their poor treatment historically by the U.S.

government and the nation's democratic war aims, they expected that their wartime patriotism would bring them a greater measure of justice. However, like African Americans, they would be disappointed.

1918–1919 Influenza Pandemic.

While fighting the war, the United States had to battle a global outbreak of deadly influenza. A highly contagious virus transmitted through the air, the disease infected around 500 million people, or about one-third of the world's population. The flu killed an estimated 50 million people globally and approximately 675,000 in the U.S. In many American cities and towns, bodies piled up due to a shortage of morticians, gravediggers, and coffins. Funerals were confined to fifteen minutes.

The origin of the influenza **pandemic** (a disease prevalent in a country, continent, or the world) remains a mystery, but at the time it was considered to have begun in Spain. Classified as an H1N1 virus, influenza came in three waves, starting in March 1918. This outbreak was relatively mild, but during the fall season a much more severe contagion struck. The third, less serious, wave broke out in the winter of 1918–1919, and by spring it had largely run its course. The virus briefly returned a year later but with comparatively little effect. The pandemic hit those in the twenty-to-forty age range especially hard, more so than in the very young and elderly. The majority of deaths occurred from pneumonia.

More American soldiers died from the flu than were killed on battlefields during World War I. Approximately 40 percent of men in the Navy and 36 percent in the Army became ill. In fact, soldiers helped spread the virus throughout Europe and the U.S. Housed in crowded military bases and transported in congested ships heading overseas and back, troops easily transmitted the disease to each other and to civilians. One of the first recorded outbreaks of the virus took place in Kansas at Camp Funston. On March 4, 1918, the first soldier reported ill at this Army training camp for soldiers preparing for assignment in Europe. Within two weeks, over 1,000 soldiers went to the hospital and 38 died. Those who survived carried the disease within the United States and to Europe as part of the American Expeditionary Force. Civilians became readily infected, including President Woodrow Wilson, who survived, and Friedrich Trump, the future president's grandfather, who did not.

African Americans were more susceptible to illnesses such as tuberculosis and pneumonia and their life expectancy was lower than whites. During the era of Jim Crow, health care for blacks was separate and unequal, leaving them at greater risk to disease. Surprisingly then, reports from black communities and public health officials indicate that African Americans contracted influenza at a lower rate than did whites for reasons that remain unclear. In contrast, the effects of the pandemic varied among Native American tribes. Less than 1 percent of Indians died from influenza in Oklahoma, Wyoming, Kansas, and Michigan, whereas 4 to 6 percent perished from the disease in Arizona, Colorado, Mississippi, New Mexico, and Utah. Navajo communities in particular were seriously affected. Despite the variations, Indians suffered heavily because the federal government failed to provide adequate health care on the reservations. Higher death rates also occurred among newly arrived immigrants from eastern and southern Europe and Mexico.

The pandemic placed a severe strain on the health care system. Many physicians and nurses were serving in the military, and medical students had to take their place. The Red Cross created a National Committee on Influenza to gather medical supplies and mobilize nurses and volunteers. President Wilson never spoke publicly about the virus nor did the U.S. Public Health Service provide much leadership; the surgeon general merely warned people to stay out of crowds and advised them to breathe fresh air. This left cities and towns with the prime responsibility of dealing with the pandemic. Local public health departments distributed masks to be worn in public, and San Francisco levied a $5 fine on individuals caught not wearing a mask. St. Louis initiated quarantines and shut down schools, churches, and theaters. In New York City, Boy Scout troops patrolled the streets warning residents not to spit on the sidewalk. In contrast, Philadelphia allowed a massive war bond parade in September 1918, causing an eruption in the number of infections and resulting in over 12,000 deaths.

Although research scientists and physicians worked hard to develop a vaccine and treatments for the flu, they did not succeed. Doctors tried almost anything they could think of to treat the ill; most prescribed aspirin and some chose quinine (used to treat malaria) or injected patients with typhoid vaccine. Other approaches degenerated into quackery, such as advising patients to sniff boric acid and baking soda to flush out the nasal cavities or ingesting hydrogen peroxide, iodine, and even low doses of toxic strychnine on the theory that some form of "internal disinfection" was necessary to cleanse the body. Whereas President Wilson had adapted progressive techniques of efficiency and order to mobilize Americans on the home front during the war, his administration failed to lead the way in applying similar methods against the pandemic. **See Primary Source Project 20: The Challenges of the 1918–1919 Influenza Pandemic, page 702.**

Waging Peace.

In January 1918, just before the onset of the pandemic and ten months before the war ended, President Wilson presented Congress with his plan for peace. Wilson bundled his ideas in the **Fourteen Points**, principles that he hoped would prevent future wars. Based on his assessment of the causes of the Great War, Wilson envisioned a generous peace treaty that included freedom of the seas, open diplomacy and the abolition of secret treaties, free trade, self-determination for colonial subjects, and a reduction in military spending. More important than any specific measure, Wilson's proposal hinged on the creation of the **League of Nations**, a body of large and small nations that would guarantee peaceful resolution of disputes and back up decisions through collective action, including the use of military force as a last resort.

Following the armistice that ended the war on November 11, 1918, Wilson personally took his message to the Paris Peace Conference, the postwar meeting of the victorious Allied nations that would set the terms of the peace. The first sitting president to travel overseas, Wilson was greeted in Paris by joyous crowds. While in Paris, Wilson contracted influenza from which he never fully recovered.

For nearly six months, Wilson tried to convince reluctant Allied leaders to accept the central components of his plan. Having exhausted themselves financially and having suffered the loss of a generation of young men, the Allies intended to scoop up the spoils of victory and make the Central Powers pay dearly. The European Allies intended to hold on to their respective colonies regardless of Wilson's call for self-determination, and as a nation that depended on a strong navy, Britain refused to limit its options concerning freedom of the seas. Perhaps Georges Clemenceau, France's president, best expressed his colleagues' skepticism about Wilson's idealistic vision: "President Wilson and his Fourteen Points bore me. Even God Almighty has only ten!"

Philadelphia Parade and the Influenza Pandemic, 1918 Despite warnings by health experts, on September 28, 1918, Philadelphia held a Liberty Loan Parade along Broad Street, which included this Naval Aircraft Factory float escorted by sailors. An estimated 200,000 onlookers lined the streets to watch the festivities, accelerating the spread of influenza that had already struck at nearby military bases. U.S. Naval History and Heritage Command Photograph

During the conference, Wilson was forced to compromise on a number of his principles in order to retain the cornerstone of his diplomacy — the establishment of the League of Nations. He abandoned his hope for peace without bitterness by agreeing to a "war guilt" clause that levied huge economic reparations on Germany for starting the war. He was willing to sacrifice some of his ideals because the league took on even greater importance in the wake of the 1917 Communist revolution in Russia. Wilson needed the league to keep the peace, giving war-ravaged and recovering nations the opportunity to choose U.S.-style economic freedom and political democracy over communism. In the end, the president won agreement for the establishment of his cherished League of Nations. The **Treaty of Versailles**, signed at the royal palace just outside Paris, authorized the league to combat aggression against any member nation through collective military action.

The Failure of Ratification. In July 1919, after enduring bruising battles in Paris, Wilson returned to Washington, D.C., only to face another wrenching struggle in the Senate over ratification of the Versailles treaty. The odds were stacked against Wilson from the start. The Republicans held a majority in the Senate, and Wilson needed the support of two-thirds of the Senate to secure ratification. Henry Cabot Lodge, the Republican chairman of the Senate Foreign Relations Committee, opposed Article X of the League of Nations covenant, which sanctioned collective security arrangements against military aggression. Lodge argued that such an alliance compromised the United States' independence in conducting its own foreign relations. Lodge had at least thirty-nine senators behind him, more than enough to block ratification. Conceding the need to protect the country's national self-interest, the president agreed to modifications to the treaty so that the Monroe Doctrine and America's obligations in the Caribbean and Central America were kept intact. Lodge, however, was not satisfied and insisted on adding fourteen "reservations" limiting compliance with the treaty, including strong language affirming Congress's right to declare war before agreeing to a League of Nations military action.

Wilson's stubbornness more than equaled Lodge's, and the president refused to compromise. Making matters worse, Wilson faced resistance from sixteen lawmakers dubbed "irreconcilables," who opposed the league under any circumstances. Mainly Republicans from the Midwest and West, they voiced the traditional U.S. rejection of entangling alliances.

To break the logjam, Wilson attempted to rally public opinion behind him. In September 1919, he embarked on a nationwide speaking tour to carry his message directly to the American people. Over a three-week period, he traveled eight thousand miles by train, keeping a grueling schedule that exhausted him. After a stop in Pueblo, Colorado, on September 25, Wilson collapsed and canceled the rest of his trip. On October 2, Wilson suffered a massive stroke that nearly killed him. The effects of the stroke, which left him partially paralyzed, emotionally unstable, and mentally impaired, dimmed any remaining hopes of compromise. The full extent of his illness was kept from the public, and his wife, Edith, ran the White House for the next eighteen months.

Still fresh from their grisly experiences with the global influenza pandemic, many Americans seemed wary of binding themselves to an international agency such as the league. On November 19, 1919, the Senate rejected the amended treaty. The following year, Wilson had one final chance to obtain ratification, but still he refused to accept reservations despite members of his own party urging compromise. In March 1920, treaty ratification failed one last time, falling just seven votes short of the required two-thirds majority. The United States never signed the Treaty of Versailles or joined the League of Nations, weakening the league and diminishing the prospects for long-term peace.

Review & Relate

- Compare the U.S. government's efforts to manage the economy and public opinion with its response to the influenza pandemic during World War I.

- How did President Wilson's wartime policies and his efforts to shape the peace that followed reflect his progressive roots?

Conclusion: A U.S. Empire

In the final decade of the nineteenth century, the United States transformed itself into an imperial power. Presidents McKinley and Roosevelt carried out the strategy outlined by Captain Mahan to enlarge the navy, construct a canal linking the Atlantic and Pacific Oceans, and acquire coaling stations and bases in the Pacific to service the fleet. U.S. officials disregarded the nationalistic aspirations of freedom fighters such as José Martí in Cuba and Emilio Aguinaldo in the Philippines in favor of the imperial spoils gained from winning the War of 1898. The United States justified intervention on moral grounds predicated on racist beliefs, much as it had in conquering the Indians during westward expansion. As a fit and manly nation, the United States felt responsible for uplifting "inferior" peoples to "civilized" standards and make them capable of self-government. This justification quickly wore thin. To crush the rebellion in the Philippines, the military engaged in atrocities that called into question the honor and virtue of the United States.

Once it achieved victory in the Philippines, the nation concentrated its efforts on maintaining territories primarily for commercial purposes. Within the few short years from 1898 to 1904, this commercial empire had fallen into place.

The Progressive Era presidents, Roosevelt and Wilson, created and sustained a U.S. empire. They disagreed significantly in approach — Roosevelt favoring force, Wilson preferring negotiations — but in practice they shared a willingness to use military power to protect national interests. These two presidents helped construct the modern American state, an expanded federal government in cooperation with responsible corporate leaders. This relationship reached its peak during World War I. In mobilizing the home front, the Wilson administration blurred the line between public and private business by expanding the reach of government over the economy and curtailing personal liberty. However, this move toward nationalization was hardly complete, as the failure of Wilson to offer a central strategy to combat the 1918 influenza pandemic shows.

In 1917, because of its heavy reliance on trade with foreign countries, especially in Europe, the United States confronted its first major international crisis of the twentieth century. Wilson reluctantly led the country into war to guarantee a world order in which reasonable nations attempted to resolve controversies through negotiation, not violence. The failure of the United States to join the League of Nations, for which the president bore much of the responsibility, shattered his own idealistic dream.

Nevertheless, the United States did not isolate itself from participation in the world. The country emerged from the war in excellent financial shape; it had become the leading foreign creditor; its industrial capacity had greatly expanded; and its commercial empire in the Caribbean and Central America remained intact. It would take another two decades for policymakers to realize that the country's refusal to support a strong collective response to expansionist aggression posed serious dangers for U.S. commerce and values.

Timeline of Events

1880–1900	U.S. creates third most powerful navy
1893	U.S. plantation owners overthrow Queen Liliuokalani of Hawaii
1895–1898	Cuban War for Independence
1898	U.S. battleship *Maine* explodes
	The War of 1898
	Anti-Imperialist League founded
1899–1902	Philippine-American War
1901	Platt Amendment passed
1904	Roosevelt Corollary announced
1909	U.S. intervenes in Nicaragua on behalf of U.S. fruit and mining companies
1914	Panama Canal opens
	World War I begins
1915	German submarine sinks the *Lusitania*
1916	Wilson sends U.S. troops into Mexico to capture Pancho Villa
1917	Zimmermann telegram
	United States enters World War I
	Espionage Act
	War Industries Board established
	Committee on Public Information established
1918	Sedition Act
	National War Labor Board established
	Germany surrenders, ending World War I
	Influenza pandemic spreads throughout the world
1919	Influenza pandemic reaches its peak and subsides
	Wilson loses battle for ratification of Treaty of Versailles

Key Terms

jingoists, *675*

Cuba Libre, *677*

yellow journalism, *678*

Teller Amendment, *680*

Platt Amendment, *680*

Anti-Imperialist League, *681*

Roosevelt Corollary, *683*

Open Door, *683*

dollar diplomacy, *685*

Mexican revolution, *687*

Zimmermann telegram, *691*

American Expeditionary Forces (AEF), *692*

War Industries Board (WIB), *693*

National War Labor Board (NWLB), *693*

Committee on Public Information (CPI), *694*

Espionage Act, *694*

Sedition Act, *695*

American Protective League (APL), *695*

pandemic, *696*

Fourteen Points, *697*

League of Nations, *697*

Treaty of Versailles, *698*

Review & Relate

1. What role did economic developments play in prompting calls for a U.S. empire? What role did social and cultural developments play?

2. Why did the United States embark on building an empire in the 1890s and not decades earlier?

3. Why did the United States go to war with Spain in 1898?

4. In what ways did the War of 1898 mark a turning point in the relationship between the United States and the rest of the world?

5. How did the United States assert its influence and control over Latin America in the early twentieth century?

6. How did U.S. policies in Latin America mirror U.S. policies in Asia?

7. In what ways, if any, did President Wilson's approach to Latin American affairs differ from that of his predecessors?

8. Why did President Wilson find it so difficult to keep the United States out of World War I?

9. Compare the U.S. government's efforts to manage the economy and public opinion with its response to the influenza pandemic during World War I.

10. How did President Wilson's wartime policies and his efforts to shape the peace that followed reflect his progressive roots?

The Challenges of the 1918–1919 Influenza Pandemic

▶ Explain how the influenza pandemic affected the United States and evaluate how Americans coped with it.

Before 1918, the United States had experienced outbreaks of diseases such as yellow fever, smallpox, cholera, and influenza. The influenza pandemic that swept through the nation and circled the globe during World War I was among the worst. More American soldiers died from this viral infection than did from gunfire, bomb blasts, and poison gas attacks on the battlefields of Europe. U.S. troops returning home transmitted the disease to civilians around the country. The United States recorded some 675,000 deaths, a tiny fraction of the estimated fifty million deaths throughout the world. The death rate from the disease among fifteen to thirty-four-year-olds was twenty times higher in 1918 than in previous years. As a result, the average life span in the U.S. dropped by ten years. This devastating illness attacked political leaders such as President Woodrow Wilson and Secretary of the Navy Franklin D. Roosevelt as well as millions of ordinary people.

At the time, the disease was known as the "Spanish Flu" or the "Grippe." Spain became stigmatized as the origin of the influenza pandemic because it remained neutral during World War I and, unlike the combatants, did not restrict its press from reporting about the spread of the disease (Source 20.10). In fact, the outbreak most likely started in Kansas and spread to military bases in Boston and Philadelphia (Source 20.6). Neither the United States nor any other nation in the world fully understood the nature of the contagion and was unprepared to cope with it. Scientists knew a good deal about bacterial infections but were just learning about viruses. Medical doctors concocted treatments; most caused little harm and a few provided a bit of relief. Seeking to profit by feeding on anxiety and inadequate knowledge, patent medicine companies and pharmacies peddled supposed cures to gullible consumers (Sources 20.8 and 20.9). The war caused a shortage of medical personnel, and the country relied heavily on nurses and medical students to take up the slack (Source 20.7). As they did in other areas on the home front, women played a major role in combating the wartime pandemic.

The United States lacked national leadership in coping with the health crisis. President Wilson was burdened first with the war and then negotiating the peace. Over the course of the pandemic, the U.S. Public Health Service learned many valuable lessons, but it left decisions mainly to local governments. They, in turn, did their best to recommend wearing masks in public, avoiding crowds, refraining from spitting on sidewalks, and staying home (Source 20.10). These suggestions were not always followed. Soldiers had to travel to carry out their duties, and people had to go to work to earn a living (in the absence of any economic assistance from the federal government). Moreover, some local leaders acted prematurely by allowing public gatherings and parades. As much as they could, Americans went about their daily lives with the disease very much on their minds. In 1918, children jumped rope to the rhyme: "I had a little bird. Its name was Enza. I opened the window, And in-flu-enza." Without a vaccine, the disease did manage to run its course by 1920, though not before leaving numerous children as orphans and many Americans suspicious of engaging with the rest of the world.

Source 20.6

Philadelphia Inquirer Describes the Crisis, 1918

In early September 1918, the Navy shipped 300 sailors, unknowingly carrying the influenza virus, from Boston to Philadelphia. Despite the subsequent outbreak of the flu among the sailors and the civilian population and ignoring medical advice, city officials refused to postpone a Liberty Loan concert and parade on September 28. These festivities attracted crowds of some 200,000 people, and within five weeks, more than 12,000 residents died. The following excerpt from the *Philadelphia Inquirer* describes the difficulties that plagued the city and shows how women were essential as frontline health workers. The Emergency Aid of Pennsylvania, a women's volunteer organization, mobilized its members to help make up for the shortage of nurses.

The return of deaths yesterday from Spanish influenza, as well as the number of new cases was greater than on any single day since the outbreak of the epidemic in this city. In the civilian population of Philadelphia the number of deaths reported yesterday was 254, of which 159 were directly due to influenza and 95 due to pneumonia superinduced by influenza. The number of new cases reported was 1480.

. . . Director Wilmer Krusen of the Department of Health and Charities, yesterday announced that forty nurses at the Philadelphia Hospital had broken down from the result of strain of overwork in caring for influenza patients at that institution. Director Krusen has made an appeal for volunteer nurses to fill in for the emergency. He stated that good use can be made at the hospital of student nurses having from a year or two of training; and said that all student nurses, so qualified, would be accepted. . . . Director Krusen announced that the wholesale drug houses of the city will be open today and deliver to hospitals all essential drugs for the treatment of influenza.

In this desperate crisis, the Emergency Aid [calls] on all its members to give their personal assistance in the care of the sick in the hospitals, All members who are free from the care of the sick at home and who are in good physical condition themselves are asked to report at the headquarters. . . .

Source: "Influenza Increase Due to Late Reports," *Philadelphia Inquirer*, October 6, 1918, 13.

Source 20.7

A Letter from a Native American, Volunteer Nurse, 1918

The first reported outbreak of influenza came in March 1918 in Haskell County, Kansas, which lies just west of the old cattle town of Dodge City. Haskell contained the United States Indian Industrial Training School, which offered an educational curriculum to assimilate Native Americans. One of its graduates, Lutiant Van Wert, who was working for the Department of Interior in Washington, D.C., volunteered to serve as a nurse at an army base in Virginia, as one of the many women signing up to help during the pandemic. She shares her experiences with her friend Louise living in Haskell. World War I had not yet ended and conspiracy theories abounded. In her letter, Lutiant shares a false story, which she believed, that German spies posed as physicians and were infecting soldiers.

Dear friend Louise:

. . . Katherine and I just returned last Sunday evening from Camp Humphrey "Somewhere in Virginia" where we volunteered to help nurse soldiers sick with the Influenza. . . .

All nurses were required to work twelve hours a day—we worked from seven in the morning to seven at night, with only a short time for luncheon and dinner.

Believe me, we were always glad when night came because we sure did get tired. We had the actual Practical [sic] nursing to do—just like the other nurses had, and were given a certain number of wards with three or four patients in each to look after. Our chief duties were to give medicines to the patients, take temperatures, fix ice packs, feed them at "eating time," rub their back or chest with camphorated sweet oil, make egg-nogs, and a whole string of other things I can't begin to name. I liked the work just fine, but it was too hard, not being used to it. When I was in the Officer's [sic] barracks, four of the officers of whom I had charge, died. Two of them were married and called for their wife nearly all the time. It was sure pitiful to see them die, I was right in the wards alone with them each time, and Oh! The first one that died sure unnerved me—I had to go to the nurses' quarters and cry it out. . . . Really Louise, Orderlies [sic] carried the dead soldiers out on stretchers at the rate of two every three hours for the first two days [we]were there. Two German spies, posing as doctors, were caught giving these Influenza germs to the soldiers and they were shot last Saturday at sunrise. . . .

Source: Letter from Lutiant Van Wert to Louise, October 17, 1918, National Archives at Kansas City, Record Group 75.

Source 20.8

Advertisement to Stop Influenza, 1918

With medical scientists unable to come up with a vaccine for the flu and doctors only able to treat the symptoms with available but insufficient treatments, enterprising — though not always honest — businesses sought to fill the void by advertising and selling "miracle drugs." One such cure-all was Miller's Antiseptic Oil, commonly called Snake Oil. A Nashville, Tennessee drug company claimed the concoction would relieve and even cure influenza, as well as a variety of other illnesses. The cost was minimal, but from one supposed testimonial, the reward was huge. Even more respectable companies, which survive to this day, such as the makers of Lysol and Vicks VapoRub, also promised that their products could help prevent a person from catching the disease if used properly.

There seems to be no question but that Miller's Antiseptic Oil, (known as Snake Oil) when rubbed on the throat and chest well greased, also inhaled thru the nose has saved thousands of lives by preventing Influenza and pneumonia. And in use by those who have already contacted the disease, Miller's Antiseptic Oil seems to make them well and strong again in no time at all.

Mr. E. E. Collins of Lyles, Tenn., writes as follows: Enclosed find 50c for a bottle of Snake Oil. A 30c bottle used by all three of my family who had Influenza certainly fixed us up. I give it full credit. I run a dormitory at an alcohol plant where there is a good deal of Influenza. Have tried Snake Oil on several cases and they have been relieved and made well again. Where doctors have lost lots of patients, we have not lost a single one.

Miller's Antiseptic Oil (known as Snake Oil) is the great pain medicine—brings almost instant relief to any kind of ache or pain such as rheumatism, neuralgia, lumbago, colds, grippe, etc. Money back if not satisfied. For sale by DeMoville-Page-Sims Drug Co., Nashville, Tenn. (adv.)

Source: "Says It Stops Influenza," *The Tennessean,* November 26, 1918, 9

Source 20.9

Dr. A. Wilberforce Williams on Fake Influenza Remedies, 1918

Although medical doctors often improvised their own treatments, they remained on the lookout for quacks who prescribed remedies that pledged to prevent or cure influenza. Physicians would have placed Snake Oil, as advertised in Source 20.8, in that category. Dr. A. Wilberforce Williams, an African American physician writing a regular health column in the *Chicago Defender*, a black newspaper, warned "Negro" readers about the folly of using harmless but unhelpful homemade remedies to prevent or cure influenza. Within systemic segregation, black institutions rose to the task of informing and caring for African Americans. Dr. Williams, a heart and lung specialist, practiced medicine in Chicago for forty-six years.

The fogies and fakers are reaping a very rich harvest in dispensing and disposing of their "sure cures" for influenza. Many people are so dull and ignorant that they will accept the uneducated, the unscientific, the untrained advice on the part of the ignorant fogy, the gad-about-grannies, the street sweepers, the sewer cleaners and various other scavengers, who claim to have a "sure cure" for all colds, *la grippe*, Spanish influenza, pneumonia, and every known disease that affects the human family.

. . . Many of the Negro people of this community have swamped the drug stores in their demand for asefatida [a pungent smelling spice] to wear in a bag around their neck as a [preventive] of influenza. . . . And so many of the [N]egro people are resorting to the wearing about their bodies raw or cooked onions, boiled or raw garlic poultice spread over their chest with red flannel to prevent and cure influenza . . . These various herbs and vegetables mentioned above and used by you have no virtue in the prevention and cure of influenza. Use common sense; be reasonable; consult and accept the advice of intelligent physicians and nurses; your health department; they are the best prepared to give you advice in the conservation of your health, in the prolongation of your life, not only now but in all times. The only virtue that we can see that may have attracted your attention from the use of asafetida, garlic or onions, is the odor, and we wish to tell you now that odors have never been known to blot out or prevent disease. . . .

Source: Dr. A. Wilberforce Williams, "Talks on Preventive Measures First Aid Remedies Hygienics and Sanitation," *Chicago Defender*, October 26, 1918, 16.

Source 20.10

→ more suggestive

U.S. Public Health Service Information on Influenza, 1919

By fall 1919, the worst of the influenza pandemic had subsided. However, still uncertain about whether the pandemic would return, the U.S. Public Health Service circulated information through newspapers and pamphlets bringing readers up-to-date with what it had learned about the infection. One of its conclusions relates to the origin of the disease, which health officials knew at this early date was not Spain. Despite this fact, the name "Spanish Flu" stuck, and many Americans continued to believe that they had been infected by outsiders.

. . . Although the recent epidemic is called "Spanish influenza," investigation has shown that it did not originate in Spain.

We know that there was undue prevalence of influenza in the United States for several years, preceding the pandemic. Because the disease occurred in a mild form, and because the public mind was focused on the war, this increased prevalence of the disease escaped attention. Not until the epidemic appeared in severe form in Boston in September 1918, did it excite any special interest. . . .

Several European observers, on the basis of experiments conducted during the recent pandemic, believe that the germ of influenza is no ordinary bacterium but belongs to a class of exceedingly small germs spoken of as "filterable viruses," because they can pass through the pores of unglazed porcelain filters.

No matter what particular kind of germ causes the epidemic, it is now known that influenza is spread directly and indirectly from person to person. Moreover, judging from experiences in other diseases, it is possible that the germ, whatever its nature, is carried about not only by those who are ill with influenza but by persons who may be entirely well. Everything which increases personal contact, therefore, should be regarded as a factor in spreading influenza. . . .

Thus, [the disease] may spread quite directly by being carried with the air along with the heavy small droplets of mucus spread by coughing, sneezing, forceful talking, and the like, by one who already has the germs of the disease. To guard against this mode of spread the use of face masks have been advocated. . . . Soiled hands, common drinking cups, improperly cleaned eating and drinking utensils in restaurants, soda fountains, etc., roller towels, infected foods, these are only a few of the common vehicles of germ transmission. . . . The use of face masks appears to make people neglect these other paths of infection, and therefore such use has not been attended with the success predicted for them. If we would be more successful in combatting influenza, greater attention must be paid to the factors just enumerated.

. . . In a disease like influenza, health authorities everywhere recognize the very close relation between its spread and overcrowding. While it is not always possible, especially in times like the present, to avoid overcrowding, people should consider the health danger and make every effort to reduce home overcrowding to a minimum. The value of fresh air through open windows cannot be over-emphasized.

Source: "Information on Influenza by the United States Public Health Service," *Lead South Dakota Daily Call*, October 17, 1919, 6,

Interpret the Evidence

1. What impact did the pandemic have on the residents of Philadelphia (Source 20.6) and how did they cope with the disease?
2. Why did so many young women volunteer during the pandemic (Source 20.7) and how did it affect them personally?
3. How did the influenza outbreak provide economic opportunities for those peddling cures and treatments (Source 20.8) and why do you think many Americans were willing to try them?
4. How did Dr. A Wilberforce Williams view homemade folk remedies for the flu (Source 20.9)? Explain whether you think his newspaper column would likely have convinced his readers.
5. What lessons did the U.S. Public Health Service learn from the pandemic (Source 20.10)? How well do you think it communicated its findings?

Put It in Context

How was the influenza pandemic affected by World War I?

The Twenties

1919–1929

Window to the Past

Aaron Douglas, Illustration, "The New Negro," 1925

The post–World War I era brought serious challenges for African Americans. Murderous white assaults on black communities in the North and South, combined with the revival of the Ku Klux Klan, placed black lives in peril. Yet African Americans displayed their resistance in a variety of ways from the Black Nationalism of Marcus Garvey to the flourishing of the arts in the Harlem Renaissance. One leading painter, Aaron Douglas, used modern art to explore the African world of his ancestors. ▶ To learn more about this primary source, see Source 21.9 on page 741.

Library of Congress, Prints and Photographs Division [LC-US262-52879J/© 2020 Heirs of Aaron Douglas/Licensed by VAGA at Artists Rights Society (ARS), NY

After reading this chapter you will be able to:

- Explain the causes of the anti-communist panic, labor unrest, and escalating racial tensions following World War I.

- Evaluate the importance of the second industrial revolution, the creation of the consumer culture, urbanization, and the federal government in promoting economic expansion.

- Describe how white and black popular culture challenged traditional morality and gender roles.

- Examine the tensions between nativists and immigrants and fundamentalism and modernism, and explain how these culture wars affected federal policies.

- Explain the dominance of the Republican Party over the Progressive and Democratic Parties and analyze the political flaws that led to the Great Depression.

Comparing American Histories

Pursuit of the American dream kept **David Curtis (D. C.) Stephenson** on the move. Born in 1891 to Texas sharecroppers, Stephenson moved with his family to the Oklahoma Territory in 1901. After quitting school at age sixteen, he drifted around for more than a decade, working for a string of newspapers and gaining a reputation as a heavy drinker. In 1915 he married and settled down; however, he soon lost his newspaper job, abandoned his pregnant wife, and hit the road working for one newspaper after another in between binges of

(left) **D. C. Stephenson** Indiana Historical Society
(right) **Ossian Sweet** Courtesy of the Burton Historical Collection, Detroit Public Library

drunkenness. His wife divorced him, and in 1917 Stephenson joined the army to fight in World War I. Despite a series of drunken brawls and sexual misadventures, he received an honorable discharge in 1919.

Stephenson remarried and settled in Indiana, where he found financial and political success. In 1920 he joined the Ku Klux Klan (KKK), the Reconstruction-era organization that had reemerged in 1915 in Georgia. The newly revived Klan spread beyond the South, targeting African Americans, recent immigrants, Jews, and Catholics as enemies of traditional Protestant family values. Stephenson directed Klan operations in twenty-three states, building a profitable empire on fear, prejudice, and get-rich-quick schemes. A few years later, however, his Klan career ended with his arrest and conviction on rape and second-degree murder charges.

Ossian Sweet also pursued the American dream. Like Stephenson, he rose from humble beginnings. The descendant of enslaved people, Sweet was born in 1895 and grew up in central Florida. Hoping to shield him from the dangers of Jim Crow, Sweet's parents sent him north when he was thirteen years old.

After attending Wilberforce University in Ohio and Howard Medical School in Washington, D.C., Sweet moved to Detroit in 1921 to open a medical practice. He married, and in 1924 the Sweets decided to buy a house in a working-class neighborhood occupied exclusively by whites. Before the Sweets moved in, their white neighbors, with Klan backing, began organizing to keep them out.

When the Sweet family moved into their house on September 8, 1925, they encountered a hostile crowd in the street. Dr. Sweet had brought some backup with him. Armed to resist the mob, the Sweets and their defenders fired their weapons at the crowd after rocks smashed through the upstairs windows of the house. When the shooting stopped and the police restored calm, one white man lay dead and another wounded. Dr. Sweet; his wife, Gladys; and the other nine occupants of his house went on trial on first-degree murder charges. Hired by the NAACP, Clarence Darrow represented the eleven defendants and after two trials — the first ended in a hung jury — won an acquittal in 1926. ∎

The American histories of Ossian Sweet and D. C. Stephenson illustrate the competing forces that shaped the 1920s. Both men achieved a measure of financial success, but they did so in the post–World War I atmosphere of growing social friction and intense racial resentments. When Sweet's parents decided to send him north, they were responding to the racial violence that plagued the South, but they were also demonstrating their belief that a better life was possible for their son. By contrast, Stephenson grew wealthy by tapping into the same racial tensions that shaped the Sweets' lives. Many whites who considered themselves "100 percent Americans" believed that racial and ethnic minorities threatened their power. The fear of Communist infiltration heightened their concerns over immigration, and changes in morality and gender roles further aroused their fears. Although the general prosperity of the period masked the tensions lying beneath the surface, it did not eliminate them. Rampant consumerism concealed the unequal prosperity fostered by Republican Party policies that later led to the Great Depression. As the experiences of D. C. Stephenson and Ossian Sweet show, the decade following the end of World War I opened up fresh avenues for economic prosperity as well as new sites for cultural clashes exacerbated by the tensions of modern America.

Social Turmoil

The return of peace in 1918 brought with it problems that would persist into the 1920s. Government efforts to suppress opposition to U.S. involvement in World War I fostered an atmosphere of fear and repression that continued after the war. The influenza epidemic that killed hundreds of thousands of Americans and millions of people around the world further heightened anxiety. Finally, the abrupt transition away from a wartime economy produced inflation, labor unrest, and escalating racial tensions.

The Red Scare, 1919–1920.
The success of the Bolshevik Revolution in Russia in 1917 and the subsequent creation of the Union of Soviet Socialist Republics terrified officials of capitalist countries in western Europe and the United States. This fear was exacerbated in 1919 with the creation of the Comintern, an association of Communists who pledged to incite revolution in capitalist countries around the world. This sparked panic over Communist-inspired radicalism known as the **Red scare**, which set the stage for the suppression of dissent.

On March 3, 1919, in *Schenck v. United States* the Supreme Court invoked the Espionage Act to uphold the conviction of Charles Schenck, the general secretary of the Socialist Party, for mailing thousands of leaflets opposing the military draft. Delivering the Court's unanimous opinion, Justice Oliver Wendell Holmes ruled that during wartime Congress has the authority to prohibit individuals from using words that create "a clear and present danger" to the safety of the country. Although the trial record failed to show that Schenck's leaflets had convinced any young men to resist conscription, the Court upheld his conviction. Later that year in *Abrams v. United States*, the Court further limited free speech by sustaining the guilty verdict of five anarchists who distributed leaflets denouncing U.S. military efforts to overthrow the Bolshevik regime.

Postwar economic problems increased the anxiety of American citizens, reinforcing officials who sought to restore order by suppressing radicals. Industries were slow to convert their plants from military to civilian production, and consumer goods therefore remained in short supply. The war had brought jobs and higher wages on the home front, and consumers who had been restrained by wartime rationing were eager to spend their savings. With demand greatly exceeding supply, however, prices soared by 77 percent. At the same time, farmers, who had benefited from wartime conditions, faced falling crop prices as European nations resumed agricultural production and the federal government ended price supports.

A series of strikes launched by labor unions in 1919 contributed to the fear that the United States was under assault by sinister, radical forces. As skyrocketing inflation undercut wages and employers launched a new round of union-busting efforts, labor went on the offensive. In 1919 more than four million workers went on strike nationwide. In September, striking Boston policemen left the city unguarded, resulting in widespread looting and violence. Massachusetts governor Calvin Coolidge sent in the National Guard to break the strike and restore order.

Public officials and newspapers decried the violence, but they also greatly exaggerated the peril. Communists and socialists did support some union activities, but few of the millions of workers who struck for higher wages and better working conditions had ties to extremists. The major prewar radical organization, the Industrial Workers of the World, never recovered from the government harassment that had crippled it during World War I. However, scattered acts of violence allowed government and business leaders to stir up anxieties about the Communist threat. On May 1, 1919, radicals sent more than thirty incendiary devices through the mail to prominent Americans, though authorities defused the bombs before they reached their targets. The following month, bombs exploded in eight cities, including one at the doorstep of the home of A. Mitchell Palmer, the attorney general of the United States.

After the attack, Palmer launched a government crusade to root out Communists. Palmer traced the source of radicalism to recent immigrants, mainly those from Russia and eastern and southern Europe. To track down suspected radicals, Palmer selected J. Edgar Hoover to head the General Intelligence Division in the Department of Justice. In November 1919, government agents in twelve cities rounded up and arrested hundreds of foreigners, including the anarchist and feminist Emma Goldman. Goldman and some 250 other people caught in the government dragnet were soon deported to Russia. Over the next few months, the **Palmer raids** continued in more than thirty cities. Authorities arrested at least four thousand suspected radicals, interrogated them without legal counsel, and held them incommunicado without stipulating the charges against them. Of the thousands arrested, the government found reason to deport 556. The raids did not uncover any extensive plots to overthrow the U.S. government, nor did they lead to the arrest of the bombers.

Explore ▶

See Palmer's justification for the raids in Source 21.1.

More deportations would have taken place had it not been for Louis F. Post. As acting secretary of labor, Post had authority over the Immigration Bureau, which handled deportations. A reformer and supporter of workers' rights, Post concluded that many of the Palmer raids had been conducted without proper search warrants and prisoners interrogated without access to a lawyer. Consequently, Post freed some 3,000 prisoners and halted further deportations despite the opposition of Palmer and Hoover.

Post's actions helped reduce public enthusiasm for the Palmer raids. In 1920 a group of pacifists, progressives, and constitutional lawyers formed the American Civil Liberties Union (ACLU) to monitor government abridgments of the Bill of Rights. Although the Palmer raids ended, the Red scare persisted. After Hoover became director of the Bureau of Investigation (later renamed the Federal Bureau of Investigation) in 1921, he continued spying and collecting information on suspected radicals and increasing his power over the next several decades.

Guided Primary Source Analysis

A. Mitchell Palmer | The Case against the Reds, 1920

Attorney General A. Mitchell Palmer was a leading architect of the Red scare. In response to the strikes and bombings throughout 1919 into early 1920, Palmer organized a series of raids against suspected Communists, anarchists, and other foreign radicals. At least four thousand people were arrested, most of whom were later released. In an article in *Forum* magazine, Palmer defended his actions and described his views on radicalism and its threat to American society.

Source 21.1

Like a prairie-fire, the blaze of revolution was sweeping over every American institution of law and order a year ago. It was eating its way into the homes of the American workman, its sharp tongues of revolutionary heat were licking the altars of the churches, leaping into the belfry of the school bell, crawling into the sacred corners of American homes, seeking to replace marriage vows with libertine laws, burning up the foundations of society.

According to Palmer, what institutions did revolutionaries threaten?

Robbery, not war, is the ideal of communism. This has been demonstrated in Russia, Germany, and in America. As a foe, the anarchist is fearless of his own life, for his creed is a fanaticism that admits no respect of any other creed. Obviously it is the creed of any criminal mind, which reasons always from motives impossible to clean thought. Crime is the degenerate factor in society.

Why does Palmer think communism is a threat?

Upon these two basic certainties, first that the "Reds" were criminal aliens, and secondly that the American Government must prevent crime, it was decided that there could be no nice distinctions drawn between the theoretical ideals of the radicals and their actual violations of our national laws. An assassin may have brilliant intellectuality, he may be able to excuse his murder or robbery with fine oratory, but any theory which excuses crime is not wanted in America. This is no place for the criminal to flourish, nor will he do so, so long as the rights of common citizenship can be exerted to prevent him.

Why doesn't Palmer think there is any practical difference between the principles of radicals and their actions?

Source: A. Mitchell Palmer, "The Case against the Reds," *Forum*, February 1920, 174–75, 185.

▌ **Put It in Context**

How did the Red Scare shape the politics and culture of the 1920s?

Racial Violence in the Postwar Era.   Racial strife also heightened postwar anxieties. Drawn by the promise of wartime industrial jobs, more than 400,000 African Americans left the South beginning in 1917 and 1918 and headed north hoping to escape poverty and racial discrimination. (By 1930 another 800,000 blacks had left the South.) This exodus became known as the **great migration**. During World War I, many blacks found work in steel production, meatpacking, shipbuilding, and other heavy industries, but most were relegated to low-paying jobs. Still, as a carpenter earning $95 a month wrote from Chicago to a friend back in Hattiesburg, Mississippi: "I should have been here 20 years ago. I just begin to feel like a man." Most African American women remained employed as domestic workers, but more than 100,000 obtained manufacturing jobs.

For many blacks, however, the North was not the "promised land" they expected. Instead, they encountered bitter opposition from white migrants from the South competing for employment and scarce housing. As black and white veterans returned from the war, racial hostilities exploded. In 1919 race riots erupted in twenty-five cities throughout the country, including one in Washington, D.C., which Ossian Sweet witnessed firsthand. The previous year, W. E. B. Du Bois of the NAACP had urged the black community to "close ranks" to fight Germany, but the racial violence against blacks in 1919 embittered him. "By the God of Heaven," Du Bois wrote, "we are cowards and jackasses if now that that war is over, we do not marshal every ounce of our brain and brawn to fight a sterner, longer, more unbending battle against the forces of hell in our own land."

The worst of these disturbances occurred in Chicago. On a hot July day, a black youth swimming at a Lake Michigan beach inadvertently crossed over into an area of water customarily reserved for whites. In response, white bathers shouted at the swimmer and hurled stones at him. The black swimmer drowned, and word of the incident quickly spread through white and black neighborhoods. For thirteen days, mobs of blacks and whites attacked each other, ransacked businesses, and torched homes. Over the course of the riots, at least 15 whites and 23 blacks died, 178 whites and 342 blacks were injured, and more than 1,000 black families were left homeless.

Two years later, on May 31 and June 1, 1921, whites launched a killing spree against the black community of Tulsa, Oklahoma. Known at the time as "the Negro Wall Street," the Greenwood district of Tulsa contained numerous black businesses and churches and was the home of African American professionals. However, status and wealth did not protect the residents of the area from the power of white supremacy. After a black man was arrested for allegedly assaulting a white woman in an elevator, white mobs gathered around the jail, threatening to lynch him. Thwarted in their attempts, a crowd of over 2,000 gun-toting whites headed into Greenwood, where a contingent of armed blacks, many of whom were World War I veterans, fought back. Outnumbered by the white vigilantes, they were forced to retreat. During the fracas, city police deployed aircraft to drop firebombs on black businesses and residences, setting Greenwood ablaze. After the smoke cleared, at least thirty-six people lay dead, twenty-six blacks and ten whites, though recent investigations place the death toll in the **Tulsa Massacre** at around 300. Some 800 victims lay in hospital beds and another 6,000 black residents were locked up in internment centers for several days. Thousands of African Americans fled the city, as thirty-five blocks remained devastated from the fires. Nevertheless, black Tulsans took the initiative to rebuild Greenwood despite white opposition.

The Tulsa Race Massacre, 1921   This photograph captures what once was a section of the thriving black business district of Greenwood in Tulsa, Oklahoma, after racist white mobs burned it down and left an estimated 300 dead. A black man surveys the charred ruins in the aftermath of the massacre. Oklahoma Historical Society/Getty Images

Review & Relate

■ What factors combined to produce the turmoil of the immediate postwar period?

■ What factors contributed to the rise in racial tensions that accompanied the transition from wartime to peacetime?

Prosperity, Consumption, and Growth

Despite the turbulence of the postwar period, the 1920s were a time of vigorous economic growth and urbanization. Between 1922 and 1927, the economy grew by 7 percent a year. Unemployment rates remained low, as producers added new workers in an effort to keep up with increasing consumer demand. Aligning themselves with big business, government officials took an active role in stimulating industrial and economic growth. The average purchasing power of wage earners soared, but many Americans were left out of this economic boom.

Government Promotion of the Economy. The general prosperity of the 1920s owed a great deal to backing by the federal government. Republicans controlled the presidency and Congress, and though they claimed to stand for principles of laissez-faire and opposed various economic and social reforms, they were willing to use governmental power to support large corporations and the wealthy.

Senator Warren G. Harding of Ohio, who was elected president in 1920, declared that he and his party wanted "less government in business and more business in government." Harding's cabinet appointments reflected this goal. Treasury Secretary Andrew Mellon, a banker and an aluminum company titan, believed that the government should stimulate economic growth by reducing taxes on the rich, raising tariffs to protect manufacturers from foreign competition, and trimming the budget. The Republican Congress enacted much of this agenda. During the Harding administration, tax rates for the wealthy, which had skyrocketed during World War I, plummeted from 66 percent to 20 percent. Mellon believed that those on the lower rungs of the economic ladder would prosper once businesspeople invested the extra money they received from tax breaks into expanding production. Supposedly, the wealth would trickle down through increased jobs and purchasing power. At the same time, Republicans turned Progressive Era regulatory agencies such as the Federal Trade Commission and the Federal Reserve Board into boosters for major corporations and financial institutions by weakening enforcement.

Secretary of Commerce Herbert Hoover had an even greater impact than Mellon in cementing the government–business partnership during the 1920s. Hoover believed that the federal government had a role to play in promoting business activities and in lessening economic suffering. He insisted on voluntary cooperation between the public and private sectors. Hoover favored the creation of trade associations in which businesses would collaborate to stabilize production levels, prices, and wages. In turn, the Commerce Department would provide helpful data and information to improve productivity and trade.

Hoover's vision fit into a larger Republican effort to weaken unions by promoting voluntary business-sponsored worker welfare initiatives. For example, under the **American Plan**, some firms established health insurance and pension plans for their workers. As early as 1914, Henry Ford provided his autoworkers over twenty-two years old "a share in the profits of the house" equal to a minimum wage of $5 a day, and he cut the workday from nine hours to eight. Unions were further damaged by a series of Supreme Court rulings that

Teapot Dome Scandal   Clifford K. Berryman, the political cartoonist for the Washington *Evening Star*, illustrates the Teapot Dome scandal, which damaged the Harding administration. Captioned "Juggernaut," this image shows Secretary of the Navy Edward Denby on the left and Secretary of the Interior Albert Fall on the right fleeing from charges of bribery and corruption that a Senate committee brought to light. Granger restricted strikes and overturned hard-won victories such as child labor legislation and minimum wage laws. By 1929 union membership had dropped from approximately five million to three million, or about 10 percent of the industrial labor market.

Scandals during the Harding presidency diminished its luster but did not stall Republican economic policy. The **Teapot Dome scandal** grabbed the most headlines. In 1921 Interior Secretary Albert Fall collaborated with Navy Secretary Edwin Denby to transfer potential oil fields to the Interior Department. Fall then parceled out these properties to private companies. As a result, Harry F. Sinclair's Mammoth Oil Company received a lease to develop the Teapot Dome section in Wyoming. In return for this handout, Sinclair delivered more than $300,000 to Fall. In the wake of congressional hearings, Fall and Sinclair were convicted on a number of criminal charges and sent to jail.

Harding's sudden death from a heart attack in August 1923 brought Vice President Calvin Coolidge to the presidency. Coolidge distanced himself from the scandals of his predecessor's administration but reaffirmed Harding's economic policies. "The chief business of the American people is business," President Coolidge remarked.

Americans Become Consumers.
The 1920s marked a period of economic expansion and general prosperity. National income rose from approximately $63 billion to $88 billion, and per capita income jumped from $641 to $847, an increase of 32 percent. The purchasing power of wage earners climbed approximately 20 percent.

This great spurt of economic growth in the 1920s resulted from technological innovation and scientific management techniques (Figure 21.1). Perhaps the greatest innovation came with the introduction of the assembly line. First used in the automobile industry

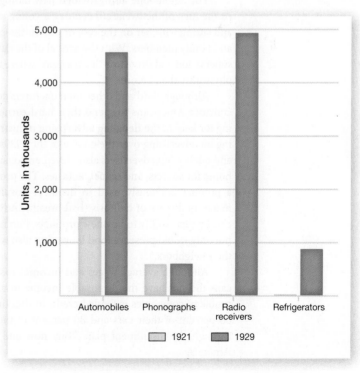

FIGURE 21.1 Production of Consumer Goods, 1921 and 1929

Rising per capita income, lower manufacturing costs, urban electrification, and advertising spurred the production of consumer goods in the 1920s. According to this figure, what were the most popular consumer goods in this period and how did they serve to bring Americans from all regions together?

before World War I, the assembly line moved the product to a worker who performed a specific task before sending it along to the next worker. Perfected by Henry Ford, this system saved enormous time, costs, and energy by emphasizing repetition, accuracy, and standardization, which allowed Ford to lower prices.

Besides the automobile, the **second industrial revolution** focused on the production of consumer-oriented goods. The electrification of urban homes created demand for a wealth of new labor-saving appliances. Refrigerators, washing machines, toasters, and vacuum cleaners appealed to middle-class housewives whose husbands could afford to purchase them. Wristwatches replaced bulkier pocket watches. Radios became the chief source of home entertainment.

Although such household items changed the lives of many Americans, the automobile had the most profound impact. Auto sales soared in the 1920s from a total of 1.5 million to 5 million, fueling the growth of related industries such as steel, rubber, petroleum, and glass. In 1929 Ford and his competitors at General Motors, Chevrolet, and Oldsmobile employed nearly 4 million workers, and around one in eight American workers toiled in factories connected to automobile production.

The automobile also changed day-to-day living patterns. Although most roads and highways consisted of dirt and contained rocks and ruts, enough were paved to extend the boundaries of suburbs farther from the city. By the end of the 1920s, around 17 percent of Americans lived in suburbia. Cars allowed families to travel to vacation destinations at greater distances from their homes, like to the resorts of Florida and the national parks in the Rocky Mountains and on the West Coast. Even the roadside landscape changed, as gas stations, diners, and motels sprang up to serve motorists.

The automobile also provided new dating opportunities for young men and women. At the turn of the twentieth century, a young man courted a woman by going to her home and sitting with her on the sofa or out on the porch under the watchful eyes of her parents and family members. With the arrival of the automobile, couples could get away from adult supervision and drive to a "lover's lane," where they could express their feelings with greater physicality than before.

Although Ford and other manufacturers succeeded in lowering prices, they still had to convince Americans to spend their hard-earned money to purchase their products. Turning for help to the fledgling advertising industry, manufacturers nearly tripled their spending on advertising over the course of the 1920s. Firms pitched their products around price and quality, but advertisers also played on consumers' unexpressed fears, unfulfilled desires, hopes for success, and sexual fantasies. The producers of Listerine mouthwash transformed a product previously used to disinfect hospitals into one that fought the dreaded but made-up disease of halitosis (bad breath). Advertisers invited consumers to measure success by their ability to buy new products. Purchasing a General Electric all-steel refrigerator not only would preserve food longer but also would enhance the owners' reputation among their neighbors.

Although average wages and incomes rose during the 1920s, the majority of Americans did not have the disposable income to afford new consumer goods. To resolve this problem, companies extended credit in dizzying amounts. By 1929 consumers purchased 60 percent of their cars and 80 percent of their radios and furniture on credit — mainly through the installment plan. "Buy now and pay later" became the motto of corporate America.

Chevrolet Advertisement, 1920s   The 1920s boom in the production of automobiles posed a challenge for business marketers and advertisers. They had to convince consumers that items once considered as luxuries were now necessities that would improve their lives. Many of these advertisements were directed at middle-class women who, as housewives, managed the family budget. The Chevrolet Motor Company aimed this advertisement at women by appealing to its car's easy handling and low price. Image Courtesy of The Advertising Archives

Urbanization.

The growth of cities helped promote the spread of the consumer-oriented economy. Increasingly clustered in urban areas, people had more convenient access to department stores and chain stores. Advertisers targeted city residents because they were easier to reach and a large middle class of shoppers provided a growing market.

The census of 1920 reported that for the first time in U.S. history a majority of Americans lived in cities. In 1910 just over 54 percent of the nation lived in small towns and villages with fewer than 2,500 people. A decade later, only 49 percent inhabited these areas. The end of World War I brought a decline in demand for American agricultural goods, and about six million residents left their farms and villages and moved to cities. By 1930 the percentage of those living in rural America dropped to 44 percent. The war had pushed large numbers of African Americans out of the rural South for jobs in the cities. Also, with war's end, immigration from southern and eastern Europe resumed.

The West grew faster than any other region of the country, and its cities boomed. From 1910 to 1930, the population of the United States increased by 33.5 percent; at the same time, the population of the West soared by nearly 59 percent. In northern California, the bay area cities of San Francisco, Oakland, and Berkeley nearly doubled in population. Seattle, Portland, Denver, and Salt Lake City also rose in prominence. After the war, western city leaders boasted of the business and employment opportunities and beautiful landscapes that awaited migrants to their urban communities (Map 21.1).

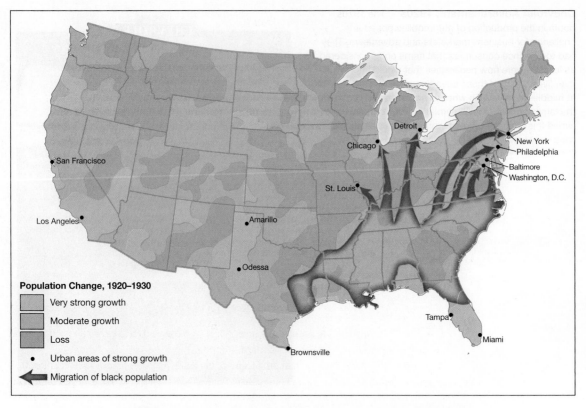

MAP 21.1   The Shift from Rural to Urban Population, 1920–1930

Throughout late nineteenth and early twentieth centuries the population of the nation had shifted from rural to urban areas. In the 1920s this migration continued, especially among African Americans in the South and Latinos in the Southwest and West. Many of these migrants from rural to urban landscapes actually stayed in the same region, particularly Latinos.

Los Angeles stood out for its growth, which skyrocketed from 319,000 residents in 1910 to over 1.2 million in 1930. The mild, sunny climate of southern California attracted midwesterners and northeasterners who were tired of rugged winters. Promoters enticed new residents to buy up real estate, which could be purchased cheaply and sold for a big profit. The city offered a dependable public transit system that connected Los Angeles and neighboring counties. During the 1920s, the motion picture industry settled here, and its movies delighted audiences throughout the nation. This urban boom boosted economic growth and, along with it, consumer spending.

Perilous Prosperity. Prosperity in the 1920s was real enough, but behind the impressive financial indicators flashed warnings that profound danger loomed ahead. Perhaps most important, the boom was accompanied by growing income inequality. A majority of workers lived below the poverty line, and farmers plunged deeper into debt. Corporate profits increased much faster than wages, resulting in a disproportionate share of the wealth going to the rich. The combined income of the top 1 percent of families was greater than

FIGURE 21.2 Income Inequality, 1923–1929

Although the U.S. economy expanded rapidly in the early 1920s, the accumulation of vast wealth among a small percentage of Americans created growing inequality. Explain the dangers this created for the overall economy in the 1920s.

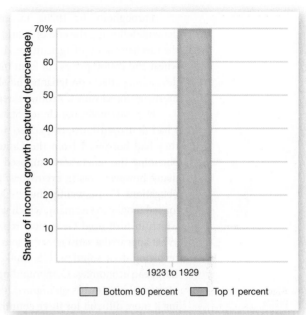

that of the 42 percent at the bottom (Figure 21.2); 66 percent lived below the income level necessary to maintain an adequate standard of living.

Income inequality was a critical problem because America's new mass-production economy depended on ever-increasing consumption, and higher income groups could consume only so much. While the expansion of consumer credit helped hide this fundamental weakness, the low wages earned by most Americans drove down demand over time. Cutbacks in demand forced manufacturers to reduce production, thereby reducing jobs and increasing unemployment, which in turn dragged down the demand for consumer goods even further. As a result, by 1926 automobile sales had begun to slow, as did new housing construction — signs of an economy heading for trouble.

At the same time, the wealthy few used their disproportionate wealth to speculate in the stock market and risky real estate ventures. To encourage investments, brokers promoted buying stocks on margin (credit) and required down payments of only a fraction of the market price. Without vigilant governmental oversight, banks and lending agencies extended credit without taking into account what would happen if a financial panic occurred and they were suddenly required to call in their loans. To make matters worse, the banking system operated on shaky financial grounds, combining savings facilities with speculative lending operations. With minimal interference from the Federal Trade Commission, businesspeople frequently managed firms in a reckless way that created a high level of interdependence among them. This interlocking system of corporate ownership and control meant that the collapse of one company could bring down many others, while also imperiling the banking houses that had generously financed them.

Rampant real estate speculation in Florida foreshadowed these dangers. In many cases, investors bought properties sight unseen, and assumed that land values would continue to increase. However, after severe storms in 1926 and 1928, land prices spiraled downward, speculators defaulted on bank loans, and financial institutions collapsed.

Throughout the 1920s, income plummeted for farmers as well. Declining world demand following the end of World War I, together with increased productivity because of the mechanization of agriculture, drove down farm prices. Between 1925 and 1929, falling wheat and cotton prices cut farm income in half. The collapse of farm prices had the most devastating effects on tenants and sharecroppers, who were forced off their lands through mortgage foreclosures. Around three million displaced farmers migrated to cities.

Internationally, the United States encountered serious economic obstacles. World War I had destroyed European economies, leaving them ill equipped to repay the $11 billion they had borrowed from the United States. Much of the Allied recovery depended on obtaining the reparations imposed on Germany at the conclusion of World War I. Germany, however, was in even worse shape than France and Britain and could not meet its obligations. Consequently, the U.S. government negotiated a deal by which American banks loaned money to Germany, which used the money to pay reparations to Britain and France, which in turn used Germany's reparations payments to repay debts owed to U.S. banks. What appeared a satisfactory resolution at the time ultimately proved a calamity. With this revolving-door solution, U.S. bankers were at the mercy of spiraling credit and unstable European economies. Compounding the problem, Republican administrations in the 1920s supported high tariffs on imports, thereby reducing foreign manufacturers' revenues, making it more difficult for these countries to pay off their debts.

Review & Relate

- Describe the relationship between business and government in the 1920s.

- Why was a high level of consumer spending so critical to 1920s prosperity, and why was the economic expansion of the 1920s ultimately unsustainable?

Challenges to Social Conventions

While most of the nation ignored growing evidence of the fragility of American prosperity, the social and cultural consequences of the second industrial revolution ushered in new, distinctly modern cultural patterns. Advertising and credit, two of the mainstays of modern capitalism, sought to bypass the time-honored virtues of saving and living within one's means. Conventional sexual standards came under assault from the growth of the film and automobile industries, which influenced clothing styles and dating practices. In addition to moral and social behavior, traditional racial assumptions came under attack. African American writers and artists condemned racism, drew on their rich racial legacies, and produced a cultural renaissance. Other blacks, led by the Jamaican immigrant Marcus Garvey, rejected the integrationist strategy of the NAACP in favor of black nationalism.

Breaking with the Old Morality. Challenges to the virtues of thrift and sacrifice were accompanied by a transformation of the moral codes of late-nineteenth-century America, especially those relating to sex. The entertainment industry played a large role in promoting relaxed attitudes toward sexual relations to a mass audience throughout the nation.

Challenging the "New Woman"   Many Americans were appalled by the look of the "New Woman" who flaunted traditional styles of dress. Municipalities passed ordinances prohibiting women from wearing bathing suits more than six inches above the knee. In this photograph taken in 1921, a fully clothed Chicago policewoman examines this bather at the beach to see if she has met the requirement. Bettmann/Getty Images

By the 1920s, Hollywood film studios had blossomed into major corporations, and movies were shown in ornate theaters in cities and towns across the country. The star system was born, and matinee idols influenced fashions and hairstyles. Female stars dressed as "flappers" and wooed audiences. Representing the liberated **new woman**, flappers sported short hair and short skirts, used ample makeup (formerly associated with prostitutes), smoked cigarettes in public, drank illegal alcoholic beverages, and gyrated to jazz tunes on the dance floor.

While Americans enjoyed new entertainment opportunities most remained faithful to traditional values. By 1929 approximately 40 percent of households owned a radio. Shows such as *The General Motors Family* and *The Maxwell House Hour* blended product advertising with family entertainment. *Amos 'n' Andy* garnered large audiences by satirizing black working-class life, which, intentionally or not, reinforced racist stereotypes. In cities like New York and Chicago, immigrants could tune in to foreign-language radio programs aimed at non-English-speaking groups, which offered listeners an outlet for preserving their ethnic identity in the face of the increasing homogeneity fostered by the national consumer culture.

The most spirited challenge to both traditional values and the modern consumer culture came from a diverse group of intellectuals known as the **Lost Generation**. Author Gertrude Stein coined the term to describe the disillusionment that many of her fellow writers and artists felt after the ravages of World War I. Already concerned about the impact of mass culture and corporate capitalism on individualism and free thought, they focused their talents on criticizing what they saw as the hypocrisy of old values and the conformity ushered in by the new. In the novel *This Side of Paradise* (1920), F. Scott Fitzgerald complained that his generation had "grown up to find all Gods dead, all wars fought, all faith in man shaken." In a series of novels, including *Main Street* (1920), *Babbitt* (1922), and *Elmer Gantry* (1927), Sinclair Lewis ridiculed the narrow-mindedness of small-town life, the empty materialism of businessmen, and the insincerity of evangelical preachers. Journalist Henry Louis (H. L.) Mencken picked up these subjects in the pages of his magazine, *The American Mercury*. From his vantage point in Baltimore, Maryland, he lampooned the beliefs and behavior of Middle America.

Scholars joined literary and social critics in challenging conventional ideas. Sigmund Freud, an Austrian psychoanalyst, shifted emphasis away from culture to individual consciousness. His disciples stressed the role of the unconscious mind and the power of the sex drive in shaping human behavior, beliefs that gained traction not only in university education but also in advertising appeals.

Scholars also discredited conventional wisdom about race. Challenging studies that purported to demonstrate the intellectual superiority of whites over blacks, Columbia University anthropologist Franz Boas argued that any apparent intelligence gap between the races resulted from environmental factors and not heredity. His student Ruth Benedict further argued that the culture of so-called primitive tribes, such as the Pueblo Indians, produced a less stressful and more emotionally connected lifestyle than that of more advanced societies.

The Harlem Renaissance.

The greatest challenge to conventional notions about race came from African Americans. The influx of southern black migrants to the North during and after World War I created a black cultural renaissance, with New York City's Harlem and the South Side of Chicago leading the way. Gathered in Harlem — with a population of more than 120,000 African Americans in 1920 and growing every day — a group of black writers paid homage to the **New Negro**, the second generation born after emancipation. These New Negro intellectuals refused to accept white supremacy. They expressed pride in their race and demanded full citizenship and participation in American society. Black writers and poets drew on themes from African American life and history for inspiration in their literary works.

The poets, novelists, and artists of the **Harlem Renaissance** captured the imagination of blacks and whites alike. Many of these artists increasingly rejected white standards of taste as well as staid middle-class black values. Writers Langston Hughes and Zora Neale Hurston in particular drew inspiration from the vernacular of African American folk life. In 1926 Hughes defiantly asserted: "We younger Negro artists who create now intend to express our dark-skinned selves without fear or shame. If white people are pleased, we are glad. If they are not, it doesn't matter." **See Primary Source Project 21: The New Negro and the Harlem Renaissance, page 739.**

Black music became a vibrant part of mainstream American popular culture in the 1920s. Musicians such as Ferdinand "Jelly Roll" Morton, Louis Armstrong, Edward "Duke" Ellington, and singer Bessie Smith developed and popularized two of America's most original forms of music — jazz and the blues. These unique compositions grew out of the everyday experiences of black life and expressed the thumping rhythms of work, pleasure, and pain. Such music did not remain confined to dance halls and clubs in black communities; it soon spread to white musicians and audiences for whom jazz rhythms meant emotional freedom and the expression of sexuality.

Augusta Savage Born in Florida, Augusta Savage joined other artists in moving to New York City in the 1920s as part of the Harlem Renaissance. She took formal art classes at the Cooper Union, working mainly in clay. In addition to the sculpture of the young boy here, Savage produced busts of W. E. B. Du Bois and Marcus Garvey. Hansel Mieth/The LIFE Picture Collection/Getty Images

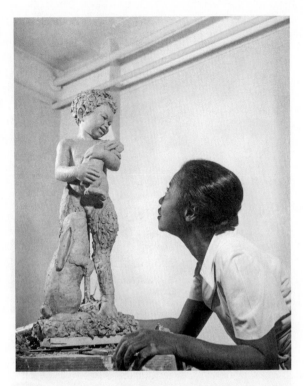

Marcus Garvey and Black Nationalism.
In addition to providing a fertile ground for African American intellectuals, Harlem became the headquarters of the most significant alternative black political vision of the 1920s. In 1916 the Jamaican-born Marcus Mosiah Garvey settled in Harlem and became the leading exponent of black nationalism. In 1914 Garvey had set up the **Universal Negro Improvement Association (UNIA)** in Jamaica, an organization through which he promoted racial separation and pride as well as economic self-help through black business ownership. Unlike the leaders of the NAACP, who sought equal access to American institutions and cooperation with whites, Garvey favored a "Back to Africa" movement that would ultimately repatriate many black Americans to their ancestral homelands on the African continent. His recently acquired Black Star Line steamship company planned to transport passengers between the United States, the West Indies, and Africa. Together with the indigenous black African majority, transplanted African Americans would help overthrow colonial rule and use their power to assist black people throughout the world.

Garvey also tapped into the racial discontent of African Americans for whom living in the United States had proved so difficult. He denounced what he saw as the accommodationist efforts of the NAACP and declared, "To be a Negro is no disgrace, but an honor, and we of the UNIA do not want to become white." Ironically, the UNIA and D. C. Stephenson's Klan agreed on the necessity of racial separation. Garvey's appeals to black manhood were accompanied by a celebration of black womanhood. He set up the Black Cross Nurses, and his wife, Amy Jacques Garvey, went beyond her husband's traditional notions of femininity to extol the accomplishments of black women in politics and

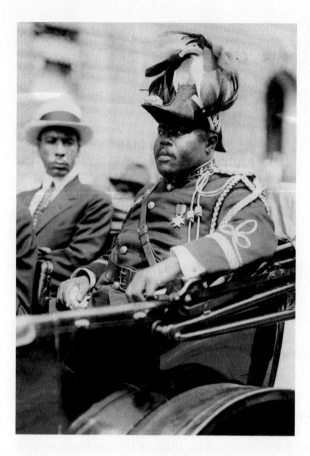

Marcus Garvey Dressed in military regalia topped off with a plumed hat, the Jamaican immigrant Marcus Garvey embodied the spirit of black nationalism after World War I. His Universal Negro Improvement Association, headquartered in Harlem, attracted a sizable following in the United States, the Caribbean, Central America, Canada, and Africa. Garvey advocated black political and economic independence. New York Daily News Archive/Getty Images

culture. Garveyism became the first mass African American movement in U.S. history and was especially effective in recruiting working-class blacks. UNIA branches were established in thirty-eight states throughout the North and South and attracted some 500,000 members.

Given his ideas and outspokenness, Garvey soon made powerful enemies. Du Bois and fellow members of the NAACP despised him. The black socialist labor leader A. Philip Randolph, who saw the UNIA program as just another form of exploitative capitalism, labeled Garvey an "unquestioned fool and ignoramus." Yet Garvey's downfall came from his own business practices. Convicted in 1925 of mail fraud related to his Black Star Line, Garvey served two years in federal prison until President Coolidge commuted his term and had the Jamaican citizen deported.

Review & Relate

■ How did new forms of entertainment challenge traditional morality and traditional gender roles?

■ Describe the black cultural and intellectual renaissance that flourished in the 1920s.

Culture Wars

Many segments of the population resisted attacks on traditional cultural and racial values. Rallying around the concepts of ethnic and racial purity, Protestant fundamentalism, and "family values," defenders of an older America attempted to roll back the tide of modernity. The enactment of prohibition was their greatest victory.

Prohibition. After decades of efforts to combat the use of alcohol, in 1919 the Eighteenth Amendment, banning its manufacture and sale, was ratified. That same year Congress passed the Volstead Act, which set up the legal machinery to enforce the amendment. Supporters claimed that prohibition would promote family stability, improve morals, and prevent crime. They took aim at the ethnically diverse culture of saloons associated with urban immigrants.

This attempt to promote traditional values proved difficult to enforce. In rural areas "moonshiners" took grain and processed it into liquor. In big cities, clubs known as speakeasies offered illegal alcohol and the entertainment to keep their customers satisfied. Treasury Department agents roamed the country destroying stills and raiding speakeasies, but liquor continued to flow. Nevertheless, prohibition did reduce alcohol consumption, but crime flourished. Gangsters paid off police, bribed judges, and turned cities into battlegrounds between rival criminal gangs, reinforcing the notion among small-town and rural dwellers that urban life eroded American values. By the end of the decade, most Americans welcomed an end to prohibition.

Nativists versus Immigrants. Prohibition reflected the surge in nativist (anti-immigrant) and racist thinking that revealed long-standing prejudices — earlier attempts at temperance reform had been largely aimed at immigrants. The end of World War I brought a new wave of Catholic and Jewish emigration from eastern and southern Europe, triggering religious prejudice among Protestants. Just as immigrants had been linked to socialism and anarchism in the 1880s and 1890s, old-stock Americans associated these immigrants with immoral behavior and political radicalism and saw them as a threat to traditional U.S. culture and values. As in the late nineteenth century, native-born workers saw immigrants as a source of cheap labor that threatened their jobs and wages.

The **Sacco and Vanzetti case** provides the most dramatic evidence of this nativism. In 1920 a botched robbery in South Braintree, Massachusetts, resulted in the murder of two employees. Police charged Nicola Sacco and Bartolomeo Vanzetti with the crime. These two Italian immigrants shared radical political views as anarchists and World War I draft evaders. The subsequent trial revolved around their foreign birth and ideology more than the facts pertaining to their guilt or innocence. The presiding judge at the trial referred to the accused as "anarchistic bastards" and "damned dagos" (a derogatory term for "Italians"). Convicted and sentenced to death, Sacco and Vanzetti lost their appeals for a new trial. Criticism of the verdict came from all over the world. Workers in Mexico, Argentina, Uruguay, France, and Morocco organized vigils and held rallies in solidarity with the condemned men. Despite such support, the two men were executed in the electric chair in 1927.

The Sacco and Vanzetti case provides an extreme example of 1920s nativism, but the anti-immigrant views that contributed to the two men's conviction and execution were commonplace during the period. For example, Henry Ford contended that immigrants did not understand "the principles which have made our [native] civilization," and he blamed the influx of foreigners for society's "marked deterioration" during the 1920s. He stirred up anti-immigrant prejudices mainly by targeting Jews. Believing that an international Jewish conspiracy was attempting to subvert Christian societies, Ford serialized in his company newspaper the so-called *Protocols of the Elders of Zion*, an anti-Semitic tract concocted in czarist Russia to justify pogroms against Jews. Ford continued to publish it even after the document was proved a fake.

Ford joined other nativists in supporting legislation to restrict immigration. In 1924 Congress passed the **National Origins Act**, a quota system on future immigration. The measure limited entry by any foreign group to 2 percent of the number of people of that nationality who resided in the United States in 1890. The statute's authors were interested primarily in curbing immigration from eastern and southern Europe, which had increased after 1890. Quotas established for northern Europe went unfilled, while those for southern and eastern Europe could not accommodate the vast number of people who sought admission. The law continued to bar East Asian immigration altogether. However, immigration from Mexico and elsewhere in the Western Hemisphere was exempted from the quotas of the Nation Origins Act because farmers in the Southwest needed Mexican laborers to tend their crops and pressured the government to excuse them from coverage. In a related measure, in 1924 Congress established the Border Patrol to control the flow of undocumented immigration from Mexico. Nevertheless, *legal* immigration to the United States from Mexico increased during the 1920s.

With immigration of those considered "undesirable" severely if not completely curtailed, some nativist reformers shifted their attention to Americanization. Speaking about immigrants, educator E. P. Cubberly said, "Our task is to break up their groups and settlements, to assimilate and amalgamate these people as a part of our American race, to implant in their children the northern-European conception of righteousness, law and order, and popular government." Business corporations conducted Americanization and naturalization classes on factory floors. Schools, patriotic societies, fraternal organizations, women's groups, and labor unions launched citizenship classes.

In the Southwest and on the West Coast, whites aimed their Americanization efforts at the growing population of Mexican Americans. Subject to segregated education, Mexican Americans were expected to speak English in their classes. Anglo school administrators and teachers generally believed that Mexican Americans were suited only for farmwork and manual trades. For Mexican Americans, therefore, Americanization meant vocational training and preparation for low-status, low-wage jobs.

To challenge discrimination against Mexican Americans, the League of United Latin American Citizens (LULAC) was formed in Corpus Christi, Texas in 1929. Mexican American veterans of World War I mainly took the lead and were soon joined by women from middle-class civic clubs. The league adopted the same nonpartisan, nonviolent, legalistic approach as did the NAACP in furthering racial equality, and campaigned to end discrimination against Mexican Americans at the ballot box, the workplace, and in schools. To this end, the league filed court cases and conducted voter registration drives. LULAC favored assimilation into American culture without Mexican Americans abandoning their heritage. Declaring its loyalty to the United States and supporting English as the official language, the league nevertheless affirmed: "We solemnly declare . . . to maintain a sincere and respectful reverence for our racial origins of which we are proud."

American Indians continued to face great challenges. During World War I, to save money the federal government had ceased appropriating funds for public health programs aimed at benefiting reservation Indians. With the war over, the government failed to restore the funds. Throughout the 1920s, rates of tuberculosis, eye infections, and infant mortality spiked among the Indian population. Boarding schools continued to promote menial service jobs for Indian students. Worse still, in Oklahoma with its large Native American population, a series of murders took place in Osage County. A 1921 federal law required members of the Osage tribe who received land allotments, many of which were atop rich oil reserves, to have a white guardian until they demonstrated "competency" to manage their parcels. Local white businessmen and lawyers made a good deal of money acting as guardians for the Osage. A federal investigation by J. Edgar Hoover's Bureau of Investigation discovered that some whites, besides engaging in fraud, committed murder to obtain the oil rights of the Osage. Only a few of the perpetrators were brought to trial and convicted. To protect this tribe, in 1925 Congress enacted a law prohibiting non-Osage from inheriting land allotments.

While these tragic events unfolded in Osage County, Congress passed landmark legislation on behalf of Native Americans. In 1924, the **Indian Citizenship Act** granted citizenship and the right to vote to all American Indians. Nevertheless, most Indians remained outside the economic and political mainstream of American society with meager government help.

Chinese residents also continued to face discrimination and segregation. The Chinese Exclusion Act remained in operation, making it difficult for nurturing family life. By 1920, Chinese men outnumbered Chinese women by seven to one. Furthermore, immigration restrictions prohibited Chinese workingmen from bringing their wives into the country. The 1924 National Origins Act made matters worse by banning all Asian women from entering the country. That same year the Supreme Court upheld the segregation of Chinese children in public schools.

Chinese communities faced problems similar to those experienced by other ethnic groups. Tensions developed between those born in China and their American-born children over assimilation. One Chinese American who grew up in San Francisco noted, "There was endless discussion about what to do about the dilemma of being *caught in between*." Many Chinese parents prohibited their children from speaking English at home and sent them to Chinese-language schools after public school. Chinese American children found cultural preservation efforts an onerous burden as they increasingly partook in America's growing consumer culture.

Despite attempts at Americanization, ethnic groups did not dissolve into a melting pot and lose their cultural identities. First-generation Americans — the children of immigrants — learned English, enjoyed American popular culture, and dressed in fashions of the day. Yet in cities around the country where immigrants had settled, ethnic enclaves remained intact and preserved the religious practices and social customs of their residents. Americanization may have watered down the "vegetable soup" of American diversity, but it did not eliminate the variety and distinctiveness of its flavors. Even the conservative U.S. Supreme Court weighed in favorably on the side of ethnic pluralism. During World War I Nebraska had enacted an anti-German measure prohibiting the teaching of any language other than English in its public schools. In *Meyer v. Nebraska* (1923), the Supreme Court struck down this law and affirmed that constitutional protections against unreasonable state restrictions applied to language minorities.

Resurrection of the Ku Klux Klan.

Nativism received its most spectacular boost from the reemergence of the Ku Klux Klan in 1915. Originally dedicated to terrorizing emancipated African Americans and their white Republican allies in the South during Reconstruction, the KKK branched out during the 1920s to the North and West. In addition to blacks, the new Klan targeted Catholics and Jews, as well as anyone who was alleged to have violated community moral values. The organization consisted of a cross section of native-born Protestants primarily from the middle and working classes who sought to reverse a perceived decline in their social and economic power. Revived by W. J. Simmons, a former Methodist minister, the new Klan celebrated its founding at Stone Mountain, Georgia, near Atlanta. There, Klansmen bowed to the twin symbols of their cause, the American flag and a burning cross that represented their fiery determination to stand up for Christian morality and against all those considered "un-American." By the mid-1920s, Klan membership totaled more than three million men and women.

Explore ▸

See Sources 21.2 and 21.3 for two perspectives on the KKK.

Not confined to rural areas, the revived Klan counted a significant following in D. C. Stephenson's Indianapolis and Ossian Sweet's Detroit, as well as in Chicago, Denver, Portland, and Seattle. Rural dwellers who had moved into cities with large numbers of black migrants and recent immigrants found solace in Klan vows to preserve "Native, white, Protestant supremacy."

The KKK also appealed to white women who desired to reestablish traditional values. In the face of challenges to conventional values, a changing sexual morality, and the flaunting of prohibition, wives joined their husbands as devoted followers. Protestant women appreciated the Klan's message condemning abusive husbands and fathers and the group's affirmation of the status of white Protestant women as the embodiment of virtue.

Like the original Klan, its successor resorted to terror tactics. Acting under cover of darkness and concealed in robes and hoods, Klansmen burned crosses to scare their victims, many of whom they beat, kidnapped, tortured, and murdered. To gain greater legitimacy and to appeal to a wider audience, the Klan participated in electoral politics. The KKK succeeded in electing governors in Georgia and Oregon, a U.S. senator from Texas, numerous state legislators, and other officials in California, Indiana, Michigan, Ohio, and Oklahoma. Politicians routinely joined the Klan to advance their careers, whether they shared its views or not.

The Klan did not go unchallenged. Organizations such as the Anti-Defamation League, founded by the Jewish service organization B'Nai B'rith in 1913, investigated and exposed the activities of anti-Semitic groups like the KKK. They were joined by the Catholic Holy Names Society, another target of the Klan, which in 1924 mobilized 10,000 marchers to Washington, D.C., to counter the Klan and promote religious tolerance. More than a dozen states, both in the North and South, passed laws aimed at the KKK, which banned the wearing of masks or hoods in public as a means of intimidation. More than these efforts, the conviction and imprisonment in 1925 of the Klan leader D. C. Stephenson for rape and murder dealt a severe blow to the KKK.

Fundamentalism versus Modernism.

Protestant fundamentalists also fought to uphold long-established values against modern-day incursions. Around 1910, two wealthy Los Angeles churchgoers had subsidized and distributed a series of booklets called *The Fundamentals*, informing readers that the Bible offered a true account of the genesis and development of humankind and the world and that its words had to be taken literally. After 1920, believers of this approach to interpreting the Bible became known as "fundamentalists." Their preachers spread the message of old-time religion through carnival-like revivals, and ministers used the new medium of radio to broadcast their sermons. Fundamentalism's appeal was strongest in the Midwest and the South—the so-called Bible belt—where residents felt deeply threatened by the secular aspects of modern life that left their conventional religious teachings open to skepticism and scorn.

Nothing bothered fundamentalist Protestants as much as Charles Darwin's theory of evolution. In *On the Origin of Species* (1859), Darwin replaced the biblical story of creation with a scientific theory of the emergence and development of life that centered on evolution and natural selection. Fundamentalists rejected this explanation and repudiated the views of fellow Protestants who attempted to reconcile Darwinian evolution with God's Word by reading the Bible as a symbolic representation of what might have happened. To combat any other interpretation but the biblical one, in 1925 lawmakers in Arkansas, Florida, Mississippi, Oklahoma, and Tennessee made it illegal to teach in public schools and colleges "any theory that denies the story of the Divine Creation of man as taught in the Bible."

Shortly after the anti-evolution law passed, the town of Dayton, Tennessee decided to take advantage of it to attract new investment to the area. The townspeople recruited John Scopes, a general science high school teacher, to defy the law by lecturing from a biology textbook that presented Darwin's theory. With help from the ACLU, which wanted to challenge the restrictive state statute on the grounds of free speech and academic freedom, Dayton turned an ordinary judicial hearing into the "trial of the century."

When court convened in July 1925, millions of people listened over the radio to the first trial ever broadcast. Reporters from all over the country descended on Dayton to keep their readers informed of the proceedings.

Clarence Darrow headed the defense team. A controversial criminal lawyer from Chicago, who in a few months would defend Ossian Sweet, Darrow doubted the existence of God. On the other side, William Jennings Bryan, three-time Democratic candidate for president and secretary of state under Woodrow Wilson, assisted the prosecution. As a Protestant fundamentalist, Bryan believed that accepting scientific evolution would undermine the moral basis of politics and that communities should have the right to determine their children's school curriculum. A minister summed up what the fundamentalists considered to be at stake: "[Darwin's theory] breeds corruption, lust, immorality, greed, and such acts of criminal depravity as drug addiction, war, and atrocious acts of genocide."

The presiding judge ruled that scientists could not take the stand to defend evolution because he considered their testimony "hearsay," given that they had not been present at the creation. The jury took only eight minutes to declare Scopes guilty, but his conviction was overturned by an appeals court on a technicality. Yet fundamentalists remained as certain as ever in their beliefs, and anti-evolution laws stayed in force until the 1970s. The trial served to highlight a cultural division over the place of religion in American society that persists to the present day.

Review & Relate

▌ What was the connection between anti-immigrant sentiment and the defense of tradition during the 1920s?

▌ Who challenged the new morality associated with modernization? Why?

Men and Women of the KKK

While the new Ku Klux Klan grew in power and visibility, many Americans also resisted and ridiculed the organization. In the first selection, journalist Gerald Johnson describes the typical KKK member. The second selection, an excerpt from the bylaws of a Maryland chapter of the Women of the Ku Klux Klan, indicates the group's devotion to the responsibilities of traditional womanhood. Nearly half a million women joined the women's auxiliaries of the KKK.

FPG/Hulton Archive/Getty Images

Source 21.2

Gerald W. Johnson | The Ku Kluxer, 1924

The Ku Klux Klan was swept beyond the racial boundaries of the Negro and flourishes now in the Middle West because it is a perfect expression of the American idea that the voice of the people is the voice of God. The belief that the average klansman is consciously affected by an appeal to his baser self is altogether erroneous. In the voice of the organizer he hears a clarion call to knightly and selfless service. It strikes him as in no wise strange that he should be so summoned; is he not, as an American citizen, of the nobility? Politics has been democratized. Social usage has been democratized. Religion has been most astoundingly democratized. Why, then, not democratize chivalry?

The klansman has already been made, in his own estimation, politically a monarch, socially a peer of the realm, spiritually a high priest. Now the Ku Klux Klan calls him to step up and for the trifling consideration of ten dollars he is made a Roland, a Lancelot, a knight-errant vowed to the succor of the oppressed, the destruction of ogres and magicians, the defense of the faith. Bursting with noble ideals and lofty aspirations, he accepts the nomination. The trouble is that this incantation doesn't work, as none of the others has worked, except in his imagination. King, aristocrat, high priest as he believes himself to be, he is neither royal, noble, nor holy. So, under his white robe and pointed hood he becomes not a Chevalier Bayard [French knight] but a thug.

Source: Gerald W. Johnson, "The Ku Kluxer," *American Mercury*, February 1924, 209–10.

Source 21.3

Women of the Ku Klux Klan, 1927

Objects and Purposes

SECTION 1. The objects of this Order shall be to unite white female persons, native-born Gentile citizens of the United States of America, who owe no allegiance of any nature or degree to any foreign government, nation, institution, sect, ruler, person, or people; whose morals are good; whose reputations and vocations are respectable; whose habits are exemplary; who are of sound minds and 18 years or more of age, under a common oath into a Sisterhood of strict regulation, to cultivate and promote patriotism toward our Civil Government; to practice an honorable clannishness toward each other; to exemplify a practical benevolence; to shield the sanctity of the home and the chastity of womanhood; to maintain forever white supremacy; to teach and faithfully inculcate a high spiritual philosophy through an exalted ritualism, and by a practical devotion to conserve, protect, and maintain the distinctive institutions, rights, privileges, principles, traditions, and ideals of a pure Americanism.

SEC. 2. To create and maintain an institution by which the present and succeeding generations shall commemorate the great sacrifice, chivalric service, and imperishable achievements of the Ku Klux Klan and the Women of the Reconstruction period of American History, to the end that justice and honor be done the sacred memory of those who wrought through our mystic society during that period, and that their valiant accomplishments be not lost to posterity; to perpetuate their faithful courage, noble spirit, peerless principles, and faultless ideals; to hold sacred and make effective their spiritual purpose in this and future generations, that they be rightly vindicated before the world by a revelation of the whole truth.

Source: Women of the KKK (Maryland) Records, Schlesinger Library, Radcliffe Institute, Harvard University, reprinted in *Modern American Women*, ed. Susan Ware (Boston: McGraw-Hill, 2002), 136–37.

Interpret the Evidence

1. How does Johnson describe the typical KKK member?
2. How do each of these statements identify the central purpose of the KKK?

▌Put It in Context

Why did the KKK and other nativist groups appeal to so many people during the 1920s?

Politics and the Fading of Prosperity

These cultural clashes tore the Democratic Party apart, leaving Republicans in command of national politics. As it attracted urban immigrants to its ranks alongside its customary base of white southerners, the Democratic Party tried to reconcile the tensions between traditional and modern America. Its failure to do so kept Republicans in power despite growing evidence of their inability to resolve serious economic problems. Although many progressives continued to press for reform, they were all but powerless to prevent the coming economic crisis.

The Battle for the Soul of the Democratic Party. The 1924 presidential election exposed serious fault lines within the Democratic Party. Since Reconstruction, Democrats had dominated the South. Southern Democrats shared fundamentalist religious beliefs and support for prohibition that usually placed them at odds with big-city Democrats. The northern urban wing of the party represented immigrants who rejected prohibition as contrary to their cultural practices. These distinctions, however, were not absolute — some rural dwellers opposed prohibition, and some urbanites supported temperance.

Delegates to the 1924 Democratic convention in New York City disagreed over a party platform and a presidential candidate. When northeastern urban delegates attempted to insert a plank condemning the Ku Klux Klan for its intolerance, they lost by a thin margin. The sizable number of convention delegates who either belonged to or had been backed by the Klan ensured the proposal's defeat.

The selection of the presidential ticket proved even more divisive. Urban Democrats favored New York governor Alfred E. Smith, who came from an Irish Catholic immigrant family and had grown up on New York City's Lower East Side. The epitome of everything that rural Democrats despised, Smith also denounced prohibition. After a fierce contest, the pride of New York City lost the nomination to John W. Davis, a West Virginia Protestant and a defender of prohibition. Left deeply divided going into the general election, Davis lost to Calvin Coolidge in a landslide (Map 21.2).

In 1928, the delicate cultural equilibrium within the Democratic Party had shifted in favor of the urban forces. With Stephenson and the Klan discredited and no longer a force in Democratic politics, the delegates nominated Al Smith as their presidential candidate.

The Republicans selected Herbert Hoover, one of the most popular men in the United States. Affectionately called "the Great Humanitarian" for his European relief efforts after World War I, Hoover served as secretary of commerce during the Harding and Coolidge administrations. His name became synonymous with the Republican

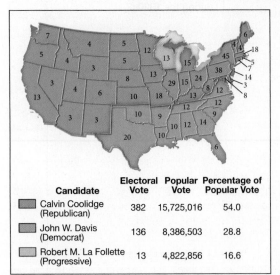

Candidate	Electoral Vote	Popular Vote	Percentage of Popular Vote
Calvin Coolidge (Republican)	382	15,725,016	54.0
John W. Davis (Democrat)	136	8,386,503	28.8
Robert M. La Follette (Progressive)	13	4,822,856	16.6

MAP 21.2 The Election of 1924

Republican Calvin Coolidge, who became president in August 1923 on the death of Warren Harding, continued Harding's policies of limited government regulation and corporate tax cuts. Coolidge easily defeated Democrat John Davis, whose strength was confined to the South. Running as the Progressive Party candidate, Senator Robert La Follette won 16 percent of the popular vote but carried only his home state of Wisconsin, with 13 electoral votes.

Explore ▶

See Sources 21.4 and 21.5 for two historians' interpretations of the effectiveness of the federal government during Prohibition.

prosperity of the 1920s. In accepting his party's nomination for president in 1928, Hoover optimistically declared: "We in America today are nearer to the final triumph over poverty than ever before in the history of the land." A Protestant supporter of prohibition from a small town, Hoover was everything Smith was not.

Hoover chose Charles Curtis as his vice-presidential running mate. Curtis's mother belonged to the Kaw Nation in Kansas. Curtis was a firm believer in Indian assimilation, and as a congressman he had successfully sponsored a bill that extended the Dawes Act to Indian territory in Oklahoma. Before campaigning for vice-president, he had served as Senate majority leader.

The outcome of the 1928 election proved predictable. Hoover trounced Smith with 58 percent of the popular vote and more than 80 percent of the electoral vote. Charles Curtis became the first vice-president of Native American ancestry. Despite the weakening economy, Smith lost usually reliable Democratic votes to religious and ethnic prejudices. The New Yorker prevailed only in Massachusetts, Rhode Island, and six southern states but failed to win his home state. A closer look at the election returns showed a significant party realignment under way. Smith succeeded in identifying the Democratic Party with urban, ethnic-minority voters and attracting them to the polls. Despite the landslide loss, he captured the twelve largest cities in the nation, all of which had gone Republican four years earlier. To break the Republicans' national dominance, the Democrats would need a candidate who appealed to both traditional and modern Americans. Smith's candidacy, though ending in defeat, laid the foundation for future Democratic political success.

Lingering Progressivism. The Democrats and Republicans were not the only parties that attracted voters in the 1920s. Some voters continued to cast their ballot for the Socialist Party. Others took the opportunity to voice their disapproval of Republican policies by voting for the remaining progressive candidates. Progressives did manage to hold on to seats in Congress, and in 1921 they helped pass the Shepherd-Towner Act, which appropriated federal funds to establish maternal and child centers. Senator Thomas J. Walsh of Montana, a progressive Democrat, led the investigation into the Teapot Dome scandal. But their efforts to restrict the power of the Supreme Court, reduce tax cuts for the wealthy, nationalize railroads, and extend agricultural relief to farmers were rebuffed by conservative legislative majorities. They did succeed in winning congressional passage of an amendment banning child labor, but it failed to win ratification by two-thirds of the states. In 1924, reformers nominated Senator Robert M. La Follette of Wisconsin to run for president on a revived Progressive Party ticket, but he came in a distant third. The Progressive Party collapsed soon after La Follette died in 1925.

Still, progressivism managed to stay alive on the local and state levels. Gifford Pinchot, a Roosevelt ally and a champion of conservation, twice won election as governor of Pennsylvania starting in 1922. Social workers continued their efforts to alleviate urban poverty and lobby for government assistance to the poor. Even at the national level, women in the Children's Bureau maintained the progressive legacy by supporting assistance to families and devising social welfare proposals. Progressivism did not disappear during the 1920s, but it did fight an uphill and often losing battle during an age of conservative political ascendancy. Its weakness contributed to the government's failure to check the worst corporate and financial practices, a failure that would play a role in the nation's economic collapse.

Financial Crash. On October 29, 1929, a day that became known as **Black Tuesday**, stock market prices tumbled. Over the previous five years, the rising market, bolstered by

The Impact of Prohibition

Prohibition, which culminated in passage of the Eighteenth Amendment (1919), pitted those who sought to combat what they considered the moral degeneracy of the modern city against those who considered the saloon an institution of immigrant cohesion. It should be recalled that Prohibition had a long history as a reform movement dating back to temperance campaigns in the mid- and late-nineteenth centuries that were aimed at promoting the economic and physical well-being of the family, particularly mothers and children. Writing five decades after Andrew Sinclair, a British historian skeptical about the war on alcohol, Lisa McGirr, a U.S. historian, takes a fresh look into the enforcement of Prohibition and the impact it had on American political culture.

Source 21.4

Andrew Sinclair | The Excesses of Prohibition, 1962

"[T]he leaders of the drys [prohibitionists] knew that they could never get a majority of the American people to give up drinking immediately. They hoped that a new generation of teetotalers would grow up from the ranks of the young, and that the protected drys would win converts among the shamed wets [drinkers]

. . . There was never any serious effort to enforce national prohibition until the early thirties, and by that time it was too late. After less than four years under the Volstead Act, it was clear that 'three tremendous popular passions' were being satisfied, 'the passion of prohibitionists for law, the passion of the drinking classes for the drink, and the passion for the largest and best-organized smuggling trade that has ever existed for money.' Once legalism had turned the possession of alcohol into a popular obsession and the sale of alcohol into a new Gold Rush, enforcement of the liquor laws had no chance.

The failure of the enforcement of the Volstead Act was due to the administrative stupidity, political graft, the federal structure of the United States, an antiquated legal system and the flaws in the act itself. These interlocking and corrigible causes for the failure were overshadowed by one overriding consideration, that the prohibition law could not be adequately enforced in the America of that time. . . . Indeed, it is doubtful that national prohibition can ever be enforced, even under a dictatorship. Alcoholic drinks have been made in every civilized society in history. . . . The job of the Prohibition Bureau was to enforce the impossible."

Andrew Sinclair, *Prohibition: The Era of Excess* (Boston: Little, Brown and Company, 1962), 182–83.

Source 21.5

Lisa McGirr | The National State and Crime Control, 2016

"The enforcement of Prohibition was notable for its magnitude and it selectivity. Not surprisingly for a movement led at its core by the well-heeled Protestant Anti-Saloon League, enforcement hit working-class, urban immigrant and poor communities hardest. It was, after all, enacted to discipline their leisure in the first place. . . . Prohibition law enforcement was anything but a dead letter. In the poor communities that bore its brunt, it contributed to a crisis of overcrowded court dockets and prisons.

. . . Even with its vast corruption, inefficacy, and insufficient funding, Prohibition marked the birth of a qualitatively new and enduring role of the federal state in crime control. The massive, flagrant violations of the law in response to the war on alcohol engendered a new public panic over crime. For the first time crime became a national problem, and a national obsession. The effort to restore law and order resulted in streamlined federal criminal record keeping, professionalized prison administration, new prison growth, and expanded and muscular federal policing, including stronger authority and a broadened purview of the FBI.

. . . Despite its baleful enforcement, Prohibition and the escalating crime it sparked permanently convinced Americans to look to the federal government for solutions to new national problems. The government did not retreat from its new role in crime control after the end of the war on alcohol. Its punitive approach to recreational narcotics persisted and expanded in new directions. . . . As broad support for the war on alcohol waned and then collapsed, key antiliquor crusaders turned their energies to the less controversial war against recreational narcotic drugs. With a second twentieth-century drug war contributing to a new crisis of overcrowded prisons and uncounted social costs, there is no better time to revisit the history of national alcohol Prohibition."

Source: Lisa McGirr, *The War on Alcohol: Prohibition and The Rise of the American State* (New York: W.W. Norton & Company, 2016), xiv, xviii, xxi, xxii.

Examine the Sources

1. Describe the major difference or differences between Sinclair's and McGirr's interpretations of Prohibition.
2. How might the difference in the times in which they wrote account for the differences in interpretation between Sinclair and McGirr?

Put It in Context

Evaluate the political and social effects that Prohibition had on the nation.

optimistic buyers, earned huge profits for investors, and the value of stocks nearly doubled. In late October, panicked sellers sent stock prices into free fall. Although only 2.5 percent of Americans owned stock, the stock market collapse had an enormous impact on the economy and the rest of the world. Because so much of the stock boom depended on generous margin requirements (a down payment of only 5 to 10 percent), when investor-borrowers got caught short by falling prices, they could not repay the financial institutions that had extended them credit. Banks and lending agencies, with their interlocking management and overextension of credit, had difficulty withstanding the turmoil unleashed by the tumbling stock market.

The 1929 crash signaled the start of the decade-long Great Depression. The seeds for this economic catastrophe had been planted far earlier. The causes stemmed from flaws in an economic system that produced a great disparity of wealth, inadequate consumption, overextension of credit both at home and abroad, and the government's unwillingness to relieve the plight of farmers. Republican administrations made matters worse by lowering taxes on the rich and raising tariffs to benefit manufacturers. The Federal Reserve Board exacerbated the situation by keeping interest rates high, thereby making it difficult for people to get loans and repay debts. The failure was not that of the United States alone; the depression affected capitalist nations throughout the world. The stock market collapse crushed whatever confidence the American public had that the unfettered law of supply and demand and laissez-faire economics could ensure prosperity.

Review & Relate

■ How did divisions within the Democratic Party contribute to Republican political dominance in the 1920s?

■ What underlying economic weaknesses led to the Great Depression?

Conclusion: The **Transitional** Twenties

The 1920s signaled the tense transition of the United States from a rural, small-town society to an urban, industrial one. Factories roared with the noise of new products aimed at the mass of American consumers. Automobiles, fueled by gasoline, traveled up and down streets and highways. Electricity powered household appliances and ran movie projectors in theaters throughout the nation. People living throughout the country had similar opportunities to buy consumer products and partake in a mass culture made possible by movies and radio. Producing for a mass market, industrial giants like Henry Ford transformed the nature of work and pleasure. The assembly line revolutionized the pace of labor and turned it into a standardized routine. The automobile transformed dating patterns and opened up new opportunities for the exploration of romance and sex.

Yet the roar of consumption and the excitement of breaking the ties of social and cultural conventions proved fleeting. Most Americans lived at or below the poverty line and earned just enough for bare necessities. They could live beyond their means through an ample supply of credit, but their poverty contrasted with the increasing concentration of wealth in the hands of the richest Americans. The stock market crash of 1929 and the ensuing Great Depression exposed the shortcomings of the corporate business world, inadequate oversight by the federal government, and an overreliance on the private sector to look after the nation's economic health.

The weaknesses of the economy were often overshadowed by the clash over cultural differences. Guardians of traditional morality and values worried about the effects of more than fifty years of industrialization, immigration, and urbanization. Issues such as the enforcement of prohibition, the teaching of evolution in the schools, and the debate about whether a Catholic should be elected president dominated political discussion, while efforts to assist farmers and workers were unsuccessful. These battles marked a turning point in U.S. history — the transition from a traditional, rural, Protestant society to an urban, ethnically and religiously diverse one. The widespread popularity of D. C. Stephenson's Ku Klux Klan throughout the South and the North demonstrated that the older America of white, northern European Protestants did not intend to relinquish political or cultural power without a struggle. At the same time, ethnic minorities represented by Al Smith had no intention of backing down. Neither did millions of African Americans, whether they joined the NAACP, as did Ossian Sweet, or supported Marcus Garvey's UNIA. During the next decade, Americans from all backgrounds would battle more than cultural threats; they would fight for their economic survival.

chapter **21** review

Timeline of Events

1915	Ku Klux Klan revived
1917–1918	Great migration begins
1917	Russian Revolution begins
1918–1920	Worldwide influenza epidemic
1919	Ratification of Eighteenth Amendment (Prohibition); Volstead Act passed
	4 million workers go on strike nationwide
	Race riots
	Radicals mail bombs
	Palmer raids begin
1919–1929	Harlem Renaissance
1920	American Civil Liberties Union (ACLU) formed
1921	J. Edgar Hoover becomes director of the Bureau of Investigation
	Teapot Dome scandal
	Tulsa Massacre
1924	Indian Citizens Act Passed
	National Origins Act passed
	Charles Dawes negotiates reduction in Germany's reparations payments
1925–1929	U.S. farm income drops by 50 percent
1925	Scopes trial
1927	Sacco and Vanzetti executed
1928	Democrat Al Smith loses presidential election to Republican Herbert Hoover
1929	Stock market crash sparks Great Depression
	Formation of League of United Latin American Citizens (LULAC)

Key Terms

Red scare, *709*

Palmer raids, *710*

great migration, *712*

Tulsa Massacre, *712*

American Plan, *714*

Teapot Dome scandal, *715*

second industrial revolution, *716*

new woman, *721*

Lost Generation, *721*

New Negro, *722*

Harlem Renaissance, *722*

Universal Negro Improvement Association (UNIA), *723*

Sacco and Vanzetti case, *725*

National Origins Act, *726*

Indian Citizenship Act, *727*

Black Tuesday, *733*

Review & Relate

1. What factors combined to produce the turmoil of the immediate postwar period?

2. What factors contributed to the rise in racial tensions that accompanied the transition from wartime to peacetime?

3. Describe the relationship between business and government in the 1920s.

4. Why was a high level of consumer spending so critical to 1920s prosperity, and why was the economic expansion of the 1920s ultimately unsustainable?

5. How did new forms of entertainment challenge traditional morality and traditional gender roles?

6. Describe the black cultural and intellectual renaissance that flourished in the 1920s.

7. What was the connection between anti-immigrant sentiment and the defense of tradition during the 1920s?

8. Who challenged the new morality associated with modernization? Why?

9. How did divisions within the Democratic Party contribute to Republican political dominance in the 1920s?

10. What underlying economic weaknesses led to the Great Depression?

The New Negro and the Harlem Renaissance

▶ Explain the political and social contexts that shaped the works of New Negro writers, artists, and performers.

In 1925 the editors of the magazine *Survey Graphic* invited Howard University sociologist Alain Locke to compile a special issue dedicated to Harlem. Locke did not suffer from a lack of source material, as the years following World War I had witnessed an unprecedented flowering of political activism and art in this majority-black section of New York City. The issue was an instant success, and Locke expanded it into a book, *The New Negro*, published that same year.

The intense activity in 1920s Harlem, which came to be known as the Harlem Renaissance, found expression in many different ways. Followers of Marcus Garvey endorsed not only black pride but also separatism. Democratic socialists such as A. Philip Randolph demanded full economic, political, and social equality for the New Negro (Source 21.6). Black writers broke ground in technique and subject matter. No topic was off-limits. Writers questioned the meaning of the American dream, as well as the significance of their shared African heritage. Poets examined African American history in all of its violence and challenged American blacks to confront the seemingly continuous rise of white supremacy in their home country. Black women challenged the gender conventions of both races. Writers and poets such as Langston Hughes, Claude McKay, Zora Neale Hurston, and Nella Larsen entered the canon of American literature (Sources 21.7 and 21.8).

The following sources offer only a glimpse of the ideas, writing, art (Source 21.9), and music (Source 21.10) that African Americans produced during the Harlem Renaissance.

Source 21.6

A. Philip Randolph and Chandler Owen | "The New Negro — What Is He?" 1919

A. Philip Randolph and Chandler Owen founded the *Messenger* in 1917 to provide an outlet for African American workers. The *Messenger* tackled issues of both race and class from a socialist perspective. It caused great controversy for its coverage of international issues, especially when it opposed U.S. involvement in World War I on pacifist grounds. The following editorial from 1920 elaborates on the definition of the New Negro and argues for fundamental changes in the structure of American life and politics.

In politics, the New Negro, unlike the Old Negro, cannot be lulled into a false sense of security with political spoils and patronage. A job is not the price of his vote. He will not continue to accept political promisory notes from a political debtor, who has already had the power, but who has refused to satisfy his political obligations. The New Negro demands political equality. He recognizes the necessity of selective as well as elective representation. He realizes that so long as the Negro votes for the Republican or Democratic party, he will have only the right and privilege to elect but not to select his representatives. And he who selects the representatives controls the representative. The New Negro stands for universal suffrage.

A word about the economic aims of the New Negro. Here, as a worker, he demands the full product of his toil. His immediate aim is more wages, shorter hours and better working conditions. As a consumer, he seeks to buy in the market, commodities at the lowest possible price.

The social aims of the New Negro are decidedly different from those of the Old Negro. Here he stands for absolute and unequivocal "*social equality*." He realizes that there cannot be any qualified equality. He insists that a society which is based upon justice can only be a society composed of *social equals*. He insists upon identity of social treatment. With respect to intermarriage, he maintains that it is the only logical, sound and correct aim for the Negro to entertain. He realizes that the acceptance of laws against intermarriage is tantamount to the acceptance of the stigma of inferiority. Besides, laws against intermarriage expose Negro women to sexual exploitation, and deprive their offspring, by white men, of the right to inherit the property of their father. Statistics show that there are nearly four million mulattoes in America as a result of miscegenation.

Source: A. Philip Randolph and Chandler Owen, "The New Negro — What Is He?" *Messenger* 2 (August 1920): 73–74.

Source 21.7

Claude McKay | "If We Must Die," 1919

Jamaican-born writer Claude McKay moved to the United States in 1912 and influenced many writers of the Harlem Renaissance. His poems focus primarily on race relations and the lives of working-class African Americans. The following poem is one of his most powerful and well-known works, written in reaction to the violence against African Americans in the summer of 1919.

If we must die, let it not be like hogs
Hunted and penned in an inglorious spot,
While round us bark the mad and hungry dogs,

Making their mock at our accursèd lot.
If we must die, O let us nobly die,
So that our precious blood may not be shed
In vain; then even the monsters we defy
Shall be constrained to honor us though dead!
O kinsmen! we must meet the common foe!
Though far outnumbered let us show us brave,
And for their thousand blows deal one death-blow!
What though before us lies the open grave?
Like men we'll face the murderous, cowardly pack,
Pressed to the wall, dying, but fighting back!

Source: Claude McKay, "If We Must Die," in *Harlem Shadows: The Poems of Claude McKay* (New York: Harcourt, Brace, 1922), 53.

Source 21.8

Langston Hughes | "The Negro Speaks of Rivers," 1921

No figure became more synonymous with the Harlem Renaissance than Langston Hughes. Poems like "The Weary Blues" (1926) and "I, Too, Sing America" (1925) simultaneously gave voice to the historical anxieties that African Americans faced and celebrated the roles of blacks in the arts. Hughes also wrote penetrating essays, such as "The Negro Artist and the Racial Mountain" (1925), which explored how African Americans might best present their art. In this poem, "The Negro Speaks of Rivers," Hughes ponders his relationship to Africa.

I've known rivers:
I've known rivers ancient as the world and older than the flow of
human blood in human veins.
My soul has grown deep like the rivers.
I bathed in the Euphrates when dawns were young.
I built my hut near the Congo and it lulled me to sleep.
I looked upon the Nile and raised the pyramids above it.
I heard the singing of the Mississippi when Abe Lincoln went down to New Orleans, and I've seen its muddy bosom turn all golden in the sunset.
I've known rivers:
Ancient, dusky rivers.
My soul has grown deep like the rivers.

Source: Langston Hughes, "The Negro Speaks of Rivers," *Crisis*, June 1921, 17.

Aaron Douglas | Illustration, *The New Negro*, 1925

Born in Topeka, Kansas, Aaron Douglas became the leading painter and illustrator of the Harlem Renaissance. He used techniques of modern art to explore themes of race and justice. This illustration appeared in Alain Locke's anthology, *The New Negro*, which contains selections by the major writers of the Harlem Renaissance.

Library of Congress, Prints and Photographs Division [LC-USZ62-52879]/© 2020 Heirs of Aaron Douglas/Licensed by VAGA at Artists Rights Society (ARS), NY

Bessie Smith | "Down-Hearted Blues," 1923

Music, particularly jazz and the blues, played a central role in the Harlem Renaissance. Born in Chattanooga, Tennessee, Bessie Smith became one of the most popular African American performers at venues like Harlem's Cotton Club. Her recording of "Down-Hearted Blues," written by Lovie Austin and Alberta Hunter, sold more than 750,000 copies and made Smith a major star of the burgeoning music industry. Its lyrics demonstrate how Smith used music to communicate ideas about relationships, gender, and sexuality.

Gee, but it's hard to love someone, when that someone don't love you,
I'm so disgusted, heartbroken too,
I've got those down-hearted blues.
Once I was crazy about a man, he mistreated me all the time,
The next man I see, he's got to promise to be mine, all mine.

Trouble, trouble, I've had it all my days,
Trouble, trouble, I've had it all my days,
It seems that trouble's going to follow me to my grave.

If I could only find the man, oh, how happy I would be,
To the Good Lord ev'ry night I pray, please send my man back to me
I've almost worried myself to death wond'ring why he went away,
But just wait and see, he's gonna want me back some sweet day.

World in a jug, the stopper's in my hand,
Got the world in a jug, the stopper's in my hand,
Going to hold it, baby, till you come under my command.

Say, I ain't never loved but three men in my life,
No, I ain't never loved but three men in my life,
'Twas my father, my brother, and the man who wrecked my life.

'Cause he mistreated me and he drove me from his door,
Yes, he mistreated me and he drove me from his door
But the Good Book says you'll reap just what you sow.

Oh, it may be a week and it may be a month or two,
Yes, it may be a week and it may be a month or two,
But the day you quit me, honey, it's coming home to you.

Oh, I walked the floor and I wrung my hands and cried,
Yes, I walked the floor and I wrung my hands and cried,
Had the down-hearted blues and couldn't be satisfied.

Source: Bessie Smith, "Down-Hearted Blues," Columbia A3844, 1923.

Interpret the Evidence

1. Compare the idea of the New Negro as presented by the editors of the *Messenger* (Source 21.6) with the ideas expressed by Claude McKay (Source 21.7).
2. Explain how Langston Hughes appeals to history to lend insight into the experiences of Africans in America (Source 21.8).
3. How does Aaron Douglas illustrate the themes Hughes presents in his poetry (Source 21.9)?
4. Examine whether Bessie Smith's lyrics (Source 21.10) provide evidence of the idea of the New Negro.

Put It in Context

Why did the Harlem Renaissance flourish in the 1920s?

Depression, Dissent, and the New Deal

1929–1940

Window to the Past

A Sharecropper's Family in Washington County, Arkansas, 1935

Photographers captured ordinary Americans as they tried to survive the hardships of the Great Depression. Through stark black-and-white photos they gave representation to those "forgotten Americans" who were, as Franklin Roosevelt put it, "ill-housed, ill-clad, ill-nourished." ▶ **To learn more about this primary source, see Source 22.8 on page 778.**

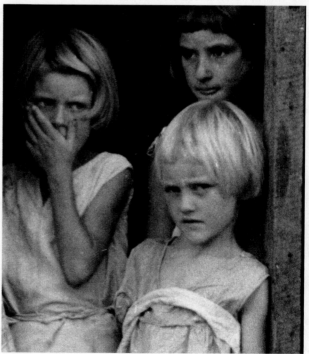

Franklin D. Roosevelt Library

After reading this chapter you will be able to:

- Evaluate the Hoover administration's response to the Great Depression and its impact on the rural poor, working people, and racial and ethnic minorities.

- Describe the major New Deal programs and assess their positive and negative effects on the groups they were designed to help.

- Explain how the New Deal expanded its scope after 1935 and why it came to an end in 1938.

Comparing American Histories

In 1901, at the age of fifteen, Anna Eleanor Roosevelt saw her uncle Theodore succeed William McKinley as president. Like other girls of her generation, Eleanor was expected to marry and become a "charming wife." Eleanor appeared well on her way toward doing so when she married her distant cousin Franklin Delano Roosevelt in 1905. Over a ten-year period, Eleanor gave birth to six children, further reinforcing her status as a traditional woman of her class.

Two events, however, altered the expected course of her life. First, thirteen years into her marriage **Eleanor Roosevelt** discovered that her husband was having an affair with her social secretary, Lucy Mercer. She did not divorce him but made it clear that she would stay with him primarily as a mother to their children and a political partner. Second, in 1921 Franklin contracted polio. Although he recovered,

he would never walk again or stand without the aid of braces. This physical hardship allowed Eleanor to gain increased political influence with Franklin. After her husband won the presidency in 1932, Eleanor did not function as a typical First Lady. She played a very public role promoting her husband's agenda, and she also took advantage of her own extensive contacts in labor unions, civil rights organizations, and women's groups to advance a variety of causes. In many ways more liberal than her husband, Eleanor was a fierce advocate for the rights of women, racial minorities, workers, and the poor. Behind the scenes, she pushed her husband to move further to the political left.

Eleanor Roosevelt's proximity to power provided her with a unique position from which to confront the problems of her day. In contrast, **Luisa Moreno** provides a striking example of an activist whose American story bears little resemblance to that of Roosevelt. A native of Guatemala, Moreno moved to Mexico and then New York City. In the midst of the Great Depression, she worked as a seamstress in a sweatshop to support her young child and unemployed husband. Like tens of thousands of people disillusioned with capitalism, in 1930 she joined the Communist Party but quit several years later.

In 1935 Moreno went to Florida to organize cigar workers for the American Federation of Labor (AFL). Despite numerous successes, she grew tired of the AFL's refusal to recruit unskilled workers and jumped to the United Cannery, Agricultural, Packing, and Allied Workers of America (UCAPAWA), an affiliate of the Congress of Industrial Organizations (CIO).

Moreno promoted the advancement of Latinos throughout the United States. In 1939 she helped create El Congreso de Pueblos de Habla Española (The Congress of Spanish-Speaking People). Besides championing equal access to jobs, education, housing, and health care, the organization pressed to end the segregation of Latinos in schools and public accommodations. Moreno was not nearly as well-known as Eleanor Roosevelt, but she worked just as hard to fight poverty, exploitation, and racial bigotry on behalf of people whom President Franklin Roosevelt called "the forgotten Americans." ∎

(*left*) **Eleanor Roosevelt** Library of Congress, Prints and Photographs Division [LC-USZ62-25812]

(*right*) **Luisa Moreno** Courtesy of Vicki Ruiz

The American histories of Eleanor Roosevelt and Luisa Moreno are very different, but both of their lives were shaped in fundamental ways by the same global catastrophe, the Great Depression. Even before the Great Depression, most Americans lived at or near the poverty level, surviving month to month. By 1933, millions of Americans had lost even this tenuous hold on economic security, as unemployment reached a record 25 percent. The Republican administration of President Herbert Hoover depended on private charity and voluntary efforts to meet the needs of downtrodden Americans afflicted by the Depression, but these efforts fell short of the vast need that grew during the Depression and left many frustrated. Proclaiming the establishment of a New Deal for America, Franklin Roosevelt expanded the power of the federal government by initiating relief, recovery, and reform measures, all the while drawing critics on the political left and right. In seeking to break from the past, Roosevelt occasionally overextended his reach, as he did in challenging the Supreme Court. Despite its successes, the New Deal did not end the depression and left racial and ethnic minorities and the rural and urban poor still suffering.

The Great Depression

Herbert Hoover had the unenviable task of assuming the presidency in 1929 just as the economy was about to crumble. Given his long history of public service, he seemed the right man for the job. Hoover, however, was unwilling to make a fundamental break with conventional economic approaches and proved unable to effectively communicate his genuine concern for the plight of the poor. Despite his sincere efforts, the depression deepened. As this happened, many Americans, made desperate by their economic plight and angered by the inadequate response of their government, took to the streets in protest.

Hoover Faces the Depression. National prosperity was at its peak when the Republican Hoover entered the White House in March 1929. Hoover brought to the presidency a blend of traditional and progressive ideas. He believed that government and business should form voluntary partnerships to work toward common goals. He argued that the government should extend its influence lightly over the economy — to encourage and persuade sensible behavior, but not to impose itself on the private sector.

The Great Depression sorely tested Hoover's beliefs. Having placed his faith in cooperation rather than coercion, the president relied on voluntarism to get the nation through hard economic times. Hoover hoped that management and labor, through gentle persuasion, would hold steady on prices and wages. In the meantime, for those in dire need, the president turned to local communities and private charities. Hoover expected municipal and state governments to shoulder the burden of providing relief to the needy, just as they had during previous economic downturns.

Hoover's remedies failed to rally the country back to good economic health. Initially, businesspeople responded positively to the president's request to maintain the status quo, but when the economy did not bounce back, they lost confidence and defected. Nor did local governments and private agencies have the funds to provide relief to all those who needed it. With tax revenues in decline, some 1,300 municipalities across the country had gone bankrupt by 1933. Benevolent societies and religious groups could handle short-term misfortunes, but they could not cope with the ongoing disaster of mass unemployment (Figure 22.1).

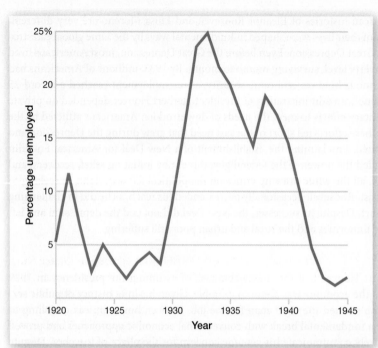

FIGURE 22.1 Unemployment, 1920–1945

Business prosperity and immigration restriction ensured low unemployment during most of the 1920s. When unemployment rose dramatically in the late 1920s, President Hoover failed to handle the crisis. During the 1930s, President Roosevelt's New Deal took initiatives to lower unemployment. What does this figure indicate about the effectiveness of New Deal programs on unemployment?

As confidence in recovery fell and the economy sank deeper into depression, President Hoover shifted direction. He persuaded Congress to lower income tax rates and to allocate an unprecedented $423 million for federal public works projects. In 1929 the president signed into law the Agricultural Marketing Act, a measure aimed at raising prices for long-suffering farmers.

Hoover's recovery efforts fell short, however. He retreated from initiating greater spending because he feared government deficits more than unemployment. With federal accounting sheets showing a rising deficit, Hoover reversed course in 1932 and joined with Congress in sharply raising income, estate, and corporate taxes on the wealthy. This effectively slowed down investment and new production, throwing millions more American workers out of jobs. The Hawley-Smoot Act, passed by Congress in 1930, made matters worse. In an effort to replenish revenues and protect American farmers and companies from foreign competition, the act increased tariffs on agricultural and industrial imports. However, other countries retaliated by raising their import duties, which hurt American companies because it diminished demand for American exports.

In an exception to his aversion to spending, Hoover lobbied Congress to create the Reconstruction Finance Corporation (RFC) to supply loans to troubled banks, railroads, and insurance companies. By injecting federal dollars into these critical enterprises, the president and lawmakers expected to produce dividends that would trickle down from the top of the economic structure to the bottom. In 1932 Congress gave the RFC a budget of $1.5 billion to employ people in public works projects, a significant allocation for those individuals hardest hit by the depression.

This departure from Republican economic philosophy failed to reach its goal. The RFC spent its budget too cautiously, and its funds reached primarily those institutions that could best afford to repay the loans, ignoring the companies in the greatest difficulty. Wealth never trickled down. Hoover was not indifferent to the plight of others, but he was incapable of breaking away from his ideological preconceptions. He refused to support expenditures for direct relief for basic needs (what today we call welfare) and hesitated to extend assistance for work relief because he believed that it would ruin individual initiative and character.

Hoover and the United States did not face the Great Depression alone; it was a world-wide calamity. By 1933 Germany, France, and Great Britain were all facing mass unemployment. In this climate of extreme social and economic unrest, authoritarian dictators came to power in a number of European countries, including Germany, Italy, Spain, and Portugal. Each claimed that his country's social and economic problems could be solved only by placing power in the hands of a single, all-powerful leader.

Hoovervilles and Dust Storms.
The depression hit all areas of the United States hard. In large cities, families crowded into apartments with no gas or electricity and little food to put on the table. In Los Angeles, people cooked their meals over wood fires in backyards. In many cities, the homeless constructed makeshift housing consisting of cartons, old newspapers, and cloth — what journalists derisively dubbed Hoovervilles. Thousands of hungry citizens wound up living under bridges in Portland, Oregon; in wrecked autos in city dumps in Brooklyn, New York, and Stockton, California; and in abandoned coal furnaces in Pittsburgh.

Soup Kitchen, 1931   At the height of the Great Depression, these unemployed men stand in a long line outside a Chicago soup kitchen waiting for a meal. Without major government relief efforts for the unemployed during the Hoover administration, such men depended mainly on the efforts of charity. In this instance, the notorious gangster Al Capone set up this establishment before going to federal prison for tax evasion in 1932. National Archives, photo no. 306-NT-165319c

Rural workers fared no better. Landlords in West Virginia and Kentucky evicted coal miners and their families from their homes in the dead of winter, forcing them to live in tents. Farmers in the Great Plains, who were already experiencing foreclosures, were little prepared for the even greater natural disaster that laid waste to their farms. In the early 1930s, dust storms swept through western Kansas, eastern Colorado, western Oklahoma, the Texas Panhandle, and eastern New Mexico, in an area that came to be known as the Dust Bowl, destroying crops and plant and animal life (Map 22.1). The storms resulted from both climatological and human causes. A series of droughts had destroyed crops and turned the earth into sand, which gusts of wind deposited on everything that lay in their path. Though they did not realize it at the time, plains farmers, by focusing on growing wheat for income, had neglected planting trees and grasses that would have kept the earth from eroding and turning into dust. **See Primary Source Project 22: The Depression in Rural America, page 776.**

As the storms continued through the 1930s, most residents — approximately 75 percent — remained on the plains. Millions, however, headed for California looking for relief from the plague of swirling dirt and hoping to find jobs in the state's fruit and vegetable fields. Although they came from several states besides Oklahoma, these migrants came to be known as "Okies," a derogatory term used by those who resented and looked down on the poverty-stricken newcomers to their communities. John Steinbeck's novel *The Grapes of Wrath* (1939) portrayed the plight of the fictional Joad family as storms and a bank foreclosure destroyed their Oklahoma farm and sent them on the road to California.

Challenges for Racial Minorities.
Given the demographics of the workforce, the overwhelming majority of Americans who lost their jobs were white men; yet racial and ethnic minorities, including African Americans, Latinos, and Asian Americans, suffered disproportionate hardship. Racial discrimination had kept these groups from achieving economic and political equality, and the Great Depression added to their woes.

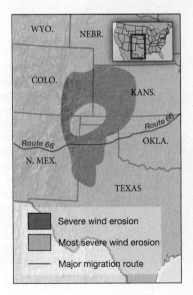

MAP 22.1 The Dust Bowl

Although "Okies" was the term used for the migrants escaping the Dust Bowl and heading to California, as depicted in John Steinbeck's classic novel *Grapes of Wrath*, Oklahoma was not the only state from where they came. Many of those who fled the terrible windstorms also journeyed from their homes in Kansas, Texas, and Colorado. Seen at the time as a natural phenomenon, the dust storms in fact originated from man-made agricultural practices that eroded the soil.

Traditionally the last hired and the first fired, blacks occupied the lowest rungs on the industrial and agricultural ladders. "The depression brought everybody down a peg or two," the African American poet Langston Hughes wryly commented. "And the Negroes had but few pegs to fall." Despite the great migration to the North during and after World War I, three-quarters of the black population still lived in the South. Mainly sharecroppers and tenant farmers, black southerners were mired in debt that they could not repay as crop prices plunged to record lows during the 1920s. As white landowners struggled to save their farms by introducing machinery to cut labor costs, they forced black sharecroppers off the land and into even greater poverty. Nor was the situation better for black workers employed at the lowest-paying jobs as janitors, menial laborers, maids, and laundresses. On average, African Americans earned $200 a year, less than one-quarter of the average wage of white factory workers.

The economic misfortune that African Americans experienced was compounded by the fact that they lived in a society rigidly constructed to preserve white supremacy. The 25 percent of blacks living in the North faced racial discrimination in employment, housing, and the criminal justice system, but at least they could express their opinions and desires by voting. By contrast, black southerners remained segregated and disfranchised by law. The depression also exacerbated racial tensions, as whites and blacks competed for the shrinking number of jobs. Lynching, which had declined during the 1920s, surged upward — in 1933 twenty-four blacks lost their lives to this form of terrorism.

Events in Scottsboro, Alabama, reflected the special misery African Americans faced during the Great Depression. Trouble erupted in 1931 when two young, unemployed white women, Ruby Bates and Victoria Price, snuck onto a freight train heading to Huntsville, Alabama. Before the train reached the Scottsboro depot, a fight broke out between black and white men on top of the freight car occupied by the two women. After the train pulled in to Scottsboro, the local sheriff arrested nine black youths between the ages of twelve and nineteen. Charges of assault quickly escalated into rape, when the women told authorities that the black men in custody had molested them on board the train.

The defendants' court-appointed attorney was less than competent and had little time to prepare his clients' cases. It probably made no difference, as the all-white male jury swiftly convicted the accused and awarded the harshest of sentences; only the youngest defendant was not given the death penalty. The Supreme Court spared the lives of the **Scottsboro Nine** by overturning their guilty verdicts in 1932 on the grounds that the defendants did not have adequate legal representation and again in 1935 because blacks had been systematically excluded from the jury pool. Although Ruby Bates had recanted her testimony and there was no physical evidence of rape, retrials in 1936 and 1937 pro-

Explore ▶

See Source 22.1 for a letter from the Scottsboro prisoners.

duced the same guilty verdicts, but this time the defendants did not receive the death penalty — a minor victory considering the charges. State prosecutors dismissed charges against four of the accused, all of whom had already spent six years in jail. Despite international protests against this racist injustice, the last of the remaining five did not leave jail until 1950.

Racism also worsened the impact of the Great Depression on Spanish-speaking Americans. Mexicans and Mexican Americans made up the largest segment of the Latino population living in the United States. Concentrated in the Southwest and California, they worked in a variety of low-wage factory jobs and as migrant laborers in fruit and vegetable fields. The depression reduced the Mexican-born population living in the United States in

Scottsboro Nine, 1933 Two years after their original conviction, the Scottsboro defendants discuss their new trial with their attorney Samuel Leibowitz in 1933 while still in prison. Flanked by two guards, they are from the left, Olen Montgomery, Clarence Norris, Willie Robertson, Andrew Wright, Ozie Powell, Eugene Williams, Charlie Weems, and Roy Wright. Haywood Patterson is seated next to Leibowitz. Known as the "Scottsboro Boys," at the time of their arrest they ranged in age from twelve to nineteen. Granger

two ways. The federal government, in cooperation with state and local governments and private businesses, deported (or what officials called "repatriation") around one million Mexicans, a majority of whom were American citizens. Los Angeles officials organized more than a dozen deportation trains transporting thousands of Mexicans to the border. Many others returned to Mexico voluntarily when demand for labor in the United States dried up.

The exodus eased off by 1933, as the number of migrants no longer posed an economic threat and the Roosevelt administration adopted more humane policies. Those who remained endured growing hardships. Relief agencies refused to provide them with the same benefits as whites. Like African Americans, they encountered discrimination in public schools, in public accommodations, and at the ballot box. Conditions remained harshest for migrant workers toiling long hours for little pay and living in overcrowded and poorly constructed housing. In both fields and factories, employers had little incentive to improve the situation because there were plenty of white migrant workers to fill their positions.

The transient nature of agricultural work and the vulnerability of Mexican laborers made it difficult for workers to organize, but Mexican Americans played a pivotal role in forming some forty agricultural unions in California during the 1930s. Mexican American laborers engaged in dozens of strikes in California and Texas. Most ended in defeat, but a few, such as a strike of pecan shellers in San Antonio, Texas, led by Luisa Moreno, won better working conditions and higher wages. Toward the end of the decade, strikers in

Guided Primary Source Analysis

Plea from the Scottsboro Prisoners, 1932

In 1931, nine black youths were arrested in Scottsboro, Alabama and charged with raping two white women. They were quickly convicted, and eight were sentenced to death. (One of the nine, Roy Wright, was twelve years old, and the prosecution did not seek the death penalty.) In this letter to the editor of the Negro Worker, a Communist magazine, the Scottsboro Nine plead their innocence and ask for help. A year had passed since their arrest and trial, which would account for their ages in the following statement recorded as between thirteen to twenty. Only those sentenced to death signed the letter. The use of the racial epithet for black people quoted in the letter reflects the pervasive racism of the era.

Source 22.1

Why do you think they mention their ages?

What tactics did Alabama officials use on the prisoners? What was their purpose?

Why do the Scottsboro prisoners repeatedly emphasize that they were workers?

We have been sentenced to die for something we ain't never done. Us poor boys have been sentenced to burn up on the electric chair for the reason that we is workers—and the color of our skin is black. We like any one of you workers is none of us older than 20. Two of us is 14 and one is 13 [12] years old.

What we guilty of? Nothing but being out of a job. Nothing but looking for work. Our kinfolk was starving for food. We wanted to help them out. So we hopped a freight—just like any one of you workers might a done—to go down to Mobile to hunt work. We was taken off the train by a mob and framed up on rape charges.

At the trial they gave us in Scottsboro we could hear the crowd yelling, "Lynch the Niggers." We could see them toting those big shotguns. Call 'at a fair trial? And while we lay here in jail, the boss-man make us watch 'em burning up other Negroes on the electric chair. "This is what you'll get," they say to us.

Working class boys, we asks you to save us from being burnt on the electric chair. We's only poor working class boys whose skin is black. . . . Help us boys. We ain't done nothing wrong.

[Signed] Andy Wright, Olen Montgomery, Ozie Powell, Charlie Weems, Clarence Norris, Haywood Patterson, Eugene Williams, Willie Robertson

Source: "Scottsboro Boys Appeal from Death Cells to the 'Toilers of the World,'" *The Negro Worker* 2, no. 5 (May 1932): 8–9.

▶ Put It in Context

Why was it unlikely that black men in Alabama could receive a fair trial on the charge of raping a white woman?

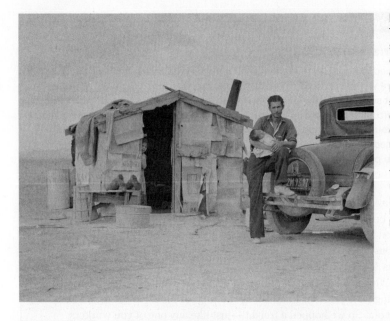

Mexican Migrant Worker, 1937
This photograph by Dorothea Lange shows a Mexican field worker on the edge of a frozen pea field in the Imperial Valley, California. Leaning on an automobile, he is holding a baby alongside a dilapidated shack. Demand for Mexican labor declined during the Great Depression as displaced farmers from the Dust Bowl moved west to take jobs formerly held by Mexicans. Government deportations further decreased the number of undocumented Mexican laborers in the United States. Library of Congress, Prints and Photographs Division, FSA/OWI Collection [LC-DIG-fsa-8b38632]

California's San Joaquin Valley won pay raises after the state labor commission concluded: "Without question civil rights of strikers have been violated." Despite these hard-fought victories, the condition of Latinos remained precarious.

On the West Coast, Asian Americans also remained economically and politically marginalized. Japanese immigrants eked out livings as small farmers, grocers, and gardeners, despite California laws preventing them from owning land. Many of their college-educated U.S.-born children found few professional opportunities available to them, and they often returned to work in family businesses. The depression magnified the problem. Like other racial and ethnic minorities, Japanese people found it harder to find even the lowest-wage jobs now that unemployed whites were willing to take them. As a result, about one-fifth of Japanese immigrants returned to Japan during the 1930s.

Chinese people suffered a similar fate. Although some 45 percent of Chinese Americans had been born in the United States and were citizens, people of Chinese ancestry remained isolated in ethnic communities along the West Coast. Discriminated against in schools and most occupations, many operated restaurants and laundries. During the depression, those Chinese who did not obtain assistance through governmental relief turned instead to their own community organizations and to extended families to help them through the hard times.

Filipino immigrants had arrived on the West Coast after the Philippines became a territory of the United States in 1901. Working as low-wage agricultural laborers, they were subject to the same kind of racial animosity as other minorities. Filipino farmworkers organized agricultural labor unions and conducted numerous strikes in California, but like their Mexican counterparts they were brutally repressed. In 1934 anti-Filipino hostility reached its height when Congress passed the Tydings-McDuffie Act. The measure accomplished two aims at once: The act granted independence to the Philippines, and it restricted Filipino immigration into the United States.

Families under Strain. With millions of men unemployed, women faced increased family responsibilities. Stay-at-home wives had to care for their children and provide emotional support for out-of-work husbands who had lost their role as the family breadwinner. Despite the loss of income, homemakers continued their daily routines of shopping, cooking, cleaning, and child rearing.

Disproportionate male unemployment led to an increase in the importance of women's income. The depression hit male-dominated industries like steel mills and automakers the hardest. As a result, men were more likely to lose their jobs than women. Although more women held on to their jobs, their often meager wages had to go further because many now had to support unemployed fathers and husbands. During the 1930s, federal and local governments sought to increase male employment by passing laws to keep married women from holding civil service and teaching positions. Nonetheless, more and more married women entered the workplace, and by 1940 the proportion of women in the job force had grown by about 25 percent.

As had been the case in previous decades, a higher proportion of African American women than white women worked outside the home in the 1930s. By 1940 about 40 percent of African American women held jobs, compared to about 25 percent of white women. Racial discrimination played a key role in establishing this pattern. Black men faced higher unemployment rates than did their white counterparts, and what work was available was often limited to the lowest-paying jobs. As a result, black women faced greater pressure to supplement family incomes. Still, unemployment rates for black women reached as high as 50 percent during the 1930s.

Despite increased burdens, most American families remained intact and discovered ways to survive the economic crisis. They pared down household budgets, made do without telephones and new clothes, and held on to their automobiles for longer periods of time. What money they managed to save they often spent on movies. Comedies, gangster movies, fantasy tales, and uplifting films helped viewers forget their troubles, if only for a few hours. Radio remained the chief source of entertainment, and radio sales doubled in the 1930s as listeners tuned in to soap operas, comedy and adventure shows, news reports, and musical programs.

Organized Protest. As the depression deepened, angry citizens found ways to express their discontent. Farmers had suffered economic hardship longer than any other group. Even before 1929, they had seen prices spiral downward, but in the early 1930s agricultural income plummeted 60 percent, and one-third of farmers lost their land (Figure 22.2). Some farmers decided that the time had come for drastic action. In the summer of 1932, Milo Reno, an Iowa farmer, created the Farm Holiday Association to organize farmers to keep their produce from going to market and thereby raise prices. Strikers from the association blocked roads and bullied other reluctant farmers by smashing their truck windshields and headlights and slashing their tires. When law enforcement officials arrested fifty-five demonstrators in Council Bluffs, thousands of farmers marched on the jail and forced their release. Despite armed attempts to prevent foreclosures and the intentional destruction of vast quantities of farm produce, the Farm Holiday Association failed to achieve its goal of raising prices.

FIGURE 22.2 Farm Foreclosures, 1932–1942

A drop of 60 percent in prices led to a wave of farm foreclosures and rural protests in the early 1930s. From 1934 on, federal programs that promoted rural electrification, crop allotments, commodity loans, and mortgage credits allowed many farmers to retain their land. What does this figure reveal about the pattern of farm foreclosures?

Disgruntled urban residents also resorted to protest. Although the Communist Party remained a tiny group of just over 10,000 members in 1932, it played a large role in organizing the dispossessed. In major cities such as New York, Communists set up unemployment councils and led marches and rallies demanding jobs and food. In Harlem, the party endorsed rent strikes by African American apartment residents against their landlords. Party members did not confine their activities to the urban Northeast. They also went south to defend the Scottsboro Nine and to organize industrial workers in the steel mills of Birmingham and sharecroppers in the surrounding rural areas of Alabama. On the West Coast, Communists unionized seamen and waterfront workers and led strikes. They also recruited writers, directors, and actors in Hollywood.

One of the most visible protests of the early 1930s centered on the Ford factory in Dearborn, Michigan. As the depression worsened after 1930, Henry Ford, who had initially pledged to keep employee wages steady, changed his mind and reduced wages. On March 7, 1932, spearheaded by Communists, three thousand autoworkers marched from Detroit to Ford's River Rouge plant in nearby Dearborn. When they reached the factory town, they faced policemen indiscriminately firing bullets and tear gas, which killed four demonstrators. The attack provoked great outrage. Around forty thousand mourners attended the funeral of the four protesters; sang the Communist anthem, the "Internationale"; and surrounded the caskets, which were draped in a red banner emblazoned with a picture of Bolshevik hero Vladimir Lenin.

Protests spread beyond Communist agitators. The federal government faced an uprising by some of the nation's most patriotic and loyal citizens — World War I veterans. Scheduled to receive a $1,000 bonus for their service, unemployed veterans could not wait until the payment date arrived in 1945. Instead, in the spring of 1932 a group of ex-soldiers from

Portland, Oregon set off on a march on Washington, D.C., to demand immediate payment of the bonus by the federal government. By the time they reached the nation's capital, the ranks of this **Bonus Army** had swelled to around twenty thousand veterans. They camped in the Anacostia Flats section of the city, constructed ramshackle shelters, and in many cases moved their families in with them.

Although many veterans eventually returned home, much of the Bonus Army remained in place until late July. When President Hoover decided to clear the capital of the protesters, violence ensued. Rather than engaging in a measured and orderly removal, General Douglas MacArthur overstepped presidential orders and used excessive force to disperse the veterans and their families. The Third Cavalry, commanded by George S. Patton, torched tents and sent their residents fleeing from the city.

In this one-sided battle, the biggest loser was President Hoover. Through four years of the country's worst depression, Hoover had lost touch with the American people. His cheerful words of encouragement fell increasingly on deaf ears. As workers, farmers, and veterans stirred in protest, Hoover appeared aloof, standoffish, and insensitive.

Review & Relate

| How did President Hoover respond to the problems and challenges created by the Great Depression? | How did different segments of the American population experience the depression? |

The **New Deal**

The nation was ready for a change, and on election day 1932, with hard times showing no sign of abating, Democratic presidential candidate Franklin Delano Roosevelt, the governor of New York, defeated Hoover easily. Roosevelt won 57 percent of the popular votes and garnered an overwhelming 472 electoral votes. He attracted a coalition of the poor: farmers and city dwellers, laborers and immigrants, northerners and southerners (the majority of African Americans did not join the coalition until 1936). Roosevelt's sizable victory provided him with a mandate to take the country in a bold new direction. However, few Americans, including Roosevelt himself, knew exactly what the new president meant to do or what his pledge of a New Deal would mean for the country.

Roosevelt Restores Confidence. As a presidential candidate, Roosevelt presented no clear, coherent policy. He did not spell out how his plans for the country would differ from Hoover's, but he did refer broadly to providing a "new deal" and bringing to the White House "persistent experimentation." Roosevelt's appeal derived more from the genuine compassion he was able to convey than from his promises. In this context, Eleanor Roosevelt's evident concern for people's suffering and her history of activism made Franklin Roosevelt even more attractive.

Instead of any fixed ideology, FDR, as he was popularly known, followed what one historian has called "pragmatic humanism." A seasoned politician who understood the need for flexibility, Roosevelt blended principle and practicality. "It is common sense," Roosevelt explained, "to take a method and try it. If it fails, admit it frankly and try another. But above all, try something." More than any president before him, FDR created an expectation among Americans that the federal government would take concrete action to improve their

Franklin Delano Roosevelt Campaigning in Kansas, 1932   New York governor Franklin D. Roosevelt promises a "new deal" to farmers in Topeka, Kansas, as he campaigns for president in 1932 as the Democratic candidate. Photographers were careful not to show that Roosevelt was unable to use his legs, which were paralyzed after he contracted polio in 1921. His son James, seated at the left, often propped up his father so that it appeared he could stand on his own, as he is doing in this photograph. Roosevelt forged a coalition of farmers and urban workers and easily defeated the incumbent Hoover. Franklin D. Roosevelt Library

lives. A Colorado woman expressed her appreciation to Eleanor Roosevelt: "Your husband is great. He seems lovable even tho' he is a 'politician.' " The New Deal would take its twists and turns, but Roosevelt never lost the support of the majority of Americans.

Starting with his inaugural address, in which he declared that "the only thing we have to fear is fear itself," Roosevelt took on the task of rallying the American people and restoring their confidence in the future. Using the power of radio to communicate directly, Roosevelt delivered regular fireside chats in which he boosted morale and informed his audience of the steps the government was taking to help solve their problems. Roosevelt's **New Deal** would provide relief, put millions of people to work, raise prices for farmers, extend conservation projects, revitalize America's financial system, and rescue capitalism.

Steps toward Recovery.
President Roosevelt took swift action on entering office. In March 1933 he issued an executive order shutting down banks for several days to calm the panic that gripped many Americans in the wake of bank failures and the loss of their

life's savings. Shortly after, Congress passed the administration's Emergency Banking Act, which subjected banks to Treasury Department inspection before they reopened, reorganized the banking system, and provided federal funds to bail out banks on the brink of closing. This assertion of federal power allowed solvent banks to reopen. Boosting confidence further, Congress passed the Glass-Steagall Act in June 1933. The measure created the **Federal Deposit Insurance Corporation (FDIC)**, insuring personal savings accounts up to $5,000, and detached commercial banks from investment banks to avoid risky speculation. The president also sought tighter supervision of the stock market. By June 1934 Roosevelt had signed into law measures setting up the Securities and Exchange Commission (SEC) to regulate the stock market and ensure that corporations gave investors accurate information about their portfolios.

The regulation of banks and the stock exchange did not mean that Roosevelt was antibusiness. He affirmed his belief in a balanced budget and sought to avoid a $1 billion deficit by cutting government workers' salaries and lowering veterans' pensions. Roosevelt also tried to keep the budget under control by ending prohibition, which would allow the government to tax alcohol sales and eliminate the cost of enforcement. The Twenty-first Amendment, ratified in 1933, ended the more than decade-long experiment with temperance.

As important as these measures were, the Roosevelt administration had much more to accomplish before those hardest hit by the depression felt some relief. Roosevelt viewed the Great Depression as a crisis analogous to war and adapted many of the bureaus and commissions used during World War I to ensure productivity and mobilize popular support to fit the current economic emergency. Many former progressives lined up behind Roosevelt, including women reformers and social workers who had worked in government and private agencies during the 1920s. At his wife Eleanor's urging, Roosevelt appointed one of them, Frances Perkins, as the first woman to head a cabinet agency—the Department of Labor.

Rehabilitating agriculture and industry stood at the top of the New Deal's priority list. Farmers came first. In May 1933 Congress passed the **Agricultural Adjustment Act**, aimed at raising prices by reducing production. The Agricultural Adjustment Administration (AAA) paid farmers subsidies to produce less in the future, and for farmers who had already planted their crops and raised livestock, the agency paid them to plow under a portion of their harvest, slaughter hogs, and destroy dairy products. By 1935 the program succeeded in raising farm income by 50 percent. Large farmers remained the chief beneficiaries of the AAA because they could afford to cut back production. In doing so, especially in the South, they forced off the land sharecroppers who no longer had plots to farm. Even when sharecroppers managed to retain a parcel of their acreage, AAA subsidies went to the landowners, who did not always distribute the designated funds owed to the sharecroppers. Though poor white farmers felt the sting of this injustice, the system of white supremacy existing in the South guaranteed that blacks suffered most.

The Roosevelt administration exhibited its boldest initiative in creating the **Tennessee Valley Authority (TVA)** in 1933, to bring low-cost electric power to rural areas and help redevelop the entire Tennessee River valley region through flood-control projects. In contrast to the AAA and other farm programs in which control stayed in private hands, the TVA owned and supervised the building and operation of public power plants. For farmers outside the Tennessee River valley, the Rural Electrification Administration helped them obtain cheap electric power starting in 1935, and for the first time tens of thousands of farmers experienced the modern conveniences that electricity brought (though most farmers would not get electric power until after World War II).

Roosevelt and Congress also acted to deal with the soil erosion problem behind the dust storms. In 1933 the Department of the Interior established a Soil Erosion Service, and two years later Congress created a permanent Soil Conservation Service in the Department of Agriculture. Although these measures would prove beneficial in the long run, they did nothing to prevent even more severe storms from rolling through the Dust Bowl in 1935 and 1936.

At the same time, Roosevelt concentrated on industrial recovery. In 1933 Congress passed the National Industrial Recovery Act, which established the **National Recovery Administration (NRA)**. This agency allowed business, labor, and the public (represented by government officials) to create codes to regulate production, prices, wages, hours, and collective bargaining. Designers of the NRA expected that if wages rose and prices remained stable, consumer purchasing power would climb, demand would grow, and businesses would put people back to work. For this plan to work, businesspeople needed to keep prices steady by absorbing some of the costs of higher wages. Businesses that joined the NRA displayed the symbol of the blue eagle to signal their patriotic participation.

However, the NRA did not function as planned, nor did it bring the desired recovery. Businesses did not exercise the necessary restraint to keep prices steady. Large manufacturers

National Recovery Administration Eagles   President Roosevelt initiated the National Recovery Administration in 1933 as the centerpiece of his New Deal to stimulate economic growth. The city of Miami Beach employed these bathing beauties to attract conventioneers and vacationers to its hotels. Under the NRA code, they worked a forty-hour week and showed their satisfaction by sporting the NRA blue eagle insignia on their backs. Bettmann/Getty Images dominated the code-making committees, and because Roosevelt had suspended enforcement of the antitrust law, they could not resist taking collective action to force smaller firms out of business. The NRA legislation guaranteed labor the right to unionize, but the agency did not vigorously enforce collective bargaining. The government failed to intervene to redress the imbalance of power between labor and management because Roosevelt depended primarily on big business to generate economic improvement. Moreover, the NRA had created codes for too many businesses, and government officials could not properly oversee them all. In 1935 the Supreme Court delivered the final blow to the NRA by declaring it an unconstitutional delegation of legislative power to the president.

Direct Assistance and Relief. Economic recovery programs were important, but they took time to take effect, and many Americans needed immediate help. Thus, relief efforts and direct job creation were critical parts of the New Deal. Created in the early months of Roosevelt's term, the Federal Emergency Relief Administration (FERA) provided cash grants to states to revive their bankrupt relief efforts. Roosevelt chose Harry Hopkins, the chief of New York's relief agency, to head the FERA and distribute its initial $500 million appropriation. On the job for two hours, Hopkins had already spent $5 million. He did not calculate whether a particular plan "would work out in the long run," because, as he remarked, "people don't eat in the long run — they eat every day."

Harold Ickes, secretary of the interior and director of the Public Works Administration (PWA), oversaw efforts to rebuild the nation's infrastructure. Funding architects, engineers, and skilled workers, the PWA built the Grand Coulee, Boulder, and Bonneville dams in the West; the Triborough Bridge in New York City; 70 percent of all new schools constructed between 1933 and 1939; and a variety of municipal buildings, sewage plants, port facilities, and hospitals.

Explore ▸

See Sources 22.2 and 22.3 for two views of direct relief.

Yet neither the FERA nor the PWA provided enough relief to the millions who faced the winter of 1933–1934 without jobs or the money to heat their homes. In response, Hopkins persuaded Roosevelt to launch a temporary program to help needy Americans get through this difficult period. Both men favored "work relief" — giving people jobs rather than direct welfare payments whenever practical. The Civil Works Administration (CWA) lasted four months, but in that brief time it employed more than 4 million people on about 400,000 projects that built 500,000 miles of roads, 40,000 schools, 3,500 playgrounds, and 1,000 airports.

One of Roosevelt's most successful relief programs was the **Civilian Conservation Corps (CCC)**, created shortly after he entered the White House. The CCC recruited unmarried men between the ages of eighteen and twenty-five for a two-year stint, putting them to work planting forests; cleaning up beaches, rivers, and parks; and building bridges and dams. Participants received $1 per day, and the government sent $25 of the $30 in monthly wages directly to their families, helping make this the most popular of all New Deal programs. The CCC employed around 2.5 million men and lasted until 1942.

New Deal Critics. Despite the unprecedented efforts of the Roosevelt administration to spark recovery, provide relief, and encourage reform between 1933 and 1935, the country remained in depression, and unemployment still hovered around 20 percent. Roosevelt found himself under attack from both the left and the right. On the right, conservatives questioned New Deal spending and the growth of big government. On the left, the

Comparative Primary Source Analysis

Letters to Eleanor Roosevelt

During the 1930s Americans wrote to President Roosevelt and the First Lady in unprecedented numbers, revealing their personal desperation and their belief that the Roosevelts would respond to their individual pleas. Though most requested government assistance, not all letter writers favored the New Deal. In the following letters written to Eleanor Roosevelt, high school student Mildred Isbell from Albertville, Alabama asks the First Lady for personal help, while Minnie Hardin of Columbus, Indiana expresses her frustration with direct relief programs.

Source 22.2

Mildred Isbell to Mrs. Roosevelt | January 1, 1936

Dear Mrs. Roosevelt,

My life has been a story to me and most of the time a miserable one. When I was 7 years old my father left for a law school and never returned. This leaving my mother and 4 children. He left us a small farm, but it could not keep us up. For when we went back to mother's people the renters would not give us part, and we were still dependent. I have been shoved to pillar to post that I feel very relieved to get off to my self.

I am now 15 years old and in the 10th grade. I have always been smart but I never had a chance as all of us is so poor. I hope to complete my education, but I will have to quit school I guess if there is no clothes can be bought. (Don't think that we are on the relief.) Mother has been a faithful servent for us to keep us to gather. I don't see how she has made it.

Mrs Roosevelt, don't think I am just begging, but that is all you can call it I guess. There is no harm in asking I guess eather. Do you have any old clothes you have throwed back. You don't realize how honored I would feel to be wearing your clothes. I don't have a coat at all to wear. The clothes may be too large but I can cut them down so I can wear them. Not only clothes but old shoes, hats, hose, and under wear would be appreciated so much. I have three brothers that would appreciate any old clothes of your boys or husband. I wish you could see the part of North Alabama now. The trees, groves, and every thing is covered with ice and snow. It is a very pretty scene. But Oh, how cold it is here. People can hardly stay comfortable.

president's critics argued that he had not done enough to topple wealthy corporate leaders from power and relieve the plight of the downtrodden.

In 1934 officials of the Du Pont Corporation and General Motors formed the American Liberty League. From the point of view of the league's founders, the New Deal was little more than a vehicle for the spread of socialism and communism. The organization spent $1 million attacking what it considered to be Roosevelt's "dictatorial" policies and his assaults on free enterprise. The league, however, failed to attract support beyond a small group of northern industrialists, Wall Street bankers, and disaffected Democrats.

Corporate leaders also harnessed Christian ministers to promote their pro-capitalism, anti–New Deal message. The United States Chamber of Commerce and the National

Source 22.3

Minnie Hardin to Mrs. Roosevelt | December 14, 1937

Mrs. Roosevelt:

I suppose from your point of view the work relief, old age pensions, slum clearance, and all the rest seems like a perfect remedy for all the ills of this country, but I would like for you to see the results, as the other half see them.

We have always had a shiftless, never-do-well class of people whose one and only aim in life is to live without work. I have been rubbing elbows with this class for nearly sixty years and have tried to help some of the most promising and have seen others try to help them, but it can't be done. We cannot help those who will not try to help themselves and if they do try, a square deal is all they need, and by the way that is all this country needs or ever has needed: a square deal for all and then, let each paddle their own canoe, or sink.

There has never been any necessity for any one who is able to work, being on relief in this locality, but there have been many eating the bread of charity and they have lived better than ever before. I have had taxpayers tell me that their children came from school and asked why they couldn't have nice lunches like the children on relief. The women and children around here have had to work at the fields to help save the crops and several women fainted while at work and at the same time we couldn't go up or down the road without stumbling over some of the reliefers, moping around carrying dirt from one side of the road to the other and back again, or else asleep.

Sources: Mildred Isbell, letter to Eleanor Roosevelt, January 1, 1936; Minnie Hardin, letter to Eleanor Roosevelt, December 14, 1937, Eleanor Roosevelt Papers, Series 190, Miscellaneous, 1937, Franklin D. Roosevelt Library.

Interpret the Evidence

1. How does each writer explain the source of poverty and the attitudes of poor people?
2. If Minnie Hardin were answering Mildred Isbell's letter, what would she say to her?

Put It in Context

How did the New Deal tackle poverty?

Association of Manufacturers allied with clergymen to challenge "creeping socialism." In 1935 the Reverend James W. Fifield founded Spiritual Mobilization and, from the pulpit of his wealthy First Congregational Church in Los Angeles, praised capitalism as a pillar of Christianity and attacked the "pagan statism" of the New Deal.

Roosevelt also faced criticism from the left. Communist Party membership reached its peak of around 75,000 in 1938, and though the party remained relatively small in numbers, it attracted intellectuals and artists whose voices could reach the larger public. Party members led unionizing drives in both the North and the South and displayed great talent and energy in organizing workers where resistance to unions was greatest. In the mid-1930s, the party followed the Soviet Union's antifascist foreign policy and joined with left-leaning, non-Communist groups, such as unions and civil rights organizations, to oppose the growing menace of fascism in Europe, particularly in Germany and Italy. As a result, the Communist Party joined New Deal liberals, unions, socialists, and civil rights advocates in the **Popular Front**, an alliance for social change rather than revolution. By the end of the decade, however, the Popular Front dissolved as the Communist Party lost credibility after the Soviet Union reversed its anti-Nazi foreign policy.

The greatest challenge to Roosevelt came from a trio of talented men who reflected diverse beliefs. Francis Townsend, a retired California physician, proposed a "Cure for Depressions." In 1934 he formed the Old-Age Revolving Pensions Corporation, whose title summed up the doctor's idea. Townsend would have the government give all Americans over the age of sixty a monthly pension of $200 if they retired and spent the entire stipend each month. Retirements would open up jobs for younger workers, and the income these workers received, along with the pension for the elderly, would pump ample funds into the economy to promote recovery. The government would fund the Townsend plan with a 2 percent "transaction" or sales tax. By 1936 Townsend Clubs had attracted about 3.5 million members throughout the country, and one-fifth of all adults in the United States signed a petition endorsing the Townsend plan.

While Townsend appealed mainly to the elderly, Charles E. Coughlin, a priest from the Detroit area, attracted Catholics and a lower-middle-class following. Father Coughlin used his popular national radio broadcasts to talk about economic and political issues. Originally a Roosevelt supporter, in 1934 Coughlin created the National Union for Social Justice and began criticizing the New Deal for catering to greedy bankers. He spoke to millions of radio listeners about the evils of the Roosevelt administration, the godless Communists who had allegedly infested it, and international bankers—coded language referring to Jews—who supposedly manipulated it. As the decade wore on, his strident anti-Semitism and his growing fondness for fascist dictatorships abroad overshadowed his economic justice message, and Catholic officials ordered him to stop broadcasting.

Huey Pierce Long of Louisiana posed the greatest political threat to Roosevelt. Unlike Townsend and Coughlin, Long had built and operated a successful political machine, first as governor and then as U.S. senator, taking on the special interests of oil and railroad corporations in his home state. Early on he had

Huey Long   This 1934 photograph shows the colorful Louisiana Senator Huey P. Long speaking at Louisiana State University. Known as the "Kingfish," Long broke with fellow Democrat Franklin D. Roosevelt for not pushing far enough in his New Deal reforms. Long's "Share Our Wealth" Plan would have provided Americans with a guaranteed annual income. Before he could challenge Roosevelt for president in 1936, Long was assassinated by a relative of a local political rival.
AP Photo

backed Roosevelt, but Long found the New Deal wanting. In 1934 Long established the Share Our Wealth society, promising to make "every man a king" by presenting families with a $5,000 homestead and a guaranteed annual income of $2,000. To accomplish this, Long proposed levying heavy income and inheritance taxes on the wealthy. Although the financial calculations behind his bold plan did not add up, Share Our Wealth clubs counted some seven million members. The swaggering senator departed from most of his segregationist southern colleagues by appealing to a coalition of disgruntled farmers, industrial workers, and African Americans. Before Long could help lead a third-party campaign for president, he was shot and killed in 1935.

Review & Relate

- What steps did Roosevelt take to stimulate economic recovery and provide relief to impoverished Americans during his first term in office?

- What criticisms did Roosevelt's opponents level against the New Deal?

The **New Deal** **Moves** to the **Left**

Facing criticism from within his own party about the pace and effectiveness of the New Deal, and with the 1936 election looming, Roosevelt moved to the left. He adopted harsher rhetoric against recalcitrant corporate leaders; beefed up economic and social programs for the unemployed, the elderly, and the infirm; and revived measures to redress the power imbalance between management and labor. In doing so, he fashioned a New Deal political coalition that would deliver a landslide victory in 1936 and allow the Democratic Party to dominate electoral politics for the next three decades.

Expanding Relief Measures. Even though the New Deal had helped millions of people, millions of others still felt left out, as the popularity of Townsend, Coughlin, and Long indicated. "We the people voted for you," a Columbus, Ohio worker wrote the president in disgust, "but it is a different story now. You have faded out on the masses of hungry, idle people. . . . The very rich is the only one who has benefited from your new deal."

In 1935 the president seized the opportunity to win his way back into the hearts of impoverished "forgotten Americans." Although Roosevelt favored a balanced budget, political necessity forced him to embark on deficit spending to expand the New Deal. Federal government expenditures would now exceed tax revenues, but New Dealers argued that these outlays would stimulate job creation and economic growth, which ultimately would replenish government coffers. Based on the highly successful but short-lived Civil Works Administration, the **Works Progress Administration (WPA)** provided jobs for the unemployed with a far larger budget, starting out with $5 billion. To ensure that the money would be spent, Roosevelt appointed Harry Hopkins to head the agency. Although critics condemned the WPA for employing people on unproductive "make-work" jobs, overall the WPA did a great deal of good. The agency constructed or repaired more than 100,000 public buildings, 600 airports, 500,000 miles of roads, and 100,000 bridges. The WPA employed about 8.5 million workers during its eight years of operation.

The WPA also helped artists, writers, and musicians. Under its auspices, the Federal Writers Project, the Federal Art Project, the Federal Music Project, and the Federal Theater

Project encouraged the production of cultural works and helped bring them to communities and audiences throughout the country. Writers Richard Wright, Ralph Ellison, Clifford Odets, Saul Bellow, John Cheever, Margaret Walker, and many others nourished both their works and their stomachs while employed by the WPA. Some painters, such as Jacob Lawrence, worked in the "easel division"; others created elaborate murals on the walls of post offices and other government buildings. Historians and folklorists researched and prepared city and state guides and interviewed black ex-slaves whose narratives of the system of bondage would otherwise have been lost.

In addition to the WPA, the National Youth Administration (NYA) employed millions of young people. Their work ranged from clerical assignments and repairing automobiles to building tuberculosis isolation units and renovating schools. Heading the NYA in Texas, the young Lyndon B. Johnson worked hard to expand educational and construction projects to unemployed whites and blacks. The Division of Negro Affairs, headed by the Florida educator Mary McLeod Bethune and the only racial minority group subsection in the NYA, ensured that African American youths would benefit from the programs sponsored by the agency.

Despite their many successes, these relief programs had a number of flaws. The WPA paid participants relatively low wages. The $660 in annual income earned by the average worker fell short of the $1,200 that a family needed to survive. In addition, the WPA limited participation to one family member. In most cases, this meant the male head of the household. As a result, women made up only about 14 percent of WPA workers, and even in the peak year

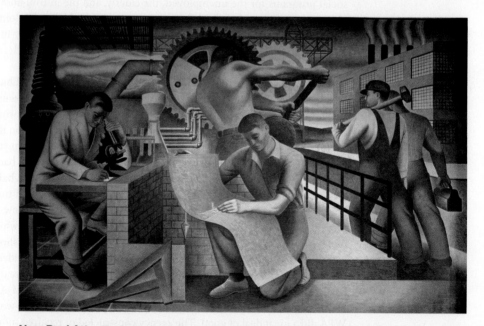

New Deal Art   The Works Progress Administration, established by the Roosevelt administration in 1935, put Americans to work amid the ongoing depression. The WPA's Federal Art Project employed artists to create stunning murals in federal buildings. This mural, painted around 1939–1940 on the Social Security Administration building in Washington, D.C., celebrates a variety of American men at work. Photographs in the Carol M. Highsmith Archive, Library of Congress, Prints and Photographs Division of 1938, the WPA hired only 60 percent of eligible women. With the exception of the program for artists, most women hired by the WPA worked in lower-paying jobs than men.

Establishing Social Security.

The elderly required immediate relief and insurance in a country that lagged behind the rest of the industrialized world in helping its aged workforce. In August 1935, the president rectified this shortcoming and signed into law the **Social Security Act**. The measure provided that at age sixty-five, eligible workers would receive retirement payments funded by payroll taxes on employees and employers. The law also extended beyond the elderly by providing unemployment insurance for those temporarily laid off from work and welfare payments for the disabled who were permanently out of a job as well as for destitute, dependent children of single parents.

The Social Security program had significant limitations. The act excluded farm, domestic, and laundry workers, who were among the neediest Americans and were disproportionately African American. The reasons for these exclusions were largely political. The president needed southern Democrats to support this measure, and as a Mississippi newspaper observed: "The average Mississippian can't imagine himself chipping in to pay pensions for able bodied Negroes to sit around in idleness." The system of financing pensions also proved unfair. The payroll tax, which imposed the same fixed percentage on all incomes, was a regressive tax, one that fell hardest on those with lower incomes. Nor did Social Security take into account the unpaid labor of women who remained in the home to take care of their children.

Even with its flaws, Social Security revolutionized the expectations of American workers. It created a compact between the federal government and its citizens, and workers

TABLE 22.1   Major New Deal Measures, 1933–1938

Year	Legislation	Purpose
1933	National Industrial Recovery Act	Government, business, labor cooperation to set prices, wages, and production codes
	Agricultural Adjustment Act	Paid farmers to reduce production to raise prices
	Civilian Conservation Corps	Jobs for young men in conservation
	Public Works Administration	Construction jobs for the unemployed
	Federal Emergency Relief Act	Relief funds for the poor
	Tennessee Valley Authority	Electric power and flood control to rural areas
	Glass-Steagall Act	Insured bank deposits and separated commercial from investment banking
1934	Securities and Exchange Commission	Regulated the stock market
1935	Social Security Act	Provided retirement pensions, unemployment insurance, aid to the disabled, and payments to women with dependent children
	Wagner Act	Guaranteed collective bargaining for unions
	Works Progress Administration	Provided jobs to 8 million unemployed
1938	Fair Labor Standards Act	Established minimum hourly wage and maximum weekly working hours

insisted that their political leaders fulfill their moral responsibilities to keep the system going. President Roosevelt recognized that the tax formula might not be economically sound, but he had a higher political objective in mind. He believed that payroll taxes would give contributors the right to collect their benefits and that "with those taxes in there, no damn politician can ever scrap my social security program."

Organized Labor Strikes Back.

In 1935 Congress passed the **National Labor Relations Act**, also known as the Wagner Act for its leading sponsor, Senator Robert F. Wagner Sr. of New York. The law created the National Labor Relations Board (NLRB), which protected workers' right to organize labor unions without owner interference. During the 1930s, union membership rolls soared from fewer than 4 million workers to more than 10 million, including more than 800,000 women. At the outset of the depression, barely 6 percent of the labor force belonged to unions, compared with 33 percent in 1940.

Government efforts boosted this growth, but these spectacular gains were due primarily to workers' grassroots efforts set in motion by economic hard times. The number of striking workers during the first year of the Roosevelt administration soared from nearly

Women's Emergency Brigade, 1937   After the United Auto Workers initiated a sit-down strike against General Motors in Flint, Michigan, for union recognition, better working conditions, and higher wages, a group of their women relatives, friends, and coworkers formed the Women's Emergency Brigade. In this February 1937 demonstration, they held the clubs that they had used to smash windows at the Chevrolet Plant occupied by the strikers.
AP Images

325,000 to more than 1.5 million. Organizers such as Luisa Moreno traveled the country to bring as many people as possible into the union movement. The most important development within the labor movement occurred in 1935, with the creation of the CIO. After the AFL, which consisted mainly of craft unions, rejected a proposal by John L. Lewis of the United Mine Workers to incorporate industrial workers under its umbrella, Lewis and representatives of seven other AFL unions defected and formed the CIO. Unlike the AFL, the new union sought to recruit a wide variety of workers without respect to race, gender, or region. Long excluded from the AFL, African American workers flocked to the CIO. Although they still encountered racial discrimination, especially in the South, they did participate in interracial organizing throughout the country. In 1937 the CIO mounted a full-scale organizing campaign. More than 4.5 million workers participated in some 4,700 strikes. Unions found new ways to protest poor working conditions and arbitrary layoffs. Members of the United Auto Workers (UAW), a CIO affiliate, launched a **sit-down strike** against General Motors (GM) in Flint, Michigan, to win union recognition, higher wages, and better working conditions. Strikers refused to work but remained in the plants, shutting them down from the inside. When the company sent in local police forces to evict the strikers on January 11, 1937, the barricaded workers bombarded the police with spare machine parts and anything that was not bolted down. The community rallied around the strikers, and wives and daughters called "union maids" formed the Women's Emergency Brigade, which supplied sit-downers with food and water and kept up their morale. Neither the state nor the federal government interfered with the work stoppage, and after six weeks GM acknowledged defeat and recognized the UAW.

The following year, the New Deal added a final piece of legislation sought by organized labor. The **Fair Labor Standards Act** (1938) established minimum wages at 40 cents an hour and maximum working hours at forty per week. By the end of the decade "big labor," as the AFL and CIO unions were known, had become a significant force in American politics and a leading backer of the New Deal.

A Half Deal for Racial Minorities.

President Roosevelt made significant gestures on behalf of African Americans. He appointed Mary McLeod Bethune and Robert Weaver to staff New Deal agencies and gathered an informal "Black Cabinet" in the nation's capital to advise him on matters pertaining to race. The Roosevelt administration also established the Civil Liberties Unit (later renamed Civil Rights Section) in the Department of Justice, which investigated racial discrimination. Eleanor Roosevelt acted as a visible symbol of the White House's concern with the plight of blacks. In 1939 Eleanor Roosevelt quit the Daughters of the American Revolution, a women's organization, when it refused to allow black singer Marian Anderson to hold a concert in Constitution Hall in Washington, D.C. Instead, the First Lady brought Anderson to sing on the steps of the Lincoln Memorial.

The New Deal inspired African Americans to form new groups, further to the left than the NAACP, in the struggle for racial and economic justice. Created in 1935, the National Negro Congress (NNC) consisted of civil rights activists, black intellectuals, black religious leaders, black and white labor organizers, Communists, and those opposed to the rise of fascism in Europe. A. Philip Randolph, a socialist and head of the Brotherhood of Pullman Car Porters, served as its president, but resigned in 1940 due to concern over increasing Communist influence. In 1937, the Southern Negro Youth Congress (SNYC), an offshoot of the NNC, formed in Richmond, Virginia. This interracial organization of young southerners,

Mary McLeod Bethune and Eleanor Roosevelt   President Roosevelt appointed prominent African Americans to positions in his administration. One member of his so-called "Black Cabinet" was Mary McLeod Bethune. A founder of the National Council of Negro Women, she served as director of Negro activities in the National Youth Administration. This 1937 photograph shows her seated next to her close friend, First Lady Eleanor Roosevelt, and Aubrey Williams, executive director of the National Youth Administration and a white southern liberal.
Bettmann/Getty Images

many of whom were college educated, conducted boycotts of businesses practicing racial discrimination in employment, conducted voter registration drives in African American communities, and promoted unions. Like the National Negro Congress, the SNYC did not exclude Communists, which drew opposition from the NAACP and other anti-Communist, civil rights organizations, following the collapse of the Popular Front. Perhaps the greatest measure of Franklin Roosevelt's impact on African Americans came when large numbers of black voters switched from the Republican to the Democratic Party in 1936, a pattern that has lasted to the present day. "Go turn Lincoln's picture to the wall," a black observer commented after the election. "That debt has been paid in full."

Yet overall the New Deal did little to break down racial inequality. President Roosevelt believed that the plight of African Americans would improve, along with that of all downtrodden Americans, as New Deal measures restored economic health. Black leaders disagreed. They argued that the NRA's initials stood for "Negroes Ruined Again" because the agency displaced black workers and approved lower wages for blacks than for whites. The AAA dislodged black sharecroppers. New Deal programs such as the CCC and those for building public housing maintained existing patterns of segregation. The Federal Housing Administration created "redlining" maps, which outlined neighborhoods where African Americans lived in red ink. This alerted banks to forgo real estate loans for those seeking to move into these communities. Owning a home is the major form of building wealth for most Americans, and redlining disadvantaged black homeownership. From 1934 to 1952, 98 percent of Federal Housing Administration loans went to whites. In addition, both the Social Security Act and the Fair Labor Standards Act omitted from coverage jobs that black and brown Americans were most likely to hold. In fact, the New Deal's big labor/big government alliance left out non-unionized industrial and agricultural workers, many of whom were African American and lacked bargaining power. Overall, "the federal government," as the historian Ira Katznelson writes, "functioned as a commanding instrument of white privilege."

This pattern of halfway reform persisted for other racial minorities. Since the end of the Indian wars in 1890, many Native Americans had lived in poverty, forced onto reservations where they were offered few economic opportunities and where whites carried out a relentless assault on their culture. By the early 1930s, American Indians earned an

The Indian New Deal   John Collier, commissioner of Indian affairs under President Roosevelt, favored a New Deal for Native Americans. An advocate for Indian culture, Collier implemented reform legislation that replaced the policy of Indian assimilation with that of self-determination. In this photo he appears with two Native Americans in the Southwest. MPI/Getty Images average income of less than $50 a year—compared with $800 for whites—and their unemployment rate was three times higher than that of white Americans. For the most part, they lived on lands that whites had given up on as unsuitable for farming or mining. The policy of assimilation established by the Dawes Act of 1887 had exacerbated the problem by depriving Indians of their cultural identities as well as their economic livelihoods. In 1934 the federal government reversed its course. Spurred on by John Collier, the commissioner of Indian affairs, Congress passed the **Indian Reorganization Act (IRA)**, which terminated the Dawes Act, authorized self-government for those living on reservations, extended tribal landholdings, and pledged to uphold native customs and language.

Although the IRA brought economic and social improvements for Native Americans, many problems remained. Despite his considerable efforts, Collier approached Indian affairs from the top down. One historian remarked that Collier had "the zeal of a crusader who knew better than the Indians what was good for them." The Indian commissioner failed to appreciate the diversity of native tribes and administered laws that contradicted Native American political and economic practices. For example, the IRA required the tribes to operate by majority rule, whereas many of them reached decisions through consensus, which respected the views of the minority. Although 174 tribes accepted the IRA, 78 tribes, including the Seneca, Crow, and Navajo, rejected it.

Decline of the New Deal.
Roosevelt's shift to the left paid political dividends, and in 1936 the president won reelection by a landslide. His sweeping victory proved to be one of the rare critical elections that signified a fundamental political realignment. Democrats replaced Republicans as the majority party in the United States, overturning thirty-six years of Republican rule. While Roosevelt had won convincingly in 1932, not until 1936 did the president put together a stable coalition that could sustain Democratic dominance for many years to come.

In 1936 Roosevelt trounced Alfred M. Landon, the Republican governor of Kansas, and Democrats increased their congressional majorities by staggering margins. The vote broke down along class lines. Roosevelt won the votes of 80 percent of union members, 81 percent of unskilled workers, and 84 percent of people on relief, compared with only 42 percent of high-income voters. Millions of new voters came out to the polls, and most of them supported Roosevelt's New Deal coalition of the poor, farmers, urban ethnic minorities, unionists, white southerners, and African Americans.

The euphoria of his triumph, however, proved short-lived. An overconfident Roosevelt soon reached beyond his electoral mandate and within two years found himself unable to extend the New Deal. In 1937 Roosevelt devised a **court-packing plan** to ensure support of New Deal legislation and asked Congress to increase the size of the Supreme Court. He justified this as a matter of reform, claiming that the present nine-member Court could not handle its workload. Roosevelt attributed a good deal of the problem to the advanced age of six of the nine justices, who were over seventy years old. Under his proposal, the president would make one new appointment for each judge over the age of seventy who did not retire so long as the bench did not exceed fifteen members. In reality, Roosevelt schemed to "pack" the Court with supporters to prevent it from declaring New Deal legislation such as Social Security and the Wagner Act unconstitutional.

Explore ▶

Compare differing interpretations of the New Deal in Sources 22.4 and 22.5.

The plan backfired. Conservatives charged Roosevelt with seeking to destroy the separation of powers enshrined in the Constitution among the executive, legislative, and judicial branches. In the end, the president failed to expand the Supreme Court, but he preserved his legislative accomplishments. In a series of rulings, the chastened Supreme Court approved Social Security, the Wagner Act, and other New Deal legislation. Nevertheless, the political fallout from the court-packing fight damaged the president and his plans for further legislative reform.

Roosevelt's court-packing plan alienated many southern Democratic members of Congress who previously had sided with the president. Traditionally suspicious of the power of the federal government, southern lawmakers worried that Roosevelt was going too far toward centralizing power in Washington at the expense of states' rights. Southern Democrats formed a coalition with conservative northern Republicans who shared their concerns about the expansion of federal power and excessive spending on social welfare programs. Their antipathy toward labor unions further bound them. Although they held a minority of seats in Congress, this **conservative coalition** could block unwanted legislation by using the filibuster in the Senate (unlimited debate that could be shut down only with a two-thirds vote). After 1938 these conservatives made sure that no further New Deal legislation passed.

Roosevelt also lost support for New Deal initiatives because of the recession of 1937, which FDR's policies had triggered. When federal spending soared after passage of the WPA and other relief measures adopted in 1935, the president lost his economic nerve for deficit spending. He called for reduced spending, which increased unemployment and slowed economic recovery. In addition, as the Social Security payroll tax took effect, it reduced the purchasing power of workers, thereby exacerbating the impact of reduced government spending. Making the situation worse, pension payments were not scheduled to begin for several years. This "recession within the depression" further eroded congressional support for the New Deal.

The country was still deep in depression in 1939. Unemployment was at 17 percent, with more than 11 million people out of work. Most of those who were poor at the start of the Great Depression remained poor. Recovery came mainly to those who were temporarily impoverished as a result of the economic crisis. The distribution of wealth remained skewed toward the top. In 1933 the richest 5 percent of the population controlled 31 percent of disposable income; in 1939 the latter figure stood at 26 percent.

Against this backdrop of persistent difficult economic times, the president's popularity began to fade. In the midterm elections of 1938, Roosevelt campaigned against Democratic conservatives in an attempt to reinvigorate his New Deal coalition. His efforts failed and upset many ordinary citizens who associated the tactic with that used by European dictators who had recently risen to power. As the decade came to a close, Roosevelt turned his attention away from the New Deal and increasingly toward a new war in Europe that threatened to engulf the entire world.

Review & Relate

▪ Why and how did the New Deal shift to the left in 1934 and 1935?

▪ Despite the president's landslide victory in 1936, why did the New Deal stall during Roosevelt's second term in office?

New Deal or Raw Deal

The long-lasting Great Depression posed major challenges for the U.S. government and its citizens. Grasping that the economic collapse was not just the ordinary rise and fall of the business cycle, Franklin Roosevelt's New Deal brought the federal government into the lives of Americans to a greater extent than ever before. Yet the New Deal did not end the depression nor did it redistribute wealth and power more equally among the various segments of the population. The historians William E. Leuchtenburg and Barton Bernstein tackle the questions of what the New Deal did and how much reform it brought to those who needed it most. Although both wrote in the 1960s, they used different standards to gauge the New Deal's achievements.

Source 22.4

William E. Leuchtenburg | The Roosevelt Reconstruction, 1963

"Franklin Roosevelt re-created the modern Presidency. He took an office which had lost much of its prestige and power in the previous twelve years and gave it an importance which went well beyond what even Theodore Roosevelt and Woodrow Wilson had done…. Under Roosevelt, the White House became the focus of all government—the fountainhead of ideas, the initiator of action, the representative of the national interest.

Despite this encroachment of government on traditional business prerogatives, the New Deal could advance impressive claims to being regarded as a 'savior of capitalism.' Roosevelt's sense of the land, of family, and of the community marked him as a man with deeply ingrained conservative traits. In the New Deal years, the government sought deliberately, in Roosevelt's words, 'to energize private enterprise.' The RFC financed business, housing agencies underwrote home financing, and public works spending aimed to revive the construction industry…. Yet such considerations should not obscure the more important point: that the New Deal, however conservative it was in some respects and however much it owed to the past, marked a radically new departure…. The New Deal achieved a more just society by recognizing groups which had been largely unrepresented—staple farmers, industrial workers, particular ethnic groups, and a new intellectual-administrative class. Yet this was still a halfway revolution; it swelled the ranks of the bourgeoisie but left many Americans—sharecroppers, slum dwellers, most Negroes—outside of the new equilibrium."

Source: William E. Leuchtenburg, *Franklin D. Roosevelt and the New Deal, 1932–1940* (New York: Harper & Row, 1963), 327, 336, 347.

Source 22.5

Barton J. Bernstein | The Conservative Achievements of Liberal Reform, 1969

"The liberal reforms of the New Deal did not transform the American system; they conserved and protected American corporate capitalism, occasionally by absorbing parts of threatening programs. There was no significant redistribution of power in American society, only limited recognition of other organized groups, seldom of unorganized peoples. Neither the bolder programs advanced by New Dealers nor the final legislation greatly extended the beneficence of government beyond the middle classes or draw upon the wealth of the few for the needs of the many. Designed to maintain the American system, liberal activity was directed toward essentially conservative goals. Experimentalism was most frequently limited to means; seldom did it extend to ends. Never questioning private enterprise, it operated within safe channels, far short of Marxism or even of native American radicalisms that offered structural critiques and structural solutions.

The New Deal was [not] . . . 'a half-way revolution,' as William Leuchtenburg concludes. Not only was the extension of representation to new groups less than full-fledged partnership, but the New Deal neglected many Americans—sharecroppers, tenant farmers, migratory workers and farm laborers, slum dwellers, unskilled workers, and unemployed Negroes. They were left outside the new order. . . . Yet by the power of rhetoric and through the appeals of political organization, the Roosevelt government managed to win or retain the allegiance of these people. Perhaps this is one of the crueler ironies of liberal politics, that the marginal men trapped in hopelessness were seduced by rhetoric, by the style and movement, of efforts seldom reaching beyond words."

Source: Barton J. Bernstein, "The New Deal: The Conservative Achievements of Liberal Reform," in *Towards a New Past: Dissenting Essays in American History*, edited by Barton J. Bernstein (New York, Vintage Books, 1969), 264, 281.

Examine the Sources

1. Compare the similarities and differences between the Leuchtenburg and Bernstein interpretations of Roosevelt and the New Deal.
2. Based on evidence in this chapter, evaluate the credibility of each interpretation.

Put it in Context

Explain why it was possible for President Roosevelt to get so much of his New Deal legislation passed.

Conclusion: New Deal Liberalism

The Great Depression produced enormous economic hardships that the Hoover administration fell far short of relieving. Although Hoover's successor, Franklin Roosevelt, failed to end the depression, in contrast he provided unprecedented economic assistance to the poor as well as the rich. The New Deal expanded the size of the federal government from 605,000 employees to more than 1 million during the 1930s. Moreover, the New Deal rescued the capitalist system, doing little to alter the fundamental structure of the American economy. Despite subjecting businesses to greater regulation, it left corporations, the stock market, farms, and banks in the hands of private enterprise. By the end of the 1930s, large corporations had more power over markets than ever before. Income and wealth remained unequally distributed, nearly to the same extent as they had been before Roosevelt took office in 1933.

Roosevelt forged a middle path between reactionaries and revolutionaries at a time when the fascist tyrants Adolf Hitler and Benito Mussolini gained power in Germany and Italy, respectively, and Joseph Stalin ruthlessly consolidated his rule in the Communist Soviet Union. By contrast, the American president expanded democratic capitalism, bringing a broader cross section of society to the decision-making table. Roosevelt's "broker state" of multiple competing interests provided for greater democracy than a government dominated exclusively by business elites. This system did not benefit those who remained unorganized and wielded little power, African Americans, Latinos, and Native Americans. The redlining policies of the Federal Housing Authority reinforced the structural racism rooted in centuries of white supremacy. Still, these marginalized groups did receive greater recognition and self-determination from the federal government. Indeed, these and other groups helped shape the New Deal. As Eleanor Roosevelt's history shows, women played key roles in campaigning for social welfare legislation. Others, like Luisa Moreno, helped organize workers and promoted ethnic pride among Latinos in the face of deportations. African Americans challenged racism and pressured the federal government to distribute services more equitably. American Indians won important democratic and cultural reforms, and though Asian Americans continued to encounter considerable discrimination on the West Coast, they joined to help each other. President Roosevelt also solidified the institution of the presidency as the focal point for public leadership. His cheerfulness, hopefulness, and pragmatism rallied millions of individuals behind him. Even after Roosevelt died in 1945, the public retained its expectation that leadership would come from the White House.

Through his programs and his force of personality, Franklin Roosevelt convinced Americans that he cared about their welfare and that the federal government would not ignore their suffering. However, he was not universally beloved: Millions of Americans despised him because they thought he was leading the country toward socialism, and he did not solve all the problems the country faced — it would take government spending for World War II to end the depression. Still, together with his wife, Eleanor, Franklin Roosevelt conveyed a sense that the American people belonged to a single community, capable of banding together to solve the country's problems, no matter how serious they were or how intractable they might seem.

Timeline of Events

1931	Scottsboro Nine tried for rape
1932–1939	Dust Bowl storms
1932	Reconstruction Finance Corporation created
	River Rouge autoworkers' strike
	Farm Holiday Association formed
	Bonus Army marches
1933	Roosevelt moves to stabilize banking and financial systems
	Agricultural Adjustment Act passed
	Federal Emergency Relief Administration created
	Tennessee Valley Authority created
	National Recovery Administration created
	Civilian Conservation Corps created
1934	Indian Reorganization Act passed
	Francis Townsend forms Old-Age Revolving Pensions Corporation
	Huey Long establishes Share Our Wealth movement
	Securities and Exchange Commission created
1935	Charles E. Coughlin organizes National Union for Social Justice
	Works Progress Administration created
	Social Security Act passed
	National Labor Relations Act passed
	Congress of Industrial Organizations founded
1937	Sit-down strike against General Motors
	Roosevelt proposes to increase the size of the Supreme Court
1938	Fair Labor Standards Act passed

Key Terms

Scottsboro Nine, *749*

Bonus Army, *755*

New Deal, *756*

Federal Deposit Insurance Corporation (FDIC), *757*

Agricultural Adjustment Act, *757*

Tennessee Valley Authority (TVA), *757*

National Recovery Administration (NRA), *758*

Civilian Conservation Corps (CCC), *759*

Popular Front, *762*

Works Progress Administration (WPA), *763*

Social Security Act, *765*

National Labor Relations Act, *766*

sit-down strike, *767*

Fair Labor Standards Act, *767*

Indian Reorganization Act (IRA), *770*

court-packing plan, *770*

conservative coalition, *771*

Review & Relate

1. How did President Hoover respond to the problems and challenges created by the Great Depression?

2. How did different segments of the American population experience the depression?

3. What steps did Roosevelt take to stimulate economic recovery and provide relief to impoverished Americans during his first term in office?

4. What criticisms did Roosevelt's opponents level against the New Deal?

5. Why and how did the New Deal shift to the left in 1934 and 1935?

6. Despite the president's landslide victory in 1936, why did the New Deal stall during Roosevelt's second term in office?

The Depression in Rural America

▶ Describe the challenges faced by rural Americans in the 1930s and explain the responses made by different individuals and groups to those problems.

During the 1930s, rural Americans' lives were devastated by the twin disasters of the Great Depression and, in the Great Plains, the most sustained drought in American history. But both crises only deepened the already difficult problems of many farmers. Agriculture in the South had long been dominated by sharecropping, a system that hampered crop diversification and left many African American tenant farmers vulnerable to exploitation by white landowners. In the Midwest, farmers had spent decades overgrazing pastures and exhausting the soil through overproduction. Prices dropped dramatically throughout the 1920s, and farmers were the only group whose incomes fell during that decade.

When the depression hit, many farmers did not have the resources to stay on their land, and farm foreclosures tripled in the early 1930s. Ferocious dust storms plagued many of the farmers who desperately struggled to hold on to their land (Source 22.6). Sharecroppers, tenant farmers, and former farm owners left their homes to find better opportunities, and a million people left the Great Plains alone (Source 22.8). Many ended up as migrant agricultural laborers in farms and orchards on the West Coast. Feeling overrun by refugees, California passed a law in 1937 making it a misdemeanor to bring into California any indigent person who was not a state resident. This law remained in effect until 1941.

Under the New Deal, the federal government acted in a number of ways to relieve the plight of farmers around the country. The Agricultural Adjustment Act attempted to raise crop prices and stabilize agricultural incomes by encouraging farmers to cut production. In doing so, however, it did little to relieve the plight of African American farmers (Source 22.7). The Farm Credit Act helped some farmers refinance mortgages at a lower rate, the Rural Electrification Administration brought electricity to farm areas previously without it, and the Soil Conservation Service advised farmers on how to properly cultivate their hillsides. The report of the Great Plains Committee (Source 22.10), another Roosevelt creation, detailed additional recommendations for helping the agricultural economy in the Midwest. In contrast, the federal government failed to protect Mexican migrant workers and instead deported a large number of them to Mexico (Source 22.9).

Source 22.6

Ann Marie Low | Dust Bowl Diary, 1934

When massive dust storms swept through the Midwest beginning in the early 1930s, they blew away the topsoil of a once productive farm region and created hazardous living conditions. Residents needed to clean and wash repetitively to perform even simple daily tasks. Ann Marie Low, a young woman living with her family in southeastern North Dakota, describes the difficulty of life in the Dust Bowl.

May 21, 1934, Monday . . .

Saturday Dad, Bud, and I planted an acre of potatoes. There was so much dirt in the air I couldn't see Bud only a few feet in front of me. Even the air in the house was just a haze. In the evening the wind died down, and Cap came to take me to the movie. We joked about how hard it is to get cleaned up enough to go anywhere.

The newspapers report that on May 10 there was such a strong wind the experts in Chicago estimated 12,000,000 tons of Plains soil was dumped on that city. By the next day the sun was obscured in Washington, D.C., and ships 300 miles out at sea reported dust settling on their decks.

Sunday the dust wasn't so bad. Dad and I drove cattle to the Big Pasture. Then I churned butter and baked a ham, bread, and cookies for the men, as no telling when Mama will be back.

May 30, 1934, Wednesday
Ethel got along fine, so Mama left her at the hospital and came to Jamestown by train Friday. Dad took us both home.

The mess was incredible! Dirt had blown into the house all week and lay inches deep on everything. Every towel and curtain was just black. There wasn't a clean dish or cooking utensil. There was no food. Oh, there were eggs and milk and one loaf left of the bread I baked the weekend before. I looked in the cooler box down the well (our refrigerator) and found a little ham and butter. It was late, so Mama and I cooked some ham and eggs for the men's supper because that was all we could fix in a hurry. It turned out they had been living on ham and eggs for two days.

. . . It took until 10 o'clock to wash all the dirty dishes. That's not wiping them—just washing them. The cupboards had to be washed out to have a clean place to put them.

Saturday was a busy day. Before starting breakfast I had to sweep and wash all the dirt off the kitchen and dining room floors, wash the stove, pancake griddle, and dining room table and chairs. There was cooking, baking, and churning to be done for those hungry men. Dad is 6 feet 4 inches tall, with a big frame. Bud is 6 feet 3 inches and almost as big-boned as Dad. We say feeding them is like filling a silo.

Mama couldn't make bread until I carried water to wash the bread mixer. I couldn't churn until the churn was washed and scalded. We just couldn't do anything until something was washed first. Every

room had to have dirt almost shoveled out of it before we could wash floors and furniture.

Source: Ann Marie Low, *Dust Bowl Diary* (Lincoln: University of Nebraska Press, 1984), 96–97.

Source 22.7

John P. Davis | A Black Inventory of the New Deal, 1935

African Americans shouldered a double burden during the Great Depression. Already victims of racial oppression, they now fell into even deeper poverty while still experiencing discrimination. Although the New Deal tried to help farmers through the Agricultural Adjustment Administration, which paid farmers to cut back production and cease farming parcels of land, it did little to improve the fortunes of black tenant farmers and sharecroppers, who were often forced off their plots to reduce production. In this excerpt from an article in the NAACP's *Crisis*, John P. Davis, a co-founder of the National Negro Congress, criticizes the New Deal's approach to solving the problems of African American farmers in the South.

The Agricultural Adjustment Administration has used cruder methods in enforcing poverty on the Negro farm population. It has made violations of the rights of tenants under crop reduction contracts easy; it has rendered enforcement of these rights impossible. The reduction of the acreage under cultivation through the government rental agreement rendered unnecessary large numbers of tenants and farm laborers. Although the contract with the government provided that the land owner should not reduce the number of his tenants, he did so. . . . Farm laborers are now jobless by the hundreds of thousands, the conservative government estimate of the decline in agricultural employment for the year 1934 alone being a quarter of a million. The larger portion of these are unskilled Negro agricultural workers— now without income and unable to secure work or relief.

But the unemployment and tenant evictions occasioned by the crop reductions policy of the A.A.A. is not all. For the tenants and sharecroppers who were retained on the plantations the government's agricultural program meant reduced income. Wholesale fraud on tenants in the payment of parity checks occurred. Tenants complaining to the Department of Agriculture in Washington have their letters referred back to the locality in which they live and trouble of serious nature often results. Even when this does not happen, the tenant fails to get his check. The remainder of the land he tills on shares with his landlord brings him only the most meagre necessities during the crop season varying from three to five months. The rest of the period for him and his family is one of "root hog or die."

Source: John P. Davis, "A Black Inventory of the New Deal," *Crisis*, May 1935, 141–42.

Source 22.8

A Sharecropper's Family in Washington County | Arkansas, 1935

The Resettlement Administration (later the Farm Security Administration) documented the plight of migrant farmworkers and sharecroppers in numerous photographs. The following photo, taken by the noted photojournalist Arthur Rothstein, depicts a sharecropper's wife and daughters in Washington County, Arkansas, in 1935.

Franklin D. Roosevelt Library

Source 22.9

Martin Torres | Protest Against Maltreatment of Mexican Laborers in California, 1934

While union organizers achieved some gains in the industrial sector, they made little headway in the agricultural fields of California despite guarantees from the National Recovery Administration. In 1934 a delegation from the Confederation of Unions of Mexican Laborers and Peasants in the State of California attended a convention of workers in Mexico and asked for assistance. In response the Mexican organization (the Mexican Regional Confederation of Labor) sent the following letter to Josephus Daniels, the U.S. ambassador to Mexico.

Several months ago ten thousand compatriots in Southern California went on a strike. . . . These compatriots had been receiving ten cents per hour and were demanding thirty and that the children who had been working for five cents should be confined in future only to scholastic labors. The rich farmers of the region were not satisfied; they armed themselves to the teeth and taking advantage of a meeting which was being held by the strikers in the town of V[i]salia, they fired their guns on them, killing two, including a Mexican who, as a member of the Honorary Commission of a nearby town, was engaged in an investigation for the Government of Mexico. The farmer assassins fled. Later, they were tried by jury and were declared free of responsibility in the crime, and in order to celebrate, the following night an orgy was held which lasted till dawn and during which could be heard only the cry of "down with the Mexican greasers!" . . .

For months five thousand Mexicans in the Imperial Valley, California, have been on strike, and under the pretext of their upholding radical ideas, notwithstanding the fact that the N.R.A. has backed the strike, they have been treated worse than beasts by the authorities and farmers. They have been incarcerated, struck, fired upon, put out of their homes with their women and children with clubs, firearms and tear bombs, and many leaders are still under arrest in the prisons of that region. . . .

The Mexican Regional Confederation of Labor consider that the acts which motivated the complaints presented by our compatriots at the XI Convention of our Organization are radically opposed to the liberal purposes of the Honorable President — Mr. Franklin D. Roosevelt — which purposes he has publicly set forth on more than one occasion, and which he has crystallized into action, in some of his principles of Government so faithfully interpreted by you as Ambassador of that Democratic Administration, setting them forth in various addresses which you have made.

[Signed] Martin Torres, April 10, 1934

Source: "Protest Against Maltreatment of Mexican Laborers in California. General Secretary Martin Torres of Mexican Regional Confederation of Labor to United States Ambassador Josephus Daniels," April 20, 1934, in *Decade of Betrayal: Mexican Repatriation in the 1930s*, by Francisco E. Balderrama and Raymond Rodríguez (Albuquerque: University of New Mexico Press, 1995), 65–68.

Source 22.10

Otis Nation | Testimony to the Great Plains Committee, 1937

In 1936 President Roosevelt established the Great Plains Committee to investigate the causes of the Dust Bowl and possible solutions for the region. The committee's report, submitted the following year, outlined how federal, state, and local government agencies could work together to restore the Great Plains to economic health. One of the witnesses the committee called to testify was Otis Nation, an organizer for the Oklahoma Tenant Farmers' Union, whose testimony follows.

Much has been written of our droughts here in Oklahoma, and how they have driven the farmers from the land. But little has been said of the other tentacles that choke off the livelihood of the small owner and the tenant. We do not wish to minimize the seriousness of these droughts and their effects on the farming population. But droughts alone would not have permanently displaced these farmers. The great majority of migrants had already become share-tenants and sharecroppers. The droughts hastened a process that had already begun. We submit the following as the cases for migratory agricultural workers:

1. *High interest rates.* Often a farmer borrows money for periods of 10 months and is charged an interest rate of 10 percent. These rates are charged when crops are good and when they fail. Through such practices the farmer loses his ownership; he becomes a tenant, then a sharecropper, then a migrant.

2. *The tenant and sharecropping system.* When share tenants are charged 33 1/3 percent of all corn or feed crops and 25 percent or more on cotton, plus 10 percent on all money borrowed at the bank, when sharecroppers are charged 50 to 75 percent of all he produces to the landlords, plus 10 percent for the bank's share on money invested; when these robbing practices are carried on in a community or a State, is it surprising that 33,241 farm families have left Oklahoma in the past 5 years?

3. *Land exhaustion, droughts, soil erosion, and the one-crop system of farming.* Lacking capital and equipment, small farmers have been unable to terrace their land or conduct other soil-conservation practices. The tenant and sharecropping system is chiefly responsible for the one-crop system. The landlord dictates what crops are to be planted — invariably cotton — and the tenant either plants it or gets off.

4. *Unstable markets.* Approximately a month and a half before the wheat harvest this year the price for this product was 93 cents here in Oklahoma City. But at harvest time the farmer sold his wheat

for 46 cents to 60 cents per bushel, depending on the grade. . . . Kaffir [a grain sorghum] was selling for $1.30 one month ago, and yesterday we sold some for 85 cents per hundred. . . .

It is obvious to all of us that farm prices are set by speculators. The farmer's losses at the market have contributed in no small part to the farmer losing his place on the land. Higher prices for farm products are quoted when the farmer has nothing to sell.

5. *Tractor farming.* In Creek County, Okla., we have the record of one land-owner purchasing 3 tractors and forcing 31 of his 34 tenants and croppers from the land. Most of these families left the State when neither jobs nor relief could be secured. This is over 10 families per machine, 10 families who must quit their profession and seek employment in an unfriendly, industrialized farming section of Arizona or California. Many of these families were even unable to become "Joads" [the fictional family in *The Grapes of Wrath*] in these other States, and had to seek relief from an unfriendly national administration and a more unfriendly State administration. . . .

. . . There are no more important problems facing us than the problem of stopping this human erosion and rehabilitating those unfortunates who have already been thrown off the land. Certainly it is un-American for Americans to be starved and dispossessed of their homes in our land of plenty. Those who seek to exploit and harass these American refugees, the migratory workers, are against our principles of democracy.

Source: U.S. Congress, House Select Committee to Investigate the Interstate Migration of Destitute Citizens (Washington, DC: U.S. Government Printing Office, 1940–1941), 2102.

Interpret the Evidence

1. Explain why women like Ann Marie Low faced particular challenges during the Dust Bowl era (Source 22.6).
2. Evaluate John P. Davis's arguments (Source 22.7) about the treatment of black farmers under the New Deal's AAA.
3. In the photograph of the Arkansas family (Source 22.8), how do the subjects seem to react to the Great Depression? Compare their plight to that of black sharecroppers.
4. Why did unions in Mexico believe that Mexican farmworkers in California would receive assistance from the federal government (Source 22.9)? Compare their assumptions with Davis's (Source 22.7).
5. How might Ann Marie Low and John P. Davis have responded to the report of the Great Plains Committee (Source 22.10)?

Put It in Context

Explain how the New Deal changed the structure of American agriculture and evaluate its effects on poor and wealthy farmers.

World War II
1933–1945

Window to the Past

Hiroshima, August 6, 1945

In the months following the death of Franklin D. Roosevelt in April 1945, President Harry S. Truman decided to give the order to drop atomic bombs on the Japanese cities of Hiroshima and Nagasaki. He considered it a military necessity to get Japan to surrender before the U.S. launched an invasion of the Japanese island, which would have resulted in the deaths of tens of thousands of American soldiers. This photograph, taken the day of the bombing, captures the tremendous devastation to Hiroshima. ▶ To learn more about this primary source, see Source 23.8 on page 815.

AP Images/Stanley Troutman

After reading this chapter you will be able to:

- Evaluate the key reasons behind U.S. intervention in World War II as well as the arguments of those who opposed it.

- Analyze the effects the war had on the U.S. economy and on the lives of women and families.

- Compare and contrast the treatment of racial minority groups and their responses on the home front.

- Explain the Allied military strategy in fighting World War II on the European and Pacific fronts, including how it affected the decision to drop the atomic bomb on Japan, U.S.-Soviet relations, and the Holocaust.

Comparing American Histories

One month after Japan attacked the U.S. naval base at Pearl Harbor on December 7, 1941, President Franklin Roosevelt approved a full-scale effort to develop an atomic bomb. As scientific director of this top-secret program, physicist **J. Robert Oppenheimer** orchestrated the work of more than 3,000 scientists, technicians, and military personnel at the Los Alamos Laboratories near Santa Fe, New Mexico. The son of German American Jews, Oppenheimer helped Jews gain asylum in the United States when the Nazis started persecuting them in the early 1930s.

On July 16, 1945, Oppenheimer and his team successfully tested their new weapon. The explosion lit up the predawn sky with a blast so powerful that it

broke a window 125 miles away. A mushroom cloud shot up 41,000 feet into the sky over ground zero, where a 1,200-foot-wide crater had formed. Oppenheimer understood that the world had been permanently transformed. Quoting from Hindu scriptures, he remembered thinking at the moment of the explosion, "I am become death, destroyer of worlds." Weeks later, in early August 1945, the United States dropped two atomic bombs on Japan, which resulted in over 200,000 deaths.

While Oppenheimer and his team remained cloistered at Los Alamos, **Fred Korematsu** and some 112,000 Japanese Americans lived in internment camps, imprisoned for no other reason than their Japanese ancestry. Born in Oakland, California, in 1919 to Japanese immigrants, Fred grew up like many first-generation Americans. His parents spoke Japanese at home and maintained the cultural traditions of their native land, while their sons learned English in public school, ate hamburgers, and played football and basketball like other children their age. Following graduation from high school, Korematsu worked on the Oakland docks as a welder.

After the 1941 bombing of Pearl Harbor, residents on the West Coast turned their anger on the Japanese and Japanese Americans living among them. As assimilated as Fred Korematsu and many other Nisei (the U.S.-born children of Japanese immigrants) had become, white Americans doubted their loyalty. As a result, Korematsu soon lost his job.

On March 21, 1942, President Roosevelt issued Executive Order 9066 authorizing military commanders on the West Coast to take any measures necessary to promote national security. On May 9, the military ordered Korematsu's family to report to Tanforan Racetrack in San Mateo, from which they would be transported to internment camps throughout the West. Although the rest of his family complied with the order, Fred refused. Three weeks later, he was arrested and then transferred to the Topaz internment camp in south-central Utah. Found guilty of violating the original evacuation order, Korematsu received a sentence of five years of probation. When he appealed his conviction to the U.S. Supreme Court in 1944, the high court upheld the verdict. ∎

(*left*) **J. Robert Oppenheimer** Agence France Presse/Getty Images
(*right*) **Fred Korematsu** National Portrait Gallery, Smithsonian Institution

The American histories of Fred Korematsu and J. Robert Oppenheimer were shaped by the profound changes brought about by war. Korematsu was subjected to the full force of anti-Japanese sentiment that followed the attack on Pearl Harbor, while Oppenheimer played a key role in developing a weapon that he believed would shorten the war.

The war that these two men experienced in such different ways marked a critical point for the United States in the twentieth century. World War II finally ended the Great Depression, cementing the trend toward government intervention in the economy that had begun with the New Deal. With the war fought almost entirely on foreign soil, the United States converted its factories to wartime production and became the "arsenal of democracy," putting millions of Americans to work in the process, including African Americans, other racial and ethnic minorities, and women. The war also provided opportunities for African Americans to press for civil rights, while at the same time the government trampled on the civil liberties of Japanese Americans. All Americans contributed to the war effort through rationing and higher taxes. Overseas, soldiers fought fierce battles in Europe, Africa, and Asia. The combined military power of the Allies, led by the United States, Great Britain, and the Soviet Union, finally defeated the Axis nations of Germany, Italy, and Japan, but not until the fighting had killed 60 to 70 million people, more than half of whom were civilians, and ushered in the Atomic Age.

The **Road** toward **War**

The end of World War I did not bring peace and prosperity to Europe. The harsh peace terms imposed on the Central Powers in 1919 left the losers, especially Germany, deeply resentful. The war saddled both sides with a huge financial debt and produced economic instability, which contributed to the Great Depression. In the Far East, Japanese invasions of China and Southeast Asia threatened America's Open Door policy (see "Opening the Door in China" in chapter 20). The failure of the United States to join the League of Nations dramatically reduced the organization's ability to maintain peace and stability. German expansionism in Europe in the late 1930s moved President Roosevelt and the nation toward war, but it took the Japanese attack on Pearl Harbor to bring the United States into the global conflict.

The Growing Crisis in Europe.

Despite its failure to join the League of Nations, the United States did not withdraw from international affairs in the 1920s. It participated in arms control negotiations; signed the Kellogg-Briand Pact, which outlawed war as an instrument of national policy but proved unenforceable; and expanded its foreign investments in Central and Latin America, Asia, the Middle East, and western Europe. In 1933 a new possibility for trade emerged when the Roosevelt administration extended diplomatic recognition to the Soviet Union (USSR).

Overall, the country did not retreat from foreign affairs so much as it refused to enter into collective security agreements that would restrain its freedom of action. To the extent that American leaders practiced isolationism, they did so mainly in the political sense of rejecting internationalist organizations such as the League of Nations, institutions that might require military cooperation to implement their decisions.

The experience of World War I had reinforced this brand of political isolationism, which was reflected in an outpouring of antiwar sentiments in the late 1920s and early

1930s. Best-selling novels like Ernest Hemingway's *Farewell to Arms* (1929), Erich Maria Remarque's *All Quiet on the Western Front* (1929), and Dalton Trumbo's *Johnny Got His Gun* (1939) presented graphic depictions of the horror and futility of war. Beginning in 1934, Senate investigations chaired by Gerald Nye of North Dakota concluded that bankers and munitions makers—"merchants of death," as one contemporary writer labeled them—had conspired to push the United States into war in 1917. Nye's hearings appealed to popular antibusiness sentiment in Depression-era America.

Following the Nye Committee hearings, Congress passed a series of **Neutrality Acts**, each designed to make it more difficult for the United States to become entangled in European armed hostilities. In 1935 Congress prohibited the sale of munitions to either warring side and authorized the president to warn Americans against traveling on passenger liners of belligerent nations. The following year, lawmakers added private loans to the ban, and in 1937 they required belligerents to pay cash for nonmilitary purchases and ship them on their own vessels—so-called cash-and-carry provisions.

Events in Europe, however, made U.S. neutrality ever more difficult to maintain. After rising to power as chancellor of Germany in 1933, Adolf Hitler revived Germany's economic and military strength despite the Great Depression. Hitler installed National Socialism (Nazism) at home and established the empire of the Third Reich abroad. The *Führer* (leader) whipped up patriotic fervor by scapegoating and persecuting Communists and Jews. To garner support for his actions, Hitler manipulated German feelings of humiliation for losing World War I and having been forced to sign the "war guilt" clause and pointed to the disastrous effects of the country's inflation-ridden economy. In 1936 Hitler sent troops to occupy the Rhineland between Germany and France in blatant violation of the Treaty of Versailles.

Hitler did not stop there. Citing the need for more space for the Germanic people to live, he pushed for German expansion into eastern Europe. In March 1938 he forced Austria to unite with Germany. In September of that year Hitler signed the Munich Accord with Great Britain and France, allowing Germany to annex the Sudetenland, the mainly German-speaking, western region of Czechoslovakia. Hitler still wanted more land and was convinced that his western European rivals would not stop him, so in March 1939 he sent German troops to invade and occupy the rest of Czechoslovakia. Hitler proved correct; Britain and France did nothing in response, a policy critics called **appeasement**.

Hitler's Italian ally, Benito Mussolini, joined him in war and conquest. In 1935 Italian troops invaded Ethiopia. The following year, both Germany and Italy intervened in the Spanish civil war, providing military support for General Francisco Franco in his effort to overthrow the democratically elected, socialist republic of Spain. While the United States and Great Britain remained on the sidelines, only the Soviet Union officially assisted the Loyalist defenders of the Spanish republic. In violation of American law, private citizens, many of whom were Communists, volunteered to serve on the side of the Spanish Loyalists and fought on the battlefield as the Abraham Lincoln Brigade. Other sympathetic Americans, such as J. Robert Oppenheimer, provided financial assistance for the anti-Franco government. Despite these efforts, Franco's forces seized control of Spain in early 1939, another victory for Hitler and Mussolini.

The Challenge to Isolationism.

As Europe drifted toward war, public opinion polls revealed that most Americans wanted to stay out of any European conflict. The president, however, thought it likely that, to protect its own economic and political interests, the

United States would eventually need to assist the Western democracies. Still, Roosevelt had to tread lightly in the face of the Neutrality Acts that Congress had passed between 1935 and 1937 and overwhelming public opposition to American involvement in Europe.

Germany's aggression in Europe eventually led to full-scale war. When Germany invaded Poland in September 1939, Britain and France declared war on Germany and Italy. Just before the invasion, the Soviet Union had signed a nonaggression agreement with Germany, which carved up Poland between the two nations and permitted the USSR to occupy the neighboring Baltic states of Latvia, Lithuania, and Estonia. Soviet leader Joseph Stalin had few illusions about Hitler's ultimate design on his own nation, but he concluded that by signing this pact he could secure his country's western borders and buy additional time. (In June 1941 the Germans broke the pact and invaded the Soviet Union.)

Roosevelt responded to the outbreak of war by reaffirming U.S. neutrality. Despite his sympathy for the Allies, which most Americans had come to share, the president stated his hope that the United States could stay out of the war: "Let no man or woman thoughtlessly or falsely talk of America sending its armies to European fields."

America First Committee Rally, 1941   Organized in 1940, the America First Committee campaigned against U.S. entry into World War II. One of its leaders, the popular aviator Charles Lindbergh, addressed a rally of 3,000 people in Ft. Wayne, Indiana on October 5, 1941. The isolationist group blamed eastern bankers, British sympathizers, and Jewish leaders for promoting war fever. The committee dissolved soon after this 1941 rally and the Japanese attack on Pearl Harbor. Everett Collection

With the United States on the sidelines, German forces marched toward victory. By the spring of 1940, German armies had launched a *Blitzkrieg* (lightning war) across Europe, defeating and occupying Denmark, Norway, the Netherlands, Belgium, and Luxembourg. With German victories mounting, committed opponents of American involvement in foreign wars organized the **America First Committee**. America First tapped into the feeling of isolationism and concern among a diverse group of Americans who did not want to get dragged into another foreign war.

The greatest challenge to isolationism occurred in June 1940 when France fell to the German onslaught and Nazi troops marched into Paris. Britain now stood virtually alone, and its position seemed tenuous. The British had barely succeeded in evacuating their forces from France by sea when the German *Luftwaffe* (air force) began a bombing campaign on London and other targets in the Battle of Britain.

The surrender of France and the Battle of Britain drastically changed Americans' attitude toward entering the war. Before Germany invaded France, 82 percent of Americans thought that the United States should not aid the Allies. After France's defeat, in a complete turnaround, some 80 percent of Americans favored assisting Great Britain in some way. However, four out of five Americans polled opposed immediate entry into the war. As a result, the politically astute Roosevelt presented U.S. assistance to Britain as a way to prevent American military intervention by allowing Great Britain to defeat the Germans on its own.

Despite public opinion, the Roosevelt administration found ways of helping Britain. On September 2, 1940, the president sent fifty obsolete destroyers to the British in return for leases on British naval bases in Newfoundland, Bermuda, and the British West Indies. Two weeks later, on September 16, Roosevelt persuaded Congress to pass the Selective Service Act, the first peacetime military draft in U.S. history, which quickly registered more than 16 million men.

This political maneuvering came as Roosevelt campaigned for an unprecedented third term in 1940. He defeated the Republican Wendell Willkie, a Wall Street lawyer who shared Roosevelt's anti-isolationist views. Both candidates accommodated voters' desire to stay out of the European war, and Roosevelt went so far as to promise American parents: "Your boys are not going to be sent into any foreign war."

Roosevelt's campaign promises did not halt the march toward war. Roosevelt succeeded in pushing Congress to pass the **Lend-Lease Act** in March 1941. With Britain running out of money and its shipping devastated by German submarines, this measure circumvented the cash-and-carry provisions of the Neutrality Acts. The United States would lend or lease equipment, but no one expected the recipients to return the used weapons and other commodities. To protect British ships carrying American supplies, the president extended naval and air patrols in the North Atlantic. In response, German submarines began sinking U.S. ships. By May 1941, Germany and the United States were engaged in an undeclared naval war.

The United States Enters the War. Financially, militarily, and ideologically, the United States had aligned itself with Britain, and Roosevelt expected that the nation would soon be formally at war. As Germany and Italy successfully expanded their empires, they endangered U.S. economic interests and democratic values. President Roosevelt believed that American security abroad was threatened by the German Nazis and Italian Fascists. After passage of the Lend-Lease Act, American and British military planners agreed that defeating Germany would become the top priority if the United States entered the war. In August 1941, Roosevelt and British prime minister Winston Churchill met in Newfoundland, where they signed the **Atlantic Charter**, a lofty statement of war aims that included principles of freedom of the seas, self-determination, free trade, and "freedom from fear and want" — ideals that laid the groundwork for the establishment of a postwar United Nations. At the same meeting, Roosevelt promised Churchill that the United States would protect British convoys in the North Atlantic as far as Iceland while the nation waited for a confrontation with Germany that would rally the American public in support of war. The president got what he wanted. After several attacks on American ships by German submarines in September and October, the president persuaded Congress to repeal the neutrality legislation of the 1930s and allow American ships to sail across the Atlantic to supply Great Britain. By December, the nation was close to open war with Germany.

The event that finally prompted the United States to enter the war, however, occurred not in the Atlantic but in the Pacific Ocean. For nearly a decade, U.S. relations with Japan had deteriorated over the issue of China's independence and maintaining the Open Door to Chinese markets. The United States did little to challenge the Japanese invasion and occupation of Manchuria in 1931, but after Japanese armed forces moved farther into China in 1937, the United States supplied arms to China.

Relations worsened in 1940 when the Japanese government signed the Tripartite Pact with Germany and Italy, which created a mutual defense agreement among the Axis powers. That same year, Japanese troops invaded northern Indochina, and Roosevelt responded by embargoing sales of products that Japan needed for war. This embargo did not deter the Japanese; in July they occupied the remainder of Indochina to gain access to the region's natural resources. The Roosevelt administration retaliated by freezing Japanese assets and cutting off all trade with Japan.

On the quiet Sunday morning of December 7, 1941, Japan attacked the U.S. Pacific Fleet stationed at Pearl Harbor in Honolulu, Hawaii. This surprise air and naval assault killed more than 2,400 Americans and seriously damaged ships and aircraft. The bombing raid abruptly ended isolationism and rallied the American public behind President Roosevelt, who pronounced December 7 "a date which will live in infamy." The next day, Congress overwhelmingly voted to go to war with Japan, and on December 11 Germany and Italy declared war on the United States in response. In little more than a year after his reelection pledge to keep the country out of war, Roosevelt sent American men to fight overseas. Still, an overwhelming majority of Americans now considered entry into the war as necessary to preserve freedom and democracy against assaults from fascist and militaristic nations.

Explore ▶

See Source 23.1 for a Japanese American perspective on the bombing of Pearl Harbor.

Review & Relate

How did American public opinion shape Roosevelt's foreign policy in the years preceding U.S. entry into World War II?

What events in Europe and the Pacific ultimately brought the United States into World War II?

Guided Primary Source Analysis

Monica Sone | Memories of Pearl Harbor

Few Americans would forget where they were or how they felt when they first learned of the Japanese attack on Pearl Harbor. The following document describes the experience of Monica Sone, a Nisei who was a student at the University of Washington in December 1941. Sone and her family were eventually placed in an internment camp in Idaho.

Source 23.1

What does this tell you about Sone's relationship to the United States?

Why was she worried?

Why did Monica and her friends think they would not be treated as Americans?

On a peaceful Sunday morning, December 7, 1941, Henry, Sumi, and I were at choir rehearsal singing ourselves hoarse in preparation for the annual Christmas recital of Handel's "Messiah." Suddenly Chuck Mizuno, a young University of Washington student, burst into the chapel, gasping as if he had sprinted all the way up the stairs.

"Listen, everybody!" he shouted. "Japan just bombed Pearl Harbor . . . in Hawaii. It's war!"

The terrible words hit like a blockbuster, paralyzing us. Then we smiled feebly at each other, hoping this was one of Chuck's practical jokes. Miss Hara, our music director, rapped her baton impatiently on the music stand and chided him, "Now Chuck, fun's fun, but we have work to do. Please take your place. You're already half an hour late."

But Chuck strode vehemently back to the door. "I mean it, folks, honest! I just heard the news over my car radio. Reporters are talking a blue streak. Come on down and hear it for yourselves."

. . . I felt as if a fist had smashed my pleasant little existence, breaking it into jigsaw puzzle pieces. An old wound opened up again, and I found myself shrinking inwardly from my Japanese blood, the blood of an enemy. I knew instinctively that the fact that I was an American by birthright was not going to help me escape the consequences of this unhappy war.

One girl mumbled over and over again, "It can't be, God, it can't be!" Someone else was saying, "What a spot to be in! Do you think we'll be considered Japanese or Americans?"

A boy replied quietly, "We'll be Japs, same as always. But our parents are enemy aliens now, you know."

A shocked silence followed.

Source: Monica Sone, *Nisei Daughter* (Boston: Little, Brown, 1953), 145–46.

Put It in Context

What does the experience of Japanese Americans during World War II indicate about constitutional guarantees of civil liberties during wartime?

The **Home-Front Economy**

The global conflict had profound effects on the American home front. World War II ended the Great Depression, restored economic prosperity, and increased labor union membership. At the same time, it smoothed the way for a closer relationship between government and private defense contractors, later referred to as the **military-industrial complex**. The war extended U.S. influence in the world and offered new economic opportunities at home. Despite fierce and bloody military battles throughout the world, Americans kept up morale by rallying around family and community.

Managing the Wartime Economy. To mobilize for war, President Roosevelt increased federal spending to unprecedented levels. Federal government employment during the war expanded to an all-time high of 3.8 million workers, setting the foundation for a large, permanent Washington bureaucracy. War orders fueled economic growth, productivity, and employment. The gross domestic product increased from the equivalent of nearly $900 billion in 1939 (in 1990 prices) to nearly $1.5 trillion (in 1990 prices) at the end of the war (Figure 23.1), union membership rose from around 9 million to nearly 15 million, and unemployment dropped from 8 million to less than 1 million. The armed forces helped reduce unemployment significantly by enlisting 12 million men and women, 7 million of whom had been unemployed.

All regions of the country experienced wartime prosperity. The industrial areas of the Northeast and Midwest once again boomed, as automobile factories converted to building tanks and other military vehicles, oil refineries processed gasoline to fuel them, steel and rubber companies manufactured parts to construct these vehicles and the weapons they carried, and textile and

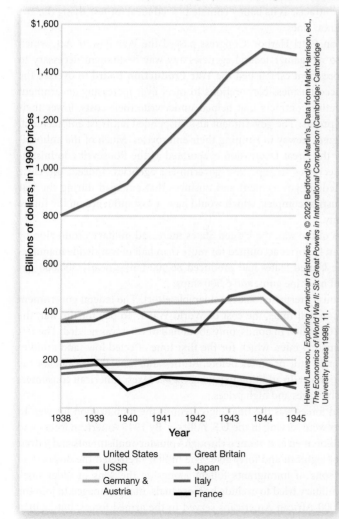

Hewitt/Lawson, *Exploring American Histories*, 4e, © 2022 Bedford/St. Martin's. Data from Mark Harrison, ed., *The Economics of World War II: Six Great Powers in International Comparison* (Cambridge: Cambridge University Press 1998), 11.

FIGURE 23.1 Real Gross Domestic Product of the Great Powers, 1938–1945

Although World War II stalled or damaged the economic productivity of most of the warring nations, the U.S. economy grew dramatically between 1938 and 1944. With all the battles taking place outside the continental United States, the demand for food, weapons, ships, airplanes, gasoline, and other items by Great Britain and other Allied powers fueled this growth. Explain why the war and not the New Deal succeeded in ending the Great Depression.

Data from Mark Harrison, ed., *The Economics of World War II: Six Great Powers in International Comparison* (Cambridge: Cambridge University Press, 1998), 11.

shoe plants furnished uniforms and boots for soldiers to wear. As farmers provided food for the nation and its allies, farm production soared. The economy diversified geographically. Fifteen million Americans—11 percent of the entire population—migrated between 1941 and 1945. The war transformed the agricultural South into a budding industrial region. The federal government poured more than $4 billion in contracts into the South to operate military camps, contract with textile factories to clothe the military, and use its ports to build and launch warships. The availability of jobs in southern cities attracted sharecroppers and tenant farmers, black and white, away from the countryside and promoted urbanization while reducing the region's dependency on the plantation economy.

No region was changed more by the war than the West. The West Coast prospered because it was the gateway to the Pacific war. The federal government established aircraft plants and shipbuilding yards in California, Oregon, and Washington, resulting in extraordinary population growth in Los Angeles, San Diego, San Francisco, Portland, and Seattle. The West's population grew three times as fast as the rest of the nation's. Los Angeles led the way in attracting defense contracts, as its balmy climate proved ideal for test-flying the aircraft that rolled off its assembly lines.

Following the attack on Pearl Harbor, Congress passed the War Powers Act, which authorized the president to reorganize federal agencies any way he thought necessary to win the war. In 1942 the president established the **War Production Board** to oversee the economy. The agency enticed business corporations to meet ever-increasing government orders by negotiating lucrative contracts that helped underwrite their costs, lower their taxes, and guarantee large profits. The government also suspended antitrust enforcement, giving private companies great leeway in running their enterprises. Much of the antibusiness hostility generated by the Great Depression evaporated as the Roosevelt administration recruited business executives to supervise government agencies. Indeed, the close relationship between the federal government and business that emerged during the war produced the military-industrial complex, which would have a vast influence on the future development of the economy.

In the first three years of the war, the United States increased military production by some 800 percent. American factories accounted for more than half of worldwide manufacturing output. By 1945 the United States had produced 86,000 tanks, nearly 300,000 airplanes, 15 million rifles and machine guns, and 6,500 ships.

Financing this enormous enterprise took considerable effort. The federal government spent more than $320 billion, ten times the cost of World War I. To pay for the war, the federal government sold $100 billion in bonds, only about half of what was needed. The rest came from increased income tax rates, which for the first time affected low- and middle-income workers, who had paid little or no tax before. At the same time, the tax rate for the wealthy was boosted to 94 percent. In addition to paying higher taxes, American consumers shouldered the burden of shortages and high prices.

Building up the armed forces was the final ingredient in the mobilization for war. In 1940 about 250,000 soldiers were serving in the U.S. military. By 1945 American forces had grown to more than 12 million men and women through voluntary enlistments and a draft of men between the ages of eighteen and forty-five. The military reflected the diversity of the U.S. population. The sons of immigrants fought alongside the sons of older-stock Americans. Although the military tried to exclude homosexuals, many managed to join the fighting forces. Some 700,000 African Americans served in the armed forces, but civilian and military officials confined them to segregated units in the army, assigned them to menial work in the navy, and excluded them from the marines. The Army Air Corps created a segregated fighting unit of black soldiers who trained at Tuskegee Institute in Alabama, and these Tuskegee airmen, like their counterparts among the ground forces, distinguished themselves in battle. Women could not fight in combat, but 140,000 joined the Women's Army Corps, and 100,000 joined the navy's WAVES (Women Accepted for Voluntary Emergency Service). In these and other service branches, women contributed mainly as nurses and performed transportation and clerical duties.

Women also played an important but secretive role in bolstering Allied military efforts. The navy and army recruited thousands of women college students and small-town school teachers to Washington, D.C., where they worked on deciphering German and Japanese diplomatic and military codes. These young, unmarried women worked very long, tedious hours during the week as well as on weekends, and succeeded in providing the U.S. military with secret information of enemy planning. In this way, they joined the efforts already begun by British female codebreakers operating at Bletchley Park, England.

The government relied on corporate executives to manage wartime economic conversion, but without the sacrifice and dedication of American workers, their efforts would have failed. The demands for wartime production combined with the departure of millions of American workers to the military created a labor shortage that gave unions increased leverage. By 1945 the membership rolls of organized labor had grown from 9 million to nearly 14 million. In 1942 the Roosevelt administration established the **National War Labor Board**, which regulated wages, hours, and working conditions and authorized the government to take over plants that refused to abide by its decisions. Unions at first refrained from striking but later in the war organized strikes to protest the disparity

Tuskegee Airmen   Twenty black pilots, among those known as the Tuskegee airmen, line up for a photograph, which they signed. The Army Air Corps created two segregated units of African American airmen, the 442nd Bombardment Group and the 99th Pursuit Squadron. The latter flew combat missions in Europe. The success of the Tuskegee airmen contributed to the postwar desegregation of the armed forces. Courtesy National Park Service, Museum Management Program and Tuskegee Airmen National Historic Site, TUAI 31 between workers' wages and corporate profits. In 1943 Congress responded by passing the Smith-Connally Act, which prohibited walkouts in defense industries and set a thirty-day "cooling-off" period before unions could go out on strike.

New Opportunities for Women.

World War II opened up new opportunities for women in the paid workforce. Between 1940 and the peak of wartime employment in 1944, the number of employed women rose by more than 50 percent, to 6 million. Given severe labor shortages caused by increased production and the exodus of male workers into the armed forces, for the first time in U.S. history married working women outnumbered single working women. At the start of the war, about half of women employees held poorly paid clerical, sales, and service jobs. Women in manufacturing labored mainly in low-wage textile and clothing factories. During the war, however, the overall number of women in manufacturing grew by 141 percent; in industries producing directly for war purposes, the

Women Workers during the War   During the war, women worked in industrial jobs in unprecedented numbers. Corporations and the federal government actively recruited women through posters and advertisements and promised women that factory work was something that would benefit them, their families, and their nation. This image spotlights two African American women, Luedell Mitchell and Lavada Cherry, real life "Rosie the Riveters," working at the El Segundo, California plant of Douglas Aircraft. As the Allies neared victory, however, the message changed, and women were urged to prepare to return to the home to open up jobs for returning soldiers. Library of Congress, 8e01286 figure jumped by 463 percent. By contrast, the number of women in domestic service dropped by 20 percent. As women moved into defense-related jobs, their incomes also improved.

As impressive as these figures are, they do not tell the whole story. First, although married women entered the job market in record numbers, most of these workers were older and without young children. Women over the age of thirty-five accounted for 60 percent of those entering the workforce. The government did little to encourage young mothers to work, and few efforts were made to provide assistance for child care for those who did. In contrast to this situation, in Great Britain child care programs were widely available. Second, openings for women in manufacturing jobs did not guarantee equality. Women received lower wages for labor comparable to the work that men performed, and women did not have the same chances for advancement. Typical union benefits, such as seniority, hurt women, who were generally the most recent hires. In fact, some contracts stipulated that women's tenure in jobs previously held by men would last only for the duration of the war.

Gender stereotypes continued to dominate the workforce and society in general. Magazine covers with the image of "Rosie the Riveter," a woman with her sleeves rolled up and her biceps bulging, became a symbol for the recruitment of women, but reality proved different. Women who took war jobs were viewed not so much as war workers but as women temporarily occupying "men's jobs" during the emergency. As the war drew to a close, public relations campaigns shifted gears and encouraged the same women they had recently recruited to prepare to return home. And nearly all of the brilliant women codebreakers in Washington, D.C., were ordered to go back home.

Everyday Life on the Home Front.
Morale on the home front remained generally high during the war, as prosperity returned and American casualties proved relatively light compared with those of other allied nations. As in World War I, the government set up an agency, the Office of War Information, to promote patriotism and urge Americans to contribute to the war effort any way they could. Schoolchildren collected scrap metal and rubber to donate to the production of military vehicles and weapons. With rationing in effect and food in short supply, the government encouraged families in towns and cities to grow "victory gardens" for their own fruits and vegetables. Mothers and daughters helped staff USO (United Service Organizations) dances and recreational activities for soldiers headquartered in the United States. Americans also contributed to the war effort by adhering to restrictions on the consumption of consumer goods. Rationing cards restricted purchases of gasoline for cars and for food such as meat, butter, and sugar.

Hollywood kept the American public entertained, and movie attendance reached a record high of more than 100 million viewers. Films portrayed the heroism of soldiers on battlefields in Guadalcanal and Bataan. They celebrated the courage of Russian allies in propaganda epics such as *Mission to Moscow* (1943) and explored the depth of personal and political loyalties in classics such as *Casablanca* (1943). Hollywood stars such as Betty Grable kept up servicemen's spirits by posing for photos that GIs pinned up in their lockers, tents, and equipment.

For many Americans, life went on, but not quite in the same way. Around 15 million Americans moved during the war, with more than half of them relocating out of state. With husbands at war and wives at work, many children became "latchkey kids" who stayed home alone after school until their mothers or fathers returned from their jobs. With less parental supervision, juvenile delinquency rose, resulting in increased teenage arrests for robbery, vandalism, and loitering. With the end of the Great Depression and with more young people working, marriage rates increased, and couples wed at a younger age. By 1945 the winding down of the war and the rapidly increasing number of marriages produced the first signs of a "baby boom." At the same time, the stresses of life during wartime, including long separations of husbands and wives, also resulted in higher divorce rates.

Review & Relate

- How did the war accelerate the trend that began during the New Deal toward increased government participation in the economy?

- How did the war affect life on the home front for the average American?

Fighting for Equality at Home

The war also had a significant impact on race relations. The fight to defeat Nazism, a doctrine based on racial prejudice and white supremacy, offered African Americans a chance to press for equal opportunity at home. By contrast, Japanese Americans experienced intensified discrimination and oppression as wartime anti-Japanese hysteria led to the internment of Japanese Americans, an erosion of their civil rights. They were freed toward the end of the war, but their incarceration left scars. Finally, Mexican Americans and American Indians benefited from wartime jobs and military service but continued to experience prejudice.

The Origins of the Civil Rights Movement. In 1941 A. Philip Randolph, the head of the Brotherhood of Sleeping Car Porters, applied his labor union experience to the struggle for civil rights. He announced that he planned to lead a 100,000-person march on Washington, D.C., in June 1941 to protest racial discrimination in government and war-related employment as well as segregation in the military. Although Randolph believed in an interracial alliance of working people, he insisted that the march should be all-black to show that African Americans could lead their own movement. Inching the country toward war, but not yet engaged militarily, President Roosevelt wanted to avoid any embarrassment the proposed march would bring to the forces supporting democracy and freedom. With his wife, Eleanor, serving as go-between, Roosevelt agreed to meet with Randolph and worked out a compromise. Randolph called off the march, and in return, on June 25, 1941, the president issued Executive Order 8802, creating the **Fair Employment Practice Committee (FEPC)**. Roosevelt refused to order the desegregation of the military, but he set up a committee to investigate inequality in the armed forces. Although the FEPC helped African Americans gain a greater share of jobs in key industries than they had before, the effect was limited because the agency did not have enforcement power.

The march on Washington movement was emblematic of rising civil rights activity. Black leaders proclaimed their own "two-front war" with the symbol of the **Double V** to represent victory against racist enemies both abroad and at home. The National Association for the Advancement of Colored People (NAACP) continued its policy of fighting racial discrimination in the courts. In 1944 the organization won a significant victory in a case from Texas, *Smith v. Allwright*, which outlawed all-white Democratic primary elections in the traditionally one-party South. As a result of the decision, the percentage of African Americans registered to vote in the South doubled between 1944 and 1948. In 1942 early civil rights activists also founded the interracial Congress of Racial Equality (CORE) in Chicago. CORE protested directly against racial inequality in public accommodations. Its members organized "sit-ins" at restaurants and bowling alleys that refused to serve African Americans. Students at Howard University in Washington, D.C., used the same tactics, with some success, to protest racial exclusion from restaurants and cafeterias in the nation's capital. Although these demonstrations did not get the national attention that postwar protests would, they constituted the prelude to the civil rights movement.

Population shifts on the home front during World War II exacerbated racial tensions, resulting in violence. As jobs opened up throughout the country at military installations and defense plants, hundreds of thousands of African Americans moved from the rural South to the urban South, the North, and the West. Cities could not handle this rapid influx of people and failed to provide sufficient housing to accommodate those who migrated in search of employment. Competition between white and black workers for scarce housing spilled over into tensions in crowded transportation and recreational facilities. In 1943 the stress caused by close wartime contact between the races exploded in more than 240 riots. The most serious one occurred in Detroit, where federal troops had to restore order after whites and blacks fought with each other following an altercation at a popular amusement park that killed thirty-four people.

Struggles for Mexican Americans. Immigration from Mexico increased significantly during the war. To address labor shortages in the Southwest and on the Pacific coast and departing from the deportation policies of the 1930s, in 1942 the United States negotiated an agreement with Mexico for contract laborers (*braceros*) to enter the country for a limited time to work as farm laborers and in factories. *Braceros* had little or no control over their living spaces or working conditions. They conducted numerous strikes for higher wages in the agricultural fields of the Southwest and Northwest. Most U.S. residents of Mexican ancestry were American citizens. Like other Americans, they settled into jobs to help fight the war, while more than 300,000 Mexican Americans served in the armed forces.

The war heightened Mexican Americans' consciousness of their civil rights. As one Mexican American World War II veteran recalled: "We were Americans, not 'spics' or 'greasers.' Because when you fight for your country in a World War, against an alien philosophy, fascism, you are an American and proud to be in America." In southern California, newspaper publisher Ignacio Lutero Lopez campaigned against segregation in movie theaters, swimming pools, and other public accommodations. He organized boycotts against businesses that discriminated against or excluded Mexican Americans. Wartime organizing led to the creation of the Unity Leagues, a coalition of Mexican American business owners, college students, civic leaders, and GIs that pressed for racial equality. In Texas, Mexican Americans joined the League of United Latin American Citizens (LULAC), a largely middle-class group that challenged racial discrimination and segregation in public accommodations. Members of the organization emphasized the use of negotiations to redress

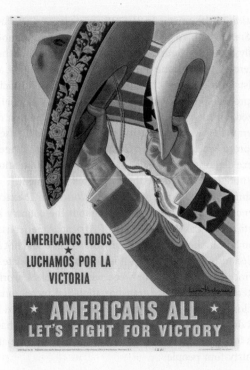

Americanos Todos Luchamos Por Victoria/Americans All Let's Fight for Victory   The Mexican American artist Leon Helguera created this poster for the Office of War Information in 1943. Helguera designed other posters to encourage unity among Spanish-speaking residents of the Southwest. He also belonged to *Los Panamericanos*, a social club in New York City whose goal was to promote friendship and solidarity between the people of the United States and Latin America. University of North Texas Libraries, UNT Digital Library

their grievances, but when they ran into opposition, they resorted to economic boycotts and litigation. The war encouraged LULAC to expand its operations throughout the Southwest.

Mexican American citizens encountered hostility from recently transplanted whites and longtime residents. Tensions were greatest in Los Angeles. A small group of Mexican American teenagers joined gangs and identified themselves by wearing zoot suits — colorful, long, loose-fitting jackets with padded shoulders and baggy pants tapered at the bottom. Not all zoot-suiters were gang members, but many outside their communities failed to make this distinction and found the zoot-suiters' dress and swagger provocative. On the night of June 4, 1943, squads of sailors stationed in Long Beach invaded Mexican American neighborhoods in East Los Angeles and indiscriminately attacked both zoot-suiters and those not dressed in this garb, setting off four days of violence. Mexican American youths tried to fight back. The **zoot suit riots** ended as civilian and military authorities restored order. In response, the Los Angeles city council banned the wearing of zoot suits in public.

American Indians.   Some twenty-five thousand Native Americans served in the military during the war, a disproportionately higher representation than their numbers in the population. Although the Iroquois nation challenged the right of the United States to draft Indians, in 1942 it separately declared war against the Axis powers. Like most other Americans, Native Americans joined up for a variety of reasons: patriotism, concern over the threat of fascism, and a desire to escape the impoverishment and drudgery of home life. The armed forces used Navajo soldiers in the Pacific theater to confuse the Japanese by sending coded messages in their tribal language. In addition to those serving in the military, another forty thousand Indians worked in defense-related industries. The migration of

Indians off reservations opened up new opportunities and fostered increased pride in the part they played in winning the war. Nevertheless, for most Indians the war did not improve their living conditions or remove hostility to their tribal identities.

The Ordeal of Japanese Americans.

World War II marked a significant crossroads for the protection of civil liberties. In general, the federal government did not repress civil liberties as harshly as it had during World War I, primarily because opposition to World War II was not nearly as great. The chief potential for radical dissent came from the Communist Party, but after the Germans attacked the Soviet Union in June 1941, Communists and their sympathizers rallied behind the war effort and did whatever they could to stifle any protest that threatened the goal of defeating Germany. On the other side of the political spectrum, after the attack on Pearl Harbor conservative isolationists in the America First Movement quickly threw their support behind the war.

Of the three ethnic groups associated with the Axis enemy—Japanese, Germans, and Italians—Japanese Americans received by far the worst treatment from the civilian population and state and federal officials. German immigrants had experienced animosity and repression on the home front during World War I but, like Italian immigrants, had generally assimilated into the wider population. In addition, German Americans and Italian Americans had spread out across the country, while Japanese Americans remained concentrated in distinct geographical pockets along the West Coast. Although German Americans and Italian Americans experienced prejudice, they had come to be considered racially white. Nevertheless, the government arrested about 1,500 Italians considered "enemy aliens" and placed around 250 of them in internment camps. It also arrested more than 11,000 Germans, some of them American citizens, who were considered a danger.

The **internment**, or forced relocation and detainment, of Italians and Germans in the United States paled in comparison with that of the Japanese. Nearly all people of Japanese descent lived along the West Coast. Government officials relocated all of those living there—citizens and noncitizens alike—to camps in Arizona, Arkansas, California, Colorado, Idaho, Texas, Utah, and Wyoming. In Hawaii, the site of the Japanese attack on Pearl Harbor, the Japanese population, nearly one-third of the territory's population, was too large to transfer and instead lived under martial law. The few thousand Japanese Americans living elsewhere in the continental United States remained in their homes.

> **Explore ▶**
>
> See Sources 23.2 and 23.3 for two views of Japanese American internment policy.

It did not matter that Fred Korematsu had been born in the United States, had a white girlfriend of Italian heritage, and counted whites among his best friends. His parents had come from Japan, and for much of the American public, his racial heritage meant that he was not a true American. As one American general put it early in the war, "A Jap's a Jap. It makes no difference whether he is an American citizen or not." Along with more than 100,000 people of Japanese descent, two-thirds of whom were American citizens, Korematsu spent most of the war held in an internment camp. Japanese Americans lost their freedom and protection under the Bill of Rights and the Fourteenth Amendment. Despite scant evidence that Japanese Americans were disloyal or harbored spies or saboteurs, U.S. officials chose to believe that as a group they threatened national security. The government established a system that questioned German Americans and Italian Americans on an individual basis if their loyalty came under suspicion. By contrast, U.S. officials identified all Japanese Americans and Japanese resident aliens with the nation

Comparative Primary Source Analysis

Japanese American Internment

In 1942 Charles Kikuchi was an American-born citizen of Japanese descent and a twenty-six-year-old graduate student when he was ordered to relocate to the Tanforan Race Track in San Bruno, California, where he and his family lived in a converted horse stable along with hundreds of others for nine months before moving to Gila River Relocation Center in Arizona. While at Tanforan he kept a vivid diary. In 1943 Kikuchi was released and moved to Chicago. A year later, the Supreme Court ruled that the detention of Japanese Americans did not violate the Constitution. Kikuchi was one of the first to be released because he agreed to move inland, but tens of thousands, like Fred Korematsu, remained interned.

Source 23.2

Charles Kikuchi │ Internment Diary, 1942

There was a terrific rainstorm last night and we have had to wade through the "slush alleys" again. Everyone sinks up to the ankles in mud. Some trucks came in today with lumber to build new barracks, but the earth was so soft that the truck sank over the hubs and they had a hell of a time pulling it out. The Army certainly is rushing things. About half of the Japanese have already been evacuated from the restricted areas in this state. Manzanar, Santa Anita, and Tanforan will be the three biggest centers. Now that S.F. [San Francisco] has been almost cleared the American Legion, the Native Sons of the Golden West, and the California Joint Immigration Committee are filing charges that the Nisei [children born in America to Japanese parents] should be disfranchised because we have obtained citizenship under false pretenses and

that "we are loyal subjects of Japan" and therefore never should have been allowed to obtain citizenship. This sort of thing will gain momentum and we are not in a very advantageous position to combat it. I get fearful sometimes because this sort of hysteria will gain momentum.

The S.F. Registrar has made a statement that we will be sent absentee ballots to which Mr. James Fisk of the Joint Immigration Committee protests greatly. Tomorrow I am going to carry a petition around to protest against their protests. I think that they are stabbing us in the back and that there should be a separate concentration camp for these so-called Americans. They are a lot more dangerous than the Japanese in the U.S. ever will or have been.

Source: John Modell, ed., *The Kikuchi Diary: Chronicle from an American Concentration Camp* (Champaign: University of Illinois Press, 1992), 73.

that had attacked Pearl Harbor, and incarcerated them. In this respect, the United States was not unique. Following the United States' lead, Canada interned its Japanese population, more than 75 percent of whom held Canadian citizenship.

For their part, Japanese Americans did their best to manage during this upheaval. They had been forced to sell their possessions and dispose of their homes and businesses quickly, either selling or renting them at very low prices or simply abandoning them. They left their neighborhoods with only what they could carry. They lived in wooden barracks divided into one-room apartments and shared communal toilets, showers, laundries, and dining

Source 23.3

Justice Hugo Black | *Korematsu v. United States*, 1944

Our task would be simple, our duty clear, were this a case involving the imprisonment of a loyal citizen in a concentration camp because of racial prejudice. Regardless of the true nature of the assembly and relocation centers—and we deem it unjustifiable to call them concentration camps with all the ugly connotations that term implies—we are dealing specifically with nothing but an exclusion order. To cast this case into outlines of racial prejudice, without reference to the real military dangers which were presented, merely confuses the issue. Korematsu was not excluded from the Military Area because of hostility to him or his race. He was excluded because we are at war with the Japanese Empire, because the properly constituted military authorities feared an invasion of our West Coast and felt constrained to take proper security measures, because they decided that the military urgency of the situation demanded that all citizens of Japanese ancestry be segregated from the West Coast temporarily, and finally, because Congress, reposing its confidence in this time of war in our military leaders—as inevitably it must—determined that they should have the power to do just this. There was evidence of disloyalty on the part of some, the military authorities considered that the need for action was great, and time was short.

Source: *Korematsu v. United States*, 323 U.S. 214, 223–24 (1944).

Interpret the Evidence

1. According to Charles Kikuchi, why did groups such as the American Legion seek to deprive the Nisei of their right to vote?
2. According to Justice Hugo Black, why were Japanese American citizens such as Kikuchi and Korematsu interned? What role did he say racial prejudice played?

Put It in Context

In what ways was internment different from when the United States suppressed civil liberties during World War I?

facilities. The camps provided schools, recreational activities, and opportunities for religious worship, except for Shintoism, the official religion of Japan. Some internees attempted to farm, but the arid land on which the camps were located made this nearly impossible. Inmates who worked at jobs within a camp earned monthly wages of $12 to $19, far less than they would have received outside the camps.

Japanese Americans responded to their internment in a variety of ways. Many formed community groups, and some expressed their reactions to the emotional upheaval by writing of their experiences or displaying their feelings through artwork. Contradicting beliefs

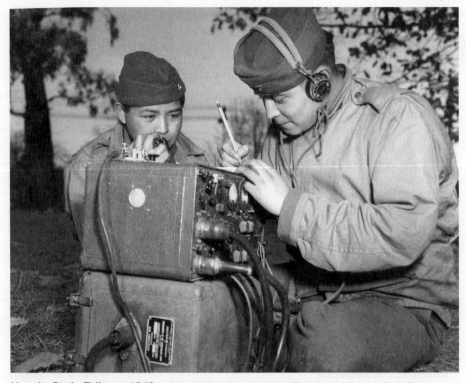

Navajo Code Talkers, 1943   Private First Class Preston Toledo and Private First Class Frank Toledo, cousins and Navajo Indians, attached to a Marine Artillery Regiment in the South Pacific, relay orders over a field radio in their native language on July 7, 1943. These "code talkers" were among the more than 400 bilingual Navajo soldiers deployed to transmit secret communications in their complex tribal language. PhotoQuest/Getty Images

that their ancestry made them disloyal or not real Americans, some 18,000 men joined the army, and many fought gallantly in some of the war's fiercest battles on the European front with the 442nd Regiment, one of the most heavily decorated units in the military. Nisei soldiers were among the first, along with African American troops, to liberate Jews from German concentration camps. Others, like Fred Korematsu, remained in the camps and challenged the legality of President Roosevelt's executive order, which had allowed military officials to exclude Japanese Americans from certain areas and evacuate them from their homes. However, the Supreme Court ruled against him and others. Finally, in December 1944, shortly after he won election to his fourth term as president, Roosevelt rescinded Executive Order 9066.

In contrast to the treatment of Japanese Americans, the status of Chinese Americans improved markedly during the war. Of the more than 100,000 Chinese living in the United States, approximately 13,000 served in the Army. Forty percent of these soldiers were not native-born citizens. With China under Japanese occupation, Congress repealed the Chinese Exclusion Act in 1943, making the Chinese, including those in the military, the first Asians who could become naturalized citizens. Chinese American men also fought in integrated military units like their Filipino peers. For the first time, the war opened up jobs to Chinese American men and women outside their ethnic economy.

Despite the violation of the civil liberties of Japanese American citizens, the majority did not become embittered against the United States. Rather, most of the internees returned to their communities after the war and resumed their lives, still intent on pursuing the American dream from which they had been so harshly excluded; however, some 8,000 Japanese Americans renounced their U.S. citizenship and repatriated to Japan in 1945. After briefly moving to Detroit, Korematsu returned to San Leandro, California, with his wife and two children. Still, Korematsu had trouble finding regular employment because he had a criminal record for violating the exclusion order. In the name of national security the government had established the precedent of incarcerating groups deemed "suspect." It took four decades for the U.S. government to admit its mistake and apologize, and in 1988 Congress awarded reparations of $20,000 to each of the 60,000 living internees. In 1998 President Bill Clinton awarded Korematsu the Presidential Medal of Freedom — the highest decoration a civilian can receive.

Review & Relate

■ What new challenges and opportunities did the war present to racial minority groups?

■ Why were Japanese Americans singled out as a particular threat to national security?

Global War

World War II pitted the "Grand Alliance" of Great Britain, the Soviet Union, the French government in exile, and the United States against the Axis powers of Germany, Japan, and Italy. From the outset, the United States deployed military forces to contain Japanese aggression, but its most immediate concern was to defeat Germany. Before battles in Europe, Asia, and four other continents concluded, more than 60 million people perished, including 405,000 Americans. Six million Jewish civilians died in the Holocaust, the Nazi regime's genocidal effort to eradicate Europe's Jewish population. Another 9 million civilians — Slavic peoples, Romani, Jehovah's Witnesses, homosexuals, the disabled, and Communists — also were systematically murdered by the Nazis. The Soviet Union experienced the greatest losses — nearly 27 million soldiers and civilians, more than two-fifths of all those killed.

War in Europe. United against Hitler, the Grand Alliance divided over how quickly to mount a counterattack directly on Germany. The Soviet Union, which bore the brunt of the fighting in trying to repel the German army's invasion, demanded the opening of a **second front** through France and into Germany to take the pressure off its forces. The British wanted to fight first in northern Africa and southern Europe, in part to remove Axis forces from territory that endangered their economic interests in the Mediterranean and the Middle East and in part to buy time to rebuild their depleted fighting strength. President Roosevelt understood the Soviet position, but worried about losing public support early in the war if the United States experienced heavy casualties. He approved his military advisers' plans for an invasion of France from England in 1943, but in the meantime he agreed with Churchill to fight the Germans and Italians on the periphery of Europe.

From a military standpoint, this circuitous approach proved successful. In October 1942 British forces in North Africa overpowered the Germans at El Alamein, pushing them out of Egypt and removing their threat to the Suez Canal. The following month, British and American troops landed in Algeria and Morocco. After some early defeats, the combined strength of British and American ground, air, and naval forces drove the Germans out of Africa in May 1943.

These military victories failed to relieve political tensions among the Allies. Although the Soviets had managed to stop the German offensive against Stalingrad, the deepest penetration of enemy troops into their country, Stalin expected the second front to begin as promised in the spring of 1943. He was bitterly disappointed when Roosevelt postponed the cross–English Channel invasion of France until 1944. To Stalin, it appeared as if his allies were looking to gain a double triumph by letting the Communists and Nazis beat each other into submission.

Instead of opening a second front in France, British, American, and Canadian troops invaded Italy from its southern tip in July 1943. Their initial victories quickly led to the removal of Mussolini and his retreat to northern Italy, where he lived under German protection (Map 23.1). Not until June 4, 1944, did the Allies occupy Rome in central Italy and force the Germans to retreat.

To overcome Stalin's dissatisfaction with the postponement of opening the second front, President Roosevelt issued orders to give the Soviets unlimited access to Lend-Lease supplies to sustain their war efforts and to care for their citizens. In November 1943, Roosevelt, Churchill, and Stalin met in Tehran, Iran. Roosevelt and Stalin seemed to get along well. Stalin agreed to deploy troops against Japan after the war in Europe ended, and Roosevelt agreed to open the second front within six months. Churchill joined Roosevelt and Stalin in supporting the creation of an international organization to ensure postwar peace.

This time the Americans and British kept their word, and the Allies finally embarked on the second-front invasion. On June 6, 1944 — called **D Day** — more than 1.5 million American, British, and Canadian troops crossed the English Channel in 4,000 boats and landed on the beaches of Normandy, France. Despite deadly machine-gun fire from German troops placed on higher ground, the Allied forces managed to establish a beachhead. The bravery and discipline of the troops, along with their superior numbers, overcame the Germans and opened the way for the Allies to liberate Paris in August 1944. By the end of the year, the Allies had regained control of the rest of France and most of Belgium.

Amid these Allied victories, Roosevelt ran for a fourth term against Republican challenger Thomas E. Dewey, governor of New York. He dumped from the campaign ticket his vice president, Henry A. Wallace, a liberal on economic and racial issues, and replaced him with Senator Harry S. Truman of Missouri, who was more acceptable to southern voters. Despite his declining health, Roosevelt won easily.

War in the Pacific. With the Soviet Union bearing the brunt of the fighting in eastern Europe, the United States shouldered the burden of fighting Japan. U.S. military commanders began a two-pronged counterattack in the Pacific in 1942. General Douglas MacArthur, whose troops had escaped from the Philippines as Japanese forces overran the islands in May 1942, planned to regroup in Australia, head north through New Guinea, and return to the Philippines. At the same time, Admiral Chester Nimitz directed the U.S. Pacific Fleet from Hawaii toward Japanese-occupied islands in the western Pacific. If all

MAP 23.1   World War II in Europe, 1941–1945

By late 1941, the Axis powers had brought most of Europe and the Mediterranean region under their control. But between 1942 and 1945, the Allied powers drove them back. Critical victories at Leningrad and Stalingrad, in North Africa, and on the beaches of Normandy forced the retreat, and then the defeat, of the Axis powers.

went well, MacArthur's ground troops and Nimitz's naval forces would combine with General Curtis LeMay's air forces to overwhelm Japan. This strategy was known as "**island-hopping.**" Accordingly, American and allied forces would leapfrog over heavily fortified Japanese positions and concentrate their resources on lightly defended Japanese islands that would provide bases capable of sustaining the campaign to attack the nation of Japan.

All went according to plan in 1942. Shortly after the Philippines fell to the Japanese, the Allies won a major victory in May in the Battle of the Coral Sea, off the northwest coast of Australia. The following month, the U.S. navy achieved an even greater victory when it defeated the Japanese in the Battle of Midway Island, northwest of Hawaii. In August, the fighting moved to the Solomon Islands, east of New Guinea, where U.S. forces waged fierce battles at Guadalcanal Island. After six months of heavy casualties on both sides, the Americans finally dislodged the Japanese. By late 1944, American, Australian, and New Zealand troops had put the Japanese on the defensive.

In 1945 the United States mounted its final offensive against Japan. In preparation for an invasion of the Japanese home islands, American marines won important battles on Iwo Jima and Okinawa, two strategic islands off the coast of Japan. The fighting proved costly — on Iwo Jima alone, the Japanese fought and died nearly to the last man while killing 6,000 Americans and wounding 20,000 others. At the same time, the U.S. Army Air Corps conducted firebomb raids over Tokyo and other major cities, killing some 330,000 Japanese civilians. These attacks were conducted by newly developed B-29 bombers, which could fly more than 3,000 miles and could be dispatched from Pacific island bases captured by the U.S. military. The purpose of this strategic bombing was to destroy Japan's economic capability to sustain the war rather than to destroy their military forces. At the same time, the navy blockaded Japan, further crippling its economy and reducing its supplies of food, medicine, and raw materials (Map 23.2). Still, the Japanese government refused to surrender and indicated its determination to resist by launching *kamikaze* attacks (suicidal airplane crashes) on American warships and airplanes.

Ending the War. With victory in sight in both Europe and the Pacific, the Allies addressed problems of postwar relations. In February 1945 Roosevelt and Churchill met with Stalin in the resort city of Yalta in the Ukraine. There they clashed over the question of the postwar government of Poland and whether to recognize the claim of the Polish government in exile in London, which the United States and Great Britain supported, or that of the pro-Soviet government, which had spent the war in the USSR. The loosely worded **Yalta Agreement**, which resulted from the conference, called for the establishment of permanent governments in Poland and the rest of eastern Europe through free elections.

Despite this controversy, the Allies left Yalta united over other issues. They renewed their commitment to establishing the United Nations, and the Soviets reaffirmed their intention to join the war against Japan three months after Germany's surrender. The Allies also reached a tentative agreement on postwar Germany. The United States, Great Britain, the Soviet Union, and France would divide the country into four zones, each occupied by one of the powers. They would further subdivide Berlin into four sectors because the capital city fell within the Soviet occupation area. As with the accord over Poland, the agreement concerning Germany created tension after the war.

The Yalta Conference concluded just as the final assault against Germany got under way. The Germans had launched one last offensive in mid-December 1944. Mobilizing troops from remaining outposts in Belgium, they attacked Allied forces in the Battle of the Bulge. After an initial German drive into enemy lines, American and British fighting men recovered and sent the Germans retreating across the Rhine River and back into Germany. Pushing from the west, American general Dwight D. Eisenhower stopped at the Elbe River, where he had agreed to meet up with Red Army troops who were charging from the east to Berlin. After an intense assault by the Soviets, the German capital of Berlin fell, and on April 25 Russian and American forces linked up in Torgau on the Elbe River. They achieved this triumph two weeks after Franklin Roosevelt died at the age of sixty-three from a cerebral hemorrhage. On April 30, 1945, with Berlin shattered, Hitler committed suicide in his bunker. A few days earlier, Italian antifascist partisans had captured and executed Mussolini in

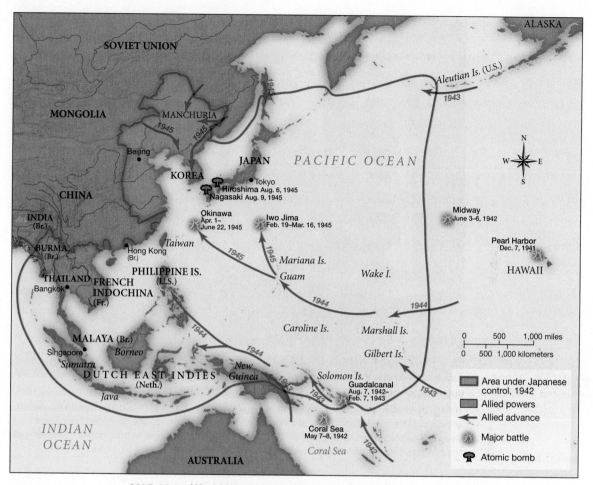

MAP 23.2   World War II in the Pacific, 1941–1945

After bombing Pearl Harbor on December 7, 1941, Japan captured the Philippines and wrenched control of Asian colonies from the British, French, and Dutch and then occupied eastern China. The Allied powers, led by U.S. forces, eventually defeated Japan by winning a series of hard-fought victories on Central Pacific islands and by bombing Hiroshima and Nagasaki.

northern Italy.   of the German government formally surrendered. The war in Europe ended the next day.

With the war over in Europe, the United States made its final push against Japan. Since 1942, J. Robert Oppenheimer and his team of scientists and engineers had labored feverishly to construct an atomic bomb. Few people knew about the top-secret **Manhattan Project**, and Congress appropriated $2 billion without knowing its true purpose.

Vice President Harry S. Truman did not learn about the details of the Manhattan Project until Roosevelt's death on April 12, and in July he found out about the first atomic test while en route to a conference in Potsdam, Germany, with Stalin and Churchill. He ordered the State Department to issue an ultimatum to the Japanese demanding their immediate surrender or else face annihilation. When Japan indicated that it would surrender if the

Roosevelt, Churchill, and Stalin at Yalta, 1945 This photograph taken in February 1945 shows, from left to right, a smiling Prime Minister Winston Churchill, President Franklin Roosevelt, and Soviet Premier Joseph Stalin at the Yalta conference in Crimea. The so-called "Big Three" allies met to discuss postwar plans for Germany and Eastern Europe. In poor health at the time of the meeting, two months later Roosevelt died of a stroke. National Archives, no. 531340

United States allowed the country to retain its emperor, Hirohito, the Truman administration refused and demanded unconditional surrender. As a further blow to Japan, Stalin was ready to send the Soviet military to attack Japanese troops in Manchuria on August 8, which would seriously weaken Japan's ability to hold out.

On August 6 the *Enola Gay*, an American B-29 bomber, dropped an atomic bomb on Hiroshima. The weapon immediately killed 80,000 civilians, and tens of thousands later died slowly from radiation poisoning. Three days later, on August 9, Japan still had not surrendered, and the Army Air Corps dropped another atomic bomb on Nagasaki, killing more than 100,000 civilians. Five days later, on August 14, Japan announced that it would surrender; the formal surrender was completed on September 2.

At the time, very few Americans questioned the decision to drop atomic bombs on Japan. Truman believed that had Roosevelt been alive, he would have authorized use of the bombs. Newly on the job, Truman hesitated to reverse a decision already reached by his predecessor. He reasoned that his action would save American lives because the U.S. military would not have to launch a costly invasion of Japan's home islands. He also felt justified in giving the order because he sought retaliation for the surprise attack on

Pearl Harbor and for Japanese atrocities against American soldiers, especially in the Philippines. **See Primary Source Project 23: The Decision to Drop the Atomic Bomb, page 813.**

Evidence of the Holocaust.
The end of the war revealed the full extent and horror of the **Holocaust** — Germany's calculated and methodical slaughter of certain religious, ethnic, and political groups. As Allied troops liberated Germany and Poland, they saw for themselves the brutality of the Nazi concentration camps that Hitler had set up to execute or work to death 6 million Jews and another 5 million "undesirables" — Slavs, Poles, Gypsies, homosexuals, the physically and mentally disabled, and Communists. At Buchenwald and Dachau in Germany and at Auschwitz in Poland, the Allies encountered the skeletal remains of inmates tossed into mass graves, dead from starvation, illness, and executions. Crematoria on the premises contained the ashes of inmates first poisoned and then incinerated. Troops also freed the "living dead," those still alive but seriously ill and undernourished.

Explore ▶

Compare different perspectives on the Roosevelt administration's response to the Holocaust in Sources 23.4 and 23.5.

Holocaust Survivors   When American troops of the 80th Army Division liberated the Buchenwald concentration camp in Germany, they found these emaciated victims of the Holocaust. Elie Wiesel (seventh from the left on the middle bunk next to the vertical post) went on to become an internationally famous writer who wrote about his wartime experiences and won the Nobel Peace Prize. H. Miller/Getty Images

Comparative Secondary Source Analysis

The Roosevelt Administration and the Holocaust

The genocide committed by the Nazis during World War II against six million European Jews stands out for its moral depravity even in the bloodiest world war in human history. In the United States, with a significant Jewish population that supported FDR, the Roosevelt administration had to deal with two problems: refugees seeking asylum and military operations against Nazi death camps. Because of the profound moral dimensions of the Holocaust, the question for historians remains whether Roosevelt could have made a greater effort on behalf of European Jews and others murdered by the Nazis. Both of the following excerpts were written well after the Holocaust. David S. Wyman's was published closer to the events of World War II and at a time when there was rising public interest in the Nazi genocide. Richard Breitman and Allan J. Lichtman do not disagree with the information Wyman presents, but they weigh the evidence differently in reaching their interpretation.

Source 23.4

David S. Wyman | FDR Abandoned the Jews, 1984

"America's response to the Holocaust was the result of action and inaction on the part of many people. In the forefront was Franklin D. Roosevelt, whose steps to aid Europe's Jews were very limited. If he had wanted to, he could have aroused substantial public backing for a vital rescue effort by speaking out on the issue. If nothing else, a few forceful statements by the President would have brought the extermination news out of obscurity and into the headlines. But he had little to say about the problem and gave no priority to rescue at all.

. . . Even when interested in rescue action, Roosevelt was unwilling to run a political risk for it, as his response to the free-ports plan showed. The WRB's [War Refugee Board] original rescue strategy depended on America setting an example to other nations by offering to open several temporary havens. The President, by agreeing to only one American camp, signaled that little was expected of any country. A more extensive free-ports program would have strained relations with Congress. It might also have cost votes, and 1944 was an election year.

. . . It appears that Roosevelt's overall response to the Holocaust was deeply affected by political expediency. Most Jews supported him unwaveringly, so an active rescue policy offered little political advantage. A pro-Jewish stance, however, could lose votes. American Jewry's great loyalty to the President thus weakened the leverage it might have exerted on him to save European Jews."

Source: David S. Wyman, *The Abandonment of the Jews: America and the Holocaust, 1941–1945* (New York: Pantheon Books, 1984), 311, 312.

Source 23.5

Richard Breitman and Allan J. Lichtman | FDR Did Not Abandon the Jews, 2013

"For most of his presidency Roosevelt did little to aid the imperiled Jews of Germany and Europe. He put other policy priorities well ahead of saving Jews and deferred to fears of an anti-Semitic backlash at home. He worried that measures to assist European Jews might endanger his political coalition at home and then a wartime alliance abroad. . . . When he engaged Jewish issues, he maneuvered, often behind the scenes. When he hesitated, other American officials with far less sympathy for Jews set or carried out policies.

Still, at times, Roosevelt acted decisively to rescue Jews, often withstanding contrary pressures from the American public, Congress, and his own State Department. . . . He was a far better president for Jews than any of his political adversaries would have been. Roosevelt defied most Republican opponents and some isolationist Democrats to lead political and military opposition to Nazi Germany's plans for expansion and world domination.

. . . The story of FDR and the Jews is ultimately a tragic one that transcends the achievements and failures of one leader. Even if FDR had been more willing to override domestic opposition and twist arms abroad, he could not have stopped the Nazi mass murder of some six million Jews. For Hitler and his followers, the annihilation of the Jews was not a diversion from the war effort, but integral to its purpose. For America and Britain, the rescue of Jews, even if practical, was ultimately subordinate to the overriding priorities of total war and unconditional surrender of the enemy."

Source: Richard Breitman and Allan J. Lichtman, *FDR and the Jews* (Cambridge, Mass., The Belknap Press of Harvard University Press, 2013), 2, 6–7.

Examine the Sources

1. Specify one major difference between Wyman's and Breitman/Lichtman's interpretation of Franklin D. Roosevelt's response to the Holocaust and explain how these historians use evidence to support their arguments.
2. Based on evidence in this chapter, evaluate the strengths and/or weaknesses of the Wyman and Breitman/Lichtman interpretations.

▌ Put It in Context

Based on what Roosevelt knew about the Holocaust at the time, how much more could he have done?

These horrific discoveries shocked the public, but evidence of what was happening had appeared early in the war. Journalists like Varian Fry had outlined the Nazi atrocities against the Jews several years before. "Letters, reports, tables all fit together. They add up to the most appalling picture of mass murder in all human history," Fry wrote in the *New Republic* magazine in 1942.

The Roosevelt administration did little in response, despite growing evidence. It chose not to send planes to bomb the concentration camps or the railroad lines leading to them, deeming it too risky militarily and too dangerous for the inmates. "The War Department," its assistant Secretary John J. McCloy wrote the director of the War Refugee Board in defending this decision, "is of the opinion that the suggested air operation is impracticable. It could be executed only by the diversion of considerable air support essential to the success of our forces now engaged in decisive operations and would in any case be of such very doubtful efficacy that it would not amount to a practical project." In a less defensible decision, the Roosevelt administration refused to relax immigration laws to allow Jews and other persecuted ethnic minorities to take refuge in the United States, and only 21,000 managed to find asylum. The State Department, which could have modified these policies, was staffed with anti-Semitic officials, and though President Roosevelt expressed sympathy for the plight of Hitler's victims, he believed that winning the war as quickly as possible was the best way to help them.

Nevertheless, even when it had been possible to rescue Jews, the United States balked. In 1939 a German liner, the SS *St. Louis*, embarked from Hamburg with 937 Jewish refugees aboard and set sail for Cuba. Blocked from entry by the Cuban government, the ship sailed for the coast of Florida, hoping to gain permission to enter the United States. However, the United States refused, maintaining that the passengers did not have the proper documents required under the Immigration Act of 1924. The ship then headed back to Europe, where the United Kingdom, Belgium, the Netherlands, and France took in the passengers. Unfortunately, in 1940, when the Nazis invaded Belgium, the Netherlands, and France and sent their Jewish residents to concentration camps, an estimated 254 of the *St. Louis* passengers died along with countless others.

Although not nearly to the same extent as in the Holocaust, the Japanese also committed numerous war atrocities. Around 50,000 U.S. soldiers and civilians became prisoners of war and about half of them were forced to work as slave laborers. From June 1942 to October 1943, the Japanese constructed a 300-mile railroad between Burma (Myanmar) and Thailand using 60,000 Allied prisoners of war and 200,000 Asian conscripts. Working under inhumane conditions, approximately 13,000 Allied prisoners of war and 80,000 Asian laborers died before the railway was completed. About 40 percent of American POWs died in Japanese captivity (in contrast only 1 percent died in Nazi camps). One reason why POWs were treated so poorly was because the Japanese believed that surrender was a cowardly act and those who did so were beneath contempt. Far more than the Americans and their allies, Chinese civilians and native residents of such countries as Burma and the Dutch East Indies (Indonesia) were brutalized and killed by the Japanese occupying forces.

Review & Relate

▪ How did the Allies win the war in Europe and in the Pacific, and how did tensions among them shape their military strategy and postwar plans?

▪ Why did the United States fail to do more to help victims of the Holocaust?

Conclusion: The Impact of World War II

Franklin Roosevelt initially charted a course of neutrality before the United States entered World War II. Roosevelt believed that the rise of European dictatorships and their expansionist pursuits throughout the world threatened American national security. He saw signs of trouble early, but responding to antiwar sentiment from lawmakers and the American public, Roosevelt waited for a blatant enemy attack before declaring war. The Japanese attack on Pearl Harbor in 1941 provided that justification.

On the domestic front, World War II accomplished what Franklin Roosevelt's New Deal could not. Prosperity and nearly full employment returned only after the nation's factories began supplying the Allies and the United States joined in the fight against the Axis powers. Mobilization for war also furthered the tremendous growth and centralization of power in the federal government that had begun under the New Deal. Washington, D.C., became the chief source of authority to which Americans looked for solutions to problems concerning economic security and financial development. The federal government showed that it would use its authority to expand equal rights for African Americans. The war swung national power against racial discrimination, and various civil rights victories during the war served as precursors to the civil rights movement of subsequent decades. The war also heightened Mexican Americans' consciousness of oppression and led them to organize for civil rights. However, in neither case, nor that of American Indians, did the war erase white prejudice.

At the same time, the federal government trampled on the civil liberties of Japanese Americans. The president succumbed to wartime antagonism against Japanese immigrants and their children. With China a wartime ally, Chinese Americans escaped a similar fate. Yet like white and black Americans, the Nisei displayed their patriotism by distinguishing themselves as soldiers on the battlefields of Europe.

The war brought women into the workforce as never before, providing a measure of independence and distancing them from their traditional roles as wives and mothers. Nevertheless, the government and private employers made it clear that they expected most female workers to give up their jobs to returning servicemen and to become homemakers once the war ended.

Finally, the war thrust the United States onto the world stage as one of the world's two major superpowers alongside the Soviet Union. This position posed new challenges. In sole possession of the atomic bomb, the most powerful weapon on the planet, and fortified by a robust economy, the United States filled the international power vacuum created by the weakening and eventual collapse of the European colonial empires. The fragile alliance that had held together the United States and the Soviet Union shattered soon after the end of World War II. The Atomic Age, which J. Robert Oppenheimer helped usher in with a powerful weapon of mass destruction, and the government oppression that Fred Korematsu endured in the name of national security did not disappear. Rather, they expanded in new directions and shaped the lives of all Americans for decades to come.

chapter **23** review

Timeline of Events

1933	United States extends diplomatic recognition to the Soviet Union
	Adolf Hitler becomes chancellor of Germany
1935–1937	Neutrality Acts
1939	Germany occupies Czechoslovakia
	Germany and Soviet Union invade Poland; World War II begins
1940	Battle of Britain begins
	Tripartite Pact signed
1941	Lend-Lease Act
	Fair Employment Practice Committee created
	Atlantic Charter signed
	Germany invades Soviet Union
December 7, 1941	Pearl Harbor bombed
December 11, 1941	Germany and Italy declare war on the United States
1942	Congress of Racial Equality established
	Manhattan Project approved
	Roosevelt orders internment of Japanese Americans
1943	Zoot suit riots
June 6, 1944	D Day invasion begins
1945	Final U.S. offensive against Japan, with victories at Iwo Jima and Okinawa
February 1945	Yalta Conference
May 1945	Germany surrenders
August 1945	U.S. drops atomic bombs on Hiroshima and Nagasaki
September 1945	Japan surrenders

Key Terms

Neutrality Acts, *784*
appeasement, *784*
America First Committee, *786*
Lend-Lease Act, *786*
Atlantic Charter, *787*
military-industrial complex, *789*
War Production Board, *790*
National War Labor Board, *791*
Fair Employment Practice Committee (FEPC), *794*
Double V, *794*
zoot suit riots, *796*
internment, *797*
second front, *801*
D Day, *802*
"island-hopping", *803*
Yalta Agreement, *804*
Manhattan Project, *805*
Holocaust, *807*

Review & Relate

1. How did American public opinion shape Roosevelt's foreign policy in the years preceding U.S. entry into World War II?

2. What events in Europe and the Pacific ultimately brought the United States into World War II?

3. How did the war accelerate the trend that began during the New Deal toward increased government participation in the economy?

4. How did the war affect life on the home front for the average American?

5. What new challenges and opportunities did the war present to racial minority groups?

6. Why were Japanese Americans singled out as a particular threat to national security?

7. How did the Allies win the war in Europe and in the Pacific, and how did tensions among them shape their military strategy and postwar plans?

8. Why did the United States fail to do more to help victims of the Holocaust?

The Decision to Drop the Atomic Bomb

▶ Evaluate the reasons the United States dropped atomic bombs on Hiroshima and Nagasaki.

The Manhattan Project — the code name given to the U.S. atomic program — was formally set up in 1942 under the direction of General Leslie Groves and physicist J. Robert Oppenheimer. The program was a massive undertaking, employing thousands of workers at sites in Chicago; Berkeley, California; Oak Ridge, Tennessee; Hanford, Washington; and, most famously, at the scientific laboratory in Los Alamos, New Mexico. It took $3 billion to create the atomic bombs. The project was so secretive that even Harry Truman didn't learn of it until he became president following Roosevelt's death.

The bombs that exploded over Hiroshima and Nagasaki in August 1945 revolutionized world history. They ended World War II, changed the nature of warfare, and altered the course of international relations. The bombs launched a nuclear arms race that continued throughout the Cold War and unleashed fears of global annihilation. Debates about whether the bombs were necessary began even before they were dropped (Sources 23.6 and 23.7). As a result of the bombing of Hiroshima and Nagasaki, some 200,000 people, mostly civilians, were killed immediately, and even more were stricken with radiation poisoning, burns, and other injuries. More than 80 percent of the buildings in each city were flattened instantly, and permanent shadows were left on walls and pavement (Sources 23.8 and 23.10).

Many aspects of Truman's decision continue to be questioned and debated, especially whether there were reasonable alternatives to dropping the two atomic bombs (Source 23.9).

Source 23.6

Petition to the President of the United States | July 17, 1945

Before the first successful test of the atomic bomb in New Mexico on June 16, 1945, code-named "Trinity," Secretary of War Henry Stimson received a memorandum from the scientific advisory panel of the Manhattan Project, including J. Robert Oppenheimer, which recommended the use of atomic weapons against Japan. However, the day after the test, as the following document shows, seventy scientists involved in the Manhattan Project wrote to President Truman arguing against the bomb's use.

Discoveries of which the people of the United States are not aware may affect the welfare of this nation in the near future. The liberation of atomic power which has been achieved places atomic bombs in the hands of the Army. It places in your hands, as Commander-in-Chief, the fateful decision whether or not to sanction the use of such bombs in the present phase of the war against Japan.

We, the undersigned scientists, have been working in the field of atomic power. Until recently we have had to fear that the United States might be attacked by atomic bombs during this war and that her only defense might lie in a counterattack by the same means. Today, with the defeat of Germany, this danger is averted and we feel impelled to say what follows:

The war has to be brought speedily to a successful conclusion and attacks by atomic bombs may very well be an effective method of warfare. We feel, however, that such attacks on Japan could not be justified, at least not unless the terms which will be imposed after the war on Japan were made public in detail and Japan were given an opportunity to surrender.

If such public announcement gave assurance to the Japanese that they could look forward to a life devoted to peaceful pursuits in their homeland and if Japan still refused to surrender our nation might then, in certain circumstances, find itself forced to resort to the use of atomic bombs. Such a step, however, ought not to be made at any time without seriously considering the moral responsibilities which are involved. . . .

If after this war a situation is allowed to develop in the world which permits rival powers to be in uncontrolled possession of these new means of destruction, the cities of the United States as well as the cities of other nations will be in continuous danger of sudden annihilation. All the resources of the United States, moral and material, may have to be mobilized to prevent the advent of such a world situation. Its prevention is at present the solemn responsibility of the United States—singled out by virtue of her lead in the field of atomic power. . . .

In view of the foregoing, we, the undersigned, respectfully petition: first, that you exercise your power as Commander-in-Chief, to rule that the United States shall not resort to the use of atomic bombs in this war unless the terms which will be imposed upon Japan have been made public in detail and Japan knowing these terms has refused to surrender; second, that in such an event the question whether or not to use atomic bombs be decided by you in the light of the considerations presented in this petition as well as all the other moral responsibilities which are involved.

Source: U.S. National Archives, Record Group 77, Records of the Chief of Engineers, Manhattan Engineer District, Harrison-Bundy file, folder #76.

President Harry S. Truman | Press Release on the Atomic Bomb, August 6, 1945

After the first atomic bomb, nicknamed "Little Boy," was dropped on Hiroshima, President Truman released the following statement to the public. In it, Truman explains the development of the bomb, its destructive power, and why it was used against Japan. This statement was made before the second bomb was dropped on Nagasaki and before Japan's surrender.

The Japanese began the war from the air at Pearl Harbor. They have been repaid many fold. And the end is not yet. With this bomb we have now added a new and revolutionary increase in destruction to supplement the growing power of our armed forces. In their present form these bombs are now in production and even more powerful forms are in development.

It is an atomic bomb. It is a harnessing of the basic power of the universe. The force from which the sun draws its power has been loosed against those who brought war to the Far East. . . .

We are now prepared to obliterate more rapidly and completely every productive enterprise the Japanese have above ground in any city. We shall destroy their docks, their factories, and their communications. Let there be no mistake; we shall completely destroy Japan's power to make war.

It was to spare the Japanese people from utter destruction that the ultimatum of July 26 was issued at Potsdam. Their leaders promptly rejected that ultimatum. If they do not now accept our terms they may expect a rain of ruin from the air, the like of which has never been seen on this earth. Behind this air attack will follow sea and land forces in such numbers and power as they have not yet seen and with the fighting skill of which they are already well aware. . . .

The fact that we can release atomic energy ushers in a new era in man's understanding of nature's forces. Atomic energy may in the future supplement the power that now comes from coal, oil, and falling water, but at present it cannot be produced on a basis to compete with them commercially. Before that comes there must be a long period of intensive research.

Source: Press Release by the White House, August 6, 1945, Ayers Papers, Truman Library.

Hiroshima | August 6, 1945

In this photograph, a survivor stands among the ruins of Hiroshima. The bomb that was dropped on the city destroyed 5 square miles and killed 70,000 to 80,000 people. Three days later, the United States dropped a second atomic bomb on Nagasaki.

AP Images/Stanley Troutman

U.S. Strategic Bombing Survey, 1946

After the war, President Truman called for a series of surveys on the effectiveness of strategic bombing campaigns in Europe and Asia and on the effects of the atomic bombs on Hiroshima and Nagasaki. The survey on the Pacific war included interviews with Japanese military and government leaders as well as information from Japanese wartime documents. It concluded that the use of the atomic bombs was unnecessary because even without them Japan would have surrendered in the fall of 1945.

4. When Japan was defeated without invasion, a recurrent question arose as to what effect the threat of a home island invasion had had upon the surrender decision. It was contended that the threat of invasion, if not the actual operation, was a requirement to induce acceptance of the surrender terms. On this tangled issue the evidence and hindsight are clear. The fact is, of course, that Japan did surrender without invasion, and with its principal armies intact. Testimony before the Survey shows that the expected "violation of the sacred homeland" raised few fears which expedited the decision to surrender beforehand. Government and Imperial household leaders felt some concern for the "destruction of the Japanese people," but the people were already being shattered by direct air attacks. Anticipated landings were even viewed by the military with hope that they would afford a means of inflicting casualties sufficiently high to improve their chances of a negotiated peace. Preparation of defenses against landings diverted certain resources from dispersal and cushioning moves which might have partially mitigated our air blows. But in Japan's then depleted state, the diversion was not significant. The responsible leaders in power read correctly the true situation and embraced surrender well before invasion was expected. . . .

6. The Hiroshima and Nagasaki atomic bombs did not defeat Japan, nor by the testimony of the enemy leaders who ended the war did they persuade Japan to accept unconditional surrender. The Emperor [Hirohito], the lord privy seal, the prime minister, the foreign minister, and the navy minister had decided as early as May of 1945 that the war should be ended even if it meant acceptance of defeat on allied terms. The war minister and the two chiefs of staff opposed unconditional surrender. The impact of the Hiroshima attack was to bring further urgency and lubrication to the machinery of achieving peace, primarily by contributing to a situation which permitted the prime minister to bring the Emperor overtly and directly into a position where his decision for immediate acceptance of the Potsdam declaration could be used to override the remaining objectors. Thus, although the atomic bombs changed no votes of the Supreme War Direction Council concerning the Potsdam terms, they did foreshorten the war and expedite the peace. . . .

There is little point in attempting more precisely to impute Japan's unconditional surrender to any one of the numerous causes which jointly and cumulatively were responsible for Japan's disaster. Concerning the absoluteness of her defeat there can be no doubt. The time lapse between military impotence and political acceptance of the inevitable might have been shorter had the political structure of Japan permitted a more rapid and decisive determination of national policies. It seems clear, however, that air supremacy and its exploitation over Japan proper was the major factor which determined the timing of Japan's surrender and obviated any need for invasion.

Based on a detailed investigation of all the facts and supported by the testimony of the surviving Japanese leaders involved, it is the Survey's opinion that certainly prior to 31 December 1945, and in all probability prior to 1 November 1945, Japan would have surrendered even if the atomic bombs had not been dropped, even if Russia had not entered the war, and even if no invasion had been planned or contemplated.

Source: United States Strategic Bombing Survey: Japan's Struggle to End the War, July 1, 1946, Elsey Papers, Truman Library.

Father Johannes Siemes | Eyewitness Account of the Hiroshima Bombing, 1945

Father Johannes Siemes, a German priest living in Japan, wrote the following eyewitness account of the Hiroshima bombing. Siemes lived less than a mile outside the city, and after the attack he went into Hiroshima to look for other priests from his order. He gave this account to Bishop Franklin Corley, an American soldier and one of the first Americans to enter the city.

More than thirty hours had gone by until the first official rescue party had appeared on the scene. We find both children and take them out of the park: six-year old girl who was uninjured, and a twelve-year old girl who had been burned about the head, hands, and legs, and who had lain for thirty hours without care in the park. The left side of her face and the left eye were completely covered with blood and pus, so that we thought that she had lost the eye. When the wound was later washed, we noted that the eye was intact and that the lids had just become stuck together. On the way home, we took another group of three refugees with us. The first wanted to know, however, of what nationality we were. They, too, feared that we might be Americans who had parachuted in. When we arrived in Nagatsuka [a Jesuit monastery in Hiroshima], it had just become dark.

We took under our care fifty refugees who had lost everything. The majority of them were wounded and not a few had dangerous burns. Father Rektor treated the wounds as well as he could with the few medicaments that we could, with effort, gather up. He had to confine himself in general to cleansing the wounds of purulent [consisting of pus] material. Even those with the smaller burns are very weak and all suffered from diarrhea. . . .

Thousands of wounded who died later could doubtless have been rescued had they received proper treatment and care, but rescue work in a catastrophe of this magnitude had not been envisioned; since the whole city had been knocked out at a blow, everything which had been prepared for emergency work was lost, and no preparation had been made for rescue work in the outlying districts. Many of the wounded also died because they had been weakened by under-nourishment and consequently lacked in strength to recover. Those who had their normal strength and who received good care slowly healed the burns which had been occasioned by the bomb. There were also cases, however, whose prognosis seemed good who died suddenly. There were also some who had only small external wounds who died within a week or later, after an inflammation of the pharynx and oral cavity had taken place. . . .

Only several cases are known to me personally where individuals who did not have external burns later died. Father Kleinsorge and Father Cieslik, who were near the center of the explosion, but who did not suffer burns, became quite weak some fourteen days after the explosion. Up to this time small incised wounds had healed normally, but thereafter the wounds which were still unhealed became worse and are to date (in September) still incompletely healed. The attending physician diagnosed it as leucopenia [a decrease in white blood cells]. There thus seems to be some truth in the statement that the radiation had some effect on the blood. I am of the opinion, however, that their generally undernourished and weakened condition was partly responsible for these findings. It was noised about that the ruins of the city emitted deadly rays and that workers who went there to aid in the clearing died, and that the central district would be uninhabitable for some time to come.

Source: Father Johannes Siemes, "Hiroshima, August 6, 1945," *Bulletin of the Atomic Scientists* 1, no. 11 (1946): 5–6.

Interpret the Evidence

1. Compare the arguments of the scientists who opposed dropping the atomic bomb on Japan (Source 23.6) with those put forward by President Truman for dropping the bombs (Source 23.7).
2. According to the strategic bombing survey, what role did the atomic bombs play in defeating Japan (Source 23.9)?
3. How does what you see in the photograph of the day after the bombing of Hiroshima (Source 23.8) compare with the eyewitness account in Source 23.10? Which do you find more powerful and why?
4. What evidence can you find in these documents that atomic power would play a critical role in shaping the postwar world?

Put It in Context

Analyze the political, military, and racial motives behind the United States' decision to drop the atomic bomb on Japan.

What were the alternatives to dropping the atomic bomb and why weren't they used?

The Opening of the Cold War

1945–1961

▶ Explore how the end of World War II and the beginning of the Cold War
influenced the postwar period. What effect did the Cold War have on American politics and society?

▶ Assess the effects of the Cold War on American society.

Window to the Past

Herblock Cartoon on McCarthyism, 1950

During the Cold War with the Soviet Union, the United States became preoccupied with searching for and punishing Communists at home. No one received more publicity in raising the alarm than did Senator Joseph R. McCarthy, a Republican from Wisconsin. Herblock (Herbert Block) coined the term "McCarthyism" in this 1950 cartoon, one of many pointing out the danger of McCarthyism to the political system and civil liberties.

▶ To learn more about this primary source, see Source 24.9 on page 852.

"You Mean I'm Supposed To Stand On That?"

A 1950 Herblock Cartoon, © The Herb Block Foundation

After reading this chapter you will be able to:

- Analyze the causes of the Cold War.

- Explain how the overall strategy of containment changed between 1948 and 1953, and describe in particular how the Korean War affected U.S. Cold War strategy and presidential power.

- Analyze the effects of the Cold War on domestic policy.

- Evaluate how the Eisenhower administration managed containment throughout the world.

Comparing American Histories

George Frost Kennan played a critical role in shaping the postwar confrontation between the United States and the Soviet Union. Kennan's views were based on extensive experience with the Soviets gained during two tours of duty serving as a diplomat at the U.S. Embassy in Moscow. During the first, from 1933 to 1937, he witnessed countless "enemies of the state" arrested, exiled, or executed in Stalin's purges. His experiences convinced him that there was little basis for a positive relationship between the United States and the Soviet Union.

Kennan's second tour as a lead U.S. diplomat in Moscow, from 1944 to 1946, came at a critical juncture in U.S.-Soviet relations. As the war drew to a close, tensions over the nature of the postwar world escalated, and by 1946 the wartime alliance had

collapsed. Against this backdrop, Kennan warned that Stalin was committed to expanding communism throughout the world and advised President Harry S. Truman to adopt a policy of *containment*. In Kennan's view, all Soviet efforts at expansion should be met with firm resistance. At the same time, the United States should take an active role in rebuilding the economies of war-torn Western European countries, thereby reducing the appeal of communism to their populations. Kennan's concept of containment would become the basis for President Truman's Cold War foreign policy.

Kennan, however, was not a rigid cold warrior. As the Cold War intensified and expanded, Kennan argued that containment would work best through political and economic rather than military means. He soon insisted that his containment strategy had been misunderstood. Increasingly, his views fell out of favor at the State Department, and Kennan left in 1950 in a disagreement with the Truman administration's growing militarization of the conflict with the Soviet Union.

Julius and Ethel Rosenberg were casualties of the Cold War that Kennan helped shape. Accused of passing military secrets to the Soviet Union, they were tried for espionage in an atmosphere of growing anti-Communist fervor. Like other young idealists during the 1930s, Ethel became disillusioned with capitalism, joined the Young Communist League, and took part in labor union organizing in her hometown of New York City. Julius attended the City College of New York, where he, too, joined the Young Communist League. Three years after they met in 1936, Julius and Ethel married and started a family.

During World War II, Julius worked for the Army Signal Corps as an engineer. In 1945 he lost his job after a security investigation revealed his Communist Party membership. Five years later, the federal government charged that during World War II the Rosenbergs had provided classified information about the construction of the atomic bomb to the Soviet Union, charges they denied.

A jury found them guilty on April 5, 1951, and the presiding judge sentenced them to death. Despite an international campaign for clemency and after unsuccessful appeals to the Supreme Court, on

(*left*) **George Kennan** Library of Congress, Prints and Photographs Division, photograph by Harris & Ewing [LC-DIG-hec-12925]

(*right*) **Ethel Rosenberg** Tallandier/Bridgeman Images

June 19, 1953, the Rosenbergs were executed. Though recent evidence has confirmed Julius Rosenberg's role as a spy, the case against Ethel remains inconclusive.

Without the heightened Cold War climate that then existed in the country, it is likely that neither would have gone to the electric chair ■

The American histories of both George Kennan and Julius and Ethel Rosenberg revolved around their views of communism and the Soviet Union. Kennan designed an approach to containing Soviet aggression based on his dealings with Stalin. The Rosenbergs believed in communism's promise of social and economic equality and saw the Soviet Union as a defense against Nazi aggression. The lives of Kennan, the Rosenbergs, and all Americans would be profoundly shaped by the epic military and ideological battle between the superpowers as the Cold War expanded from the late 1940s through the 1950s, bringing with it increased interventions abroad, fear of communism within the United States, and changes in the executive power of the presidency.

The **Origins** of the
Cold War 1945–1947

The wartime partnership between the United States and the Soviet Union (USSR) was an alliance of necessity. The two nations joined forces to combat Nazi aggression, putting aside ideological differences and a history of mutual distrust. As long as the Nazi threat existed, the alliance held, but as the war ended and attention turned to the postwar world, the allies became adversaries. The two nations did not engage directly in war, but they entered into a prolonged struggle for political, economic, and military dominance known as the **Cold War**.

Mutual Misunderstandings. The roots of the Cold War stretched back several decades. After the Bolshevik Revolution of 1917, the United States refused to grant diplomatic recognition to the Soviet Union and sent troops to Russia to support anti-Bolshevik forces seeking to overturn the revolution, an effort that failed. At the same time, the American government, fearing Communist efforts to overthrow capitalist governments, sought to wipe out communism in the United States by deporting immigrant radicals during the Red scare (see "The Red Scare, 1919–1920" in chapter 21). The United States continued to deny diplomatic recognition to the USSR until 1933, when President Roosevelt reversed this policy. Nevertheless, relations between the two countries remained uneasy.

World War II brought a thaw in tensions. President Roosevelt went a long way toward defusing Stalin's concerns at the Yalta Conference in 1945. The Soviet leader viewed the Eastern European countries that the USSR had liberated from the Germans, especially Poland, as a buffer to protect his nation from future attacks by Germany. Roosevelt understood Stalin's reasoning and recognized political realities: The Soviet military already occupied Eastern Europe, a state of affairs that increased Stalin's bargaining position. Still, the president attempted to balance Soviet influence by insisting that the Yalta Agreement include a guarantee of free elections in Eastern Europe.

By contrast, Roosevelt's successor, Harry S. Truman, took a much less nuanced approach to U.S.-Soviet relations than his predecessor. Stalin's ruthless purges within the Soviet Union in the 1930s and 1940s convinced Truman that the Soviet dictator was paranoid and extremely dangerous. He believed that the Soviets threatened "a barbarian invasion of Europe," and he intended to deter it. In his first meeting with Soviet foreign minister Vyacheslav Molotov in April 1945, Truman rebuked the Russians for failing to support free elections in Poland. Molotov, recoiling from the sharp tone of Truman's remarks, replied: "I have never been talked to like that in my life."

Despite this rough start, Truman did not immediately abandon the idea of cooperation with the Soviet Union. At the Potsdam Conference in Germany in July 1945, Truman and Stalin agreed on several issues. The two leaders reaffirmed the concept of free elections in Eastern Europe; Soviet troop withdrawal from the oil fields of northern Iran, which bordered the USSR; and the partition of Germany (and Berlin itself) into four Allied occupation zones.

Within six months of the war's end, however, relations between the two countries soured. The United States was the only nation in the world with the atomic bomb and boasted the only economy reinvigorated by the war. As a result, the Truman administration believed that it held the upper hand against the Soviets. With this in mind, the State Department offered the Soviets a $6 billion loan, which the country needed to help rebuild its war-ravaged economy. But when the Soviets undermined free elections in Poland in 1946 and established a compliant government, the United States withdrew the offer. Soviet troops also remained in northern Iran, closing off the oil fields to potential capitalist enterprises. The failure to reach agreement over international control of atomic energy proved the last straw. The United States wanted to make sure it would keep its atomic weapons, while the Soviets wanted the United States to destroy its nuclear arsenal. Clearly, the former World War II allies did not trust each other.

Truman had significantly underestimated the strength of the Soviet position. The Soviets were well on their way toward building their own atomic bomb, negating the Americans' nuclear advantage. The Soviets could also ignore the enticement of U.S. economic aid by taking resources from East Germany and mobilizing the Russian people to rebuild their country's industry and military. On February 9, 1946, Stalin delivered a tough speech to rally Russians to make sacrifices to enhance national security. By asserting that communism was "a better form of organization than any non-Soviet social system," he implied, according to George Kennan, that capitalist nations could not coexist with communism and that future wars were unavoidable unless communism triumphed over capitalism.

Whether Stalin meant this speech as an unofficial declaration of a third world war was not clear, but U.S. leaders interpreted it this way. A few days after Stalin spoke, Kennan sent an 8,000-word telegram from the U.S. Embassy in Moscow to Washington, blaming the Soviets for stirring up international tensions and confirming that Stalin could not be trusted. The following month, on March 15, former British prime minister Winston Churchill gave a speech in Truman's home state of Missouri. Declaring that "an iron curtain has descended across the Continent" of Europe, Churchill observed that "there is nothing [the Russians] admire so much as strength, and there is nothing for which they have less respect than for . . . military weakness." This comment reaffirmed Truman's sentiments expressed the previous year: "Unless Russia is faced with an iron fist and strong language another war is in the making." The message was clear: Unyielding resistance to the Soviet Union was the only way to avoid another world war.

Not all Americans agreed with this view. Led by Roosevelt's former vice president Henry Wallace, who served as Truman's secretary of commerce, critics voiced concern about taking a "hard line" against the Soviet Union. Stalin was pursuing a policy of expansion, they agreed, but for limited reasons. Wallace claimed that the Soviets merely wanted to protect their borders by surrounding themselves with friendly countries, just as the United States had done by establishing spheres of influence in the Caribbean. Except for Poland and Romania, Stalin initially accepted an array of governments in Eastern Europe, allowing free elections in Czechoslovakia, Hungary, and, to a lesser extent, Bulgaria. Only as Cold War tensions escalated did the Soviets tighten control over all of Eastern Europe. Critics such as Wallace considered this outcome the result of a self-fulfilling prophecy; by misinterpreting Soviet motives, the Truman administration pushed Stalin to counter the American hard line with a hard line of his own.

Explore ▸

See Source 24.1 for Henry Wallace's criticism of aggressive behavior toward the Soviet Union.

Thus, after World War II, the United States came to believe that the Soviet Union desired world revolution to spread communism, a doctrine hostile to free market individualism. At the same time, the Soviet Union viewed the United States as seeking to make the world safe for capitalism, thereby reducing Soviet chances to obtain economic resources and rebuild its war-shattered economy. Each nation tended to see the other's actions in the most negative light and to see global developments as a zero-sum game, one in which every victory for one side was necessarily a defeat for the other.

The Truman Doctrine.

By 1947 U.S.-Soviet relations had reached a new low. International arms control had proved futile, the United States had gone to the United Nations to pressure the Soviets to withdraw from Iran, and the rhetoric from both sides had become warlike. From the American vantage point, Soviet actions to expand communism in Eastern Europe appeared to threaten democracies in Western Europe. By contrast, the Soviets viewed the United States as seeking to extend economic control over nations close to their borders and to weaken communism in the Soviet Union.

Events in Greece allowed Truman to take the offensive and apply Kennan's policy of containment. To maintain access to the Middle East and its Asian colonies, the United Kingdom considered it vitally important to keep Greece within its sphere of influence. In 1946 a civil war broke out in Greece between the right-wing monarchy and a coalition of insurgents consisting of members of the wartime anti-Nazi resistance, Communists, and non-Communist opponents of the repressive government. Exhausted by the war and in desperate financial shape, the British turned to the United States for help.

The Truman administration believed that the presence of Communists among the Greek rebels meant that Moscow was behind the insurgency. In fact, Stalin was not aiding the Greek revolutionaries; the assistance came from the Communist leader of Yugoslavia, Josip Broz (known then as Marshall Tito), who acted independently of the Soviets and would soon break with them. Following Kennan's lead in advocating containment, Truman incorrectly believed that all Communists around the world were ultimately controlled by the Kremlin.

While Truman was convinced that the United States had to intervene in Greece to contain the spread of communism, he still had to convince the Republican-controlled Congress and the American people to go along. To overcome potential opposition to its plans, the Truman administration exaggerated the danger of Communist influence in Greece. Truman sent Undersecretary of State Dean Acheson to testify before a congressional committee that, "like apples in a barrel infected by one rotten one, the corruption of Greece would infect Iran and all to the east." The administration's presentation of the issues to the

Guided Primary Source Analysis

Henry Wallace | The Way to Peace, 1946

By the late 1940s, tensions between the two superpowers threatened to erupt into armed conflict. Opinion within the U.S. government about how to respond to this challenge ranged widely: Some urged cooperation, while others argued for aggressive confrontation with the Soviet Union. In the following selection, Secretary of Commerce Henry Wallace criticizes aggressive responses to the Soviet Union.

Source 24.1

"Getting tough" never bought anything real and lasting—whether for schoolyard bullies or businessmen or world powers. The tougher we get, the tougher the Russians will get.

Throughout the world there are numerous reactionary elements which had hoped for Axis victory—and now profess great friendship for the United States. Yet, these enemies of yesterday and false friends of today continually try to provoke war between the United States and Russia. They have no real love of the United States. They only long for the day when the United States and Russia will destroy each other. We must not let our Russian policy be guided or influenced by those inside or outside the United States who want war with Russia. This does not mean appeasement. . . .

The real peace treaty we now need is between the United States and Russia. On our part, we should recognize that we have no more business in the political affairs of Eastern Europe than Russia has in the political affairs of Latin America, Western Europe, and the United States. We may not like what Russia does in Eastern Europe. Her type of land reform, industrial expropriation, and suppression of basic liberties offends the great majority of the people of the United States. But whether we like it or not the Russians will try to socialize their sphere of influence just as we try to democratize our sphere of influence. . . .

Russia must be convinced that we are not planning for war against her and we must be certain that Russia is not carrying on territorial expansion or world domination through native Communists faithfully following every twist and turn in the Moscow party line. But in this competition, we must insist on an open door for trade throughout the world. There will always be an ideological conflict—but that is no reason why diplomats cannot work out a basis for both systems to live safely in the world side by side.

Source: Henry Wallace, "The Way to Peace," in *The Annals of America* (Chicago: Encyclopedia Britannica, 1968), 16:372–73.

According to Wallace, why do some countries want the United States to confront the Soviet Union?

How does recognition of a nation's spheres of influence affect Wallace's thinking?

What does Wallace indicate the United States would gain from pursuing peace with the Soviet Union?

Put It in Context

Why do you think American foreign policy leaders rejected Wallace's perspective in the postwar period?

American public was even more dramatic. On March 12, 1947, Truman gave a speech to a joint session of Congress that was broadcast over national radio to millions of listeners. He interpreted the civil war in Greece as a titanic struggle between freedom and totalitarianism that threatened the free world. "I believe," the president declared, "that it must be the policy of the United States to support free peoples who are resisting attempted subjugation by armed minorities or by outside pressures." Truman's rhetoric stretched the truth on many counts — the armed minorities to which the president referred had fought Nazi totalitarianism; the Soviets did not supply the insurgents; and the right-wing monarchy, propped up by the military, was hardly democratic. Nevertheless, Truman achieved his goal of frightening both lawmakers and the public, and Congress appropriated $400 million in military aid to fortify the existing governments of Greece and neighboring Turkey.

The **Truman Doctrine**, which pledged to protect democratic countries and contain the expansion of communism, was the cornerstone of American foreign policy throughout the Cold War. The United States committed itself to shoring up governments, whether democratic or dictatorial, as long as they were avowedly anti-Communist. Americans believed that the rest of the world's nations wanted to be like the United States and therefore would not willingly accept communism, which they thought could be imposed only from the outside by the Soviet Union and never reasonably chosen from within.

Although Truman misread Soviet intentions with respect to Greece, Stalin's regime had given him cause for worry. Soviet actions that imposed communism in Poland, along with the USSR's refusal to withdraw troops from the Baltic states of Latvia, Lithuania, and Estonia, reinforced the president's concerns about Soviet expansionism and convinced many in the U.S. government that Stalin had no intention of abiding by his wartime agreements. Difficulties in negotiating with the Soviets about international control of atomic energy further worried American foreign-policy makers about Russian designs for obtaining the atomic bomb.

The Marshall Plan and Economic Containment.

U.S. diplomat George Kennan's version of containment called for economic and political aid to check Communist expansion. In this context, to forestall Communist inroads and offer humanitarian assistance to Europeans facing homelessness and starvation, the Truman administration offered economic assistance to the war-torn continent. In doing so, the United States also hoped to guarantee increased trade with Europe. In a June 1947 speech that drew heavily on Kennan's ideas, Secretary of State George Marshall sketched out a plan to provide financial assistance to Europe. Although he invited any country, including the Soviet Union, that experienced "hunger, poverty, desperation, and chaos" to apply for aid, Marshall did not expect Stalin to ask for assistance. To do so would require the Soviets to supply information to the United States concerning the internal operations of their economy and to admit to the failure of communism.

Following up Marshall's speech, Truman asked Congress in December 1947 to authorize $17 billion for European recovery. With conservative-minded Republicans still in control of Congress, the president's spending request faced steep opposition. The Soviet Union inadvertently came to Truman's political rescue. Stalin interpreted the proposed **Marshall Plan** of economic assistance as a hostile attempt by the United States to gain influence in Eastern Europe. To forestall this possibility, in late February 1948 the Soviets

Explore ▶

See Sources 24.2 and 24.3 for the reactions of the United States and Soviet Union to the Marshall Plan.

extinguished the remaining democracy in Eastern Europe by engineering a Communist coup in Czechoslovakia. Congressional lawmakers viewed this action as further proof of Soviet aggression. In April 1948, they approved the Marshall Plan, providing $13 billion in economic assistance to sixteen European countries over the next five years.

Review & Relate

▪ Why did American policymakers believe that containing Communist expansion should be the foundation of American foreign policy?

▪ What role did mutual misunderstandings and mistrust play in the emergence of the Cold War?

The **Cold War Hardens,** 1948–1953

After 1947 the Cold War intensified. Both sides increased military spending and took measures to enhance their military presence around the world. Fueled by growing distrust, the Soviet Union and the United States engaged in inflammatory rhetoric that added to the danger the conflict posed to world peace. In 1950 the United States, in cooperation with the United Nations, sent troops to South Korea to turn back an invasion from the Communist North. Truman took advantage of Cold War hostilities to expand presidential power through increased military spending and the creation of a vast national intelligence network.

Military Containment. The New Deal and World War II had increased the power of the president and his ability to manage economic and military crises. The Cold War further strengthened the presidency and shifted the balance of governmental power to the executive branch, creating what has been called the **imperial presidency**.

As the Cold War heated up, Congress granted the president enormous authority over foreign affairs and internal security. The National Security Act, passed in 1947, created the Department of Defense as a cabinet agency (replacing the Department of War), consolidated control of the various military services under its authority, and established the Joint Chiefs of Staff, composed of the heads of the army, navy, air force, and marines. To advise the president on military and foreign affairs, the act set up the **National Security Council (NSC)**, a group presided over by the national security adviser and consisting of the secretaries of state, defense, the army, the navy, and the air force and any others the president might appoint.

In addition to this panel, the National Security Act established the Central Intelligence Agency (CIA) as part of the executive branch. The CIA was given the responsibility of coordinating intelligence gathering and conducting espionage abroad to counter Soviet spying operations. Another new intelligence agency, the National Security Agency, created in 1949, monitored overseas communications through the latest technological devices. Together, these agencies enhanced the president's ability to conduct foreign affairs with little congressional oversight and out of public view.

By 1948 the Truman administration had decided that an economically healthy Germany, with its great industrial potential, provided the key to a prosperous Europe and consequently a depression-proof United States. Rebuilding postwar Germany would also fortify the eastern boundary of Europe against Soviet expansion. In mid-1948 the United States, the United Kingdom, and France consolidated their occupation zones, created the Federal Republic of Germany (West Germany), and initiated economic reforms to stimulate a speedy recovery. The Soviet Union saw a strong Germany as a threat to its national security and responded by closing the access roads from the border of West Germany to Berlin, located in the Soviet zone of East Germany, which effectively cut off the city from the West.

The Soviet blockade of West Berlin turned the Cold War even colder. Without provisions from the United States and its allies in West Germany, West Berliners could not survive. In an effort to break the blockade, Truman ordered a massive airlift, during which American and British planes transported more than 2.5 million tons of supplies to West Berlin. After nearly a year of these flights, the **Berlin airlift** ended in the spring of 1949 when the Russians lifted the blockade.

Meanwhile, in November 1948 Truman won election for a second term. He drew opposition from critics on his left and right for his handling of the Cold War, challenging both his aggressiveness toward the Soviets and his increased spending for containment. Nevertheless, most Americans stood behind his anti-Communist foreign policy as the Cold War continued.

The Berlin Airlift   This group of West Berliners waits anxiously as an American C-47 cargo plane prepares to land at Tempelhof Airfield to deliver food in July 1948. The Soviets had blockaded ground transportation to the Allied sector of West Berlin, prompting President Truman to airlift supplies. Three years after the war ended, the photograph shows Germany still in ruins.
Walter Sanders/The LIFE Picture Collection/Getty Images

Comparative Primary Source Analysis

The Marshall Plan and the Soviet Union

Shortly after Secretary of State George Marshall proposed the Marshall Plan to grant economic assistance to Europe, France and the United Kingdom invited Soviet leaders to a conference in Paris to discuss their response to General Marshall's offer. The following selections present Marshall's plan and Soviet foreign minister Vyacheslav Molotov's reaction to it.

Source 24.2

George C. Marshall | The Marshall Plan, 1947

The truth of the matter is that Europe's requirements for the next three or four years of foreign food and other essential products—principally from America—are so much greater than her present ability to pay that she must have substantial additional help or face economic, social, and political deterioration of a very grave character.

Aside from the demoralizing effect on the world at large and the possibilities of disturbances arising as a result of the desperation of the people concerned, the consequences to the economy of the United States should be apparent to all. It is logical that the United States should do whatever it is able to do to assist in the return of normal economic health in the world, without which there can be no political stability and no assured peace. Our policy is directed not against any country or doctrine but against hunger, poverty, desperation and chaos. Its purpose should be the revival of a working economy in the world so as to permit the emergence of political and social conditions in which free institutions can exist. Such assistance, I am convinced, must not be on a piecemeal basis as various crises develop. Any assistance that this

Government may render in the future should provide a cure rather than a mere palliative. Any government that is willing to assist in the task of recovery will find full co-operation I am sure, on the part of the United States Government. Any government which maneuvers to block the recovery of other countries cannot expect help from us. Furthermore, governments, political parties, or groups which seek to perpetuate human misery in order to profit therefrom politically or otherwise will encounter the opposition of the United States.

. . . It would be neither fitting nor efficacious for this Government to undertake to draw up unilaterally a program designed to place Europe on its feet economically. This is the business of the Europeans. The initiative, I think, must come from Europe. The role of this country should consist of friendly aid in the drafting of a European program and of later support of such a program so far as it may be practical for us to do so. The program should be a joint one, agreed to by a number, if not all European nations.

Source: Speech by George C. Marshall, "European Initiative Essential to Economic Recovery," June 5, 1947, *Department of State Bulletin* 16, no. 415 (1947): 1159–60.

The two superpowers kept the conflict alive when each fashioned military alliances to keep the other at bay. In April 1949, the United States joined eleven European countries in the **North Atlantic Treaty Organization (NATO)**. A peacetime military alliance, NATO established a collective security pact in which an attack on one member was viewed as an

Source 24.3

Vyacheslav Molotov | Soviet Objections to the Marshall Plan, 1947

When efforts are directed toward Europe helping herself in the first place and developing her economic potentialities as well as the exchange of goods between countries, such efforts are in conformity with the interests of the countries of Europe. When, however, it is stated . . . that the decisive hold on the rehabilitation of the economic life of European countries should belong to the United States and not to the European countries themselves, such a position stands in contradiction to the interests of European countries since it might lead to a denial of their economic independence, which denial is incompatible with national sovereignty.

The Soviet delegation believes that internal measures and the national efforts of each country should have a decisive importance for the countries of Europe and not make calculations for foreign support which should be of secondary importance. The Soviet Union has always counted above all on its own powers and is known to be on a steady way of progress of its economic life.

The first form of cooperation is based on the development of political and economic relations between states possessing equal rights and in that case their national sovereignty does not suffer from foreign interference.

Such is the democratic basis for international cooperation which brings nations closer together and facilitates the task of their mutual aid.

Source: U.S. Department of State, *A Decade of American Foreign Policy: Basic Documents, 1941–1949* (Washington, DC: Department of State Printing Office, 1985), 969.

Interpret the Evidence

1. Why does George Marshall believe the United States should help in the reconstruction of Europe? What roles do self-interest and humanitarianism play?
2. Why does Vyacheslav Molotov think that accepting U.S. assistance would be against the interests of European countries?
3. How do their views differ on the definition of international cooperation?

Put It in Context

How did the Marshall Plan contribute to tensions between the superpowers during the Cold War?

attack on all (Map 24.1). In 1949 the Russians followed suit by organizing the Council for Mutual Economic Assistance to help their satellite nations rebuild and six years later by creating the Warsaw Pact military alliance, the respective counterparts in Eastern Europe to the Marshall Plan and NATO.

MAP 24.1 The Cold War in Europe, 1945–1955

In 1946, the four major victorious wartime allies divided Germany and Berlin into distinct sectors, leading to increasing conflict. Between 1949 and 1955, the descent of what Winston Churchill called the "iron curtain" of communism and the creation of rival security pacts headed by the United States and the Soviet Union hardened these postwar divisions into the Cold War.

Amid the growing militarization of the Cold War, 1949 brought two new shocks to the United States and its allies. First, in September the Russians successfully tested an atomic bomb. Second, Communist forces within China led by Mao Zedong and Zhou Enlai succeeded in overthrowing the U.S.-backed government of Jiang Jieshi and creating the People's Republic of China. These two events convinced many in the United States that the threat posed by communism was escalating rapidly.

In response, the National Security Council met to reevaluate U.S. strategy in fighting the Cold War. In April 1950 the NSC recommended to Truman that the United States intensify its containment policy both abroad and at home. The document it handed over to the president, entitled **NSC-68**, spelled out the need for action in ominous language. "The Soviet Union, unlike previous aspirants to hegemony," NSC-68 warned, "is animated by a new fanatic faith, antithetical to our own, and seeks to impose its absolute authority over the rest of the world. It is in this context that this Republic and its citizens . . . stand in their deepest peril." NSC-68 proposed that the United States develop an even more powerful nuclear weapon, the hydrogen bomb; increase military spending; and continue to negotiate NATO-style alliances around the globe. Departing from the original guidelines for the CIA, the president's advisers proposed that the United States engage in "covert means" to foment and support "unrest and revolt in selected strategic [Soviet] satellite countries." At home, they added, the government should prepare Americans for the Communist danger by enhancing internal security and civil defense programs.

Truman agreed with many of the principles behind NSC-68 but worried about the cost of funding it. Though the Democrats controlled both houses of Congress, there was little sentiment to raise taxes and slash the economic programs established during the New Deal. However, circumstances abruptly changed when, in June 1950, shortly after the president received the NSC report, Communist North Korea invaded U.S.-backed South Korea. In response to this attack, Truman took the opportunity to put into practice key recommendations of NSC-68.

The Korean War. Korea emerged from World War II divided between U.S. and Soviet spheres of influence. Above the 38th parallel, the Communist leader Kim Il Sung ruled North Korea with support from the Soviet Union. Below that latitude, the anti-Communist leader Syngman Rhee governed South Korea. The United States supported Rhee, but in January 1950 Secretary of State Dean Acheson commented that he did not regard South Korea as part of the vital Asian "defense perimeter" protected by the United States against Communist aggression. Truman had already removed remaining American troops from the country the previous year. On June 25, 1950, an emboldened Kim Il Sung sent military forces to invade South Korea, seeking to unite the country under his leadership.

Following the invasion Korea took on new importance to American policymakers. If South Korea fell, the president believed, Communist leaders would be "emboldened to override nations closer to our own shores." Thus the Truman Doctrine was now applied to Asia as it had previously been applied to Europe. This time, however, American financial aid would not be enough. It would take the U.S. military to contain the Communist threat.

Truman did not seek a declaration of war from Congress. Instead, he chose a multinational course of action. With the Soviet Union boycotting the United Nations over its refusal to admit the Communist People's Republic of China, on June 27, 1950, the United States obtained authorization from the UN Security Council to send a peacekeeping force to Korea. Fifteen other countries joined UN forces, but the United States supplied the bulk of the troops, as well as their commanding officer, General Douglas MacArthur. In reality, MacArthur reported to the president, not the United Nations.

Before MacArthur could mobilize his forces, the North Koreans had penetrated most of South Korea, except for the port of Pusan on the southwest coast of the peninsula. In a daring counterattack, on September 15, 1950, MacArthur dispatched land and sea forces to capture Inchon, northwest of Pusan on the opposite coast, to cut off North Korean supply lines. Joined by UN forces pushing out of Pusan, MacArthur's Eighth Army troops chased the enemy northward back over the 38th parallel.

Now Truman had to make a key decision. MacArthur wanted to invade North Korea, defeat the Communists, and unify the country. Instead of sticking to his original goal of containing Communist aggression against South Korea, Truman succumbed to the lure of

U.S. Racial Integration of the Military in Korea, 1950   In 1948, President Truman issued an executive order to desegregate the armed forces. During the Korean War African American soldiers served in integrated combat units. On the top left of this November 20, 1950, photo, Sergeant First Class Major Cleveland, the African American squad leader of this racially integrated unit fighting with the 2nd Infantry Division, points out a Communist-led North Korean position to his machine gun crew. Corbis/Getty Images

liberating all of Korea from the Communists. MacArthur received permission to proceed, and on October 9 his forces crossed into North Korea. Within three weeks, UN troops marched through the country until they reached the Yalu River, which bordered China. With the U.S. military massed along their southern perimeter, the Chinese warned that they would send troops to repel the invaders if the Americans crossed the Yalu. Both General MacArthur and Secretary of State Acheson, guided by CIA intelligence, discounted this threat. The intelligence, however, was faulty. Truman approved MacArthur's plan to cross the Yalu, and on November 27, 1950, China sent more than 300,000 troops south into North Korea. Within two months, Communist troops regained control of North Korea, allowing them once again to invade South Korea. On January 4, 1951, the South Korean capital of Seoul fell to Chinese and North Korean troops (Map 24.2).

By the spring of 1951, the war had degenerated into a stalemate. UN forces succeeded in recapturing Seoul and repelling the Communists north of the 38th parallel. This time, with the American public anxious to end the war and with the presence of the Chinese promising an endless, bloody predicament, the president sought to replace combat with diplomacy. The American objective would be containment, not Korean unification.

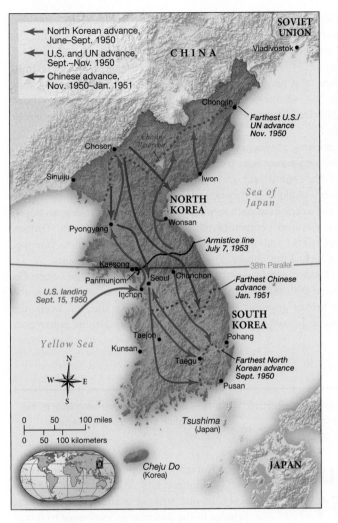

MAP 24.2 The Korean War, 1950–1953

Considered a "police action" by the United Nations, the Korean War cost the lives of nearly 37,000 U.S. troops. Approximately 1 million Koreans were killed, wounded, or missing. Each side pushed deep into enemy territory, but neither could achieve victory. When hostilities ceased in 1953, a demilitarized zone near the original boundary line separated North and South Korea.

Truman's change of heart infuriated General MacArthur, who was willing to risk an all-out war with China and to use nuclear weapons to win. After MacArthur spoke out publicly against Truman's policy by remarking, "There is no substitute for victory," the president removed him from command on April 11, 1951. Even with the change in strategy and leadership, the war dragged on for two more years, until July 1953, when a final armistice agreement was reached. By that time, the Korean War had cost the United States close to 37,000 lives and $54 billion.

The Korean War and the Imperial Presidency.

The Korean War boosted the imperial presidency by allowing the president to bypass Congress and the Constitution to initiate wars in the name of "police actions." The war permitted Truman to expand his powers as commander in chief and augmented the strength of the national security state over which he presided. As a result of the Korean conflict, the military draft became a regular feature of American life for young men over the next two decades. The expanded peacetime military was active around the globe, operating bases in Europe, Asia, and the Middle East. During the war, the military budget rose from $13.5 billion to $50 billion, strengthening the connection between economic growth and permanent mobilization to fight the Cold War. The war also permitted President Truman to reshape foreign policy along the lines sketched in NSC-68, including the extension of U.S. influence in Southeast Asia. Consequently, he authorized economic aid to support the French against Communist revolutionaries in Vietnam.

Yet the power of the imperial presidency did not go unchecked. Congress deferred to Truman on key issues of military policy, but on one important occasion the Supreme Court stepped in to restrain him. The central issue grew out of a labor dispute in the steel industry. In 1952 the United Steel Workers of America threatened to go on strike for higher wages, which would have had a serious impact on war production as well as the economy in general. On May 2, after the steel companies refused the union's demands, Truman announced the government seizure and operation of the steel mills to keep them running. He argued that as president he had the "inherent right" to take over the steel plants.

The steel companies objected and brought the matter before the Supreme Court. On June 2, 1952, the Court ruled against Truman. It held that the president did not have the intrinsic authority to seize private property, even during wartime. For the time being, the Supreme Court affirmed some limitations on the unbridled use of presidential power even during periods of war.

Review & Relate

- What were the causes and consequences of the militarization of the containment strategy in the late 1940s and early 1950s?

- How did the Korean War contribute to the centralization of power in the executive branch?

Combating Communism at Home, 1945–1954

The Korean War heightened fear of the threat of Communist infiltration in American society. In one striking example, the presiding judge in the Rosenbergs' espionage trial sentenced them to death because he believed their actions "caused . . . the Communist aggression in Korea, with the resultant casualties exceeding 50,000." For most of Truman's second administration, fear of Communist subversion within the United States consumed domestic politics. Increasing evidence of Soviet espionage fueled this anti-Communist obsession. In an atmosphere of fear, lawmakers and judges blurred the distinction between actual Soviet spies and political radicals who were merely attracted to Communist beliefs. In the process, these officials trampled on individual constitutional freedoms.

Loyalty and the Second Red Scare.

The postwar fear of communism echoed earlier anti-Communist sentiments. The government had initiated the repressive Palmer raids during the Red scare following World War I, which led to the deportation of immigrants sympathetic to the Communist doctrines of the Russian Revolution (see "The Red Scare, 1919–1920" in chapter 21). In 1938 conservative congressional opponents of the New Deal established the **House Un-American Activities Committee (HUAC)** to investigate domestic communism, which they tied to the Roosevelt administration. Much of anticommunism, however, was bipartisan. In 1940 Roosevelt signed into law the Smith Act, which prohibited teaching or advocating the "duty, necessity, desirability, or propriety of overthrowing or destroying any government in the United States by force or violence" or belonging to any group with that aim. At the same time, President Roosevelt secretly authorized the FBI to monitor and wiretap individuals suspected of violating the act.

The Cold War produced the second Red scare. Just two weeks after his speech announcing the Truman Doctrine in March 1947, the president signed an executive order creating the **Federal Employee Loyalty Program**. Under this program, a board investigated federal employees to see if "reasonable grounds [existed] to suspect disloyalty." Soviet espionage was, in fact, a cause for legitimate concern. Spies operated in both Canada and the United States during and after World War II, and they had infiltrated the Manhattan Project.

The loyalty board concentrated its attention on individuals who espoused dissenting views on a variety of issues. It failed to uncover a single verifiable case of espionage or find even one actual Communist in public service. This lack of evidence did not stop the board from dismissing 378 government employees for their political beliefs and personal behavior. Some employees were fired because they were homosexuals and considered susceptible to blackmail by foreign agents. (Heterosexual men and women who were having extramarital affairs were not treated in the same manner.) The accused rarely faced their accusers and at times did not learn the nature of the charges against them. This disregard for due process of law spread as loyalty boards at state and municipal levels questioned and fired government employees, including public school teachers and state university professors.

Congress also investigated communism in the private sector, especially in industries that shaped public opinion. In 1947 HUAC broadened the anti-Red probe from Washington to Hollywood. Convinced that the film industry had come under Communist influence and threatened to poison the minds of millions of moviegoers, HUAC conducted hearings that attracted much publicity. HUAC cited for contempt ten witnesses, among them directors and screenwriters, for refusing to answer questions about their political beliefs and associations. These and subsequent hearings assumed the form of a ritual. The committee already had information from the FBI about the witnesses; HUAC really wanted the accused to confess their Communist heresy publicly and to show contrition by naming their associates. Those who did not comply were considered "unfriendly" witnesses and were put on an industry blacklist that deprived them of employment. **See Primary Source Project 24: McCarthyism and the Hollywood Ten, page 849.**

HUAC grabbed even bigger headlines in 1948. With Republicans in charge of the committee, they launched a probe of Alger Hiss, a former State Department official in the Roosevelt administration who had accompanied the president to the Yalta Conference. The hearings resulted from charges brought by former Soviet spy Whittaker Chambers that Hiss had passed him classified documents. Hiss denied the allegations, and President Truman dismissed them as a distraction. In fact, Democrats viewed the charges as a politically motivated attempt by Republicans to characterize the Roosevelt and Truman administrations as having been riddled with Communists.

Following Truman's victory in the 1948 presidential election, first-term Republican congressman Richard M. Nixon kept the Hiss affair alive. A member of HUAC, Nixon went to Chambers's farm and discovered a cache of State Department documents that Chambers had stored for safekeeping. Armed with this evidence, Nixon reopened the case. While the statute of limitations for espionage from the 1930s had expired, the federal government had enough evidence to prosecute Hiss for perjury—lying under oath about passing documents to Chambers. One trial produced a hung jury, but a second convicted Hiss; he was sentenced to five years in prison.

Hiss's downfall tarnished the Democrats, as Republicans charged them with being "soft on communism." It did not matter that Truman was a cold warrior who had advanced the doctrine of containment to stop Soviet expansionism or that he had instituted the federal loyalty program to purge Communists from government. In fact, in 1949 Truman tried to demonstrate his cold warrior credentials by authorizing the Justice Department to prosecute twelve high-ranking officials of the Communist Party for violating the Smith Act. In the 1951 decision in *Dennis v. United States*, the Supreme Court upheld the conviction of the Communist leaders on the grounds that they posed a "clear and present danger" to the United States by advocating the violent overthrow of the government. With no evidence of an immediate danger of a Communist uprising, the justices decided that "the gravity of the [Communist] evil" was enough to warrant conviction.

In 1950 the Truman administration also prosecuted Julius and Ethel Rosenberg. Unlike the *Dennis* case, which involved political beliefs, the Rosenbergs were charged with espionage. When the Russians successfully tested an atomic bomb in 1949, anyone accused of helping them obtain this weapon became "Public Enemy Number One." The outbreak of the Korean War the following year, in which tens of thousands of soldiers died, made the Rosenbergs appear as conspirators to murder. After a lengthy trial in 1951, the couple received the death penalty, rather than a possible thirty-year sentence, undoubtedly because they refused to confess and because the trial took place during the war.

By 1950 the anti-Communist crusade included Democrats and Republicans, liberals and conservatives. Liberals had the most to lose because conservatives could easily brand them as ideologically tainted. In his successful campaign to become a U.S. senator from California in 1950, Richard Nixon had accused his opponent, the liberal Democrat Helen Gahagan Douglas, of being "pink down to her underwear," not quite a Red but close enough. Liberal civil rights and civil liberties groups as well as labor unions were particularly vulnerable to such charges and rushed to rid their organizations of suspected Communists. Such efforts did nothing, however, to slow down conservative attacks. In 1950 Republicans supported legislation proposed by Senator Pat McCarran, a conservative Democrat from Nevada, which required Communist organizations to register with the federal government, established detention camps to incarcerate radicals during national emergencies, and denied passports to American citizens suspected of Communist affiliations. The severity of the entire measure proved too much for President Truman, and he vetoed it. Reflecting the bipartisan consensus on the issue, the Democratic-controlled Congress overrode the veto.

McCarthyism.
Joseph Raymond McCarthy, a Republican senator from Wisconsin, took advantage of the phenomenon of postwar anticommunism, which was already in full swing from 1947 to 1950, and served as its most public and feared voice from 1950 until 1954. Senator McCarthy used his position as the head of the Permanent Investigation Subcommittee of the Committee on Government Operations to harass current and former government officials and employees who, he claimed, collaborated with the Communist conspiracy. He had plenty of assistance from members of his own party who considered

McCarthy a potent weapon in their battle to reclaim the White House. Robert A. Taft, the respected conservative Republican senator from Ohio, told McCarthy "to keep talking and if one case doesn't work [you] should proceed with another." The press also courted the young senator by giving his charges substantial coverage on the front pages of daily newspapers and then shifting the story to the back pages when McCarthy's claims turned out to be false. McCarthy bullied people, exaggerated his military service, drank too much, and did not pull his punches in making speeches — but his anti-Communist tirades fit into mainstream Cold War politics.

Aware of the power of the Communists-in-government issue, McCarthy gave a speech in February 1950 in Wheeling, West Virginia. Waving sheets of paper in his hand, the senator announced that he had "the names of 205 men known to the Secretary of State as being members of the Communist Party and who nevertheless are still working and shaping the policy of the State Department." McCarthy cared more about the message than about the truth. As he continued campaigning for Republican congressional candidates across the country, he kept changing the number of alleged Communists in the government. When Senator Millard Tydings of Maryland, a Democrat who headed the Senate Foreign

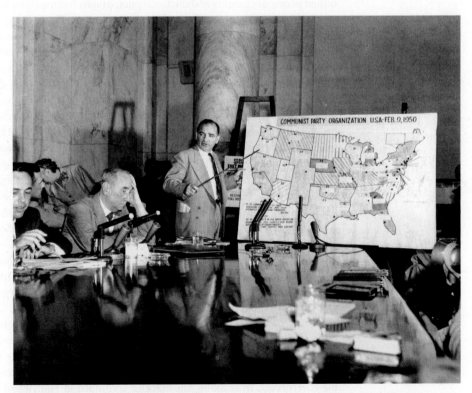

Senator Joseph R. McCarthy, 1954   Senator Joseph R. McCarthy, Republican from Wisconsin, testifies against the U.S. army during the televised army-McCarthy hearings on June 9, 1954. McCarthy stands before a map that charts alleged Communist activity in the United States. Seated next to McCarthy is Joseph N. Welch, the attorney for the army, who called McCarthy a "cruelly reckless character assassin." Bettmann/Getty Images

Relations Committee, launched an investigation of McCarthy's charges, he concluded that they were irresponsible and unfounded.

This finding did not stop McCarthy; if anything, it emboldened him to go further. He accused Tydings of being "soft on communism" and campaigned against his reelection in 1952. Tydings's defeat in the election scared off many critics from openly confronting McCarthy. McCarthy won reelection to the Senate, and when Republicans once again captured a majority in Congress, he became chair of the Permanent Investigations Subcommittee. Not only did he make false accusations and smear witnesses with anti-Communist allegations, he also dispatched two aides to travel to Europe and purge what they considered disreputable books from the shelves of overseas libraries sponsored by the State Department.

McCarthy stood out among anti-Communists for his brazen tactics. McCarthy publicly hurled charges so astounding, especially coming from a U.S. senator, that people thought there must be something to them. He specialized in the "multiple untruth," a concoction of allegations so complex and convoluted that it was impossible to refute them simply or quickly. By the time the accusations could be discredited, the damage was already done. The senator bullied and badgered witnesses, called them names, and if necessary furnished phony documents and doctored photographs linking them to known Communists.

In 1954 McCarthy finally went too far. After one of his aides got drafted and the army refused to give him a special commission, McCarthy accused the army of harboring Communists at Camp Kilmer and Fort Monmouth in New Jersey. To sort out these charges and to see whether the army had acted appropriately, McCarthy's own Senate subcommittee conducted an investigation, with the Wisconsin senator stepping down as chair. For two months, the relatively new medium of television broadcast live the army-McCarthy hearings, during which the cameras showed viewers for the first time how reckless McCarthy had become. As his public approval declined, the Senate decided that it could no longer tolerate McCarthy's outrageous behavior. The famous television journalist Edward R. Murrow ran an unflattering documentary on McCarthy on his evening program on CBS, which further cast doubt on the senator's character and veracity. In December 1954 the Senate voted to censure McCarthy for conduct unbecoming a senator, having violated senatorial decorum by insulting colleagues who criticized him. McCarthy retained his seat on the subcommittee and all his Senate prerogatives, but he never again wielded substantial power. In 1957 he died from acute hepatitis, a disease related to alcoholism.

The anti-Communist consensus did not end with the execution of the Rosenbergs in 1953 or the censure of Joseph McCarthy in 1954. Even J. Robert Oppenheimer, "the father of the atomic bomb," came under scrutiny. In 1954 the Atomic Energy Commission revoked Oppenheimer's security clearance for suspected, though unproven, Communist affiliations. That same year, Congress passed the Communist Control Act, which required "Communist infiltrated" groups to register with the federal government. Federal, state, and municipal governments required employees to take a loyalty oath affirming their allegiance to the United States and disavowing support for any organization that advocated the overthrow of the government. In addition, the blacklist continued in Hollywood throughout the rest of the decade. After the Supreme Court declared racial segregation in public schools unconstitutional in 1954, a number of southern states, including Florida and Louisiana, set up committees to investigate Communist influence in the civil rights movement. In a case concerning civil liberties, the Supreme Court still upheld HUAC's authority to investigate communism and to require witnesses who came before it to answer questions about their affiliations. Yet the Court did put a stop to the anti-Communist momentum. In 1957 the high court dealt a severe blow to enforcement of the Smith Act by ruling in *Yates v. United States* that the Justice Department could not prosecute someone for merely advocating an abstract doctrine favoring the violent overthrow of the government. In response, Congress tried, but failed, to limit the Supreme Court's jurisdiction in cases of this sort.

Although attacks against radicals in this period came to be known as **McCarthyism**, J. Edgar Hoover and the FBI did more to fuel the anti-Communist hysteria of the second Red scare than did the Wisconsin senator. Hoover and his bureau did even greater damage than McCarthy because they used their broad reach to disperse the information from Communist-hunters throughout the government in order to suppress any perceived anti-Communist activity. The FBI was involved in criminal prosecutions in the *Dennis* and *Rosenberg* cases, supplied evidence to congressional committees and loyalty boards, and wiretapped suspected targets and used undercover agents to monitor and harass them. The FBI under the long tenure of J. Edgar Hoover perpetuated a zealous policy of anticommunism in this era.

Review & Relate

■ Why did fear of Communists in positions of influence escalate in the late 1940s and early 1950s?

■ Why was McCarthyism much more powerful than Joseph McCarthy?

The **Cold War** Expands, **1953–1961**

With the end of the Korean War in 1953, the United States and the Soviet Union each spent huge sums of money and manpower building up their arsenal of nuclear weapons and military forces. They did not engage directly on the battlefield, but they attempted to spread their influence around the world while protecting their spheres of influence closer to their borders. The growing presence of nuclear weapons hung over diplomatic crises wherever they emerged, occasionally prompting the leaders of the two most powerful nations to seek an accommodation.

Explore ▸

Read differing interpretations of the causes of the Cold War in Sources 24.4 and 24.5.

Nuclear Weapons and Containment. In foreign affairs, President Dwight D. Eisenhower perpetuated Truman's containment doctrine while at the same time espousing the contradictory principle of "rolling back" communism in Eastern Europe. However, when Hungarians rose up against their Soviet-backed regime in 1956, the U.S. government did little in response. Rather than pushing back communism, the Eisenhower administration expanded the doctrine of containment around the world by entering into treaties to establish regional defense pacts.

Eisenhower's commitment to fiscal discipline had a profound effect on his foreign policy. The president worried that the alliance among government, defense contractors, and research universities — which he dubbed "the military-industrial complex" — would bankrupt the economy and undermine individual freedom. With this in mind, he

Comparative Secondary Source Analysis

Causes of the Cold War

Historians have debated the causes of the Cold War for more than seven decades. Interpretations have cast responsibility on the Soviet Union, the United States, or both. Historians have emphasized a variety of approaches from economic, political, and institutional to cultural, psychological, and ideological. The following excerpts present two schools of thought: the revisionist, first proposed by the historian William Appleman Williams, who argued that the United States was at fault for the Cold War, and the post-revisionist, articulated initially by the historian John Lewis Gaddis, who believed that neither the United States nor the USSR was solely to blame for the cause of the Cold War.

Source 24.4

William Appleman Williams | Expanding the Economic Open Door, 1959

"The leaders who succeeded [Franklin] Roosevelt understood neither the dilemma nor the need to alter their outlook. A handful of them thought briefly of stabilizing relations with the Soviet Union on the basis of economic and political agreements, but even that tiny minority saw the future in terms of continued open-door [access to overseas markets] expansion. The great majority rapidly embarked upon a program to force the Soviet Union to accept America's traditional conception of itself and the world. This decision represented the final stage in the transformation of the policy of the open door from a utopian idea into an ideology, from an intellectual outlook for changing the world into one concerned with preserving it in the traditional mold.

American leaders had internalized, and had come to *believe*, the theory and the morality of open-door expansion. Hence they seldom thought it necessary to explain or defend the approach. Instead, they *assumed* the premises and concerned themselves with exercising their apparent freedom to deal with the necessities defined by such an outlook. As far as American leaders were concerned, the philosophy and practice of open-door expansion had become, in both its missionary and economic aspects, *the* view of the world. Those who did not recognize and accept that fact were not only wrong, but they were incapable of thinking correctly."

Source: William Appleman Williams, *The Tragedy of American Diplomacy* (Cleveland: The World Publishing Company, 1959), 150–51.

implemented the **New Look** strategy, which placed a higher priority on building a nuclear arsenal and delivery system than on the more expensive task of maintaining and deploying armed forces on the ground throughout the world. Nuclear missiles launched from the air by air force bombers or fired from submarines would give the United States, as Secretary of Defense Charles Wilson asserted, "a bigger bang for the buck." With the nation now armed with nuclear weapons, the Eisenhower administration threatened "massive retaliation" in the event of Communist aggression.

The New Look may have saved money and slowed the rate of defense spending, but it had serious flaws. First, it placed a premium on "brinksmanship," taking Communist enemies to the precipice of nuclear destruction, risking the death of millions, and hoping the

Source 24.5

John Lewis Gaddis | Competing Ideologies, 1972

"Moscow's position would not have seemed so alarming to American officials . . . had it not been for the Soviet Union's continued commitment to an ideology dedicated to the overthrow of capitalism throughout the world. Hopes that the United States might cooperate successfully with the USSR after the war had been based on the belief, encouraged by Stalin himself, that the Kremlin had given up its former goal of exporting Communism. . . . It seems likely that Washington policy makers mistook Stalin's determination to ensure Russian security through spheres of influence for a renewed effort to spread communism outside the borders of the Soviet Union. . . . But [Stalin] failed to make the limited nature of his objectives clear.

Revisionists are correct in emphasizing the importance of internal constraints, but they have defined them too narrowly: by focusing so heavily on economics, they neglect the profound impact of the domestic political system on the conduct of American foreign policy. . . . The delay in opening the second front, nonrecognition of Moscow's sphere of influence in Eastern Europe, and the decision to retain control of the atomic bomb can all be explained far more plausibly by citing the Administration's need to maintain popular support for its policies rather than by dwelling upon requirements of the economic order . . . , Stalin's paranoia, together with the bureaucracy of institutionalized suspicion with which he surrounded himself, made the situation much worse."

Source: John Lewis Gaddis, *The United States and the Origins of the Cold War, 1941–1947* (New York: Columbia University Press, 1972), 354–55, 359.

Examine the Sources

1. Describe one major difference between Williams's and Gaddis's interpretations of the causes of the Cold War.
2. Based on evidence in this chapter, evaluate the strengths and weaknesses of each interpretation.

Put It in Context

Explain why the Cold War began so soon after World War II ended.

---

other side would back down. Second, massive retaliation did not work for small-scale conflicts. For instance, in the event of a confrontation in Berlin, would the United States launch nuclear missiles toward Germany and expose its European allies in West Germany and France to nuclear contamination? Third, the buildup of nuclear warheads provoked an arms race by encouraging the Soviet Union to do the same. Peace depended on the superpowers terrifying each other with the threat of nuclear annihilation — that is, if one country attacked the other, retaliation was guaranteed to result in shared obliteration. This strategy was known as **mutually assured destruction**, and its acronym — **MAD** — summed up its nightmarish qualities. As each nuclear power increased its capacity to destroy the other many

Bomb Shelter, 1954   The successful test of an atomic bomb by the Soviets in 1949 followed by the Korean War prompted many Americans to begin preparing for a possible nuclear attack. This Houston, Texas family, including their dog, pose in their bomb shelter stocked with food, first aid supplies, weapons, and ammunition. John Dominis/The LIFE Picture Collection/Getty Images

times over, the potential for mistakes and errors in judgment increased, threatening a nuclear holocaust that would leave little to rebuild. (See Table 24.1.)

National security concerns occupied a good deal of the president's time. Fearing that a Soviet nuclear attack could wipe out nearly a third of the population before the United States could retaliate, the Eisenhower administration stepped up civil defense efforts. Schoolchildren took part in "duck and cover" drills, in which teachers shouted "Take cover" and students hid under their desks. In the meantime, both the United States and the Soviet Union began producing intercontinental ballistic missiles armed with nuclear warheads. They also stepped up aboveground tests of nuclear weapons, which contaminated the atmosphere with dangerous radioactive particles.

Despite doomsday rhetoric of massive retaliation, Eisenhower generally relied more on diplomacy than on military action. Stalin's death in 1953 and his eventual replacement by Nikita Khrushchev in 1955 permitted détente, or a relaxation of tensions, between the two superpowers. In July 1955 Eisenhower and Khrushchev, together with British and French leaders, gathered in Geneva to discuss arms control. Nothing concrete came out of this

TABLE 24.1 Nuclear Warheads, United States, Soviet Union, United Kingdom, 1945–1960

Country	1945	1950	1955	1960
United States	2	299	2,422	18,638
Soviet Union	0	5	200	1,605
United Kingdom	0	0	14	42

Source: Robert S. Norris & Hans M. Kristensen (2010). Global Nuclear Weapons Inventories, 1945–2010, *Bulletin of the Atomic Scientists*, 66:4, 77–83, DOI: 10.2968/066004008

The Cold War launched a nuclear arms race between the United States and its British ally and the Soviet Union. By 1960, the United States had lost its nuclear monopoly, but together with the United Kingdom its nuclear stockpile of warheads vastly outnumbered that of the Soviet Union.

summit, but Eisenhower and Khrushchev did ease tensions between the two nations. In a speech to Communist officials two years later, Khrushchev denounced the excesses of Stalin's totalitarian rule and reinforced hopes for a new era of peaceful coexistence between the Cold War antagonists. In 1958, Vice President Richard Nixon visited the Soviet Union, the first top elected official to do so since the onset of the Cold War, as a sign of warming relations between the two nations. Nixon and Khrushchev attended a U.S. exhibition in Moscow on July 24, 1959, where the two leaders debated the relative merits of capitalism and communism, while looking at an American kitchen that displayed the latest household appliances. This so-called "Kitchen Debate" did not dissuade Khrushchev from making a twelve-day visit to the United States later that year. Yet peaceful coexistence remained precarious. Just as President Eisenhower was about to begin his own tour of the Soviet Union in 1960, the Soviets shot down an American U-2 spy plane flying over their country. Eisenhower canceled his trip, and tensions resumed.

Decolonization

Between 1945 and 1960, three dozen new states in Asia, Africa, and the Middle East gained independence from their European colonial rulers. In addition, the United States granted full independence to the Philippines in 1946. This **decolonization** movement coincided with the freezing of Cold War relations between the United States and the Soviet Union. Both Presidents Truman and Eisenhower feared that as these former European colonies won their independence, the Soviets would seek to gain influence over them and swing the global balance of power to its side. In this battle over the allegiance of

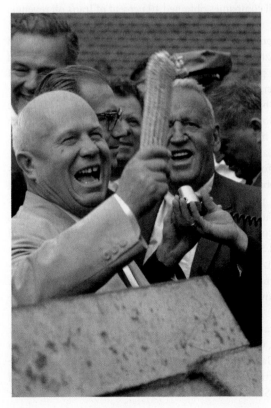

the newly freed and developing nations (what was called at the time the Third World), both the United States and the USSR jockeyed for position to win them over by offering economic and technical aid. While the United States promoted its democratic ideology, the Soviets countered with the argument that communism represented the masses and stood against imperialism.

The decolonization movement reconfigured the composition of the United Nations. In 1946, there were 35 member states in the world organization. As a result of decolonization, by 1961, membership in the UN had jumped to 104. Most of these new developing nations sought to rebuild their fragile economic and political systems and reclaim their cultural identities. These liberated countries remained wary of their former colonizers, most of whom were allied with the United States during the Cold War. Consequently, the United States had to walk a fine line between accommodating its European partners and gaining the trust of developing nations.

Khrushchev Visits the U.S., 1959   During a brief thaw in the Cold War, Soviet Premier Nikita Khrushchev visits the U.S. and tours the country. Here he laughs as he holds up a corn cob during a visit to the farm of Roswell Garst (standing to his right) in Coon Rapids, Iowa on September 23, 1959. Hank Walker/The LIFE Picture Collection/Getty Images

The difficulties proved challenging. Confronting the problem of Cold War alignments, these developing nations chose neutrality. At the **Bandung Conference** in Indonesia in 1955, twenty-nine Asian and African nations, many of them recently liberated, condemned continued colonization, particularly control in North Africa by France, a close U.S. ally, and asserted their intention to remain non-aligned with either side in the Cold War. The U.S. government took a dim view of this meeting and refused to send representatives. Especially worrisome to the United States, the Communist Chinese government made serious overtures to form closer relations with these nations.

Interventions in the Middle East, Latin America, and Africa. While relations between the Soviet Union and the United States thawed and then cooled during the Eisenhower era, the Cold War expanded into new regions. The efforts of Iranian, Guatemalan, and Cuban leaders to seize control of their countries' resources mirrored the surge of nationalism that swept through former European colonies in the 1950s. The United States frequently took a heavy handed approach when it suspected newly decolonized nations were edging to the side of the Soviets. In a manner first suggested in NSC-68, the Eisenhower administration deployed the CIA to help topple governments considered pro-Communist as well as to promote U.S. economic interests. For example, after Prime Minister Mohammed Mossadegh of Iran nationalized foreign oil corporations in 1953, the CIA engineered a successful coup that ousted his government and installed the pro-American shah Mohammad Reza Pahlavi in his place. Mossadegh was not a Communist, but by overthrowing him American oil companies obtained 40 percent of Iran's oil revenue.

In 1954 the economics of fruit and shipping replaced oil as the catalyst for U.S. intervention into a third-world nation within its own sphere of influence. The elected socialist regime of Jacobo Arbenz Guzmán in Guatemala had seized 225,000 acres of land held by the United Fruit Company, a powerful American company in which Secretary of State John Foster Dulles and his brother, CIA director Allen Dulles, held stock. According to the Dulles brothers, the land's seizure by the Guatemalan government posed a threat to the nearby Panama Canal. Eisenhower allowed the CIA to hatch a plot that resulted in a coup d'état, or government overthrow, that installed a right-wing military regime in Guatemala, which safeguarded both the Panama Canal and the United Fruit Company.

The success of the CIA's covert efforts in Guatemala prompted the Eisenhower administration to plan a similar action in Cuba, ninety miles off the coast of Florida. In 1959 Fidel Castro led an uprising and came to power in Cuba after overthrowing the American-backed dictator Fulgencio Batista. A Cuban nationalist in the tradition of José Martí, Castro sought to regain full control over his country's economic resources, including those owned by U.S. corporations. He appropriated $1 billion worth of American property and signed a trade agreement with the Soviet Union. To consolidate his political rule, Castro jailed opponents and installed a Communist regime. In 1960 President Eisenhower authorized the CIA to design a clandestine operation to overthrow the Castro government, but he left office before the invasion could occur.

Developing nations seeking to practice neutrality during the Cold War did so at their own peril. Such was the case in Egypt, which achieved independence from Great Britain in 1952. Two years later, under General Gamal Abdel Nasser, the country sought to modernize its economy by building the hydroelectric Aswan Dam on the Nile River. Nasser welcomed financial backing from the United States and the Soviet Union, but the Eisenhower administration refused to contribute so long as the Egyptians accepted Soviet assistance. In 1956 Nasser, falling short of funds, sent troops to take over the Suez Canal, the waterway run by Great Britain and through which the bulk of Western Europe's oil was shipped. He intended to pay for the dam by collecting tolls from canal users. In retaliation, Britain and France, the two European powers most affected by the seizure, invaded Egypt on October 29, 1956. Locked in a struggle with Egypt and other Arab nations since its creation in 1948, Israel joined in the attack. The invading forces — all U.S. allies — had not warned the Eisenhower administration of their plans. Coming at the same time as the Soviet crackdown against the Hungarian revolution, the British-French-Israeli assault placed the United States in the difficult position of condemning the Soviets for intervening in Hungary while its anti-Communist partners waged war in Suez. Instead, Eisenhower cooperated with the United Nations to negotiate a cease-fire and engineer a pullout of the invading forces in Egypt. Ultimately, the Soviets proved the winners in this Cold War skirmish. The Suez invasion revived memories of European imperialism and fueled anti-Western sentiments and pan-Arab nationalism (a sense of unity among Arabs across national boundaries), which worked to the Soviets' advantage.

The Eisenhower administration soon moved to counter growing Soviet power in the region. In 1957, to throttle increasing Communist influence in the Middle East, Congress approved the **Eisenhower Doctrine**, which gave the president a free hand to use U.S. military forces in the Middle East "against overt armed aggression from any nation controlled by International Communism." In actuality, the Eisenhower administration proved more concerned with protecting access to oil fields from hostile Arab nationalist leaders than with any Communist incursion. In 1958, when an anti-American, non-Communist regime came to power in Iraq, the president sent 14,000 marines to neighboring Lebanon to prevent a similar outcome there.

Just before Eisenhower left office in January 1961, his administration intervened in a civil war in the newly independent Congo. This former colony of Belgium held valuable mineral resources, which Belgium and the United States coveted. After the Congo's first prime minister, Patrice Lumumba, stated his intentions to remain neutral in the Cold War, President Eisenhower and CIA director Allen Dulles declared him unreliable in the conflict with the Soviet Union. With the support of Belgian military troops and encouragement from the United States, the resource-rich province of Katanga seceded from the Congo in 1960. After the Congolese military, under the leadership of Joseph Mobuto, overthrew Lumumba's government, the CIA launched an operation that culminated in the execution of Lumumba on January 17, 1961. Several years later, Mobuto became president of the country, changed its name to Zaire, and allied with the West.

Early Intervention in Vietnam, 1954–1960.

One offshoot of the Korean War was increased U.S. intervention in Vietnam, resulting in profound, long-term consequences. By the 1950s, Vietnamese revolutionaries (the Vietminh) had been fighting for independence from the French for decades. They were led by Ho Chi Minh, a revolutionary who had studied Communist doctrine in the Soviet Union but was not controlled by the Soviets. In fact, he modeled his 1945 Vietnamese Declaration of Independence on that of the United States. In 1954 the Vietminh defeated the French at the Battle of Dien Bien Phu. With the backing of the United States, the Soviet Union, and China, both sides agreed to divide Vietnam at the seventeenth parallel and hold free elections to unite the country in 1956.

The Battle of Dien Bien Phu, 1954   This photograph shows Vietnamese soldiers resting in a trench at Dien Bien Phu, site of the pivotal battle at which French colonial forces were defeated. Fighting began on March 13, 1954, and ended on May 7, when French troops surrendered. This photo, like most of those taken of the battle, was restaged shortly after the action, mainly for propaganda purposes. AFP/Getty Images

President Dwight Eisenhower, who had brought the Korean War to a close in 1953, believed that if Vietnam fell to the Communists, the rest of Southeast Asia and Japan would "go over very quickly" like "a row of dominoes," threatening American strategic power in the Far East as well as free access to Asian markets. Convinced that Ho Chi Minh and his followers would win free elections, in 1955 the Eisenhower administration supported the anti-French, anti-Communist Ngo Dinh Diem to lead South Vietnam and then backed his regime's refusal to hold national elections in 1956. The anti-Communist interests of the United States had trumped its democratic promises. With the country now permanently divided, Eisenhower funneled economic aid to Diem to undertake needed land reforms that would strengthen his government and weaken the appeal of Ho Chi Minh. The president also dispatched CIA agents and military advisers to support the South Vietnamese government. However, Diem used most of the money to consolidate his power rather than implement reforms, which only widened opposition to his regime from Communists and non-Communists alike. This prompted Ho Chi Minh in 1959 to support the creation in the South of the National Liberation Front, or **Vietcong**, to wage a military insurgency against Diem. By the end of the decade, the Eisenhower administration had created a major diplomatic problem with no clear plan for its resolution.

Review & Relate

▪ In what ways did the Eisenhower administration continue the Cold War policies of President Truman? In what ways did it depart from his predecessor?

▪ How did U.S. intervention in Vietnam reflect the policy of containment?

Conclusion: The **Cold War** and **Anticommunism**

Anticommunism remained a potent weapon in political affairs as long as the Cold War operated in full force. When George Kennan designed the doctrine of containment in 1946 and 1947, he had no idea that it would lead to permanent military alliances such as NATO or to a war in Korea. He viewed the Soviet Union as an unflinching ideological enemy, but he believed that it should be contained through economic rather than military means. Despite his launching of the Marshall Plan and providing aid to the Greeks through the Truman Doctrine, President Truman soon departed from Kennan's vision by militarizing containment. Beginning with NATO and continuing with the Korean War, the Truman administration put into operation around the world the heightened military plans called for by NSC-68. Hard-line Cold War rhetoric portrayed the struggle as a battle between good and evil. Born out of different perceptions of national interests and mutual misunderstandings of the other side's actions, the Cold War became frozen in the language of competing moralistic assumptions and self-righteousness. Within this context, though some Americans rallied to obtain clemency for the Rosenbergs, most considered that they got just what they deserved.

The Eisenhower administration continued the policy of containment inherited from Truman. Eisenhower brought the Korean War to an end and attempted to slow down the rate of military spending. Nevertheless, in the name of checking Communist aggression, his administration did not hesitate to intervene in Latin America, the Middle East, Africa, and Southeast Asia. Both the United States and the Soviet Union built up their nuclear arsenals and developed speedier ways by air and sea to deliver these deadly weapons against each other. Occasionally, foreign crises riveted the attention of Americans on the perils of atomic brinksmanship with the Soviets, but the sheer horror of the possibility of nuclear war helped the two major Cold War powers avoid escalating existing conflicts into nuclear destruction. Such brinksmanship did little to quell mounting fears of Communist infiltration and espionage at home in the United States. Those fears led to the second Red scare, as well as a strengthened presidency, one given more powers with which to combat communism and maintain national security. Cold War spending helped boost the American economy, but the renewed prosperity it brought masked some serious trouble brewing at home over civil rights and teenage culture.

chapter **24** review

Timeline of Events

1938	House Un-American Activities Committee (HUAC) established
1945	Potsdam Conference
1946	Kennan telegram outlines containment strategy
	Churchill's "iron curtain" speech
1947	Truman Doctrine articulated
	National Security Act passed
	Central Intelligence Agency (CIA) established
	Truman creates Federal Employee Loyalty Program
1948–1949	Berlin blockade and airlift
	Alger Hiss affair
1948	Marshall Plan approved
1949	National Security Agency established
	Communists win Chinese civil war
	North Atlantic Treaty Organization (NATO) formed
	Soviet Union successfully tests atomic weapon
1950–1953	Korean War
1950–1954	McCarthy's anti-Communist crusade
1950	NSC-68 issued
1953	Julius and Ethel Rosenberg executed for espionage
	U.S. supports overthrow of Iranian government
1954	French defeated in Vietnam
	U.S. supports overthrow of Guatemalan government
1955	U.S. supports Ngo Diem in South Vietnam
1955	Bandung Conference of Non-Aligned Nations
1956	Suez crisis
1958	U.S. troops sent to Lebanon
1959	Fidel Castro takes power in Cuba
	The Vietcong formed
1961	U.S. intervenes in the Congo

Key Terms

Cold War, *821*

Truman Doctrine, *825*

Marshall Plan, *825*

imperial presidency, *826*

National Security Council (NSC), *826*

Berlin airlift, *827*

North Atlantic Treaty Organization (NATO), *828*

NSC-68, *830*

House Un-American Activities Committee (HUAC), *834*

Federal Employee Loyalty Program, *835*

McCarthyism, *839*

New Look, *840*

mutually assured destruction (MAD), *841*

decolonization, *843*

Bandung Conference, *844*

Eisenhower Doctrine, *845*

Vietcong, *846*

Review & Relate

1. Why did American policymakers believe that containing Communist expansion should be the foundation of American foreign policy?

2. What role did mutual misunderstandings and mistrust play in the emergence of the Cold War?

3. What were the causes and consequences of the militarization of the containment strategy in the late 1940s and early 1950s?

4. How did the Korean War contribute to the centralization of power in the executive branch?

5. Why did fear of Communists in positions of influence escalate in the late 1940s and early 1950s?

6. Why was McCarthyism much more powerful than Joseph McCarthy?

7. In what ways did the Eisenhower administration continue the Cold War policies of President Truman? In what ways did it depart from his predecessor?

8. How did U.S. intervention in Vietnam reflect the policy of containment?

McCarthyism and the Hollywood Ten

▶ Evaluate the power of McCarthyism by explaining why so few people challenged McCarthy, HUAC, and other anti-Communist investigators.

In 1947 the House Un-American Activities Committee (HUAC) began a headline-grabbing investigation of Hollywood, hoping to expose Communist influence in the Screen Writers Guild and pro-Communist messages in films. HUAC first called a number of "friendly" witnesses, such as actors Ronald Reagan (Source 24.6) and Gary Cooper, writer Ayn Rand, and movie studio heads Walt Disney and Jack Warner. These witnesses affirmed the presence of Communists in the film industry, though they were careful also to affirm their own anti-Communist beliefs. HUAC then called ten "unfriendly" witnesses who were suspected of being Communists (Source 24.7). They invoked the First Amendment's protection of free speech (or the right not to speak) and free association and refused to answer the committee's questions. The "Hollywood Ten," as they became known, included one director and nine writers, and all were held in contempt of Congress and given fines and jail sentences.

Over the next ten years, thousands of writers, actors, directors, producers, and technicians were blacklisted and lost their jobs (Sources 24.8 and 24.10). Although some were able to continue working under pseudonyms (especially writers), others had to leave the United States to find work; many were forced to look for employment outside the entertainment industry. There were personal consequences, too: Some marriages and families broke apart from the strain, and a few individuals were even driven to suicide. Nevertheless, others fought back. The cartoonist Herbert Lawrence Block (Herblock) ridiculed the attack on civil liberties (Source 24.9).

Source 24.6

Ronald Reagan | Testimony before HUAC, 1947

Ronald Reagan's acting career began in the late 1930s and included numerous starring roles, mostly in B movies. During World War II, he served in the Public Relations Unit of the Army Air Corps, where he helped produce hundreds of training films. Reagan was the president of the Screen Actors Guild during HUAC's Hollywood investigations, and he testified before the committee. Robert Stripling was the committee's chief investigator.

MR. STRIPLING Mr. Reagan, what is your feeling about what steps should be taken to rid the motion-picture industry of any Communist influences, if they are there?

MR. REAGAN Well, sir . . . 99 percent of us are pretty well aware of what is going on, and I think within the bounds of our democratic rights, and never once stepping over the rights given us by democracy, we have done a pretty good job in our business of keeping those people's activities curtailed. After all, we must recognize them at present as a political party. On that basis we have exposed their lies when we came across them, we have opposed their propaganda, and I can certainly testify that in the case of the Screen Actors Guild we have been eminently successful in preventing them from, with their usual tactics, trying to run a majority of an organization with a well organized minority.

So that fundamentally I would say in opposing those people that the best thing to do is to make democracy work. In the Screen Actors Guild we make it work by insuring everyone a vote and by keeping everyone informed. I believe that, as Thomas Jefferson put it, if all the American people know all of the facts they will never make a mistake.

Whether the party should be outlawed, I agree with the gentlemen that preceded me that that is a matter for the Government to decide. As a citizen I would hesitate, or not like, to see any political party outlawed on the basis of its political ideology. We have spent 170 years in this country on the basis that democracy is strong enough to stand up and fight against the inroads of any ideology. However, if it is proven that an organization is an agent of a power, a foreign power, or in any way not a legitimate political party, and I think the Government is capable of proving that, if the proof is there, then that is another matter.

I do not know whether I have answered your question or not. I . . . would like at this moment to say I happen to be very proud of the industry in which I work; I happen to be very proud of the way in which we conducted the fight. I do not believe the Communists have ever at any time been able to use the motion-picture screen as a sounding board for their philosophy or ideology. I think that will continue as long [as] the people in Hollywood continue as they are, which is alert, conscious of it, and fighting.

Source: House Un-American Activities Committee, *Hearings Regarding the Communist Infiltration of the Motion Picture Industry*, 80th Cong., 1st sess. (Washington, DC: Government Printing Office, 1947), 216–17.

Source 24.7

John Howard Lawson | Testimony before HUAC, 1947

Playwright and screenwriter John Howard Lawson was a founding member of the Screen Writers Guild. He was also a member of the American Communist Party and served as the party's cultural commissar in Hollywood, and many of his films included leftist political themes. In 1947 Lawson appeared before HUAC. The following selection shows several attempts by the committee to force Lawson's compliance. Like the other Hollywood Ten, Lawson was imprisoned and blacklisted for refusing to answer HUAC's questions or detail his political affiliations.

MR. LAWSON I am glad you have made it perfectly clear that you are going to threaten and intimidate the witnesses, Mr. Chairman. (The chairman pounding gavel.)

MR. LAWSON I am an American and I am not at all easy to intimidate, and don't think I am. (The chairman pounding gavel.)

MR. STRIPLING Mr. Lawson, I repeat the question. Have you ever held any position in the Screen Writers Guild?

MR. LAWSON I have stated that the question is illegal. But it is a matter of public record that I have held many offices in the Screen Writers Guild. I was its first president, in 1933, and I have held office on the board of directors of the Screen Writers Guild at other times. . . .

MR. STRIPLING Mr. Lawson, are you now, or have you ever been a member of the Communist Party of the United States?

MR. LAWSON In framing my answer to that question I must emphasize the points that I have raised before. The question of communism is in no way related to this inquiry, which is an attempt to get control of the screen and to invade the basic rights of American citizens in all fields.

MR. McDOWELL Now, I must object—

MR. STRIPLING Mr. Chairman—(The chairman pounding gavel.)

MR. LAWSON The question here relates not only to the question of my membership in any political organization, but this committee is attempting to establish the right—(The chairman pounding gavel.)

MR. LAWSON (continuing) Which has been historically denied to any committee of this sort, to invade the rights and privileges and immunity of American citizens, whether they be Protestant, Methodist, Jewish, or Catholic, whether they be Republicans or Democrats or anything else.

THE CHAIRMAN (pounding gavel) Mr. Lawson, just quiet down again. Mr. Lawson, the most pertinent question that we can ask is whether or not you have ever been a member of the Communist Party. Now, do you care to answer that question?

MR. LAWSON You are using the old technique, which was used in Hitler Germany in order to create a scare here—

THE CHAIRMAN (pounding gavel) Oh—

MR. LAWSON In order to create an entirely false atmosphere in which this hearing is conducted—(The chairman pounding gavel.)

MR. LAWSON In order that you can then smear the motion-picture industry, and you can proceed to the press, to any form of communication in this country.

THE CHAIRMAN You have learned—

MR. LAWSON The Bill of Rights was established precisely to prevent the operation of any committee which could invade the basic rights of Americans. . . .

THE CHAIRMAN (pounding gavel) We are going to get the answer to that question if we have to stay here for a week. Are you a member of the Communist Party, or have you ever been a member of the Communist Party?

MR. LAWSON It is unfortunate and tragic that I have to teach this committee the basic principles of American—

THE CHAIRMAN (pounding gavel) That is not the question. That is not the question. The question is: Have you ever been a member of the Communist Party?

MR. LAWSON I am framing my answer in the only way in which any American citizen can frame his answer to a question which absolutely invades his rights.

THE CHAIRMAN Then you refuse to answer that question; is that correct?

MR. LAWSON I have told you that I will offer my beliefs, affiliations, and everything else to the American public, and they will know where I stand.

THE CHAIRMAN (pounding gavel) Excuse the witness—

MR. LAWSON As they do from what I have written.

THE CHAIRMAN (pounding gavel) Stand away from the stand—

MR. LAWSON I have written Americanism for many years, and I shall continue to fight for the Bill of Rights, which you are trying to destroy.

THE CHAIRMAN Officers, take this man away from the stand—(Applause and boos.)

THE CHAIRMAN (pounding gavel) There will be no demonstrations. No demonstrations, for or against. Everyone will please be seated.

Source: House Un-American Activities Committee, *Hearings Regarding the Communist Infiltration of the Motion Picture Industry*, 80th Cong., 1st sess. (Washington, DC: Government Printing Office, 1947), 292–95.

Source 24.8

The Waldorf Statement and the Introduction of the Blacklist, 1947

After the Hollywood Ten were cited for contempt, the movie studios established a policy of blacklisting "unfriendly" witnesses called before congressional committees. After meeting at the Waldorf Astoria in New York, on December 3, 1947, the Motion Picture Association of America issued the following statement.

Members of the Association of Motion Picture Producers deplore the action of the 10 Hollywood men who have been cited for contempt by the House of Representatives. We do not desire to prejudge their legal rights, but their actions have been a disservice to their employers and have impaired their usefulness to the industry.

We will forthwith discharge or suspend without compensation those in our employ, and we will not reemploy any of the 10 until such time as he is acquitted or has purged himself of contempt and declares under oath that he is not a Communist.

On the broader issue of alleged subversive and disloyal elements in Hollywood, our members are likewise prepared to take positive action.

We will not knowingly employ a Communist or a member of any party or group which advocates the overthrow of the government of the United States by force or by any illegal or unconstitutional methods.

In pursuing this policy, we are not going to be swayed by hysteria or intimidation from any source. We are frank to recognize that such a policy involves dangers of hurting innocent people. Creative work at its best cannot be carried on in an atmosphere of fear. We will guard against this danger, this risk, this fear.

The absence of a national policy, established by Congress, with respect to employment of Communists in private industry makes our task difficult. Ours is a nation of laws. We request Congress to enact legislation to assist American industry to rid itself of subversive, disloyal elements.

Nothing subversive or un-American has appeared on the screen, nor can any number of Hollywood investigations obscure the patriotic services of the 30,000 loyal Americans employed in Hollywood who have given our government invaluable aid to war and peace."

Source: "Film Industry's Policy Defined," *Daily Variety*, November 26, 1947, 3.

Herblock | "You Mean I'm Supposed to Stand on That," 1950

Editorial cartoonist Herbert Lawrence Block, who wrote under the name "Herblock," was a fierce critic of McCarthy — both the man and the movement — and coined the term *McCarthyism* on March 29, 1950, weeks after Senator McCarthy's first anti-Communist speech in Wheeling, West Virginia. The following cartoon, published in the *Washington Post*, shows four prominent Republican senators, Robert Taft, Styles Bridges, Kenneth Wherry, and George Gabrielson, pushing the Republican Party behind McCarthy.

"You Mean I'm Supposed To Stand On That?"

Lillian Hellman | Letter to HUAC, 1952

Playwright Lillian Hellman, who was known for her devotion to leftist causes, was called to testify before HUAC in May 1952. Before her appearance, Hellman wrote the following letter to John Wood, the chairman of HUAC, explaining her willingness to answer questions about herself as long as she was not asked to testify against anyone else. Her request was denied. Hellman was blacklisted after invoking the Fifth Amendment during her HUAC appearance.

Dear Mr. Wood:

As you know, I am under subpoena to appear before your committee on May 21, 1952.

I am most willing to answer all questions about myself. I have nothing to hide from your committee and there is nothing in my life of which I am ashamed. I have been advised by counsel that under the fifth amendment I have a constitutional privilege to decline to answer any questions about my political opinions, activities, and associations, on the grounds of self-incrimination. I do not wish to claim this privilege. I am ready and willing to testify before the representatives of our Government as to my own opinions and my own actions, regardless of any risks or consequences to myself.

But I am advised by counsel that if I answer the committee's questions about myself, I must also answer questions about other people and that if I refuse to do so, I can be cited for contempt. My counsel tells me that if I answer questions about myself, I will have waived my rights under the fifth amendment and could be forced legally to answer questions about others. This is very difficult for a layman to understand. But there is one principle that I do understand: I am not willing, now or in the future, to bring bad trouble to people who, in my past association with them, were completely innocent of any talk or any action that was disloyal or subversive. I do not like subversion or disloyalty in any form and if I had ever seen any I would have considered it my duty to have reported it to the proper authorities. But to hurt innocent people whom I knew many years ago in order to save myself is, to me, inhuman and indecent and dishonorable. I cannot and will not cut my conscience to fit this year's fashions, even though I long ago came to the conclusion that I was not a political person and could have no comfortable place in any political group.

I was raised in an old-fashioned American tradition and there were certain homely things that were taught to me: To try to tell the truth, not to bear false witness, not to harm my neighbor, to be loyal to my country, and so on. In general, I respected these ideals of Christian honor and did as well with them as I knew how. It is my belief that you will agree with these simple rules of human decency and will not expect me to violate the good American tradition from which they spring. I would, therefore, like to come before you and speak of myself.

I am prepared to waive the privilege against self-incrimination and to tell you everything you wish to know about my views or actions if your committee will agree to refrain from asking me to name other people. If the committee is unwilling to give me this assurance, I will be forced to plead the privilege of the fifth amendment at the hearing.

A reply to this letter would be appreciated.

Sincerely yours,
Lillian Hellman

Source: House Un-American Activities Committee, *Hearings Regarding Communist Infiltration of the Hollywood Motion-Picture Industry*, 82nd Cong., 2nd sess. (Washington, DC: Government Printing Office, 1952), 3545–46.

Interpret the Evidence

1. Explain how Ronald Reagan (Source 24.6) views the threat communism poses to American society and how that threat should be handled.

2. Assess the way movie producers (Source 24.8) draw the line between artistic expression and blacklisting.

3. Explain how the Herblock cartoon (Source 24.9) depicts McCarthyism and the support of the Republican Party for it.

4. Compare the testimonies of John Howard Lawson and Lillian Hellman (Sources 24.7 and 24.10). What are their chief objections to testifying before HUAC?

Put It in Context

Why did anti-Communist investigations dominate politics after World War II?

Troubled Innocence

1945–1961

The Commercial Appeal/ZUMApress.com

Window to the Past

The Desegregation of Central High School, 1957

After two decades of economic depression and world war, the 1950s saw a return of peace and prosperity. However, for African Americans the 1950s were a time of challenges and conflicts. This photo of Elizabeth Eckford walking through a hostile crowd in Little Rock, Arkansas exhibits the dignity of one teenager in the struggle for racial equality. ▶ **To learn more about this primary source, see Source 25.8 on page 888.**

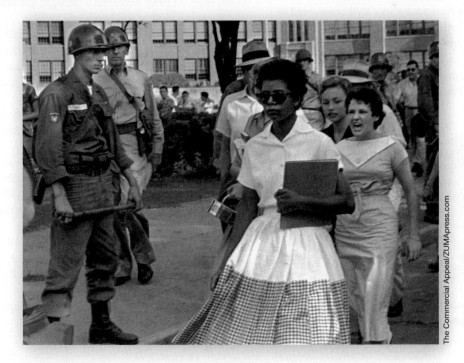

After reading this chapter you will be able to:

- Explain the problems of converting from World War II to peacetime and describe the causes and effects of the postwar economic boom.

- Analyze how the 1950s popular culture reflected the expanding consumer-oriented economy and explain the challenges to mainstream culture posed by teenagers, women, and the Beat generation.

- Examine the growth of the civil rights movement and identify the strategies used to challenge segregation and discrimination in the 1950s.

- Evaluate the impact of President Eisenhower's domestic policies and accomplishments on the Republican Party and the nation.

Comparing American Histories

Alan Freed shook up American youth culture in the 1950s by rebranding black music and making it popular with white teenagers. In 1951, at the age of twenty-nine, Aldon (Alan) James Freed was a white disc jockey, or "deejay," spinning records at a Cleveland, Ohio, radio station. He played rhythm and blues, an African American music style considered by many whites as "race music" that was only suitable for blacks. Calling himself Moondog, Freed howled like a dog and used sound effects to rattle his radio listeners. Although he initially appealed mainly to a black audience, Freed's radio show and live concerts

(*left*) **Alan Freed** Michael Ochs Archives/Getty Images
(*right*) **Grace Metalious** Everett Collection

of music he dubbed rock 'n' roll soon attracted white teenagers.

In 1954 Freed moved to New York City, where his evening rock 'n' roll radio broadcast became a number one hit with a broad audience. Three years later, he hosted a nationally televised rock 'n' roll program, but only briefly. The American Broadcasting Company canceled Freed's show after four telecasts because of outrage from affiliate stations in the South after the black singer Frankie Lymon was shown dancing with a white girl.

The television incident was only the start of Freed's professional problems. In 1960 Freed was brought before a congressional committee investigating "payola," a common practice among deejays of receiving gifts from record companies in exchange for playing their records. His career sank further when, in 1962, Freed was convicted of commercial bribery by New York State. Impoverished and struggling with alcoholism, Freed died in 1965 at the age of forty-three.

Like Alan Freed, **Grace Metalious** sent shock waves through American popular culture in the 1950s. Metalious grew up in poverty in Manchester, New Hampshire. In 1943, while still a teenager, she married and became a mother and housewife. In 1956 Metalious published her first novel, *Peyton Place*, and the book sold more than three million copies the first year. Considered provocative and racy because of its discussion of sex, rape, and incest, the novel punctured myths about the straitlaced life of small-town America. It criticized small-minded conformity that enforced a double standard of sexual behavior on women.

Despite the book's popularity, Metalious was never seen as a serious writer. Detractors described her as an untalented author who disseminated filth. Metalious could not reconcile her success with the criticism she received and, like Alan Freed, increasingly turned to alcohol for comfort. In 1964, just eight years after publication of *Peyton Place*, she died at age thirty-nine of cirrhosis of the liver. Both Metalious and Freed challenged notions of conventional taste, and both found their lives upended by the backlash their work inspired. ■

The American histories of Alan Freed and Grace Metalious, both of whom attacked conformity, were made possible by the emergence of a mass-consumption economy fueled by technological innovation. The end of World War II had produced economic, social, and political challenges for Americans; however, the economic boom of the 1950s allowed many Americans to overcome them. A large number of families moved into the middle class and out to suburbia. Yet not everyone felt satisfied, and critics expressed their disapproval in diverse ways. Young people challenged their parents' culture. Writers and musicians experimented with freer forms of artistic expression and attacked the conformity they associated with mainstream America. And African Americans and other marginalized groups challenged racial segregation directly in the Supreme Court and through powerful community protests.

Peacetime Transition and the Boom Years

The notoriety of Grace Metalious and Alan Freed came at a time of renewed economic growth and prosperity in the United States. Although confronted with family upheaval, labor disruptions, and economic constraints immediately following the war, by 1950 Americans had more disposable income than they had enjoyed in decades. While President Truman struggled to hold together the New Deal coalition, consumers responded enthusiastically to the wide range of products that advertisers promised would improve their lives. The search for the good life propelled middle-class families from cities to the suburbs. At the same time, a postwar baby boom added millions of children to the population and created a market to supply them with goods from infancy and childhood to adolescence.

Peacetime Challenges, 1945–1948.

Before Americans could work their way toward prosperity, they faced considerable challenges. Immediately after the war, consumers experienced shortages and high prices, businesses complained about tight regulations, and labor unions sought higher wages and a greater voice in companies' decision making. The return to peace also occasioned debates about whether married women should continue to work outside the home.

By mid-1946, 9 million American soldiers had returned to a changed world. The war had exerted pressures on traditional family life as millions of women had left home to work jobs that men had vacated. Most of the 150,000 women who served in the military received their discharge, and like their male counterparts they hoped to obtain employment. Many other women who had tasted the benefits of wartime employment also wanted to keep working and were reluctant to give up their positions to men.

The war disrupted other aspects of family life as well. During the war, husbands and wives had spent long periods apart, resulting in marital tensions and an increased divorce rate. The relaxation of parental authority during the war led to a rise in juvenile delinquency, which added to the anxieties of adults. In 1948 the noted psychiatrist William C. Menninger observed, "While we alarm ourselves with talk of . . . atom bombs, we are complacently watching the disintegration of our family life." Some observers worried that the very existence of the traditional American family was in jeopardy.

Economic Conversion and Labor Discontent.

Even before the war ended, the U.S. government took some steps to meet postwar economic challenges. In 1944, for

The GI Bill   Attending Pennsylvania State College under the GI Bill of Rights, William Oskay, Jr. pays $28 a month for the trailer home in which he is studying at a desk made from orange crates. Mrs. Oskay plays with their young daughter in the background. To gain extra money for clothing and entertainment, the enterprising Oskay sells sandwiches in fraternity houses, earning $3 or $4 a night. Bettmann/Getty Images

example, Congress passed the **Servicemen's Readjustment Act**, commonly known as the **GI Bill**, which offered veterans educational opportunities and financial aid as they adjusted to civilian life. Nevertheless, veterans, like other Americans, faced shortages in the supply of housing and consumer goods and high prices for available commodities.

President Harry Truman ran into serious difficulty handling these and other problems. In the years immediately following the war, incomes fell, undermined by inflation and reduced overtime hours. As corporate profits rose, workers in the steel, automobile, and fuel industries struck for higher wages and a greater voice in company policies. Truman responded harshly. Labor had been one of Franklin Roosevelt's strongest allies, but his successor put that relationship in jeopardy. In 1946 the federal government took over railroads and threatened to draft workers into the military until they stopped striking. Truman took a tough stance, but in the end union workers received a pay raise, though it did little to relieve inflation.

Political developments forced Truman to change course with the labor unions. In the 1946 midterm elections, Republicans won control of Congress. Stung by this defeat, Truman sought to repair the damage his anti-union policies had done to the Democratic Party coalition. In 1947 Congress passed the **Taft-Hartley Act**, which hampered the ability of unions to organize and limited their power to strike if larger national interests were seen to be at stake. Seeking to regain labor's support, Truman vetoed the measure. Congress, however, overrode the president's veto, and the Taft-Hartley Act became law.

Truman, the New Deal Coalition, and the Election of 1948.

Truman's handling of domestic and foreign affairs brought out several challengers for the 1948 election. Much of the opposition came from his own party. From the left, former Democratic vice president Henry Wallace ran on the Progressive Party ticket, backed by disgruntled liberals who opposed Truman's hard-line Cold War policies. From the right, Democratic governor Strom Thurmond of South Carolina campaigned mainly on preserving racial segregation in the South and headed up the States' Rights Party, known as the Dixiecrats. Both Wallace and Thurmond threatened to take Democratic votes from the president. However, Truman's strongest challenge came from the popular Republican governor of New York, Thomas E. Dewey.

Up against overwhelming odds, Truman managed to win the presidency. He out-campaigned Dewey, while Wallace and Thurmond failed to draw significant votes away from Truman. He succeeded in holding together the New Deal coalition of labor, racial and ethnic minority groups, farmers, and liberals and winning enough votes in the South to come out ahead.

By this time, most liberals had moved closer to the political center. Rejecting what they considered the ideological dogmatism of the extreme left and right, they favored a strong anti-Communist policy abroad and supported a brand of reform capitalism at home that encouraged economic growth rather than a redistribution of wealth to lift Americans into the middle class. In doing so, they also sought to avoid the political fallout from charges of Communist sympathizers-in-government hurled by Republicans.

Economic Boom. While the United States faced political challenges, the economy flourished in the decade and a half after the Second World War. Between 1945 and 1960, the gross national product (GNP) soared 250 percent and per capita income (total income divided by the population) grew 35 percent. During this fifteen-year period, the average real income (actual purchasing power) for American workers increased by as much as it had during the fifty years preceding World War II. Equally striking, 60 percent of Americans achieved middle-class status, and the number of salaried office workers rose 61 percent. Factory workers also experienced gains. Union membership leaped to the highest level in U.S. history, reaching nearly 17 million.

The affluence of the 1950s was much more equally distributed than the prosperity of the 1920s had been. As the middle class grew, the top 5 percent of wealthy families dropped in the percentage of total income they earned from 21.3 percent to 19 percent. Though poverty remained a persistent problem, the rate of poverty decreased, falling from 34 percent in 1947 to 22.1 percent in 1960 (Figure 25.1). A college education served as a critical marker of

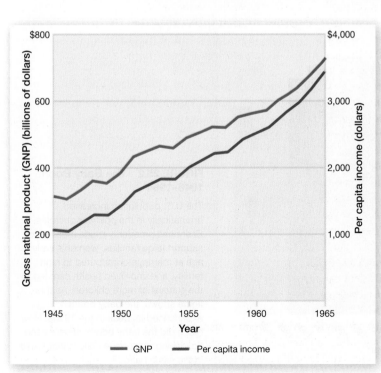

FIGURE 25.1 Economic Growth, 1945–1965

As industries shifted from war equipment to consumer goods, productivity remained high. More Americans entered the middle class in the two decades following World War II, while rising union membership ensured higher incomes for the working class. As a result, the purchasing power of most Americans increased in the immediate postwar period. What factors promoted the growth of the middle class in the 1950s?

middle-class status. Traditionally, colleges and universities had been accessible only to the upper class. That began to change between 1940 and 1960 as the number of high school students who entered college more than doubled.

The market for consumer goods skyrocketed. TV sets became a household staple in the 1950s, and by 1960, 87 percent of Americans owned a television. Americans also continued to purchase automobiles—75 percent owned a car. With gas supplies plentiful and the price per gallon less than 30 cents, automakers concentrated on size, power, and style to compete for buyers. With more cars on the road, motel chains such as Holiday Inn sprang up along the highways. Fast-food establishments proliferated to feed motorists and their families.

Baby Boom.   During the postwar years, with traditional gender roles largely reinstated and the economy booming, nuclear families began to grow. In the 1940s and 1950s the average age at marriage was younger than it had been in the 1930s. On average, men married for the first time at the age of just under twenty-three, and 49 percent of women married by nineteen. Couples also produced children at an astonishing rate. In the 1950s, the growth rate in the U.S. population approached that of India (Figure 25.2).

Explore ▶

See Source 25.1 for Adlai Stevenson's speech at Smith explaining why a woman's place is in the home.

Marriage and parenthood reflected a culture spurred by the Cold War. Public officials and the media urged young men and women to build nuclear families in which the father held a paying job and the mother stayed at home and raised her growing family. Doing so would strengthen the moral fiber of the United States in its battle against Soviet communism.

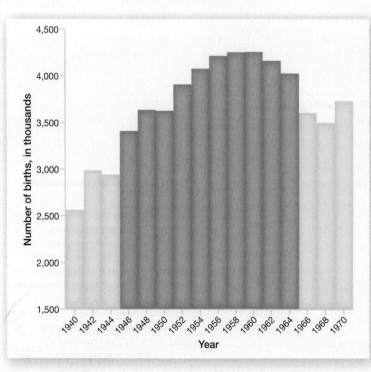

FIGURE 25.2   The Baby Boom, 1946–1964

The U.S. population increased dramatically in the postwar decades. Economic prosperity made it easier to support large families, women's early age at marriage contributed to high fertility, and improved health care led to the survival of more children. As this figure shows, the baby boom experienced its peak in the 1950s. How much did the baby boom influence the flourishing of teenage culture that arose in the same period?

Guided Primary Source Analysis

Adlai E. Stevenson | "A Purpose for Modern Woman," 1955

Adlai E. Stevenson was governor of Illinois and Democratic presidential candidate in 1952 and 1956. A liberal Democrat, he nevertheless shared the conventional view of the relationship between the sexes. In his 1955 commencement address at all-female Smith College, he argued that women, however educated they were, should embrace their duty as housewives.

Source 25.1

According to Stevenson, what role do educated housewives have to play?

Why does he believe educated women feel frustrated?

What does he think women can accomplish?

Women, especially educated women, have a unique opportunity to influence us, man and boy, and to play a direct part in the unfolding drama of our free society. But I am told that nowadays the young wife or mother is short of time for such subtle arts, that things are not what they used to be; that once immersed in the very pressing and particular problems of domesticity, many women feel frustrated and far apart from the great issues and stirring debates for which their education has given them understanding and relish. Once they read Baudelaire. Now it is the *Consumers' Guide*. Once they wrote poetry. Now it's the laundry list. Once they discussed art and philosophy until late in the night. Now they are so tired they fall asleep as soon as the dishes are finished. . . . They had hoped to play their part in the crisis of the age. But what they do is wash the diapers. . . .

In modern America the home is not the boundary of a woman's life. There are outside activities aplenty. But even more important is the fact, surely, that what you have learned and can learn will fit you for the primary task of making homes and whole human beings in whom the rational values of freedom, tolerance, charity and free inquiry can take root.

Source: Adlai E. Stevenson, "A Purpose for Modern Woman," *Woman's Home Companion*, September 1955, 30–31.

Put It in Context

How were women's roles influenced by economic and social developments after World War II?

Parents could also look forward to their children surviving diseases that had resulted in many childhood deaths in the past. In the 1950s, children received vaccinations against diphtheria, whooping cough, and tuberculosis before they entered school. The most serious illness affecting young children remained the crippling disease of polio, or infantile paralysis. In 1955 Dr. Jonas Salk developed a successful injectable vaccine against the disease. On April 12, 1955, news bulletins interrupted scheduled television programs to announce Salk's breakthrough, and, as one writer recalled, "citizens rushed to ring church bells and fire sirens, shouted, clapped, sang, and made every kind of joyous noise they could." By the mid-1960s polio was no longer a public health menace in the United States.

Changes in Living Patterns.

With larger families and larger family incomes came an increased demand for better housing. The economic and demographic booms encouraged migration out of the cities so that growing families could have their own homes, greater space, and a healthier environment. To meet this demand, the federal government offered Americans opportunities to purchase their own homes. The Federal Housing Administration, created in the 1930s, provided long-term mortgages to qualified buyers at low interest rates. After the war, the Veterans Administration offered even lower mortgage rates and did not require substantial down payments for ex-GIs. The federal government also cooperated by building highways that allowed drivers to commute to and from the suburbs. By 1960 nearly 60 million people, one-third of the nation's population, lived in suburbs.

William Levitt, a thirty-eight-year-old veteran from Long Island, New York, devised the formula for attracting home buyers to the suburbs. In 1948, Levitt remarked: "No man who owns his own house and lot can be a Communist. He has too much to do." After World War II, Levitt, his father, and his brother saw opportunity in the housing crunch and pioneered the idea of adapting Henry Ford's mass-production principles to the housing industry. To build his subdivision of **Levittown** in Hempstead, Long Island, twenty miles from Manhattan, he bulldozed 4,000 acres of potato fields and brought in trucks that dumped piles of building materials at exact intervals of sixty feet. Specialized crews then moved from pile to pile, each performing their assigned job. In July 1948, Levitt's workers constructed 180 houses a week, or 36 a day, in two shifts. Mass-production methods kept prices low, and Levitt quickly sold his initial 17,000 houses and soon built other subdivisions in Pennsylvania and New Jersey. With Levitt leading the way, the annual production of new single-family homes nearly doubled from 937,000 in 1946 to 1.7 million in 1950.

Although millions of Americans took advantage of opportunities to move to the suburbs, Levitt closed his subdivisions to African Americans. He was supported by the Federal Housing Administration, which guaranteed financing for sales of housing in "all-white" communities. Many whites moved out of the cities because they were prejudiced against the growing number of southern blacks who migrated north during World War II and the influx of Puerto Ricans who came to the United States after the war. Many communities in the North adopted restrictive covenants, which prohibited resale of homes to blacks and members of other racial and ethnic minority groups, including Hispanics, Jews, and Asian Americans. Although the Supreme Court outlawed restrictive covenants in *Shelley v. Kraemer* (1948), housing discrimination remained prevalent in urban and suburban neighborhoods. Real estate brokers steered buyers from these marginalized groups away from white communities, and banks refused to lend money to black purchasers who sought to move into white locales, an illegal policy called redlining.

Nevertheless, a few African Americans succeeded in cracking suburban racial barriers, but at great risk. In August 1957, a black couple, William Myers, an electrical engineer, and his wife Daisy, managed to buy a house in Levittown, Pennsylvania. Once the Myers moved in, they faced two weeks of intimidation and assaults from mobs of hostile white community residents. When local police refused to protect them, the governor dispatched state

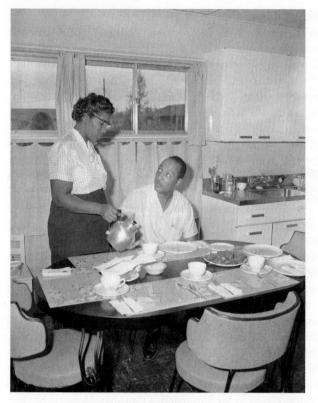

William and Daisy Myers Integrate Levittown, 1957   Daisy Myers serves coffee to her husband William in their new $12,150 ranch-style house in Levittown, Pennsylvania. The first black family to move into this all-white community, on August 19, 1957, the Myers braved two weeks of threatening protests by their new neighbors and proclaimed: "We're here to stay," and they did. AP Images/Sam Myers

troopers to keep them safe. Although the Myers succeeded in remaining in Levittown, their experience underscored the racially discriminatory housing practices that existed in the North.

No sections of the nation expanded faster than the West and the South. Attracted by the warmer climate and jobs in the defense, petroleum, and chemical industries, transplanted Americans swelled the populations of California, Texas, and Florida. The advent of air conditioning also made such moves much more feasible. California's population increased the most, adding nearly six million new residents between 1940 and 1960, including a large influx of Asians and Latinos. In 1957, in a sign of the times, New York City lost two of its baseball teams, the New York Giants and the Brooklyn Dodgers, to San Francisco and Los Angeles. This migration to the **Sun Belt**, as the southern and western states would be called, transformed the political and social landscapes of the nation.

Review & Relate

■ How did the conversion from war to peacetime affect the economy, society, and politics in the United States?

■ What factors contributed to the economic and population growth of the 1950s, and how did they contribute to suburbanization and the growth in the Sun Belt?

The **Culture** of the **1950s**

In the 1950s, new forms of popular culture developed as the United States confronted difficult political, diplomatic, and social issues. Amid this turmoil, television played a large role in shaping people's lives, reflecting their desire for success and depicting the era as a time of innocence. The rise of teenage culture as a powerful economic force also influenced this portrayal of the 1950s. Teenage tastes and consumption patterns reinforced the impression of a simpler and more carefree time. Religion painted a similar picture, as attendance at houses of worship rose. Still, the decade held a more complex social reality. Cultural rebels — writers, actors, and musicians — emerged to challenge mainstream values. Women did not always act the suburban parts that television and society assigned them, and religion seemed to serve more of a communal, social function than an individual, spiritual one.

The Rise of Television.

Few postwar developments had a greater impact on American society and politics than the advent of television. The three major television networks — the Columbia Broadcasting System (CBS), the National Broadcasting Company (NBC), and the American Broadcasting Company (ABC) — offered programs nationwide that appealed to mainstream tastes while occasionally challenging the public with serious drama, music, and documentaries. During the 1950s, television networks began to feature presidential campaign coverage, from the national nominating conventions to election-day vote tallies, and political advertisements began to fill the airwaves.

If some Americans recall the 1950s as a time of innocence, they have in mind television shows that depicted white families entertaining themselves, mediating quarrels peacefully, and relying on the wisdom of parents. In *The Adventures of Ozzie and Harriet*, the Nelsons raised two clean-cut sons. In *Father Knows Best*, the Andersons — a father and mother and their three children — lived a tranquil life in the suburbs, and the father solved whatever dilemmas arose. The same held true for the Cleaver family on *Leave It to Beaver*. Television portrayed working-class families in grittier fashion on shows such as *The Life of Riley*, whose lead character worked at a factory, and *The Honeymooners*, whose male protagonists were a bus driver and a sewer worker. Nevertheless, like their middle-class counterparts, these families stayed together and worked out their problems despite their more challenging financial circumstances.

By contrast, African American families received little attention on television. Black female actors usually appeared as maids, and the one show that featured an all-black cast, *The Amos 'n' Andy Show*, highlighted the racial stereotypes of the period. American Indians faced similar difficulties. Few appeared on television, and those who did served mainly as targets for "heroic" cowboys defending the West from "savage" Indians. One exception was Tonto, the Lone Ranger's sidekick. Played by Jay Silverheels, a Canadian Mohawk, he challenged the false image of the "hostile Indian" by showing his loyalty to his white partner and his commitment to the code of "civilized" justice.

Wild Ones on the Big Screen.

If parents expected young people to behave like Ozzie and Harriet Nelson's sons, the popular culture industry provided teenagers with alternative role models. In *Rebel Without a Cause* (1955), actor James Dean portrayed a seventeen-year-old filled with anguish about his life. A sensitive but misunderstood young man, he muses that he wants "just one day when I wasn't all confused . . . [when] I wasn't ashamed of everything . . . [when] I felt I belonged some place." *The Wild One* (1954), which starred Marlon Brando, also popularized youthful angst. The leather-outfitted leader of a motorcycle gang, Brando rides into a small town, hoping to shake it up. When asked by a local resident, "What are you rebelling against?" he coolly replies, "Whaddya got?" Real gangs did exist on the streets of New York and other major cities. Composed of working-class youth from various ethnic and racial backgrounds, these gangs were highly organized, controlled their neighborhood turfs, and engaged in "rumbles" (fights) with intruders.

Hollywood rarely portrayed women as rebels, but instead as mothers, understanding girlfriends, and dutiful wives. If they sought a career, like many of the women played by actor Doris Day, they pursued it only as long as necessary to meet the right man. The film industry also perpetuated an image of a tantalizing woman who utilized her attributes to seduce and outwit men. Marilyn Monroe in *The Seven Year Itch* (1955) and Elizabeth Taylor in *Cat on a Hot Tin Roof* (1958) both portrayed female characters as sexual beings.

Rebel Without a Cause, 1955   James Dean starred in the movie *Rebel Without a Cause*, playing Jim Stark, a troubled teenager seeking an escape from his middle-class, suburban life. The movie explored the conflict between parents and teenagers, what we call today "the generation gap." Dean's outfit of leather jacket and blue jeans and his anguished demeanor both reflected and shaped teenage culture. Everett Collection

The Influence of Teenage Culture. In 1941 *Popular Science* magazine coined the term *teenager*, and by the middle of the next decade members of this age group viewed themselves not as prospective adults but as a distinct group with its own identity, patterns of behavior, and tastes. Postwar prosperity provided teenagers with money to support their own choices and styles. In 1959 *Life* magazine found that teenagers had $10 billion at their disposal, "a billion more than the total sales of GM [General Motors]." **See Primary Source Project 25: Teenagers in Postwar America, page 886.**

Teenagers owned 10 million record players, more than 1 million TV sets, and 13 million cameras. They spent 16 percent of their disposable income on entertainment, particularly the purchase of rock 'n' roll records. The comic book industry also attracted a huge audience among teenagers by selling inexpensive, illustrated, and easy-to-read pulp fiction geared toward romance and action adventure.

Public high schools reinforced teenage identity. Following World War II, high school attendance exploded. In 1930, 50 percent of white children attended high school; thirty years later, the figure had jumped to 90 percent. The percentage of black youths attending high school also grew, doubling from 1940 to 1960. For the first time, many white middle-class teenagers saw the fashions and heard the language of working-class youths close up and both emulated and feared what they encountered.

More than anything else, rock 'n' roll music set teenagers apart from their elders. The pop singers of the 1940s and early 1950s — such as Frank Sinatra, Perry Como, Rosemary Clooney, and Patti Page, who had appealed to both adolescents and parents — lost much of their teenage audience after 1954 to rock 'n' roll, with its heavy downbeat and lyrics evoking teenage passion and sexuality. Black artists such as Chuck Berry, Little Richard, and Antoine "Fats" Domino popularized the sound of classic, up-tempo rock.

Although blacks pioneered the sound of rhythm and blues, the music entered the mainstream largely through white artists. Born in Tupelo, Mississippi, and living in Memphis, Tennessee, Elvis Presley adapted the fashion and sensuality of black performers to his own style. Elvis's snarling singing and pelvic gyrations excited young people, both black and white, while upsetting their parents. In an era when matters of sex remained private or were not discussed at all and when African Americans were still treated as second-class citizens, a white man singing "black" music and shaking his body to its frenetic tempo caused alarm. When Elvis sang on the popular *Ed Sullivan Show* in 1956, cameras were allowed to show him only from the waist up to uphold standards of decency.

The Lives of Women.   Throughout the 1950s, movies, women's magazines, mainstream newspapers, and medical and psychological experts informed women that only by embracing domesticity could they achieve personal fulfillment. Dr. Benjamin Spock's best-selling *Common Sense Book of Baby and Child Care* (1946) advised mothers that their children would reach their full potential only if wives stayed at home and watched over their offspring. In another best seller, *Modern Women: The Lost Sex* (1947), Ferdinand Lundberg and Marynia Farnham called the independent woman "a contradiction in terms." A 1951 study of corporate executives found that most businessmen viewed the ideal wife as one who devoted herself to her husband's career. College newspapers described female undergraduates who were not engaged by their senior year as "distraught." Certainly many women professed to find domestic lives fulfilling, but many others experienced anxiety and depression. Far from satisfied, these women suffered from what the social critic Betty Friedan would later call "a problem that has no name," a malady that derived from the unrewarding roles women were expected to play.

Although most married women with families did not work during the 1950s, the proportion of working wives doubled from 15 percent in 1940 to 30 percent in 1960, with the greatest increase coming among women over the age of thirty-five. Married women were more likely to work if they were African American or came from working-class immigrant families. Moreover, women's magazines offered readers a more complex message than domesticity. Alongside articles about and advertisements directed at stay-at-home mothers, these periodicals profiled career women, such as white Maine senator Margaret Chase Smith, black educator Mary McLeod Bethune, and sports figures such as white golf and tennis great Babe (Mildred) Didrikson Zaharias. At the same time, working women played significant roles in labor unions, where they fought to reduce disparities between men's and women's income and provide a wage for housewives, recognizing the importance of their unpaid work to maintaining families. Many other women joined clubs and organizations like the Young Women's Christian Association (YWCA), where they engaged in charitable and public service activities. Some participated in political organizations, such as Henry Wallace's Progressive Party, and peace groups, such as the Women's International League for Peace and Freedom, to campaign against the violence caused by racial discrimination at home and Cold War rivalries abroad.

Religious Revival.   Along with marriage and the family, religion experienced a revival in the postwar United States. The arms race between the United States and the Soviet Union heightened the dangers of international conflict for ordinary citizens, and the social and

Women in the Home and in the Workplace   In the 1950s married women were encouraged to stay at home. Modern appliances like this refrigerator (left) supposedly made housework less difficult, but wives had to spend a great deal of time keeping it fully stocked and attending to other household chores. With all the new devices at their disposal, wives were expected to keep the home neat and spotless, while caring for their children. But not all married women stayed at home and tended the family. Margaret Chase Smith (above) was an influential Republican senator from Maine who took on Senator Joseph McCarthy in Congress and challenged his harsh anti-Communist methods. Here she is engaged in serious deliberations with Democratic majority leader Lyndon B. Johnson at a Senate hearing in 1957. Left: George Marks/Retrofile/Getty Images; Above: Robert W. Kelley/The LIFE Picture Collection/Getty Images

economic changes that accompanied the Cold War intensified personal anxiety. Church-going underscored the contrast between the United States, a religious nation, and the "god-less" communism of the Soviet Union. The link between religion and Americanism prompted Congress in 1954 to add "under God" to the pledge of allegiance and to make "In God We Trust" the national motto. A good American, one magazine proclaimed, could not be "un-religious."

Americans worshipped in growing numbers. Between 1940 and 1950, church and synagogue membership rose by 78 percent, and more than 95 percent of the population professed a belief in God. Yet religious affiliation appeared to reflect a greater emphasis on togetherness than on specific doctrinal beliefs. It offered a way to overcome isolation and embrace community in an increasingly alienating world.

Television spread religiosity into millions of homes. The Catholic bishop Fulton J. Sheen spoke to a weekly television audience of ten million and alternated his message of "a life worth living" with attacks on atheistic Communists. The Methodist minister Norman Vincent Peale, also a popular TV figure, combined traditional religious faith with self-help remedies prescribed in his best-selling book *The Power of Positive Thinking* (1952). The Reverend Billy Graham, from Charlotte, North Carolina, preached about the unhappiness caused by personal sin at huge outdoor crusades, which were broadcast on television.

Beats and Other Nonconformists. As many Americans migrated to the suburbs, spent money on leisure and entertainment, and cultivated religion, a small group of
young poets, writers, intellectuals, musicians, and artists attacked mainstream politics and
culture. Known as **Beats** (derived from "beaten down"), they offered stinging critiques of
what they considered the sterility and conformity of white middle-class society. In 1956
Allen Ginsberg began his epic poem *Howl* with the line "I saw the best minds of my generation destroyed by madness, starving hysterical naked." In his novel *On the Road* (1957), Jack
Kerouac praised the individual who pursued authentic experiences and mind-expanding
consciousness through drugs, sexual experimentation, and living in the moment. At a time
when whiteness was a standard of beauty and virtue, the Beats and authors such as Norman
Mailer looked to African Americans as cultural icons, embracing a sense of spontaneity and
coolness they attributed to blacks. The Beats formed their own artistic enclaves in New
York City's Greenwich Village and San Francisco's North Beach and Haight-Ashbury
districts.

The Beat writers frequently read their poems and prose to the rhythms of jazz,
reflecting both their affinity with African American culture and the innovative explorations
taking place in music. From the big bands of the 1930s and 1940s, postwar jazz musicians

The Beat Generation   The literary rebels of the Beat Generation questioned the dominant
values of the 1950s. They attacked materialism and conventional sexual morality. They explored
Eastern religions as an alternative to Christianity and Judaism, and experimented with
psychedelic drugs to reach a higher consciousness. This photograph captures the rebels-to-be
as they attended Columbia University in the mid-1940s. From left to right are Hal Chase, Jack
Kerouac, Allen Ginsberg, and William S. Burroughs. Allen Ginsberg/Corbis/Getty Images

formed smaller trios, quartets, and quintets and experimented with sounds more suitable for serious listening than for dancing. The bebop rhythms of trumpeter Dizzy Gillespie and alto saxophonist Charlie Parker revolutionized jazz, as did trumpeter Miles Davis and tenor saxophonist John Coltrane, who experimented with more complex and textured forms of this music and took it to new heights. Like rock 'n' roll musicians, these black artists broke down racial barriers as their music attracted white audiences.

Homosexuals also attempted to live nonconformist lifestyles, albeit clandestinely. According to studies by researcher Dr. Alfred Kinsey of Indiana University, homosexuals made up approximately 10 percent of the adult population. During World War II, gay men and lesbians had the opportunity to meet other homosexuals in the military and in venues that attracted gay soldiers. Though homosexuality remained taboo and public displays of same-sex sexuality were criminalized, politically radical gay men organized against homophobia after the war. In 1951 they formed the Mattachine Society in Los Angeles, which then spread to the East Coast. In 1954 a group of lesbians founded the Daughters of Bilitis in San Francisco. Because of police harassment, most homosexuals refused to reveal their sexual orientation, which made sense practically but reduced their ability to counter anti-homosexual discrimination.

Kinsey also shattered myths about conformity among heterosexuals. In *Sexual Behavior in the Human Female* (1953), he revealed that 50 percent of the women he interviewed had had sexual intercourse before marriage, and 25 percent had had extramarital affairs. Kinsey's findings were supported by other data. Between 1940 and 1960, the frequency of out-of-wedlock births among all women rose from 7.1 newborns to 21.6 newborns per thousand women of childbearing age. The sexual relations that Grace Metalious depicted in *Peyton Place* reflected what many Americans practiced but did not talk about. The brewing sexual revolution went public in 1953 with the publication of *Playboy* magazine, founded by Hugh Hefner. Through a combination of serious articles and photographs of nude women, the magazine provided its chiefly male readers with a guide to pursuing sexual pleasure and a sophisticated lifestyle.

Like Metalious, many writers denounced the conformity and shallowness they found in suburban America. Novelist Sloan Wilson wrote about the alienating experience of suburban life in *The Man in the Gray Flannel Suit* (1955). In J. D. Salinger's novel *Catcher in the Rye* (1951), the young protagonist, Holden Caulfield, mocks the phoniness of the adult world while ending up in a mental institution. Journalists and scholars joined in the criticism, and they tapped into a growing feeling, especially among a new generation of young people, of the dangers of a mass culture based on standardization, compliance, and bureaucratization.

Review & Relate

- What trends in American popular culture did the television shows and popular music of the 1950s reflect?

- How did artists, writers, and social critics challenge the mainstream politics and culture of the 1950s?

The **Growth** of the **Civil Rights Movement**

African Americans wanted what most other Americans desired after World War II — the opportunity to make a decent living, buy a nice home, raise a healthy family, and get the best education for their children. Yet blacks faced much greater obstacles than did whites in obtaining these dreams, particularly in the Jim Crow South. Determined to eliminate racial injustices, black Americans mounted a campaign against white supremacy in the decades after World War II. African Americans increasingly viewed their struggle as part of an international movement of black people in Africa and other non-whites in the Middle East and Asia to obtain their freedom from Western colonial rulers. Embracing similar hopes, Asian Americans and Latinos pursued their own struggles for equality.

Explore ▶

See Sources 25.2 and 25.3 for two views of the meaning and importance of the civil rights movement.

The Rise of the Southern Civil Rights Movement.
With the war against Nazi racism over, African Americans expected to win first-class citizenship in the United States. During World War II, blacks waged successful campaigns to pressure the federal government to tackle discrimination and organizations such as the Congress of Racial Equality (CORE) and the NAACP attacked racial injustice. African American veterans, such as Medgar Evers in Mississippi, returned home to the South determined to build on these victories, especially by extending the right to vote. Yet African Americans found that most whites resisted demands for racial equality.

In 1946 violence surfaced as the most visible evidence of many white people's determination to preserve the traditional racial order. A race riot erupted in Columbia, Tennessee, in which blacks were killed and black businesses were torched. In South Carolina, Isaac Woodard, a black veteran still in uniform and on his way home on a bus, got into an argument with the white bus driver. When the local sheriff arrived, he pounded Woodard's face with a club, permanently blinding the ex-GI. In Mississippi, Senator Theodore Bilbo, running for reelection in the Democratic primary, told white audiences that they could keep blacks from voting "by seeing them the night before" the election. Groups such as the NAACP and the National Association of Colored Women demanded that the president take action to combat this reign of terror.

In December 1946, President Truman responded by issuing an executive order creating the President's Committee on Civil Rights. While the committee conducted its investigation, in April 1947, Jackie Robinson became the first black baseball player to enter the major leagues. This accomplishment proved to be a sign of changes to come.

After extensive deliberations, the committee, which consisted of blacks and whites, northerners and southerners, issued its report, *To Secure These Rights*, on October 29, 1947. Placing the problem of "civil rights shortcomings" within the context of the Cold War, the report argued that racial inequality and unrest could only aid the Soviets in their global anti-American propaganda efforts. "The United States is not so strong," the committee asserted, "the final triumph of the democratic ideal not so inevitable that we can ignore what the world thinks of us or our record." A far-reaching document, the report called for racial desegregation in the military, interstate transportation, and education, as well as extension of the right to vote. The following year, under pressure from African American activists, President Truman signed an executive order to desegregate the armed forces.

Even without federal action, African Americans moved to obtain civil rights. The anti-Communist attacks in the late 1940s and early 1950s against liberal and left-wing groups had damaged a number of interracial organizations, including the National Negro Congress and the Southern Negro Youth Congress. However, NAACP branches and local civic groups remained in the South to challenge white supremacy. These organizations dispatched black women and men to conduct voter registration drives throughout major cities and small towns in the South. By 1954, the percentage of black registered voters in the South had leaped from 3 percent in 1940 to 20 percent. These black freedom efforts, though fruitful, were very dangerous. In 1951, Harry T. Moore, the leader of the NAACP in Florida who had spearheaded voter registration campaigns, was killed along with his wife when the Ku Klux Klan detonated a bomb under their house. .

School Segregation and the Supreme Court. Led by the NAACP, African Americans also launched a prolonged assault on school segregation. First the association filed lawsuits against states that excluded blacks from publicly funded law schools and universities. After victories in Missouri and Maryland, the group's chief lawyer, Thurgood Marshall, convinced the Supreme Court in 1950 to disband the separate law school that Texas had established for blacks and admit them to the University of Texas Law School. At the same time, the Court eliminated separate facilities for black students at the University of Oklahoma graduate school and ruled against segregation in interstate rail transportation.

Before African Americans could attend college, they had to obtain a good education in public schools. Black schools typically lacked the resources provided to white schools, and the NAACP understood that southern officials would never live up to the "separate but equal doctrine" asserted in *Plessy v. Ferguson* (1896). African Americans sought to integrate schools not because they wanted their children to sit next to white students, but because they believed that integration offered the best and quickest way to secure quality education.

On May 17, 1954, in *Brown v. Board of Education of Topeka, Kansas*, the Supreme Court overturned *Plessy*. In a unanimous decision read by Chief Justice Earl Warren, the Court concluded that "in the field of public education the doctrine of 'separate but equal' has no place. Separate educational facilities are inherently unequal." This ruling undercut the legal foundation for segregation and officially placed the law on the side of those who sought racial equality. Nevertheless, the ruling did not end the controversy; in fact, it led to more battles over segregation. In 1955 the Court issued a follow-up opinion calling for implementation with "all deliberate speed." But it left enforcement of *Brown* to federal district courts in the South, which consisted mainly of white southerners who espoused segregationist views. As a result, southern officials emphasized "deliberate" rather than "speed" and slowed the implementation of the *Brown* decision.

The Montgomery Bus Boycott. The *Brown* decision encouraged African Americans to protest against other forms of racial discrimination. In 1955 in Montgomery, Alabama, the Women's Political Council, a group of middle-class and professional black women, petitioned the city commission to improve bus service for black passengers. Among other things, they wanted blacks not to have to give up their seats to white passengers who boarded the bus after black passengers did. Their requests went unheeded until December 1, 1955, when Rosa Parks, a black seamstress and an NAACP activist, refused to

The Civil Rights Movement and Its Opponents

As the civil rights movement began to tear down the walls of racial segregation and disfranchisement, southern segregationists resisted these efforts. In 1956, 101 southern congressmen issued a manifesto, which is excerpted in the first document here, rejecting the *Brown v. Board of Education* (1954) Supreme Court decision. By 1960 the pace of the civil rights movement had quickened, and young people formed organizations such as the Student Nonviolent Coordinating Committee (SNCC) to challenge racial inequality and white supremacy. In the second document, Ella Baker, a longtime activist and adviser to SNCC, sketches out her views on the meaning of the movement.

Source 25.2

The Southern Manifesto, 1956

We regard the decision of the Supreme Court in the school cases as a clear abuse of judicial power. It climaxes a trend in the Federal Judiciary undertaking to legislate, in derogation of the authority of Congress, and to encroach upon the reserved rights of the states and the people. . . .

This unwarranted exercise of power by the Court, contrary to the Constitution, is creating chaos and confusion in the States principally affected. It is destroying the amicable relations between the white and Negro races that have been created through ninety years of patient effort by the good people of both races. It has planted hatred and suspicion where there has been heretofore friendship and understanding.

Without regard to the consent of the governed, outside agitators are threatening immediate and revolutionary changes in our public-school systems. If done, this is certain to destroy the system of public education in some of the States. . . .

We pledge ourselves to use all lawful means to bring about a reversal of this decision which is contrary to the Constitution and to prevent the use of force in its implementation.

Source: "Declaration of Constitutional Principles," *Congressional Record*, 84th Congress, 2d Session, March 12, 1956, 4460–61.

give up her seat to a white man. Parks's arrest rallied civic, labor, and religious groups and sparked a bus boycott that involved nearly the entire black community. Instead of riding buses, black commuters walked to work or joined car pools. White officials refused to capitulate and fought back by arresting leaders of the **Montgomery Improvement Association**,

Source 25.3

Ella Baker | "Bigger Than a Hamburger," 1960

The Student Leadership Conference made it crystal clear that current sit-ins and other demonstrations are concerned with something much bigger than a hamburger or even a giant-sized Coke.

Whatever may be the difference in approach to their goal, the Negro and white students, North and South, are seeking to rid America of the scourge of racial segregation and discrimination— not only at lunch counters, but in every aspect of life.

In reports, casual conversations, discussion groups, and speeches, the sense and the spirit of the following statement that appeared in the initial newsletter of the students at Barber-Scotia College, Concord, N.C., were re-echoed time and again: "We want the world to know that we no longer accept the inferior position of second-class citizenship. We are willing to go to jail, be ridiculed, spat upon, and even suffer physical violence to obtain First Class Citizenship."

By and large, this feeling that they have a destined date with freedom, was not limited to a drive for personal freedom, or even freedom for the Negro in the South. Repeatedly it was emphasized that the movement was concerned with the moral implications of racial discrimination for the "whole world" and the "Human Race."

This universality of approach was linked with a perceptive recognition that "it is important to keep the movement democratic and to avoid struggles for personal leadership."

It was further evident that desire for supportive cooperation from adult leaders and the adult community was also tempered by apprehension that adults might try to "capture" the student movement. The students showed willingness to be met on the basis of equality, but were intolerant of anything that smacked of manipulation or domination.

This inclination toward group-centered leadership, rather than toward a leader-centered group pattern of organization, was refreshing indeed to those of the older group who bear the scars of the battle, the frustrations and the disillusionment that come when the prophetic leader turns out to have heavy feet of clay.

Source: Ella Baker, "Bigger Than a Hamburger," *Southern Patriot*, June 1960, 4.

Interpret the Evidence

1. Why do the signers of the Southern Manifesto condemn the *Brown* decision?
2. According to Ella Baker, why are the goals of the civil rights movement "bigger than a hamburger"?
3. How does Baker define "rights" differently than the signers of the Southern Manifesto?

Put It in Context

How did the new generation of young civil rights activists challenge both southern segregationists and older civil rights advocates?

the organization that coordinated the protest. Other whites hurled insults at blacks and engaged in violence. After more than a year of conflict, the Supreme Court ruled in favor of the complete desegregation of Montgomery's buses.

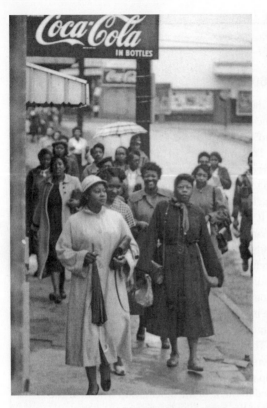

Montgomery Bus Boycott, 1956   Two months after African American residents of Montgomery, Alabama, began their boycott of the city buses to protest segregation and mistreatment, the black community kept up its boycott despite violence and intimidation. Black women had made up the majority of bus riders, and this photograph, taken on February 1, 1956, shows many of them walking to work or to stores for shopping. Don Cravens/Getty Images

Out of this landmark struggle, Martin Luther King Jr. emerged as the civil rights movement's most charismatic leader. His personal courage and power of oratory inspired nearly all segments of the African American community. Twenty-six years old at the time of Parks's arrest, King was the pastor of the prestigious Dexter Avenue Baptist Church. Though King was familiar with the nonviolent methods of the Indian revolutionary Mohandas Gandhi and the civil disobedience of the nineteenth-century writer Henry David Thoreau, he drew his inspiration and commitment to these principles mainly from black church and secular leaders such as A. Philip Randolph and Bayard Rustin. King understood how to convey the goals of the civil rights movement to sympathetic white Americans, but his vision and passion grew out of black communities. At the outset of the Montgomery bus boycott, King noted proudly of the boycott: "When the history books are written in future generations, the historians will have to pause and say 'There lived a great people — a Black people — who injected new meaning and dignity into the veins of civilization.' "

The Montgomery bus boycott made King a national civil rights leader, but it did not guarantee him further success. In 1957 King and a like-minded group of southern black ministers formed the **Southern Christian Leadership Conference (SCLC)** to spread nonviolent protest throughout the region, but except in a few cities, such as Tallahassee, Florida, additional bus boycotts did not take hold.

White Resistance to Desegregation.

Segregationists responded forcefully to halt black efforts to eliminate Jim Crow. In 1956, 101 southern congressmen issued a manifesto denouncing the 1954 *Brown* opinion and pledging to resist it through "lawful means." Other white southerners went beyond the law. In 1957 a federal court approved a plan submitted by the Little Rock, Arkansas School Board to integrate Central High School. However, the state's governor, Orval Faubus, obstructed the court ruling by sending the state National Guard to keep out nine black students chosen to attend Central High. Faced with blatant state resistance to federal authority, President Eisenhower placed the National Guard under federal control and sent in the 101st Airborne Division to restore order after a mob blocked the students from entering the school. These black pioneers, who became known as the **Little Rock Nine**, attended classes for the year under the protection of the National Guard but still encountered considerable harassment from white students. In defiance of the high court, other school districts, such as Prince Edward County, Virginia, chose to close their public schools rather than desegregate. By the end of the decade, public schools in the South remained mostly segregated.

The white South used other forms of violence and intimidation to preserve segregation. The third incarnation of the Ku Klux Klan (KKK) appeared after World War II to strike back at growing African American challenges to white supremacy. This terrorist group threatened, injured, and killed blacks they considered "uppity." Following the *Brown* decision, segregationists also formed the White Citizens' Council (WCC). The WCC drew members largely from businessmen and professionals. The WCC generally intimidated blacks by threatening to fire them from jobs or denying them credit from banks. In Alabama, WCC members launched a campaign against radio stations playing the kind of rock 'n' roll music that Alan Freed popularized in New York City because they believed that it fostered close interracial contact.

The WCC and the KKK created a racial climate in the deep South that encouraged whites to believe they could get away with murder to defend white supremacy. In the summer of 1955, Emmett Till, a fourteen-year-old from Chicago who was visiting his great-uncle in Mississippi, was killed because he allegedly flirted with a white woman in a country store. Although the two accused killers were brought to trial, an all-white jury quickly acquitted them. The white woman, Carolyn Bryant, later admitted that her accusations were false.

The Sit-Ins. With boycotts petering out and white violence rising, African Americans, especially high school and college students, developed new techniques to confront discrimination, including sit-ins, in which protesters seat themselves in a strategic spot and refuse to move until their demands are met or they are forcibly evicted. These mass protests really got off the ground in February 1960, when four students at historically black North Carolina A&T University in Greensboro initiated sit-ins at the whites-only lunch counters in Woolworth and Kress department stores. Their demonstrations sparked similar efforts throughout the Southeast (Map 25.1).

A few months after the sit-ins began, a number of participants formed the **Student Nonviolent Coordinating Committee (SNCC)**. The organization's young members sought to challenge racial segregation in the South and to create interracial communities based on economic equality and political democracy. This generation of black and white sit-in veterans came of age in the 1950s at a time when Cold War democratic rhetoric and the Supreme Court's *Brown* decision raised their expectations for racial equality. Yet these young activists, including the Alabamian teenager and future congressman John Lewis, often saw their hopes dashed by southern segregationist resistance, including the murder of Emmett Till, which both horrified and helped mobilize them to fight for black equality.

Explore ▸

For differing perspectives on when the civil rights movement began, read Sources 25.4 and 25.5.

Civil Rights Struggles in the North. Northern racism was systemic and powerful, but often invisible. Residential segregation reinforced racial segregation in public neighborhood schools. Banks used redlining to map out neighborhoods where African Americans could not obtain home mortgages. Public service jobs in many police and fire departments favored the descendants of white immigrants who had first held these posts in the late nineteenth century. Because blacks were commonly the last hired by most employers, seniority rules worked against them when it came to cutting jobs. When private

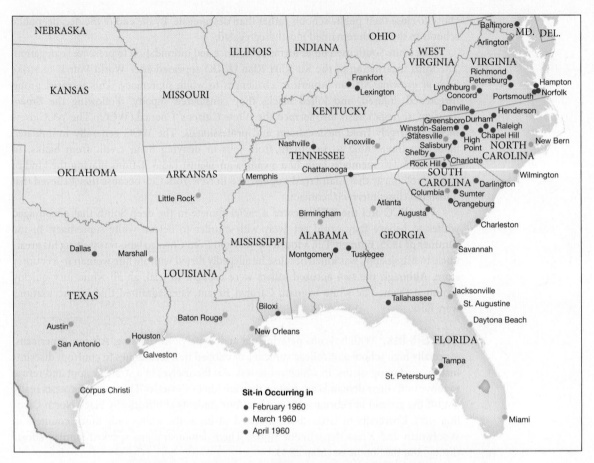

MAP 25.1   Lunch Counter Sit-Ins, February–April 1960

After starting slowly in the late 1950s, lunch counter sit-ins exploded in 1960 following a sit-in by college students in Greensboro, North Carolina. Within three months, sit-ins erupted in fifty-eight cities across the South. The participation of high school and college students revitalized the civil rights movement and led to the formation of the Student Nonviolent Coordinating Committee in April 1960.

businesses hired African Americans, they usually placed them in the lowest wage positions. Some labor unions also practiced discrimination by excluding blacks from joining, while others confined them to the lowest job categories.

Northern blacks also encountered discrimination in public accommodations. Public swimming pools in Pittsburgh, Denver, Cleveland, and Buffalo, among other cities, barred African Americans. Many restaurants refused to serve blacks. Palisades Amusement Park, overlooking the Hudson River from New Jersey, was off-limits to African Americans, as was the main amusement park in Cincinnati. Even with a paycheck, one observer remarked, black workers "couldn't enjoy themselves, in terms of theaters and other things. . . . They couldn't use their money for purposes of themselves or their families."

Despite widespread racial discrimination in the entire country, there were significant differences between the North and South. Most northern blacks could vote, and cities such as Chicago and New York had elected African Americans to municipal offices and to Congress. Children living in adjacent black and white neighborhoods attended public schools together. The City College of New York, a free public university, admitted African Americans, including Colin Powell, the future secretary of state. Blacks rode on public transportation without the Jim Crow restrictions imposed in the South. Lynching was rare in the North, though the Ku Klux Klan flourished in the region in the 1920s. In addition, northern civil rights advocates made gradual inroads against racial discrimination. In the 1950s New York City passed a fair housing law and California created a fair employment practices commission.

Civil Rights Struggles in the West.
World War II sparked a migration of African Americans to the West as part of the larger population movement to the Sun Belt. From 1940 to 1960, the black population in the region jumped from 4.9 to 5.4 percent of the total population and numbered more than 1.2 million. In the West, as in the North, the black population explosion brought unwarranted attention from police. African Americans who walked through white neighborhoods often found themselves targeted and confronted by white policemen. William Parker, the Los Angeles police chief, summed up the attitude of his department: "Any time that a person is in a place other than his place of residence or where he is conducting business . . . it might be a cause for inquiry." This attitude gave police license to engage in racial profiling.

Encountering various forms of racial discrimination, African Americans waged boycotts and sit-ins of businesses that refused blacks equal service in Lawrence, Kansas and Albuquerque, New Mexico. Perhaps the most significant protest occurred in Oklahoma City. In August 1958, the teenagers of the NAACP Youth Council and their adult adviser, Clara M. Luper, led sit-ins to desegregate lunch counters in downtown stores. Having succeeded in integrating a dozen facilities, the movement waged a six-year struggle to end discrimination in public accommodations throughout the city.

Other marginalized groups in the postwar West also struggled for equality. For Mexican Americans World War II inspired such challenges. In southern California, they formed Unity Leagues to protest segregation, and they often joined with African American groups in addressing discrimination. In 1947, the League of United Latin American Citizens (LULAC) won a case in federal court in *Mendez v. Westminster* prohibiting separate public schools for Mexican-American students. Spurred on by such efforts, Mexican Americans in 1949 succeeded in electing Edward Roybal to the Los Angeles City Council, the first American of Mexican descent to serve on that body since 1888. In Texas LULAC succeeded through litigation and boycotts in desegregating movie theaters, swimming pools, restaurants, and other public accommodations. LULAC also brought an end to discrimination in jury selection. Once Jackie Robinson integrated baseball in 1947, he opened the way for Afro-Hispanic ballplayers. Two years later, Orestes "Minnie" Miñoso, an Afro-Cuban, made it to the major leagues, playing for the Cleveland Indians.

World War II helped advance civil rights for Chinese Americans. In 1943 Congress repealed the exclusion law and followed up by passing the War Brides Act in 1945, which resulted in the admission of 6,000 Chinese women to the United States. However, the fall of China to the Communists in 1949 and the beginning of the Korean War the next year posed

Comparative Secondary Source Analysis

When Did the Civil Rights Movement Begin?

The "classical" phase of the civil rights movement spans the years from *Brown v. Board of Education* (1954) to the death of Martin Luther King Jr. (1968). Critics of this timeline contend that it places too much emphasis on national events and national leaders, almost all of whom were men. Instead, they find a longer civil rights movement that stretches back to the 1930s and 1940s and includes women, working people, and radicals. The following debate between two historians raises the larger question of when historical periods begin and end. Writing within several years of each other, Jacquelyn Dowd Hall and Steven F. Lawson reach different conclusions based on contrasting conceptions of the civil rights struggle as a social movement.

Source 25.4

Jacquelyn Dowd Hall | The Long Civil Rights Movement, 2005

"Another force also rose from the caldron of the Great Depression and crested in the 1940s: a powerful social movement sparked by the alchemy of laborites, civil rights activists, progressive New Dealers, and black and white radicals, some of whom were associated with the Communist party . . . signals the movement's commitment to building coalitions, the expansiveness of the social democratic vision, and the importance of its black radical and laborite leadership. A national movement with a vital southern wing, civil rights unionism was not just a precursor of the modern civil rights movement. It was its decisive first phase.

The link between race and class lay at the heart of the movement's political imagination. . . . [C]ivil rights unionists sought to combine protection from discrimination with universalistic social welfare policies and individual rights with labor rights. For them, workplace democracy, union wages, and fair and full employment went hand in hand with open, affordable housing, political enfranchisement, educational equity, and an enhanced safety net, including health care for all. . . . Extending the New Deal and reforming the South were two sides of the same coin. . . . To challenge the southern Democrats' congressional stranglehold, the movement had to enfranchise black and white southern workers and bring them into the house of labor, thus creating a constituency on which the region's emerging pro-civil rights, pro-labor politicians could rely."

Source: Jacquelyn Dowd Hall, "The Long Civil Rights Movement and the Political Uses of the Past," *Journal of American History* 91 (March 2005), 1245–46.

new challenges to Chinese communities on the West Coast. Although organizations such as the Six Companies of San Francisco denounced Communist China and pledged their loyalty to the United States, Cold War witch-hunts targeted the Chinese. With the Chinese Communists fighting against the United States in Korea, some regarded Chinese people in America with suspicion. "People would look at you in the street and think," one Chinese woman recalled, "'Well you're one of the enemy.'" The federal government established a

Source 25.5

Steven F. Lawson | The Short Civil Rights Movement, 2011

"There was a genuine movement for social change in the South during the New Deal era, but it took on a different shape from the civil rights movement that followed in the next two decades. Civil rights unions . . . performed the work of extending civil rights and laid the groundwork for what followed, but this remained distinct from the civil rights movement. . . . Class mattered more than race, and critics targeted capitalism as the source of black oppression. . . . [O]nly through a restructuring of corporate capitalism would genuine economic democracy emerge and white supremacy collapse. Although African American progressives actively participated in unions . . . the leadership and membership of these organizations in the South consisted mainly of whites. . . . These activists were courageous, visionary, and essential, but they composed only a tiny fraction of the southern population. Their influence should be neither ignored nor exaggerated.

. . . By the time of the *Brown* decision and [Emmett] Till's murder, African Americans possessed the institutional structures necessary to mobilize to close the gap between their expectations of change and the brutal reality of white supremacy. At the national level the NAACP led the way, followed by the SCLC, CORE, and SNCC. Indeed, after *Brown*, state-led efforts to destroy the NAACP, considered the most radical of black organizations by southern white authorities, spurred the creation of new protest organizations locally and throughout the South. Black churches, civic associations, and informal community networks added organizational muscle to the demands for racial equality during the 1950s and 1960s. Without these structures . . . the yearning for civil rights would not have grown into a movement, and people would not have taken action against the power of state-supported white supremacy."

Source: Steven F. Lawson, "Long Origins of the Short Civil Rights Movement, 1954-1968," in *Freedom Rights: New Perspectives on the Civil Rights Movement*, edited by Daniel McGuire and John Dittmer (Lexington, Kentucky: University Press of Kentucky, 2011), 14–15, 19, 22–23.

Examine the Sources

1. Describe the major difference between the Hall and Lawson interpretations of when the civil rights movement began.
2. Despite this difference, what similarities in their arguments can you find?

Put It in Context

Historians often look for major turning points, after which there was notable change from before. Why does it matter what turning points historians select for when the civil rights movement began and ended?

"Confession Program" by which Chinese people illegally in the country would be allowed to stay if they came forward, acknowledged their loyalty to the United States, and provided information about friends and relatives. Some 10,000 Chinese in San Francisco participated in this program.

Despite these hardships, Chinese Americans made great economic strides. Chinatowns shrank in population as their upwardly mobile residents moved to the suburbs. By 1959

Chinese Americans had a median family income of $6,207, compared with $5,660 for all Americans.

During the late 1940s and 1950s, Japanese Americans attempted to rebuild their lives following their wartime evacuation and internment. Overall, they succeeded. Many returned to the West Coast and although they found their neighborhoods occupied by other ethnic groups and their businesses in other hands, they took whatever jobs they could find and stressed education for their children. The McCarran-Walter Immigration Act of 1952 made it possible for Japanese aliens to become U.S. citizens. In addition, California repealed its Alien Land Law of 1913, which prohibited noncitizen Japanese from purchasing land. In 1955 about 40,000 Japanese Americans lived in Los Angeles, a figure slightly higher than the city's prewar population. Like other Americans, they began moving their families to suburbs such as Gardena, a half-hour ride from downtown Los Angeles. The federal government neither apologized for its wartime treatment of the Japanese nor awarded them financial compensation for their losses; this would happen three decades later.

Review & Relate

- What strategies did African Americans adopt in the 1940s and 1950s to fight segregation and discrimination? How did other racial and ethnic minorities pursue equality?

- How and why did white southerners resist efforts to end segregation?

Domestic Politics in the Eisenhower Era

Despite the existence of civil rights protesters, rock 'n' roll upstarts, intellectual dissenters, and sexual revolutionaries, the 1950s seemed to many a tranquil, even dull period. This impression owes a great deal to the leadership of President Dwight D. Eisenhower. Serving two terms from 1953 to 1961, Eisenhower, or "Ike" as he was affectionately called, convinced the majority of Americans that their country was in good hands regardless of political turbulence at home and heated international conflicts abroad. By 1960, however, the nation was ready for a new generation of leadership.

Modern Republicanism. President Eisenhower, a World War II hero, radiated strength and trust, qualities the American people found very attractive as they rebuilt their lives and established families in the 1950s. In November 1952, Eisenhower coasted to victory over the Democratic candidate Adlai Stevenson, winning 55 percent of the popular vote and 83 percent of the electoral vote. The Republicans managed to win slim majorities in the Senate and the House, but within two years the Democrats regained control of Congress.

Eisenhower adopted **Modern Republicanism**, which tried to fit the traditional Republican Party ideals of individualism and fiscal restraint within the broad framework of Franklin Roosevelt's New Deal. As Eisenhower wrote to his brother, "Should any political party attempt to abolish social security, unemployment insurance, and eliminate labor laws and farm programs, you would not hear of that party again in our political history." With

Democrats in control of Congress after 1954, Republicans agreed to raise Social Security benefits and to include coverage for some ten million additional workers. Congress and the president retained another New Deal mainstay, the minimum wage, and increased it from 75 cents to $1 an hour. Departing from traditional Republican criticism of big government, the Eisenhower administration added the Department of Health, Education, and Welfare to the cabinet in 1953.

In 1956 the Eisenhower administration sponsored the **National Interstate and Defense Highway Act**, which provided funds for the construction of 42,500 miles of roads throughout the country, boosting both suburbanization and national defense. In order to build this highway network, planners designed a road system that tore through black urban neighborhoods. Residents in the path of these highways lost their homes, businesses, churches, and entertainment centers. During the first twenty years of interstate highway construction over one million people, including 475,000 families, most of them African Americans, were displaced. An example of structural racism, the highway legislation produced longterm socio-economic effects.

In 1958 Eisenhower signed into law the National Defense Education Act, which provided federal aid for instruction in science, math, and foreign languages and graduate fellowships and loans for college students. He portrayed the new law as a way to catch up with the Soviets, who the previous year had successfully launched the first artificial satellite, called *Sputnik*, into outer space.

For six of Eisenhower's eight years in office, the president had to work with Democratic majorities in Congress. Overall, he managed to forge bipartisan support for his proposals, most significantly civil rights. Under his administration's leadership, Republicans joined with Democrats, led by Senate Majority Leader Lyndon B. Johnson, to pass the first pieces of civil rights legislation since Reconstruction. In 1957 and 1960, Eisenhower signed into law two bills that extended the authority of the federal government to file court challenges against southern election officials who blocked African Americans from registering to vote. However, southern Democratic senators thwarted Congress from passing even stronger voting measures or acts that would have enforced school desegregation.

Eisenhower administration policy, however, did not work to the benefit of Native Americans. The federal government reversed many of the reforms instituted during the New Deal. In the 1950s the Bureau of Indian Affairs (BIA) adopted the policy of termination and relocation of Indian tribes. Those tribes deemed to have achieved the most "progress," such as the Flatheads of Montana, the Klamaths of Oregon, and the Hoopas of northern California, were treated as ordinary American citizens, which resulted in termination of their federal benefits and transfer of their tribal lands to state and local governments. The National Congress of American Indians fought unsuccessfully against this program.

The government also relocated Indians to urban areas. Between 1952 and 1960, the BIA encouraged more than 30,000 Indians to move from reservations to cities. The Indian population of Los Angeles grew to 25,000, including members of the Navajo, Sioux, and Cherokee nations. Although thousands of Indians took advantage of the relocation program, many had difficulty adjusting to urban life and fell into poverty.

The Eisenhower administration also repatriated undocumented Mexican laborers. The *bracero* program instituted in 1942, had permitted immigration from Mexico into the United States, but large agricultural growers sought an even greater supply of cheap labor.

When Mexicans crossed the border illegally, simply seeking work, Mexico complained because it also needed a larger supply of agricultural workers. American labor groups protested that illegal immigrants took jobs away from Americans. In 1954, Eisenhower's Immigration and Naturalization Service rounded up undocumented Mexicans, mainly in Texas and California, and returned them to Mexico. Those deported often suffered harsh conditions, and seven deportees drowned after they jumped ship. "Operation Wetback," as the program was dubbed using a derogatory term for Mexicans, forced an estimated 250,000 to 1.3 million Mexicans to leave the United States.

The same year as the deportations began, the U.S. Supreme Court ruled in favor of Mexican Americans in *Hernandez v. Texas* (1954). The justices decided unanimously that the equal protection clause of the Fourteenth Amendment protects Mexican Americans as a distinct nationality group. The court found that a Texas county had deprived a defendant of his constitutional rights in a criminal trial, because the state systematically excluded Mexican Americans from serving on juries. Moreover, the case marked the first time in history that Mexican American attorneys — Carlos C. Cadena, Gustavo C. Garcia, and Johnny Herrara — argued before the Supreme Court.

The Election of 1960.
Even after serving two terms, Eisenhower remained popular. However, he could not run for a third term, barred by the Twenty-second Amendment (1951), and Vice President Richard M. Nixon ran as the Republican candidate for president in 1960. Unlike Eisenhower, Nixon was not universally liked or respected. His reputation for unsavory political combat drew the scorn of Democrats, especially liberals. And Nixon had to fend off charges that Republicans, as embodied in the seventy-year-old Eisenhower, were out-of-date and out of new ideas.

The Democratic candidate for president in 1960, Senator John F. Kennedy of Massachusetts, promised to instill renewed "vigor" in the White House and get the country moving again. Yet Kennedy did not differ much from his Republican rival on domestic and foreign policy issues. While Kennedy employed a rhetoric of high-minded change, he had

Deporting Mexican Americans   A group of Mexican immigrants who had come to the United States to work without proper documentation are rounded up and marched off by U.S. officials across the border to Mexico. The largest number of deportations occurred during the Eisenhower Administration's "Operation Wetback." Loomis Dean/The LIFE Picture Collection via Getty Images

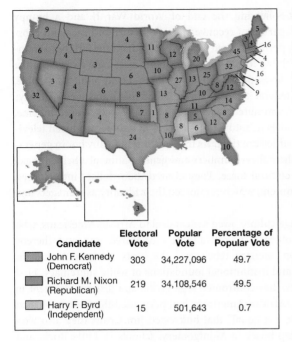

Candidate	Electoral Vote	Popular Vote	Percentage of Popular Vote
John F. Kennedy (Democrat)	303	34,227,096	49.7
Richard M. Nixon (Republican)	219	34,108,546	49.5
Harry F. Byrd (Independent)	15	501,643	0.7

MAP 25.2 The Election of 1960

The 1960 presidential candidates differed little on major policy issues. John F. Kennedy gained the White House by winning back black voters who had supported Eisenhower, gaining crucial support from Catholic voters across the country, and appearing more presidential on the first televised debate in history. Still, his margin of victory was razor thin.

not compiled a distinguished record in the Senate. Moreover, his family's fortune had paved the way for his political career, and he had earned a well-justified reputation in Washington as a playboy and womanizer.

The outcome of the 1960 election turned on several factors. The country was experiencing a slight economic recession, reviving memories in older voters of the Great Depression, which had begun with the Republican Herbert Hoover in power. In addition, presidential candidates faced off on television for the first time, participating in four televised debates. TV emphasized visual style and presentation. In the first debate, with Nixon having just recovered from a stay in the hospital and looking haggard, Kennedy convinced a majority of viewers that he possessed the presidential bearing for the job. Nixon performed better in the next three debates, but the damage had been done. Still, Kennedy had to overcome considerable religious prejudice to win the election. No Catholic had ever won the presidency, and the prejudices of Protestants, especially in the South, threatened to divert critical votes from Kennedy's Democratic base. While many southern Democrats supported Nixon, Kennedy balanced out these defections by gaining votes from the nation's Catholics, especially in northern states rich in electoral votes (Map 25.2).

Race also exerted a critical influence. Nixon and Kennedy had similar records on civil rights, and if anything, Nixon's was slightly stronger. However, on October 19, 1960, when Atlanta police arrested Martin Luther King Jr. for participating in a restaurant sit-in, Kennedy sprang to his defense, whereas Nixon kept his distance. Kennedy telephoned the civil rights leader's wife to offer his sympathy and used his influence to get King released from jail. As a result, Kennedy won back for Democrats 7 percent of black voters who had supported Eisenhower in 1956. Kennedy triumphed by a margin of less than 1 percent of the popular vote, underscoring the importance of the African American electorate.

Review & Relate

■ Why did Eisenhower adopt a moderate domestic agenda? What were his most notable domestic accomplishments and failures?

■ Why did Kennedy win the 1960 presidential election?

Conclusion: Postwar Politics and Culture

Following the end of World War II and a bumpy period of reconversion, the return of peace and prosperity fostered a baby boom that sent families scrambling for new housing and increasingly away from the cities. Suburbs grew as housing developers such as William Levitt built affordable, mass-produced homes and as the federal government provided loans and new highways that allowed suburban residents to commute to their urban jobs. With increased income, consumers purchased the latest models in automobiles as well as newly introduced televisions, reshaping how they spent their leisure time. As the wartime and baby boom generations entered their teenage years, their sheer numbers and general affluence helped make them a significant economic and cultural force. They poured their dollars into clothes, music, and other forms of entertainment, which reinforced their identity as teenagers and set them apart from adults.

The increasingly distinct teenage culture owed a great deal to African Americans, who contributed to the development of rock 'n' roll and revolutionized jazz and thereby influenced cultural challenges from teenage rebels and the beats. African Americans focused on tearing down the legal and institutional foundations of white supremacy. First in the courts and then in the streets, they confronted segregation and disfranchisement in the South. By the end of the 1950s, African Americans had persuaded the Supreme Court to reverse the doctrine of "separate but equal" that buttressed Jim Crow; they also won significant victories in desegregating buses in Montgomery, schools in Little Rock, and lunch counters in Greensboro. Black teenagers reinvigorated the civil rights movement through their boldness and energy, opening the path for even greater racial changes in the coming decade. In the North and West, African Americans faced a more subtle and enduring form of Jim Crow — **systemic racism** contained in housing practices, education, and criminal justice institutions. Other marginalized groups, inspired by the civil rights movement, pursued equal rights for themselves. In addition to struggles over racial equality, the 1950s witnessed serious tensions at home. Teenage cultural rebellion, sexual revolution, and McCarthyite witch-hunts, in addition to a bloody war in Korea, confronted the citizens of Alan Freed's and Grace Metalious's America. Nevertheless, the popular image of the 1950s as a tranquil and innocent period persists, with President Eisenhower remaining a symbol for the age. He provided moderate leadership that helped the country adjust to dramatic changes. His critics complained that the nation had lost its spirit of adventure, misplaced its ability to distinguish between community and conformity, failed to live up to ideals of racial and economic justice, and relinquished its primary place in the world. Nevertheless, most Americans emerging from decades of depression and war felt satisfied with the new lives they were building: They still liked Ike.

When the Republican Eisenhower left office in 1961, a new decade began with a Democratic president in charge. Yet the challenges that Eisenhower had faced and the diplomatic, social, and cultural forces that propelled them had not diminished. During the following years, many of the young people who had benefited from the peace and prosperity of the 1950s would lead the way in questioning the role of the United States in world affairs and its commitment to democracy, freedom, and equality at home.

Timeline of Events

1940–1960	Migration to Sun Belt swells region's population
1944	Servicemen's Readjustment Act (GI Bill)
1945–1960	U.S. gross national product soars 250 percent; 60 percent of Americans achieve middle-class status; union membership reaches new high
1947	Taft-Hartley Act
	President's Committee on Civil Rights issues *To Secure These Rights*
	Jackie Robinson becomes the first black baseball player to enter the major leagues
1954–1958	Eisenhower adopts Modern Republicanism and expands domestic programs
1954	*Brown v. Board of Education of Topeka, Kansas* Supreme Court ruling
	Operation Wetback
1955–1956	Montgomery bus boycott
1955	Jonas Salk develops polio vaccine
	Emmett Till murdered
1956	Grace Metalious publishes *Peyton Place*
	National Interstate and Defense Highway Act
1957	Martin Luther King Jr. and other black ministers form Southern Christian Leadership Conference (SCLC)
	School desegregation in Little Rock, Arkansas, enforced
	Soviet Union launches *Sputnik*
1960	Student Nonviolent Coordinating Committee (SNCC) formed

Key Terms

Servicemen's Readjustment Act (GI Bill), *858*

Taft-Hartley Act, *858*

Levittown, *862*

Sun Belt, *863*

Beats, *868*

To Secure These Rights, *870*

Brown v. Board of Education of Topeka, Kansas, *871*

Montgomery Improvement Association, *872*

Southern Christian Leadership Conference (SCLC), *874*

Little Rock Nine, *874*

Student Nonviolent Coordinating Committee (SNCC), *875*

Modern Republicanism, *880*

National Interstate and Defense Highway Act, *881*

systemic racism, *884*

Review & Relate

1. How did the conversion from war to peacetime affect the economy, society, and politics in the United States?

2. What factors contributed to the economic and population growth of the 1950s, and how did they contribute to suburbanization and the growth in the Sun Belt?

3. What trends in American popular culture did the television shows and popular music of the 1950s reflect?

4. How did artists, writers, and social critics challenge the mainstream politics and culture of the 1950s?

5. What strategies did African Americans adopt in the 1940s and 1950s to fight segregation and discrimination? How did other racial and ethnic minorities pursue equality?

6. How and why did white southerners resist efforts to end segregation?

7. Why did Eisenhower adopt a moderate domestic agenda? What were his most notable domestic accomplishments and failures?

8. Why did Kennedy win the 1960 presidential election?

Teenagers in Postwar America

▶ Examine how teenagers affected the U.S. economy, culture, and politics in the postwar period (1945–1961).

"There are many different opinions about just what is the most exclusive club in America these days," observed Dick Clark in his 1959 book *Your Happiest Years* (Source 25.6). But for Clark, the most exclusive and important club was the one he called "Teenagers of America, Inc." Still, for Clark and most other Americans that club was exclusively white—African American, Latino, and Asian teenagers rarely appear in a positive light. Indeed, Clark's appraisal of American society in 1959 may have been self-serving—after all, his career hinged largely on appealing to teen audiences—but he was not alone in his belief in the significance of teenagers in postwar American society.

Even now, pop culture often portrays the 1950s as a simpler time when girls wore poodle skirts and swooned over Elvis Presley (Source 25.7), while boys raced hot-rod cars and took their dates to the malt shop. In this vision, teens were concerned with little more than increasing their popularity, "going steady," and watching *American Bandstand*. As the following documents illustrate, there is much to support this interpretation of postwar teen culture. Young people made rock 'n' roll into an enduring and lucrative entertainment industry, shaped the advertising and manufacture of products, and were the focus of numerous television shows and movies.

But there are other, more complicated images of teen life in this era. For one, juvenile delinquency was seen by many as a serious problem. Actor James Dean's *Rebel Without a Cause* competed with singer Pat Boone's squeaky-clean haircut and white shoes. In 1959 actor Sandra Dee portrayed both a perky Malibu surfer in *Gidget* and an unwed pregnant teen in *A Summer Place*. Teens also grew up under the looming threat of the Cold War, the Korean War, and McCarthyism. African Americans helped popularize rock 'n' roll, but in Little Rock, Arkansas, and elsewhere in the South, black teenagers risked their lives to desegregate public schools (Source 25.8).

The following sources consider different aspects of teen life and postwar culture in the 1950s. They also illustrate teenagers in the 1950s who had more on their minds than just dating and having a good time (Sources 25.9 and 25.10).

Source 25.6

Dick Clark | *Your Happiest Years,* 1959

By 1959 Dick Clark was a nationally popular disc jockey and host of television's *American Bandstand*. Always seen in a suit and tie, Clark, with his clean-cut good looks, projected a more wholesome vision of rock 'n' roll than did many of his contemporaries, such as Alan Freed. Clark's advice book for teenagers includes instructions on manners, makeup, and getting along with parents and other teens, as well as advice on romantic relationships.

We've mentioned before that it is very important to build a wide circle of friends, both fellows and girls. There are two reasons for this, but one is basic to dating. That is, the more fellows or girls you meet, the better the possibility that one or two might consider you what we called "date bait." The other reason, and it's a long shot, is that having a wide circle of friends, you meet more different types of people and learn how to adjust to them. This pays off after the teen years are past and you are either at work or away at school. But in order to get yourself into this teenage world of dating, let's just say you'll grow very lonely if you lock yourself away from eligible fellows or girls.

You've joined the staff of the school paper, or you are a member of a crowd of fellows that seem to attract a liberal following of the fair sex to your athletic contests. Or, on the distaff [female] side, you've a fine collection of girl friends—they're especially fine if they have at least one or two brothers of dating age. If you haven't quite reached that stage of teenage paradise yet, there are such events as community dances, or mixed school or church activities, that bring manly blips on your radarscope. In other words, you've gotten out of your shell and into the teenage swim. Don't be shy. You know that all the other fellows and girls your own age feel the same way you do. Remember, no self-pity. Braces on your teeth can't dim the glow of a sparkling personality, and neither can a shortage of new dresses or suits be an alibi for what is really a lack of effort on your part. Your fellow teenagers are eager to find sincere friends, and if you can prove that you are one then you definitely classify as "date bait." There is a phrase that I heard from General Carlos P. Romulo, the Philippines' famed patriot and Ambassador to the United States, and I think it applies here. "A stranger," the General said, "is a friend that I haven't met." It's a wonderful application of the Golden Rule, and it's one sentence that can carry a teenager through a lot of embarrassing uncertainty.

Accepting your fellow teenagers as friends, known or unknown, is another step toward that all-important phone call or whispered conference in the hall at school. You know the one I mean. It may begin, "Uh, Margie . . . uh, this Saturday night . . . uh, well, some of us were. . . ." And a date is born.

Source: Dick Clark, *Your Happiest Years* (New York: Random House, 1959), 100–101.

Source 25.7

Charlotte Jones | Letter on Elvis, 1957

Nothing highlighted the growing generation gap more than rock 'n' roll. When Elvis Presley burst onto the music scene in the mid-1950s, adults criticized his music and gyrating hips, while teenage boys dressed to imitate his style, and teenage girls screamed and fainted at his concerts. In 1957 Charlotte Jones, an admiring fan, wrote the following letter to the conservative newspaper columnist George Sokolsky in response to Sokolsky's criticism of Presley's popularity.

There are too many people saying that Elvis is going to die out. When Elvis dies out is when the sun quits burning.

You say everybody is forgotten that is once great; George Washington has never been forgotten and nobody can be as great a president or as long remembered as he. Nobody can ever take his place or do what he did. Well, it's the same with Elvis. He'll always be remembered and nobody has ever [done] or ever will do the same thing as Elvis has.

Elvis is the king of popularity and we (teens of America) love him and we'll see he lives forever. Not his body but his name. Adults won't admit he's so great, because they're jealous! They know that their top singers weren't as great as Elvis. They're mad because their taste isn't quite as good as ours.

Look at James Dean, been dead for a year and he's bigger now than he ever was.

God gifted Elvis to us and you oughta thank him, not tear down the greatest thing the world has ever known: Elvis Presley!!!!!!

Scornfully yours,
Charlotte Jones

P.S.: And if you're over 30, you're old. You're certainly not young.

Source: George E. Sokolsky, "Teenager Puts Rap on Suggestion Elvis on Way Out," *Milwaukee Sentinel*, March 11, 1957, 5.

The Desegregation of Central High School, 1957

In 1957 nine black teenagers attempted to desegregate Central High School in Little Rock, Arkansas, pursuant to a federal court order. This photograph captures fifteen-year-old Elizabeth Eckford, one of the Little Rock Nine, surrounded by an angry white crowd on the first day of school. The photo also shows an enraged white student, Hazel Bryan, shouting at her to go home. Neither Eckford nor the other black students managed to attend school that day, but they entered Central High after President Eisenhower sent in federal troops to protect them.

The Commercial Appeal/ZUMApress.com

Gloria Lopez-Stafford | A Mexican American Childhood in El Paso, Texas, 1949

Born in 1937, Gloria Lopez-Stafford grew into her teenage years in the 1950s. While African Americans were fighting for integrated schools in neighboring Arkansas, Lopez-Stafford and her friends attended interracial schools. Still, as she relates in the following excerpt from her memoir, attending classes with whites did not necessarily satisfy Mexican American youths.

"Remember the Alamo!"

The banner slogan was draped across the blackboard of my social studies class in El Paso, Texas. The black letters jumped off the white background. The slogan on the banner was appropriate because the elementary school was named after Sam Houston, first president of the Texas Republic. . . .

It was September and we were going to the auditorium to see the movie, *The Battle of the Alamo*. Texas history was the course of study for the year and the whole week before the film we made salt maps of the state. I was very proud of my carved Ivory soap model of the Alamo. . . .

That year, my class at Houston School was about half Anglo and half Mexican. . . . *The Battle of the Alamo* was an old film, very dark and gray. The battle brought together small, overdressed Mexican men and big white men dressed in buckskins. As you probably know, the battle was fierce and it was won by a villain named Antonio López de Santa Anna. He was portrayed as a small ruthless man who made martyrs of the Anglos that day at the Alamo. There were 187 Anglos killed and 600 Mexicans killed.

After the film was over, the dark shades on the windows were lifted and the lights turned on. I felt uncomfortable as I looked around the auditorium. . . . I avoided the looks of my friends because I couldn't understand my confused feelings. I felt sick. I was painfully aware of being Mexican. And it wouldn't be the last time that year.

. . . I walked back quietly until my friend Linda ran up to me. Linda's family was from Monterrey

[Mexico] and she didn't live far from me.

"Gloria, who did you cheer for?" she asked in a quiet tone. I looked at her and looked around before I answered. "The Mexicans," I replied softly. Linda shrieked, "Me too." . . .

When we were back in the classroom, the teacher stood in front of the room directly beneath the banner. She was a slender, very white woman with sky blue eyes. . . . "The men at the Alamo were heroes—true Texans," she said in a soft voice. . . .

"Yeah. And Texas is for Texans," yelled a voice at the back of the classroom. . . . Even though I was born in Mexico, I had been a Texan since I was two years old. I am also a Mexican. Joe pushed me from behind and uttered a chant of mockery. My friend José across the aisle slugged him. He gestured to Joe with his fists to leave me alone. . . . Angry and confused, I put my head down so that no one could see me cry.

Source: Gloria López-Stafford, *A Place in El Paso: A Mexican American Childhood* (Albuquerque: University of New Mexico Press, 1996), 3–5.

"Why No Chinese American Delinquents?" 1955

Asian Americans had faced a great deal of prejudice from whites, especially on the West Coast. However, after World War II, the hard work and striving of Japanese and Chinese Americans to succeed reversed the traditional prejudices of many white Americans toward them, especially the younger generation. As the following magazine article shows, whereas teenagers in general were a source of concern for older Americans, Chinese teenagers were perceived as a "model minority."

Not long ago, a New York City judge wrote to the *New York Times* saying that not in the seventeen years he had been on the bench had a Chinese-American teen-ager been brought before him on a juvenile-delinquency charge. The judge said that he queried his colleagues on the matter and they, too, expressed their astonishment. They said that not one of the estimated 10,000 Chinese-American teenagers, to their knowledge, had ever been haled into court on a depredation, narcotics, speeding, burglary, vandalism, stickup, purse-snatching or mugging accusation. A check with San Francisco, where there is a large colony of Chinese-Americans, tells the same story. The same holds true of Chicago, where the police report "excellent" behavior on the part of Chinese-American youngsters.

P. H. Chang, Chinese consul-general in New York City, was asked to comment on this warm and amazing return. He said simply, "I have heard this story many times from many judges. They tell me that none of our people are ever brought before them for juvenile delinquency. They were surprised, but I was not. Why?

"I will tell you why I think this is so. Filial piety, the love for parents, is a cardinal virtue my people have brought over from the China that was once free. A Chinese child, no matter where he lives, is brought up to recognize that he cannot shame his parents. To do so would relegate him to worse than oblivion, for his parents would disown him and he would be cast free and alone from our traditions that go back many, many centuries.

"Before a Chinese child makes a move, be stops to think what the reaction on his parents will be. Will

they be proud or will they be ashamed? That is the sole question he asks himself. The answer comes readily, and thus he knows what is right and wrong.

"Above all other things, the Chinese teen-ager is anxious to please his parents before he pleases himself. Our family households work on the theory that the parents are wise and seasoned, and if the children follow the same course, they can do no wrong."

Today, there are some 100,000 Chinese-Americans in the United States, of whom 90 percent live in New York City, Chicago and San Francisco. Most are small businessmen in the import trade who deal with their own people in their own communities. Most, no matter whether wealthy or poor, maintain a strict, family-style home. Mealtimes are ceremonial affairs which must be attended by every member of the family. Holidays are celebrated in family style. Schooling, the reverence for religion and decorum, plus reverence for elders and family tradition, are the prime movers in developing the child from infancy.

Interpret the Evidence

1. Analyze which information in these documents confirms or challenges commonly held beliefs about teenagers in the 1950s.
2. Compare the assumptions about adults and teenagers in Sources 25.6 and 25.10. How do they differ, either in tone or in content, from those written *by* teens (Sources 25.7 and 25.9)?
3. Evaluate what Sources 25.7 and 25.10 tell us about generational differences.
4. Assess what these sources, especially 25.8, tell us about racial and ethnic differences among teenagers in the postwar era.

Put It in Context

How did the economy, politics, and culture of the postwar period (1945–1960) influence teen life in this era?

Liberalism and Its Challengers

1960–1973

Window to the Past

Nancy Ellin, Letter Describing Freedom Summer, 1964

In 1964, white and black volunteers spent a summer in Mississippi attempting to register voters and establishing Freedom Schools. Often surrounded by danger, they wrote letters to family and friends, such as the letter here, explaining the work they did, problems they encountered, and the courage of local blacks. ▶ To learn more about this primary source, see Source 26.7 on page 927.

June 30

Dear Dr. and Mrs. Ellin,

It was nice to get your letter today; we hope you will write often. I'm sure Joe will write to you any minute now, but I thought I might as well, too.

We got here OK, though we were frightened most of the way, quite unnecessarily. It was the people who came down in integrated cars who had the unpleasant time - refused service, cars following them, etc. We came down with a very nice girl who just graduated from Smith and who did quite a bit of driving.

We are currently hard at work getting the Freedom Schools organized. Joe and another boy have everyone typing up stencils of the Constitution, the Declaration of Independence, etc. The school enrollment is over 150; we are having official registration Thursday. The philosophy is to take everyone who comes; we will be teaching adults in the evening. There are 10 teachers, 8 more expected from New York City on Thursday. We also intend to recruit a few local people.

I, too, am sorry things came to such a pass. We felt terrible about causing you all such anguish, but we felt the decision was ours to make, and though we were very afraid and doubtful at Oxford, we made the decision to come. You must know that you were not the only parents who were worried, and some kids did drop out, one from our group, in fact, who was underage and couldn't get his parents' consent. Now that we are here we feel more than ever that coming here was the right things to do. Even if we don't teach a singlechild (and I think the odds are heavily against that) we still will have accomplished

After reading this chapter you will be able to:

- Evaluate President Kennedy's approaches to liberalism at home and in foreign affairs.

- Explain how the civil rights movement succeeded in convincing the federal government to enact the Civil Rights Act of 1964 and the Voting Rights Act of 1965.

- Describe the major legislative accomplishments of the Great Society.

- Explain why U.S. intervention in Vietnam escalated in the 1960s.

- Examine the challenges to liberalism from the political left and right and analyze their similarities and differences.

Comparing American Histories

As attorney general of California at the outset of World War II, **Earl Warren** helped convince President Franklin D. Roosevelt to order the relocation of 110,000 Japanese Americans. After the war, as governor, he continued to fight against perceived threats to national security by joining the anti-Communist crusade. In 1953 President Dwight D. Eisenhower appointed Warren to be chief

(*left*) **Earl Warren** Collection of the Supreme Court of the United States
(*right*) **Bayard Rustin** Library of Congress, Prints and Photographs Division [LC-USZ62-118986]

justice of the United States, a choice that many observers saw as a safe conservative pick.

As chief justice, however, Warren defied expectations and instead led the Supreme Court in a liberal direction. In 1954 Warren wrote the landmark opinion ordering school desegregation in *Brown v. Board of Education of Topeka, Kansas*. The Warren Court did not shrink from controversy, and its rulings expanding the rights of accused criminals, banning prayer in public school classrooms, and upholding birth control as a right of privacy evoked harsh criticism from the police, religious fundamentalists, and conservative politicians.

Unlike Earl Warren, **Bayard Rustin** worked outside of regular political and social channels to achieve change. Rustin joined the Young Communist League in the 1930s because of its commitment to economic justice, racial equality, and international peace. As a committed pacifist, however, Rustin quit the organization in 1941 when the party supported U.S. intervention in World War II and retreated on its fight against racial discrimination during the war.

In 1942 Rustin helped found the Congress of Racial Equality (CORE), an interracial organization that pioneered nonviolent, direct-action protests against racial bias. Rustin was imprisoned from 1943 to 1946 for declining to perform alternative service after he refused to register for the military draft. Following his release, in 1947 Rustin helped plan and lead the Journey of Reconciliation, which challenged segregation on interstate buses in the South. In the 1950s and 1960s, he became an adviser to Martin Luther King Jr. and a major strategist in the civil rights movement.

Rustin remained active in various causes throughout his life. One of his last efforts was perhaps his most personal: the struggle against antigay prejudice. Rustin had to conceal his sexual identity at a time when the public and his political allies rejected homosexuals. In the 1980s, as the gay liberation movement grew more vocal, Rustin spoke out for tolerance and equality until his death in 1987. ■

The American histories of Earl Warren and Bayard Rustin demonstrate the complexity of social change. The federal government had the power to encourage social movements by interpreting the Constitution, enacting legislation, and enforcing the law in a manner that eliminated barriers to racial, sexual, and political equality. Yet federal action would not have happened without the pressure applied by activists like Rustin. As president, Lyndon Johnson took action with his Great Society programs, but his escalation of the war in Vietnam divided his party and generated opposition from young activists on the left. At the same time, efforts to promote equality and social justice, along with the military stalemate in Vietnam, produced a strong reaction from conservatives who sought to roll back liberal gains; pursue their own policies of small government, low taxes, and self-reliance; and bring about an end to the war.

The Politics
of Liberalism

Hoping to build on the legacy of the New Deal, liberals sought to increase the role of the federal government in the economy, education, and health care. Most liberals supported a staunchly anti-Communist foreign policy, differing with Republicans more over means than over ends. Indeed, when Democrats recaptured the White House in 1960, they seized opportunities in Cuba and Southeast Asia to vigorously challenge the expansion of Soviet influence.

Kennedy's New Frontier.
With victory in World War II and the revival of economic prosperity, liberal thinkers regained confidence in capitalism. Many saw the postwar American free-enterprise system as different from the old-style capitalism that had existed before Franklin Roosevelt's New Deal. In their view, this new "reform capitalism," or democratic capitalism, created abundance for all and not just for the elites. Rather than pushing for the redistribution of wealth, liberals now called on the government to help create conditions conducive to economic growth and increased productivity. The liberal economist John Kenneth Galbraith argued in *The Affluent Society* (1958) that increased public investments in education, research, and development were the key to American prosperity and progress.

These ideas guided the thinking of Democratic politicians such as Senator John F. Kennedy of Massachusetts. Elected president in 1960, the forty-three-year-old Kennedy brought good looks, charm, a beautiful wife, and young children to the White House. Kennedy pledged a **New Frontier** to battle "tyranny, poverty, disease, and war," but lacking strong majorities in Congress, he contented himself with making small gains on the New Deal's foundation. Congress expanded unemployment benefits, increased the minimum wage, extended Social Security benefits, and raised appropriations for public housing, but Kennedy's caution disappointed many liberals.

Kennedy, the Cold War, and Cuba.
The Kennedy administration showed greater zeal in fighting the Cold War abroad. The president believed that America's reform capitalism should become a global model. Communism, like fascism before it, posed a fundamental threat to American interests and to other countries' ability to emulate the economic miracle of the United States. The faith of liberals in U.S. ingenuity, willpower, technological superiority, and moral righteousness encouraged them to reshape the "free world" in America's image.

President Kennedy's first Cold War battle took place in Cuba. Before his election, Kennedy learned of a secret CIA plan, devised by the Eisenhower administration, to topple Fidel Castro from power. After becoming president, Kennedy approved the scheme that Eisenhower had set in motion.

The operation ended disastrously. On April 17, 1961, the invasion force of between 1,400 and 1,500 Cuban exiles, trained by the CIA, landed by boat at the Bay of Pigs on Cuba's southwest coast. Kennedy refused to provide backup military forces for fear of revealing the U.S. role in the attack. Castro's troops defeated the insurgents in three days. CIA planners had underestimated Cuban popular support for Castro, falsely believing that the invasion would inspire a national uprising against the Communist regime. The Kennedy administration had blundered into a bitter foreign policy defeat (Map 26.1).

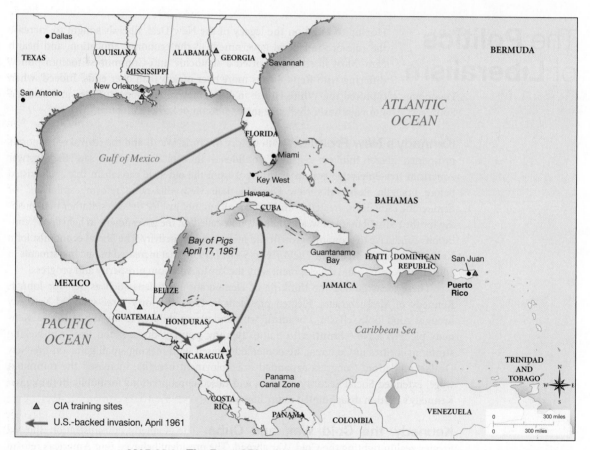

MAP 26.1   The Bay of Pigs Invasion, 1961

President Kennedy launched the Bay of Pigs invasion on April 17, 1961 to topple the Communist regime of Fidel Castro. The CIA secretly trained Cuban exiles in locations in the southern United States, Central America, and the Caribbean. After three days of fighting, the invasion failed and turned Castro into a national hero, thereby strengthening his leadership. Fearing further U.S. aggression, Castro turned to the Soviet Union to install missiles in Cuba for protection.

Two months later, Kennedy met Soviet leader Nikita Khrushchev at a summit meeting in Vienna. Khrushchev took advantage of the president's embarrassing defeat in Cuba to press his own demands. After the confrontational summit meeting raised tensions between the superpowers, Kennedy persuaded Congress to increase the defense budget, dispatch additional troops to Europe, and bolster civil defense. In August, the Soviets responded by constructing a wall through Berlin, making it more difficult for refugees to flee from East Berlin to West Berlin.

Despite the Bay of Pigs disaster, the United States continued its efforts to topple the Castro regime. Such attempts were uniformly unsuccessful, but a wary Castro invited the Soviet Union to install short- and intermediate-range missiles in Cuba to protect the country against any U.S. incursion. On October 22, 1962, Kennedy went on national television to inform the American people that the Soviets had placed missiles in Cuba. The Kennedy administration decided to blockade Cuba to prevent Soviet ships from supplying the deadly warheads that would make the missiles fully operational. If Soviet ships defied the blockade, the president would order air strikes on its island neighbor. Ordinary Americans nervously contemplated the very real possibility of nuclear destruction.

On the brink of nuclear war, both sides chose compromise. Khrushchev agreed to remove the missiles, and Kennedy pledged not to invade Cuba and secretly promised to dismantle U.S. missile sites in Turkey aimed at the Soviet Union. Kennedy and Khrushchev, having stepped back from the edge of nuclear holocaust, worked to ease tensions further. In 1963 they signed a Partial Nuclear Test Ban Treaty — which prohibited atmospheric but not underground testing — and installed an electronic "hot line" to ensure swift communications between Washington and Moscow.

Explore ▶

See Source 26.1 for one cartoonist's commentary on the Soviet removal of missiles from Cuba.

Kennedy sought to balance his hard-line, anti-Communist policies with new outreach efforts to inspire developing nations to follow a democratic path. The Peace Corps program sent thousands of volunteers to teach and advise developing nations, and Kennedy's Alliance for Progress supplied economic aid to emerging democracies in Latin America.

Review & Relate

▌ How did President Kennedy's domestic agenda reflect the liberal political ideology of the early 1960s?

▌ Evaluate Kennedy's and Khrushchev's actions in the Cuban missile crisis. How was war averted?

The **Civil Rights Movement Intensifies, 1961–1968**

At home, the most critical issue facing the nation in the early 1960s was the intensification of the civil rights movement. As a candidate, Kennedy had promised vigorous action on civil rights, but as president he did little to follow through on his promises. With southern Democrats occupying key positions in Congress and threatening to block any civil rights proposals, Kennedy sought to mollify this critical component of his political base. Following Kennedy's death in 1963, President Johnson succeeded in breaking the legislative logjam and signed into law three major pieces of civil rights legislation.

Guided Primary Source Analysis

Edmund Valtman | The Cuban Missile Crisis, 1962

For thirteen days in October 1962, the world held its breath while U.S. president John F. Kennedy and Soviet premier Nikita Khrushchev traded threats over the presence of nuclear weapons in Cuba. Khrushchev eventually backed down and removed the missiles. Two days after the crisis ended, the following cartoon by Edmund Valtman appeared in the *Hartford Times*.

Source 26.1

Why might Khrushchev tell Castro, "This hurts me more than it hurts you!"?

What does the placement of the missiles suggest about their importance to Cuba?

What does the position of both characters suggest about the power relationship between Castro and Khrushchev?

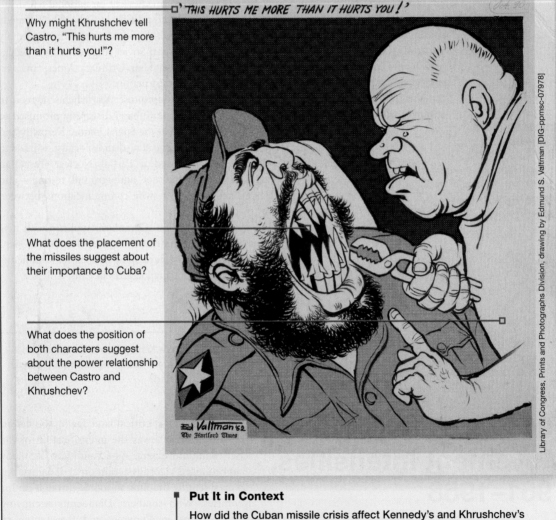

'THIS HURTS ME MORE THAN IT HURTS YOU !'

Ed Valtman '62
The Hartford Times

Library of Congress, Prints and Photographs Division, drawing by Edmund S. Valtman [DIG-ppmsc-07978]

▌**Put It in Context**

How did the Cuban missile crisis affect Kennedy's and Khrushchev's thinking about the Cold War?

He did so under considerable pressure from the civil rights movement. At the height of their triumphs, however, many civil rights activists became increasingly skeptical of nonviolence and integration and turned to the self-determination of black power.

Freedom Rides.

Similar to Bayard Rustin's efforts in the 1940s to challenge discrimination, the Congress of Racial Equality took action. CORE mounted racially integrated **Freedom Rides** to test whether facilities in the South were complying with the 1960 Supreme Court ruling that outlawed segregated bus and train stations serving passengers who were traveling interstate. CORE alerted the Justice Department and the FBI of its plans for May 4, 1961, but the riders received no protection when Ku Klux Klan–dominated mobs in Anniston and Birmingham, Alabama attacked two of its buses, seriously wounding several activists.

After safety concerns forced CORE to forgo the rest of the trip, members of the Student Nonviolent Coordinating Committee (SNCC) rushed to Birmingham to continue the bus rides. The Kennedy administration urged them to reconsider, but Diane Nash, a SNCC founder, explained that although the group realized the peril of resuming the journey, "we can't let them stop us with violence. If we do, the movement is dead." When the replenished busload of riders reached Montgomery on May 20, they were brutally assaulted by a mob. Dr. Martin Luther King Jr. subsequently held a rally in a Montgomery church, where white mobs threatened the lives of King and the Freedom Riders inside the building. Faced with the prospect of more bloodshed, the Kennedy administration dispatched federal marshals to the scene and persuaded the governor to call out the Alabama National Guard to ensure the safety of everyone in the church.

The president and his brother, Attorney General Robert Kennedy, worked out a compromise to let the rides continue with minimal violence, and with minimal publicity. The Cold War worked in favor of the protesters. With the Soviet Union publicizing the violence against Freedom Riders in the South, the Kennedy administration attempted to preserve America's image abroad by persuading the Interstate Commerce Commission to issue an order prohibiting segregated transportation facilities. Still, southern whites resisted. When Freedom Riders encountered opposition in Albany, Georgia, in the fall of 1961, SNCC workers remained in Albany and helped local leaders organize residents against segregation and other forms of racial discrimination. Even with the assistance of Dr. King and the Southern Christian Leadership Conference (SCLC), the Albany movement stalled.

Kennedy Supports Civil Rights.

Despite the setback in Albany, the civil rights movement kept up pressure on other fronts. In September 1962 Mississippi governor Ross Barnett tried to thwart the registration of James Meredith as an undergraduate at the University of Mississippi. Barnett's obstruction precipitated a riot on campus, and President Kennedy dispatched army troops and federalized the Mississippi National Guard to restore order, but not before two bystanders were killed.

The following year, King and the SCLC joined the Reverend Fred Shuttlesworth's movement in Birmingham, Alabama, in its battle against discrimination, segregation, and police brutality. With the white supremacist Eugene "Bull" Connor in charge of law enforcement, civil rights protesters, including children from age six to sixteen, encountered violent resistance, vicious police dogs, and high-powered water hoses. Connor ordered mass arrests, including Dr. King's, prompting the minister to write his famous "Letter from

Birmingham Jail," in which he justified the use of nonviolent direct action. Seeking to defuse the crisis, President Kennedy sent an emissary in early May 1963 to negotiate a peaceful solution that granted concessions to Birmingham blacks and ended the demonstrations. On Sunday, September 15, 1963, however, the Ku Klux Klan dynamited Birmingham's Sixteenth Street Baptist Church, a freedom movement staging ground. The blast killed four young girls attending services.

Even before this brutal bombing, the president had finally embraced the nation's duty to guarantee equal rights regardless of race. On June 11, 1963, shortly after negotiating the Birmingham agreement, Kennedy delivered a nationally televised address. He acknowledged that the country faced a "moral crisis" heightened by the events in Birmingham, and he noted the difficulty of preaching "freedom around the world" while "this is a land of the free except for Negroes." He proposed congressional legislation to end segregation in public accommodations, increase federal power to promote school desegregation, and broaden the right to vote.

Events on the day Kennedy delivered his powerful speech reinforced the need for swift action. Earlier that morning, Alabama governor George C. Wallace stood in front of the administration building at the University of Alabama to block the entrance of two black undergraduates. To uphold the federal court decree ordering their admission, Kennedy deployed federal marshals and the Alabama National Guard, and Wallace, having dramatized his point, stepped aside. However, victory soon turned into tragedy. That evening Medgar Evers, the head of the NAACP in Mississippi, was shot and killed in the driveway of his Jackson home by the white supremacist Byron de la Beckwith. (Following two trials, de la Beckwith remained free until 1994, when he was retried and convicted for Evers's murder.)

Congress was still unwilling to act. To increase pressure on lawmakers, civil rights organizations held the **March on Washington for Jobs and Freedom** on August 28, 1963, carrying out an idea first proposed by A. Philip Randolph in 1941 (see "The Origins of the Civil Rights Movement" in chapter 23). With Randolph as honorary chair, his associate Bayard Rustin directed the proceedings as 250,000 black and white peaceful protesters rallied in front of the Lincoln Memorial. Two speakers in particular caught the attention of the crowd. John Lewis, the chairman of SNCC, expressed the frustration of blacks with both the Kennedy administration and Congress. "The revolution is at hand. . . . We will not wait for the President, nor the Justice Department, nor Congress," Lewis asserted. "But we will take matters into our own hands." In a more conciliatory tone, King delivered a speech expressing his dream for racial and religious brotherhood. Still, King issued a stern warning to "those who hope that the Negro needed to blow off steam and will now be content. . . . There will be neither rest nor tranquility in America until the Negro is granted his citizenship rights."

If civil rights leaders hoped to elicit additional support from the Kennedy administration, their hopes were dashed. On November 22, 1963, Lee Harvey Oswald shot President Kennedy as he rode in an open motorcade in Dallas, Texas. The assassination prompted an outpouring of public grief. In death, Kennedy achieved immense popularity, yet he left many problems unresolved. His legislative agenda, including civil rights, remained unfulfilled. It was up to Vice President Lyndon Johnson to step into the breach.

Freedom Summer and Voting Rights.
Following Kennedy's death, President Johnson took charge of the pending civil rights legislation. Under his leadership, a bipartisan coalition passed the **Civil Rights Act of 1964**. The law prohibited discrimination in

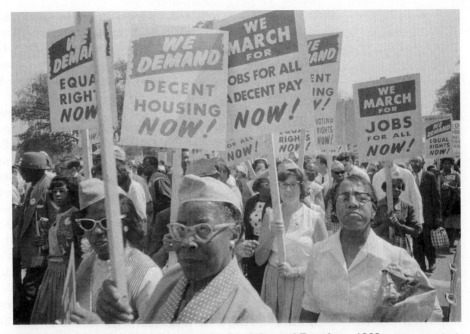

Women and the March on Washington for Jobs and Freedom, 1963   Although black women played central roles in grassroots organizing within the civil rights movement, they received far less attention on the national stage than did male leaders, such as Martin Luther King Jr. and A. Philip Randolph. At the historic 1963 March on Washington, women, black and white, turned out in large numbers, as this photograph shows, but they were not chosen to give any of the major speeches or march at the front of the line with the leading men. Wally McNamee /Corbis/Getty Images

public accommodations, increased federal enforcement of school desegregation and the right to vote, and created the Community Relations Service, a federal agency authorized to help resolve racial conflicts. The act also contained a final measure to combat employment discrimination on the basis of race and sex.

Yet even as President Johnson signed the Civil Rights Act into law on July 2, black freedom forces launched a new initiative to secure the right to vote in the South. The 1964 act contained a voting rights provision but did little to address the main problems of the discriminatory use of literacy tests and poll taxes and the biased administration of registration procedures that kept the majority of southern blacks from registering. Beatings, killings, acts of arson, and arrests became a routine response to voting rights efforts. Although the Justice Department filed lawsuits against recalcitrant voter registrars and police officers, the government refused to send in federal personnel or instruct the FBI to safeguard vulnerable civil rights workers.

To focus national attention on this problem, SNCC, CORE, the NAACP, and the SCLC launched the **Freedom Summer** project in Mississippi. They assigned eight hundred volunteers from around the nation, mainly white college students, to work with local black community organizers on voter registration drives and in "freedom schools" to improve education for rural black youngsters. White supremacists fought back against what they perceived as an enemy invasion. In late June 1964, the Ku Klux Klan, in collusion with local law enforcement officials, killed three civil rights workers. This tragedy provoked national outrage, and President Johnson pressed the usually uncooperative FBI to find the culprits, which it did. However, civil rights workers continued to encounter white violence and harassment throughout Freedom Summer. **See Primary Source Project 26: Freedom Summer, page 926.**

One outcome of the Freedom Summer project was the creation of the **Mississippi Freedom Democratic Party (MFDP)**. Because the regular state Democratic Party excluded blacks, the civil rights coalition formed an alternative Democratic Party open to everyone. In August 1964 the mostly black MFDP sent a delegation to the Democratic National Convention, meeting in Atlantic City, New Jersey, to challenge the seating of the all-white delegation from Mississippi. One MFDP delegate, Fannie Lou Hamer, who had lost her job for her voter registration activities, offered passionate testimony that was broadcast on television. President Johnson then hammered out a compromise that gave the MFDP two at-large seats, seated members of the regular delegation who took a loyalty oath, and prohibited racial discrimination in the future by any state Democratic Party. While both sides rejected the deal, four years later an integrated delegation, which included Hamer, represented Mississippi at the Democratic National Convention in Chicago.

Freedom Summer highlighted the problem of disfranchisement, but it took further demonstrations in Selma, Alabama, to resolve it. After state troopers shot and killed a black voting rights demonstrator in February 1965, Dr. King called for a march from Selma to the capital, Montgomery, to petition Governor Wallace to end the violence and allow blacks to vote. On Sunday, March 7, as black and white marchers, including John Lewis, left Selma, the sheriff's forces sprayed them with tear gas, beat them, and sent them running for their lives. A few days later, a white clergyman who had joined the protesters was killed by a group of white thugs. On March 21, following another failed attempt to march to Montgomery, King finally led protesters on the fifty-mile hike to the state capital, where they arrived safely four days later. Still, after the march, the Ku Klux Klan murdered a white female marcher from Michigan.

Events in Selma prompted President Johnson to take action. On March 15 he addressed a joint session of Congress and told lawmakers and a nationally televised audience that the black "cause must be our cause too." On August 6, 1965, the president signed the **Voting Rights Act**, which banned the use of literacy tests for voter registration, authorized a federal lawsuit against the poll tax (which succeeded in 1966), empowered federal officials to register disfranchised voters, and required seven southern states to submit any voting changes to Washington before they went into effect. With strong federal enforcement of the law, by 1968 a majority of black southerners and nearly two-thirds of black Mississippians could vote (Figure 26.1).

These civil rights victories had exacted a huge toll on the movement. SNCC and CORE came to distrust Presidents Kennedy and Johnson for failing to provide protection for voter registration workers. Furthermore, Johnson's attempt to broker a compromise at the 1964 Atlantic City Convention convinced MFDP supporters that the liberal president had sold them out. The once united movement showed signs of splintering.

Civil Rights and Black Power.

Increasingly after 1964, SNCC and CORE began exploring new ways of seeking freedom through strategies of black self-determination and self-defense. They were greatly influenced by Malcolm X. Born Malcolm Little, he had engaged in a life of crime, which landed him in prison. Inside jail, he converted to the Nation of Islam, a religious sect based partly on Muslim teachings and partly on the belief

FIGURE 26.1 Black Voter Registration in the South, 1947–1976

After World War II, the percentage of black adults registered to vote in the South slowly but steadily increased, largely as a result of grassroots voting drives. Despite the Kennedy administration's support for voter registration drives, a majority of southern blacks remained prohibited from voting in 1964. The passage of the 1965 Voting Rights Act removed barriers such as literacy tests and poll taxes, strengthened the federal government's enforcement powers, and enabled more than 60 percent of southern blacks to vote by the late 1960s. Compare the growth of black voter registration during the Eisenhower (1953–1961), Kennedy (1961–1963), and Johnson (1963–1969) administrations. Source: Data from David Garrow, *Protest at Selma* (New Haven, CT: Yale University Press, 1978), and U.S. Department of Commerce, Bureau of the Census, *Statistical Abstract of the United States*, 1976.

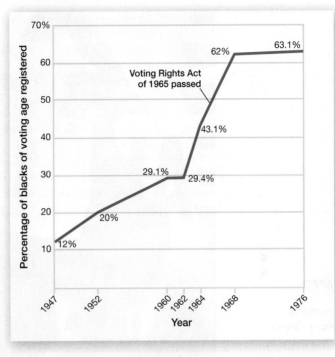

that white people were devils (not a doctrine associated with orthodox Islam). After his release from jail, Malcolm rejected his "slave name" and substituted the letter X to symbolize his unknown African forebears. Minister Malcolm helped convert thousands of disciples in black neighborhoods by denouncing whites and encouraging blacks to embrace their African heritage and beauty as a people. Favoring self-defense over nonviolence, he criticized civil rights leaders for failing to protect their communities. After 1963, Malcolm X broke away from the Nation of Islam, visited the Middle East and Africa, and accepted the teachings of traditional Islam. He moderated his anti-white rhetoric but remained committed to black self-determination. He had already influenced the growing number of disillusioned young black activists when, in 1965, members of the Nation of Islam murdered him, apparently in revenge for challenging the organization.

Black militants, echoing Malcolm X's ideas, challenged racial liberalism. They renounced the principles of integration and nonviolence in favor of black power and self-defense. Instead of welcoming whites within their organizations, black radicals believed that African Americans had to assert their independence from white America. In 1966 SNCC expelled white members and created an all-black organization. Stokely Carmichael, SNCC's chairman, proclaimed "black power" as the central goal of the freedom struggle and linked the cause of African American freedom to revolutionary conflicts in Cuba, Africa, and Vietnam.

Despite differences in tactics and philosophy, both the civil rights and black power movements grew out of the broader African American freedom struggle and sought full citizenship for African Americans without diminishing their black cultural heritage. Many civil rights leaders emerged from black universities, churches, and civic groups. Black power activists such as Stokely Carmichael had gained experience working in southern black communities during the civil rights movement. In addition, both movements maintained contact with African liberation struggles and supported their anti-colonial efforts.

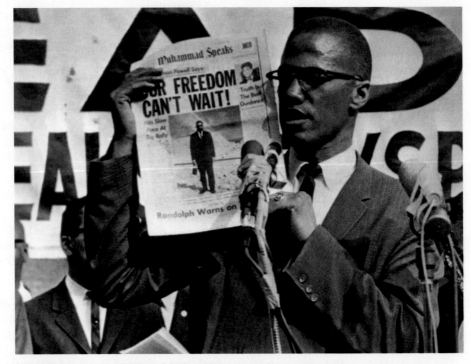

Malcolm X   A charismatic minister in the Nation of Islam, Malcom X preached a fiery message of black nationalism and self-defense, ideas that later merged into the ideology of black power. Though his message drew criticism from liberal whites and black civil rights leaders, Malcolm X appealed to many African Americans. In this July 27, 1963 rally in Harlem, he holds up a copy of *Muhammed Speaks*, the Nation of Islam newspaper. Underwood Archives/Getty Images

Black power gained notoriety against a backdrop of riots in black neighborhoods, which erupted across the nation starting in the mid-1960s: in Harlem and Rochester, New York, in 1964; in Los Angeles in 1965; and in Cleveland, Chicago, Detroit, Newark, and Tampa in the following two years. Urban blacks, many in the North and West, faced problems of high unemployment, dilapidated housing, and police mistreatment that civil rights legislation had done nothing to correct. While many whites perceived the uprisings solely as an exercise in criminal behavior, many blacks viewed the violence as an expression of political discontent—as rebellions, not riots. Even nonviolence proponents such as Dr. King recognized the source of frustration behind the uprisings. "In the final analysis," King explained in 1967, "a riot is the language of the unheard. . . . Social justice and progress are the absolute guarantors of riot prevention." The Kerner Commission, appointed by President Johnson to assess urban disorders and chaired by Governor Otto Kerner of Illinois, concluded in 1968 that white racism remained at the heart of the problem: "Our nation is moving toward two societies, one black, one white — separate and unequal."

New groups emerged to take up the cause of black power. In 1966 Huey P. Newton and Bobby Seale, college students in Oakland, California, formed the **Black Panther Party**. Dressed in black leather, sporting black berets, and carrying guns, the Panthers appealed mainly to black men. The Panthers also sought to make improvements in their neighborhoods. They established day care centers and health facilities, often run by women, which gained the admiration of many in their communities. Much of this good work was overshadowed by violent confrontations with the police, which led to the deaths of Panthers in shootouts and the imprisonment of key party officials. By the early 1970s, government crackdowns on the Black Panthers had destabilized the organization and reduced its influence.

The assassination of Martin Luther King Jr. in 1968 furthered black disillusionment. King was shot and killed by James Earl Ray in Memphis, where he was supporting demonstrations by striking sanitation workers. In the wake of his murder, riots erupted in hundreds of cities throughout the country. Little noticed amid the fiery turbulence, President Johnson signed into law the 1968 Fair Housing Act, the final piece of civil rights legislation of his term.

Review & Relate

- How did civil rights activists pressure state and federal government officials to enact their agenda?

- How were the civil rights and black power movements similar and in what ways were they different?

Federal Efforts toward Social Reform, 1964–1968

President Johnson's liberal accomplishments reached beyond civil rights, and he drew on Kennedy's legacy and his own considerable political skills to win passage of the most important items on the liberal agenda. While Johnson pressed ahead in the legislative arena, Chief Justice Earl Warren's Supreme Court issued rulings that extended social justice to marginalized people and favored those who believed in a firm separation of church and state, free speech, and a right to privacy.

The Great Society. In an address at the University of Michigan on May 22, 1964, President Johnson sketched out his dream for the **Great Society**, one that "rests on abundance and liberty for all. It demands an end to poverty and racial injustice, to which we are totally committed in our time."

Besides poverty and race, he outlined three broad areas in need of reform: education, the environment, and cities. Toward this end, the Elementary and Secondary School Act (1965) was the most far-reaching federal law ever passed. It provided federal funds directly to public schools to improve their quality. The Model Cities program (1966) set up the Department of Housing and Urban Affairs, which coordinated efforts at urban planning and rebuilding neighborhoods in decaying cities. The Department of Transportation sought to ensure a fast, safe, and convenient transportation system. In addition, the president pushed Congress to pass hundreds of environmental protection laws, including those dealing with air and water pollution, waste disposal, the use of natural resources, and the preservation of wildlife and wilderness areas.

The War on Poverty came with passage of the Economic Opportunity Act of 1964. Through this measure, Johnson wanted to offer the poor "a hand up, not a handout." Among its major components, the law provided job training, food stamps, rent supplements, redevelopment of depressed rural areas, remedial education (later to include the preschool

President Johnson Signs Medicare into Law, 1965 On July 30, 1965, President Johnson signed the Medicare bill, the health insurance program for elderly Americans. The ceremony took place at the Truman Library in Independence, Missouri, and former President Harry S. Truman received the first Medicare card. In 1945, Truman had first proposed national health insurance, but Congress rejected it. Standing to the right immediately behind Johnson (seated on the left) and Truman (seated on the right) are (from left to right) Lady Bird Johnson, the president's wife; Vice President Hubert Humphrey; and Bess Truman, the former president's wife. LBJ Library photo

program Head Start), a domestic Peace Corps called Volunteers in Service to America (VISTA), and a Community Action Program that empowered the poor to shape policies affecting their own communities. Between 1965 and 1968, expenditures targeted for the poor doubled, from $6 billion to $12 billion. The antipoverty program helped reduce the proportion of poor people from 20 percent in 1963 to 13 percent five years later, and it helped reduce the rate of black poverty from 40 percent to 20 percent during this same period.

Johnson intended to fight the War on Poverty through the engine of economic growth, which would create new jobs for the unemployed without redistributing wealth. With this in mind, he persuaded Congress to enact significant tax cuts. Johnson's tax cut, which applied across the board, stimulated the economy and sent the gross national product soaring from $591 billion in 1963 to $977 billion by the end of the decade. Despite the gains made, many liberals believed that Johnson's spending on the War on Poverty did not go far enough. Whatever the shortcomings, Johnson campaigned on his antipoverty and civil rights record in his bid to recapture the White House in 1964. His Republican opponent, Senator Barry M. Goldwater of Arizona, personified the conservative right wing of the Republican Party. The Arizona senator condemned big government, supported states' rights, and accused liberals of not waging the Cold War forcefully enough. His aggressive conservatism appealed to his grassroots base in small-town America, especially in southern California, the Southwest, and the South. His tough rhetoric, however, scared off moderate Republicans, resulting on election day in a landslide for Johnson as well as considerable Democratic majorities in Congress.

Flush with victory, Johnson pushed Congress to move quickly. Among its accomplishments, the Eighty-ninth Congress (1965–1967) subsidized health care for the elderly and the poor by creating Medicare and Medicaid, expanded voting rights for African Americans in the South, raised the minimum wage, and created national endowments for the fine arts and the humanities. The 1965 Immigration Act repealed discriminatory national origins quotas established in 1924, resulting in a shift of immigration from Europe to Asia and Central and South America (Table 26.1). With immigration on the rise, President Johnson signed into law the 1968 Bilingual Education Act, which provided federal funds to improve education for students who spoke little or no English.

The Warren Court. The Warren Court reflected this high tide of liberalism. In 1967, the justices overturned state laws prohibiting interracial marriages. A year later, fourteen years after the *Brown* decision, they ruled that school districts in the South could no longer

TABLE 26.1 Major Great Society Measures, 1964–1968

Year	Legislation or Order	Purpose
1964	Civil Rights Act	Prohibited discrimination in public accommodations, education, and employment
	Economic Opportunity Act	Established War on Poverty agencies: Head Start, VISTA, Job Corps, and Community Action Program
1965	Elementary and Secondary Education Act	Federal funding for elementary and secondary schools
	Medical Care Act	Provided Medicare health insurance for citizens sixty-five years and older and Medicaid health benefits for the poor
	Voting Rights Act	Banned literacy tests for voting, authorized federal registrars to be sent into seven southern states, and monitored voting changes in these states
	Executive Order 11246	Required employers to take affirmative action to promote equal opportunity and remedy the effects of past discrimination
	Immigration and Nationality Act	Abolished quotas on immigration that reduced immigration from non-Western and southern and eastern European nations
	Water Quality Act	Established and enforced federal water quality standards
	Air Quality Act	Established air pollution standards for motor vehicles
	National Arts and Humanities Act	Established National Endowment of the Humanities and National Endowment of the Arts to support the work of scholars, writers, artists, and musicians
1966	Model Cities Act	Approved funding for the rehabilitation of inner cities
1967	Executive Order 11375	Expanded affirmative action regulations to include women
1968	Civil Rights Act	Outlawed discrimination in housing
1968	Bilingual Education Act	Provided bilingual education for students of limited English-speaking ability

maintain racially exclusive schools and must desegregate immediately. In a series of cases, the Warren Court ensured fairer legislative representation for blacks and whites by removing the disproportionate power that rural districts had held over urban districts.

The Supreme Court's most controversial rulings dealt with the criminal justice system, religion, and private sexual practices. Strengthening the rights of criminal defendants, the justices ruled in *Gideon v. Wainwright* (1963) that states had to provide indigents accused of felonies with an attorney, and in *Miranda v. Arizona* (1966) they ordered the police to advise suspects of their constitutional rights. The Court also moved into controversial territory concerning school prayer, contraception, and pornography. In 1962 the Court outlawed a nondenominational Christian prayer recited in New York State schools as a violation of the separation of church and state guaranteed by the First Amendment. Three years later, in *Griswold v. Connecticut*, the justices struck down a state law that banned the sale of contraceptives because such laws, they contended, infringed on an individual's right to privacy. In a 1966 case the justices ruled that states could not prohibit what they deemed pornographic material unless it was "utterly without redeeming social value," a standard that opened the door for the dissemination of sexually explicit books, magazines, and films. These verdicts unleashed a firestorm of criticism, especially from religious groups that accused the Warren Court of undermining traditional values of faith and decency.

Review & Relate

▪ What problems and challenges did Johnson's Great Society legislation target?

▪ In what ways did the Warren Court's rulings advance the liberal agenda?

The **Vietnam War,** 1961–1969

While substantial progress was made on civil rights and liberal reforms at home, the Kennedy and Johnson administrations enjoyed far less success in fighting communism abroad. Following the overthrow of French colonial rule in Vietnam in 1954, the Cold War spread to Southeast Asia, where the United States applied the doctrine of containment (see "Early Intervention in Vietnam, 1954–1960" in chapter 24). Mistaking the situation in Vietnam as a war of outside Communist aggression, the United States deployed hundreds of thousands of troops to fight in what was, instead, a civil war.

Kennedy's Intervention in South Vietnam. President Kennedy believed that if Communists toppled one regime in Asia it would produce a "domino effect," with one country after another falling to the Communists. Kennedy also believed that aggressive nations that attacked weaker ones threatened world peace unless they were challenged.

Kennedy's containment efforts in Vietnam ran into difficulty because the United States did not control the situation on the ground. The U.S.-backed president of South Vietnam, Ngo Dinh Diem, had spent more than $1 billion of American aid on building up military and personal security forces to suppress political opposition rather than implement the economic and political reforms that he had promised. In 1961 Kennedy sent military advisers to help the South Vietnamese fight the Communists, but the situation deteriorated in 1963 when the Catholic Diem prohibited the country's Buddhist majority from holding religious celebrations. In protest, Buddhist monks committed suicide by setting themselves on fire, a grisly display captured on television news programs in the United States. With political opposition mounting against Diem and with the war going poorly, the Kennedy administration endorsed a military coup to replace the Diem government. On November 1, 1963, the coup leaders removed Diem from office, assassinated the deposed president and key members of his regime, and installed a military government.

Diem's death, however, did little to improve the war against the Communists. The National Liberation Front (Vietcong), Communist political and military forces living in South Vietnam and sponsored by Ho Chi Minh, had more support in the rural countryside than did the South Vietnamese government. The rebels promised economic and political reforms and recruited local peasants opposed to the corruption and ruthlessness of the Diem regime. The Kennedy administration committed itself to supporting Diem's successor, but by late November 1963 Kennedy seemed torn between sending more American troops and finding a way to negotiate a peace.

Johnson Escalates the War in Vietnam.

When Lyndon Johnson took office after Kennedy's assassination, there were 16,000 American military personnel in Vietnam. Privately, Johnson harbored reservations about fighting in Vietnam, but he feared appearing soft on communism and was concerned that a demonstration of weakness would jeopardize congressional support for his domestic plans. Although Johnson eventually concluded that more U.S. forces had to be sent to Vietnam, he waited for the right moment to rally Congress and the American public behind an escalation of the war.

That moment came in August 1964. On August 2, North Vietnamese gunboats attacked an American spy ship sixty miles off the North Vietnamese coast in the Gulf of Tonkin. Two days later, another U.S. destroyer reported coming under torpedo attack, but because of stormy weather the second ship was not certain that it had been fired on. Neither ship suffered any damage. Despite the considerable uncertainty about what actually happened with the second ship, Johnson seized the opportunity to urge Congress to authorize military action. On August 7 Congress passed the **Gulf of Tonkin Resolution**, which provided the president with unlimited power to make military decisions regarding Vietnam.

After winning election in 1964, President Johnson stepped up U.S. military action. In March 1965, with North Vietnamese forces flooding into the South, the president initiated a massive bombing campaign called Operation Rolling Thunder. For more than three years, American planes dropped a million tons of bombs on North Vietnam, more than the total amount the United States used in World War II. Despite this massive firepower, the operation proved ineffective. A largely agricultural country, North Vietnam did not have the type of industrial targets best suited for air attacks. It stored its vital military resources underground and was able to reconstruct rudimentary bridges and roads to maintain the flow of troops into the South within hours after U.S. bombers had pounded them.

Responding to the need to protect American air bases and the persistent ineffectiveness of the South Vietnamese military, Johnson deployed ever-increasing numbers of ground troops to Vietnam. Troop levels rose from 16,000 in 1963 to 536,000 in 1968. The U.S. military also deployed napalm bombs, which spewed burning jellied gasoline, and Agent Orange, a chemical that denuded the Vietnamese countryside and produced long-term adverse health effects for those who came in contact with it, including American soldiers. These attacks added to the resentment of South Vietnamese peasants and helped the Vietcong gain new recruits.

The United States confronted a challenging guerrilla war in Vietnam. The Vietcong fought at night and blended in during the day as ordinary residents of cities and villages.

My Lai Massacre, 1968   On March 16, 1968, U.S. army soldiers killed hundreds of unarmed civilians — most of them women, children, and the elderly — in the village of My Lai. The soldiers left bodies piled in ditches that ran around the village. The massacre became public in 1969, but only one soldier was convicted by a military tribunal. Ronald S. Haeberle/The LIFE Images Collection/Getty Images

They did not provide a visible target, and they recruited women and men of all ages, making it difficult for U.S. ground forces to distinguish friend from foe. In the end, the U.S. military effort alienated the population they were designed to safeguard.

On the ground, frustration also bred racism, as many American soldiers could not relate to the Vietnamese way of life and dismissed the enemy as "gooks." This attitude helped push some troops over the line between legitimate warfare and murder. Frustrated by rising casualties from an enemy they could not see, some American soldiers indiscriminately burned down villages and killed noncombatant civilians. Such contemptible behavior peaked in March 1968 when an American platoon murdered between 347 and 504 unarmed Vietnamese civilians in the village of My Lai, an event that came to be known as the My Lai massacre.

The My Lai carnage came in the wake of the **Tet Offensive**. On January 31, 1968, the Buddhist New Year of Tet, some 67,000 Communist forces mounted a surprise offensive throughout South Vietnam that targeted major population centers (Map 26.2). For six hours, a suicide squadron of Vietcong surrounded the U.S. Embassy in Saigon. U.S. forces finally repelled the Tet Offensive, but the battle proved psychologically costly to the United States. Following it, the most revered television news anchor of the era, Walter Cronkite of CBS, turned against the war and expressed the doubts of a growing number of viewers when he announced: "To say that we are mired in stalemate seems the only reasonable, yet unsatisfactory conclusion."

MAP 26.2   The Vietnam War, 1968

The United States wielded vastly more military personnel and weaponry than the Vietcong and North Vietnamese but faced a formidable challenge in fighting a guerrilla war in a foreign country. Massive American bombing failed to defeat the North Vietnamese or stop their troop movements and supply lines along the Ho Chi Minh Trail. The 1968 Tet Offensive demonstrated the shortcomings in the U.S. strategy.

Tet marked the beginning of the end of the war's escalation. On March 31, 1968, President Johnson ordered a halt to the bombing campaign and called for peace negotiations. He also stunned the nation by announcing that he would not seek reelection. By the time Johnson left the White House in 1969, peace negotiations had stalled and some 36,000 Americans had died in combat, along with 52,000 South Vietnamese troops. The escalation of the war had exacted another high price as well: It created a crisis of public confidence in government and turned many ordinary Americans into dissenters against the political establishment.

Review & Relate

▌ Why did Kennedy and Johnson escalate the Vietnam War?

▌ How did the reality of the war on the ground compare with the political and military assumptions for fighting it?

Challenges to the Liberal Establishment

Even at its peak in the 1960s, liberalism faced major challenges from both the left and the right. Young activists became impatient with what they saw as the slow pace of social progress and were increasingly distressed by the escalation of the Vietnam War. At the same time, the right was disturbed by the failure of the United States to win the war as well as by the liberal reforms they believed diminished individual initiative and benefited racial minorities at the expense of the white middle class. Conservatives depicted the left as unpatriotic and out of step with mainstream American values. By 1969 Richard M. Nixon, a political conservative, had captured the White House.

The New Left. The civil rights movement had inspired many young people to activism. Combining ideals of freedom, equality, and community with direct-action protest, civil rights activists offered a model for those seeking to address a variety of problems, including the threat of nuclear devastation, the loss of individual autonomy in a corporate society, racism, poverty, sexism, and environmental degradation. The formation of SNCC in 1960 illuminated the possibilities for personal and social transformation and offered a movement culture founded on democracy.

Tom Hayden helped apply the ideals of SNCC to predominantly white college campuses. After spending the summer of 1961 registering voters in Mississippi and Georgia, the University of Michigan graduate student returned to campus eager to recruit like-minded students who questioned America's commitment to democracy.

Hayden became an influential leader of the **Students for a Democratic Society (SDS)**, which advocated the formation of a "New Left." They considered the "Old Left," which revolved around attraction to the Communist Party, as autocratic and no longer relevant. "We are people of this generation," SDS proclaimed, "bred in at least modest comfort, housed now in universities, looking uncomfortably to the world we inherit." In its **Port Huron Statement** (1962), SDS condemned mainstream liberal politics, Cold War foreign policy, racism, and research-oriented universities that cared little for their undergraduates. It called for the adoption of "participatory democracy," which would return power to the people. In an ironic twist, the framers of the manifesto picked up the rhetoric of the moderate Republican president, Dwight Eisenhower, in condemning the military-industrial complex. "Not only is ours the first generation to live with the possibility of world-wide cataclysm," the statement declared, "it is the first to experience the actual social preparation for cataclysm, the general militarization of American society." The attack on the military-industrial complex and the unrestrained power of the executive branch to conduct foreign and military policy would become a staple of New Left protest.

The New Left never consisted of one central organization; after all, many protesters challenged the very idea of centralized authority. In fact, SDS did not initiate the New Left's most dramatic early protest. In 1964 the University of California at Berkeley banned political activities just outside the main campus entrance in response to CORE protests against racial bias in local hiring. When CORE defied the prohibition, campus police arrested its leader, prompting a massive student uprising. Student activists then formed the **Free Speech Movement (FSM)**, which held rallies in front of the administration building, culminating in a nonviolent, civil rights–style sit-in. When California governor Edmund "Pat" Brown dispatched state and county police to evict the demonstrators, students and faculty

The Berkeley Free Speech Movement   Mario Savio, a student leader at the University of California at Berkeley and a Freedom Summer volunteer, stands among demonstrators sitting in at Sproul Hall on December 3, 1964, to protest university curbs on free speech. A day earlier, Savio had declared: "There's a time when the operation of the machine becomes so odious . . . you've got to put your bodies upon the gears . . . and you've got to make it stop." AP Photo/Robert Houston

joined in protest and forced the university administration to yield to FSM's demands for amnesty and reform. By the end of the decade, hundreds of demonstrations had erupted on campuses throughout the nation.

The Vietnam War accelerated student radicalism, and college campuses provided a strategic setting for antiwar activities. Like most Americans in the mid-1960s, undergraduates had only a dim awareness of U.S. activity in Vietnam. Yet all college men were eligible for the draft once they graduated and lost their student deferment. As more troops were sent to Vietnam, student protesters launched a variety of campaigns and demonstrations. Others resisted the draft by fleeing to Canada. Most college students, however, were not activists — between 1965 and 1968, only 20 percent of college students attended demonstrations. The activist minority, however, received extensive media attention and helped raise awareness about the difficulty of waging the Vietnam War abroad and maintaining domestic tranquility at home.

By the end of 1967, as the number of troops in Vietnam approached half a million, protests increased. Antiwar sentiment had spread to faculty, artists, writers, businesspeople, and elected officials. In April Martin Luther King Jr. delivered a powerful antiwar address at Riverside Church in New York City. "The world now demands," King declared, "that we admit that we have been wrong from the beginning of our adventure in Vietnam, that we have been detrimental to the life of the Vietnamese people." As protests spread and the government clamped down on dissenters, some activists substituted armed struggle for nonviolence. SDS split into factions, with the most prominent of them, the Weathermen, going underground and adopting violent tactics.

The Counterculture.

The New Left's challenge to liberal politics attracted many students, and the **counterculture's** rejection of conventional middle-class values of work, sexual restraint, and rationality captivated even more. Cultural rebels emphasized living in the present, seeking immediate gratification, expressing authentic feelings, and reaching a higher consciousness through mind-altering drugs. Despite differences in approach, both the New Left and the counterculture expressed concerns about modern technology, bureaucratization, and the possibility of nuclear annihilation and sought new means of creating political, social, and personal liberation.

Rock 'n' roll became the soundtrack of the counterculture. In 1964 Bob Dylan's song "The Times They Are A-Changin' " became an anthem for youth rebellion. That same year, the Beatles, a British quartet influenced by 1950s black and white rock 'n' rollers, toured the United States and revolutionized popular music. Originally singing melodic compositions of teenage love and angst, the Beatles embraced the counterculture and began writing songs about alienation and politics, flavoring them with the drug-inspired sounds of psychedelic music. Although most of the songs that reached the top ten on the record charts did not undermine traditional values, the music of groups like the Beatles, the Rolling Stones, the Who, the Grateful Dead, Jefferson Airplane, and the Doors spread counterculture messages.

The counterculture viewed the elimination of sexual restrictions as essential for transforming personal and social behavior. The 1960s generation did not invent sexual freedom, but it did a great deal to shatter time-honored moral codes of monogamy, fidelity, and moderation. Promiscuity—casual sex, group sex, extramarital affairs, public nudity—and open-throated vulgarity tested public tolerance. Within limits, the broader culture reflected these changes. The Broadway production of the musical *Hair* showed frontal nudity, the movie industry adopted ratings of "X" and "R" that made films with nudity and profane language available to a wider audience, and new television comedy shows featured sketches with risqué content.

With sexual conduct in flux, society had difficulty maintaining the double standard of behavior that privileged men over women. The counterculture gave many women a chance to enjoy sexual pleasure that had long been denied them. The availability of birth control pills for women, introduced in 1960, made much of this sexual freedom possible. Although sexual liberation still carried more risks for women than for men, increased openness in discussing sexuality allowed many women to gain greater control over their bodies and their relationships.

Liberation Movements.

The varieties of political protest and cultural dissent emboldened other oppressed groups to emancipate themselves. Women, Latinos, Native Americans, and gay Americans all launched liberation movements.

Despite passage of the Nineteenth Amendment in 1920, which gave women the right to vote, women did not have equal access to employment, wages, or education or control over reproduction. Nor did they have sufficient political power to remove these obstacles to full equality. Yet by 1960 nearly 40 percent of all women held jobs, and women made up 35 percent of college enrollments. The social movements of the 1960s—attracted large numbers of women. Groups like SNCC empowered female staff in community-organizing projects, and women also played central roles in antiwar efforts, leading many to demand their own movement for liberation.

The women's liberation movement also built on efforts of the federal government to address gender discrimination. In 1961 President Kennedy appointed the **Commission on the Status of Women**. The commission's report, *American Women*, issued in 1963, reaffirmed the primary role of women in raising the family but cataloged the inequities women faced in the workplace. In 1963 Congress passed the Equal Pay Act, which required employers to give men and women equal pay for equal work. The following year, the 1964 Civil Rights Act opened up further opportunities when it prohibited sexual bias in employment and created the Equal Employment Opportunity Commission (EEOC).

In 1963 Betty Friedan published a landmark book, *The Feminine Mystique*, which questioned society's prescribed gender roles and raised the consciousness of mostly college-educated women. In *The Feminine Mystique*, she described the post-college isolation and alienation experienced by her female friends who got married and stayed home to care for their children. However, not all women saw themselves reflected in Friedan's book. Many working-class women and those from African American and other racial and ethnic minority families had not had the opportunity to attend college or stay home with their children, and younger college women had not yet experienced the burdens of domestic isolation.

In October 1966, Betty Friedan and like-minded women formed the **National Organization for Women (NOW)**. With Friedan as president, NOW dedicated itself to moving society toward "true equality for all women in America, and toward a fully equal partnership of the sexes." NOW called on the EEOC to enforce women's employment rights more vigorously and favored passage of an Equal Rights Amendment (ERA), paid maternity leave for working women, the establishment of child care centers, and reproductive rights. Although NOW advocated job training programs and assistance for impoverished women, it attracted a mainly middle-class white membership. Some blacks were among its charter members, but most African American women chose to concentrate first on eliminating racial barriers that affected black women and men alike.

> **Explore ▶**
>
> Compare two historians' perspectives on second wave feminism in Sources 26.4 and 26.5.

Young women, black and white, had also faced discrimination, sometimes in unexpected places. Even within the civil rights movement women were not always treated equally, often being assigned clerical duties. Men held a higher status within the antiwar movement because women were not eligible for the draft. Ironically, men's claims of moral advantage justified many of them in seeking sexual favors. "Girls say yes to guys who say no," quipped draft-resisting men who sought to put women in their traditional place.

As a result of these experiences, some women formed their own "consciousness-raising" groups to share their experiences of oppression in the family, the workplace, the university, and movement organizations. These women's liberationists went beyond NOW's emphasis on legal equality and attacked male domination, or patriarchy, as a crucial source of women's subordination. They criticized the nuclear family and cultural values that glorified women as the object of male sexual desires, and they protested creatively against discrimination. In 1968 radical feminists picketed the popular Miss America contest in Atlantic City, New Jersey, and set up a "Freedom Trash Can" into which they threw undergarments and cosmetics. Radical groups such as the Redstockings condemned all men as oppressors and formed separate female collectives to affirm their identities as women. In contrast, other feminists attempted to build the broadest possible coalition. In 1972 Gloria Steinem, a founder of NOW, established *Ms.* magazine in hope of attracting readers from across the feminist political spectrum. The magazine featured women's art and poetry alongside articles on sisterhood, child rearing, and abortion.

In 1973 feminists won a major battle in the Supreme Court over a woman's right to control reproduction. In ***Roe v. Wade***, the high court ruled that states could not prevent a woman from obtaining an abortion in the first three months of pregnancy but could impose

The Miss America Pageant Protest, 1968 In fighting for gender equality, the women's movement that emerged in the 1960s challenged all aspects of the male-dominated culture that considered women as sex objects. On September 7, 1968, feminists targeted the Miss America contest in Atlantic City, New Jersey. Protesters believed the pageant degraded women by producing a sex-driven ideal of femininity. An unidentified member of the Women's Liberation Party drops a brassiere, a garment protesters considered an instrument "of female torture," in the trash barrel. AP Images

some limits in the next two trimesters. In furthering the constitutional right of privacy for women, the justices classified abortion as a private medical issue between a patient and her doctor. This decision marked a victory for a woman's right to choose to terminate her pregnancy, but it also stirred up a fierce reaction from women and men who considered abortion to be the murder of an unborn child.

Latinas joined the feminist movement, often forming their own organizations, but they, like black women, also joined men in struggles for racial equality and advancement. During the 1960s, the size of the Spanish-speaking population in the United States tripled from three million to nine million. They were a diverse group who hailed from many countries and backgrounds. In the 1950s, Cesar Chavez had emerged as the leader of oppressed Mexican farmworkers in California. In seeking the right to organize a union and gain higher wages and better working conditions, Chavez shared King's nonviolent principles. In 1962, along with Dolores Huerta, a fellow labor leader, Chavez formed the National Farm Workers Association, and in 1965 the union called a strike against California grape growers, one that attracted national support and finally succeeded after five years.

Another leader who fought for social and economic justice for Mexican Americans was Reies Tijerina. Beginning in the late 1950s in New Mexico, Tijerina, a Pentecostal minister, organized Mexican Americans to seek the return of lands confiscated by Anglos in violation of the 1848 Treaty of Guadalupe Hidalgo between the United States and Mexico. In 1963, Tijerina formed *La Alianza Federal de Mercedes* (Federal Alliance of Land Grants) and broadened his agenda to include first-class citizenship, economic opportunity, and the right

Reies Tijerina and the Poor People's Campaign, 1968 Reies Tijerina (left), the Mexican American leader, stands alongside Native American leader Al Bridges (center) and the Reverend Ralph Abernathy (right), Martin Luther King Jr.'s successor. They are in Washington, D.C., preparing for the Poor People's March and encampment at the National Mall in front of the Capitol. Bettmann/Getty Images

to speak Spanish. In 1966 Tijerina led *Alianza* members in a takeover of government land in New Mexico's Carson National Forest. The next year they waged an armed raid on the Tierra Amarilla courthouse in northern New Mexico, attempting to make a citizen's arrest of the local district attorney for violating their civil rights and denying their claims to land grants. In 1970, the federal government convicted Tijerina on charges stemming from the courthouse raid, and he was sentenced to prison. As a result, the *Alianza* declined.

Young Mexican Americans, especially those in cities such as Los Angeles, supported Chavez, Huerta, and Tijerina and challenged moderate political leaders who favored cultural assimilation. Borrowing from the Black Panthers, Mexican Americans formed the Brown Berets, a self-defense organization. In 1969 some 1,500 activists gathered in Denver and declared themselves *Chicanos* (from *mejicano*, the Spanish word for "Mexican"), a term that expressed their cultural pride and identity. Chicanos created a new political party, **La Raza Unida (The United Race)**, to promote their interests, and the party and its allies sponsored demonstrations to fight for jobs, bilingual education, and the creation of Chicano studies programs in colleges. Chicano and other Spanish-language communities also took advantage of the protections of the Voting Rights Act, which in 1975 was amended to include sections of the country — from New York to California to Florida and Texas — where Hispanic literacy in English and voter registration were low.

Puerto Ricans organized the Young Lords Party (YLP). Originating as a youth gang in Chicago in 1969, the group soon spread to New York City. Like the Black Panthers, the organization established inner-city breakfast programs and medical clinics. The YLP supported bilingual education in public schools, condemned U.S. imperialism, favored independence for Puerto Rico, and supported women's reproductive rights. Under the leadership of José Cha Cha Jiménez, the Young Lords became a national organization.

Native Americans also joined the upsurge of activism. By 1970 some 800,000 people identified themselves as American Indians, many of whom lived in poverty on reservations. They suffered from inadequate housing, high alcoholism rates, low life expectancy, staggering unemployment, and lack of education. Conscious of their heritage as the first Americans, they determined to halt their deterioration by asserting pride in "red power" and established the **American Indian Movement (AIM)** in 1968. The following year, Indians occupied the abandoned prison island of Alcatraz in San Francisco Bay, where they remained until 1971. Among their demands, they offered to buy the island for $24 in beads and cloth — a reference to the purchase of Manhattan Island in 1626 — and turn it into an Indian educational and cultural center. In 1972 AIM occupied the headquarters of the Federal Bureau of Indian Affairs in Washington, D.C. Demonstrators also seized the village of Wounded Knee, South Dakota, the scene of the 1890 massacre of Sioux residents by the U.S. army, to dramatize the impoverished living conditions on reservations. They held on for more than seventy days with eleven hostages until a shootout with the FBI ended the confrontation, killing one protester and wounding another.

Explore ▶

See Sources 26.2 and 26.3 for statements on Chicano and American Indian protests.

The results of the red power movement proved mixed. Demonstrations focused media attention on the plight of Native Americans but did little to address their needs in meaningful ways. Nevertheless, courts became more sensitive to Indian claims and protected mineral and fishing rights on reservations.

One of the biggest obstacles faced by radical liberation movements came from federal and local governments. The FBI used its Counter Intelligence Program (COINTELPRO) to infiltrate these groups and stir up distrust and factionalism within them. In 1969, tipped off by an informer, the FBI joined with the Chicago Police Department in an armed, pre-dawn raid against Black Panthers, resulting in the shooting and killing of the popular leaders Fred Hampton and Mark Clark.

Asian American college students on the West Coast fought their own liberation struggle. At the University of California, Berkeley, and San Francisco State University, they participated in demonstrations against the Vietnam War and racism. In 1968 Asian American students at San Francisco State joined the Third World Liberation Front and, along with the Black Student Union, went on strike for five months, succeeding in the establishment of programs in Asian American and Black studies.

The children of newly arrived Chinese immigrants faced different problems, struggling in public schools that taught exclusively in English. Established in 1969, the Chinese for Affirmative Action filed a lawsuit against San Francisco school officials for discriminating against students with limited English-language skills. In *Lau v. Nichols* (1974), the Supreme Court upheld the group's claim, accelerating opportunities for bilingual education.

During this period many Japanese American high school and college students learned for the first time about their parents' and grandparents' internment during World War II. Like other activists, they expressed pride in their ethnic heritage and joined in efforts to publicize the injustices that earlier generations had endured. The activism of this third generation of Japanese helped convince the moderate Japanese American Citizens League in 1970 to endorse reparations for the internees, the first step in an ultimately successful two-decade effort.

Homosexuals were also marginalized and discriminated against in American society. Estimated at 4.5–5.5 percent of the population, gay men and lesbians remained largely invisible to the rest of society. In the 1950s, gay men and women created their own political and cultural organizations and frequented bars and taverns outside mainstream commercial culture, but most lesbians and gay men, like Bayard Rustin, hid their identities. There were, however, notable exceptions. During the early 1960s Frank Kameny, a member of the Mattachine Society, a group founded in the 1950s to protect the rights of gay men, led protesters in picketing the White House, the Pentagon, the United Nations, and the United States Civil Service Commission. Kameny had been fired by the federal government in the 1950s because he was gay.

In 1969, gay men and lesbians turned more militant in asserting their collective grievances. Police regularly cracked down on gay bars like the Stonewall Tavern in New York City's Greenwich Village. But on June 27, 1969, gay patrons battled back. The *Village Voice* called the **Stonewall riots** "a kind of liberation, as the gay brigade emerged from the bars, back rooms, and bedrooms of the Village and became street people." In the manner of black power, the New Left, and radical feminists, homosexuals organized the Gay Liberation Front, voiced pride in being gay, and demanded equality of opportunity regardless of sexual orientation.

As with other oppressed groups, LGBT people achieved victories slowly and unevenly. In the decades following the 1960s, they faced discrimination in employment, could not marry or receive domestic benefits, and were subject to violence for public displays of affection.

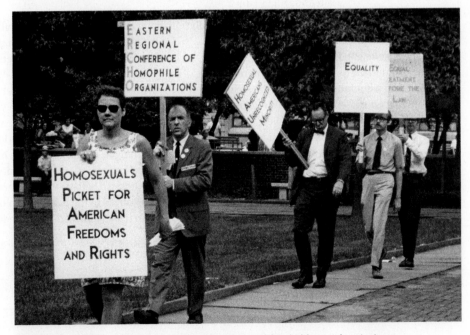

Gay Pride, 1969 Beginning in 1965, gay rights activists held annual protests on Independence Day, July 4, in Philadelphia to remind people that gay citizens (what would later be called the LGBTQ community) did not benefit from civil rights protections. In this fifth annual "reminder," protesters picket Independence Hall where the Declaration of Independence and the U.S. Constitution were adopted. Leading the lesbian and gay protesters were Barbara Gittings of the Daughters of Bilitis and Frank Kameny of the Mattachine Society. Nancy Tucker/Lesbian Herstory Educational Foundation

Chicano and Native American Freedom Movements

In April 1969, a group of students met at the University of California at Santa Barbara and formed the Movimiento Estudiantil Chicano de Aztlán (MEChA; Chicano Student Movement of Aztlán). MEChA organizers drafted "El Plan de Santa Barbara," excerpted in Document 26.2, which set out their basic philosophy and objectives. The same year, eighty-nine California college students representing a number of different tribes of American Indians seized Alcatraz Island located in San Francisco Bay and presented their grievances, which are excerpted in Source 26.3, to the American government. They claimed that under a Sioux Treaty of 1868, Alcatraz belonged to the Indians.

Source 26.2

Chicano Student Movement of Aztlán, 1969

For decades Mexican people in the United States struggled to realize the "American Dream." And some — a few — have. But the cost, the ultimate cost of assimilation, required turning away from *el barrio* [one's neighborhood] and *la colonia* [one's community]. In the meantime, due to the racist structure of this society, to our essentially different life style, and to the socioeconomic functions assigned to our community by Anglo-American society — as suppliers of cheap labor and a dumping ground for the small-time capitalist entrepreneur — the *barrio* and *colonia* remained exploited, impoverished, and marginal.

As a result, the self-determination of our community is now the only acceptable mandate for social and political action; it is the essence of Chicano commitment. Culturally, the word *Chicano*, in the past a pejorative and class-bound adjective, has now become the root idea of a new cultural identity for our people. It also reveals a growing solidarity and the development of a common social praxis [customary conduct]. The widespread use of the term *Chicano* today signals a rebirth of pride and confidence. *Chicanismo* simply embodies an ancient truth: that man is never closer to his true self as when he is close to his community.

Chicanismo draws its faith and strength from two main sources: from the just struggle of our people and from an objective analysis of our community's strategic needs. We recognize that without a strategic use of education, an education that places value on what we value, we will not realize our destiny. Chicanos recognize the central importance of institutions of higher learning to modern progress, in this case, to the development of our community. But we go further: we believe that higher education must contribute to the information of a complete man who truly values life and freedom.

Source: Carlos Muñoz Jr., *Youth, Identity, Power: The Chicano Movement* (London: Verso, 1989), 191–92.

Source 26.3

The Alcatraz Proclamation, 1969

We, the native Americans, re-claim the land known as Alcatraz Island in the name of all American Indians *by right of discovery.*

We wish to be fair and honorable in our dealings with the Caucasian inhabitants of this land, and hereby offer the following treaty:

We will purchase said Alcatraz Island for 24 dollars ($24) in glass beads and red cloth, a precedent set by the white man's purchase of a similar island about 300 years ago. We know that $24 in trade goods for these 16 acres is more than was paid when Manhattan Island was sold, but we offer that land values have risen over the years. Our offer of $1.24 per acre is greater than the 47 cents per acre the white men are now paying the California Indians for their land. We will give to the inhabitants of this island a portion of that land for their own, to be held in trust by the American Indian Government—for as long as the sun shall rise and the rivers go down to the sea—to be administered by the Bureau of Caucasian Affairs (BC). We will further guide the inhabitants in the proper way of living. We will offer them our religion, our education, our life-ways in order to help them achieve our level of civilization and thus raise them and all their white brothers up from their savage and unhappy state. We offer this treaty in good faith and wish to be fair and honorable in our dealings with the white men.

. . . In the name of all Indians, therefore, we reclaim this island for Indian nations, for all these reasons. We feel this claim is just and proper, and that this land should rightfully be granted to us for as long as the rivers run and the sun shall shine. Signed, Indians of All Tribes, November 19, 1969, San Francisco, California

Source: Camilla Townsend, ed., *American Indian History: A Documentary Reader* (Malden, MA: Wiley-Blackwell, 2009), 186–88.

Interpret the Evidence

1. Why does MEChA focus on the use of the term *Chicano*, and what does it hope to gain by its usage?
2. Why do the Alcatraz protesters believe they are being fair to the United States?
3. What connections do Chicano and Indian protesters make between cultural awareness and political activism?

Put It in Context

How did the civil rights and black power movements influence other freedom movements?

The Revival of Conservatism.
These diverse social movements did a great deal to change the political and cultural landscapes of the United States, but they did not go unchallenged. Many white Americans worried about black militancy, opposed liberalism, and were even more dismayed by the radical offshoots they spawned. Conservatives soon attracted support from many Americans who did not see change as progress. Many believed that the political leadership of the nation did not speak for them about what constituted a great society.

The brand of conservatism that emerged in the 1960s united libertarian support for a laissez-faire political economy with opposition to social welfare policies and moralistic concerns for defeating communism and defending religious devotion, moral decency, and family values. Conservatives believed that the United States had to escalate the struggle against the evil of godless communism anywhere it posed a threat in the world, but they opposed internationalism as represented in the United Nations.

Conservative activists built on the foundation erected by writers such as William F. Buckley, the creator of the *National Review*, an influential journal of conservative ideas, and the novelist Ayn Rand. They also incorporated the ideas of the Reverend Billy Joe Hargis's Christian Crusade and Dr. Frederick Charles Schwartz's Christian Anti-Communist Crusade, both formed in the early 1950s. These groups promoted conspiracy theories about how the eastern liberal establishment intended to sell the country out to the Communists by supporting the United Nations, foreign aid, Social Security, and civil rights. The John Birch Society packaged these ideas in periodicals and radio broadcasts throughout the country and urged readers and listeners to remain vigilant to attacks against their freedom.

In the late 1950s and early 1960s, the conservative revival grew, mostly unnoticed, at the grassroots level in the suburbs of southern California and the Southwest. Bolstered by the postwar economic boom that centered around military research and development, these towns in the Sun Belt attracted college-educated engineers, technicians, managers, and other professionals from the Midwest Rust Belt seeking new economic opportunities. These migrants brought with them Republican loyalties as well as conservative political and moral values. Women played a large part in conservative causes, especially in protesting against public school curricula that they perceived as un-Christian and un-American. Young housewives built an extensive network of conservative study groups.

The conservative revival also found fertile recruiting ground on college campuses. In October 1960 some ninety young conservatives met at William Buckley's estate in Sharon, Connecticut to draw up a manifesto of their beliefs. "In this time of moral and political crisis," the framers of the Sharon Statement declared, "the foremost among the transcendent values is the individual's use of his God-given free will, whence derives his right to be free from the restrictions of arbitrary force." Based on this principle, the manifesto affirmed the conservative doctrines of states' rights, the free market, and anticommunism. Participants at the conference formed the **Young Americans for Freedom (YAF)**, which six months later boasted 27,000 members. In 1962 the YAF filled Madison Square Garden to listen to a speech by the one politician who excited them: Republican senator Barry M. Goldwater of Arizona.

Goldwater's book *The Conscience of a Conservative* (1960) attacked New Deal liberalism and advocated abolishing Social Security; dismantling the Tennessee Valley Authority, the government-owned public power utility; and eliminating the progressive income tax. His firm belief in states' rights put him on record against the ruling in *Brown v. Board of Education* and prompted him to vote against the Civil Rights Act of 1964, positions that won him increasing support from conservative white southerners. However, Goldwater's advocacy of small government did not prevent him from supporting increased military spending to halt the spread of communism. The senator may have anticipated growing concerns about government excess, but his defeat in a landslide to Lyndon Johnson in the 1964 presidential election indicated that most voters perceived Goldwater's brand of conservatism as too extreme.

The election of 1964 also brought George C. Wallace onto the national stage as a leading architect of the conservative revival. As Democratic governor of Alabama, the segregationist Wallace had supported states' rights and opposed federal intervention to reshape social and political affairs. Wallace began to attract white northerners fed up with rising black militancy, forced busing to promote school integration, and open housing laws to desegregate their neighborhoods. Running in the Democratic presidential primaries in 1964, the Alabama governor garnered 34 percent of the votes in Wisconsin, 30 percent in Indiana, and 43 percent in Maryland.

More so than Goldwater, Wallace united a populist message against the political establishment with concern for white working-class Americans. Wallace voters identified with the governor as an "outsider." Many of them also backed Wallace for attacking privileged college students who, he claimed, mocked patriotism, violated sexual taboos, and looked down on hardworking, churchgoing, law-abiding Americans. How could "all those rich kids—from the fancy suburbs," one father wondered, "[avoid the draft] when my son has to go over there and maybe get his head shot off?" Both George Wallace and Barry Goldwater waged political campaigns against liberals for undermining the economic freedom of middle- and working-class whites and coddling what they considered "racial extremists" and "countercultural barbarians."

Review & Relate

◾ How did organizations on the left challenge social, cultural, and economic norms in the 1960s?

◾ What groups were attracted to the 1960s conservative movement? Why?

Race and Class in Second Wave Feminism

The civil rights and black liberation movements helped inspire the re-emergence of feminism in the 1960s and 1970s, but the ongoing relationship between feminism and race-based liberation movements was complicated and often fraught. This was especially true for the women's liberation movement, which in the 1960s was one wing of second wave feminism (the first wave originated in the nineteenth century and culminated in the adoption of the women's suffrage amendment in 1920). Second wave feminism attracted multiple generations of women that espoused diverse solutions to various forms of sexism. While many scholars highlight the tensions and conflicts between white feminists and women activists of color, they often differ on the degree of antagonism and the extent of common ground. In reading these selections by Anne Valk and Linda Gordon, keep in mind that Valk's is based specifically on a community study of Washington, D.C., whereas Gordon's is an analysis of feminism in general.

Source 26.4

Anne Valk | Feminist Interactions, 2008

"By the late 1960s a distinct movement to end women's gender-based oppression emerged that was philosophically and strategically tied to, but also separate from, contemporaneous struggles for black liberation. . . . As this predominantly white women's movement evolved to fight for reproductive and sexual freedom, its participants drew on—and reacted to—the ideas and approaches generated within movements . . . [such as] African American liberation. At the same time, participants in campaigns for racial liberation and economic justice responded to arguments and priorities advanced within women's liberation organizations, adopting and adapting some while rejecting others. . . . But . . . women of color . . . resisted the notion of a universal sisterhood and contended that no single approach could guarantee the liberation of all women, . . . Black feminism also challenged white feminists and proponents of racial liberation to understand the intersectional nature of racism, sexism, and class oppression.

. . . . Although acknowledging the important influence that the civil rights, student, and anti-war movements played on the emergence of second-wave feminism, [early] studies have typically treated the histories of these movements separately. As a result, much of this scholarship has obscured the continuous and fruitful interactions that occurred even when each movement declared its independence from the others. . . . Many recent studies, however, have focused on African American's women's activism for racial and sexual liberation, thereby challenging the view that feminism was exclusively a white women's movement; yet even this scholarship treats black and white women's activities as largely separate and generally antagonistic. . . . [T]his book acknowledges the divisions that occurred between various movements and groups, but still aims to understand the cross-fertilization of ideas that took place. . . . [It] includes both women who explicitly identified themselves as feminists and . . . those who fought to elevate women's status in their own communities and in the larger society through movements for economic justice and black liberation."

Source: Anne Valk, *Radical Sisters: Second-Wave Feminism and Black Liberation in Washington, D.C.* (Urbana: University of Illinois Press, 2008), 3, 4–5.

Source 26.5

Linda Gordon | Race, Class, and Feminism, 2014

"One fissure within women's liberation . . . was never bridged; its dominant white and middle-class composition gave rise to accusations of racism and privilege directed at it. The confidence, the articulateness, even the vocabularies of the college-educated women who dominated many feminist groups in the 1970s often functioned to silence working-class women. . . . Sisterhood talk and a one size-fits-all feminist program were not harmless; in reflecting the class and race upbringings and cultures of those who dominated the movement, middle-class women built walls around themselves. Despite their best intentions and despite their conscious opposition to racism, their priorities and assumptions sometimes blinded them to the situation of women of color and poorer women. . . . Middle-class whites did not take sufficiently into account the situation of women who experienced racism, low wages, ill health, and dangerous neighborhoods. Those poor and working-class women, in turn, frequently felt that the women's liberation movement did not represent them—even though many of them were feminist in the generic sense that they recognized women as disadvantaged."

Source: Linda Gordon, "The Women's Liberation Movement," in *Feminism Unfinished: A Short, Surprising History of American Women's Movements*, by Dorothy Sue Cobble, Linda Gordon, and Astrid Henry (New York: Liveright Publishing Corporation, 2014), 92–93.

Examine the Sources

1. Where do Valk and Gordon agree and differ in their understandings of the relations between white women and women of color in second wave feminism and women's liberation?
2. Drawing upon evidence in this chapter, how would you evaluate the strengths and weaknesses of Valk's and Gordon's interpretations?

Put It in Context

How did racial and gender differences shape the New Left and the distinct liberation movements that emerged in the 1960s and 1970s?

Conclusion: Liberalism and Its Discontents

The presidencies of John Kennedy and Lyndon Johnson marked the high point of liberal reform as well as Cold War military interventionism. Kennedy's New Frontier and Johnson's Great Society expanded the power of the national state to provide both compassionate government and bureaucratic regulation. Liberalism permitted greater freedom for racial, ethnic, and sexual minorities; expanded educational opportunities for the disadvantaged; reduced poverty; extended health care for the elderly; and began to clean up the environment. However, these expensive programs drew opposition from conservatives who saw big government as a threat to fiscal responsibility and individual liberty. Kennedy and Johnson's escalation of the Vietnam War fractured the liberal coalition of the 1960s and overshadowed their domestic accomplishments.

Kennedy and Johnson did not achieve their liberal agenda by themselves. The civil rights movement, with activists like Bayard Rustin, pushed the federal government into action. In addition, Earl Warren's Supreme Court affirmed the constitutionality of major pieces of reform legislation and charted a new course for expanding the guarantees of the Bill of Rights.

Although the Vietnam War tarnished liberalism, the struggles of African Americans, Asian Americans, women, Chicanos, Native Americans, and LGBT people continued. Indeed, the civil rights movement spurred other exploited groups to seek greater freedom, and they flourished in the late 1960s and early 1970s despite the waning of liberalism.

Liberalism began to unravel during the 1960s as its policies and programs prompted powerful attacks from radicals and conservatives alike. Indeed, over the next twenty-five years conservatives mobilized the American electorate and gained power by attacking liberal political, economic, and cultural values.

Timeline of Events

1960	Young Americans for Freedom founded
1961	Kennedy sends military advisers to South Vietnam
	Bay of Pigs invasion
	Freedom Rides
	Soviets build Berlin Wall
1962	Port Huron Statement
	Cuban missile crisis
1963–1968	U.S. troops in Vietnam rise from 16,000 to 536,000
1963	Betty Friedan publishes *The Feminine Mystique*
	Partial Nuclear Test Ban Treaty
	March on Washington for Jobs and Freedom
	John F. Kennedy assassinated; Lyndon B. Johnson becomes president
1964–1966	Great Society domestic programs enacted
1964	Civil Rights Act of 1964
	Freedom Summer
	Gulf of Tonkin Resolution
1965	Operation Rolling Thunder begins
	Voting Rights Act
1966	Black Panther Party formed
	National Organization for Women (NOW) formed
1967	Raid on Tierra Amarilla by Reies Tijerina and *La Alianza Federal de Mercedes*
1968	American Indian Movement (AIM) founded
	Martin Luther King Jr. assassinated
	Tet Offensive begins
1969	Stonewall Riots
1973	*Roe v. Wade* Supreme Court decision

Key Terms

New Frontier, *893*

Freedom Rides, *897*

March on Washington for Jobs and Freedom, *898*

Civil Rights Act of 1964, *898*

Freedom Summer, *899*

Mississippi Freedom Democratic Party (MFDP), *900*

Voting Rights Act, *900*

Black Panther Party, *902*

Great Society, *903*

Gulf of Tonkin Resolution, *907*

Tet Offensive, *908*

Students for a Democratic Society (SDS), *910*

Port Huron Statement, *910*

Free Speech Movement (FSM), *910*

counterculture, *912*

Commission on the Status of Women, *912*

National Organization for Women (NOW), *913*

Roe v. Wade, *913*

La Raza Unida (The United Race), *915*

American Indian Movement (AIM), *916*

Stonewall riots, *917*

Young Americans for Freedom (YAF), *920*

Review & Relate

1. How did President Kennedy's domestic agenda reflect the liberal political ideology of the early 1960s?

2. Evaluate Kennedy's and Khrushchev's actions in the Cuban missile crisis. How was war averted?

3. How did civil rights activists pressure state and federal government officials to enact their agenda?

4. How were the civil rights and black power movements similar and in what ways were they different?

5. What problems and challenges did Johnson's Great Society legislation target?

6. In what ways did the Warren Court's rulings advance the liberal agenda?

7. Why did Kennedy and Johnson escalate the Vietnam War?

8. How did the reality of the war on the ground compare with the political and military assumptions for fighting it?

9. How did organizations on the left challenge social, cultural, and economic norms in the 1960s?

10. What groups were attracted to the 1960s conservative movement? Why?

Freedom Summer

▶ Explain the aims of civil rights workers in Mississippi in 1964 and evaluate the extent to which they achieved them.

In June 1964 white college students gathered at the Western College for Women in Oxford, Ohio to train for a massive voter registration project in Mississippi (Source 26.6). Freedom Summer, as it was called, was organized by the Student Nonviolent Coordinating Committee, the Congress of Racial Equality, the National Association for the Advancement of Colored People, and the Southern Christian Leadership Conference. Working under an umbrella organization, the Congress of Federated Organizations (COFO), the project focused on political rights, particularly the right to vote. COFO set up freedom schools, which taught voter literacy, organizing techniques, and basic reading and writing skills (Source 26.7). The decision to use white volunteers was a deliberate one to put more activists on the ground and, more important, draw national attention to the cause. The activities of Freedom Summer volunteers provoked violence and resistance (Source 26.8). The most well-known acts of violence were the murders of three civil rights workers: James Chaney, a local black activist; and Michael Schwerner and Andrew Goodman, two northern whites.

Also, black activists formed the interracial Mississippi Freedom Democratic Party (MFDP), which sent its own delegates to the Democratic National Convention in Atlantic City, New Jersey and sought official recognition by the convention to replace the all-white delegation (Source 26.9). Offered a compromise, the MFDP refused it and returned home but supported Lyndon Johnson's election (Source 26.10).

Although few black Mississippians successfully registered to vote and the MFDP was denied official recognition at the Democratic National Convention, Freedom Summer did publicize the plight of black communities in Mississippi and throughout the South, and this publicity contributed to the passage of the Voting Rights Act of 1965.

Source 26.6

Prospectus for Mississippi Freedom Summer, 1964

Civil rights organizers carefully prepared for Freedom Summer, knowing that such a large campaign against intransigent disfranchisement in Mississippi would require extensive planning and coordination. The following selection is from an internal document of the Student Nonviolent Coordinating Committee that summarizes the purpose and strategies of Freedom Summer. It highlights the goals of voter registration and freedom schools.

It has become evident to the civil rights groups involved in the struggle for freedom in Mississippi that political and social justice cannot be won without the massive aid of the country as a whole, backed by the power and authority of the federal government. Little hope exists that the political leaders of Mississippi will steer even a moderate course in the near future . . . ; in fact, the contrary seems true: as the winds of change grow stronger, the threatened political elite of Mississippi becomes more intransigent and fanatical in its support of the status quo.

. . . A program is planned for this summer which will involve the massive participation of Americans dedicated to the elimination of racial oppression. Scores of college students, law students, medical students, teachers, professors, ministers, technicians, folk artists, and lawyers from all over the country have already volunteered to work in Mississippi this summer—and hundreds more are being recruited. . . .

Why this summer?

Mississippi at this juncture in the movement has received too little attention—that is, attention to what the state's attitude really is. . . . Either the civil rights struggle has to continue, as it has for the past few years, with small projects in selected communities with no real progress on any fronts, or [there must be a] task force of such a size as to force either the state and the municipal governments to change their social and legal structures, or the Federal Government to intervene on behalf of the constitutional rights of its citizens.

Since 1964 is an election year, the clear-cut issue of voting rights should be brought out in the open. Many SNCC and CORE workers in Mississippi hold the view that Negroes will never vote in large numbers until Federal marshals intervene. . . . [M]any Americans must be made to realize that the voting rights they so often take for granted involve considerable risk for Negroes in the South. . . . Major victories in Mississippi, recognized as the stronghold of racial intolerance in the South, would speed immeasurably the breaking down of legal and social discrimination in both North and South. . . .

Direction of the Project: . . .

Voter Registration: This will be the most concentrated level of activity. Voter registration workers will be involved in an intensive summer drive to encourage as many Negroes as possible to register. . . . Finally, registration workers will assist in the campaigns of Freedom candidates who are expected to run for seats in all five of the State's congressional districts and for the seat of Senator John Stennis, who is up for re-election.

Freedom Schools:

1. *General Description.* About 25 Freedom Schools are planned, of two varieties: day schools in

about 20–25 towns (commitments still pending in some communities) and one or two boarding, or residential, schools on college campuses. Although the local communities can provide school buildings, some furnishings, and staff housing (and, for residential schools, student housing), all equipment, supplies, and staff will have to come from outside. . . . In the schools, the typical day will be hard study in the morning, an afternoon break (because it's too hot for an academic program), and less formal evening activities.

Source: Prospectus for the Mississippi Freedom Summer, Miller (Michael J.) Civil Rights Collection, McCain Library and Archives, University of Southern Mississippi.

Source 26.7

Nancy Ellin | Letter Describing Freedom Summer, 1964

Setting up freedom schools throughout Mississippi was a key project of Freedom Summer. The schools in Hattiesburg were staffed by many northern white volunteers, including Nancy and Joseph Ellin. Both originally from New York City, Nancy and Joseph met at Yale University. The following selection is from a letter written by Nancy to Joseph's parents shortly after Nancy and Joseph arrived in Mississippi.

June 30

Dear Dr. and Mrs. Ellin,

. . . We got here OK, though we were frightened most of the way, quite unnecessarily. It was the people who came down in integrated cars who had the unpleasant time—refused service, cars following them, etc. We came down with a very nice girl who just graduated from Smith [College] and who did quite a bit of driving.

We are currently hard at work getting the Freedom Schools organized. Joe and another boy have everyone typing up stencils of the Constitution, the Declaration of Independence, etc. The school enrollment is over 150; we are having official registration Thursday. The philosophy is to take everyone who comes; we will be teaching adults in the evening. There are 10 teachers, 8 more expected from New York City on Thursday. We also intend to recruit a few local people.

. . . We felt terrible about causing you all such anguish, but we felt the decision was ours to make, and though we were very afraid and doubtful at Oxford [in Ohio], we made the decision to come. You must know that you were not the only parents who were worried, and some kids did drop out, one from our group, in fact, who was underage and couldn't get his parents' consent. Now that we are here we feel more than ever that coming here was the right thing to do. Even if we don't teach a single child (and I think the odds are heavily against that) we still will have accomplished something in showing the people of Hattiesburg that they should not hate whites. Even our own group leaders, Carolyn and Arthur Reese, who are Detroit Negroes (schoolteachers), were very anti-white until Oxford, Ohio. Things here are pretty horrible. The Negro section, where we are, smells and looks more than a little like India. The house we are staying in (free) is pretty good-sized but very dilapidated—creaky floors, etc. It has a bathroom—some don't. Our landlady is registered; her husband has tried but hasn't made it yet. Everyone agrees that things here would be much worse right this minute if it weren't for our presence and the pressure exerted on the [government] on our behalf by our rich Northern parents. Negroes in the movement tend to lose their jobs. We feel—rightly or wrongly—that our place is here, in the heart of the struggle. No man is an island. . . .

. . . Another job we have before us is organizing the library—there are tremendous quantities of books. We haven't had much contact yet, aside from smiles and handshakes, with the regular Negro community, so I haven't much else to report. The leaders we have met are terrific.

Thank Mary and everyone for praying for us.

Love,
Nancy

Source: Letter from Joseph and Nancy Ellin to Dr. and Mrs. Ellin, Joseph and Nancy Ellin Freedom Summer Collection, McCain Library and Archives, University of Southern Mississippi.

White Southerners Respond to Freedom Summer, 1964

As Freedom Summer activists began arriving in Mississippi, newspapers throughout the South ran editorials and articles condemning the volunteers. The following article appeared in a South Carolina newspaper and is representative of the ways in which white southerners characterized Freedom Summer. It mentions the National Council of Churches, a federation of white and black Christian churches that supported many civil rights and peace causes in the postwar era, including Freedom Summer.

This week the vanguard of a youthful army left the rolling hill country of southwestern Ohio, where volunteers had spent several weeks being indoctrinated and incensed, for the flat Delta land of Mississippi. The Summer Project, a joint effort of the Student Non-Violent Coordinating Committee (SNICK) and the National Council of Churches, was on the march. . . .

"The real aim of SNICK and the other more extreme Negro organizations is to secure the military occupation of Mississippi by federal troops." This is not the expressed judgment of Mississippi Governor Paul Johnson or even of Senator James Eastland. The words are those of Joseph Alsop, the liberal columnist. Mr. Alsop, however much he may desire civil rights for Negroes, knows that no good can come from this Summer Project, controlled as it is by the most militant of the many civil rights groups and the one whose ranks include, according to Mr. Alsop, more than a few dedicated Communists.

. . . The crusade leaders say publicly that the main thrust of the summer invasion will be directed at voter discrimination in Mississippi, where only 6.6 percent of Negroes of voting age are registered to vote. Such an effort, conducted with forbearance and directed at helping the Negro improve himself, might produce some good. Judging by the record, however, SNICK is short on forbearance and uncommonly long on making trouble. Nor is the National Council of Churches likely to provide much in the way of restraint.

"The main problem at this point," [according to the Council,] "is the concentration of wealth among the few, e.g., on an average, 5 percent of the farms control 50 percent of all the farmland."

Voting? This has nothing to do with voting. The Council is speaking of agrarian reform of the sort that socialists promote.

From this, the goals of the Summer Project appear to be two-fold: first, indoctrination in socialist economics; second, military occupation of Mississippi if that can be arranged. This is no longer a struggle of black and white. If the reports of even the most liberal observers are to be believed, the Reds predominate and the nation can anticipate a long, hot summer indeed.

Source: "'Freedom' to the Delta," *Charleston Post*, June 24, 1964.

Source 26.9

Fannie Lou Hamer | Address to the Democratic National Convention Credentials Committee, 1964

At the 1964 Democratic National Convention, Mississippi Freedom Democratic Party members attempted to unseat the official all-white Mississippi delegation. Fannie Lou Hamer testified before the credentials committee in front of a national television audience, but that coverage ended when President Johnson quickly held a press conference to divert attention from the controversy. In the following selection, Hamer tells of her arrest in Winona, Mississippi as she traveled home from a voter registration workshop.

was carried to the county jail and put in the booking room. They left some of the people in the booking room and began to place us in cells.

And it wasn't too long before three white men came to my cell. One of these men was a state highway patrolman and he asked me where I was from. And I told him Ruleville. He said, "We are going to check this." And they left my cell and it wasn't too long before they came back. He said, "You's from Ruleville all right," and he used a curse word. And he said, "We are going to make you wish you was dead."

I was carried out of that cell into another cell where they had two Negro prisoners. The state highway patrolmen ordered the first Negro to take the blackjack [police baton]. The first Negro prisoner ordered me, by orders from the state highway patrolman, for me to lay down on a bunk bed on my face.

And I laid on my face and the first Negro began to beat. And I was beat by the first Negro until he was exhausted. I was holding my hands behind me at that time on my left side, because I suffered from polio when I was six years old. After the first Negro had beat until he was exhausted, the state highway patrolman ordered the second Negro to take the blackjack. The second Negro began to beat and I began to work my feet, and the state highway patrolman ordered the first Negro [who] had beat me to sit on my feet — to keep me from working my feet. I began to scream and one white man got up and began to beat me in my head and tell me to hush.

One white man — my dress had worked up high — he walked over and pulled my dress, I pulled my dress down, and he pulled my dress back up.

. . . All of this is on account of we want to register, to become first-class citizens. And if the Freedom Democratic Party is not seated now, I question America. Is this America, the land of the free and the home of the brave, where we have to sleep with our telephones off of the hooks because our lives be threatened daily, because we want to live as decent human beings, in America? Thank you.

Source: Megan Parker Brooks and David W. Houck, eds., *The Speeches of Fannie Lou Hamer: To Tell It Like It Is* (Jackson: University Press of Mississippi, 2011), 44–45.

Lyndon B. Johnson | Monitoring the MFDP Challenge, 1964

To maintain party unity and white southern support, President Johnson instructed Senator Hubert Humphrey of Minnesota, a respected liberal, to work out a compromise over the MFDP challenge. In this telephone conversation on August 9, 1964 with Walter Reuther, the head of the United Auto Workers and a power broker at the convention, an irritated Johnson explains his reasoning for working out a deal.

JOHNSON If you and Hubert Humphrey have got any leadership, you'd get Joe Rauh [MFDP lawyer] off that damn television. The only thing that can really screw us good is to seat that group of challengers from Mississippi. . . . He said he's going to take it to the convention floor. Now there's not a damn vote that we get by seating these folks. What we want to do is elect some Congressmen to keep 'em from repealing this [1964 Civil Rights] act. And who's seated at this convention don't amount to a damn. Only reason I would let Mississippi [all-white delegation] come in is because I don't want to run off fourteen border states, like Oklahoma and Kentucky. . . . Incidentally this Governor [Mississippi governor Paul Johnson] has done everything I've asked him to do in Mississippi. We've broken that case [the Chaney, Schwerner, and Goodman murders]. I talk to him two or three times a week. Now he's not for [me]. But I can't say that he hasn't listened to us and he hasn't cooperated.

REUTHER Exactly. . . . We'll lose Mississippi, but the impact on the other Southern states—

JOHNSON That's all I'm worried about. . . . I've got to carry Georgia. . . . I've got to carry Texas. . . . We don't want to cut off our nose to spite our face. If they give us four years, I'll guarantee the Freedom delegation somebody representing views like that will be seated four years from now. But we can't do it all before breakfast.

Source: Michael R. Beschloss, ed., *Taking Charge: The Johnson White House Tapes, 1963–1964* (New York: Simon and Schuster, 1997), 510–11.

Interpret the Evidence

1. Describe the role white volunteers played in the Freedom Summer project (Source 26.7) and explain the advantages and disadvantages they brought to Mississippi.

2. Examine the arguments the *Charleston Post* (Source 26.8) made to discredit Freedom Summer. Compare these arguments to the goals for the project as expressed in the Freedom Summer Prospectus (Source 26.6).

3. Evaluate the testimony of Fannie Lou Hamer (Source 26.9) as a means to gain support for the Mississippi Freedom Democratic Party.

4. Explain President Johnson's views toward seating the MFDP delegation (Source 26.10) and evaluate whether they were consistent with his vision of the Great Society.

Put It in Context

Evaluate the successes and failures of Freedom Summer.

The Swing toward Conservatism

1968–1980

Window to the Past

Phyllis Schlafly, "What's Wrong with 'Equal Rights' for Women?" 1972

The conservative writer and political organizer Phyllis Schlafly spoke out forcefully against the women's liberation movement and its supposedly antifamily values. Believing that American women were happy and fulfilled raising families, she used her *Report* to rally readers against the Equal Rights Amendment and other aspects of feminism. ▶ To learn more about this primary source, see Source 27.7 on page 963.

The

Phyllis Schlafly Report

VOL. 5, NO. 7   Box 618, ALTON, ILLINOIS 62002   FEBRUARY, 1972

What's Wrong With "Equal Rights" for Women?

Permission from Phyllis Schlafly

After reading this chapter you will be able to:

- Compare how President Nixon handled the Vietnam War and the Cold War.

- Evaluate the extent to which President Nixon shaped conservatism and the forces that led to his downfall.

- Evaluate President Carter's successes and failures in domestic and foreign politics.

- Explain how liberal activists addressed the issues of clean energy, equal rights for women, racial equality, and nuclear proliferation in the 1970s.

- Explain the rise of the New Right and compare it to Richard Nixon's approach to conservatism.

Comparing American Histories

Louise Day Hicks fought against liberal notions of racial justice, thereby rallying support for conservatism. Born in 1916, Louise Day grew up in a relatively comfortable Irish Catholic home in South Boston. The daughter of a prominent judge, Hicks never moved far away from her working-class Irish community. Yet she crossed boundaries that most women of her age and neighborhood did not reach. A wife and a mother, she graduated from Boston University Law School in 1955, one of only nine women enrolled in her class of 232.

In 1961, Hicks entered the political arena, winning election to the Boston School Committee as "the only mother on the ballot." She became identified with the cause that would define her public career: opposition to racial integration in schools. Segregation existed in northern schools because of public policies that reinforced housing segregation and kept blacks from moving into white ethnic neighborhoods. Hicks refused to acknowledge the existence of this kind of segregation and lashed out at "racial agitators" and "pseudo-liberals."

In the late 1960s and 1970s, she rode to higher office on the white backlash to racial integration, first as a congresswoman and then as president of the Boston City Council. When a federal judge ordered busing to desegregate city schools in 1974, Hicks founded Restore Our Alienated Rights (ROAR). The group's protests created a good deal of havoc but failed to stop the court ruling. Through all this, Hicks remained a Democrat, but many of her white, working-class supporters in Boston and elsewhere joined the growing conservative coalition shaping the Republican Party.

Pauli Murray took a different path to advocate for her political beliefs. The descendant of Africans, Europeans, and Native Americans, Murray spent her life challenging racial and gender discrimination. Born Anna Pauline Murray in 1910 and orphaned at the age of thirteen, she moved to Durham to live with her mother's family. After graduating college in New York City, she applied for admission to the University of North Carolina Law School. Rejected by the all-white university, Murray moved to Washington, D.C., to attend historically black Howard University Law School, where she led demonstrations against segregated public accommodations in the city. In the decade following her graduation in 1944, she wrote a book about state segregation laws, which the NAACP cited in support of its successful arguments in *Brown v. Board of Education* (1954).

In the 1960s and 1970s, Murray devoted much of her energy toward issues of race and gender. President John F. Kennedy appointed her to a federal commission to investigate the status of women. Murray helped launch the National Organization for Women, supported the Equal Rights Amendment, and coined the term "Jane Crow" to define the dual racial and gender discrimination black women faced. In the

(*left*) **Pauli Murray** Bettmann/Getty Images
(*right*) **Louise Day Hicks** AP Images

1970s, the pioneering Murray carved out a new career path by becoming the first African American woman ordained as an Episcopal priest.

Throughout her life, Murray wrestled with her sexual identity. Although she had married (and divorced) a man, she shared intimate relationships with women. Having lived before the emergence of the transgender movement, Murray, who thought of her inner self as male, would most likely have identified as queer. ■

The American histories of Louise Day Hicks and Pauli Murray reveal that while conservatism grew in the late 1960s and 1970s, liberalism persisted. Elected in 1968 in the conservative backlash to radical dissent, Richard Nixon ended the war in Vietnam and withdrew from the war on poverty. Although the Watergate scandal briefly interrupted conservative momentum, New Right conservatism continued to grow throughout the 1970s. It meshed traditional conservative support for lower taxes, deregulation, and anti-unionism with cultural and racial resentments. Still, liberalism survived the rise of conservatism. The women's movement and black freedom struggle turned in new directions. The environmental movement accelerated amidst several man-made disasters. The reduction of overseas oil supplies propelled interest in finding alternative sources of energy. Nevertheless, the political balance between conservatism and liberalism began tipping toward the right.

Nixon: War and Diplomacy, 1969–1974

In winning the presidency in 1968, Richard Nixon paid close attention to international affairs. Having pledged to end the war in Vietnam, it took him another four years to do so. A fierce anti-Communist, Nixon considered himself a realist in foreign affairs. He was concerned more with a stable world order than with promoting American ideals. Nixon and Secretary of State Henry Kissinger worked to establish closer relations with both the Communist People's Republic of China and the Soviet Union. While the Soviet Union and China competed for influence in Asia, Nixon exploited this conflict to keep these nuclear powers divided. His administration brought a thaw in Cold War relations, but he was less successful in navigating Arab-Israeli hostilities in the Middle East, a misstep that caused pain for consumers of gasoline and oil at home.

The Election of 1968. Nineteen sixty-eight was a turbulent year. In February, police shot indiscriminately into a crowd gathered for civil rights protests at South Carolina State University in Orangeburg, killing three students. In March, student protests at Columbia University led to a violent confrontation with the New York City police. On April 4, the murder of Martin Luther King Jr. sparked an outburst of rioting by blacks in more than one hundred cities throughout the country. The assassination of Democratic presidential aspirant Robert Kennedy in June further heightened the mood of despair. Adding to the unrest, demonstrators gathered in Chicago in August at the Democratic National Convention to press for an antiwar plank in the party platform. Thousands of protesters were beaten and arrested by Chicago police officers. Many Americans watched in horror as television networks broadcast the bloody clashes, but a majority of viewers sided with the police rather than the protesters.

Similar protests occurred around the world. In early 1968, university students outside Paris protested educational policies and what they perceived as their second-class status. When students at the Sorbonne in Paris joined them in the streets, police attacked them viciously. In June, French president Charles de Gaulle sent in tanks to break up the strikes but also instituted political and economic reforms. Protests erupted during the spring in Prague, Czechoslovakia, where President Alexander Dubček vowed to reform the Communist regime by initiating "socialism with a human face." In August the Soviet Union sent its military into Prague to crush the reforms, bringing this brief experiment in freedom remembered as the "Prague Spring" to a violent end. During the same year, student-led demonstrations erupted in Yugoslavia, Poland, West Germany, Italy, Spain, Japan, and Mexico.

It was against this backdrop of global unrest that Richard Nixon ran for president against the Democratic nominee Hubert H. Humphrey and the independent candidate, George C. Wallace, the segregationist governor of Alabama and a popular archconservative. To outflank Wallace on the right, Nixon declared himself the "law and order" candidate, a phrase that became a code for reining in black militancy. To win southern supporters, he pledged to ease up on enforcing federal civil rights legislation and oppose forced busing to achieve racial integration in schools. He criticized antiwar protesters and promised to end the Vietnam War with honor. Seeking to identify the Democratic party with social and cultural radicalism, Nixon geared his campaign message to the "silent majority" of voters — what one political analyst characterized as "the unyoung, the unpoor, and unblack." This conservative message appealed to many Americans who were fed up with domestic uprisings and war abroad.

> **Explore ▶**
>
> See Source 27.1 for a statement by Richard Nixon on his conservative agenda.

Although Nixon won 301 electoral votes, 110 more than Humphrey, none of the three candidates received a majority of the popular vote (Map 27.1, page 936). Yet Nixon and Wallace together garnered about 57 percent of the popular vote, a dramatic shift to the right compared with Lyndon Johnson's landslide victory just four years earlier. The New Left had given way to an assortment of old and new conservatives, overwhelmingly white, who were determined to contain, if not roll back, the Great Society.

The Failure of Vietnamization.

Vietnam plagued Nixon as it had his Democratic predecessor. Despite intimations during the campaign that he had a secret plan to end the war, Nixon's approach to Vietnam turned out to look much the same as Johnson's. Henry Kissinger, who served first as national security adviser and then as secretary of state, continued peace talks with the North Vietnamese, which Johnson had initiated. Over the next four years, Nixon and Kissinger devised a strategy that removed U.S. ground forces and turned over greater responsibility for the fighting to the South Vietnamese army, a process called **Vietnamization**.

Vietnamization did not mean an end to U.S. belligerence in the region. In 1969, at the same time that American troop levels were being drawn down, the president ordered secret bombing raids in Cambodia, a neutral country adjacent to South Vietnam that contained enemy forces and parts of the Ho Chi Minh Trail. Meant to pressure the North Vietnamese into accepting U.S. peace terms, the bombing accomplished little. In April 1970 Nixon ordered the invasion of Cambodia, which destabilized the country and eventually brought to power the Communist organization Khmer Rouge, which later slaughtered two million Cambodians. In 1971 the United States sponsored the South Vietnamese invasion of Laos, a neighboring country that harbored North Vietnamese troops and supply lines, which again

Richard Nixon | Speech Accepting the Republican Nomination for President, August 8, 1968

After a decade of upheaval, the 1968 Republican candidate Richard Nixon, as the following passage from his address at the Republican National Convention shows, appealed to conservatives by supporting their demands for a smaller federal government, maintaining law and order, and cutting expenditures for social welfare programs.

Source 27.1

[T]o those who say that law and order is the code word for racism, there and here is a reply:

Our goal is justice for every American. If we are to have respect for law in America, we must have laws that deserve respect.

Just as we cannot have progress without order, we cannot have order without progress, and so, as we commit to order tonight, let us commit to progress.

How does Nixon reply to the claim that "law and order" is a code term for racism?

And this brings me to the clearest choice among the great issues of this campaign.

For the past five years we have been deluged by government programs for the unemployed; programs for the cities; programs for the poor. And we have reaped from these programs an ugly harvest of frustration, violence and failure across the land.

According to Nixon, what is the source of the nation's economic and social problems?

And now our opponents will be offering more of the same—more billions for government jobs, government housing, government welfare.

I say it is time to quit pouring billions of dollars into programs that have failed in the United States of America. . . .

But for those who are able to help themselves—what we need are not more millions on welfare rolls—but more millions on payrolls in the United States of America.

Instead of government jobs, and government housing, and government welfare, let government use its tax and credit policies to enlist in this battle the greatest engine of progress ever developed in the history of man—American private enterprise.

Let us enlist in this great cause the millions of Americans in volunteer organizations who will bring a dedication to this task that no amount of money could ever buy. . . .

Black Americans, no more than white Americans, they do not want more government programs which perpetuate dependency.

They don't want to be a colony in a nation.

They want the pride, and the self-respect, and the dignity that can only come if they have an equal chance to own their own homes, to own their own businesses, to be managers and executives as well as workers, to have a piece of the action in the exciting ventures of private enterprise.

How does Nixon view African Americans?

Source: Richard M. Nixon, "Address Accepting the Presidential Nomination at the Republican National Convention in Miami Beach, Florida," August 8, 1968, in John T. Woolley & Gerhard Peters, *The American Presidency Project*, http://www.presidency.ucsb.edu/ws/?pid=25968.

Put It in Context

How does Nixon's speech reflect conservative ideology?

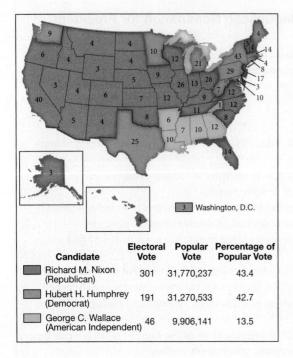

MAP 27.1   The Election of 1968

Democratic presidential candidate Hubert Humphrey lost across the South as white voters turned to Republican Richard Nixon or segregationist George Wallace. Many working-class whites in the North and West also shifted their allegiance to these "law and order" candidates, rejecting the civil rights and antipoverty agendas promoted by President Johnson and blaming Democrats for the turmoil over the Vietnam War.

Candidate	Electoral Vote	Popular Vote	Percentage of Popular Vote
Richard M. Nixon (Republican)	301	31,770,237	43.4
Hubert H. Humphrey (Democrat)	191	31,270,533	42.7
George C. Wallace (American Independent)	46	9,906,141	13.5

yielded no battlefield gains. Finally, in December 1972, shortly before Christmas, the United States carried out a massive eleven-day bombing campaign of targets in North Vietnam meant to force the North Vietnamese government to reach a peace accord.

The intense bombing of North Vietnam did end formal U.S. involvement in the war. An agreement signed on January 27, 1973 stipulated that the United States would remove all American troops, the North Vietnamese would return captured U.S. soldiers, and North and South Vietnam would strive for peaceful national unification. This agreement did not bring peace and the war in Vietnam continued. In 1975 North Vietnamese and Vietcong forces captured Saigon, resulting in a Communist victory. This outcome came at a terrible cost. Some 58,000 American soldiers, 215,000 South Vietnamese soldiers, 1 million North Vietnamese and Vietcong soldiers, and an estimated 4 million South and North Vietnamese civilians were killed in the conflict.

The Nixon administration's war efforts generated great controversy at home. The invasion of Cambodia touched off widespread campus demonstrations in May 1970. At Kent State University in Ohio, four student protesters were shot and killed by the National Guard. Large crowds of antiwar demonstrators descended on Washington in 1969 and 1971, though the president refused to heed their message. Nevertheless, the American public, and not just radicals, had turned against the war. By 1972 more than 70 percent of those polled believed that the Vietnam War was a mistake. Growing numbers of Vietnam veterans also spoke out against the war. Contributing to this disillusionment, in 1971 the *New York Times* and the *Washington Post* published a classified report known as the **Pentagon Papers**. This document confirmed that the Kennedy and Johnson administrations had misled the public about the origins and nature of the Vietnam War. Congress

The Fall of Saigon, 1975   On April 29, 1975, the day before Communist troops took control of Saigon, crowds of South Vietnamese, many of whom had supported the United States, scramble to climb the wall of the U.S. Embassy. They were making a desperate attempt to get to evacuation helicopters, but with space limited on available aircraft, many of these people were left behind. AP Images/Neal Ulevich

reflected growing disapproval for the war by repealing the Gulf of Tonkin Resolution in 1970 after the Cambodian invasion. In 1973 Congress passed the **War Powers Act**, which required the president to consult with Congress within forty-eight hours of deploying military forces and to obtain a declaration of war from Congress if troops remained on foreign soil beyond sixty days.

The Cold War Thaws. Although the Vietnam War remained controversial for Nixon, his efforts toward easing tensions with the country's Cold War adversaries proved more successful, through a policy known as **détente**. Through secret negotiations, Kissinger prepared the way for Nixon to visit mainland China in 1972. After blocking the People's Republic of China's admission to the United Nations for twenty-two years, the United States announced that it would no longer oppose China's entry to the world organization.

The closer relations between China and the United States worried the USSR. Although both were Communist nations, the Soviet Union and China had pursued their own ideological and national interests. To check growing Chinese influence with the United States, Soviet premier Leonid Brezhnev invited President Nixon to Moscow in May 1972, the first time an American president had visited the Soviet Union since 1945. The main topic of discussion concerned arms control, and with the Soviet Union eager to make a deal in the aftermath of Nixon's trip to China, the two sides worked out the historic **Strategic Arms Limitation Treaty (SALT I)**, the first to curtail nuclear arms production during the Cold

War. The pact restricted the number of antiballistic missiles that each nation could deploy and froze the number of intercontinental ballistic missiles and submarine-based missiles for five years.

Throughout the world, the United States chose to support dictatorship over democracy when its strategic or economic interests were at stake. In Chile, the United States overthrew the democratically elected socialist president Salvador Allende after he nationalized U.S. properties. In 1973 the Central Intelligence Agency (CIA) backed an operation that led to the murder of Allende, and the coup brought nearly two decades of dictatorial rule to that country. Under Nixon's leadership, the United States also supported repressive regimes in Nicaragua, South Africa, the Philippines, and Iran.

Crisis in the Middle East and at Home.
Nixon's diplomatic initiatives, however, failed to resolve festering problems in the Middle East. Since its victory in the Six-Day War of 1967, Israel had occupied territory once controlled by Egypt and Syria as well as the former Palestinian capital of Jerusalem. On October 6, 1973, during the start of the Jewish High Holidays of Yom Kippur, Egyptian and Syrian troops, fortified with Soviet arms, launched a surprise attack on Israel. An Israeli counterattack, reinforced by a shipment of $2 billion of American weapons, repelled Arab forces, and the Israeli military stood ready to destroy the Egyptian army. To avoid a complete breakdown in the balance of power, the United States and the Soviet Union agreed to broker a cease-fire that left the situation the same as before the war.

U.S. involvement in the struggle between Israel and its Arab enemies exacerbated economic troubles at home. On October 17, 1973, in the midst of the Yom Kippur War, the **Organization of Petroleum Exporting Countries (OPEC)** imposed an oil embargo on the United States as punishment for its support of Israel. In 1960 the Persian Gulf countries of Saudi Arabia, Iran, Iraq, and Kuwait together with Venezuela had formed OPEC and used its control of petroleum supplies to set world prices. As a result of the embargo, the price of oil skyrocketed. The effect of high oil prices rippled through the economy, leading to increased inflation and unemployment. The crisis lasted until May 1974, when OPEC lifted its embargo following six months of diplomacy by Kissinger.

Review & Relate

- Compare Nixon's policies toward Vietnam with those toward the Soviet Union and China.

- How did Nixon's Middle East policy affect Americans at home?

Nixon and Politics, 1969–1974

Nixon had won the presidency in 1968 by forging a conservative coalition behind him and blaming liberals for the radical excesses of the 1960s. Nixon won reelection in 1972, but his victory was short-lived. In an effort to ensure an overwhelming victory, the Nixon administration engaged in illegal activities that subsequently came to light and forced the president to resign.

Pragmatic Conservatism. On the domestic front, Nixon had pledged during his 1968 campaign to "reverse the flow of power and resources from the states and communities to Washington." He kept his promise by dismantling Great Society programs, cutting funds for the War on Poverty, and eliminating the Office of Economic Opportunity. In 1972 the president adopted a program of revenue sharing, which transferred federal tax revenues to the states to use as they wished. Hoping to rein in the liberal Warren Court, Nixon nominated conservative justices to the Supreme Court.

However, in several areas Nixon departed from conservatives who favored limited government. In 1970 he persuaded Congress to pass the Environmental Protection Act, which strengthened federal oversight of industrial activities affecting the natural environment throughout the country. In 1972 the federal government increased its responsibility for protecting the health and safety of American workers through the creation of the Occupational Safety and Health Administration (OSHA). The Consumer Products Safety Commission was established to provide added security for the buying public. The president also signed a law banning cigarette advertising on radio and television because of the link between smoking and cancer.

Nixon also applied a pragmatic approach to racial issues. In general, he supported "benign neglect" and rejected new legislative attempts to use busing to promote school desegregation. In this way, Nixon courted southern conservatives in an attempt to deter George Wallace from mounting another third-party challenge in 1972. Still, Nixon made efforts to further civil rights. Expanding **affirmative action** programs begun under the Johnson administration, he adopted plans that required construction companies and unions to recruit racial minority workers according to their percentage in the local labor force. His support of affirmative action was part of a broader approach to encourage "black capitalism," a concept designed to convince African Americans to seek opportunity within the free-enterprise system rather than through government handouts. Moreover, in 1970 Nixon signed the extension of the 1965 Voting Rights Act, which lowered the voting age from twenty-one to eighteen for national elections. Support for the measure reflected the impact of the Vietnam War: If young men could fight at eighteen, then they should be able to vote at eighteen. In 1971 the Twenty-sixth Amendment was ratified to lower the voting age for state and local elections as well.

The Nixon Landslide and Watergate Scandal, 1972–1974.

By appealing to voters across the political spectrum, Nixon won a monumental victory in 1972. The president invigorated the "silent majority" by demonizing his opponents and encouraging Vice President Spiro Agnew to aggressively pursue his strategy of polarization. Agnew called protesters "kooks" and "social misfits" and attacked the media and Nixon critics with heated rhetoric. As Nixon had hoped, George Wallace ran in the Democratic primaries. Wallace won impressive victories in the North as well as the South, but his campaign ended after an assassination attempt left him paralyzed. With Wallace out of the race, the Democrats helped Nixon look more centrist by nominating George McGovern, a liberal antiwar senator from South Dakota.

Winning in a landslide, Nixon captured more than 60 percent of the popular vote and nearly all of the electoral votes. Nonetheless Democrats retained control of Congress. Nixon would have little time to savor his victory, for within the next two years his conduct in the campaign would come back to destroy his presidency.

In the early hours of June 17, 1972, five men broke into Democratic Party headquarters in the Watergate apartment complex in Washington, D.C. What appeared initially as a routine robbery turned into the most infamous political scandal of the twentieth century. It was eventually revealed that the break-in had been authorized by the Committee for the Re-Election of the President in an attempt to steal documents from the Democrats.

President Nixon may not have known in advance the details of the break-in, but he did authorize a cover-up of his administration's involvement. Nixon ordered his chief of staff, H. R. Haldeman, to get the CIA and FBI to back off from a thorough investigation of the incident. To silence the burglars at their trials, the president promised them $400,000 and hinted at a presidential pardon after their conviction.

Nixon embarked on the cover-up to protect himself from revelations of his administration's other illegal activities. Several of the Watergate burglars belonged to a secret band of operatives known as "the plumbers," which had been formed in 1971 and authorized by the president to find and plug up unwelcome information leaks from government officials. On their first secret operation, the plumbers broke into the office of military analyst Daniel Ellsberg's psychiatrist to look for embarrassing personal information with which to discredit Ellsberg, who had leaked the *Pentagon Papers*. The president had other unsavory matters to hide. In an effort to contain leaks about the administration's secret bombing of Cambodia in 1969, the White House had illegally wiretapped its own officials and members of the press.

Watergate did not become a major scandal until months after the 1972 election. The trial judge forced one of the burglars to reveal the men's backers. This revelation led two *Washington Post* reporters, Bob Woodward and Carl Bernstein, to investigate the link between the administration and the plumbers. With the help of Mark Felt, a top FBI official whose identity long remained secret and whom the reporters called "Deep Throat," Woodward and Bernstein exposed the true nature of the crime. The Senate created a special committee in February 1973 to investigate the scandal. White House counsel John Dean, whom Nixon had fired, testified about discussing the cover-up with the president and his closest advisers. His testimony proved accurate after the committee learned that Nixon had secretly taped all Oval Office conversations. When the president refused to release the tapes to a special prosecutor, the Supreme Court ruled against him.

With Nixon's cover-up revealed, and impeachment and conviction likely, Nixon resigned on August 9, 1974. The scandal took a great toll on the administration: Attorney General John Mitchell and Nixon's closest advisers, H. R. Haldeman and John Ehrlichman, resigned, and twenty-five government officials went to jail. Watergate also damaged the office of the president, leaving Americans wary and distrustful.

Vice President Gerald Ford served out Nixon's remaining term. The Republican representative from Michigan had replaced Vice President Spiro Agnew after Agnew resigned in 1973 following charges that he had taken illegal kickbacks while governor of Maryland. Ford chose Nelson A. Rockefeller, the moderate Republican governor of New York, as his vice president; thus, neither man had been elected to the office he now held. President Ford's most controversial and defining act took place shortly after he entered the White House. Explaining to the country that he wanted to quickly end the "national nightmare" stemming from Watergate, Ford pardoned Nixon for any criminal offenses he might have committed as president. Rather than healing the nation's wounds, this preemptive pardon polarized Americans and cost Ford considerable political capital.

Nixon Supporters Rally during Watergate, 1974   On July 29, 1974, while the House Judiciary Committee was voting to recommend the impeachment of President Nixon, his supporters held a prayer vigil in front of the Capitol. Although 57 percent of Americans thought Nixon should be removed from office, Nixon did retain support from the Republican rank and file, as this protest shows. Nevertheless, on August 9, he resigned. Keystone/Getty Images

Review & Relate

■ Describe the conservative coalition that brought Nixon to power.

■ How did Nixon appeal to conservatism and how much did he depart from it?

The **Presidency** of **Jimmy Carter, 1976–1980**

Though deeply disillusioned by Vietnam and the Watergate scandal, most Americans hoped that, with these disasters behind them, better times lay ahead. This was not to be. Under the leadership of the Democratic president Jimmy Carter, the economy worsened as oil-producing nations in the Persian Gulf and Latin America raised the price of petroleum. Carter's efforts to revive the economy and rally the country behind energy conservation were ineffective. In foreign policy President Carter sought to negotiate with the Soviets over arms reduction while at the same time challenging them to do more to protect human rights. In practice, Carter found this balancing act difficult to sustain, and despite his desire to find ways to cooperate with the Soviets, relations between the superpowers deteriorated over the course of his term in office. Despite successful diplomatic efforts in the Middle East, trouble in the Persian Gulf added to the Carter administration's woes.

Jimmy Carter and the Limits of Affluence.

Gerald Ford received the Republican presidential nomination in 1976 and ran against James Earl (Jimmy) Carter, a little-known former governor of Georgia, who used his "outsider" status to his advantage. Shaping his campaign with Watergate in mind, Carter stressed personal character over economic issues. As a moderate, post-segregationist governor of Georgia, Carter won the support of the family of Martin Luther King Jr. and other black leaders. Carter needed all the help he could get and eked out a narrow victory.

The greatest challenge Carter faced once in office was a faltering economy. America's consumer-oriented economy depended on cheap energy, a substantial portion of which came from sources outside the United States (Figure 27.1). Due to the 1973 OPEC oil embargo on the United States, the price of oil had skyrocketed. By the time Carter became president, American automobile drivers who had paid 30 cents a gallon for gas in 1970 were paying several times that amount.

Energy concerns helped reshape American industry. With energy prices rising, American manufacturers sought ways to reduce costs by moving their factories to nations that offered cheaper labor and lower energy costs. This outmigration of American manufacturing had two significant consequences. First, it weakened the American labor movement, particularly in heavy industry. In the 1970s, union membership dropped from 28 to 23 percent of the workforce and continued to decline over the next

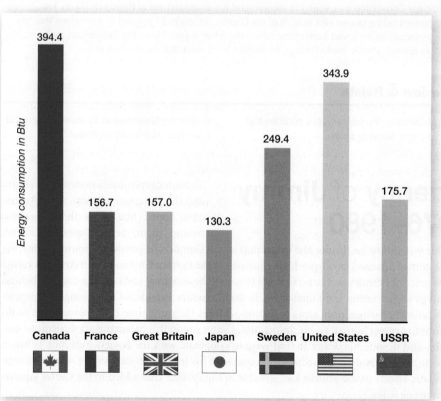

FIGURE 27.1 Global Per Capita Energy Consumption

Next to Canada, in 1980 the United States consumed the largest amount of energy per capita, measured in British thermal units (Btu), among the major industrialized nations in the world. The source of most of this energy came (and still comes) from such fossil fuels as coal and oil. Greenhouse gas emissions from this fuel production and consumption have created an environmental hazard in the above nations, and those like China and India that experienced rapid industrialization in the decades following 1980. Besides industrialization, what other factors influence per capita energy consumption?

Gas Shortages, 1973   Long lines of motorists descend on a gas station in Portland, Oregon, a scene replayed throughout the nation. OPEC's 1973 oil embargo during the Yom Kippur War caused gas shortages and soaring prices in the United States. As this December 1973 photograph shows, motorists scrambled to find available supplies at gas stations, creating long lines. PF-(usna)/ Alamy Stock Photo

decade. Second, this process of deindustrialization accelerated a significant population shift that had begun during World War II from the old industrial areas of the Northeast and the Midwest (the Rust Belt) to the South and the Southwest (the Sun Belt), where cheaper costs and lower wages were enormously attractive to businesses (Map 27.2). Only 14 percent of southern workers were unionized in a region with a long history of opposition to labor organizing. Sun Belt cities such as Houston, Atlanta, Phoenix, and San Diego flourished, while steel and auto towns in Ohio, Michigan, and Pennsylvania decayed.

These monumental shifts in the American economy produced widespread pain. Higher gasoline prices affected all businesses that relied on energy, leading to serious inflation. To maintain their standard of living in the face of rising inflation and stagnant wages, many Americans went into debt, using a new innovation, the credit card, to borrow collectively more than $300 billion. The American economy had gone through inflationary spirals before, but they were usually accompanied by high employment, with wages helping to drive up prices. In the 1970s, however, rising prices were accompanied by growing unemployment, a situation that economists called "stagflation." With both inflation and unemployment occurring at the same time, economists were confounded, and many Americans felt they had lost control over their economy (Figure 27.2).

President Carter tried his best to find a solution. To reduce dependency on foreign oil, in 1977 Carter devised a plan for energy self-sufficiency, which he called the "moral equivalent of war." Critics called the proposal weak. A more substantial accomplishment came on August 4, 1977, when Carter signed into law the creation of the Department of Energy, with responsibilities covering research, development, and conservation of energy. In 1978, he backed the **National Energy Act**, which set gas emission standards for automobiles and provided incentives for installing alternate energy systems, such as solar and wind power, in homes and public buildings. He also supported congressional legislation to spend $14 billion for public sector jobs as well as to cut taxes by $34 billion, which reduced unemployment but only temporarily.

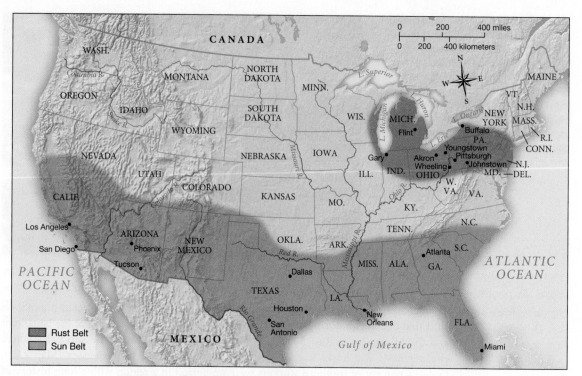

MAP 27.2   The Sun and Rust Belts

Dramatic economic and demographic shifts during the 1970s led to industrial development and population growth in the "Sun Belt" in the South and Southwest at the expense of the "Rust Belt" in the Northeast and Midwest. As manufacturers sought cheap, non-unionized labor, they moved factories to the South or overseas while defense industries and agribusiness fueled growth from Texas to California.

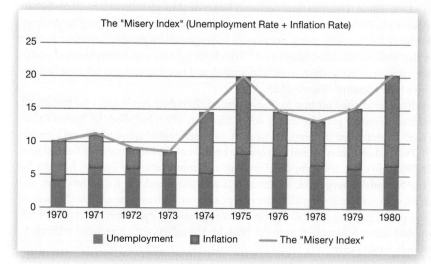

FIGURE 27.2   United States Unemployment Rate and Inflation Rate (the "Misery Index"), 1970–1980

The misery index is calculated by adding the unemployment rate to the annual rate of inflation. It measures how the average person is doing economically. High rates of unemployment and inflation drive up the misery index, indicating overall economic suffering. How do you explain the spike in the misery index in 1975 and 1980?

In many other respects Carter embraced conservative principles. Believing in fiscal restraint, he rejected liberal proposals for national health insurance and more expansive employment programs. Instead, he signed into law bills deregulating the airline, banking, trucking, and railroad industries, measures that appealed to conservative proponents of free market economics.

The Perils of Détente.

In the area of foreign policy Carter departed from Nixon. Whereas Nixon was a realist who considered the U.S. role in world affairs as an exercise in power politics, Carter was an idealist who made human rights a cornerstone of his foreign policy. Unlike previous presidents who had supported dictatorial governments as long as they were anti-Communist, Carter intended to hold such regimes to a higher moral standard. The Carter administration cut off military and economic aid to repressive regimes in Argentina, Uruguay, and Ethiopia. Still, Carter was not entirely consistent in his application of moral standards to diplomacy. Important U.S. allies around the world such as the Philippines, South Korea, and South Africa were hardly models of democracy, but national security concerns kept the president from severing ties with them.

One way that Carter tried to set an example of responsible moral leadership was by signing an agreement to return control of the Panama Canal Zone to Panama at the end of 1999. The treaty that President Theodore Roosevelt negotiated in 1903 gave the United States control over this ten-mile piece of Panamanian land forever. Panamanians resented this affront to their sovereignty, and Carter considered the occupation a vestige of colonialism.

The president's pursuit of détente with the Soviet Union was less successful. In 1978 the Carter administration extended full diplomatic recognition to China. After the fall of China to the Communists in 1949, the United States had supported Taiwan, an island off the coast of China, as an outpost of democracy against mainland China. In abandoning Taiwan by recognizing China, Carter sought to drive a greater wedge between China and the Soviet Union. Nevertheless, Carter did not give up on cooperation with the Soviets. In June 1979 Carter and Soviet leader Leonid Brezhnev signed **SALT II**, a new strategic arms limitation treaty. Six months later, however, the Soviet Union invaded Afghanistan to bolster its pro-Communist Afghan regime. President Carter viewed this action as a violation of international law and a threat to Middle East oil supplies, and he therefore persuaded the Senate to drop consideration of SALT II. In addition, Carter obtained from Congress a 5 percent increase in military spending, reduced grain sales to the USSR, and led a boycott of the 1980 Olympic Games in Moscow.

Of perhaps the greatest long-term importance was President Carter's decision to authorize the CIA to provide covert military and economic assistance to Afghan rebels resisting the Soviet invasion. Chief among these groups were the *mujahideen*, or warriors who wage jihad. Although portrayed as freedom fighters, these Islamic fundamentalists (including a group known as the Taliban) did not support democracy in the Western sense. Among the mujahideen who received assistance from the United States was Osama bin Laden, a Saudi Arabian Islamic fundamentalist.

Challenges in the Middle East.

Before President Carter attempted to restrain the Soviet Union in Afghanistan, he did have some notable diplomatic successes. Five years after the 1973 Yom Kippur War, with relations between Israel and its Arab

Afghan Mujahideen, January 1980   On December 25, 1979, Soviet troops invaded Afghanistan to suppress mujahideen guerrillas who were trying to overthrow the nation's secular, pro-Soviet regime. These rebel forces were among the guerrillas who defeated the Soviets after a decade of warfare and eventually established an Islamic theocracy. Pascal Manoukian/Sygma/GettyImages

neighbors in a deadlock, Carter invited the leaders of Israel and Egypt to the United States. Following two weeks of discussions in September 1978 at the presidential retreat at Camp David, Maryland, Israeli prime minister Menachem Begin and Egyptian president Anwar Sadat reached an agreement on a "framework for peace." For the first time in its history, Egypt would extend diplomatic recognition to Israel in exchange for Israel's agreement to return the Sinai peninsula to Egypt, which Israel had captured and occupied since 1967. Carter facilitated Sadat's acceptance of the **Camp David accords** by promising to extend foreign aid to Egypt. The treaty, however, left unresolved controversial issues between Israelis and Arabs concerning the establishment of a Palestinian state and control of Jerusalem.

Whatever success Carter had in promoting peace in the Middle East suffered a serious setback in the Persian Gulf nation of Iran. In 1953 the CIA had helped overthrow Iran's democratically elected president, replacing him with a monarch and staunch ally, Mohammad Reza Pahlavi, the shah of Iran. For more than two decades, the shah ruled Iran with U.S. support, seeking to construct a modern, secular state allied with the United States. In doing so, he used repressive measures against Islamic fundamentalists, deploying his secret police to imprison, torture, and exile dissenters. In 1979 revolutionary forces headed by Ayatollah Ruholla Khomeini, an Islamic fundamentalist exiled by the shah, overthrew his government. Khomeini intended to end the growing secularism in Iran and reshape the nation according to strict Islamic law.

When the deposed shah needed treatment for terminal cancer, President Carter invited him to the United States for medical assistance as a humanitarian gesture, despite warnings from the Khomeini government that it would consider this invitation a hostile action. On November 4, 1979, the ayatollah ordered fundamentalist Muslim students to seize the U.S. Embassy in Tehran and hold its fifty-two occupants hostage until the United States returned the shah to Iran to stand trial. President Carter retaliated by freezing all Iranian assets in American banks, breaking off diplomatic relations, and imposing a trade embargo. As the impasse dragged on and with the presidential election of 1980 fast approaching, Carter launched a failed rescue attempt to free the hostages. Seeking to humiliate the president further, Khomeini released the hostages on January 20, 1981, the inauguration day of Carter's successor, Ronald Reagan.

Review & Relate

- How effective was President Carter in domestic politics?

- How did events in the Middle East, the Persian Gulf, and Afghanistan challenge the objectives of the Carter administration?

The **Persistence** of **Liberalism** in the **1970s**

Many of the changes sought by liberals and radicals during the 1960s had entered the political and cultural mainstreams in the 1970s. The counterculture, with its long hairstyles and colorful clothes, also entered the mainstream, and rock continued to dominate popular music. Some Americans experimented with recreational drugs, and the remaining sexual taboos of the 1960s fell away. Many parents became resigned to seeing their daughters and sons living with boyfriends or girlfriends before getting married. And many of those same parents divorced their spouses.

Popular Culture. The antiwar movement and counterculture influenced popular culture in many ways. Rock musicians such as Bruce Springsteen, Jackson Browne, and Billy Joel sang of loss, loneliness, urban decay, and adventure. The film *M*A*S*H* (1970), though dealing with the Korean War, was a thinly veiled satire of the horrors of the Vietnam War, and in the late 1970s filmmakers began producing movies specifically about Vietnam and the toll the war took on ordinary Americans who served there. The television sitcom *All in the Family* gave American viewers the character of Archie Bunker, an opinionated, white, blue-collar worker, in a comedy that dramatized the contemporary political and cultural wars as conservative Archie taunted his liberal son-in-law with politically incorrect remarks about racial minorities, feminists, and liberals.

Women's Movement. In the 1970s the women's movement gained strength, but it also attracted powerful opponents. The 1973 Supreme Court victory for abortion rights in *Roe v. Wade* did not end the controversy. In 1976 Congress responded to abortion opponents by passing legislation prohibiting the use of federal funds for impoverished women seeking to terminate unintended pregnancies.

Feminists engaged in other debates in this decade, often clashing with more conservative women. The National Organization for Women (NOW) and its allies succeeded in getting thirty-five states out of a necessary thirty-eight to ratify the **Equal Rights Amendment (ERA)**, which prevented the abridgment of "equality of rights under law . . . by the United States or any State on the basis of sex." Pauli Murray, one of the founders of NOW, summed up the argument for why black women needed the ERA. "The Negro woman has suffered more than the addition of sex discrimination to race discrimination," Murray declared. "She . . . remains on the lowest rank of social and economic status in the United States."

In response, conservative women activists formed their own movement to block ratification. Phyllis Schlafly founded the Stop ERA organization to prevent the creation of a "unisex society." Despite the inroads made by feminists, traditional notions of femininity appealed to many women and to male-dominated legislatures. The remaining states refused to ratify the ERA, thus killing the amendment in 1982, when the ratification period expired.

Despite the failure to obtain ratification of the ERA, feminists achieved significant victories. In 1972 Congress passed the Educational Amendments Act. Title IX of this law prohibited colleges and universities that received federal funds from discriminating on the basis of sex, leading to substantial advances in women's athletics. Many more women sought relief against job discrimination through the Equal Employment Opportunity Commission, resulting in major victories. In the case of *Reed v. Reed* (1971) Ruth Bader Ginsburg, an attorney for the American Civil Liberties Union, convinced the Supreme Court that the Equal Protection Clause of the Fourteenth Amendment prohibited differential treatment based on sex. From 1973 to 1976, Ginsburg won another five cases before the Supreme Court, thereby reshaping the Fourteenth Amendment as an instrument for gender equality.

NOW membership continued to grow, and the number of battered women's shelters and rape crisis centers multiplied in towns and cities across the country. Women saw their ranks increase on college campuses, in both undergraduate and professional schools. Women also began entering politics in greater numbers, especially at the local and state levels. At the national level, women such as Shirley Chisholm and Geraldine Ferraro of New York, Louise Day Hicks of Massachusetts, Barbara Jordan of Texas, and Patricia Schroeder of Colorado won seats in Congress.

At the same time, women of color sought to broaden the definition of feminism to include struggles against race and class oppression as well as sex discrimination. In 1974 a group of black feminists, led by author Barbara Smith, organized the Combahee River Collective and proclaimed: "We . . . often find it difficult to separate race from class from sex oppression because in our lives they are most often experienced simultaneously." Chicana and other Latina feminists also sought to extend women's liberation beyond the confines of the white middle class. In 1987 feminist poet and writer Gloria Anzaldúa wrote: "Though I'll defend my race and culture when they are attacked by non-mexicanos . . . I abhor some of my culture's ways, how it cripples its women . . . our strengths used against us, lowly [women] bearing humility with dignity."

Explore ▶

See Sources 27.2 and 27.3 for two views of feminism by women of color.

Environmentalism. Another outgrowth of 1960s liberal activism that flourished in the 1970s was the effort to clean up and preserve the environment. The publication of Rachel Carson's *Silent Spring* in 1962 had renewed awareness of what Progressive Era reformers called conservation. Carson expanded the concept of conservation to include ecology, which addressed the relationships of human beings and other organisms to their environments. By exploring these connections, she offered a revealing look at the devastating effects of pesticides on birds and fish, as well as on the human food chain and water supply.

This new environmental movement not only focused on open spaces and national parks but also sought to publicize urban environmental problems. By 1970, 53 percent of Americans considered air and water pollution to be one of the top issues facing the country, up from only 17 percent five years earlier.

Not everyone embraced environmentalism. As the **Environmental Protection Agency (EPA)** toughened emission standards, automobile manufacturers complained that the regulations forced them to raise prices and hurt an industry that was already feeling the threat of foreign competition, especially from Japan. Workers were also affected, as declining sales forced companies to lay off employees. Similarly, passage of the Endangered Species Act of 1973 pitted timber companies in the Northwest against environmentalists. The new law prevented the federal government from funding any projects that threatened the habitat of animals at risk of extinction.

Several disasters heightened public demands for stronger government oversight of the environment. In 1978 women living near Love Canal outside Niagara Falls, New York complained about unusually high rates of illnesses and birth defects in their community. Investigations revealed that their housing development had been constructed on top of a toxic waste dump. This discovery spawned grassroots efforts to clean up this area as well as other contaminated communities. In 1980 President Carter and Congress responded by passing the Comprehensive Environmental Response, Compensation, and Liability Act (known as Superfund) to clean up sites contaminated with hazardous substances. Further inquiries showed that the presence of such poisonous waste dumps disproportionately affected racial minorities and the poor. Critics called the placement of these waste locations near African American and other racial and ethnic minority communities "environmental racism" and launched a movement for environmental justice.

Three Mile Island Nuclear Power Plant, 1979   On March 28, 1979, the Three Mile Island nuclear power plant, outside Harrisburg, Pennsylvania, started leaking radioactive steam that contaminated the surrounding area. The governor called for a voluntary evacuation within a twenty-mile distance. The cooling tower of the nuclear plant stands behind an abandoned playground, where children had been playing only days earlier. AP Images/Barry Thumma, File

Comparative Primary Source Analysis

Women of Color and Feminism

Although women of color participated in predominantly white feminist groups, they faced economic and social problems that middle-class white women did not. At the first National Chicana Conference, participants highlighted issues that ranged beyond gender while advocating sexual freedom, legalized abortion, free child care, and cultural self-determination. The black feminist Combahee River Collective contended that sexism had many sources: capitalism, racism, patriarchy, and enforced heterosexuality. Both groups proclaimed racial solidarity with men of color but recognized the difficulties of forging alliances with them.

Source 27.2

Workshop Resolutions │ First National Chicana Conference, 1971

SEX AND THE CHICANA

. . . I. Sex is good and healthy for both Chicanos and Chicanas and we must develop this attitude.

II. We should destroy the myth that religion and culture control our sexual lives.

III. We recognize that we have been oppressed by religion and that the religious writing was done by *men* and interpreted by *men*. Therefore, for those who desire religion, they should interpret their Bible, or Catholic rulings according to their own feelings, what they think is right, without any guilt complexes.

IV. Mothers should teach their sons to respect women as human beings who are equal in every respect. *No double standard.*

V. Women should go back to the communities and form discussion and action groups concerning sex education.

VI. Free, legal abortions and birth control for the Chicano community, controlled by *Chicanas*. As Chicanas we have the right to control our own bodies. . . .

RESOLUTIONS:

. . . Whereas: The need for self-determination and the right to govern their own bodies is a necessity for the freedom of all people, therefore, BE IT RESOLVED: That the National Chicana Conference go on record as supporting free

family planning and free and legal abortions for all women who want or need them.

III. Whereas: Due to socio-economic and cultural conditions, Chicanas are often heads of households, i.e., widows, divorcees, unwed mothers, or deserted mothers, or must work to supplement family income, and

Whereas: Chicana motherhood should not preclude educational, political, social, and economic advancement, and

Whereas: There is a critical need for a 24-hour child-care center in Chicano communities, therefore,

BE IT RESOLVED: That the National Chicana Conference go on record as recommending that every Chicano community promote and set up 24-hour day-care facilities, and that it be further resolved that these facilities will reflect the concept of La Raza as the united family, and on the basis of brotherhood (La Raza), so that men, women, young and old assume the responsibility for the love, care, education, and orientation of all the children of Aztlan [ancestral homeland of pre-Columbian Mexicans].

Source: Mirta Vidal, *Chicanas Speak Out, Women: New Voice of La Raza* (New York: Pathfinder Press, 1971), 13–16, http://library.duke.edu /digitalcollections/wlmpc_wlmms01005/.

Source 27.3

Combahee River Collective | *A Black Feminist Statement*, 1977

The major source of difficulty in our political work is that we are not just trying to fight oppression on one front or even two, but instead to address a whole range of oppressions. We do not have racial, sexual, heterosexual, or class privilege to rely upon, nor do we have even the minimal access to resources and power that groups who possess any one of these types of privilege have.

. . . The reaction of black men to feminism has been notoriously negative. They are, of course, even more threatened than black women by the possibility that black feminists might organize around our own needs. They realize that they might not only lose valuable and hard-working allies in their struggles but that they might also be forced to change their habitually sexist ways of interacting with and oppressing black women. Accusations that black feminism divides the black

struggle are powerful deterrents to the growth of an autonomous black women's movement.

One issue that is of major concern to us and that we have begun to publicly address is racism in the white women's movement. As black feminists we are made constantly and painfully aware of how little effort white women have made to understand and combat their racism, which requires among other things that they have a more than superficial comprehension of race, color, and black history and culture. Eliminating racism in the white women's movement is by definition work for white women to do, but we will continue to speak to and demand accountability on this issue.

Source: Zillah R. Eisenstein, ed., *Capitalist Patriarchy and the Case for Socialist Feminism* (New York: Monthly Press, 1978), 367–69, 371–72.

Interpret the Evidence

1. In what ways were Chicana and African American feminist views of the sources of sexism the same, and in what ways were they different?
2. Why do these African American feminists criticize their white counterparts?

Put It in Context

How did racial and ethnic diversity within the feminist movement shape women's issues in the 1970s?

The burgeoning environmental movement worried that potential accidents in nuclear energy plants would pour radioactive contaminants into the environment and endanger surrounding communities. In 1976, over 1,400 activists were arrested protesting the construction of a nuclear power plant in Seabrook, New Hampshire. Some of the worst fears of the anti-nuclear movement nearly came to pass in March 1979 at the Three Mile Island nuclear power plant near Harrisburg, Pennsylvania. A broken valve at the plant leaked coolant and threatened the meltdown of the reactor's nuclear core. As officials quickly evacuated residents from the surrounding area, employees at the plant narrowly averted catastrophe by fixing the problem before an explosion occurred.

Racial Struggles Continue. The struggle for racial equality did not end with the 1960s. The coalition of civil rights organizations had disintegrated, but the National Association for the Advancement of Colored People remained active, as did local organizations in communities nationwide. Following passage of the 1965 Voting Rights Act, electoral politics became the new form of activism. In 1970 Congress placed a permanent ban on literacy tests for voting. By 1992 there were more than 7,500 black elected officials in the United States. Many of them had participated in the civil rights movement and subsequently worked to gain for their constituents the economic benefits that integration and affirmative action had not yet achieved. In 1975, Congress renewed the Voting Rights Act and added provisions safeguarding the ballot for language minorities, including holding bilingual elections.

The issue of school busing highlighted the persistence of racial discrimination. In the fifteen years following *Brown v. Board of Education*, few schools had been integrated. Starting in 1969, the U.S. Supreme Court ruled that genuine racial integration of the public schools must no longer be delayed. In 1971 the Court went even further in *Swann v. Charlotte-Mecklenburg Board of Education* by requiring school districts to bus pupils to achieve integration. Cities such as Charlotte, North Carolina; Lexington, Kentucky; and Tampa, Florida, embraced the ruling and carefully planned for it to succeed.

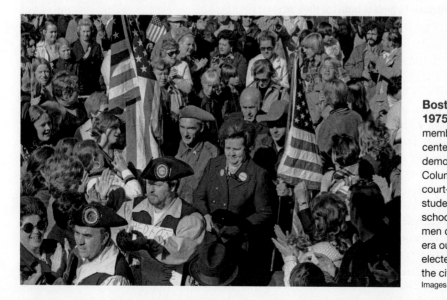

Boston Anti-busing March, 1975   Boston City Council member Louise Day Hicks (in center) arrives to address a large demonstration in South Boston's Columbus Park to protest federal court-ordered busing of black students to all-white neighborhood schools, Joining her were some men dressed in Revolutionary War era outfits. In 1976, Hicks was elected first women president of the city council. Spencer Grant/Getty Images

The decision was more controversial in other municipalities around the nation and it exposed racism as a national problem. In many northern communities racially discriminatory housing policies created segregated neighborhoods and, thus, segregated schools. When white parents in the Detroit suburbs objected to busing their children to inner-city, predominantly black schools, the Supreme Court in 1974 departed from the *Swann* case and prohibited busing across distinct school district boundaries. This ruling created a serious problem for integration efforts because many whites were fleeing the cities and moving to the suburbs where few blacks lived.

As the conflict over school integration intensified, violence broke out in communities throughout the country. In Boston, Massachusetts, busing opponents led by Louise Day Hicks tapped into the racial and class resentments of the largely white working-class population of South Boston, which was paired with the black community of Roxbury for busing, leaving mainly middle- and upper-class white communities unaffected. In the fall of 1974, battles broke out inside and outside the schools. Despite the violence, schools stayed open, and for the next three decades Boston remained under court order to continue busing.

Along with busing, affirmative action generated fierce controversy. From 1970 to 1977, with the acceleration of affirmative action programs, the number of African Americans attending college doubled, constituting nearly 10 percent of the student body, a few percentage points lower than the proportion of blacks in the national population. Though the average black family still earned a lower income than the average white family, black family income as a percentage of white family income had grown from 55.1 percent in 1965 to 61.5 percent ten years later. African Americans, however, still had a long struggle ahead to attain income and wages equal to whites. The situation was even worse for those who did not reach middle-class status: About 30 percent of African Americans slid deeper into poverty during the decade.

The case of Allan Bakke shaped the policy of affirmative action. In 1973, Bakke was rejected for admission into the medical school at the University of California at Davis. Of the one hundred available spaces in the incoming class, the university awarded sixteen spots to racial minorities, as part of its affirmative action policy to recruit a more racially and ethnically diverse student body. Contending that the policy amounted to reverse discrimination, Bakke sued the University of California at Davis. "I realize that the rationale for these quotas is that they attempt to atone for past racial discrimination," Bakke complained. "But insisting on a new racial bias in favor of minorities is not a just situation." In 1978, in *Regents of the University of California v. Bakke*, the U.S. Supreme Court struck down racial quotas as a component of affirmative action, but the justices permitted the use of race as one criterion in higher education admissions.

Despite the persistence of economic and educational inequality, many whites believed that affirmative action placed them at a disadvantage with blacks in the educational and economic marketplaces. In particular, many white men condemned policies that they thought recruited blacks at their expense. Polls showed that although most whites favored equal treatment of blacks, they disapproved of affirmative action as a form of "reverse discrimination." The furor over affirmative action did not end with the *Bakke* case, and over the next three decades affirmative action opponents succeeded in narrowing the use of racial considerations in employment and education.

Beyond voting rights, education, and affirmative action, one of the biggest concerns for African Americans remained treatment by the criminal justice system. Police officers patrolled black neighborhoods and arrested their residents disproportionately; trial juries convicted blacks disproportionately, and judges gave higher sentences disproportionately to

African Americans. The lopsided imprisonment rates of blacks (and Latinos) played a substantial role in giving the United States the highest incarceration figures in the world.

A prisoner rights movement emerged. In September 1971 mainly black and Latino inmates at the Attica Correctional Facility, near Batavia, New York, rose up in protest of their treatment. Subject to overcrowding, censorship, and religious discrimination (against Muslims), more than 1,200 inmates overpowered their guards and seized forty-two prison staff. Influenced by the liberationist philosophies of Malcolm X and Martin Luther King Jr., and inspired by the revolutionary prisoner rights activists George Jackson and Angela Davis, the Attica rebels sought a variety of prison reforms. After peaceful negotiations collapsed over the issue of granting amnesty to the insurgents, Governor Nelson Rockefeller sent state troopers to regain control of the prison. The armed assault ended the rebellion and resulted in the deaths of thirty-three inmates and ten correctional officers. The Attica insurrection sparked awareness not just of prisoner rights but of systemic racism in criminal justice programs.

Mexican Americans Challenge Discrimination. During the late 1960s and 1970s, Mexican Americans campaigned for educational equality. School districts disproportionately assigned Mexican Americans into classes for the learning disabled and assigned them to vocational rather than college preparatory tracks. Mexican American students in East Los Angeles, San Antonio, Denver, and Houston conducted walkouts in protest of the lack of resources provided their schools.

Mexican American parents in San Antonio sued their school district, contending that financing education through property taxes placed their children at a disadvantage. They argued that the teacher-student ratio in their schools was substantially higher and the availability of books for pupils substantially lower compared to conditions in wealthier school districts. In *San Antonio Independent School District v. Rodriguez* (1973), however, the Supreme Court ruled that financing school systems through property taxes was not unconstitutional. Despite the unfavorable outcome, the case raised greater awareness about disparities in educational funding, and many states attempted to equalize school spending.

Mexican American college students also pressed their demands for equal rights. Formed in 1969, the Movimiento Estudiantil Chicano de Aztlán (Chicano Student Movement of Aztlán), known as MEChA, sought to promote Mexican

Chicano Power, 1970   The Brown Berets was a militant Chicano group supporting farm workers, educational and criminal justice reform, and antiwar activities. In this February 28, 1970 photo, two Chicana women stand together in Los Angeles, wearing matching uniforms during a National Chicano Moratorium Committee march in opposition to the war in Vietnam. David Fenton/Getty Images

American empowerment through political action. In the 1970s chapters arose on college campuses in Los Angeles, San Diego, and Riverside, California, and spread to Washington, Oregon, Colorado, Arizona, and Indiana. MEChA placed a premium on higher education in order to "contribute to the information of a complete person who truly values life and freedom." The organization embraced the idea of *Chicanismo*, a political and cultural identity signaling a "rebirth of pride and confidence." These student radicals condemned Anglos for exploiting cheap Mexican labor and turning their *barrios* (neighborhoods) into colonies.

Review & Relate

- How and why did the social and cultural developments of the 1960s continue to create conflict and controversy in the 1970s?

- Evaluate the strengths and weaknesses of liberalism in the 1970s.

The **New Right** Rises

Explore ▶

Read Sources 27.4 and 27.5 for two different perspectives on the New Right.

The backlash against affirmative action and the ERA confirmed that liberal reformers were losing ground to conservatives. By the end of the 1970s, liberalism had become identified with special interests and elitism. At the same time, the pragmatic conservatism of Richard Nixon was being displaced by a harder edged brand of conservatism called the **New Right**. The New Right was founded on the budding conservatism of the 1960s as represented in the Sharon Statement and the presidential candidacy of Barry Goldwater. In the 1970s it expanded for a variety of reasons: the revolt against higher taxes, the backlash against the growth of the federal government, the disillusionment of former liberal intellectuals, and the growth of the Christian Right.

Tax Revolt. In the 1970s, working- and middle-class white resentment centered on big government spending and higher taxes. During that decade, taxation claimed 30 percent of the gross national product, up 6 percent from 1960. Although Americans still paid far less in taxes than their counterparts in Western Europe, Americans objected to raising state and federal taxes. Leading the tax revolt was the Sun Belt state of California. In a 1978 referendum, California voters passed Proposition 13, a measure that reduced property taxes and placed strict limits on the ability of local governments to raise them in the future. In the wake of Proposition 13, a dozen states enacted similar measures.

Economic conservatives also set their sights on reducing the federal income tax. They supported cutting personal and corporate taxes by a third in the belief that reducing taxes would encourage new investment and job creation. "Supply-side" economists argued that lowering tax rates would actually boost tax receipts: With lower taxes, companies and investors would have more capital to invest, leading to expanded job growth; with increased employment, more people would be paying taxes. At the same time, supply-side conservatives called for reduced government spending, especially in the social service sector, to ensure balanced budgets and to eliminate what they saw as unnecessary spending on domestic programs.

Comparative Secondary Source Analysis

The Rise of the New Right

Historians have attempted to trace the politicization of conservative Christians in the 1970s in support of the Republican Party. Some emphasize opposition among Christian evangelicals to feminism, abortion, gay rights, and a variety of other social issues. Other historians focus on the racial concerns that galvanized the New Right, as evidenced in the independent presidential candidacy of George Wallace, segregationist governor of Alabama, in 1968. In the excerpts below, Dan T. Carter and Daniel K. Williams offer different perspectives on the New Right, the former highlighting its racial origins and the latter its social and cultural foundations.

Source 27.4

Dan T. Carter, George Wallace | Race, and the New Right, 1996

"Historians of the American left have made much of the way in which the civil rights movement influenced the social movements of the 1960s and 1970s, inspiring, for example, the women's rights movement and the politics of sexual liberation. But the movement's counterrevolutionary effects are equally important. In the three decades following the emergence of George Wallace, the rhetoric of racial politics evolved: from the issues of public accommodations to school desegregation, busing, housing, quotas, and struggles over job discrimination, and proposals for economic affirmative action.

. . . Economic and social conservatives—particularly those who have been lifelong opponents of racial bigotry—have bridled at the

attempt to link what neoconservatives have called the 'new majoritarianism' of the 1980s with the politics of race. Nevertheless, I think it is fair to say that even though the streams of racial and economic conservatism have sometimes flowed in separate channels, they ultimately joined in the political coalition that reshaped American politics from the 1970s through the mid-1990s. . . . [George] Wallace's sensitivity to being 'looked down on' and his identity as a beleaguered white southerner strengthened his appeal to white ethnic minorities and working class Americans."

Source: Dan T. Carter, *From George Wallace to Newt Gingrich: Race in the Conservative Counterrevolution, 1963–1994* (Baton Rouge: Louisiana State University Press, 1996), xiii–xiv, 12.

Neoconservatism. The New Right also benefited by the defection of disillusioned liberals. Labeled **neoconservatives**, intellectuals such as Irving Kristol, Norman Podhoretz, and Nathan Glazer reversed course and condemned the Great Society programs that they had originally supported. They believed that federal policies, such as affirmative action, had aggravated rather than improved the problems government planners intended to solve. They considered the New Left's opposition to the Vietnam War and its disapproval of foreign intervention a threat to national security.

Christian Conservatism. Perhaps the greatest spark igniting the New Right came from religious and social conservatives, mainly evangelical Christians and Catholics. Evangelicals

Source 27.5

Daniel K. Williams | The Christian Right, 2010

"During . . . the late 1960s, conservative Protestants succeeded not only in making alliances with Republican politicians, but in changing the agenda of the party. This time, they focused more on the culture wars than the Cold War. Conservative Protestants who mobilized against feminism, abortion, pornography, and gay rights acquired control of the Republican Party, partly because of their long-standing alliances with Republican politicians, but perhaps more important because of the united front that they presented, and because of demographic and political shifts that favored evangelicals. . . . The sexual revolution, sex education, race riots, the counterculture, increases in drug use, and the beginning of the feminist movement convinced them that the nation had lost its Christian identity and that the family was under attack.

The end of the civil rights movement facilitated the formation of the Christian political coalition, because it enabled fundamentalists and evangelicals who had disagreed over racial integration to come together. After the passage of federal civil rights legislation and the end of nationally publicized civil rights marches, fundamentalists such as Jerry Falwell accepted the reality of racial integration and began forging political alliances with mainstream Republicans who would have been embarrassed by their segregationist rhetoric only a few years earlier. At the same time, moderate evangelicals who had once cautiously supported the civil rights movement reacted in horror to the race riots and began taking more conservative stances on civil rights. Both fundamentalists and evangelicals embraced Richard Nixon's call for 'law and order.' "

Source: Daniel Williams, *God's Own Party: The Making of the Christian Right* (New York: Oxford University Press, 2010), 3, 5, 6.

Examine the Sources

1. Describe the major difference between Carter's and Williams's interpretations of the New Right.
2. Based on evidence in this chapter, evaluate the extent to which this difference reflects a contrast of perspectives as opposed to a disagreement over facts.

Put It in Context

To what extent was the rise of the New Right in the 1970s a reaction to racial, moral, and economic concerns?

considered themselves to have been "born again" — literally experiencing Jesus Christ's saving presence inside of them. By the end of the 1970s, evangelical Christians numbered around 50 million, about a quarter of the population. The Christian Right opposed abortion, gay rights, and sex education; attacked Supreme Court rulings banning prayer in the public schools; denounced Charles Darwin's theory of evolution in favor of divine creationism; supported the traditional role of women as mothers and homemakers; and backed a hard-line, anti-Communist stand against the Soviet Union. Certainly not all evangelical Christians held all of these beliefs; for example, President Carter, a born-again Christian, did not. Still, conservative Christians believed that the liberals and radicals of the 1960s had spread the secular creed of individual rights and personal fulfillment at the expense of established Christian values.

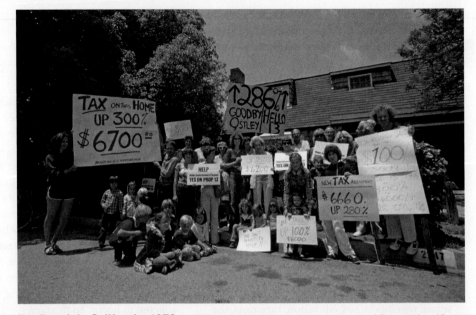

Tax Revolt in California, 1978.   California residents gather in support of Proposition 13, a state constitutional amendment that proposed a cap on property tax rates. The amendment also required a two-thirds vote by any local or state government to increase taxes in the future. The initiative passed overwhelmingly by a state-wide vote on June 6, 1978. Tony Korody/Sygma/Getty Images

Social conservatives worried that the traditional nuclear family was in danger, as households consisting of married couples with children declined from 30 percent in the 1970s to 23 percent thirty years later, and the divorce rate soared. The number of unmarried couples living together doubled over the last quarter of the twentieth century. In 1970, 26.4 percent of infants were born to single mothers; by 1990 the rate had risen to 43.8. This increase was part of a trend in developed countries worldwide. Moreover, social conservatives united in fierce opposition to abortion, which the Supreme Court legalized in *Roe v. Wade*. They argued that an unborn fetus is a person and therefore has a right to life protected by the Constitution.

The direct impetus pushing conservative evangelicals into politics came when the Internal Revenue Service (IRS) removed tax-exempt status from a fundamentalist Christian college. Bob Jones University in South Carolina defended racial segregation on biblical grounds, but under pressure from the federal government began admitting some African American students in the mid-1970s. However, the school continued practicing discrimination by prohibiting interracial dating. In 1976, when the IRS revoked the university's tax-exempt status, conservative Christians charged that the federal government was interfering with religious freedom. This sparked a grassroots political campaign to rally Christian evangelicals around a host of grievances.

Television became an even greater instrument in the hands of New Right Christian preachers in the 1970s and 1980s. The Reverend Pat Robertson of Virginia founded the

Christian Broadcasting Network, and ministers such as Jerry Falwell used the airwaves to great effect. What distinguished Falwell and Robertson from earlier evangelists like Billy Graham was their fusion of religion and electoral politics. In 1979 Falwell founded the Moral Majority, an organization that backed political candidates who supported a "family values" social agenda. Within two years of its creation, the Moral Majority counted four million members who were eager to organize in support of New Right politicians. The New Right also lined up advocacy groups such as the American Enterprise Institute and the Heritage Foundation to generate and promote conservative ideals. The alliance of economic, intellectual, and religious conservatives offered a formidable challenge to liberalism. **See Primary Source Project 27: The New Right and Its Critics, page 962.**

Review & Relate

- Explain the rise of the New Right in the 1970s.

- How did Christian evangelicals influence the New Right?

Conclusion: The Swing toward Conservatism

The election of President Richard M. Nixon signaled discontent with the liberal policies and radical excesses of the 1960s. However, this conservative victory proved short-lived, as Nixon was forced to resign in disgrace as a result of the Watergate scandal. Before his resignation in 1973, Nixon had displayed a pragmatic conservatism that dismantled parts of the Great Society while at the same time signing into law measures that extended environmental protection and voting rights, including those for eighteen-year-olds. He issued executive orders expanding affirmative action.

The return of Democrats to the White House in 1977 did not restore 1960s-style liberalism. The presidential administration of Jimmy Carter acknowledged the conservative notions of limited government and a deregulated market economy while embracing key conservative social values, such as faith in God and prayer. Although Carter departed from conservatives on some key issues concerning the economy, race, and gender, he did not portray himself as the heir of the liberal ideals promoted by Franklin Roosevelt, Harry Truman, and Lyndon Johnson.

The movement toward conservatism grew slowly and sporadically. Nixon's pragmatic conservatism may have stalled in Washington, D.C., but in cities and states around the nation conservatives with a more rigid ideological bent than Nixon rallied their forces. The 1970s marked the rise of the New Right, which joined defectors from liberalism and exponents of conservative free market, anti-government principles with white members of the working class resentful of racial change, anti-abortion advocates, and proponents of right-wing Christian beliefs. The New Right sought to transform the politics of resentment toward the culture of the 1960s into the politics of revivalism, convincing many that traditional values once again might guide the nation.

The move to the right, however, did not stifle liberalism or dissent. For much of the 1970s, Democrats controlled Congress and although the Supreme Court shifted in a more conservative direction, the Court did not reject the precedents established by the Warren Court. The justices upheld abortion rights and, in the *Bakke* case, they limited affirmative action but did not overturn its constitutional foundation. Civil rights reformers, feminists such as Pauli Murray, environmentalists, and antinuclear activists continued to press their concerns and achieve victories. Nevertheless, racial problems persisted as conservatives attacked affirmative action and school busing to promote integration. Many of these battles shifted northward, as white, working-class, grassroots activists such as Louise Day Hicks fought against busing in particular and more generally against liberal elites, who, they believed, ignored them.

In foreign affairs, President Nixon ushered in a period of détente with the Soviet Union and the opening of diplomatic relations with Communist China. He brought an end to American military participation in Vietnam, but did so with less than honor. Throughout the rest of the world, Nixon pursued a muscular foreign policy, which often left the United States siding with dictators. His Middle East strategy in the 1973 Yom Kippur War produced a damaging gasoline crisis at home, which would be felt for years. Jimmy Carter built on Nixon's spirit of cooperation with the Soviet Union and China, only to see it end with renewed conflict with the Soviets. Where Nixon and previous presidents had failed, Carter succeeded in brokering a peace treaty between Egypt and Israel. However, his popularity plummeted after Iranian revolutionaries seized the American Embassy in Teheran and held its fifty-two occupants hostage for 444 days despite a failed rescue attempt.

Conservatism experienced its political ups and downs in the 1970s, but by the end of the decade it stood on the edge of transforming the political landscape of the nation. It remained for Ronald Reagan to lead the New Right forward.

Timeline of Events

Key Terms

Review & Relate

1. Compare Nixon's policies toward Vietnam with those toward the Soviet Union and China.

2. How did Nixon's Middle East policy affect Americans at home?

3. Describe the conservative coalition that brought Nixon to power.

4. How did Nixon appeal to conservatism and how much did he depart from it?

5. How effective was President Carter in domestic politics?

6. How did events in the Middle East, the Persian Gulf, and Afghanistan challenge the objectives of the Carter administration?

7. How and why did the social and cultural developments of the 1960s continue to create conflict and controversy in the 1970s?

8. Evaluate the strengths and weaknesses of liberalism in the 1970s.

9. Explain the rise of the New Right in the 1970s.

10. How did Christian evangelicals influence the New Right?

The New Right and Its Critics

▶ Analyze the arguments of the proponents and critics of the New Right and compare the respective audiences they are aimed at reaching.

The New Right had much in common with its Old Right forebear. Both stood for small government, lower taxes, and deregulation of the economy (Source 27.6). Each viewed labor unions as a danger to free enterprise and believed in a states' rights approach to handling civil rights conflicts. In foreign affairs they took a strong anti-Communist position in challenging the Soviet Union. During the 1950s, groups of conservative religious crusaders put forth right-wing political principles within a Christian framework, but the stridency of their critiques and their penchant for conspiracy theories pushed them to the fringes of political acceptability.

The grassroots conservative movement that propelled Barry Goldwater into national prominence in 1964 gained momentum in the 1970s. It forged a national coalition of economic and social conservatives; militant anti-Communists; and disaffected Democrats, especially in the South. Linking them was their hostility to Great Society programs, Vietnam War protesters, inner-city uprisings, affirmative action, feminism, and challenges to traditional cultural values (Sources 27.7 and 27.9). The New Right coalition that emerged in the 1970s differed in one key respect from its conservative predecessor: It successfully incorporated the religious right as a main partner. By 1980, the political landscape had moved to the right, and Christian conservatives, unlike those in the 1950s, were considered respectable and legitimate.

Defenders of liberalism did not remain silent in the face of conservative arguments. They attacked New Right economics for its trickle-down tax cuts, which benefited the wealthy at the expense of the poor and the middle class, and for failing properly to fund education, scientific research and technological development, energy conservation, and environmental protection. They also criticized social conservatives for opposing the Equal Rights Amendment (Source 27.8) and denounced the Moral Majority for attempting to impose its religious values on a secular society (Source 27.10).

Source 27.6

Proposition 13, California, 1978

Howard Jarvis, a conservative Republican lobbyist, spearheaded a taxpayer revolt in California for lower, fixed property taxes. He devised Proposition 13 and gained sufficient signatures to place it on the ballot as a referendum initiative. In 1978 California voters adopted the measure by an overwhelming majority and set off a national movement for property tax relief.

Section 1.

(a) The maximum amount of any ad valorem [according to value] tax on real property shall not exceed one percent (1%) of the full cash value of such property. The one percent (1%) tax to be collected by the counties and apportioned according to law to the districts within the counties. . . .

Section 2.

. . . (b) The fair market value base may reflect from year to year the inflationary rate not to exceed two percent (2%) for any given year or reduction as shown in the consumer price index or comparable data for the area under taxing jurisdiction.

Section 3.

From and after the effective date of this article, any changes in State taxes enacted for the purpose of increasing revenues collected pursuant thereto whether by increased rates or changes in methods of computation must be imposed by an Act passed by not less than two-thirds of all members elected to each of the two houses of the Legislature, except that no new ad valorem taxes on real property, or sales or transaction taxes on the sales of real property may be imposed.

Section 4.

Cities, Counties and special districts, by a two-thirds vote of the qualified electors of such district, may impose special taxes on such district, except ad valorem taxes on real property or a transaction tax or sales tax on the sale of real property within such City, County or special district.

Source: Howard Jarvis Taxpayers Association, "The Original Proposition 13," accessed December 4, 2015, http://www.hjta.org /propositions/proposition-13/.

Source 27.7

Phyllis Schlafly | "What's Wrong with 'Equal Rights' for Women?" 1972

A long-standing conservative activist, Phyllis Schlafly was an attorney, wife, and mother of six children. She had campaigned for Barry Goldwater in 1964 and successfully led the antifeminist forces against the Equal Rights Amendment in the 1970s. In the excerpt below she explains her views on women.

Of all the classes of people who ever lived, the American woman is the most privileged. We have the most rights and rewards, and the fewest duties. Our unique status is the result of a fortunate combination of circumstances.

1. We have the immense good fortune to live in a civilization which respects the family as the basic unit of society. This respect is part and parcel of our laws and our customs. It is based on the fact of life — which no legislation or agitation can erase — that women have babies and men don't.

If you don't like this fundamental difference, you will have to take up your complaint with God because He created us this way. The fact that women, not men, have babies is not the fault of selfish and domineering men, or of the establishment, or of any clique of conspirators who want to oppress women. It's simply the way God made us. . . .

The Financial Benefits of Chivalry

2. The second reason why American women are a privileged group is that we are the beneficiaries of a tradition of special respect for women which dates from the Christian Age of Chivalry. The honor and respect paid to Mary, the Mother of Christ, resulted in all women, in effect, being put on a pedestal. . . .

In other civilizations, such as the African and the American Indian, the men strut around wearing feathers and beads and hunting and fishing (great sport for men!), while the women do all the hard, tiresome drudgery including the tilling of the soil (if any is done), the hewing of wood, the making of fires, the carrying of water, as well as the cooking, sewing and caring for babies.

This is not the American way because we were lucky enough to inherit the traditions of the Age of Chivalry. In America, a man's first significant purchase is a diamond for his bride, and the largest financial investment of his life is a home for her to live in. American husbands work hours of overtime to buy a fur piece or other finery to keep their wives in fashion, and to pay premiums on their life insurance policies to provide for her comfort when she is a widow (benefits in which he can never share). . . .

The Real Liberation of Women

3. The third reason why American women are so well off is that the great American free enterprise system has produced remarkable inventors who have lifted the backbreaking "women's work" from our shoulders.

In other countries and in other eras, it was truly said that "Man may work from sun to sun, but woman's work is never done." . . . Our American free enterprise system has given us the gigantic food and packaging industry and beautiful supermarkets, which provide an endless variety of foods, prepackaged for easy carrying and a minimum of waiting. In America, women have the freedom from the slavery of standing in line for daily food.

Thus, household duties have been reduced to only a few hours a day, leaving the American woman with plenty of time to moonlight. She can take a full or part-time paying job, or she can indulge to her heart's content in a tremendous selection of interesting educational or cultural or homemaking activities. . . .

Women's Libbers Do NOT Speak for Us

The "women's lib" movement is *not* an honest effort to secure better jobs for women who want or need to work outside the home. This is just the superficial sweet-talk to win broad support for a radical "movement." Women's lib is a total assault on the role of the American woman as wife and mother, and on the family as the basic unit of society.

Source: *The Phyllis Schlafly Report* 5, no. 7 (February 1972): 1–4.

Source 27.8

Gloria Steinem | Testimony on the Equal Rights Amendment, May 6, 1970

Gloria Steinem is a feminist writer, founding editor of *MS.* Magazine, and political activist. In 1970, she testified before the Senate Committee on the Equal Rights Amendment.

During 12 years of working for a living, I have experienced much of the legal and social discrimination reserved for women in this country. I have been refused service in public restaurants, ordered out of public gathering places, and turned away from apartment rentals; all for the clearly stated, sole reason that I am a woman. And all without the legal remedies available to blacks and other racial minorities. I have been excluded from professional groups, writing assignments on so-called "unfeminine" subjects such as politics, full participation in the Democratic Party, jury duty, and even from such small male privileges as discounts on airline fares. Most important to me, I have been denied a society in which women are encouraged, or even allowed to think of themselves as first-class citizens and responsible human beings.

. . . The truth is that all our problems stem from the same sex based myths. . . . Like racial myths, they have been reflected in our laws. Let me list a few.

That woman are biologically inferior to men. In fact, an equally good case can be made for the reverse. Women live longer than men, even when the men are not subject to business pressures. Women survived Nazi concentration camps better, keep cooler heads in emergencies currently studied by disaster-researchers, are protected against heart attacks by their female sex hormones, and are so much more durable at every stage of life that nature must conceive 20 to 50 percent more males in order to keep the balance going. However, I don't want to prove the superiority of one sex to another. That would only be repeating a male mistake.

. . . Women suffer this second class treatment from the moment they are born. They are expected to be, rather than achieve, to function biologically rather than learn. A brother, whatever his intellect, is more likely to get the family's encouragement and education money, while girls are often pressured to conceal ambition and intelligence, to "Uncle Tom."

. . . Another myth, that children must have full-time mothers. American mothers spend more time with their homes and children than those of any other society we know about. In the past, joint families, servants, a prevalent system in which grandparents raised the children, or family field work in the agrarian systems—all these factors contributed more to child care than the labor-saving devices of which we are so proud.

The truth is that most American children seem to be suffering from too much mother, and too little father. Part of the program of Women's Liberation is a return of fathers to their children. If laws permit women equal work and pay opportunities, men will then be relieved of their role as sole breadwinner. Fewer ulcers, fewer hours of meaningless work, equal responsibility for his own children: these are a few of the reasons that Women's Liberation is Men's Liberation too.

Source: *The "Equal Rights" Amendment, Hearings before the Subcommittee on Constitutional Amendments of the Committee on the Judiciary United States Senate Ninety-First Congress, Second Session, on S. J. Res. 61 5–7 May 1970* (Washington, DC: U.S. Government Printing Office, 1970), 335–37.

Source 27.9

Paul Weyrich | Building the Moral Majority, 1979

Paul Weyrich, a conservative Republican from Wisconsin and founder of the Heritage Foundation think tank, orchestrated the formation of the Moral Majority. A devout Catholic, he sought to unite Christians in a crusade against abortion and other liberal causes, as the following excerpt shows.

Because of the strong political reaction against abortion, the necrophiliac agenda for euthanasia, limiting the number of children a family may have (population control) and other overt antifamily schemes has been slowed down considerably. . . .

What the right-to-life movement has managed to put together on the abortion issue is only a sample of what is to come when the full range of family and educational issues becomes the focus of debate in the 1980s.

The homosexual rights advocates, genetic engineers and militant secular humanists who insist on their religion in the schools had better understand what is happening.

The threat to the family has caused leaders of various denominations to put aside their sectarian differences and, for the first time in decades, agree on basic principles worth fighting for. . . . [T]he pro-family movement is a recognition that the moral majority must be put together as a coalition—because our very right to worship as we choose, to bring up our families in some kind of moral order, to educate our children free from the interference of the state, to follow the commands of Holy Scripture and the Church are at stake.

Source: Paul Weyrich, "Building the Moral Majority," *Conservative Digest*, August 1979, 18–19.

Source 27.10

A. Bartlett Giamatti | The Moral Majority Threatens Freedom, 1981

One of the Moral Majority's sharpest critics was A. Bartlett Giamatti, a Renaissance scholar, president of Yale University (1978–1986), and subsequently commissioner of Major League Baseball. In an excerpt from the speech he originally gave to Yale's incoming freshman class in 1981, Giamatti attacked the Religious Right for its dogmatism and threat to personal freedom.

A self-proclaimed "Moral Majority," and its satellite or client groups, cunning in the use of a native blend of old intimidation and new technology, threatens the values [of freedom]. Angry at change, rigid in the application of chauvinistic slogans, absolutistic in morality, its members threaten through political pressure or public denunciation whoever dares to disagree with their authoritarian positions. . . .

From the maw of this "morality" come those who presume to know what justice for all is; come those who presume to know what books are fit to read; which television programs are fit to watch; which textbooks will serve for all the young; come spilling those who presume to know what only God knows, which is when human life begins. . . . There is no debate, no discussion, no dissent. They know. There is only one set of overarching political and spiritual and social beliefs; whatever view does not conform to these views is by definition relativistic, negative, secular, immoral, against the family, anti-free enterprise, un-American. What nonsense.

. . . For what [these groups] claim they espouse—love of country, a regard for the sanctity of life and the importance of the family, a belief in high standards of personal conduct, a conviction that we derive our values from a transcendent being, a desire to assert that free enterprise is better than state ownership and state control—are not evil or pernicious beliefs. Quite the contrary. They are the kernels of beliefs held dear, in various ways, by me and by millions of other Americans. You should not scorn these ideas simply because some extremists claim, whether sincerely or hypocritically, to have captured these beliefs for themselves. The point is,

the rest of us hold to ideas of family, country, belief in God, *in different ways*. The right to differ, and to see things differently, is our concern.

Source: A. Bartlett Giamatti, "A Liberal Education and the New Coercion," *A Free and Ordered Space: The Real World of the University* (New York: W. W. Norton, 1990), 110–17.

Interpret the Evidence

1. Explain the goals of Proposition 13 (Source 27.6), and how its provisions attempt to achieve them.
2. Compare Phyllis Schlafly's (Source 27.7) views of American women with those of Gloria Steinem (Source 27.8). Why do they reach different conclusions?
3. Describe the perceived dangers that united religious conservatives in the Moral Majority (Source 27.9).
4. Compare the ideas of A. Bartlett Giamatti (Source 27.10) and the Moral Majority (Source 27.9). Describe the areas of disagreement and agreement.

Put It in Context

How did the New Right shape the political and social landscapes of the United States in the 1970s?

The Triumph of Conservatism, the End of the Cold War, and the Rise of the New World Order

1980–1992

Window to the Past

United States Conference of Catholic Bishops, Pastoral Letter on War and Peace, 1983

Many Americans worried over President Reagan's buildup of the U.S. nuclear arsenal against the Soviet Union and called on both sides to initiate a nuclear weapons freeze. In 1983 U.S. Catholic bishops wrote this pastoral letter (excerpted below) with recommendations to lessen the threat of nuclear war. ▶ To learn more about this primary source, see Source 28.3 on page 983.

2. We support efforts to achieve deep cuts in the arsenals of both superpowers; efforts should concentrate first on systems which threaten the retaliatory forces of either major power.

3. We support early and successful conclusion of negotiations of a comprehensive test ban treaty.

4. We urge new efforts to prevent the spread of nuclear weapons in the world, and to control the conventional arms race, particularly the conventional arms trade.

After reading this chapter you will be able to:

- Assess the impact of Reaganomics and the ability of Presidents Reagan and Bush to deliver on the New Right's agenda.

- Analyze Ronald Reagan's role in ending the Cold War and fighting international terrorism.

- Describe how George H. W. Bush managed the end of the Cold War, and evaluate how he established a New World Order between the United States and the rest of the world.

Comparing American Histories

As secretary of state, **George Pratt Shultz** presided over the end of the Cold War. A skilled mediator, Shultz believed in hard-nosed diplomacy, asserting that "negotiations are a euphemism for capitulation if the shadow of power is not cast across the bargaining table." Upon graduating from Princeton with an economics degree in 1942, Shultz joined the Marine Corps and served in the Pacific during World War II. After the war, he earned a Ph.D. in industrial economics and taught at the Massachusetts Institute of Technology and the University of Chicago. In 1955 he joined President Eisenhower's Council of Economic Advisors, the first of many government posts he would fill in the Kennedy, Johnson, and Nixon administrations before he left government for the corporate world.

(*left*) **George Shultz** U.S. Department of State
(*right*) **Demetria Martinez** Copyright: The Albuquerque Journal. Reprinted with permission.

In 1982 Shultz returned to Washington to serve as President Ronald Reagan's secretary of state. Like Reagan, Shultz believed that the United States needed to reassert itself as a global power and rebound from the insecurity and self-doubt that followed the Vietnam War. The president believed that a tough approach would bring peace, and he revived the fiery rhetoric and military preparedness of the darkest days of the Cold War. Reagan and Shultz also sided with anti-Communist dictators in Nicaragua and El Salvador who brutally repressed their political opponents. As an economist, Shultz doubted that the Soviet Union was financially able to sustain its military strength, and his predictions proved correct. Faced with an escalating arms race, a fresh group of Soviet leaders decided to pursue peaceful relations.

While President Reagan and Secretary of State Shultz advocated confrontation with the Soviet Union, **Demetria Martinez** took a very different approach to foreign affairs. Born in Albuquerque, New Mexico in 1960, Martinez came from a family with roots in Mexico. Her maternal grandmother, Lucy Jamarillo, migrated to New Mexico after the Mexican Revolution of 1910, and in the 1940s was elected county clerk in Albuquerque. Demetria's parents were educators, and her father, Ted, was the first Mexican American elected to the Albuquerque school board.

Demetria Martinez chose creative writing and journalism rather than electoral politics as a career. Following graduation from Princeton University in 1982, she returned to New Mexico and became a religion reporter for the *Albuquerque Journal*. As a journalist she came into contact with the **Sanctuary Movement**, a network of religious groups that provided asylum for undocumented immigrants from Central America. As part of a newspaper assignment in 1986, she travelled to Juarez, Mexico to interview two pregnant El Salvadoran women who sought sanctuary in the United States. Martinez and the two women crossed over the border to El Paso and then drove separately to Albuquerque. Martinez declined to write the story because she feared that U.S. immigration officials would find out the identity of the women and deport them. Instead she wrote a poem, "Nativity: For Two Salvadoran Women, 1986–1987."

Martinez became a catalyst for the Sanctuary Movement after she was indicted and tried by the federal government for criminal violation of immigration laws. Denying that she had illegally smuggled the two women into the United States and defending her right as a journalist under the First Amendment to interview the Salvadorans, she was acquitted by the jury.

Martinez went on to become an educator and prize-winning poet and author. She continues to promote Chicana causes and social justice through her writing and teaching. ■

The American histories of George Shultz and Demetria Martinez were shaped by decades of Cold War strife overseas and in Central America. Shultz and Martinez, however, stood on opposite sides. Advised by Secretary of State Shultz, President Ronald Reagan employed harsher anti-Soviet rhetoric than at any time since the early 1960s and accelerated the buildup of the military. With the end of the Cold War and the collapse of the Soviet Union and its empire, the United States became the world's sole superpower. At the same time, the United States had to operate in an increasingly globalized world and face tests of its strength in Central America, the Middle East, and the Persian Gulf. In contrast, Martinez directed her efforts toward publicizing the plight of refugees who tried to escape from Cold War era conflicts in El Salvador.

Not only did Reagan transform diplomatic relationships with the Soviet Union, he reshaped the nation's political priorities. The president implemented anti-union measures and signed legislation granting large tax cuts as well as reductions in spending for programs that helped the poor and needy. His administration also relaxed government regulations over business and succeeded in tipping the Supreme Court to the right through its conservative appointments. Social conservatives, too, made headway during the 1980s by defeating the Equal Rights Amendment.

The Reagan Revolution

The election of former California governor Ronald Reagan as president in 1980 reflected the spectacular growth in political power of the New Right. Reagan pushed the conservative economic agenda of lower taxes and business deregulation alongside the New Right's concern for traditional religious and family values. His presidency installed conservatism as the dominant political ideology for the remainder of the twentieth century.

Reagan and Reaganomics.

A former movie actor, Reagan had transformed himself from a New Deal Democrat into a conservative Republican politician when he ran for governor of California in 1966. As governor, he implemented conservative ideas of free enterprise and small government and denounced Johnson's Great Society for threatening private property and individual liberty. His support for conservative economic and social issues carried him to the presidency.

Explore ▶

For Ronald Reagan's view of America, see Source 28.1.

In 1980 Reagan handily beat Jimmy Carter and John Anderson, a moderate Republican who ran as an independent candidate (Map 28.1). The high unemployment and inflation of the late 1970s worked in Reagan's favor. Reagan appealed to a coalition of conservative Republicans and disaffected Democrats, promising to cut taxes and reduce

Guided Primary Source Analysis

Ronald Reagan | First Inaugural Address, January 20, 1981

In the 1980s, as the nation reeled in the aftermath of Watergate and the Vietnam War as well as the more immediate crises of oil shortages and stagflation, Ronald Reagan promised voters that better times were coming. In his first inaugural address, Reagan reasserted his pledges to lower taxes, reduce the size of the federal government, and restore American pride. By 1984 Reagan and his supporters were ready to claim victory, seeing in the return of economic growth vindication of their ideas and optimism.

Source 28.1

According to Reagan, what are the sources of the nation's economic problems?

The business of our nation goes forward. These United States are confronted with an economic affliction of great proportions. We suffer from the longest and one of the worst sustained inflations in our national history. It distorts our economic decisions, penalizes thrift, and crushes the struggling young and the fixed-income elderly alike. It threatens to shatter the lives of millions of our people.

Idle industries have cast workers into unemployment, human misery, and personal indignity. Those who do work are denied a fair return for their labor by a tax system which penalizes successful achievement and keeps us from maintaining full productivity. . . .

How does Reagan view the role of government in solving society's problems?

In this present crisis, government is not the solution to our problem; government is the problem. From time to time, we've been tempted to believe that society has become too complex to be managed by self-rule, that government by an elite group is superior to government for, by, and of the people. Well, if no one among us is capable of governing himself, then who among us has the capacity to govern someone else? All of us together, in and out of government, must bear the burden. The solutions we seek must be equitable, with no one group singled out to pay a higher price. . . .

How does Reagan view the relationship between the federal and state governments?

It is my intention to curb the size and influence of the Federal establishment and to demand recognition of the distinction between the powers granted to the Federal Government and those reserved to the States or to the people. All of us need to be reminded that the Federal Government did not create the States; the States created the Federal Government.

Now, so there will be no misunderstanding, it's not my intention to do away with government. It is rather to make it work—work with us, not over us; to stand by our side, not ride on our back. Government can and must provide opportunity, not smother it; foster productivity, not stifle it.

Source: Michael Waldman, ed., *My Fellow Americans: The Most Important Speeches of America's Presidents, from George Washington to George W. Bush* (Naperville, IL: Sourcebooks, 2003), 247–49.

Put It in Context

Why did conservatism rise to political power in the 1980s?

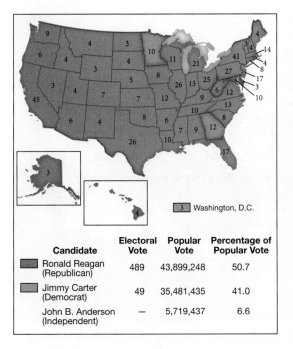

MAP 28.1   The Election of 1980

Ronald Reagan won 50.7 percent of the popular vote in the 1980 election, but his margin of victory over Jimmy Carter was much greater in the electoral vote. Reagan won the votes of the South and many disaffected Democrats in the urban North. A third-party candidate, John Anderson of Illinois, won 6.6 percent of the popular vote, demonstrating significant disapproval with both major parties.

3 | Washington, D.C.

Candidate	Electoral Vote	Popular Vote	Percentage of Popular Vote
Ronald Reagan (Republican)	489	43,899,248	50.7
Jimmy Carter (Democrat)	49	35,481,435	41.0
John B. Anderson (Independent)	—	5,719,437	6.6

spending, and to end affirmative action. The 1980 and subsequent presidential elections demonstrated the rising political, economic, and social influence of the American South and West, especially as these regions continued their rapid population growth by drawing migrants from other areas of the nation. Finally, he energized members of the religious right, who flocked to the polls to support Reagan's demands for voluntary prayer in the public schools, defeat of the Equal Rights Amendment, and a constitutional amendment to outlaw abortion. In fact, the religious right attracted its most ardent supporters from the South and West.

Reagan's first priority was stimulating the stagnant economy. The president's strategy, known as **Reaganomics**, reflected the ideas of supply-side economists and conservative Republicans. Reagan subscribed to the idea of trickle-down economics in which the gains reaped at the top of a strong economy would trickle down to the benefit of those below, thus reducing the need for large government social programs. Stating that "government is not the solution to our problem; government is the problem," Reagan asked Congress for a huge income tax cut of 30 percent over three years, a reduction in spending for domestic programs of more than $40 billion, and new monetary policies to lower rising rates for loans.

The president did not operate in isolation from the rest of the world. He learned a great deal from Margaret Thatcher, the British prime minister who took office two years before Reagan. Thatcher combated inflation by slashing welfare programs, selling off publicly owned companies, and cutting back health and education programs. An advocate of supply-side economics, Thatcher reduced income taxes on the wealthy by more than 50 percent to encourage new investment. West Germany also moved toward the right under Chancellor Helmut Kohl, who reined in welfare spending. In the 1980s Reaganomics and Thatcherism dominated the United States and the two most powerful nations of Western Europe.

Ronald Reagan Campaigns for President, 1980   Pledging to make America great again, Republican presidential candidate Ronald Reagan greets supporters at a senior citizens' retirement community in Seal Beach, California. During his 1980 campaign, Reagan expressed the cardinal tenet of antigovernment conservatism: "Government is like a baby, an alimentary canal with a big appetite at one end and no sense of responsibility at the other." AP Images/Walter Zeboski

In March 1981 Reagan survived a nearly fatal assassin's bullet. More popular than ever after his recovery, the president persuaded the Democratic House and the Republican Senate to pass his economic measures in slightly modified form in the **Economic Recovery Tax Act**. These cuts in taxes and spending did not produce the immediate results Reagan sought — unemployment rose to 9.6 percent in 1983 from 7.1 percent in 1980. However, the government's tight money policies, as engineered by the Federal Reserve Board, reduced inflation from 14 percent in 1980 to 4 percent in 1984. By 1984 the unemployment rate had fallen to 7.5 percent, while the gross national product grew by a healthy 4.3 percent, an indication that the recession, and the stagflation that came with it, had subsided.

The success of Reaganomics came at the expense of the poor and the lower middle class. The president reduced spending for food stamps, school lunches, Aid to Families with Dependent Children (welfare), and Medicaid, while maintaining programs that middle-class voters relied on, such as Medicare and Social Security. Rather than diminishing the government, the savings that came from reduced social spending went into increased military appropriations. Together with lower taxes, these expenditures benefited large corporations that received government military contracts and favorable tax write-offs.

As a result of Reagan's economic policies, financial institutions and the stock market ·rned huge profits. The Reagan administration relaxed antitrust regulations, encouraging corporate mergers to a degree unseen since the Great Depression. Fueled by falling interest rates, the stock market created wealth for many investors. The number of millionaires doubled during the 1980s, as the top 1 percent of families gained control of 42 percent of the nation's wealth and 60 percent of corporate stock. Reflecting this phenomenal accumulation of riches, television produced melodramas depicting the lives of oil barons (such as *Dallas* and *Dynasty*), whose characters lived glamorous lives filled with intrigue and extravagance. In *Wall Street* (1987), a film that captured the money ethic of the period, the main character utters the memorable line summing up the moment: "Greed, for lack of a better word, is good. Greed is right. Greed works."

Contrary to the promises of Reaganomics, the wealth did not trickle down and the gap between the rich and the poor widened. During the 1980s, the nation's share of poor people rose from 11.7 percent to 13.5 percent, representing 33 million Americans. Severe cutbacks in government social programs such as food stamps worsened the plight of the poor. Poverty disproportionately affected women and racial minorities. The number of homeless people grew to as many as 400,000 during the 1980s. The middle class also diminished from a high of 53 percent of families in the early 1970s to 49 percent in 1985.

The Reagan administration's relaxed regulation of the corporate sector also contributed to the unbalanced economy. The president aided big business by challenging labor unions. In 1981 air traffic controllers went on strike to gain higher wages and improved safety conditions. In response, the president fired the strikers who refused to return to work, and in their place he hired new controllers. Reagan's anti-union actions encouraged a decline in union membership throughout the 1980s, with union membership falling to 16 percent, its lowest level since the New Deal. Without union protection, wages failed to keep up with inflation, further increasing the gap between rich and poor.

Reagan continued the business deregulation initiated under Carter. Federal agencies concerned with environmental protection, consumer product reliability, and occupational safety saw their key functions shifted to the states, which made them less effective. Reagan also extended banking deregulation, which encouraged savings and loan institutions (S&Ls) to make risky loans to real estate ventures. When real estate prices began to tumble, savings and loan associations faced collapse and Congress appropriated over $100 billion to rescue them. Notwithstanding deregulation and small-government rhetoric, the number of federal government employees actually increased under Reagan by 200,000.

Reagan's landslide victory over Democratic candidate Walter Mondale in 1984 sealed the national political transition from liberalism to conservatism. Voters responded overwhelmingly to the improving economy, Reagan's defense of traditional social values, and his boundless optimism about America's future. Despite the landslide, the election was notable for the nomination of Representative Geraldine Ferraro of New York as Mondale's Democratic running mate, the first woman to run on a major party ticket for national office.

Reagan's second term did not produce changes as significant as did his first term. Democrats still controlled the House and in 1986 recaptured the Senate. The Reagan administration focused on foreign affairs and the continued Cold War with the Soviet Union, thus escalating defense spending. Most of the Reagan economic revolution continued as before, but with serious consequences. The federal deficit mushroomed, and by 1989 the nation was saddled with a $2.8 trillion debt, a situation that jeopardized the country's financial independence and the economic well-being of succeeding generations.

The president further reshaped the future through his nominations to the U.S. Supreme Court. Starting with the choice of Sandra Day O'Connor, the Court's first female justice, in 1981, Reagan's appointments moved the Court in a more conservative direction. The elevation of Associate Justice William Rehnquist to chief justice in 1986 reinforced this trend, which would have significant consequences for decades to come.

The Implementation of Social Conservatism.   Throughout his two terms, President Reagan pushed the New Right's social agenda. Conservatives blamed political liberalism for what they saw as a decline in family values. Their solution was a renewed focus on conservative Christian principles. In addition to trying to remove evolution and sex education from the classroom and bring in prayer, the New Right stepped up its opposition to abortion and imposed limits on reproductive rights. The Reagan administration required family planning agencies seeking federal funding to notify parents of children under age eighteen before dispensing birth control, cut off financial aid to international organizations supporting abortion, and provided funds to promote sexual abstinence. Despite these efforts, conservatives could not convince the Supreme Court to overturn *Roe v. Wade*. However, they did see the Equal Rights Amendment go down to defeat in 1982 when it failed to get the required two-thirds approval from the states.

Social conservatives also felt threatened by more tolerant views of homosexuality. The gay rights movement, which began in the 1960s, strengthened during the 1970s as thousands of gay men and lesbians made known their sexual orientation, fought discrimination, and expressed pride in their sexual identity. Then, in the early 1980s, physicians traced an outbreak of a deadly illness among gay men to a virus that attacked the immune system (human immunodeficiency virus, or HIV), making it vulnerable to infections that were usually fatal. This disease, called **acquired immune deficiency syndrome (AIDS)**, was transmitted through bodily fluids during sexual intercourse, through blood transfusions,

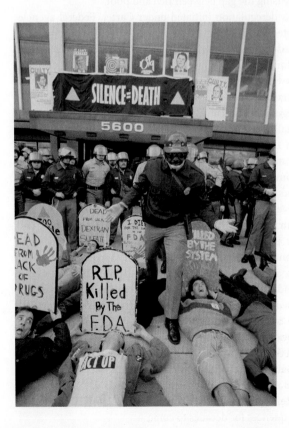

ACT UP Protest, 1988   Amid the AIDS epidemic in the gay community, the militant group AIDS Coalition to Unleash Power (ACT UP) campaigned for better funding of programs to fight the disease. This photo shows ACT UP protesters blocking the entrance to the headquarters of the Food and Drug Administration in Rockville, Maryland on Oct. 11, 1988. A police officer steps into the group, and some fifty of the protesters were arrested. AP Images/J. Scott Applewhite

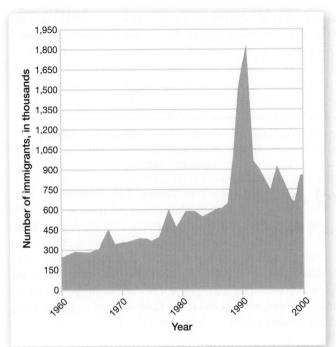

FIGURE 28.1 Immigrant Arrivals to the United States, 1960–2000

Immigration to the United States rose dramatically in the 1970s and 1980s, peaking in the early 1990s. Between 1970 and 2000, nearly 21 million immigrants arrived in the United States, mainly from Mexico, Central America, the Caribbean, and eastern and southern Asia. How do you explain the rise in immigration after 1965? Source: Data from 2000 Statistical Yearbook of the Immigration and Naturalization Service

and by intravenous drug use. Scientists could not explain why the disease initially showed up among gay men in the United States; however, New Right critics insisted that AIDS was a plague visited on sexual deviants by an angry God. As the epidemic spread beyond the gay community, gay rights organizers and their heterosexual allies raised research money and public awareness. By the early 1990s, medical advances had begun to extend the lives of AIDS patients and manage the disease.

Increased immigration also troubled social conservatives as another reflection of the general societal breakdown. The number of immigrants to the United States rose dramatically in the 1970s and 1980s following the relaxation of foreign quota restrictions after 1965 (Figure 28.1). During these decades, immigrants came mainly from Mexico, Central America, the Caribbean, and eastern and southern Asia and tended to settle in California, Florida, Texas, New York, and New Jersey. By 1990 one-third of Los Angeles's and New York City's populations were foreign-born, figures similar to the high numbers of European immigrants at the turn of the twentieth century.

Confronted by anti-immigrant attacks from the New Right, Reagan walked a fine line on immigration. In 1982, the U.S. Supreme Court in *Plyler v. Doe* ruled that a county in Texas could not withhold funds from the education of children of undocumented Mexican immigrants. In 1986 Reagan supported the **Immigration Reform and Control Act**, which extended amnesty to undocumented aliens residing in the United States for a specified period. It permitted them to acquire legal status, while penalizing employers who hired new illegal workers. The measure allowed Reagan and the Republicans to appeal to Latino voters in the Sun Belt states while convincing the New Right that the administration intended to halt further undocumented immigration.

The president disagreed with New Right critics who questioned whether culturally diverse people could assimilate into American society. To the contrary, Reagan appointed Lauro F. Cavazos, a sixth generation Texan, as secretary of education, the first Latino to hold a cabinet position.

Review & Relate

- What was Reaganomics, and what were its most important long-term consequences?

- How did conservative ideas shape the social, cultural, and political landscape of the 1980s and 1990s?

Reagan and the End of the Cold War, 1981–1988

President Reagan and Secretary of State George Shultz believed that the Cold War would be won only after the United States achieved military supremacy over the Soviet Union. Reagan also took strong measures to fight communism around the globe, from Central America to the Middle East. Yet military superiority alone would not defeat the Soviet Union. A shift of leadership within the USSR, as well as a worldwide protest movement for nuclear disarmament, helped bring an end to the Cold War and prepare the way for the dissolution of the Soviet empire.

"The Evil Empire." In running for president in 1980, Reagan wrapped his hard-line anti-Communist message in the rhetoric of peace. "I've called for whatever it takes to be so strong that no other nation will dare violate the peace," he told the Veterans of Foreign Wars Convention on August 18, 1980. Once in the White House, Reagan left no doubt about his anti-Communist stance. He called the Soviet Union "the evil empire," regarding it as "the focus of evil in the modern world." The president planned to confront that evil with both words and deeds, backing up his rhetoric with a massive military buildup.

In a show of economic might, Reagan proposed the largest military budget in American history. The defense budget grew by about 7 percent per year, increasing from $157 billion in 1981 to around $282 billion in 1988. Reagan clearly intended to win the Cold War by outspending the Soviets, even if it meant running up huge deficits that greatly burdened the U.S. economy.

Reagan was unyielding in his initial dealings with the Soviet Union, and negotiations between the superpowers moved slowly and unevenly. The Reagan administration's "zero option" proposal called for the Soviets to dismantle all of their intermediate-range missiles in exchange for the United States agreeing to refrain from deploying any new medium-range missiles. The administration presented this option merely for show, expecting the Soviets to reject it. However, in 1982, after the Soviets accepted the principle of "zero option," Reagan sent negotiators to begin Strategic Arms Reduction Talks (START). Influenced by antinuclear protests in Europe, which had a great impact on European governments, the Americans proposed shelving the deployment of 572 Pershing II and cruise missiles in Europe in return for the Soviets' dismantling of Eastern European–based intermediate-range ballistic missiles that were targeted at Western Europe. The Soviets viewed this offer as perpetuating American nuclear superiority and rejected it.

Relations between the two superpowers deteriorated in September 1983 when a Soviet fighter jet shot down a South Korean passenger airliner, killing 269 people. The Soviets charged that the plane had veered off course and violated their airspace. Although the disaster resulted mainly from Soviet mistakes, Reagan chose to condemn this attack as further proof of the malign intentions of the USSR. The United States sent additional missiles to bases in West Germany, Great Britain, and Italy; in response, the Soviets abandoned the disarmament talks and replenished their nuclear arsenal in Czechoslovakia and East Germany. More symbolically, the Soviets boycotted the 1984 Olympic Games in Los Angeles, in retaliation for the U.S. boycott of the Olympics in Moscow four years earlier. As the two adversaries swung from peace talks to threats of nuclear confrontation, one European journalist observed: "The second Cold War has begun."

Human Rights and the Fight against Communism.

The Reagan administration extended its Cold War position throughout the world, emphasizing anticommunism often at the expense of human rights. Reagan embraced the distinction made by his ambassador to the United Nations, Jeane Kirkpatrick, between non-Communist "authoritarian" nations, which were acceptable, and Communist "totalitarian" regimes, which were not.

Reagan considered the South African government an example of an acceptable authoritarianism, even though it practiced apartheid (white supremacy and racial separation) and torture. The fact that the South African Communist Party had joined the fight against apartheid reinforced Reagan's desire to support the white-minority, anti-Communist government. Interested in the country's vast mineral wealth, Reagan opted for what he called "constructive engagement" with South Africa, rather than condemn its racist practices. The Reagan administration did so even as protesters across the United States and the world spoke out against South Africa's repressive white-majority government and campaigned for divestment of public and corporate funds from South African companies. After years of pressure from the divestment movement on college campuses and elsewhere, in 1986 Congress passed the Comprehensive Anti-Apartheid Act, which prohibited new trade and investment in South Africa. President Reagan vetoed it, but Congress overrode the president's veto.

The president also exploited the fear of communism in Central America and the Caribbean, where for nearly a century the United States had guarded its sphere of influence. During the 1980s, the United States continued its economic isolation of Cuba via the trade embargo, and it sought to prevent other Communist or leftist governments from emerging in Central America and the Caribbean.

In the late 1970s Nicaraguan revolutionaries, known as the National Liberation Front or Sandinistas, had overthrown the tyrannical government of General Anastasio Somoza, a brutal dictator. President Jimmy Carter, who had originally supported Somoza's overthrow, halted all aid to Nicaragua in 1980 after the Sandinistas began nationalizing foreign companies and drawing closer to Cuba. Under Reagan, Secretary of State Shultz suggested a U.S. invasion of Nicaragua, reflecting the administration's belief that the revolution in Nicaragua had been sponsored by Moscow. Instead Reagan adopted a more indirect approach. In 1982 he authorized the CIA to train approximately two thousand guerrilla forces outside the country, known as Contras (Counterrevolutionaries), to overthrow the Sandinista government. Although Reagan praised the Contras as "the moral equivalent of our Founding Fathers," the group consisted of pro-Somoza reactionaries as well as anti-Marxist democrats who blew up bridges and oil dumps, burned crops, and killed civilians. In 1982 Congress, unwilling to support such actions, passed the **Boland Amendment**, which prohibited direct aid to the Contras. In the face of congressional opposition, Reagan and his advisers came up with a plan that would secretly fund the efforts of their military surrogates in Nicaragua. Reagan ordered the CIA and the National Security Council (NSC) to raise money from anti-Communist leaders abroad and wealthy conservatives at home. This effort, called "Project Democracy," raised millions of dollars, and by 1985 the number of Contra troops had swelled from 10,000 to 20,000. In violation of federal law, CIA director William Casey also authorized his agency to continue training the Contras in assassination techniques and other methods of subversion.

Elsewhere in Central America, the Reagan administration supported a corrupt right-wing government in El Salvador that, in an effort to put down an insurgency, sanctioned military death squads and killed forty thousand people during the 1980s. Despite the failings and abuses of the El Salvadoran government, Reagan insisted that Communist regimes in Nicaragua and Cuba were behind the Salvadoran insurgents. The United States sent more than $5 billion in aid to El Salvador and trained its military leaders to combat guerrilla forces (Map 28.2).

In addition to financing guerrilla wars in Central America, on October 25, 1983 Reagan sent 7,000 marines to invade the tiny Caribbean island of Grenada. After a coup toppled the leftist government of Maurice Bishop, who had received Cuban and Soviet aid, the United States stepped in, ostensibly to protect American medical school students in Grenada from political instability following the coup. A pro-American government was installed. The swift action in Grenada boosted Reagan's popularity.

While many Americans supported Reagan's strong anti-Communist stance, others opposed to the president's policy mobilized protests. Marches, rallies, and teach-ins were organized in cities and college campuses nationwide. U.S.-sponsored wars also drove many people to flee their dangerous, poverty-stricken countries and seek asylum in the United States. Between 1984 and 1990, 45,000 Salvadorans and 9,500 Guatemalans applied for asylum in the United States, but because the United States supported the established

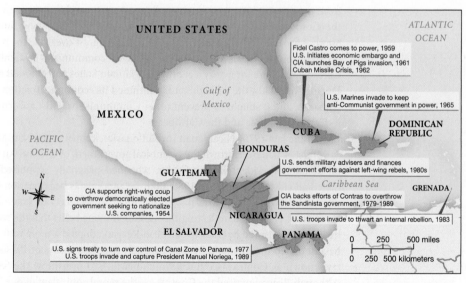

MAP 28.2 The United States in Central America and the Caribbean, 1954–1989

The United States had intervened in Central America and the Caribbean since the late 1890s to protect its sphere of interest. With the onset of the Cold War in the late 1940s, the United States intervened in the internal affairs of these nations to thwart what it viewed as the threat of Communist aggression, even if this meant supporting dictatorial regimes. As a result of such conflicts in the 1980s, many immigrants from Central America sought political asylum in the United States, mainly in Texas, New Mexico, Arizona, and California.

governments in those two nations, nearly all requests for refugee status were denied. Approximately five hundred American churches and synagogues established a sanctuary movement to provide safe haven for those fleeing Central American civil wars. Demetria Martinez's trial and acquittal in 1988 for allegedly smuggling undocumented immigrants into the United States gave a big boost to the sanctuary cause. Like other Christians, she was influenced by "liberation theology," a movement developed by Catholic clergymen in Latin America to promote social justice and political freedom.

In contrast, many other Americans, especially in California and Texas, began to view the influx of refugees from Central America with alarm. This immigration, both legal and illegal, meant an increase in medical and educational costs for state and local communities, which taxpayers considered a burden.

Fighting International Terrorism.
Two days before the Grenada invasion in 1983, the U.S. military suffered a grievous blow halfway around the world. In the tiny country of Lebanon, wedged between Syrian occupation on its northern border and the Palestine Liberation Organization's (PLO) fight against Israel to the south, a civil war raged between Christians and Muslims. Reagan believed that stability in the region was in America's national interest. In 1982 the Reagan administration sent 800 marines, as part of a multilateral force that included French and Italian troops, to keep the peace. On October 23, 1983, a suicide bomber drove a truck into a marine barracks, killing 241 soldiers. Reagan withdrew the remaining troops.

The removal of troops did not end threats to Americans in the Middle East. Terrorism had become an ever-present danger, especially since the Iranian hostage crisis in 1979–1980. In 1985, 17 American citizens were killed in terrorist assaults, and 154 were injured. In one of those attacks, commandos of the Palestine Liberation Organization hijacked the Italian liner *Achille Lauro*, which was cruising from Egypt to Israel. One of the 450 passengers, the wheelchair-bound, elderly Jewish American Leon Klinghoffer, was murdered and thrown overboard. After three days, Egyptian authorities negotiated an end to the terrorist hijacking.

In response to the 1985 PLO cruise ship attack, the Reagan administration targeted the North African country of Libya for retaliation. Its military leader, Muammar al-Qaddafi, supported the Palestinian cause and provided sanctuary for terrorists. The Reagan administration had placed a trade embargo on Libya, and Secretary of State Shultz remarked: "We have to put Qaddafi in a box and close the lid." In 1986, after the bombing of a nightclub in West Berlin killed 2 American servicemen and injured 230, Reagan charged that Qaddafi was responsible. In late April the United States retaliated by sending planes to bomb the Libyan capital of Tripoli. Following the bombing, Qaddafi took a much lower profile against the United States. Reagan had demonstrated his nation's military might despite the retreat from Lebanon (Map 28.3).

In the meantime, the situation in Lebanon remained critical as the strife caused by civil war led to the seizing of American hostages. By mid-1984, seven Americans in Lebanon had been kidnapped by Shi'ite Muslims financed by Iran. Since 1980, Iran, a Shi'ite nation, had been engaged in a protracted war with Iraq, which was ruled by military leader Saddam Hussein and his Sunni Muslim party, the chief rival to the Shi'ites. With relations between the United States and Iran having deteriorated in the aftermath of the 1979 coup, the Reagan administration backed Iraq in this war. The fate of the hostages in Lebanon, however, motivated Reagan to make a deal with Iran. In late 1985 Reagan's national security adviser, Robert McFarlane, negotiated secretly with an Iranian intermediary for the United States to sell antitank missiles to Iran in exchange for the Shi'ite government using its influence to induce the Muslim kidnappers to release the hostages.

MAP 28.3 The United States in the Middle East, 1978–1991

The United States has historically needed access to the rich oil reserves of the Middle East. From the 1970s to the 1990s, both Democratic and Republican administrations were committed to the security of Israel, supportive of Afghan rebels fighting Soviet invaders, and opposed to the rising power of Islamic regimes. These principles often led to contradictory policies that further embroiled the United States in Middle East affairs.

Had the matter ended there, the secret deal might never have come to light. However, NSC aide Lieutenant Colonel Oliver North developed a plan to transfer the proceeds from the arms-for-hostages deal to fund the Contras in Nicaragua and circumvent the Boland Amendment, which prohibited direct aid to the rebels. Despite opposition from Secretary of State Shultz, Reagan liked North's plan, although the president seemed vague about the details, and some $10 million to $20 million of Iranian money flowed into the hands of the Contras.

In 1986 information about the **Iran-Contra affair** came to light. **See Primary Source Project 28: The Iran-Contra Affair, page 999.** In the summer of 1987, televised Senate hearings exposed much of the tangled, covert dealings with Iran. In 1988 a special federal prosecutor indicted NSC adviser Vice Admiral John Poindexter (who had replaced McFarlane), North, and several others on charges ranging from perjury to conspiracy to obstruction of justice. Reagan took responsibility for the transfer of funds to the Contras, but he managed to weather the political crisis.

The Nuclear Freeze Movement.

Reagan's tough talk and military buildup against the Soviet Union ignited protests against nuclear weapons in the United States and Europe.

Ronald Reagan and Mikhail Gorbachev, 1987   After once calling the Soviet Union "the evil empire," President Ronald Reagan sits alongside Soviet leader Mikhail Gorbachev to sign the Intermediate-range Nuclear Forces (INF) agreement in the East Room of the White House on December 8, 1987. The agreement marked a turning point in the Cold War. Ronald Reagan Presidential Library

At the end of the Carter administration, the United States had promised NATO that it would station new missiles in England, Italy, West Germany, and Belgium. Reagan's decision to implement this policy sparked enormous protest. One such protest came in 1981 when women peace activists set up camp at Greenham Common in England outside of one of the military bases prepared to house the arriving missiles, one of twenty such camps in England. At the Greenham Common peace camp, protesters sang, danced, and performed skits to affirm women's solidarity for peace. Women came together not only to promote disarmament but also to empower themselves and create supportive communities dedicated to peace.

These activities were part of a larger **nuclear freeze movement** that began in 1980. Its proponents called for a "mutual freeze on the testing, production, and deployment of nuclear weapons and of missiles and aircraft designed primarily to deliver nuclear weapons." Grassroots activists also held town meetings throughout the United States to mobilize ordinary citizens to speak out against nuclear proliferation. In 1982 some 750,000 people rallied in New York City's Central Park to support a nuclear freeze resolution presented at the United Nations. Despite opposition from the United States and its NATO allies, measures favoring the freeze easily passed in the UN General Assembly. In the 1982 elections, peace groups placed nonbinding, nuclear freeze referenda on local ballots, which passed with wide majorities.

The following year, the Seneca Falls Women's Encampment for a Future of Peace and Justice set up operations in western New York next to an army depot that stored nuclear missiles. On July 30, 1983, peace activist Barbara Deming led a march of seventy-five female activists into the small town of Waterloo. Several miles into the walk the marchers found their way blocked by a few hundred counter-demonstrators brandishing American flags and chanting, "Commies, go home!" The peace activists then sat down in nonviolent protest, and the police arrested Deming and fifty-three other protesters. Congress rejected the demonstrators' call for an "immediate freeze."

Explore ▶

See Sources 28.2 and 28.3 to read about two nuclear freeze efforts.

The Nuclear Freeze Movement

In 1982, 30 percent of American voters considered nuclear freeze referenda in ten states and thirty-seven cities and counties. The nuclear freeze movement called on the United States and the Soviet Union to mutually halt the production, testing, and deployment of nuclear weapons. A nonbinding referendum in New Jersey passed overwhelmingly in every county. In addition to initiating ballot measures, the nuclear freeze campaign won the support of the Catholic Church, which issued a pastoral letter in 1983.

Source 28.2

New Jersey Referendum on Nuclear Freeze, 1982

Public Question No. 1: Freeze on Nuclear Arms Escalation

Do you support a mutual United States–Soviet Union nuclear weapons "freeze" and urge the government of the United States:

   (1) to propose to the government of the Soviet Union that both countries immediately agree to a mutual, verifiable halt of all further testing, production and deployment of nuclear warheads, missiles, and delivery systems as a first step toward mutual, balanced reduction, and

   (2) to apply the money saved to human needs and tax reduction?

Interpretive Statement

"This non-binding referendum, if approved by the public, would demonstrate the voters' support of a nuclear weapons freeze and would direct the Secretary of State to transmit the results of these voters' opinions on this question to the President of the United States, the Speaker of the House of Representatives and President of the United States Senate no later than twenty (20) days after the conclusion of the election."

Source: "New Jersey Nuclear Freeze Ballot," 1982, http://www .njelections.org/election-results/1982-public-questions.pdf.

Yet the antinuclear movement in the United States and in Europe influenced Reagan. According to a 1982 public opinion poll, 57 percent of Americans favored an immediate nuclear freeze. Reagan acknowledged that he was more inclined to reconsider deploying missiles abroad because European leaders felt pressure from protesters in their home countries. The freeze movement inside and outside the United States created a favorable climate in which the president and Soviet leaders could negotiate a genuine plan for nuclear disarmament by the end of the decade.

Source 28.3

United States Conference of Catholic Bishops | Pastoral Letter on War and Peace, 1983

What are we saying? Fundamentally, we are saying that the decisions about nuclear weapons are among the most pressing moral questions of our age. While these decisions have obvious military and political aspects, they involve fundamental moral choices. In simple terms, we are saying that good ends (defending one's country, protecting freedom, etc.) cannot justify immoral means (the use of weapons which kill indiscriminately and threaten whole societies). We fear that our world and nation are headed in the wrong direction. More weapons with greater destructive potential are produced every day. More and more nations are seeking to become nuclear powers. In our quest for more and more security we fear we are actually becoming less and less secure. . . .

On Promoting Peace

1. We support immediate, bilateral verifiable agreements to halt the testing, production, and deployment of new nuclear weapons systems. This recommendation is not to be identified with any specific political initiative.

2. We support efforts to achieve deep cuts in the arsenals of both superpowers; efforts should concentrate first on systems which threaten the retaliatory forces of either major power.

3. We support early and successful conclusion of negotiations of a comprehensive test ban treaty.

4. We urge new efforts to prevent the spread of nuclear weapons in the world, and to control the conventional arms race, particularly the conventional arms trade.

5. We support, in an increasingly interdependent world, political and economic policies designed to protect human dignity and to promote the human rights of every person, especially the least among us.

Source: "The Challenge of Peace: God's Promise and Our Response," United States Conference of Catholic Bishops, 1983.

Interpret the Evidence

1. What did voters in New Jersey hope to accomplish with a nonbinding referendum? Do you think the nonbinding nature of the measure made much difference to the outcome of the vote?
2. Why did the Catholic Church take such a strong position in support of the nuclear freeze? How do its goals compare with those of the New Jersey referendum?

Put It in Context

What impact did the nuclear freeze movement have on the Cold War?

The Road to Nuclear De-escalation.

Ronald Reagan won reelection in 1984 by a landslide. Following his enormous victory, Reagan softened his militant stance and became more amenable to negotiating with the USSR. Reagan espoused conservative principles during his presidency, but he refused to let rigid dogma interfere with more pragmatic considerations to foster peace. Having earned political capital from his long fight against communism, he was prepared, as president, to spend it. By the time President Reagan left office, little remained of the Cold War.

In the mid-1980s, powerful changes were sweeping through the Soviet Union. In September 1985, Mikhail Gorbachev became general secretary of the Communist Party and head of the Soviet Union. Gorbachev introduced a program of economic and political reform. Through **glasnost** (openness) and **perestroika** (restructuring), the Soviet leader hoped to reduce massive state control over the declining economy and to extend democratic elections, as well as freedom of speech and freedom of the press. Gorbachev understood that the success of his reforms depended on reducing Cold War tensions with the United States and slowing the arms escalation that was bankrupting the Soviet economy. Gorbachev's *glasnost* brought the popular American musical performer Billy Joel to the Soviet Union in August 1987, staging the first rock concert in the country.

The changes that Gorbachev brought to the internal affairs of the Soviet Union carried over to the international arena. From 1986 to 1988, the Soviet leader negotiated in person with the American president, something that had not happened during Reagan's first term. In 1986 at a summit in Reykjavik, Iceland, the two leaders agreed to cut the number of strategic nuclear missiles in half. In 1987 the two sides negotiated an Intermediate Nuclear Forces Treaty, which provided for the destruction of existing intermediate-range missiles and on-site inspections to ensure compliance. The height of détente came in December 1987, when Gorbachev traveled to the United States to take part in the treaty-signing ceremony. Reagan no longer referred to the USSR as "the evil empire," and Gorbachev impressed Americans with his personal charm. The following year, Reagan flew to the Soviet Union, hugged Gorbachev at Lenin's Tomb, and told reporters, "They've changed," referring to the once and not-so-distant "evil empire." Citizens of the two adversarial nations breathed a collective sigh of relief; at long last, the icy terrain of the Cold War appeared to be melting.

Explore ▶

Compare Sources 28.4 and 28.5 for two historians' interpretations of the end of the Cold War.

Review & Relate

How did anticommunism shape Ronald Reagan's foreign policy?

What role did ordinary citizens play in prompting the superpowers to move toward nuclear de-escalation?

The **Presidency** of George H. W. Bush, 1989–1993

After Reagan left office, his two-term vice president, George H. W. Bush, generally carried on his conservative legacy at home and abroad. While sharing most of Reagan's views, Bush called for a "kinder, gentler nation" in dealing with social justice and the environment. When Bush became president in 1989, he also encountered a very different Soviet Union from the one Reagan had faced a decade earlier and one that produced new challenges. The USSR was undergoing an internal revolution, which allowed Bush and the United States to take on a new role in a world that was no longer divided between capitalist and Communist nations and their allies. Globalization became the hallmark of the post–Cold War era, replacing previously dualistic economic and political systems, with mixed consequences. Following the collapse of the old world order, local and regional conflicts long held in check by the Cold War broke out along religious, racial, and ethnic lines.

"Kinder and Gentler" Conservatism.

In his 1988 presidential campaign against Michael Dukakis, the Democratic governor of Massachusetts, Bush defended conservative principles when he promised, "Read my lips: No new taxes." The Republican candidate attacked Dukakis for his liberal positions and accused him of being soft on crime. Bush also affirmed his own opposition to abortion and support for gun rights and the death penalty.

Once in office Bush had to deal with problems that he inherited from his predecessor. Reagan's economic programs and military spending had left the nation with a mounting federal budget deficit and fears over inflation. Attempts to ward off inflation by raising interest rates had slowed economic growth. Then the real estate market faltered, resulting in the failure of a third of the nation's saving and loans associations. To make matters worse, oil prices spiked in 1990 after President Bush ordered the invasion of Iraq. As a result, the nation fell back into recession. Unemployment rose from 5.3 percent when Bush took office in 1989 to 7.5 percent by 1992, and state and local governments had difficulty paying for the educational, health, and social services that the Reagan and Bush administrations had transferred to them. To reverse the downward spiral, Bush abandoned his "no new taxes" pledge. In 1990 he supported a deficit reduction package that included more than $130 billion in new taxes, but which failed to solve the economic problems and angered Reagan conservatives. He also departed from anti-government conservatives when he signed the Americans with Disabilities Act (1990), extending a range of protections to some 40 million Americans with physical and mental handicaps.

Bush had a mixed record on the environment. In 1989 the oil tanker *Exxon Valdez* struck a reef off the coast of Alaska, dumping nearly 11 million gallons of oil into Prince William Sound. This disaster created pressure for stricter environmental legislation. In 1990 the president signed the Clean Air Act, which reduced emissions from automobiles and power plants. Bush refused to go further, and in 1992 he opposed international efforts to limit carbon dioxide emissions, greenhouse gases that contribute to climate change.

Bush courted conservatives in his nomination of Clarence Thomas in 1991 to fill the Supreme Court vacancy left by Justice Thurgood Marshall, the first African American justice. Thomas belonged to a rising group of conservative blacks who shared Republican views supporting private enterprise and the free market system and opposing affirmative action. As chief of the Equal Employment Opportunity Commission (EEOC) under Reagan, Thomas had generally weakened the agency's enforcement of racial and gender equality in the workplace. He also opposed abortion and denounced welfare. During the course of Thomas's Senate confirmation hearing, Anita Hill, Thomas's assistant at the EEOC, testified before the Senate Judiciary Committee and a nationally televised audience that Thomas had made unwanted sexual advances to her on and off the job, which she quit in 1983. Hill's charges of sexual harassment did not stop his confirmation. Thomas became one of the most conservative members of the Court. Membership in women's political associations — such as Emily's List, founded in 1984, and the Fund for a Feminist Majority, founded in 1987 — soared following Hill's testimony.

Bush made less controversial but noteworthy appointments aimed at appealing to racial minority voters. He retained Lauro Cavazos as secretary of education and selected Manuel Lujan Jr. of New Mexico as secretary of the interior. Republicans maintained their political efforts to appeal to Latinos, particularly Mexican Americans, and broaden the base of their party.

Anita Hill Testifies Against the Supreme Court Nomination of Clarence Thomas, 1991   Anita F. Hill is sworn-in to testify before the Senate Judiciary Committee on the confirmation of Clarence Thomas to the U.S. Supreme Court by chairman Joseph Biden, a Democrat from Delaware, on October 11, 1991. Hill claimed Thomas had sexually harassed her when she had worked for him in the early 1980s. There was no woman serving on the Judiciary Committee at that time. Shutterstock

The Breakup of the Soviet Union. Bush's first year in office coincided with upheavals in the Soviet-controlled Communist bloc, with Poland leading the way. In 1980 Polish dockworker Lech Walesa had organized **Solidarity**, a trade union movement conducting a series of popular strikes that forced the Communist government to recognize the group. Solidarity had ten million members and attracted various opponents of the Communist regime, including working-class democrats, Catholics, and nationalists who favored breaking ties with the Soviet Union. In 1981 Soviet leaders, disturbed by Solidarity's growing strength, forced the Polish government to crack down on the organization, arrest Walesa, and ban Solidarity. In 1989 Walesa and Solidarity seized on the changes ushered in by Mikhail Gorbachev's *glasnost* in the USSR to press their demands for democracy in Poland. The Soviets refused to intervene, and Poland conducted its first free elections since the beginning of the Cold War, electing Lech Walesa as president of the country. In July 1989, Gorbachev further broke from the past and announced that the Soviet Union would respect the national sovereignty of all the nations in the Warsaw Pact, which the Soviet Union had controlled since the late 1940s.

Gorbachev's proclamation spurred the end of communism throughout Eastern Europe. Within the next year, Soviet-sponsored regimes fell peacefully in Hungary and Czechoslovakia, replaced by elected governments. Bulgaria held free elections, which brought reformers to power. Only in Romania did Communist rulers put up a fight. There, it took a violent popular uprising to topple the brutal dictator Nicolae Ceausescu. The Baltic states of Latvia, Lithuania, and Estonia, which the Soviets had incorporated into the USSR at the outset of World War II, also regained their independence, sparking the political breakup of the Soviet Union itself.

Perhaps the most striking symbolism in the dismantling of the Soviet empire came in Germany, a country that had been divided between East and West states since 1945. With Communist governments collapsing around them, East Germans demonstrated against the regime of Erich Honecker. With no Soviet help forthcoming, Honecker decided to open the border between East and West Germany. On November 9, 1989, East and West Germans flocked to the Berlin Wall and jubilantly joined workers in knocking down the concrete barricade that divided the city. A year later, East and West Germany merged under the democratic, capitalist Federal Republic of Germany.

Gorbachev also brought an end to the costly nine-year Soviet-Afghan War. When the Soviets withdrew their last troops on February 15, 1989, they left Afghanistan in shambles. One million Afghans had perished, and another 5 million fled the country for Pakistan and Iran, resulting in the political destabilization of Afghanistan. Following a civil war, the Taliban, a group of Sunni Muslim fundamentalists, came to power in the mid-1990s and established a theocratic regime that, among other things, strictly regulated what women could wear in public and denied them educational and professional opportunities. The Taliban also provided sanctuary for many of the mujahideen rebels who had fought against the Soviets, including Osama bin Laden, who would use the country as a base for his al-Qaeda organization to promote terrorism against the United States.

Meanwhile, the Soviet Union disintegrated. Free elections were held in 1990, which ironically threatened Gorbachev's own power by bringing non-Communists to local and national political offices. Although an advocate of economic reform and political openness, Gorbachev remained a Communist and was committed to preserving the USSR. Challenges to Gorbachev came from both ends of the political spectrum. Boris Yeltsin, his former protégé, led the non-Communist forces that wanted Gorbachev to move more quickly in adopting capitalism; on the other side, hard-line generals in the Soviet army disapproved of Gorbachev's reforms and his cooperation with the United States. On August 18, 1991, a group of hard-core conspirators staged a coup against Gorbachev, placed him under house arrest, and surrounded the parliament building with troops. Yeltsin, the president of the Russian Republic, rallied fellow legislators and Muscovites against the plotters and brought the uprising to a peaceful end. Several months later, in early December, Yeltsin and the leaders of the independent republics of Belarus and Ukraine formed the Commonwealth of Independent States (CIS), consisting of the Russian Federation and eleven of fifteen former Soviet states. Shortly after, the CIS removed the hammer and sickle, the symbol of communism, from its flag.

Under these circumstances, on December 25, 1991, Gorbachev resigned. The next day, the Soviet legislative body passed a resolution dissolving the USSR. With the Soviet Union dismantled, Yeltsin, as head of the Russian Federation and the CIS, expanded the democratic and free market reforms initiated by Gorbachev (Map 28.4).

Before Gorbachev left office, he completed one last agreement with the United States to curb nuclear arms. In mid-1991, just before conspirators staged their abortive coup, Gorbachev met with President Bush, who had traveled to Moscow to sign a strategic arms reduction treaty. Under this pact, each side agreed to reduce its bombers and missiles by

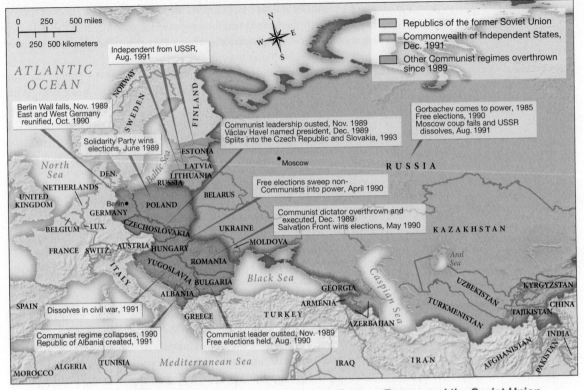

MAP 28.4   The Fall of Communism in Eastern Europe and the Soviet Union, 1989–1991

The collapse of Communist regimes in Eastern Europe was due in part to political and economic reforms initiated by Soviet premier Mikhail Gorbachev, including agreements with the United States to reduce nuclear arms. These changes inspired demands for free elections that were supported by popular uprisings, first in Poland and then in other former Soviet satellites.

one-third and to trim its conventional military forces. This accord led to a second strategic arms reduction treaty. Gorbachev's successor, Boris Yeltsin, met with Bush in January 1993, and the two agreed to destroy their countries' stockpile of multiple-warhead intercontinental missiles within a decade.

Globalization and the New World Order.

With the end of the Cold War, cooperation replaced economic and political rivalry between capitalist and Communist nations in a new era of **globalization** — the extension of economic, political, and cultural interconnections among nations through commerce, migration, and communication. In 1976 the major industrialized democracies had formed the Group of Seven (G7). Consisting of the United States, the United Kingdom, France, West Germany, Italy, Japan, and Canada, the G7 nations met annually to discuss common problems related to issues of global concern, such as trade, health, energy, the environment, and economic and social development. After the fall of communism, Russia joined the organization, which became known as G8. This group

Globalization, 1980s Following the efforts of Presidents Nixon, Ford, and Carter to normalize relations with Communist China, companies established commercial enterprises there, including American fast-food chain restaurants. Here a Chinese soldier, standing beside a replica of Colonel Sanders, picks up his order at the bike ride-up window of a Kentucky Fried Chicken restaurant. Dave Bartruff/Getty Images

of countries represented only 14 percent of the globe's population but produced 60 percent of the world's economic output.

Globalization was accompanied by the extraordinary growth of multinational (or transnational) corporations — companies that operate production facilities or deliver services in more than one country. Between 1970 and 2000, the number of such firms soared from 7,000 to well over 60,000. By 2000 the 500 largest corporations in the world generated more than $11 trillion in revenues, owned more than $33 trillion in assets, and employed 35.5 million people. American companies left their cultural and social imprint on the rest of the world. Walmart greeted shoppers in more than 1,200 stores outside the United States, and McDonald's changed global eating habits with its more than 1,000 fast-food restaurants worldwide. As American firms penetrated other countries with their products, foreign companies changed the economic landscape of the United States. For instance, by the twenty-first century Japanese automobiles, led by Toyota and Honda, captured a major share of the American market, surpassing Ford and General Motors, once the hallmark of the country's superior manufacturing and salesmanship.

Comparative Secondary Source Analysis

The End of the Cold War

After forty years of conflict, the Cold War appeared to come to an abrupt end. President Reagan entered the White House in 1981 as a staunch cold warrior and left eight years later as a negotiator of peace with the Soviet Union. Fortunately, he had a willing partner in the new head of the USSR, Mikhail Gorbachev. John Spanier and Beth Fischer each wrote the excerpts below within a decade of the end of the Cold War. They approach the subject from different perspectives: one focused on the Soviet Union and the other on the United States.

Source 28.4

John Spanier | Gorbachev Needed to End the Cold War, 1992

"The rapidity of the change in the two superpowers relationship was certainly astounding. . . . Soviet policy was at a high point in the 1970s . . . The apparent successes of the Soviet Union were, however, deceptive. Two reasons account for what was, in fact, a flawed policy. One was the failure of the Soviet economy. The economic growth rate, 5 percent in the 1960s, and only 2 percent by the early 1970s, was standing still at virtually 0 percent a decade later. Capable of producing a plentiful supply of weapons, the Soviet economy was characterized by an absence of consumer goods and food. . . . A second reason for the Soviet turnabout was the cost of . . . [its] foreign policy. . . . The continuous arms buildup across the board and Moscow's expansionist activities in the third world produced fear and suspicion of Soviet intentions. . . . The Reagan administration's hard-line policies made Soviet foreign policy even more costly, thereby contributing to Gorbachev's awareness that the Soviet Union faced a systemic crisis.

Gorbachev therefore changed priorities and launched his program of *glasnost* (openness) and *perestroika* (restructuring) to revitalize Soviet society and the economy. . . . Opposition to Gorbachev was . . . fueled by the fear that the loosening of central controls could be harmful, if not fatal, politically. . . . In other words, the fundamental structural reforms required by the Soviet Union might threaten not only the party's sole control of power but also Moscow's imperial control over its own vast country. . . . The Soviet Union faced the real possibility of becoming the Soviet *Dis*union . . . the Soviet political system had become the greatest obstacle to economic modernization. That is why, preoccupied at home, Gorbachev needed to end the Cold War."

Source: John Spanier, *American Foreign Policy Since World War II, Twelfth Revised Edition* (Washington, D.C., 1992), 346, 347, 349, 350.

Globalization also affected popular culture and media. In the 1990s reality shows, many of which originated in Europe, became a staple of American television. The Swedish series *Expedition Robinson* was converted into *Survivor*, pitting contestants against each other in remote areas of the globe. At the same time, American programs such as *Cheers* and *Friends* were shown as reruns all over the world. As cable channels proliferated, American viewers of Hispanic or Asian origin could watch programs in their native languages. The Cable News Network (CNN), the British Broadcasting Corporation (BBC), and

Source 28.5

Beth Fischer | Reagan Ends the Cold War, 1997

"Washington did not merely respond to changes within the Soviet Union. In fact, the Reagan administration began seeking rapprochement with the Kremlin *before* the Soviets began to reform. The White House switched to a more conciliatory policy toward Moscow in January 1984 – fifteen months before Gorbachev became leader of the Soviet Union, and more than two years before the introduction of *glasnost* and *perestroika*.

. . . [T]he Reagan administration's stated policy toward Moscow was especially hard-line through October 1983. . . . Only ten weeks later, however, Washington reversed course. On January 16, 1984, President Reagan delivered an address on super-power relations that proved to be a turning point in his administration's approach to the Kremlin. With this speech, Reagan began seeking a rapprochement. . . . Reagan warned of the dangers of war, and declared that the United States posed no threat to the security of the Soviet Union. Throughout 1984 and 1985, others within the administration echoed Reagan's calls for 'cooperation and understanding' between the superpowers, and underscored that Washington 'posed no threat' to Soviet security.

The policy changes that Reagan introduced in 1984 are striking for a number of reasons. Most importantly, they are remarkable because they were implemented before the Soviets began to reform. [In 1984] . . . the old guard within the Kremlin was still fighting the cold war. The conventional view that Washington responded to changes within the Soviet Union is therefore inaccurate."

Source: Beth A. Fischer, *The Reagan Reversal: Foreign Policy and the End of the Cold War* (Columbia: University of Missouri Press, 1997), 2, 3, 4.

Examine the Sources

1. Where do Spanier and Fischer agree and disagree in their interpretations of the end of the Cold War?
2. Based on the evidence in this chapter, explain whose interpretation you find more convincing.

Put It in Context

What are the problems of writing history so close to the events that are taking place?

Al Jazeera, an Arabic-language television channel, competed for viewers with specially designed international broadcasts.

Globalization also had negative consequences. Organized labor in particular suffered a severe blow. By 2004 union membership in the United States had dropped to 12.5 percent of the industrial workforce. Fewer and fewer consumer goods bore the label "Made in America," as multinational companies shifted manufacturing jobs to low-wage workers in developing countries. Many of these foreign workers earned more than the prevailing wages in their countries, but by Western standards their pay was extremely low. There were few or no regulations governing working conditions or the use of child labor, and many foreign factories resembled the sweatshops of early-twentieth-century America. Not surprisingly, workers in the United States could not compete in this market. Furthermore, China, which by 2007 had become a prime source for American consumers, failed to regulate the quality of its products closely. Chinese-made toys, including the popular Thomas the Train, showed up in U.S. stores with excessive lead paint and had to be returned before endangering millions of children.

Globalization also posed a danger to the world's environment. As poorer nations sought to take advantage of the West's appetite for low-cost consumer goods, they industrialized rapidly, with little concern for the excessive pollution that accompanied their efforts. The desire for wood products and the expansion of large-scale farming eliminated one-third of Brazil's rain forests. The health of indigenous people suffered wherever globalization-related manufacturing appeared. In Taiwan and China, chemical byproducts of factories and farms turned rivers into polluted sources of drinking water and killed the rivers' fish and plants.

The older industrialized nations added their share to the environmental damage. Americans consumed electricity and gas produced overwhelmingly from coal and petroleum. The burning of fossil fuels by cars and factories released greenhouse gases, which has raised the temperature of the atmosphere and the oceans and contributed to the phenomenon known as global warming or climate change. Nearly all scientists believe that global warming threatens the stability of animal species and of human societies across the planet. However, after the industrialized nations of the world signed the Kyoto Protocol in 1998 to curtail greenhouse-gas emissions, the U.S. Senate refused to ratify it. Critics of the agreement maintained that it did not address the newly emerging industrial countries that polluted heavily and thus was unfair to the United States.

Globalization also highlighted health problems such as the AIDS epidemic. By the outset of the twenty-first century, approximately 33.2 million people worldwide suffered from the disease, though the number of new cases diagnosed annually had dropped to 2.5 million from more than 5 million a few years earlier. Africa remained the continent with the largest number of AIDS patients and the center of the epidemic. Increased education and the development of more effective pharmaceuticals to treat the illness reduced cases and prolonged the lives of those affected by the disease. Though treatments were more widely available in prosperous countries like the United States, agencies such as the United Nations and the World Health Organization, together with nongovernmental groups such as Partners in Health, were instrumental in offering relief in developing countries.

Managing Conflict after the Cold War. The end of the Cold War left the United States as the only remaining superpower. Though Reagan's Cold War defense spending had created huge deficits, the United States emerged from the Cold War with its economic and military strength intact. With the power vacuum created by the breakup of the Soviet Union, the question remained how the United States would use its strength to preserve world order and maintain peace.

Events in China showed the limitations of American military might. In May 1989, university students in Beijing and other major cities in China held large-scale protests to demand political and economic reforms in the country. Some 200,000 demonstrators consisting of students, intellectuals, and workers gathered in the capital city's huge Tiananmen Square, where they constructed a papier-mâché figure resembling the Statue of Liberty and sang songs borrowed from the African American civil rights movement. Deng Xiaoping, Mao Zedong's successor, cracked down on the demonstrations by declaring martial law and dispatching the army to disperse the protesters. Peaceful activists were mowed down by machine guns and stampeded by tanks. In response, President Bush merely issued a temporary ban on sales of weapons and nonmilitary items to China. When outrage over the Tiananmen Square massacre subsided, the president restored normal trade relations.

Flexing military muscle in Panama, however, was more feasible for the Bush administration than doing so in China. During the 1980s, the United States had developed a precarious relationship with Panamanian general Manuel Noriega. Although Noriega channeled aid to the Contras with the approval and support of the CIA, he angered the Reagan administration by maintaining close ties with Cuba. Noriega cooperated with the U.S. Drug Enforcement Agency in halting shipments of cocaine from Latin America headed for the United States at the same time that he helped Latin American drug kingpins launder their profits. In 1988 two Florida grand juries indicted the Panamanian leader on charges of drug smuggling and bribery, pressuring President Reagan to cut off aid to Panama and to ask Noriega to resign. Not only did Noriega refuse to step down, but he also nullified the results of the 1989 presidential election in Panama and declared himself the nation's "maximum leader."

After the United States tried unsuccessfully to foment an internal coup against Noriega, in 1989 the Panamanian leader proclaimed a "state of war" between the United States and his country. On December 28, 1989, President Bush launched Operation Just Cause, sending some 27,000 marines to invade Panama. Bush justified the invasion as necessary to protect the Panama Canal and the lives of American citizens, as well as to halt the drug traffic promoted by Noriega. In reality, the main purpose of the mission was to overthrow and capture the Panamanian dictator. The United States easily defeated its much weaker enemy. The U.S. government installed a new regime, and the marines captured Noriega and sent him to Florida to stand trial on the drug charges. In 1992 he was found guilty and sent to prison.

The Bush administration deployed much more military force in Iraq. Maintaining a steady flow of oil from the Persian Gulf was vital to U.S. strategic interests. During the prolonged Iraq-Iran War in the 1980s, the Reagan administration had switched allegiance from one belligerent to the other to ensure that neither side emerged too powerful. Though the administration had orchestrated the arms-for-hostages deal with Iran, it had also courted the Iraqi dictator Saddam Hussein. U.S. support for Hussein ended in 1990, after Iraq sent 100,000 troops to invade the small oil-producing nation of Kuwait, on the southern border of Iraq.

President Bush responded aggressively. He warned the Iraqis that their invasion "will not stand." Oil was at the heart of the matter. Hussein needed to revitalize the Iraqi economy, which was devastated after a decade of war with Iran. Bush feared that the Iraqi dictator would also attempt to overrun Kuwait's neighbor Saudi Arabia, an American ally, thereby giving Iraq control of half of the world's oil supply. Bush was also concerned that an emboldened Saddam Hussein would then upset the delicate balance of power in the Middle East and pose a threat to Israel by supporting the Palestinians. The Iraqis were rumored to be quickly developing nuclear weapons, which Hussein could use against Israel.

Rather than act unilaterally, President Bush organized a multilateral coalition against Iraq. Secretary of State James Baker persuaded the United Nations to adopt a resolution calling for Iraqi withdrawal from Kuwait and imposing economic sanctions. Thirty-eight nations, including the Arab countries of Egypt, Saudi Arabia, Syria, and Kuwait, contributed 160,000 troops, roughly 24 percent of the 700,000 allied forces that were deployed in Saudi Arabia in preparation for an invasion if Iraq did not comply.

With military forces stationed in Saudi Arabia, Bush gave Hussein a deadline of January 15, 1991 to withdraw from Kuwait or else risk attack. However, the president faced serious opposition at home against waging a war for oil. Demonstrations occurred throughout the nation, and most Americans supported the continued implementation of economic sanctions, which were already causing serious hardships for the Iraqi people. In the face of widespread opposition, the president requested congressional authorization for military operations against Iraq. After long debate, Congress narrowly approved Bush's request.

Saddam Hussein let the deadline pass. On January 16, **Operation Desert Storm** began when the United States launched air attacks on Baghdad and other key targets in Iraq. After a month of bombing, Hussein still refused to capitulate, so a ground offensive was launched on February 24, 1991. More than 500,000 allied troops moved into Kuwait and easily drove Iraqi forces out of that nation; they then moved into southern Iraq. The vastly outmatched Iraqi army, worn out from its ten-year war with Iran, was quickly defeated. Desperate for help, Hussein ordered the firing of Scud missiles on Israel to provoke it into war, which he hoped would drive a wedge between the United States and its Arab allies. Despite sustaining some casualties, Israel refrained from retaliation. The ground war ended within one

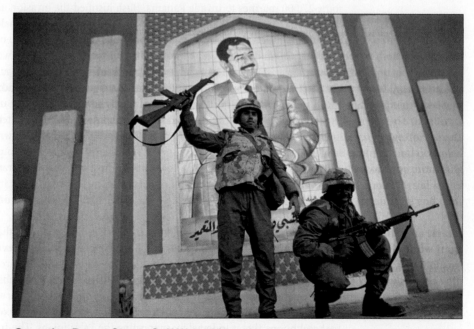

Operation Desert Storm, Gulf War, 1991   American soldiers stand in front of an image of Iraqi President Saddam Hussein before preparing to tear it down in late February 1991. The troops were part of the forces that defeated the Iraqi army that had invaded and occupied Kuwait in August 1990. HIRES/MERILLON/Gamma-Rapho via Getty Images hundred hours, and Iraq surrendered. An estimated 100,000 Iraqis died; by contrast, 136 Americans perished (see Map 28.3).

With the war over quickly, President Bush resisted pressure to march to Baghdad and overthrow Saddam Hussein. Bush's stated goal had been to liberate Kuwait; he did not wish to fight a war in the heart of Iraq. The administration believed that such an expedition would involve house-to-house, urban guerrilla warfare. Marching on Baghdad would also entail battling against Hussein's elite Republican Guard, not the weaker conscripts who had put up little resistance in Kuwait. Bush's Arab allies opposed expanding the war, and the president did not want to risk losing their support. Finally, getting rid of Hussein might make matters worse by leaving Iran and its Muslim fundamentalist rulers the dominant power in the region.

Operation Desert Storm preserved the U.S. lifeline to oil in the Persian Gulf and succeeded because of its limited military objectives. President Bush and his advisers understood that the United States had triumphed because it had pieced together a genuine coalition of nations, including Arab ones, to coordinate diplomatic and military action. Military leaders had a clear and defined mission — the liberation of Kuwait — as well as adequate troops and supplies. When they carried out their purpose, the war was over. The Bush administration had applied the Cold War policy of limited containment in dealing with Hussein. This successful U.S. military intervention in the Middle East provided President Bush an opportunity to address other explosive issues in the region. Following the end of the Iraq war, Bush set in motion the peace process that brought the Israelis and Palestinians together to sign a 1993 agreement providing for eventual Palestinian self-government in the Gaza Strip and the West Bank. For the first time the United States officially recognized Yasser Arafat, the head of the PLO, whom both the Israelis and the Americans had considered a terrorist.

In several areas of the globe, the move toward democracy that had begun in the late 1980s proceeded peacefully into the 1990s. The oppressive, racist system of apartheid fell in South Africa, and antiapartheid activist Nelson Mandela was released after twenty-seven years in prison to become president of the country in 1994. In 1990 the dictator Augusto Pinochet stepped down as president of Chile and ceded control to a democratically elected candidate. That same year, the pro-Communist Sandinista government lost at the polls in Nicaragua, and in 1992 the ruling regime in El Salvador signed a peace accord with the rebels.

The 1992 Election.

Despite his successes abroad, Bush's popularity plunged at home. After the president dispatched American troops and defeated Iraqi military forces in Kuwait in 1991, his approval rating stood at a whopping 89 percent. In sharp contrast, Bush's poll number plummeted to 34 percent in 1992. This precipitous decline resulted mainly from his inability to revive the sagging economy.

Bush ran for reelection against Governor William Jefferson (Bill) Clinton of Arkansas. Learning from the mistakes of Michael Dukakis as well as the successes of Reagan, Clinton ran as a centrist Democrat who promised to reduce the federal deficit by raising taxes on the wealthy and who supported conservative social policies such as the death penalty, tough measures against crime, and welfare reform. Though he did pledge to extend health care and opposed discrimination against homosexuals, Clinton relied on his mainstream southern Democratic credentials to deflect any claims that he was a liberal. Bush also faced a challenge from the independent candidate Ross Perot, a wealthy self-made businessman from Texas, whose campaign against rising government deficits won 19 percent of the popular vote, mostly at Bush's expense. In turn, Clinton defeated the incumbent by a two-to-one electoral margin.

Review & Relate

- What role did George H. W. Bush play in shaping the post–Cold War world?

- How did the end of the Cold War contribute to the growth of globalization?

Conclusion: Conservative Ascendancy and the End of the Cold War

The election of President Ronald Reagan represented the culmination of conservative ideas first set in motion by Republican Barry Goldwater's campaign for the White House in 1964. He emerged out of southern California where the movement to lower property taxes, increase community control over school curricula, rein in student protesters, disband affirmative action, and dismantle liberal programs had gained momentum in the 1960s and 1970s. First as governor of California and then as president, Reagan spearheaded the New Right movement. Although Reagan did not have a Republican-controlled Congress to work with throughout his presidency (Republicans held the Senate but not the House), he did succeed in reshaping government policies along more conservative lines.

Reagan's New Right regime bestowed a mixed legacy. The Reagan-Bush administrations reduced inflation and revived economic growth. But they also burdened the country with worrisome budget deficits and with fiscal and monetary policies that encouraged widespread, imprudent speculation on Wall Street and increased the power of giant corporations over political and economic life. Tax and spending cuts further enriched the wealthy but hurt the poor and the middle class. Americans learned about dangers to the environment and took some measures to correct them, but generally refused to alter their lifestyles. African Americans and women broke through barriers that denied them equal access to education and politics, but they confronted white male opposition to further progress. Although the sanctuary movement, highlighted by the trial of Demetria Martinez, provided refuge for undocumented immigrants from Central America fleeing political persecution and poverty, it encountered serious opposition from conservatives distressed by the economic and cultural consequences of immigration from south of the border.

Conservatives came to power amid major changes occurring in foreign affairs, most notably the proliferation and then the cessation of the Cold War. Some unlikely people were responsible for ending the Cold War. President Reagan, a militant anti-Communist crusader, together with his pragmatic and steady secretary of state, George Shultz, guided the United States through a policy of heightened military preparedness to push the Soviet Union toward peace. It was a dangerous gambit, but it worked; diplomacy rather than armed conflict prevailed. Reagan's Cold War strategy succeeded in part because during the 1980s a leader amenable to peace, Mikhail Gorbachev, governed the Soviet Union. He envisioned the end of the Cold War as a means of bringing political and economic reform to his beleaguered and bankrupt nation. What Reagan and Gorbachev began, their successors, George H. W. Bush and Boris Yeltsin, completed: the Cold War came to a conclusion, and the Soviet Union dismantled its empire and incorporated a measure of democracy and capitalism into Russia.

The activism of ordinary people around the world also helped transform the relationship between the superpowers. Antinuclear protesters in Western Europe and the United States kept up pressure on Western leaders to make continued nuclear expansion unacceptable. In Eastern Europe, Polish dockworker Lech Walesa and other fighters for democracy broke from the Soviet orbit and tore down the bricks and barbed-wire fences of the iron curtain.

The United States emerged as the winner of the Cold War, thereby gaining dominance as the world's sole superpower. Yet this did not necessarily guarantee peace. In assuming this preeminent role, the United States faced new threats to international security from governments and insurgents seeking to rebuild nations along ethnic and religious lines in the Middle East and the Persian Gulf. The collapse of the Soviet empire created a power vacuum that would be filled by a variety of unchecked and combustible local and regional forces intent on challenging the political and economic dominance of the United States. President Bush responded to such crises in Iraq and Panama decisively, but his response to China's crackdown at Tiananmen Square was far more tepid.

At the same time, globalization presented new opportunities and posed additional challenges. It promoted more international cooperation and freer trade among nations. Globalization also fostered greater communication and cultural exchanges around the world. However, globalization brought many problems as well. Rapid industrialization and exploration of new sources of wealth accelerated the environmental dangers of air and water pollution, climate change, and the destruction of primeval forests. As globalization shrank the world economically and culturally, the United States became the chief target of those who wanted to contain the influence of Western values. Terrorism, which transcended national borders, replaced communism as the leading enemy of the United States and its allies.

chapter 28 review

Timeline of Events

1981	Passage of the Economic Recovery Tax Act
1982	Boland Amendment passed
	750,000 attend nuclear freeze rally in New York City
	Ratification period expires for Equal Rights Amendment
1983	Suicide bomb attack in Lebanon kills 241 U.S. soldiers
	U.S. invasion of Grenada
1987	Senate hearings on Iran-Contra affair
	Intermediate Nuclear Forces Treaty signed
1989	Tiananmen Square protests
	Fall of the Berlin Wall
1990	Bush signs Americans with Disabilities Act and Clean Air Act
1990–1991	Soviet Union dismantled
1991	U.S. pushes Iraq out of Kuwait
1993	Second Strategic Arms Reduction Treaty signed

Key Terms

Sanctuary Movement, 968

Reaganomics, 971

Economic Recovery Tax Act, 972

acquired immune deficiency syndrome (AIDS), 974

Immigration Reform and Control Act, 975

Boland Amendment, 977

Iran-Contra affair, 980

nuclear freeze movement, 981

glasnost, 984

perestroika, 984

Solidarity, 986

globalization, 988

Operation Desert Storm, 994

Review & Relate

1. What was Reaganomics, and what were its most important long-term consequences?

2. How did conservative ideas shape the social, cultural, and political landscape of the 1980s and 1990s?

3. How did anticommunism shape Ronald Reagan's foreign policy?

4. What role did ordinary citizens play in prompting the superpowers to move toward nuclear de-escalation?

5. What role did George H. W. Bush play in shaping the post–Cold War world?

6. How did the end of the Cold War contribute to the growth of globalization?

The Iran-Contra Affair

▸ Evaluate the role President Reagan and his administration played in secretly funding anti-revolutionary forces in Nicaragua and explain whether you think Congress reached the correct conclusion about the president's responsibility.

On November 3, 1986, the Lebanese magazine *Ash-Shiraa* revealed a secret arms-for-hostages deal between the United States and Iran. As the affair unfolded, it was revealed that the profits from these arms sales had been illegally diverted to aid anti-Sandinista rebels (called Contras) in Nicaragua. For the next year, the Iran-Contra affair, as it was known, played out in the press as questions of governmental conspiracy, abuse of power, and a White House cover-up swirled around the Reagan administration.

Since the early 1980s, the CIA had been funding, arming, and training groups of dissident forces opposing the leftist Nicaraguan government. After Congress passed the Boland Amendment, which prohibited further aid to the Contras, the Reagan administration then looked for other ways to continue its support for the rebels, eventually funneling money from the Iranian arms sales (Sources 25.6 and 25.7).

Less than a month after the story broke, President Reagan appointed a three-person commission to investigate the allegations. Unsatisfied with the commission's work, the U.S. Senate and House of Representatives established a joint investigative committee and held hearings in the summer of 1987 (Sources 28.9 and 28.10). Both the presidential commission and the congressional committee concluded that neither Reagan nor Vice President George H. W. Bush was aware of the illegal funding of the Contras, though Reagan was sharply criticized

as a poor administrator who needed to exert more control over his staff (Source 28.8).

Several of Reagan's top officials were eventually indicted on a variety of felony accounts, including lying to Congress, destroying evidence, and obstructing justice. In all, eleven men were convicted or pleaded guilty. In late 1992, then-President George H. W. Bush pardoned six men indicted or convicted as part of the Iran-Contra affair.

Source 28.6

The Boland Amendments, 1982 and 1984

Alarmed at the CIA's involvement in the Nicaraguan civil war, Congress passed a measure in 1982 to limit funding and support for these activities. Offered by Edward Boland, a Democratic representative from Massachusetts, the Boland Amendment prohibited the CIA or any other government agency from providing military aid or advice to the Contra rebels. When the Reagan administration found ways to evade the amendment, in 1984 Congress adopted a stronger version as part of an appropriations bill.

1982 Amendment

A substitute amendment to the Harkin amendment [which also prohibited support of military activity in Nicaragua] to prohibit the CIA or Defense Department to use funds of the bill to furnish military equipment, military training or advice, or other support for military activities, to any group or individual, not part of a country's armed forces, for the purpose of overthrowing the government of Nicaragua or provoking a military exchange between Nicaragua and Honduras. The Harkin amendment has prohibited support of any military activity in Nicaragua.

Source: House Amendment 974, 97th Congress (1981–1982).

1984 Amendment

No appropriations or funds made available pursuant to this joint resolution to the Central Intelligence Agency, the Department of Defense, or any other agency or entity of the United States involved in intelligence activities may be obligated or expended for the purpose or which could have the effect of supporting, directly or indirectly, military or paramilitary operations in Nicaragua by any nation, group, organization, movement or individual.

Source: Pub. L. No. 98–441, 98 Stat. 1699 (Oct. 3, 1984).

Source 28.7

CIA Freedom Fighter's Manual, 1983

The CIA's support for the Contras included training in sabotage to disrupt the Nicaraguan government and society. In 1983 the CIA prepared the Freedom Fighter's Manual and air-dropped thousands of pamphlets over Nicaragua. Promising "minimal risk for the combatant," the manual's advice ranged from passive and mundane techniques — such as showing up late for work, spreading false rumors, and plugging up toilets with sponges — to more aggressive methods of sabotage, shown here.

PUT NAILS ON ROADS AND HIGHWAYS

REGAR CLAVOS EN LOS CAMINOS Y CARRETERAS

PUT DIRT INTO GASOLINE TANKS

TIERRA

ECHARLE TIERRA AL TANQUE DE GASOLINA

COLOCAR CLAVOS JUNTO A LOS NEUMÁTICOS DE VEHÍCULOS ESTACIONADOS

PUT NAILS NEXT TO THE TIRES OF PARKED VEHICLES

ECHAR AGUA EN EL TANQUE DE GASOLINA

AGUA

PUT WATER IN GASOLINE TANKS

Ronald Reagan | Speech on the Iran-Contra Affair, 1987

President Reagan appointed a commission headed by Senator John Tower to investigate the allegations concerning the sale of arms to Iran in exchange for the release of hostages in Lebanon and the subsequent channeling of funds to support the Contras in Nicaragua. The commission's report, released in February 1987, concluded that while Reagan should have been more directly aware of the actions of his advisers, he was not aware of the illegal diversion of funds to the Contras. A few weeks after the Tower Commission released its report, President Reagan went on television and spoke about the Iran-Contra affair.

First, let me say I take full responsibility for my own actions and for those of my administration. As angry as I may be about activities undertaken without my knowledge, I am still accountable for those activities. As disappointed as I may be in some who served me, I'm still the one who must answer to the American people for this behavior. And as personally distasteful as I find secret bank accounts and diverted funds—well, as the Navy would say, this happened on my watch.

Let's start with the part that is the most controversial. A few months ago I told the American people I did not trade arms for hostages. My heart and my best intentions still tell me that's true, but the facts and the evidence tell me it is not. As the Tower board reported, what began as a strategic opening to Iran deteriorated, in its implementation, into trading arms for hostages. This runs counter to my own beliefs, to administration policy, and to the original strategy we had in mind. There are reasons why it happened, but no excuses. It was a mistake. . . .

Now, another major aspect of the Board's findings regards the transfer of funds to the Nicaraguan contras. The Tower board wasn't able to find out what happened to this money, so the facts here will be left to the continuing investigations of the court-appointed Independent Counsel and the two congressional investigating committees. I'm confident the truth will come out about this matter,

as well. As I told the Tower board, I didn't know about any diversion of funds to the contras. But as President, I cannot escape responsibility.

Much has been said about my management style, a style that's worked successfully for me during 8 years as Governor of California and for most of my Presidency. The way I work is to identify the problem, find the right individuals to do the job, and then let them go to it. I've found this invariably brings out the best in people. They seem to rise to their full capability, and in the long run you get more done. . . .

Now, what should happen when you make a mistake is this: You take your knocks, you learn your lessons, and then you move on. That's the healthiest way to deal with a problem. This in no way diminishes the importance of the other continuing investigations, but the business of our country and our people must proceed. I've gotten this message from Republicans and Democrats in Congress, from allies around the world, and—if we're reading the signals right—even from the Soviets. And of course, I've heard the message from you, the American people. You know, by the time you reach my age, you've made plenty of mistakes. And if you've lived your life properly—so, you learn. You put things in perspective. You pull your energies together. You change. You go forward.

Source: "Address to the Nation on the Iran Arms and Contra Aid Controversy," March 4, 1987, http://www.pbs.org/wgbh/americanexperience/features/primary-resources/reagan-iran-contra.

Oliver North | Testimony to Congress, July 1987

As the Iran-Contra affair intensified, Lieutenant Colonel Oliver North appeared before the joint congressional committee in the summer of 1987 and admitted his role as a chief operator in the Iran-Contra affair. He also confessed that he had lied to Congress and had shredded incriminating documents, but he defended himself as a soldier in service to his country. North was eventually indicted and convicted on three felony counts, though his conviction was overturned on appeal.

QUESTION: Is it correct to say that following the enactment of the Boland Amendment, our support for the war in Nicaragua did not end and that you were the person in the United States Government who managed it?

ANSWER: Starting in the spring of 1984, well before the Boland proscription of no appropriated funds made available to the D.O.D. [Department of Defense] and the C.I.A. etc., I was already engaged in supporting the Nicaraguan resistance and the democratic outcome in Nicaragua. I did so as part of a covert operation. It was carried out starting as early as the spring of '84, when we ran out of money and people started to look in Nicaragua, in Honduras and Guatemala, El Salvador, and Costa Rica for some sign of what the Americans were really going to do, and that that help began much earlier than the most rigorous of the Boland proscriptions. And yes, it was carried out covertly, and it was carried out in such a way as to insure that the heads of state and the political leadership in Nicaragua—in Central America—recognized the United States was going to meet the commitments of the President's foreign policy.

And the President's foreign policy was that we are going to achieve a democratic outcome in Nicaragua and that our support for the Nicaraguan freedom fighters was going to continue, and that I was given the job of holding them together in body and soul. And it slowly transitioned into a more difficult task as time went on and as the C.I.A. had to withdraw further and further from that support, until finally we got to the point in October when I was the only person left talking to them. . . .

QUESTION: Do you know whether or not the President was aware of your activities seeking funds and operational support for the contras, from third countries?

ANSWER: I do not know.

QUESTION: Were you ever—

ANSWER: I assumed that he did.

QUESTION: . . . What was the basis of your assumption?

ANSWER: Just that there was a lot going on and it was very obvious that the Nicaraguan resistance survived—I sent forward innumerable documents, some of which you've just shown us as exhibits, that demonstrated that I was keeping my superiors fully informed, as to what was going on.

Source: "Iran-Contra Hearings: 'I Came Here to Tell You the Truth'; The Colonel States His Case: Country and Orders above All," *New York Times*, July 8, 1987, A8.

Source 28.10

George Mitchell | Response to Oliver North, 1987

Maine senator George Mitchell joined the joint House and Senate committee investigating the Iran-Contra affair in 1987. During Oliver North's testimony, Mitchell listened to North's characterization of his activities and support for the Contras as the true patriotic course of action. In Mitchell's response to North, he discusses the meaning of patriotism in a democratic society.

You have talked here often and eloquently about the need for a democratic outcome in Nicaragua. There is no disagreement on that. There is disagreement as how best to achieve that objective. Many Americans agree with the President's policy; many do not. Many patriotic Americans, strongly anti-Communist, believe there's a better way to contain the Sandinistas, to bring about a democratic outcome in Nicaragua and to bring peace to Central America.

And many patriotic Americans are concerned that in the pursuit of democracy abroad we not compromise it in any way here at home. You and others have urged consistency in our policies, you have said repeatedly that if we are not consistent our allies and other nations will question our reliability. That is a real concern. But if it's bad to change policies, it's worse to have two different policies at the same time: one public policy and an opposite policy in private. It's difficult to conceive of a greater inconsistency than that. It's hard to imagine anything that would give our allies more cause to consider us unreliable than that we say one thing in public and secretly do the opposite. And that's exactly what was done when arms were sold to Iran and arms were swapped for hostages.

. . . You talked about your background and it was really very compelling, and is obviously one of the reasons why the American people are attracted to you.

Let me tell you a story from my background. Before I entered the Senate, I had the great honor of serving as a federal judge. In that position I had great power. The one I most enjoyed exercising was the power to make people American citizens. From time to time I presided at what we call naturalization ceremonies; they're citizenship ceremonies. These are people who came from all over the world, risked their lives, sometimes left their families and their fortunes behind to come here. They had gone through the required procedures, and I, in the final act, administered to them the oath of allegiance to the United States, and I made them American citizens. To this moment, to this moment it was the most exciting thing I've ever done in my life.

Ceremonies were always moving for me because my mother was an immigrant, my father the orphan son of immigrants. Neither of them had any education, and they worked at very menial tasks in our society. But because of the openness of America, because of equal justice under law in America, I sit here today a United States Senator. And after every one of these ceremonies I made it a point to speak to these new Americans, I asked them why they came, how they came, and their stories, each of them, were inspiring. I think you would be interested and moved by them given the views you have expressed on this country.

And when I asked them why they came they said several things, mostly two. The first is they said we came because here in America everybody has a chance, opportunity. And they also said over and over again, particularly people from totalitarian societies, we came here because here in America you can criticize the government without looking over your shoulder. Freedom to disagree with the government.

Now, you have addressed several pleas to this committee, very eloquently. None more eloquent than last Friday when in response to a question by Representative [Richard] Cheney you asked that Congress not cut off aid to the Contras for the love of God and for the love of country. I now address a plea to you. Of all the qualities which the American people find compelling about you, none is more impressive than your obvious deep devotion to this country. Please remember that others share that devotion and recognize that it is possible for an American to disagree with you on aid to the Contras and still love God and still love this country just as much as you do.

Although he's regularly asked to do so, God does not take sides in American politics. And in America, disagreement with the policies of the government is not evidence of lack of patriotism.

. . . Indeed, it is the very fact that Americans can criticize their government openly and without fear of reprisal that is the essence of our freedom, and that will keep us free.

Now, I have one final plea. Debate this issue forcefully and vigorously as you have and as you surely will, but, please, do it in a way that respects the patriotism and the motives of those who disagree with you, as you would have them respect yours.

Source: Iran-Contra Investigation, Joint Hearings Part II, July 10, 13, and 14, 1987: Continued Testimony of Oliver L. North and Robert C. McFarlane, 31–46.

Interpret the Evidence

1. Compare the 1982 and 1984 versions of the Boland Amendment (Source 28.6). How does the wording of the second version clarify Congress's original intent?

2. What, if anything, surprises you about the Freedom Fighter's Manual (Source 28.7)? Why would it focus on these specific activities, and do you think they were effective?

3. Evaluate Reagan's explanation of his Iran-Contra involvement (Source 28.8) and compare it to Oliver North's testimony (Source 28.9).

4. How does Senator George Mitchell (Source 28.10) define patriotism differently than Oliver North (Source 28.9)?

Put It in Context

Compare the Iran-Contra affair with Watergate ("The Nixon Landslide and Watergate Scandal, 1972–1974" in chapter 27). How did Reagan's presidency survive such a scandal when Nixon's did not?

The Challenges of a Globalized World

1993 to the present

Window to the Past

Anti-Muslim discrimination, 2011

The September 11, 2001 terror attacks sparked an outbreak of anti-Muslim sentiment. The Patriot Act and attacks on Muslims reflected this hostility. This editorial cartoon by Angelo Lopez nearly a decade after 9/11 illustrates the complicated position of mainstream Muslims in the United States and the Persian Gulf. ▸ **To learn more about this primary source, see Source 29.8 on page 1044.**

Angelo Lopez

After reading this chapter you will be able to:

- Assess the impact of computer technology, globalization, and immigration on the United States.
- Evaluate President Clinton's responses to domestic and global issues.
- Explain the impact of the 9/11 attacks on President Bush's foreign policy and describe his compassionate conservatism at home.
- Analyze the reasons for Barack Obama's election as president and explain the challenges that faced his administration.
- Explain how Donald Trump reshaped the presidency.

Comparing American Histories

William Henry Gates III started tinkering with computers at age thirteen. As a teenager in 1969, the enterprising Gates and some friends set up a business to make computerized traffic counters to gauge the speed of vehicles, for which they earned $20,000.

His brilliant mind and entrepreneurial inclinations led Gates to enroll at Harvard and then to drop out after spending more time at the university's computer center than he did in class. In 1974 he became interested in microcomputers as an alternative to large conventional computers. A year later, Gates formed a computer software company called Microsoft, envisioning the microcomputer on office desktops and in homes throughout America.

(*left*) **Bill Gates** Dursun Aydemir/Anadolu Agency/Getty Images
(*right*) **Alicia Garza** Kim White/Getty Images

Bill Gates succeeded beyond all expectations. In 1980 Microsoft collaborated with International Business Machines (IBM) to create a software package for IBM's new line of personal computers. In 1986 Microsoft became a publicly traded company on the New York Stock Exchange. Within a decade, Gates became the richest man in America, and like industrial titans a century earlier, he donates generously to fund philanthropic activities worldwide. In 2000, along with his wife, he set up the Bill and Melinda Gates Foundation, the largest private foundation in the world, which seeks to extend health care, fight diseases such as malaria, tuberculosis, and HIV/AIDS, and promote economic development in poor and developing countries around the globe.

Digital technology played an important part in the life of **Alicia Garza** and the movement she helped found, **Black Lives Matter (BLM)**. Born in 1981, Alicia Schwartz Garza was raised by her African American mother and her Jewish stepfather in the San Francisco Bay area. She graduated from the University of California, San Diego with a degree in anthropology and sociology, and she became a community organizer. She came out as queer, and in 2008, she married Malachi Garza, a trans-male activist.

BLM grew out of Garza's 2013 Facebook post following the acquittal of a white Florida man who shot and killed Trayvon Martin, an unarmed black teenager who was about the same age as Garza's younger brother. Her post concluded: "Black people. I love you. I love us. Our lives matter." From the last three words emerged the hashtag, Black Lives Matter, and along with Patrisse Cullors and Opal Tometi, Garza built a social media platform that sparked the creation of the BLM movement.

The 2014 killing of another unarmed black youth, Michael Brown, by a policeman in Ferguson, Missouri, fueled BLM protests. In 2015, Garza led a Freedom Ride to Ferguson, which helped propel Black Lives Matter chapters throughout the country and internationally. As writer and activist, Alicia Garza continues to promote racial, gender, and economic equality on behalf of communities of color, LGBTQ (lesbian, gay, bisexual, transgender, queer), and the poor. ■

The American histories of Bill Gates and Alicia Garza were deeply affected by the twin forces of digital technology and systemic racism. Computers, the Internet, and cell phone technology reformulated commerce and social relations, furthering the globalization that emerged after the Cold War. Google, the Web, Facebook, and Twitter became household words and broke down domestic and global barriers that earlier technologies had not penetrated. Computer technology revolutionized political communication and organization, mobilized ordinary citizens into action, and expanded opportunities for disgruntled and oppressed citizens of foreign countries to overthrow despotic rulers. At the same time, the al-Qaeda terror attacks of September 11, 2001 placed the United States and its allies on a permanent war footing, resulting in wars against terrorism in Iraq and Afghanistan and increased surveillance of suspected terrorists and citizens alike. Amid these upheavals, Americans broke new ground by electing their first black president. Still, the nation faced historic burdens of institutionalized racism, as spotlighted in the wave of police killings of unarmed black citizens from Trayvon Martin to George Floyd. The 2016 election of Donald Trump as president underscored the political, economic, and cultural divisions that continued to divide the country and highlighted the challenges digital technology posed for national unity and security. Trump proved unable to handle a series of public health, economic, and racial crises and was defeated by Joseph Biden in the 2020 election.

Transforming American Society

The 1990s marked a period of great economic growth and technological advancement in the United States. Computers stood at the center of the technological revolution of the late twentieth and early twenty-first centuries, allowing both small and large businesses to reach new markets and transform the workplace. Digital technology also altered the way individuals worked, purchased goods and services, communicated, and spent their leisure time. As the Internet connected Americans to the rest of the world, corporate leaders embraced globalization as the key to economic prosperity. They put together business mergers so that their companies could operate more powerfully in the international market. Government officials generally supported their efforts by reducing regulations on business and financial practices. Globalization not only thrust American business enterprises outward but also brought a new population of immigrants to the United States.

The Computer Revolution. The first working computers were developed for military purposes during World War II and the Cold War and were enormous in size and cost. Engineers began to resolve the size issue with the creation of transistors. Invented in the late 1940s, these small electronic devices came into widespread use in running computers during the 1960s. The design of integrated circuits in the 1970s led to the production of microcomputers in which a silicon chip the size of a nail head did the work once performed by huge computers. Bill Gates was not the only one to recognize the potential market of microcomputers for home and business use. Steve Jobs, like

Gates a college dropout, founded Apple Computer Company in 1976, Microsoft's biggest competitor.

Microchips and digital technology found a market beyond home and office computers. Over the last two decades of the twentieth century, computers came to operate everything from standard appliances such as televisions and telephones, to new electronic devices such as CD players, fax machines, and cell phones. Computers controlled traffic lights on the streets and air traffic in the skies. They changed the leisure patterns of youth: Many young people preferred to play video games indoors than to engage in outdoor activities. Consumers purchased goods online, and companies such as Amazon sold merchandise through the Internet without any retail stores. Soon computers became the stars of movies such as *The Matrix* (1999), *A.I. Artificial Intelligence* (2001), and *Iron Man* (2008).

The Internet — an open, global series of interconnected computer networks that transmit data, information, electronic mail, and other services — grew out of military research in the 1970s, when the Department of Defense constructed a system of computer servers connected to one another throughout the United States. The main objective of this network was to preserve military communications in the event of a Soviet nuclear attack. At the end of the Cold War, the Internet was repurposed for nonmilitary use, linking government, academic, business, and organizational systems. In 1991 the World Wide Web came into existence as a way to access the Internet and connect documents and other resources to one another through hyperlinks. In 2020 over 85 percent of people in the United States used the Internet, up from 50 percent in 2000. Internet use worldwide leapt ten fold, from nearly 361 million people in 2000 to over 4.6 billion in 2020.

The Changing American Population.
As the technological revolution transformed the United States, an influx of immigrants began to alter the composition of the American population. The population of the United States grew from 202 million to 331 million between 1970 and 2020, and immigrants accounted for some 28 million of the increase.

Most newcomers in the 1980s and 1990s arrived from Latin America and South and East Asia. Relatively few Europeans (approximately 2 million) moved to the United States, though their numbers increased after the collapse of the Soviet empire in the early 1990s. Poverty and political unrest pushed migrants out of Mexico, Central America, and the Caribbean. At the beginning of the twenty-first century, Latinos (35 million) had surpassed African Americans (34 million) as the nation's largest racial minority group. With the arrival of Caribbean and African immigrants, black America was also becoming more diverse.

In addition to the 16 million immigrants who came from south of the U.S. border, another 9 million headed eastward from Asia, including Chinese, South Koreans, and Filipinos, together with refugees from Vietnam and Cambodia. By 2010 an estimated 3.18 million Indians from South Asia lived in the United States, most arriving after the 1960s. Indian Americans became the third-largest Asian American group behind Chinese and Filipinos. Another 1 to 2 million people came from predominantly Islamic nations such as Pakistan, Lebanon, Iraq, and Iran (Figure 29.1).

Explore ▶

See Source 29.1 for one immigrant's experience in low-wage factory work.

FIGURE 29.1 Immigrant Growth by Home Region, 1981–2010

In the late twentieth and early twenty-first centuries, immigration to the United States increased significantly, especially from North America (which in this figure includes Mexico, Central America, and the Caribbean). Asians formed the second largest group of immigrants, while Africans arrived in small but growing numbers. Compare each region's percentage of immigration in 1991 with 2010 and present the conclusions you can draw.

Source: Data from *2015 Yearbook of Immigration Statistics, Office of Immigration Statistics, U.S. Department of Homeland Security, December 2016.*

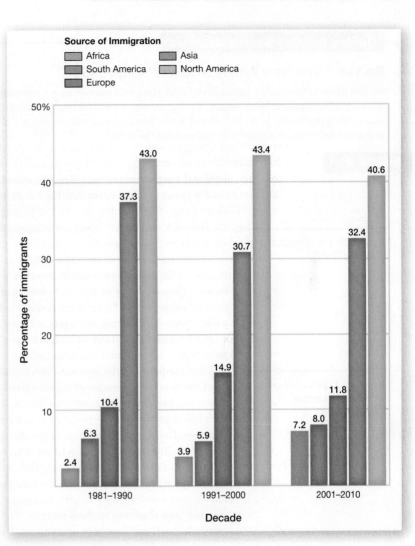

Review & Relate

- How did computers change life in the United States at the turn of the millennium?

- How has globalization affected immigration in recent decades?

Political Polarization and Globalization in the Clinton Years

The first president born after 1945, President Bill Clinton had to deal with the challenges facing the post–Cold War world. He embraced globalization as the key to economic prosperity and showed his readiness to promote and defend U.S. national security. Despite achieving general prosperity and peace, Clinton could not escape the political polarization that divided the American electorate, and his tenure in office only intensified this schism.

Guided Primary Source Analysis

Bo Yee | The New American Sweatshop, 1994

Bo Yee came to the United States from Hong Kong and worked as a seamstress. When her employer laid off workers without paying back wages, Yee joined with a local immigrant women's organization to fight for outstanding payments. In a 1994 interview she described conditions in the California garment factory where she was paid $5 to create dresses that retailed for $175.

Source 29.1

Why did Yee come to the United States?

I started working at a factory a month after I got here. I immigrated to the US because of my two sons. They were not going to be happy in Hong Kong after the 1997 changeover [the transfer of Hong Kong from the United Kingdom to China]. My husband did not want to come to the US but he did come in 1985.

How did Yee's boss get workers to exploit themselves?

I started working at Lucky Sewing Company in June 1986. Working there was like being a prisoner in a sealed cage. All the windows were locked. They wouldn't let you go to the bathroom. They had "No loud talking" signs posted. There were about 20 of us there working ten hours a day, seven days a week, endlessly, without rest. Most of the workers were from mainland China, although some came from Hong Kong and there were a few Latinos. The boss' wife created a tense, competitive atmosphere between the workers. She would praise some people and downgrade others. Because of my experience, I can work faster than newer workers from China who are not as skillful. They would sacrifice their lunch and break time to catch up. I hated the way the boss made us compete. There were three of us in one department who had to produce 200 pieces. They would push us to see who could finish first. They were getting people to exploit themselves. How disgusting! I hate this!

I couldn't communicate with the Latino workers, but you can have fun without speaking each other's language. You motion. You use body language and whatever method you can. The relations with Latinos were better. We were not forced to compete with each other.

How did working in this factory change Yee's opinion of the United States?

I thought America was a very advanced country, but working in sweatshops here, I see that the garment industry is very backward compared to Hong Kong.

Source: Miriam Ching Yoon Louie, *Sweatshop Warriors: Immigrant Women Workers Take On the Global Factory* (Cambridge, MA: South End Press, 2001), 49–50.

▌ Put It in Context

Compare the factory Yee describes to sweatshops that existed a century earlier in the United States as described in chapter 18.

Politics during the Clinton Administration.
Born in Arkansas in 1946, William Jefferson (Bill) Clinton served five terms as Democratic governor of his home state. As governor, Clinton spoke out for equal opportunity, improved education, and economic development. After defeating President George H. W. Bush in 1992, Clinton entered the White House.

In 1993 Clinton sought to reverse a number of Reagan-Bush policies. He persuaded Congress to raise taxes on wealthy individuals and corporations, while his administration reduced defense spending following the end of the Cold War. Taken together, these measures stimulated a robust economic growth of 4 percent annually, established over 22 million jobs, lowered the national debt, and created a budget surplus. Clinton further departed from his Republican predecessors by signing executive orders expanding federal assistance for legal abortion. He also approved the 1993 Family and Medical Leave Act, which allowed parents to take up to twelve weeks of unpaid leave to care for newborn children without risk of losing their jobs. The president had less success opening the military to gay men and lesbians, though many already served secretly. His policy of "don't ask, don't tell" permitted lesbian, gay, and bisexual individuals to serve in the armed forces so long as they kept their sexual orientation a secret, a compromise that failed to end discrimination. The Clinton administration's most stinging defeat came when Congress failed to pass universal medical coverage.

Clinton tried to appeal to voters across the political spectrum on other issues. He signed a tough anticrime law that funded the recruitment of an additional 100,000 police officers to patrol city streets, while supporting gun control legislation. Although the prison population had been on the rise before the 1990s, Clinton's anticrime bill accelerated the rate of incarceration and had a disproportionate effect on African Americans and Latinos. Managing to overcome the powerful lobby of the National Rifle Association, in 1993 Clinton signed the Brady Bill, which imposed a five-day waiting period to check the background of gun buyers.

Conservatives were fiercely opposed to Clinton on several fronts. Right-wing talk radio hosts criticized the president and his wife, Hillary Rodham Clinton, a lawyer and leader in the effort to reform health care. Conservatives blamed the Clintons for all they considered wrong in society — feminism, abortion, affirmative action, and secularism. Criticism of pre-presidential dealings in a controversial real estate project known as White-water prompted the appointment in 1994 of a special prosecutor to investigate allegations of impropriety.

Facing conservative antagonism, the president and the Democratic Party fared poorly in the 1994 congressional elections, losing control of both houses of Congress. Republicans, led by House Minority Leader Newt Gingrich of Georgia, championed the **Contract with America**. This document embraced conservative principles, including a constitutional amendment for a balanced budget, reduced welfare spending, lower taxes, and term limits for lawmakers. It also marked a shift toward rigid partisan divisions in Congress. The election underscored the increasing influence of white evangelical Christians, who voted in large numbers for Republican candidates.

Stung by this defeat, Clinton tried to outmaneuver congressional Republicans by shifting rightward and championing welfare reform. In 1996 he signed the **Personal Responsibility and Work Opportunity Reconciliation Act**. It replaced the Aid to Families with Dependent Children provision of the Social Security law, the basis for welfare in the United

Celebrating the Contract with America On April 7, 1995, Speaker of the House Newt Gingrich holds up a copy of the *Contract with America* on the steps of the U.S. Capitol. The document helped Republicans win the mid-term congressional elections in 1994, the first time they controlled both houses of Congress since 1953. Gingrich is joined by some 160 House Republicans to celebrate the completion of the Republicans' 100-day promise of change. However, their legislative efforts to achieve the contract's proposals were mixed. Richard Ellis/AFP/Getty Images

States since the New Deal, with a new measure that required adult welfare recipients to find work within two years or lose the benefits provided to families earning less than $7,700 annually. The law also placed a lifetime limit of five years on these federal benefits. Also in 1996, the president approved the Defense of Marriage Act, which denied married same-sex couples the federal benefits granted to heterosexual married couples, including Social Security survivor's benefits.

In adopting such positions as welfare reform and antigay legislation, Clinton angered many of his liberal supporters but ensured his reelection in 1996. Running against Republican senator Robert Dole of Kansas and the independent candidate Ross Perot, Clinton captured 49 percent of the popular vote and 379 electoral votes. Dole received 41 percent of the vote, and Perot came in a distant third.

Declining support from his liberal base did not seriously undermine President Clinton, but sexual indiscretions nearly brought him down. Starting in 1995, Clinton had engaged in consensual sexual relations with Monica Lewinsky, a twenty-two-year-old White House intern. Clinton denied these charges under oath, but when Lewinsky testified about their sexual encounters, the president recanted his earlier statements. After an independent prosecutor concluded that Clinton had committed perjury and obstructed justice, the Republican-controlled House voted to impeach the president on December 19, 1998. However, on February 12, 1999, Republicans in the Senate failed to muster the necessary two-thirds vote to convict Clinton on the impeachment charges.

These impeachment efforts did not deter Clinton from improving the country's economy. In the midst of the sex scandal in 1998, the unemployment rate fell to 4.3 percent, the lowest level since the early 1970s. The rate of home ownership reached a record-setting 66 percent. As the "misery index" — a compilation of unemployment and inflation — fell, the gross domestic product grew by more than $250 billion. In 1999 the stock market's Dow Jones average reached a historic high of 10,000 points. That same year the president signed into law a measure that freed banks to merge commercial, investment, and insurance services, prohibited since 1933, giving them enormous leeway in undertaking profitable but risky ventures. The Clinton administration boasted that its economic policies had succeeded in canceling the Reagan-Bush budget deficit, yielding a surplus for the fiscal year 2000. This boom, however, did not affect everyone equally. African Americans and Latinos lagged behind whites economically; and the gap between rich and poor widened as the wealthiest 13,000 American families earned as much income as the poorest 20 million.

Global Challenges. Clinton embraced economic cooperation in Europe. In 1993 western European nations formed the European Union (EU), which encouraged free trade and investment among member nations. In 1999 the EU introduced a common currency, the euro, which nineteen nations have now adopted.

Clinton encouraged the formation of a similar economic partnership in North America. In 1993, together with the governments of Mexico and Canada, the U.S. Congress ratified the **North American Free Trade Agreement (NAFTA)**. The agreement removed tariffs and other obstacles to commerce and investment among the three countries to encourage trade. Between 1994 and 2004, trade among NAFTA nations increased by nearly 130 percent. Although Mexico saw a significant drop in poverty rates and a rise in real income, NAFTA harmed some workers in the United States. From 1994 to 2007, net manufacturing jobs dropped by 3,654,000 as U.S. companies outsourced their production to Mexico, with its low wage and benefits structure. However, many more manufacturing jobs were lost to automation.

Clinton also actively promoted globalization through the World Trade Organization (WTO). Created in 1995, the WTO consists of more than 150 nations and seeks "to ensure that trade flows as smoothly, predictably, and freely as possible." The policies of the WTO generally benefit wealthier nations, such as the United States. From 1978 to 2000, the value of U.S. exports and imports jumped from 17 percent to 25 percent of the gross domestic product.

As the first president elected in the post–Cold War era, Clinton faced numerous foreign policy challenges during his two terms in office. No longer did the problems facing the United States result from customary military aggression by one nation against another; rather, the greatest threats came from the implosion of national governments into factionalism and genocide and the rise of Islamic extremists.

President Clinton responded boldly to violence in the Balkans, an area considered vital to U.S. national security. In 1989 Yugoslavia splintered after the ruling Communist regime crumbled. The predominantly Roman Catholic states of Slovenia and Croatia declared their independence from the largely Russian Orthodox Serbian population in Yugoslavia. In 1992 the mainly Muslim territory of Bosnia-Herzegovina also broke away, despite protests by its substantial Serbian population (Map 29.1). A civil war erupted between Serb and Croatian minorities and the Muslim-dominated Bosnian government. Supported by Slobodan Milošević, the leader of the neighboring province of Serbia, Bosnian Serbs wrested control of large parts of the region and slaughtered tens of thousands of Muslims through

AUSTRIA

HUNGARY

SLOVENIA
1991

CROATIA
1991

ROMANIA

VOJVODINA

BOSNIA-
HERZEGOVINA
1992

SERBIA
2006

Adriatic
Sea

KOSOVO
2008

BULGARIA

ITALY

MONTENEGRO
2006

MACEDONIA
1991

ALBANIA

GREECE

0   100   200 miles

0   100   200 kilometers

N
W   E
S

——— Yugoslavia, 1945–1991

1991   Date of independence

MAP 29.1   The Breakup of Yugoslavia, 1991–2008

With the collapse of Communist control of Yugoslavia in 1989, the country splintered along ethnic and religious lines, eventually forming seven separate nations. A civil war between Serbia and Croatia ended in 1995, but Serbs then attacked Muslims in Bosnia and Kosovo.

what they euphemistically called **ethnic cleansing**. In 1995 Clinton sponsored NATO bombing raids against the Serbs, dispatched 20,000 American troops as part of a multilateral peacekeeping force, and brokered a peace agreement. In 1999 renewed conflict erupted when Milošević's Serbian government attacked the province of Kosovo to eliminate its Albanian Muslim residents. Clinton and NATO initiated air strikes and placed troops on the ground that preserved Kosovo's independence.

The United States faced an even graver danger from Islamic extremists intent on waging a religious struggle (jihad) and establishing a transnational religious caliphate. The United States' close relationship with Israel placed it high on the list of terrorist targets, along with pro-American Muslim governments in Egypt, Pakistan, and Indonesia. In 1993 Islamic militants orchestrated the bombing of the World Trade Center's underground garage, killing six people and injuring more than one thousand. Five years later, terrorists blew up American embassies in Kenya and Tanzania, killing hundreds and injuring thousands of local workers and residents. In retaliation, Clinton ordered air strikes against terrorist bases in Sudan and Afghanistan. In 2000, al-Qaeda terrorists blew a gaping hole in the side of the USS *Cole*, a U.S. destroyer anchored in Yemen, killing seventeen American sailors. Terrorism would continue to plague the United States.

Review & Relate

■ How did conflicts between Democrats and Republicans affect President Clinton's accomplishments?

■ Explain the new post–Cold War foreign policy threats that President Clinton faced.

The **Presidency** of **George W. Bush**

In 2000 Americans celebrated the new millennium, looking forward with hope for the future. Yet within three years, the country endured a bruising presidential election, experienced unprecedented terrorism at home, and engaged in two wars abroad. President George W. Bush left the country as politically divided as his predecessor had.

Bush and Compassionate Conservatism. In 2000 the Democratic candidate, Vice President Al Gore, ran against George W. Bush, the Republican governor of Texas and son of the forty-first president. Gore ran on the coattails of the Clinton prosperity while Bush campaigned as a "compassionate conservative." Ralph Nader, an anti-corporate activist, ran under the banner of the Green Party, formed in 1991 to support environmentalism and social justice.

Although Gore won a narrow plurality of the popular vote (48.4 percent, compared with 47.8 percent for Bush and 2.7 percent for Nader), Bush won a slim majority of the electoral votes: 271 to 267. The key state in this Republican victory was Florida, where Bush led Gore by fewer than 500 popular votes. Counties with high proportions of African Americans and lower-income residents, who were more likely to support Gore, encountered significant difficulties and outright discrimination in voting. When litigation over the recount reached the U.S. Supreme Court in December 2000, the Court, which included conservative justices appointed by Ronald Reagan and George H. W. Bush, proclaimed Bush the winner.

George W. Bush appealed to his conservative political base by governing as boldly as if he had received a resounding electoral mandate. The president promoted the agenda of the evangelical Christian wing of the Republican Party. He spoke out against same-sex marriage, abortion, and federal support for stem cell research, a scientific procedure that used discarded embryos to find cures for diseases. Bush created a special office in the White House to coordinate faith-based initiatives, providing religious institutions with federal funds for social service activities without violating the First Amendment's separation of church and state.

Attending to the faithful made for good politics. At the turn of the twenty-first century, a growing number of churchgoers were joining megachurches. These congregations, mainly Protestant, each contained 2,000 or more worshippers. Between 1970 and 2005, the number of megachurches jumped from 50 to more than 1,300. Joel Osteen—the evangelical pastor of Lakewood Church in Houston, Texas—drew average weekly audiences of 43,000 people, with sermons available in English and Spanish. Such religious leaders held sway with large groups of voters who could be mobilized to significant political effect.

While courting people of faith, Bush also acknowledged economic conservatives. Congress gave the president tax-cut proposals to sign in 2001 and 2003, measures that favored the wealthiest Americans. Yet to maintain a balanced budget, the cardinal principle of fiscal conservatism, these tax cuts would have required a substantial reduction in spending, which Bush and Congress chose not to do. Furthermore, continued deregulation of business encouraged unsavory activities that resulted in corporate scandals and risky financial practices.

At the same time, Bush showed the compassionate side of his conservatism. His cabinet appointments reflected racial, ethnic, and sexual diversity. They included African

Americans as secretary of state (Colin Powell) and national security adviser (Condoleezza Rice, who later succeeded Powell as secretary of state). His Latino appointments included Alberto Gonzalez as attorney general, Carlos Gutierrez as secretary of commerce, and Mel Martinez as secretary of housing and urban affairs. Compassionate conservatism also included educational reform for those attending school in underprivileged areas. In addition, in 2003 Bush signed into law the Medicare Prescription Drug, Improvement, and Modernization Act, which aimed to lower the cost of prescription drugs to some 40 million senior citizens enrolled in Medicare.

The Iraq War. President Bush spent less time on domestic issues when events vaulted him into the role of wartime president. On September 11, 2001, four commercial jets were hijacked by al-Qaeda operatives recruited by Osama bin Laden, and used as weapons to attack the World Trade Center and the Pentagon, killing 2,996 people. Bush then launched a war on terror, one that led to protracted and costly conflicts in Afghanistan and Iraq and the erosion of civil liberties at home. As part of that effort, in 2002 Congress created a cabinet-level superagency, the Department of Homeland Security, responsible for developing a national strategy against further terrorist threats. Two years

President Bush at Ground Zero   On September 14, 2001, President George W. Bush toured the wreckage of the destroyed World Trade Center. Standing on a pile of rubble, he heard firefighters, police officers, and other rescuers shout, "USA, USA." He responded: "I can hear you. The rest of the world hears you. And the people who knocked these buildings down will hear all of us soon." Courtesy George W. Bush Presidential Library and Museum. (P7365-23a) © Tribune Content Agency, LLC. All Rights Reserved. Reprinted with permission.

later, Congress created the Office of the Director of National Intelligence to coordinate the work of security agencies more effectively.

In the immediate aftermath of the September 11 terrorist attacks, Bush acted decisively. The president dispatched U.S. troops to Afghanistan, whose Taliban leaders refused to turn over Osama bin Laden and other terrorists operating training centers in the country. A combination of anti-Taliban warlords and U.S. military forces toppled the Taliban regime and installed a pro-American government; however, the elusive bin Laden escaped into a remote area of Pakistan.

On the home front, the war on terror prompted passage of the **Patriot Act** in October 2001. The measure expanded the authority of law enforcement and immigration officials in detaining and deporting immigrants suspected of terrorism-related acts. The act also gave law enforcement agencies nearly unlimited authority to wiretap telephones, retrieve e-mail messages, and search the medical, financial, and library borrowing records of individuals, including U.S. citizens, suspected of involvement in terrorism overseas or at home. The computer age provided terrorist networks like al-Qaeda with the means to communicate quickly across national borders and to raise money and launder it into safe bank accounts online. Computer technology also gave U.S. intelligence agencies ways to monitor these communications and transactions.

Amid rising anti-Muslim sentiments, the overwhelming majority of Americans supported the Patriot Act. In the weeks and months following September 11, some people committed acts of violence against mosques, Arab American community centers and businesses, and individual Muslims and people they thought were Muslims. Despite some criticism of its harsh provisions, the Patriot Act was renewed in 2006 with only minor changes.

The Bush administration sought to expand the war on terror to reshape the politics of the Middle East and Persian Gulf along pro-American lines. In doing so, the United States and its European allies would ensure the flow of cheap oil to satisfy the energy demands of consumers in these countries. Furthermore, by replacing authoritarian regimes with democratic governments, the president envisioned a domino effect that would lead to the toppling of reactionary leaders. In crafting this strategy, Bush departed from the well-established, post–World War II policy of containing enemies short of going to war. Instead, the **Bush Doctrine** proposed undertaking preemptive war against despotic governments deemed a threat to U.S. national security, even if that danger was not imminent.

President Bush declared in January 2002 that Iraq was part of an "axis of evil," along with Iran and North Korea. Bush considered Saddam Hussein, the Iraqi dictator, undependable to protect U.S. oil interests in the region. Removing him, Bush believed, would also open a path to overthrowing the radical Islamic government of neighboring Iran, which had embarrassed the United States in 1979 and remained its sworn enemy.

Over the next two years, Bush convinced Congress and a majority of the American people that Iraq presented an immediate danger to the United States by falsely connecting Saddam Hussein to the 9/11 al-Qaeda terrorists. The president also accused Iraq of being well advanced in building and stockpiling "weapons of mass destruction," despite evidence to the contrary. **See Primary Source Project 29: The Uses of September 11, page 1042.**

In March 2003, after a congressional vote of approval, U.S. military aircraft unleashed massive bombing attacks on Baghdad. Contrary to the approach taken by the first President Bush in the 1991 Gulf War, the United States did not wait for any overt act of aggression and created merely a nominal alliance of nations with only Great Britain supplying significant combat troops. Within weeks Hussein went into hiding, prompting Bush to declare that "major combat operations" had ended in Iraq.

This triumphant declaration proved premature. Hussein was captured several months later, but despite the presence of 130,000 U.S. and 30,000 British troops, the war dragged on. More American soldiers (over 4,000) died after the president proclaimed victory than had died during the invasion. The perception of the United States as an occupying power destabilized Iraq, leading to a civil war between the country's Shi'ite Muslim majority, which had been persecuted under Saddam Hussein, and its Sunni religious minority, which Hussein represented. In the northern part of the nation, the Kurdish majority, another group brutalized by Hussein, also battled Sunnis. Al-Qaeda forces, which previously had been absent from the country, joined the fray.

> **Explore ▶**
>
> Compare President Bush's optimistic view of the war's end with a reporter's description of life in war-torn Iraq the following year in Sources 29.2 and 29.3.

At the same time, Bush instituted the policy of incarcerating suspected al-Qaeda rebels in the U.S. military base in Guantánamo, Cuba, without due process of the law. The facility housed more than six hundred men classified as "enemy combatants," who were subject to extreme interrogation and were deprived of legal counsel.

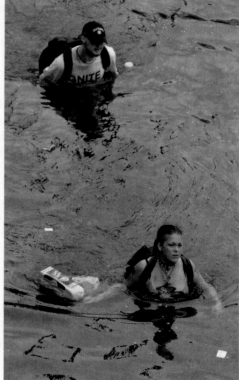

Two Perceptions of New Orleans Looting Some members of the media were guilty of racial profiling in their reporting of the aftermath of Hurricane Katrina. Compare the original caption for the photo on the left ("A young man walks through chest-deep floodwater after looting a grocery store in New Orleans") with the one on the right ("Two residents wade through chest-deep water after finding bread and soda from a local grocery store after Hurricane Katrina came through the area in New Orleans"). Racial identity appears to be the only distinction between who was "looting" and who was "finding." (above): AP Photo/Dave Martin; (right): Chris Graythen/Getty Images

Amid a protracted war in Iraq, President Bush won reelection in 2004 by promising to stay the course and deter further terrorism. Although the Democratic presidential candidate, Senator John Kerry of Massachusetts, criticized Bush's handling of Iraq, Bush eked out a victory, winning a slight majority of the popular vote (50.7 percent).

Bush's Second Term. Over the next four years President Bush's credibility suffered. Several issues — sectarian violence in Iraq, mounting death tolls, and the failures of the U.S.-supported Iraqi government — turned the majority of Americans against the war. Little changed, however, as American troops remained in Iraq and Afghanistan. The war on terror had become a permanent part of life in the United States.

With turmoil also continuing in the Persian Gulf, the threat of nuclear proliferation grew. Iraq did not have nuclear weapons in actuality, but Iran was developing nuclear capabilities. Iranian leaders claimed that they wanted nuclear technology for peaceful purposes, but the Bush administration believed that Iran's real purpose was to build nuclear devices to attack Israel and establish its supremacy in the region.

Bush's handling of a major natural disaster further diminished his popularity. On August 29, 2005, **Hurricane Katrina** slammed into Louisiana and Mississippi. This powerful storm devastated New Orleans, a city with a population of nearly 500,000, a majority of whom were African American. The flood surge caused levees to break, deluging large areas of the city and trapping 50,000 residents. Not only did local and state officials respond slowly and ineptly to the crisis, but so, too, did the federal government.

The flooding killed at least 1,800 residents of the Gulf coast, New Orleans's population dropped by around 130,000 residents, and critics blamed the president for his lack of leadership and slow response to the disaster.

Review & Relate

■ How did President Bush put compassionate conservatism into action?

■ How did the war on terror affect American foreign policy in the Bush administration?

The **Challenges** **Faced** by **President** **Barack Obama**

The world was economically interconnected and fully concerned with combating terror when a severe recession began in 2008. Looking for new hope, many Americans rallied behind the presidential candidacy of Barack Obama. Obama's election ushered in reforms, but his victory did not eliminate the nation's deep political and cultural divisions or eradicate pervasive economic and social inequality.

Comparative Primary Source Analysis

The War in Iraq

After U.S. forces ousted Saddam Hussein, on May 1, 2003, President Bush addressed the nation from the USS *Abraham Lincoln* and proclaimed that major combat operations in Iraq had ended. However, civil war broke out between rival religious sects of Sunni and Shi'ite Muslims. Many Iraqis viewed the United States as an occupying power despite efforts to reconstruct the war-torn nation and promote free elections. In an e-mail to friends in the United States, *Wall Street Journal* correspondent Farnaz Fassihi presents a frank assessment of the deteriorating conditions in Baghdad in September 2004.

Source 29.2

George W. Bush | Declaration of Victory in Iraq, May 1, 2003

Major combat operations in Iraq have ended. In the battle of Iraq, the United States and our allies have prevailed. And now our coalition is engaged in securing and reconstructing that country. . . .

Operation Iraqi Freedom was carried out with a combination of precision and speed and boldness the enemy did not expect and the world had not seen before. From distant bases or ships at sea, we sent planes and missiles that could destroy an enemy division or strike a single bunker. Marines and soldiers charged to Baghdad across 350 miles of hostile ground, in one of the swiftest advances of heavy arms in history. You have shown the world the skill and the might of the American Armed Forces. . . . America is grateful for a job well done. . . .

We have difficult work to do in Iraq. We're bringing order to parts of that country that remain dangerous. We're pursuing and finding leaders of the old regime, who will be held to account for their crimes. We've begun the search for hidden chemical and biological weapons and already know of hundreds of sites that will be investigated. We're helping to rebuild Iraq, where the dictator built palaces for himself instead of hospitals and schools. And we will stand with the new leaders of Iraq as they establish a Government of, by, and for the Iraqi people.

The transition from dictatorship to democracy will take time, but it is worth every effort. Our coalition will stay until our work is done. And then we will leave, and we will leave behind a free Iraq.

Source: *Public Papers of the Presidents of the United States: George W. Bush, 2003* (Washington, DC: U.S. Government Printing Office), 410–13.

The Great Recession. In 2008 the boom times of the previous decade came to a sudden halt. The stock market's Dow Jones average, which had hit a high of 14,000, fell 6,000 points, the steepest percentage drop since 1931. Americans who had invested their money in the stock market lost trillions of dollars. The gross domestic product fell by about 6 percent, a loss too great for the economy to absorb quickly. Millions of Americans lost their jobs, and many forfeited their homes when they could no longer afford to pay their

Source 29.3

Farnaz Fassihi | Report from Baghdad, 2004

Being a foreign correspondent in Baghdad these days is like being under virtual house arrest. Forget about the reasons that lured me to this job: a chance to see the world, explore the exotic, meet new people in far away lands, discover their ways, and tell stories that could make a difference.

Little by little, day-by-day, being based in Iraq has defied all those reasons. I am house bound. I leave when I have a very good reason to and a scheduled interview. I avoid going to people's homes and never walk in the streets. I can't go grocery shopping any more, can't eat in restaurants, can't strike a conversation with strangers, can't look for stories, can't drive in anything but a full armored car, can't go to scenes of breaking news stories, can't be stuck in traffic, can't speak English outside, can't take a road trip, can't say I'm an American, can't linger at checkpoints, can't be curious about what people are saying, doing, feeling. And can't and can't. There has been one too many close calls, including a car bomb so near our house that it blew out all the windows. So now my most pressing concern every day is not to write a kick-ass story but to stay alive and make sure our Iraqi employees stay alive. In Baghdad I am a security personnel first, a reporter second. . . .

Iraqis like to call this mess "the situation." When asked "how are things?" they reply: "the situation is very bad."

What they mean by situation is this: the Iraqi government doesn't control most Iraqi cities, there are several car bombs going off each day around the country killing and injuring scores of innocent people, the country's roads are becoming impassable and littered by hundreds of landmines and explosive devices aimed to kill American soldiers, there are assassinations, kidnappings, and beheadings. The situation, basically, means a raging barbaric guerilla war. . . . As for reconstruction: firstly it's so unsafe for foreigners to operate that almost all projects have come to a halt. After two years, of the $18 billion Congress appropriated for Iraq reconstruction only about $1 billion or so has been spent and a chunk has now been reallocated for improving security, a sign of just how bad things are going here.

Source: Lisa Grunwald and Stephen J. Adler, eds., *Women's Letters: America from the Revolutionary War to the Present* (New York: Dial Press, 2005), 758–60.

Interpret the Evidence

1. From President Bush's perspective, what had the United States accomplished in Iraq?
2. How does Fassihi's report challenge the Bush administration's views on the Iraq War?

Put It in Context

How did the September 11 attacks influence the decision to invade Iraq?

---

mortgages. Unemployment jumped from 4.9 percent in January 2008 to 7.6 percent a year later. Confronted by this spiraling disaster, President Bush approved a $700 billion bailout plan to rescue the nation's largest banks and brokerage houses.

The causes of the **Great Recession** were many and had developed over a long period. Since the Reagan presidency, the federal government had relaxed regulation of the financial industry, while the Federal Reserve Bank encouraged excessive borrowing by keeping interest rates low and relaxed its oversight of Wall Street practices that placed ordinary investors' money at risk. Investment houses developed elaborate computer models that produced new and risky kinds of financial instruments, which went unregulated. Insurance companies such as American International Group marketed so-called credit default swaps as protection for risky securities, exacerbating the financial crisis.

The economy might have experienced a less severe downturn if there had been greater economic equality to bolster consumer spending. Instead, wealth remained concentrated in relatively few hands. In 2007 the top 1 percent of households owned 34.6 percent of all privately held wealth, and the next 19 percent held 50.5 percent. The other 80 percent of Americans owned only 15 percent of the wealth. This maldistribution of wealth made it extremely difficult to support an economy that required ever-expanding purchasing power and produced steadily rising personal debt (Figure 29.2).

With the interdependence of economies through globalization, the Great Recession spread rapidly throughout the world. Great Britain's banking system teetered on the edge of collapse. Other nations in the European Union (EU), most notably Greece and Spain, verged on bankruptcy and had to be rescued by stronger EU nations. Even in China, where the economy had boomed as a result of globalization, businesses shut down and unemployment rose as global consumer demand declined.

Obama and the Great Recession.
In the midst of the Great Recession, the United States held the 2008 presidential election. The Republican candidate, John McCain, was a Vietnam War hero and a three-term senator from Arizona. His Democratic opponent,

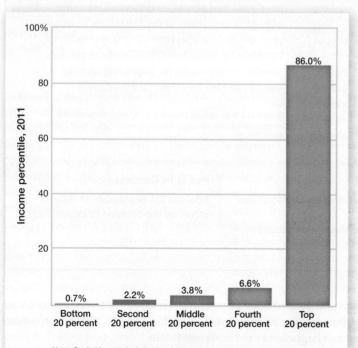

Note: Capital income includes taxable and nontaxable interest income, as well as income from dividends, capital gains, and corporate tax liability. Capital income does not include earned income in the form of salaries and wages.

FIGURE 29.2 Wealth Inequality (Capital Income), 2011

The decline of American manufacturing and the expansion of the low-wage service sector, combined with the rise of high-tech industries and unregulated investment banking, led to growing disparities of wealth in the early twenty-first century. Disparities exist even within the top 20th percentile, as the top 1 percent controlled more than half of all capital income in 2011. Compare the top 20 percent and the bottom 20 percent of Americans with respect to capital income.

Barack Obama, had served four years in the Senate from Illinois. For their vice presidential running mates, McCain chose Sarah Palin, the first-term governor of Alaska, and Obama selected Joseph Biden, the senior senator from Delaware.

Obama overcame racial prejudices in the country by speaking eloquently about his background — the son of a black immigrant from Kenya and the grandson of a white World War II veteran from Kansas. The former community organizer also succeeded in building a nationwide, grassroots political movement through digital technology. He raised an enormous amount of campaign money from ordinary donors through the Internet and used Web sites and text messaging to mobilize his supporters. Moreover, the public blamed the Bush administration for the recession, and Obama offered hope for economic recovery. Obama captured 53 percent of the popular vote, obtaining a majority of votes from African Americans, Latinos, women, and the young, who turned out in record numbers, and a comfortable 365 electoral votes. The Democrats also scored big victories in the House and Senate.

Explore ▶

Read Sources 29.4 and 29.5 for two different interpretations of President Obama.

President Obama stemmed the tide of the Great Recession and turned its course toward economic recovery. He continued the Bush administration's bailout of collapsing banks and investment firms and expanded it to include American automobile companies. In 2009 the president supported passage of an economic stimulus plan that provided federal funds to state and local governments to create jobs and keep their employees on the public payroll.

In addition to restoring the economy, President Obama dealt with the health care problems that disproportionately affected the poor. He pushed Congress to pass the **Patient Protection and Affordable Care Act ("Obamacare")** in 2010, a measure mandating that all Americans had to obtain health insurance or face a tax penalty and that no one could be denied coverage for a preexisting condition. He also signed into law repeal of President Clinton's "don't ask, don't tell" policy, which discriminated against lesbian, gay, and bisexual service members in the military.

The 2010 Revolt against Obama.
Despite such accomplishments, President Obama continued to encounter vigorous political opposition. Most Republican lawmakers refused to support his economic stimulus and health care reform bills. A group of Republican conservatives formed the **Tea Party movement** and attacked the president as a "socialist" for what they perceived as an effort to expand federal control over the economy and diminish individual liberty. The rise of the Tea Party intensified the partisanship within the country and added to the growing gridlock in Washington, D.C. The Tea Party flexed its electoral muscle in the 2010 midterm elections, successfully campaigning for Republican congressional and gubernatorial candidates who supported its positions. As a result, Republicans regained control of the House while the Democratic majority in the Senate narrowed.

Obama also encountered political difficulties from the left. Although the president saved the financial system from collapse, at the end of 2011 unemployment dropped from 10.2 percent to a still high 8.5 percent. With millions of people still out of work, a resurgent Wall Street rewarded its managers and employees with big financial bonuses. Large corporations earned millions of dollars in profits but did not create new jobs. In 2011 protesters in cities around the nation launched the Occupy Wall Street movement, which attacked corporate greed, economic inequality, and government ineffectiveness. High unemployment and crushing student loan debt and massive cuts in spending on education, social services, and infrastructure inspired many of these activists.

President Obama, Healer-in-Chief, 2015 In this June 26, 2015 photo, President Barack Obama sings "Amazing Grace" during his eulogy for the Reverend Clementa Pinckney in Charleston, South Carolina. Pinckney was one of the nine people murdered by a white supremacist shooter at Mother Emanuel African Methodist Episcopal Church in Charleston on June 17. AP Photo/David Goldman

Obama's Second Term. With unemployment remaining high, economic growth moving at a slow pace, and a number of European nations unable to pay mounting debts, the economy loomed as the top issue in the 2012 presidential election. The Republican nominee, Mitt Romney, the former governor of Massachusetts, appealed to conservative voters by opposing Obamacare and embracing the social agenda of the Christian Right. Despite the slower-than-expected economic recovery, Obama won reelection by holding together his coalition of African American, Latino, female, young, and lower-income voters.

During President Obama's second term, the economy showed greater improvement. The unemployment rate dropped to 4.9 percent in February 2016, the lowest figure in eight years. From 2010 to 2014, the gross domestic product grew steadily by an average of more than 2 percent, and the strengthening economy cut the budget deficit significantly. However, as the economy recovered from recession, real wages declined and income and wealth inequality widened. The top 1 percent gained about 95 percent of the income growth since 2009, and the top 10 percent held its highest share of income since World War I. One reason for this widening gap was that since 2000 the United States lost 5 million good-paying manufacturing jobs, and many of the jobs created by the recovery were low-wage service positions, whereas the wealthiest Americans benefited from the soaring stock market and rising capital gains. Making the problem worse, union membership continued its long-term decline, eliminating the major vehicle for workers to increase their wages.

In two other areas, gay rights and the environment, the Obama administration made great strides. Initially Obama had supported civil unions rather than same-sex marriage, but in 2012 he declared his support for it. The following year, the Supreme Court struck down the 1996 Defense of Marriage Act, thereby extending recognition of same-sex marriage. Finally, in 2015, in ***Obergefell v. Hodges*** the Court legalized same-sex marriage nationwide. (In *Bostock v. Clayton County* [2020], the Court ruled that the Civil Rights Act of 1964 protects employees from discrimination because of sexual orientation or gender identity.) With respect to the environment, the Obama administration took climate change seriously, encouraged fuel efficiency and clean energy production, bolstered the Environmental Protection Agency, and extended protection of significant cultural and natural landmarks.

Latinos and Immigration. In the twenty-first century, Latinos constituted the chief source of immigration into the United States. This group consisted of Mexicans, Central and South Americans, and those from the Caribbean islands of Cuba, the Dominican Republic, and Puerto Rico (whose residents are U.S. citizens). In 2010, some 50 million Latinos lived in the United States, and many of these residents made the economy run by

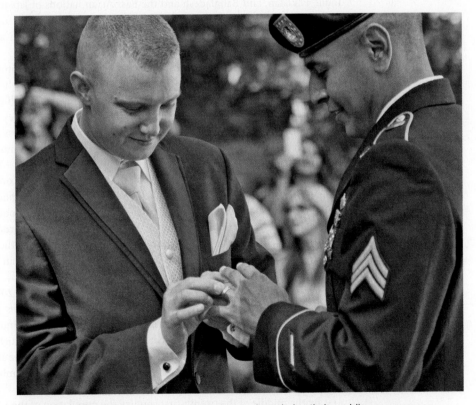

Same-Sex Marriage   A gay couple exchange rings during their wedding ceremony on August 11, 2012, in Cedar Springs, Washington. The state of Washington allowed same-sex marriage three years before the U.S. Supreme Court, in 2015, ruled it legal nationwide under the Equal Protection Clause of the Fourteenth Amendment. AP Photo/The News Tribune, Peter Haley taking low wage jobs in service industries and agriculture. The influx in Latino immigration resulted in a rise in poverty in many Latino communities. In 2010, the poverty rate of Latinos was twice the national average and hovered at 30 percent. Still, Latinos held political office and proved successful in many areas of economic and cultural life. President Obama appointed four Latinos to serve in his cabinet, Hilda Solis, Ken Salazar, Thomas Perez, and Julian Castro.

Most Latinos favored immigration reform, especially the protection of undocumented children brought by their parents into the country. Congress had failed to pass the Development, Relief, and Education for Alien Minors (DREAM) Act, first introduced in 2001, which would have provided an opportunity for the children of undocumented immigrants in the United States to gain legal residency status. To protect these so-called "dreamers," in 2012 President Obama instituted the **Deferred Action for Childhood Arrivals (DACA)** policy, which allows children who have entered the country illegally to receive a renewable two-year extension of their residence in the United States along with eligibility for work permits.

Asian Americans.

Immigrants continued to arrive from the South Asian countries of India, Pakistan, and Bangladesh and the East Asian nations of Japan, South Korea, Philippines, China, Vietnam, and Cambodia. Most came for economic opportunity, others for political reasons. By 2012, about 75 percent of Asian American adults had been born overseas.

In 2016, the Asian American population of 21 million constituted 6.5 percent of the total U.S. population, up from 1 percent in 1965. They tended to be better educated than any other immigrant group. Their higher educational levels paid off economically. In 2007, their median income of $66,000 was higher than that of whites. They were more likely than any ethnic group to live in mixed neighborhoods and marry across racial lines. President Obama appointed three Asian Americans to his cabinet, Eric Shinseki, Steven Chu, and Gary Locke.

Asian Americans were a diverse group. Those from South Korea, Japan, China, and India came from different backgrounds than those from Laos, Cambodia, and Bangladesh. Not all became successful, and many, particularly those from Cambodia and Laos, suffered from the same economic problems as did other marginalized groups. The income gap within the Asian American population was greater than for any other ethnic group. From 1970 to 2016, the difference in the standard of living between Asian Americans at the top and the bottom of the income ladder nearly doubled.

California modeled diversity as a result of immigration. By 2016, 27 percent of the state's population was foreign-born. The majority of Californians consisted of Latinos, Asian Americans, and African Americans, with whites in the minority. Immigrants also flocked to the Southwest and to northeastern and midwestern cities like New York City, Jersey City, Chicago, and Detroit. They fanned out across the Southeast, adding to the growing populations of Atlanta, Raleigh-Durham, Charlotte, Columbia, and Memphis and providing these cities with an unprecedented ethnic mixture.

By the middle of the twenty-first century the population of the United States may look much different than it did at the beginning. In 2012 the U.S. Census Bureau reported that nonwhite babies made up the majority of births for the first time. If the current trends in immigration and birthrates continue, the percentage of Latinos and Asian Americans in the nation will increase, while that of whites and blacks will decline. In addition, the racial and ethnic composition of the population has been transformed through intermarriage. In 2010 the Census Bureau disclosed that one of seven new marriages, or 14.6 percent, was interracial or interethnic. In 1961, when Barack Obama was born, the figure for interracial marriages was less than 0.1 percent. In an increasingly globalized nation, debates over immigration, race, and citizenship will continue.

African Americans and Systemic Racism.

During his two terms, President Obama selected seven African Americans to positions in his cabinet, reflecting the racial and ethnic diversity reshaping contemporary America. Particularly noteworthy, he chose Eric Holder (2009–2015) and Loretta Lynch (2015–2017) to serve as attorney general. He also appointed a black woman, Susan Rice, to the key post of national security adviser.

Despite the political recognition gained by African Americans, racial conflicts continued to erupt. Blacks had long-standing grievances with the criminal justice system as a result of systemic racism. Whereas most whites saw police officers as protectors, blacks viewed them with suspicion or as threats to their safety. The 2013 acquittal of a white man in the killing of Trayvon Martin in Sanford, Florida triggered outrage. A series of subsequent police killings of unarmed blacks in Ferguson, Missouri; Cleveland, Ohio; Staten Island, New York; and Baltimore, Maryland launched Black Lives Matter, co-founded by Alicia Garza. As a result of federal investigations, in 2015 the Justice Department found a pattern of systemic racism in the Ferguson and Cleveland police departments and negotiated settlements that instituted reforms. Nevertheless, persistent problems remained not only in policing but in prison sentencing. The enforcement of drug laws put blacks at a serious disadvantage. Judges handed down longer sentences for possession of crack cocaine, more commonly used among inner city residents, than powder cocaine, more likely used by suburban whites. Over 28 percent of African American men can expect to be incarcerated over their lifetime, while whites have a 4 percent chance of imprisonment. The "prison-industrial complex" grew as states spent more money on building new prisons than on higher education. Disproportionate black imprisonment perpetuated the cycle of poverty and disfranchisement, as released African American felons had difficulty finding jobs and getting their right to vote restored.

African Americans also faced renewed barriers to voting. The Supreme Court in *Shelby v. Holder* (2013) ruled that a critical enforcement provision of the 1965 Voting Rights Act was no longer valid. In the wake of this decision, Republican state legislatures adopted voter identification requirements and voter suppression measures that made it more difficult for African Americans, Latinos, and Native Americans to cast ballots.

The Native American Struggle Continued.

In 2020 nearly 7 million Native Americans lived in the United States. They continued to push for maintaining their tribal sovereignty at the same time as exercising their rights as U.S. citizens. Recent court victories had given them greater control over their internal affairs, including education and law enforcement. For example, in *McGirt v. Oklahoma* (2020) the Supreme Court ruled that most of the eastern portion of Oklahoma, including Tulsa, remains by treaty within the Indian nations of the Muscogee (Creek), Cherokee, Choctaw, Chickasaw, and Seminole. Native Americans living there are subject to tribal or federal courts rather than state jurisdiction. In addition, Indians have also established a network of thirty-eight tribal colleges, integrating indigenous traditions into their curriculum. In 2010, nearly 200,000 indigenous students were enrolled in colleges.

Most Native Americans, however, lived in poverty. Although the courts have given tribes control over gambling casinos, a lucrative enterprise, the jobs that gaming creates are low paying, and some reservations face unemployment rates of 80 percent. Indians on remote reservations did not have access to health facilities. Indigenous tribes continued to battle corporations over development of oil pipelines near their land and access to natural resources.

President Obama sought closer cooperation between the federal government and Native Americans. He convened annual White House Tribal Nations conferences. The president established the White House Council on Indian Affairs and appointed a record number of Native Americans to positions in his administration, among them Karen Driver of the Fond du lac Band (Chippewa); Tracy Goodluck, an Oneida/Muscogee; and Gina Jackson, a Te-Moak Western Shoshone. Despite this recognition, Native Americans remained a vulnerable population.

Obama and the World.

Throughout Obama's two terms, his administration faced serious tests of its international leadership. In 2008 the president appointed Hillary Clinton, the former first lady and a senator from New York, as his secretary of state. The U.S. military increased combat troop withdrawals from Iraq and turned over security for the country to the newly elected Iraqi government. At the same time, the Obama administration stepped up the war in Afghanistan by increasing U.S. troop levels, which led to a rise in casualties. In 2011 he achieved dramatic success when U.S. special forces killed Osama bin Laden in his hideout in Pakistan. By 2016, with John Kerry now his secretary of state, the president had withdrawn most combat soldiers from Afghanistan. Yet Iraq remained unstable, and the outcome of the war against the Taliban in Afghanistan proved uncertain. Despite bin Laden's death, radical jihadists continued to pose a serious danger.

Other international challenges continued as well. From 2006 to 2013, instability in Asia, the Middle East, and the Persian Gulf also heightened U.S. security concerns and underscored the difficulties of achieving lasting peace in these regions (Map 29.2).

The Middle East posed the greatest threat with the rise of a new militant organization known as the **Islamic State of Iraq and Syria (ISIS)**. An offshoot of al-Qaeda, it grew out of the sectarian violence following the overthrow of Saddam Hussein in Iraq. ISIS took over parts of Syria and Iraq, prompting the United States and some Arab nations to launch air strikes against its forces.

The civil war in Syria had profound effects on the rest of the world. Starting in 2010, millions of Syrians fled their homes, and tens of thousands sought refuge in western Europe and the United States. This movement of refugees, greater than at any time since World War II, overwhelmed those European countries to which they first came — Greece, Hungary, and the Czech Republic. The EU split over how to manage the crisis. In 2015 President Obama pledged to accept 10,000 Syrian refugees into the United States during 2016, but that number paled in comparison to the numbers who needed safe havens. Meanwhile, the humanitarian crisis of providing food, shelter, and medical attention to the refugees grew.

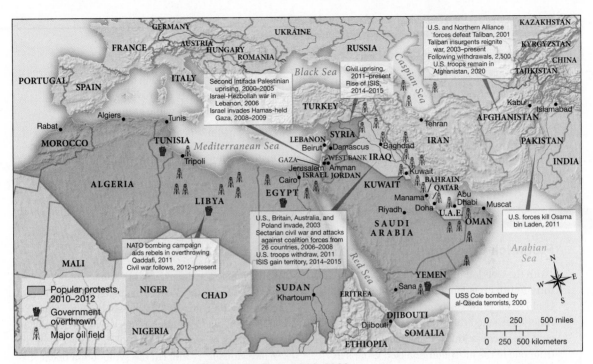

MAP 29.2 The Middle East, 2000–2020

Since 2000 the Middle East has been marked by both terrorism and democratic uprisings. After 9/11 the United States tried to transform Iraq and Afghanistan by military might, which led to prolonged wars. Yet popular rebellions in 2011, led by young people and fueled by new technology, created hope that change was possible. However, as of 2016 the military had regained power in Egypt, and Libya had descended into civil war. Syria remained involved in a brutal civil war. The terrorist, military organization ISIS captured sections of Syria as well as territory in Iraq, but in 2017 they were driven out of most of this territory by Syrian government, Russian, and American-backed military forces.

Antiterrorist surveillance within the United States provoked growing controversy. Under the Patriot Act, the National Security Agency (NSA) began collecting and storing phone records of U.S. citizens. The NSA did not listen to the calls, but it drew on this bulk data to track suspected terrorists. In 2015, Congress passed legislation curtailing this massive, clandestine operation, which restored some balance between national security and individual privacy. On other foreign fronts, President Obama launched bold departures. In 2014 he set in motion the normalization of diplomatic relations with Cuba and, the following year, along with several other world powers, negotiated an agreement with Iran on restricting its nuclear program. In contrast, relations with Russia deteriorated. In 2014 Russia, led by Vladimir Putin, annexed its former territory of the Crimea and in 2015 provided military support for pro-Russian separatists in Ukraine. In response the United States and the EU imposed economic sanctions on Russia but declined to take military action. Later in 2015 Russia sent military forces to Syria to support the government of the dictator Bashar al-Assad, a long-time ally, and fight his opponents, both ISIS and rebels backed by the United States.

Comparative Secondary Source Analysis

The Election of Barack Obama

The election of Barack Obama as president in 2008 raised great expectations among many Americans. The first African American president faced the difficult challenge of proving to whites that he would be the president of all the people—a "post-racial" president—while at the same time assuring blacks that he would continue to fight for their interests and further the legacy of the civil rights movement. Writing during Obama's presidency, African American scholars Frederick C. Harris and Randall Kennedy reach different conclusions about Obama's attempts to achieve this delicate balance.

Source 29.4

Frederick C. Harris | Decline of Black Politics, 2012

"With the election of Barack Obama as the forty-fourth president of the United States, one could easily draw the conclusion that black America reached the pinnacle of political empowerment–a journey that has taken blacks from one of the most marginalized groups in American history (alongside Native Americans) to a key constituency that helps to elect a man of African descent to lead the nation. . . . Far from black America gaining greater influence in American politics, Obama's ascendency to the White House actually signals a decline of a politics aimed at challenging racial inequality head on.

. . . In the age of Obama . . . the majority of black voters have struck a bargain with Obama.

In exchange for the president's silence on community-focused interests, black voters are content with a governing philosophy that helps 'all people' and a politics centered on preserving the symbol of a black president and family in the White House. . . . Indeed, the symbol of a black president is not a trivial matter. Yet, the grand bargain granting black pride in exchange for silence on race-specific issues and the marginalization of targeted policies by the Obama administration have left much to be desired."

Source: Frederick C. Harris, *The Price of the Ticket: Barack Obama and the Rise and Decline of Black Politics* (Oxford: Oxford University Press, 2012), x, xii.

The United States also faced global economic and environmental challenges. As China flourished economically, American workers lost jobs, and the Chinese amassed a nearly $200 billion trade surplus with the United States. In addition, the growth of manufacturing and the market economy in China resulted in the rising consumption of oil and gasoline. The increase in carbon emissions in China and other parts of Asia contributed to the problem of climate change, which ultimately threatens the delicate balance between the natural environment and human societies across the planet. Global warming in the past half century has resulted mainly from emissions of greenhouse gases into the atmosphere and the erosion of the ozone layer. Climbing temperatures cause the melting of glaciers, a rise in the sea level, extreme fluctuations of weather with severely damaging storms, and famines. Disruptions in

Source 29.5

Randall Kennedy | The Importance of Symbolism, 2011

"Most African Americans eschew the demanding racial politics of Obama's detractors on the black left. . . . Blacks have, for the most part, been remarkably savvy, patient, and loyal in terms of their relationship to the Obama administration. They appreciate that Obama must accommodate a wide range of competing demands. They expect him to do what he can, consistent with political practicalities, to push the country's agenda in a progressive direction. . . . [T]hey defer to Obama because they trust him.

. . . [T]ime and again people of all sorts have demonstrated the transcendent importance of symbolism in their lives: the liberty to sit anywhere on a bus unhampered by a color line or the freedom to eat a hamburger at a lunch counter unburdened by caste restrictions. Most African Americans gratefully appreciate that the simple fact of a black man occupying the presidency has irrevocably transformed the United States. . . . Having received so little for so long, blacks are happy to have someone in the White House with whom they can fully identify and who fully identifies with them, even if he is unwilling to advance any set of federal initiatives that could plausibly be labeled a 'black agenda.' "

Source: Randall Kennedy, *The Persistence of the Color Line: Racial Politics and the Obama Presidency* (New York: Pantheon Books, 2011), 33, 34, 35.

Examine the Sources

1. Describe the similarities and differences in Harris's and Kennedy's interpretations of President Obama's relationship with African Americans.
2. How does the fact that Harris and Kennedy are interpreting current events present both opportunities and problems for them?

Put It in Context

What difference did it make for race relations for an African American to get elected president?

industrial and agricultural production caused by storms and the subsequent expense of rebuilding have already had a negative impact on the U.S. and world economies. In December 2015 the United States joined 194 nations, including China and India, in signing the Paris Climate Agreement to reduce greenhouse gas emissions produced from fossil fuels.

Review & Relate

What were the causes and consequences of the Great Recession?

What effects did the election and presidency of Barack Obama have on American politics, society, and the United States' relationship to the world?

The **Presidency** of **Donald Trump**

As Barack Obama's second term drew to a close in 2016, Americans elected Donald Trump to succeed him. The Republican Trump defeated the Democratic candidate Hillary Rodham Clinton, preventing her from becoming the first woman elected president. Despite this triumph, Trump and the Republican-controlled Congress found governing difficult.

The 2016 Election. A New York City real estate tycoon and a reality television host, Trump had never held political office or engaged in public service. In contrast, Hillary Clinton had an extensive record of public and political service: first lady, U.S. senator from New York, and secretary of state.

Running as an antiestablishment outsider, Trump adopted the slogan "Make America Great Again." He embraced right-wing, nativist populism against Mexican, Central American, and Muslim immigrants and opposed free trade agreements that he concluded shipped jobs overseas. As part of his "America First" stance, he criticized international military alliances such as NATO, a major component of U.S. foreign policy since World War II. His well-publicized moral lapses notwithstanding, Trump appealed to white Christian evangelicals by stating his opposition to abortion and pledging to appoint conservative judges to the Supreme Court who would overturn *Roe v. Wade.*

His nativist rhetoric echoed the beliefs of white nationalism, including neo-Nazis, the Ku Klux Klan, and whites who believed they were losing ground to other racial or ethnic groups. Obama's presidency had brought to a boil white racial resentments and provided fuel for Trump's candidacy. Even before running for president, Trump had called into question Obama's U.S. citizenship, despite substantial proof to the contrary, claiming that he had been born in Kenya and therefore was ineligible to become president. During the campaign, Trump appealed to white racial bitterness by attacking an American-born judge of Latino heritage and the Muslim parents of a dead war hero who criticized Trump for his racial and religious intolerance. He also stoked the flames of ethnic prejudice by calling unauthorized Mexican immigrants "rapists" and promising to build a wall between the U.S. and Mexican border and make the Mexican government pay for it.

Trump's appeal to certain segments of the U.S. electorate did not operate in a vacuum. Throughout western Europe anti-immigrant, right-wing nationalist parties were gaining ground. In a 2016 referendum, voters in the United Kingdom chose to withdraw from the European Union, a move known as Brexit (British exit). Nativist, anti-Muslim parties grew stronger in France, Germany, Austria, the Netherlands, and Scandinavia, though none gained control of their governments as they did in Hungary, Poland, and the Czech Republic.

Late in the campaign, when the online Web site WikiLeaks published e-mails stolen from the accounts of the Democratic National Committee and Hillary Clinton's campaign director, Trump tried to use them to his advantage. Seventeen U.S. intelligence agencies later concluded that Russian state-sponsored agents had hacked the accounts and given the e-mails to WikiLeaks. Russian hackers had pilfered the records in an attempt to promote negative publicity about the Clinton campaign and sow discord within the American electorate. Trump refused to acknowledge Russian meddling and instead praised Russia's authoritarian leader, Vladimir Putin.

Despite losing the popular vote by nearly 3 million ballots, Trump won in the Electoral College, 304–227. Trump captured six states that Obama had won in 2012, and the outcome turned on a total of 78,000 votes in Pennsylvania, Michigan, and Wisconsin. Trump's nativist agenda, along with sexist and white-identity appeals, resonated especially with older white men, residents of small towns and rural areas, workers who had lost their jobs to automation and globalization, and those who had less than a college education. Even a majority of white women (53 percent) gave Trump a slight edge, though Clinton did remain overwhelming popular among African American women.

Racial and cultural resentments proved most significant in the outcome. White attitudes toward African Americans, recent immigrants, and Muslims were the main indicators in determining support for Trump. The president-elect did not create these racial, ethnic, and religious resentments, but he exploited and legitimized them.

The Trump Presidency.   From the outset of his administration, women like BLM's co-founder Alicia Garza played a leading role in challenging President Trump. The president's misogynist behavior and rhetoric mobilized millions of women and male allies to march in Washington, D.C., and major cities around the nation and the world to reject Trump's views and affirm that "women's rights are human rights." His election also inspired many women to run for political office.

The rage against Trump and his defeat of the first female, major-party candidate for president inspired a collective uprising against sexual degradation of women. "When Trump won the election, I felt a crushing sense of powerlessness," one woman declared. "And then I realized that I had to do something." Social media provided a means for women's activism.

Women's March on Washington, D.C., 2017   About 500,000 demonstrators gather in the nation's capital on January 21, 2017, a day after President Trump's inauguration, to attend the Women's March on Washington. Refusing to remain silent after the election of a man they considered a misogynist, marchers supported a wide range of goals including gender equality, reproductive freedom, racial equality, worker rights, immigration reform, health care expansion, and environmental protection. Mario Tama/Getty Images

Originated by Tarana Burke, an African American social activist, and promoted by the actress Alyssa Milano, the **#MeToo movement** linked tens of millions of women who shared on Twitter and Facebook their stories of rape, sexual harassment, and sexual assault. As a result, by the end of 2017, numerous women had come forward with complaints of sexual misconduct by media, entertainment, and sports celebrities, corporate executives, and politicians of both political parties, often leading to the swift firing or resignation of these men.

Once in the White House, Trump did not reverse course and become more "presidential." Rather, he continued to subvert the norms of American politics. He used his Twitter account to insult those who disagreed with him, including fellow Republicans. He viewed all criticism as personal, and attacked the mainstream media as "the enemy of the American people," claiming it promoted "fake news."

President Trump had some success in achieving his agenda. Although Congress narrowly rejected his signature campaign promise to repeal and replace the Affordable Care Act, the president won passage of a Republican tax cut law that disproportionately favored corporations and the wealthy. The economic recovery that had begun under the Obama administration continued during the first three years of Trump's administration. The stock market soared, and unemployment figures tumbled to 3.6 percent. The president also secured ratification of his appointments of Neil Gorsuch, Brett Kavanaugh, and Amy Coney Barrett to the Supreme Court, thereby reinforcing the conservative majority on the bench. In 2018 he signed into law the First Step Act, a bipartisan reform measure aimed at reducing mass incarceration and the length of mandatory criminal sentencing. As commander-in-chief, the president furnished American military support to defeat ISIS in Iraq and Syria, forcing it to withdraw from major cities under its control.

Trump achieved even more by issuing executive orders. He managed to put into effect a ban on immigrants from primarily Muslim nations. He revoked Obama's DACA order allowing so-called "dreamers," to remain indefinitely. His administration cancelled the provisional residency permits of more than 200,000 immigrants from El Salvador, Haiti, and Honduras who had fled to the U.S. following natural disasters in their countries. The children subsequently born into these families were American citizens, and the deportation of one or both of their parents would create a humanitarian crisis. Cracking down on asylum-seeking Central American immigrants at the southern border with Mexico, in 2018 the Trump administration initiated a "zero tolerance" policy. **U.S. Immigration and Customs Enforcement (ICE)** agents separated over 5,000 children from their parents who faced deportation and locked them up in crowded and unsafe holding facilities. In 2018, a federal judge ordered the reunification of the separated families.

Trump used his executive power to weaken health care coverage as well as loosen protections for consumers and the environment. He appointed individuals to head cabinet offices and regulatory agencies who favored limited governance and privatization of public services, while denying scientific evidence of man-made global warning. He withdrew the United States from the Paris Climate Agreement; rolled back Obama-initiated trade and travel relations with Cuba; and decertified the Iran Nuclear Agreement. He issued some seventy executive orders either reversing or curtailing environmental and climate regulations he considered burdensome to the fossil fuel industry and other businesses. Trump took these actions in the face of ecological disasters resulting from climate change. Warmer temperatures in California, Oregon, and Washington State dried out forests, causing in 2020 a series of extensive fires that threatened life, property, and natural resources.

While many of these policies provoked outrage, the Trump presidency fueled greater controversy over issues of race. White nationalists became emboldened by Trump's election, and he in turn provided encouragement by choosing not to condemn them forcefully or consistently. At a rally in Charlottesville, Virginia, Nazis and Ku Klux Klan members paraded across the University of Virginia campus mocking Jews and other racial or ethnic groups. They were there to oppose removal of Confederate monuments, which offended African Americans and others for honoring the war to maintain slavery. When an anti-fascist protester was run down and killed by an automobile driven by a white nationalist, President Trump squandered the moral authority of his office by equating the white nationalist demonstrators with those who opposed them. During Trump's term, right-wing, white supremacist, anti-Semitic extremists posed the greatest threat of domestic terrorism.

Of greater concern to his presidency was the investigation into Russian interference in the 2016 election. Two congressional committees and a special prosecutor appointed by the Justice Department, Robert Mueller, looked into Russian hacking and possible collusion between members of the Trump campaign and Kremlin-sponsored operatives seeking to damage Hillary Clinton's campaign. One of the targets of the investigation was General Michael Flynn, who was forced to resign as National Security Advisor shortly after taking office. He subsequently pled guilty to lying to the FBI about his contacts with Russia (Trump later pardoned him). In 2019, Mueller reported that although the Trump campaign "welcomed" Russian interference in the election, there was no conclusive evidence that the campaign had "conspired" with Russian agents in their illegal activities. Nevertheless, Mueller found that Trump may have obstructed justice in attempting to thwart investigations into Russian interference, but he accepted the Justice Department's legal opinion that a sitting president could not be indicted on criminal charges. Despite evidence to the contrary, Trump called the charge of Russian interference a "hoax" perpetrated by his opponents to delegitimize his election.

Trump escaped criminal charges following the **Mueller Report**, but his subsequent actions led to impeachment. In July 2019, he telephoned the president of Ukraine and asked him to dig up political dirt on former vice president Joe Biden, a possible Democratic opponent in the 2020 election, and his son for alleged corrupt activities in that country. In return, Trump indicated that he would release military assistance to the Ukrainian government to aid in its war against Russian-sponsored insurgents. The 2018 congressional elections had brought Democrats control of the House of Representatives. After investigating whether Trump had solicited foreign interference from Ukraine for his own political gain, a majority of the House voted along partisan lines to impeach the president for obstructing justice and obstructing Congress. With Republicans still a majority of the Senate, in February 2020 Democrats fell far short of winning the two-thirds vote necessary to convict Trump and remove him from office.

Pandemic, Protests, and Politics.
In 2020, Trump faced a deadly threat to his presidency. Early in the year, the outbreak in China of a new virus, **COVID-19**, erupted into a worldwide pandemic, potentially as deadly as the 1918 influenza contagion. After the United States reported its first cases in late January, Trump banned air travel to China and European countries struck by the disease, but it was too late. At the end of February 2021, a year after the pandemic started, the United States experienced over 28 million cases and over 500,000 deaths, leading the world in the largest number of infections and deaths. With

4 percent of the global population, the United States counted 26 percent of the over 111 million worldwide coronavirus cases and 21 percent of the deaths.

The president made a bad situation worse. His administration was unprepared with a detailed plan to deal with the pandemic despite warnings from scientists. From the beginning, he played down the severity of the deadly virus claiming that he "didn't want to create panic." He misled the public by claiming the disease would quickly disappear. He refused to mobilize the full resources of the federal government and left it up to the states to deal with the crisis. He advocated a variety of treatments and drugs that either were of dubious value or potentially caused harmful side effects. Ignoring many of the recommendations of his health advisers, particularly the wearing of masks in close quarters and avoiding large gatherings, in October the president caught the virus and had to be hospitalized. Still, he continued to downplay the danger of the pandemic even as infections and deaths skyrocketed, and he placed his efforts behind "Operation Warp Speed," which he launched to encourage pharmaceutical companies to develop a vaccine. In December 2020 the Federal Drug Administration approved the first vaccines, but it would take many months for the general public to be inoculated.

The pandemic caused the most severe economic downturn since the Great Depression. The Gross Domestic Product fell sharply, and by December the unemployment rate, after briefly rising to over 14 percent, hovered around 7 percent, with higher figures for African Americans, Latinos, Native Americans, and women. The president and Congress twice reached a bipartisan agreement on legislation that provided funds to keep businesses afloat and extend unemployment payments, but never agreed on any wider plan to combat the disease.

COVID-19 underscored the systemic racism that plagued the United States. Marginalized groups and people of color tended to work in service and agricultural jobs that did not permit them to do telework at home, thus placing them at greater risk. Blacks, Latinos, and indigenous people suffered from disproportionately higher infection and death rates. They were more vulnerable because socioeconomic conditions, often a legacy of discrimination, forced them to live in dense, segregated housing through which the disease spread rapidly. They had more limited access to adequate health care, a higher level of distrust of the medical community, and relatedly a higher incidence of pre-existing conditions that made the effects of the virus more devastating.

The pandemic was not the only crisis that African Americans and other racial and ethnic minorities faced. While the country locked down from the virus, black people rose up to protest police brutality. Joined by a younger generation of whites, Latinos, and indigenous people, they challenged the pernicious effects of structural racism in the criminal justice system. The killings of Breonna Taylor by Louisville police and George Floyd by Minneapolis police sparked this uprising. Taylor died from gunfire after three police officers broke into her apartment mistakenly believing a suspected drug dealer was inside. When George Floyd was arrested, one policeman placed his knee on his neck as Floyd lay on the ground shouting that he could not breathe. Meanwhile three other police officers stood by and watched Floyd die over the course of nine minutes. Bystanders videoed this, and millions watched in horror on television news programs and the Internet.

There had been police killings before but these incidents fueled outrage long bottled up. Led by Black Lives Matter, interracial demonstrations erupted around the country. Most protests were peaceful, but frustration turned rage into sporadic violence. Support grew for BLM. Minneapolis made substantial reforms in its policing, and Louisville reached a

Helen H. Richardson/MediaNews Group/The Denver Post via Getty Images

George Floyd and Breonna Taylor, Black Lives Matter, 2020 The police killings of George Floyd and Breonna Taylor sparked interracial demonstrations throughout the nation with the rallying cry of "Black Lives Matter." In the photo on the top, on June 7, 2020, public school students walk peacefully by a mural of George Floyd painted on a wall in Denver, Colorado. In the photo on the bottom, taken on September 21, 2020, Tamika Palmer, mother of Breonna Taylor, stands in front of a mural of her daughter at Jefferson Square Park in Louisville, Kentucky, where protesters had demonstrated peacefully since Taylor's killing by police on March 13. Brandon Bell/Getty Images

$12 million civil settlement with Breonna Taylor's family and promised to initiate police reforms. Government officials in the South removed Confederate monuments that glorified the institutional segregation and disfranchisement of the Jim Crow era. In contrast, President Trump condemned the protesters, called for law and order against "agitators" and "anarchists," defended retaining Confederate memorials, and sent in federal troops to tear-gas demonstrators.

The 2020 election took place amidst the swirl of pandemic, protests, and economic distress. These challenges proved too much for Donald Trump to overcome. His opponent, the former vice president Joseph Biden of Delaware, and his running mate, Senator Kamala Harris of California, triumphed. An African American and South Asian, Harris became the first woman vice president. The Biden-Harris ticket won by more than seven million popular votes and swept to victory in the Electoral College by a vote of 306–232.

Trump responded by falsely charging widespread election fraud. He sought to overturn the results of the election through frivolous court challenges and by pressuring Republicans in swing states and in Congress to reject Biden's victory and re-install him as president. On January 6, 2021, at a rally in Washington, D.C., President Trump incited a crowd to storm the Capitol and block the certification of the electoral votes for Biden and Harris. The violent mob invaded the Capitol, resulting in five deaths, before city police ended the insurrection. A week later, in a bipartisan vote, the House of Representative impeached Trump for inciting an insurrection, making him the only president in history to be impeached twice. Following Biden's inauguration, the Senate conducted the impeachment trial but fell short of the two-thirds vote to convict Trump. Although seven Republicans joined fifty Democrats — the largest bipartisan majority for conviction in history — the overwhelming majority of Republican senators voted in Trump's favor.

Review & Relate

- Explain how Donald Trump was elected president and describe the differences between campaigning for office and governing.

- Explain how the pandemic and protests influenced American politics and society during the Trump administration.

Conclusion: Technology, Terror, and Pandemic in a Global Society

Since 1993 Americans have faced new forms of globalization, new technologies, and new modes of warfare. The computer revolution begun by Bill Gates and others helped change the way Americans gather information, communicate ideas, purchase goods, and conduct business. It has also shaped national and international conflicts. The September 11, 2001 attacks on the World Trade Center and the Pentagon demonstrated that terrorists could use computers and digital equipment to wreak havoc on the most powerful nation in the world. And Barack Obama's 2008 presidential campaign, protesters demonstrating against various Middle East dictatorships, and leaders such as Alicia Garza and Tarana Burke of the Black Lives Matter and #MeToo movements also wielded technology to promote their causes. On the other hand, in the interest of combating terrorism, the U.S. government has used this technology to monitor the activities of citizens it considers a threat to national security, thereby raising concerns about civil liberties.

The Bush administration responded to the 9/11 terrorist attacks by fighting wars in Iraq and Afghanistan. President Obama ended the Iraq War and steadily withdrew troops from Afghanistan, but neither administration was able to build stable governments in these countries. The rise of ISIS, which grew out of the fighting in Iraq, posed an even greater danger than did al-Qaeda to stability in the Middle East and the spread of terrorism throughout the world. At the same time, the United States and its allies faced a militarily revitalized Russia seeking to extend its influence in Ukraine and Syria, once again heightening the prospect of confrontation between the world's major nuclear powers.

Along with the computer revolution, globalization has encouraged vast economic transformations throughout the world. Presidents as politically different as Bill Clinton and George W. Bush supported deregulation, free trade, and other policies that fostered corporate mergers and allowed businesses to reach beyond U.S. borders for cheap labor, raw materials, and new markets. While the 1990s witnessed the fruits of the new global economy, in 2008 the dangers of financial speculation and intertwined national economies became strikingly clear with the onset of the Great Recession. This economic collapse has underscored the inequalities of wealth that continue to widen, aggravated by racial, ethnic, and gender disparities.

The Obama administration succeeded in ending the worst features of the recession and at the same time managed to extend health care coverage to the country's most vulnerable citizens. Yet Obama faced increased partisan congressional gridlock that made further reforms concerning immigration, job creation, racial justice, energy consumption, and the environment impossible. Indeed, it took the federal courts to extend marriage equality nationwide.

The election of Donald Trump in 2016 demonstrated that despite the accomplishments of the Obama administration, many Americans felt left out or fearful of that progress. Trump waged a political campaign based on racial, economic, and cultural grievances that carried over from the campaign into his presidency. Although Trump lost to Joe Biden in 2020, these divisions in the nation remain sharper than at any time since the turbulent 1960s. The cult of Donald Trump — Trumpism — continued its hold on the Republican Party.

It should be kept in mind that throughout its history, the United States has shown great strength in finding solutions to its problems. The nation has incorporated diverse populations into its midst, redefined old cultural identities and created new ones, expanded civil rights and civil liberties, extended economic opportunities, and joined other nations to fight military aggression and address other international concerns. The nation will have to draw on these strengths and continue to innovate and adapt to change if it expects to exert leadership in the world and maintain its greatness in the twenty-first century.

chapter **29** review

Timeline of Events

1975	Microsoft formed
1976	Apple Computer Company formed
1980–1990s	Immigration surges from Mexico, Central America, the Caribbean, and South and East Asia
1991	World Wide Web created
1994	Contract with America announced; Republicans win control of Congress
1996	Personal Responsibility and Work Reconciliation Act passed
	Defense of Marriage Act passed
1998	President Clinton impeached
2000	Supreme Court rules in favor of George W. Bush in contested presidential election
2001	September 11 attacks on World Trade Center and Pentagon
	U.S. troops invade Afghanistan; Patriot Act passed
2003–2011	War in Iraq
2005	Hurricane Katrina
2008	Great Recession begins
	Barack Obama elected president
	Tea Party movement formed

2010	Patient Protection and Affordable Care Act ("Obamacare")
2011	Osama bin Laden killed
	Occupy Wall Street movement formed
	Black Lives Matter movement formed
2012	Deferred Action for Childhood Arrivals (DACA) policy
2015	Supreme Court legalizes same-sex marriage nationwide
	Agreement signed by 195 nations to lower greenhouse gas emissions
	Agreement with Iran restricting its nuclear weapons program
2016	Donald Trump elected president
2017	Women's March on Washington and formation of #MeToo movement
2019	First impeachment of President Trump
2020	Coronavirus pandemic
2021	George Floyd and Breonna Taylor killings and Black Lives Matter protests for racial justice
	Joseph Biden and Kamala Harris elected president and vice president
	Trump incites insurrection at the Capitol and is impeached again

Key Terms

Review & Relate

1. How did computers change life in the United States at the turn of the millennium?
2. How has globalization affected business consolidation and immigration in recent decades?
3. How did conflicts between Democrats and Republicans affect President Clinton's accomplishments?
4. Explain the new post–Cold War foreign policy threats that President Clinton faced.
5. How did President Bush put compassionate conservatism into action?
6. How did the war on terror affect American foreign policy in the Bush administration?
7. What were the causes and consequences of the Great Recession?
8. What effects did the election and presidency of Barack Obama have on American politics, society, and the United States' relationship to the world?
9. Explain how Donald Trump was elected president and describe the differences between campaigning for office and governing.
10. Explain how the pandemic and protests influenced American politics and society during the Trump administration.

The Uses of September 11

▶ How do the authors of these primary sources use the 9/11 attacks for different purposes?

The terrorist attacks on the morning of September 11, 2001 killed three thousand people and left the American nation reeling. Millions spent that morning and the days that followed glued to their television sets, watching repeated images of the World Trade Center, the Pentagon, and scattered wreckage in Pennsylvania. Police and firefighters flocked to the Pentagon and Ground Zero to aid in rescue and recovery efforts. It was quickly discovered that the terrorist organization al-Qaeda, under the direction of Osama bin Laden, had carried out the attacks.

Americans reacted to the events in various ways, and official responses were immediate. The Bush administration launched the war on terror, which included the creation of the Department of Homeland Security, passage of the Patriot Act, and the invasion of Afghanistan, actions that resulted in heightened government surveillance of both its citizens and adversaries (Source 29.9). In the aftermath of the attacks, more than eighty thousand Arabs and Muslims living in the United States were fingerprinted and registered with the federal government (Sources 29.7 and 29.8). President Bush, believing that Saddam Hussein was linked to al-Qaeda, ordered an American invasion of Iraq in the spring of 2003.

In the wake of the 9/11 attacks, individuals and communities nationwide responded with an outpouring of grief (Source 29.6). Communities held ceremonies, candlelight vigils, and marches. Impromptu memorials appeared in New York City and Washington, D.C., and photos of the missing filled subway stations and parks. In 2011, ten years after the attacks, the National September 11 Memorial and Museum opened and presented personal stories and artifacts to find meaning in the events of that day (Source 29.10).

Source 29.6

Diana Hoffman | "The Power of Freedom," 2002

The September 11 attacks inspired thousands of poems, essays, and songs that expressed sorrow for the victims and resolve that the tragedy would make America a stronger nation. The following poem by Diana Hoffman, which reflects these sentiments, appeared on a memorial Web site in 2002.

I know you're celebrating
what your evil deeds have wrought
But with the devastation
something else you've also brought
For nothing is more powerful
than Americans who unite
Who put aside their differences
and for freedom fight
Each defenseless victim whose
untimely death you caused
And every fallen hero

whose brave life was lost
Has only served to strengthen
our national resolve
Each freedom-loving citizen
will surely get involved
You've galvanized our nation
into a force so strong
We'll end your reign of terror
although the fight is long
For every heart that's broken
ten million will stand tall
and every tear that's falling
is the mortar for it all
And when this war is over
one thing I know is sure
Our country will be greater
and our freedom will endure

Source: Diana Hoffman, "The Power of Freedom," Never Forgotten Poems, accessed October 16, 2015, http://911neverforget.tripod.com/neverforgotten/id3.html.

Source 29.7

Khaled Abou El Fadl | Response to September 11, 2001

Arab Americans and Muslims became targets of violence, racial profiling, surveillance, and even deportation in the wake of the September 11 attacks. Khaled Abou El Fadl is a law professor at the University of California at Los Angeles and a leading expert on Islamic law. In the following reflection, he recalls how he felt on September 11 and how being a Muslim shaped his response to the attacks.

My reaction very soon after it happened was anguished hope that Muslims were not involved in this. And actually I remember very distinctly sort of a degree of feeling ashamed about having that hope, because you would like to respond to something like this at a human and universal level. You would like to feel like, Muslim or not Muslim, this is just terrible, period. It's really irrelevant who has done this. But because of what I knew, what it's going to mean for Muslims, I knew

that the sort of hyphenation of whether a Muslim did this or not was going to make a big difference for me, for my friends, for my family, for my son. That's a reality. And the agony of it has not subsided because the worst fears, that this is going to open a door of much suffering for many human beings, has fully materialized. . . .

The word *fear* describes everything. There is fear of fellow citizens being killed. There is fear that you yourself will be the subject of a terrorist attack. Terrorism doesn't have an exemption clause for Arabs or Muslims. If I was on that plane that day, the fact that I was Arab or Muslim wouldn't have made an iota of difference. So you run the risk of being the victim of a terrorist attack as much as any other member of society. But you now also run the risk of being blamed for it, just simply by the fact that you're Arab or Muslim. . . .

We belong on this plane and on our seat, you don't. You're here because we allow you to be here. It's as if it's a privilege. You're different, it's a privilege that you are allowed on this plane. And when I started wearing suits and ties consistently, regardless of how long or short the flight is, I've noticed that the treatment has gotten better. But it's always anxiety producing, not just for the normal security concerns, but because it's an unknown sum. You just don't know whether you're going to run into someone who's going to say something rude, something hurtful, whether you're going to sit next to someone who asks to change seats, which has happened to me, because they don't feel comfortable sitting next to you. Every time you pick up something from your travel bag, or you take out a magazine, or take out a book, they look like they're going to have a heart attack. Or constantly staring at you. It's just, it's an extremely anxiety producing experience and the irony of it is that if, God forbid, there is a terrorist attack, and I am on a plane, I'm just like everyone else, I die just like everyone else.

Source: "Face to Face: Stories from the Aftermath of Infamy," ITVS Interactive, accessed October 15, 2015, http://archive.itvs.org/facetoface/stories/khaled.html.

Anti-Muslim Discrimination, September 7, 2010

The terrorist attacks on September 11 incited anti-Muslim sentiment among many Americans. Although President Bush made it clear that the enemy was al-Qaeda and not Muslims in general, the passage of the Patriot Act and the roundup and deportation of Arab and Muslim immigrants reflected an underlying hostility to Muslim Americans. This cartoon by Angelo Lopez appeared in the *Tri-City Voice*, a California weekly newspaper, around the ninth anniversary of 9/11. With nearly a decade of perspective, it highlights the harsh dilemma of mainstream Muslims both in the United States and the Persian Gulf.

Angelo Lopez

Edward Snowden | Interview, 2014

The attacks on September 11 created the need for more reliable intelligence gathering. The latest advances in computer technology aided in this effort. However, as time passed, many critics worried that the government had exceeded the limits of legitimate constitutional bounds and posed a threat to individual freedom. Edward Snowden worked as an intelligence contractor for the National Security Administration (NSA). Following 9/11, the NSA was one of many government agencies conducting information on suspected terrorists. In 2013 Snowden leaked thousands of classified documents to the *Guardian* newspaper revealing the NSA's worldwide secret surveillance program, including the gathering of bulk data on the telephone conversations of many Americans. In the following interview with the *Guardian*, Snowden explains his motivations.

We constantly hear the phrase "national security" but when the state begins . . . broadly intercepting the communications, seizing the communications by themselves, without any warrant, without any suspicion, without any judicial involvement, without any demonstration of probable cause, are they really protecting national security or are they protecting state security?

What I came to feel—and what I think more and more people have seen at least the potential for—is that a regime that is described as a national security agency has stopped representing the public interest and has instead begun to protect and promote state security interests. And the idea of western democracy as having state security bureaus, just that term, that phrase itself, "state security bureau," is kind of chilling. . . .

Generally, it's not the people at the working level you need to worry about. It's the senior officials, it's the policymakers who are shielded from accountability, who are shielded from oversight and who are allowed to make decisions that affect all of our lives without any public input, any public debate, or any electoral consequences because their decisions and the consequences of the decisions are never known.

Because of the advance of technology, storage becomes cheaper and cheaper year after year and when our ability to store data outpaces the expense of creating that data, we end up with things that are no longer held for short-term periods, they're held for long-term periods and then they're held for a longer term period. At the NSA for example, we store data for five years on individuals. And that's before getting a waiver to extend that even further.

Source: Alan Rusbridger and Ewen MacAskill, "Edward Snowden Interview," *Guardian*, July 18, 2014, mhttp://www.theguardian.com/world/2014/jul/18/-sp-edward-snowden-nsa-whistleblower-interview-transcript, accessed December 14, 2015.

Alice M. Greenwald | Message from the Director of the 9/11 Memorial Museum

After eight years of construction, the National September 11 Memorial and Museum opened to the public on May 21, 2014, at the site of the World Trade Center attacks. The museum documents the history of the events surrounding 9/11 and does so through exhibits of artifacts and personal stories. By 2016, more than 4 million people had visited the museum. In the following statement, the director of the museum explains its historical mission.

Our visitors have a voice in this Museum, reinforcing the idea that each of us is engaged in the making of history. Whether telling one's own 9/11 story, recording a remembrance for someone who was killed in the attacks, or adding an opinion about some of the more challenging questions raised by 9/11, visitors can contribute their own stories to the Museum in our on-site recording studio. What they record will be added to the Museum archive, and excerpts may be integrated into media exhibits on an ongoing basis.

The core creative team responsible for the 9/11 Museum spent years deliberating over how to shape a memorial museum that would offer a safe environment in which to explore difficult history. While the events of 9/11 are the foundation of the experience, the Museum does more than facilitate learning. It is a place where an encounter with history connects visitors to the shared human impacts of this event, transforming what can seem like the anonymous abstractions of terrorism and mass murder into a very personal sense of loss.

As much about "9/12" as it is about 9/11, the Museum provides a case study in how ordinary people acted in extraordinary circumstances, their acts of kindness, compassion and generosity of spirit demonstrating the profoundly constructive effect we can have on each other's lives by the choices we make, even in the face of unspeakable destruction. The 9/11 Memorial Museum takes you on a journey into the heart of memory as an agent of transformation, empowering each of us to seek a deeper understanding of what it means to be a human being living in an interdependent world at the start of the 21st century.

Source: Alice M. Greenwald, "Message from the Museum Director," 2014, 9/11 Memorial, http://www.911memorial.org /message-museum-director, accessed October 16, 2015.

Interpret the Evidence

1. Compare and contrast the audiences that Diana Hoffman (Source 29.6) and Khaled Abou El Fadl (Source 29.7) aim at reaching.
2. How does the political cartoon (Source 29.8) portray the plight of mainstream Muslims in the United States and abroad? How did the legacy of 9/11 affect this dilemma?
3. How does Edward Snowden justify his actions in leaking classified documents from the NSA (Source 29.9)? How does his behavior signify that for many Americans the lessons of 9/11 are lessening in importance and other considerations have become more significant?
4. How does the 9/11 Memorial Museum draw on history to chronicle September 11 (Source 29.10)? What would you include in the museum for the sake of historical accuracy?

Put It in Context

How did the attacks on September 11 change America?

The Declaration of Independence

In Congress, July 4, 1776.

The unanimous Declaration of the thirteen United States of America

When in the course of human events, it becomes necessary for one people to dissolve the political bands which have connected them with another, and to assume, among the powers of the earth, the separate and equal station to which the laws of nature and of nature's God entitle them, a decent respect to the opinions of mankind requires that they should declare the causes which impel them to the separation.

We hold these truths to be self-evident, that all men are created equal; that they are endowed by their Creator with certain unalienable rights; that among these, are life, liberty, and the pursuit of happiness. That, to secure these rights, governments are instituted among men, deriving their just powers from the consent of the governed; that, whenever any form of government becomes destructive of these ends, it is the right of the people to alter or to abolish it, and to institute a new government, laying its foundation on such principles, and organizing its powers in such form, as to them shall seem most likely to effect their safety and happiness. Prudence, indeed, will dictate that governments long established, should not be changed for light and transient causes; and, accordingly, all experience hath shown, that mankind are more disposed to suffer, while evils are sufferable, than to right themselves by abolishing the forms to which they are accustomed. But, when a long train of abuses and usurpations, pursuing invariably the same object, evinces a design to reduce them under absolute despotism, it is their right, it is their duty, to throw off such government and to provide new guards for their future security. Such has been the patient sufferance of these colonies, and such is now the necessity which constrains them to alter their former systems of government. The history of the present King of Great Britain is a history of repeated injuries and usurpations, all having, in direct object, the establishment of an absolute tyranny over these States. To prove this, let facts be submitted to a candid world: He has refused his assent to laws the most wholesome and necessary for the public good.

He has forbidden his governors to pass laws of immediate and pressing importance, unless suspended in their operation till his assent should be obtained; and, when so suspended, he has utterly neglected to attend to them.

He has refused to pass other laws for the accommodation of large districts of people, unless those people would relinquish the right of representation in the legislature; a right inestimable to them, and formidable to tyrants only.

He has called together legislative bodies at places unusual, uncomfortable, and distant from the depository of their public records, for the sole purpose of fatiguing them into compliance with his measures.

He has dissolved representative houses repeatedly for opposing, with manly firmness, his invasions on the rights of the people.

He has refused, for a long time after such dissolutions, to cause others to be elected; whereby the legislative powers, incapable of annihilation, have returned to the people at large for their exercise; the state remaining in the mean-time exposed to all the danger of invasion from without, and convulsions within.

He has endeavoured to prevent the population of these States; for that purpose, obstructing the laws for naturalization of foreigners, refusing to pass others to encourage their migration hither, and raising the conditions of new appropriations of lands.

He has obstructed the administration of justice, by refusing his assent to laws for establishing judiciary powers.

He has made judges dependent on his will alone, for the tenure of their offices, and the amount and payment of their salaries.

He has erected a multitude of new offices, and sent hither swarms of officers to harass our people, and eat out their substance.

He has kept among us, in times of peace, standing armies, without the consent of our legislature.

He has affected to render the military independent of, and superior to, the civil power.

He has combined, with others, to subject us to a jurisdiction foreign to our Constitution, and unacknowledged by our laws; giving his assent to their acts of pretended legislation:

For quartering large bodies of armed troops among us:

For protecting them by a mock trial, from punishment, for any murders which they should commit on the inhabitants of these States:

For cutting off our trade with all parts of the world:

For imposing taxes on us without our consent:

For depriving us, in many cases, of the benefit of trial by jury:

For transporting us beyond seas to be tried for pretended offences:

For abolishing the free system of English laws in a neighboring province, establishing therein an arbitrary government, and enlarging its boundaries, so as to render it at once an example and fit instrument for introducing the same absolute rule into these colonies:

For taking away our charters, abolishing our most valuable laws, and altering, fundamentally, the powers of our governments:

For suspending our own legislatures, and declaring themselves invested with power to legislate for us in all cases whatsoever.

He has abdicated government here, by declaring us out of his protection, and waging war against us.

He has plundered our seas, ravaged our coasts, burnt our towns, and destroyed the lives of our people.

He is, at this time, transporting large armies of foreign mercenaries to complete the works of death, desolation, and tyranny, already begun, with circumstances of cruelty and perfidy scarcely paralleled in the most barbarous ages, and totally unworthy the head of a civilized nation.

He has constrained our fellow citizens, taken captive on the high seas, to bear arms against their country, to become the executioners of their friends, and brethren, or to fall themselves by their hands.

He has excited domestic insurrections amongst us, and has endeavored to bring on the inhabitants of our frontiers, the merciless Indian savages, whose known rule of warfare is an undistinguished destruction of all ages, sexes, and conditions.

In every stage of these oppressions, we have petitioned for redress; in the most humble terms; our repeated petitions have been answered only by repeated injury. A prince, whose character is thus marked by every act which may define a tyrant, is unfit to be the ruler of a free people.

Nor have we been wanting in attention to our British brethren. We have warned them, from time to time, of attempts made by their legislature to extend an unwarrantable jurisdiction over us. We have reminded them of the circumstances of our emigration and settlement here. We have appealed to their native justice and magnanimity, and we have conjured them, by the ties of our common kindred, to disavow these usurpations, which would inevitably interrupt our connections and correspondence. They, too, have been deaf to the voice of justice and consanguinity. We must, therefore, acquiesce in the necessity which denounces our separation, and hold them as we hold the rest of mankind, enemies in war, in peace, friends.

We, therefore, the representatives of the United States of America, in general Congress assembled, appealing to the Supreme Judge of the world for the rectitude of our intentions, do, in the name, and by authority of the good people of these colonies, solemnly publish and declare, that these united colonies are, and of right ought to be, free and independent states: that they are absolved from all allegiance to the British Crown, and that all political connection between them and the state of Great Britain is, and ought to be, totally dissolved; and that, as free and independent states, they have full power to levy war, conclude peace, contract alliances, establish commerce, and to do all other acts and things which independent states may of right do. And, for the support of this declaration, with a firm reliance on the protection of Divine Providence, we mutually pledge to each other our lives, our fortunes, and our sacred honor.

The foregoing Declaration was, by order of Congress, engrossed, and signed by the following members:

JOHN HANCOCK

New Hampshire
Josiah Bartlett
William Whipple
Matthew Thornton

Massachusetts Bay
Samuel Adams
John Adams
Robert Treat Paine
Elbridge Gerry

Rhode Island
Stephen Hopkins
William Ellery

Connecticut
Roger Sherman
Samuel Huntington
William Williams
Oliver Wolcott

New York
William Floyd
Phillip Livingston
Francis Lewis
Lewis Morris

New Jersey
Richard Stockton
John Witherspoon
Francis Hopkinson
John Hart
Abraham Clark

Pennsylvania
Robert Morris
Benjamin Rush
Benjamin Franklin
John Morton
George Clymer
James Smith
George Taylor

James Wilson
George Ross
Caesar Rodney
George Read
Thomas M'Kean

Maryland
Samuel Chase
William Paca
Thomas Stone
Charles Carroll, of
Carrollton

North Carolina
William Hooper
Joseph Hewes
John Penn

South Carolina
Edward Rutledge
Thomas Heyward, Jr.

Thomas Lynch, Jr.
Arthur Middleton

Virginia
George Wythe
Richard Henry Lee
Thomas Jefferson
Benjamin Harrison
Thomas Nelson, Jr.
Francis Lightfoot Lee
Carter Braxton

Georgia
Button Gwinnett
Lyman Hall
George Walton

Resolved, That copies of the Declaration be sent to the several assemblies, conventions, and committees, or councils of safety, and to the several commanding officers of the continental troops; that it be proclaimed in each of the United States, at the head of the army.

The Articles of Confederation and Perpetual Union

Agreed to in Congress, November 15, 1777.
Ratified March 1781.

Between the states of New Hampshire, Massachusetts Bay, Rhode Island and Providence Plantations, Connecticut, New York, New Jersey, Pennsylvania, Delaware, Maryland, Virginia, North Carolina, South Carolina, Georgia.*

Article 1

The stile of this confederacy shall be "The United States of America."

Article 2

Each State retains its sovereignty, freedom and independence, and every power, jurisdiction, and right, which is not by this confederation expressly delegated to the United States, in Congress assembled.

Article 3

The said states hereby severally enter into a firm league of friendship with each other for their common defence, the security of their liberties and their mutual and general welfare; binding themselves to assist each other against all force offered to, or attacks made upon them, or any of them, on account of religion, sovereignty, trade, or any other pretence whatever.

Article 4

The better to secure and perpetuate mutual friendship and intercourse among the people of the different states in this union, the free inhabitants of each of these states, paupers, vagabonds, and fugitives from justice excepted, shall be entitled to all privileges and immunities of free citizens in the several states; and the people of each State shall have free ingress and regress to and from any other State, and shall enjoy therein all the privileges of trade and commerce, subject to the same duties, impositions, and restrictions, as the inhabitants thereof respectively; provided, that such restrictions shall not extend so far as to prevent the removal of property, imported into any State, to any other State of which the owner is an inhabitant; provided also, that no imposition, duties, or restriction, shall be laid by any State on the property of the United States, or either of them. If any person guilty of, or charged with treason, felony, or other high misdemeanor in any State, shall flee from justice and be found in any of the United States, he shall, upon demand of the governor or executive power of the State from which he fled, be delivered up and removed to the State having jurisdiction of his offence. Full faith and credit shall be given in each of these states to the records, acts, and judicial proceedings of the courts and magistrates of every other State.

Article 5

For the more convenient management of the general interests of the United States, delegates shall be annually appointed, in such manner as the legislature of each State shall direct, to meet in Congress, on the 1st Monday in November in every year, with a power reserved to each State to recall its delegates, or any of them, at any time within the year, and to send others in their stead for the remainder of the year.

*This copy of the final draft of the Articles of Confederation is from the *Journals of the Continental Congress*, 9:907–925, November 15, 1777.

No State shall be represented in Congress by less than two, nor by more than seven members; and no person shall be capable of being a delegate for more than three years in any term of six years; nor shall any person, being a delegate, be capable of holding any office under the United States, for which he, or any other for his benefit, receives any salary, fees, or emolument of any kind.

Each State shall maintain its own delegates in a meeting of the states, and while they act as members of the committee of the states.

In determining questions in the United States, in Congress assembled, each State shall have one vote.

Freedom of speech and debate in Congress shall not be impeached or questioned in any court or place out of Congress: and the members of Congress shall be protected in their persons from arrests and imprisonments, during the time of their going to and from, and attendance on Congress, except for treason, felony, or breach of the peace.

Article 6

No State, without the consent of the United States, in Congress assembled, shall send any embassy to, or receive any embassy from, or enter into any conference, agreement, alliance, or treaty with any king, prince, or state; nor shall any person, holding any office of profit or trust under the United States, or any of them, accept of any present, emolument, office or title, of any kind whatever, from any king, prince, or foreign state; nor shall the United States, in Congress assembled, or any of them, grant any title of nobility.

No two or more states shall enter into any treaty, confederation, or alliance, whatever, between them, without the consent of the United States, in Congress assembled, specifying accurately the purposes for which the same is to be entered into, and how long it shall continue.

No state shall lay any imposts or duties which may interfere with any stipulations in treaties entered into by the United States, in Congress assembled, with any king, prince, or state, in pursuance of any treaties already proposed by Congress to the courts of France and Spain.

No vessels of war shall be kept up in time of peace by any State, except such number only as shall be deemed necessary by the United States, in Congress assembled, for the defence of such State or its trade; nor shall any body of forces be kept up by any State, in time of peace, except such number only as, in the judgment of the United States, in Congress assembled, shall be deemed requisite to garrison the forts necessary for the defence of such State; but every State shall always keep up a well regulated and disciplined militia, sufficiently armed and accoutred, and shall provide, and constantly have ready for use, in public stores, a due number of field pieces and tents, and a proper quantity of arms, ammunition and camp equipage.

No State shall engage in any war without the consent of the United States, in Congress assembled, unless such State be actually invaded by enemies, or shall have received certain advice of a resolution being formed by some nation of Indians to invade such State, and the danger is so imminent as not to admit of a delay till the United States, in Congress assembled, can be consulted; nor shall any State grant commissions to any ships or vessels of war, nor letters of marque or reprisal, except it be after a declaration of war by the United States, in Congress assembled, and then only against the kingdom or state, and the subjects thereof, against which war has been so declared, and under such regulations as shall be established by the United States, in Congress assembled, unless such State be infested by pirates, in which case vessels of war may be fitted out for that occasion, and kept so long as the danger shall continue, or until the United States, in Congress assembled, shall determine otherwise.

Article 7

When land forces are raised by any State for the common defence, all officers of or under the rank of colonel, shall be appointed by the legislature of each State respectively, by whom such forces shall be raised, or in such manner as such State shall direct; and all vacancies shall be filled up by the State which first made the appointment.

Article 8

All charges of war and all other expences, that shall be incurred for the common defence or general welfare, and allowed by the United States, in Congress assembled, shall be defrayed out of a common treasury, which shall be supplied by the several states, in proportion to the value of all land within each State, granted to or surveyed for any person, as such land and the buildings and improvements thereon shall be estimated according to such mode as the United States, in Congress assembled, shall, from time to time, direct and appoint.

The taxes for paying that proportion shall be laid and levied by the authority and direction of the legislatures of the several states, within the time agreed upon by the United States, in Congress assembled.

Article 9

The United States, in Congress assembled, shall have the sole and exclusive right and power of determining on peace and war, except in the cases mentioned in the 6th article; of sending and receiving ambassadors; entering into treaties and alliances, provided that no treaty of commerce shall be made, whereby the legislative power of the respective states shall be restrained from imposing such imposts and duties on foreigners as their own people are subjected to, or from prohibiting the exportation or importation of any species of goods or commodities whatsoever; of establishing rules for deciding, in all cases, what captures on land or water shall be legal, and in what manner prizes, taken by land or naval forces in the service of the United States, shall be divided or appropriated; of granting letters of marque and reprisal in times of peace; appointing courts for the trial of piracies and felonies committed on the high seas, and establishing courts for receiving and determining, finally, appeals in all cases of captures; provided, that no member of Congress shall be appointed a judge of any of the said courts.

The United States, in Congress assembled, shall also be the last resort on appeal in all disputes and differences now subsisting, or that hereafter may arise between two or more states concerning boundary, jurisdiction or any other cause whatever; which authority shall always be exercised in the manner following: whenever the legislative or executive authority, or lawful agent of any State, in controversy with another, shall present a petition to Congress, stating the matter in question, and praying for a hearing, notice thereof shall be given, by order of Congress, to the legislative or executive authority of the other State in controversy, and a day assigned for the appearance of the parties by their lawful agents, who shall then be directed to appoint, by joint consent, commissioners or judges to constitute a court for hearing and determining the matter in question; but, if they cannot agree, Congress shall name three persons out of each of the United States, and from the list of such persons each party shall alternately strike out one, the petitioners beginning, until the number shall be reduced to thirteen; and from that number not less than seven, nor more than nine names, as Congress shall direct, shall, in the presence of Congress, be drawn out by lot; and the persons whose names shall be so drawn, or any five of them, shall be commissioners or judges to hear and finally determine the controversy, so always as a major part of the judges who shall hear the cause shall agree in the determination; and if either party shall neglect to attend at the day appointed, without shewing reasons which Congress shall judge sufficient, or, being present, shall refuse to strike, the Congress shall proceed to nominate three persons out of each State, and the secretary of Congress shall strike in behalf of such party absent or refusing; and the judgment and sentence of the court to be appointed, in the manner before prescribed, shall be final and conclusive; and if any of the parties shall refuse to submit to the authority of such court, or to appear or defend their claim or cause, the court shall nevertheless proceed to pronounce sentence or judgment, which shall, in like manner, be final and decisive, the judgment or sentence and other proceedings begin, in either case, transmitted to Congress, and lodged among the acts of Congress for the security of the parties concerned: provided, that every commissioner, before he sits in judgment, shall take an oath, to be administered by one of the judges of the supreme or superior court of the State where the cause shall be tried, "well and truly to hear and determine the matter in question, according to the best of his judgment, without favour, affection, or hope of reward:" provided, also, that no State shall be deprived of territory for the benefit of the United States.

All controversies concerning the private right of soil, claimed under different grants of two or more states, whose jurisdictions, as they may respect such lands and the states which passed such grants, are adjusted, the said grants, or either of them, being at the same time claimed to have originated antecedent to such settlement of jurisdiction, shall, on the petition of either party to the Congress of the United States, be finally determined, as near as may be, in the same manner as is before prescribed for deciding disputes respecting territorial jurisdiction between different states.

The United States, in Congress assembled, shall also have the sole and exclusive right and power of regulating the alloy and value of coin struck by their own authority, or by that of the respective states; fixing the standard of weights and measures throughout the United States; regulating the trade and managing all affairs with the Indians not members of any of the states; provided that the legislative right of any State within its own limits be not infringed or violated; establishing and regulating post offices from one State to another throughout all the United States, and exacting such postage on the papers passing through the same as may be requisite to defray the expences of the said office; appointing all officers of the land forces in the service of the United States, excepting regimental officers; appointing all the officers of the naval forces, and commissioning all officers whatever in the service of the United States; making rules for the government and regulation of the said land and naval forces, and directing their operations.

The United States, in Congress assembled, shall have authority to appoint a committee to sit in the recess of Congress, to be denominated "a Committee of the States," and to consist of one delegate from each State, and to appoint such other committees and civil officers as may be necessary for managing the general affairs of the United States, under their direction; to appoint one of their number to preside; provided that no person be allowed to serve in the office of president more than one year in any term of three years; to ascertain the necessary sums of money to be raised for the service of the United States, and to appropriate and apply the same for defraying the public expences; to borrow money or emit bills on the credit of the United States, transmitting, every half year, to the respective states, an account of the sums of money so borrowed or emitted; to build and equip a navy; to agree upon the number of land forces, and to make requisitions from each State for its quota, in proportion to the number of white inhabitants in such State; which requisitions shall be binding; and thereupon, the legislature of each State shall appoint the regimental officers, raise the men, and cloathe, arm, and equip them in a soldier-like manner, at the expence of the United States; and the officers and men so cloathed, armed, and equipped, shall march to the place appointed and within the time agreed on by the United States, in Congress assembled; but if the United States, in Congress assembled, shall, on consideration of circumstances, judge proper that any State should not raise men, or should raise a smaller number than its quota, and that any other State should raise a greater number of men than the quota thereof, such extra number shall be raised, officered, cloathed, armed, and equipped in the same manner as the quota of such State, unless the legislature of such State shall judge that such extra number cannot be safely spared out of the same, in which case they shall raise, officer, cloathe, arm, and equip as many of such extra number as they judge can be safely spared. And the officers and men so cloathed, armed, and equipped, shall march to the place appointed and within the time agreed on by the United States, in Congress assembled.

The United States, in Congress assembled, shall never engage in a war, nor grant letters of marque and reprisal in time of peace, nor enter into any treaties or alliances, nor coin money, nor regulate the value thereof, nor ascertain the sums and expences necessary for the defence and welfare of the United States, or any of them: nor emit bills, nor borrow money on the credit of the United States, nor appropriate money, nor agree upon the number of vessels of war to be built or purchased, or the number of land or sea forces to be raised, nor appoint a commander in chief of the army or navy, unless nine states assent to the same; nor shall a question on any other point, except for adjourning from day to day, be determined, unless by the votes of a majority of the United States, in Congress assembled.

The Congress of the United States shall have power to adjourn to any time within the year, and to any place within the United States, so that no period of adjournment be for a longer duration than the space of six months, and shall publish the journal of their proceedings monthly, except such parts thereof, relating to treaties, alliances or military operations, as, in their judgment, require secrecy; and the yeas and nays of the delegates of each State on any question shall be entered on the journal, when it is desired by any delegate; and the delegates of a State, or any of them, at his, or their request, shall be furnished with a transcript of the said journal, except such parts as are above excepted, to lay before the legislatures of the several states.

Article 10

The committee of the states, or any nine of them, shall be authorized to execute, in the recess of Congress, such of the powers of Congress as the United States, in Congress assembled, by the consent of nine states, shall, from time to time, think expedient to vest them with; provided, that no power be delegated to the said committee, for the exercise of which, by the articles of confederation, the voice of nine states, in the Congress of the United States assembled, is requisite.

Article 11

Canada acceding to this confederation, and joining in the measures of the United States, shall be admitted into and entitled to all the advantages of this union; but no other colony shall be admitted into the same, unless such admission be agreed to by nine states.

Article 12

All bills of credit emitted, monies borrowed and debts contracted by, or under the authority of Congress before the assembling of the United States, in pursuance of the present confederation, shall be deemed and considered as a charge against the United States, for payment and satisfaction whereof the said United States and the public faith are hereby solemnly pledged.

Article 13

Every State shall abide by the determinations of the United States, in Congress assembled, on all questions which, by this confederation, are submitted to them. And the articles of this confederation shall be inviolably observed by every State, and the union shall be perpetual; nor shall any alteration at any time hereafter be made in any of them, unless such alteration be agreed to in a Congress of the United States, and be afterwards confirmed by the legislatures of every State.

These articles shall be proposed to the legislatures of all the United States, to be considered, and if approved of by them, they are advised to authorize their delegates to ratify the same in the Congress of the United States; which being done, the same shall become conclusive.

The Constitution of the United States*

Agreed to by Philadelphia Convention, September 17, 1787. Implemented March 4, 1789.

Preamble

We the people of the United States, in order to form a more perfect union, establish justice, insure domestic tranquility, provide for the common defense, promote the general welfare, and secure the blessings of liberty to ourselves and our posterity, do ordain and establish this Constitution for the United States of America.

Article I

Section 1. All legislative powers herein granted shall be vested in a Congress of the United States, which shall consist of a Senate and a House of Representatives.

Section 2. The House of Representatives shall be composed of members chosen every second year by the people of the several States, and the electors in each State shall have the qualifications requisite for electors of the most numerous branch of the State Legislature.

No person shall be a Representative who shall not have attained to the age of twenty-five years, and been seven years a citizen of the United States, and who shall not, when elected, be an inhabitant of that State in which he shall be chosen.

Representatives and direct taxes shall be apportioned among the several States which may be included within this Union, according to their respective numbers, *which shall be determined by adding to the whole number of free persons, including those bound to service for a term of years and excluding Indians not taxed, three-fifths of all other persons.* The actual enumeration shall be made within three years after the first meeting of the Congress of the United States, and within every subsequent term of ten years, in such manner as they shall by law direct. The number of Representatives shall not exceed one for every thirty thousand, but each State shall have at least one Representative; and until such enumeration shall be made, *the State of New Hampshire shall be entitled to choose three, Massachusetts eight, Rhode Island and Providence Plantations one, Connecticut five, New York six, New Jersey four, Pennsylvania eight, Delaware one, Maryland six, Virginia ten, North Carolina five, South Carolina five, and Georgia three.*

*Passages no longer in effect are in italic type.

When vacancies happen in the representation from any State, the Executive authority thereof shall issue writs of election to fill such vacancies.

The House of Representatives shall choose their Speaker and other officers; and shall have the sole power of impeachment.

Section 3.   The Senate of the United States shall be composed of two Senators from each State, *chosen by the legislature thereof,* for six years; and each Senator shall have one vote.

Immediately after they shall be assembled in consequence of the first election, they shall be divided as equally as may be into three classes. The seats of the Senators of the first class shall be vacated at the expiration of the second year, of the second class at the expiration of the fourth year, and of the third class at the expiration of the sixth year, so that one-third may be chosen every second year; and if vacancies happen by resignation or otherwise, during the recess of the legislature of any State, the Executive thereof may make temporary appointments until the next meeting of the legislature, which shall then fill such vacancies.

No person shall be a Senator who shall not have attained to the age of thirty years, and been nine years a citizen of the United States, and who shall not, when elected, be an inhabitant of that State for which he shall be chosen.

The Vice-President of the United States shall be President of the Senate, but shall have no vote, unless they be equally divided.

The Senate shall choose their other officers, and also a President pro tempore, in the absence of the Vice-President, or when he shall exercise the office of President of the United States.

The Senate shall have the sole power to try all impeachments. When sitting for that purpose, they shall be on oath or affirmation. When the President of the United States is tried, the Chief Justice shall preside: and no person shall be convicted without the concurrence of two-thirds of the members present.

Judgment in cases of impeachment shall not extend further than to removal from the office, and disqualification to hold and enjoy any office of honor, trust or profit under the United States: but the party convicted shall nevertheless be liable and subject to indictment, trial, judgment and punishment, according to law.

Section 4.   The times, places and manner of holding elections for Senators and Representatives shall be prescribed in each State by the legislature thereof; but the Congress may at any time by law make or alter such regulations, except as to the places of choosing Senators.

The Congress shall assemble at least once in every year, and such meeting *shall be on the first Monday in December, unless they shall by law appoint a different day.*

Section 5.   Each house shall be the judge of the elections, returns and qualifications of its own members, and a majority of each shall constitute a quorum to do business; but a smaller number may adjourn from day to day, and may be authorized to compel the attendance of absent members, in such manner, and under such penalties, as each house may provide.

Each house may determine the rules of its proceedings, punish its members for disorderly behavior, and with the concurrence of two-thirds, expel a member.

Each house shall keep a journal of its proceedings, and from time to time publish the same, excepting such parts as may in their judgment require secrecy; and the yeas and nays of the members of either house on any question shall, at the desire of one fifth of those present, be entered on the journal.

Neither house, during the session of Congress, shall, without the consent of the other, adjourn for more than three days, nor to any other place than that in which the two houses shall be sitting.

Section 6. The Senators and Representatives shall receive a compensation for their services, to be ascertained by law and paid out of the treasury of the United States. They shall in all cases except treason, felony and breach of the peace, be privileged from arrest during their attendance at the session of their respective houses, and in going to and returning from the same; and for any speech or debate in either house, they shall not be questioned in any other place.

No Senator or Representative shall, during the time for which he was elected, be appointed to any civil office under the authority of the United States, which shall have been created, or the emoluments whereof shall have been increased, during such time; and no person holding any office under the United States shall be a member of either house during his continuance in office.

Section 7. All bills for raising revenue shall originate in the House of Representatives; but the Senate may propose or concur with amendments as on other bills.

Every bill which shall have passed the House of Representatives and the Senate, shall, before it become a law, be presented to the President of the United States; if he approve he shall sign it, but if not he shall return it with objections to that house in which it shall have originated, who shall enter the objections at large on their journal, and proceed to reconsider it. If after such reconsideration two-thirds of that house shall agree to pass the bill, it shall be sent, together with the objections, to the other house, by which it shall likewise be reconsidered, and, if approved by two-thirds of that house, it shall become a law. But in all such cases the votes of both houses shall be determined by yeas and nays, and the names of the persons voting for and against the bill shall be entered on the journal of each house respectively. If any bill shall not be returned by the President within ten days (Sundays excepted) after it shall have been presented to him, the same shall be a law, in like manner as if he had signed it, unless the Congress by their adjournment prevent its return, in which case it shall not be a law.

Every order, resolution, or vote to which the concurrence of the Senate and House of Representatives may be necessary (except on a question of adjournment) shall be presented to the President of the United States; and before the same shall take effect, shall be approved by him, or being disapproved by him, shall be repassed by two-thirds of the Senate and House of Representatives, according to the rules and limitations prescribed in the case of a bill.

Section 8. The Congress shall have power

To lay and collect taxes, duties, imposts, and excises, to pay the debts and provide for the common defense and general welfare of the United States; but all duties, imposts and excises shall be uniform throughout the United States;

To borrow money on the credit of the United States;

To regulate commerce with foreign nations, and among the several States, and with the Indian tribes;

To establish an uniform rule of naturalization, and uniform laws on the subject of bankruptcies throughout the United States;

To coin money, regulate the value thereof, and of foreign coin, and fix the standard of weights and measures;

To provide for the punishment of counterfeiting the securities and current coin of the United States;

establish post offices and post roads;

To promote the progress of science and useful arts by securing for limited times to authors and inventors the exclusive right to their respective writings and discoveries;

To constitute tribunals inferior to the Supreme Court;

To define and punish piracies and felonies committed on the high seas and offences against the law of nations;

To declare war, grant letters of marque and reprisal, and make rules concerning captures on land and water;

To raise and support armies, but no appropriation of money to that use shall be for a longer term than two years;

To provide and maintain a navy;

To make rules for the government and regulation of the land and naval forces;

To provide for calling forth the militia to execute the laws of the Union, suppress insurrections and repel invasions;

To provide for organizing, arming, and disciplining the militia, and for governing such part of them as may be employed in the service of the United States, reserving to the States respectively the appointment of the officers, and the authority of training the militia according to the discipline prescribed by Congress;

To exercise exclusive legislation in all cases whatsoever, over such district (not exceeding ten miles square) as may, by cession of particular States, and the acceptance of Congress, become the seat of the government of the United States, and to exercise like authority over all places purchased by the consent of the legislature of the State, in which the same shall be, for erection of forts, magazines, arsenals, dock-yards, and other needful buildings;—and

To make all laws which shall be necessary and proper for carrying into execution the foregoing powers, and all other powers vested by this Constitution in the government of the United States, or in any department or officer thereof.

Section 9.   *The migration or importation of such persons as any of the States now existing shall think proper to admit shall not be prohibited by the Congress prior to the year one thousand eight hundred and eight; but a tax or duty may be imposed on such importation, not exceeding ten dollars for each person.*

The privilege of the writ of habeas corpus shall not be suspended, unless when in cases of rebellion or invasion the public safety may require it.

No bill of attainder or ex post facto law shall be passed.

No capitation, or other direct, tax shall be laid, unless in proportion to the census or enumeration herein before directed to be taken.

No tax or duty shall be laid on articles exported from any State.

No preference shall be given by any regulation of commerce or revenue to the ports of one State over those of another; nor shall vessels bound to, or from, one State be obliged to enter, clear, or pay duties in another.

No money shall be drawn from the treasury, but in consequence of appropriations made by law; and a regular statement and account of the receipts and expenditures of all public money shall be published from time to time.

No title of nobility shall be granted by the United States: and no person holding any office of profit or trust under them, shall, without the consent of the Congress, accept of any present, emolument, office, or title, of any kind whatever, from any king, prince, or foreign state.

Section 10.   No State shall enter into any treaty, alliance, or confederation; grant letters of marque and reprisal; coin money; emit bills of credit; make anything but gold and silver coin a tender in payment of debts; pass any bill of attainder, ex post facto law, or law impairing the obligation of contracts, or grant any title of nobility.

No State shall, without the consent of Congress, lay any imposts or duties on imports or exports, except what may be absolutely necessary for executing its inspection laws: and the net produce of all duties and imposts, laid by any State on imports or exports, shall be for the use of the treasury of the United States; and all such laws shall be subject to the revision and control of the Congress.

No State shall, without the consent of Congress, lay any duty of tonnage, keep troops, or ships of war in time of peace, enter into any agreement or compact with another State, or with a foreign power, or engage in war, unless actually invaded, or in such imminent danger as will not admit of delay.

Article II

Section 1.   The executive power shall be vested in a President of the United States of America. He shall hold his office during the term of four years, and, together with the Vice-President, chosen for the same term, be elected as follows:

Each State shall appoint, in such manner as the legislature thereof may direct, a number of electors, equal to the whole number of Senators and Representatives to which the State may be entitled in the Congress; but no Senator or Representative, or person holding an office of trust or profit under the United States, shall be appointed an elector.

The electors shall meet in their respective States, and vote by ballot for two persons, of whom one at least shall not be an inhabitant of the same State with themselves. And they shall make a list of all the persons voted for, and of the number of votes for each; which list they shall sign and certify, and transmit sealed to the seat of government of the United States, directed to the President of the Senate. The President of the Senate shall, in the presence of the Senate and House of Representatives, open all the certificates, and the votes shall then be counted. The person having the greatest number of votes shall be the President, if such number be a majority of the whole number of electors appointed; and if there be more than one who have such majority, and have an equal number of votes, then the House of Representatives shall immediately choose by ballot one of them for President; and if no person have a majority, then from the five highest on the list said house shall in like manner choose the President. But in choosing the President the votes shall be taken by States, the representation from each State having one vote; a quorum for this purpose shall consist of a member or members from two-thirds of the States, and a majority of all the States shall be necessary to a choice. In every case, after the choice of the President, the person having the greatest number of votes of the electors shall be the Vice-President. But if there should remain two or more who have equal votes, the Senate shall choose from them by ballot the Vice-President.

The Congress may determine the time of choosing the electors, and the day on which they shall give their votes; which day shall be the same throughout the United States.

No person except a natural-born citizen, *or a citizen of the United States at the time of the adoption of this Constitution,* shall be eligible to the office of President; neither shall any person be eligible to that office who shall not have attained to the age of thirty-five years, and been fourteen years a resident within the United States.

In cases of the removal of the President from office or of his death, resignation, or inability to discharge the powers and duties of the said office, the same shall devolve on the Vice-President, and the Congress may by law provide for the case of removal, death, resignation, or inability, both of the President and Vice-President, declaring what officer shall then act as President, and such officer shall act accordingly, until the disability be removed, or a President shall be elected.

The President shall, at stated times, receive for his services a compensation, which shall neither be increased nor diminished during the period for which he shall have been elected, and he shall not receive within that period any other emolument from the United States, or any of them.

Before he enter on the execution of his office, he shall take the following oath or affirmation:—"I do solemnly swear (or affirm) that I will faithfully execute the office of the President of the United States, and will to the best of my ability preserve, protect and defend the Constitution of the United States."

Section 2.   The President shall be commander in chief of the army and navy of the United States, and of the militia of the several States, when called into the actual service of the United States; he may require the opinion, in writing, of the principal officer in each of the executive departments, upon any subject relating to the duties of their respective offices, and he shall have power to grant reprieves and pardons for offenses against the United States, except in cases of impeachment.

He shall have power, by and with the advice and consent of the Senate, to make treaties, provided two-thirds of the Senators present concur; and he shall nominate, and by and with the advice and consent of the Senate, shall appoint ambassadors, other public ministers and consuls, judges of the Supreme Court, and all other officers of the United States, whose appointments are not herein otherwise provided for, and which shall be established by law: but Congress may by law vest the appointment of such inferior officers, as they think proper, in the President alone, in the courts of law, or in the heads of departments.

The President shall have power to fill up all vacancies that may happen during the recess of the Senate, by granting commissions which shall expire at the end of their next session.

Section 3.   He shall from time to time give to the Congress information of the state of the Union, and recommend to their consideration such measures as he shall judge necessary and expedient; he may, on extraordinary occasions, convene both houses, or either of them, and in case of disagreement between them, with respect to the time of adjournment, he may adjourn them to such time as he shall think proper; he shall receive ambassadors and other public ministers; he shall take care that the laws be faithfully executed, and shall commission all the officers of the United States.

Section 4.   The President, Vice-President and all civil officers of the United States shall be removed from office on impeachment for, and on conviction of, treason, bribery, or other high crimes and misdemeanors.

Article III

Section 1.   The judicial power of the United States shall be vested in one Supreme Court, and in such inferior courts as the Congress may from time to time ordain and establish. The judges, both of the Supreme and inferior courts, shall hold their offices during good behavior, and shall, at stated times, receive for their services a compensation which shall not be diminished during their continuance in office.

Section 2.   The judicial power shall extend to all cases, in law and equity, arising under this Constitution, the laws of the United States, and treaties made, or which shall be made, under their authority;—to all cases affecting ambassadors, other public ministers and consuls;—to all cases of admiralty and maritime jurisdiction;—to controversies to which the United States shall be a party;—to controversies between two or more States;—between a State and citizens of another State;—between citizens of different States;—between citizens of the same State claiming lands under grants of different States, and between a State, or the citizens thereof, and foreign states, citizens or subjects.

In all cases affecting ambassadors, other public ministers and consuls, and those in which a State shall be party, the Supreme Court shall have original jurisdiction. In all the other cases before mentioned, the Supreme Court shall have appellate jurisdiction, both as to law and fact, with such exceptions, and under such regulations, as the Congress shall make.

The trial of all crimes, except in cases of impeachment, shall be by jury; and such trial shall be held in the State where said crimes shall have been committed; but when not committed within any State, the trial shall be at such place or places as the Congress may by Law have directed.

Section 3.   Treason against the United States shall consist only in levying war against them, or in adhering to their enemies, giving them aid and comfort. No person shall be convicted of treason unless on the testimony of two witnesses to the same overt act, or on confession in open court.

The Congress shall have power to declare the punishment of treason, but no attainder of treason shall work corruption of blood, or forfeiture except during the life of the person attainted.

Article IV

Section 1.   Full faith and credit shall be given in each State to the public acts, records, and judicial proceedings of every other State. And the Congress may by general laws prescribe the manner in which such acts, records, and proceedings shall be proved, and the effect thereof.

Section 2.   The citizens of each State shall be entitled to all privileges and immunities of citizens in the several States.

A person charged in any State with treason, felony, or other crime, who shall flee from justice, and be found in another State, shall on demand of the executive authority of the State from which he fled, be delivered up, to be removed to the State having jurisdiction of the crime.

No Person held to service or labor in one State, under the laws thereof, escaping into another, shall, in consequence of any law or regulation therein, be discharged from such service or labor, but shall be delivered up on claim of the party to whom such service or labor may be due.

Section 3.   New States may be admitted by the Congress into this Union; but no new State shall be formed or erected within the jurisdiction of any other State; nor any State be formed by the junction of two or more States, or parts of States, without the consent of the legislatures of the States concerned as well as of the Congress.

The Congress shall have power to dispose of and make all needful rules and regulations respecting the territory or other property belonging to the United States; and nothing in this Constitution shall be so construed as to prejudice any claims of the United States, or of any particular State.

Section 4.   The United States shall guarantee to every State in this Union a republican form of government, and shall protect each of them against invasion; and on application of the legislature, or of the executive (when the legislature cannot be convened), against domestic violence.

Article V

The Congress, whenever two-thirds of both houses shall deem it necessary, shall propose amendments to this Constitution, or, on the application of the legislatures of two-thirds of the several States, shall call a convention for proposing amendments, which, in either case, shall be valid to all intents and purposes, as part of this Constitution, when ratified by the legislatures of three-fourths of the several States, or by conventions in three-fourths thereof, as the one or the other mode of ratification may be proposed by the Congress; *provided that no amendments which may be made prior to the year one thousand eight hundred and eight shall in any manner affect the first and fourth clauses in the ninth section of the first article;* and that no State, without its consent, shall be deprived of its equal suffrage in the Senate.

Article VI

All debts contracted and engagements entered into, before the adoption of this Constitution, shall be as valid against the United States under this Constitution, as under the Confederation.

This Constitution, and the laws of the United States which shall be made in pursuance thereof; and all treaties made, or which shall be made, under the authority of the United States, shall be the supreme law of the land; and the judges in every State shall be bound thereby, anything in the Constitution or laws of any State to the contrary notwithstanding.

The Senators and Representatives before mentioned, and the members of the several State legislatures, and all executive and judicial officers, both of the United States and of the several States, shall be bound by oath or affirmation to support this Constitution; but no religious test shall ever be required as a qualification to any office or public trust under the United States.

Article VII

The ratification of the conventions of nine States shall be sufficient for the establishment of this Constitution between the States so ratifying the same.

Done in convention by the unanimous consent of the States present, the seventeenth day of September in the year of our Lord one thousand seven hundred and eighty-seven and of the Independence of the United States of America the twelfth. In witness whereof we have hereunto subscribed our names.

GEORGE WASHINGTON, President and Deputy from Virginia

New Hampshire
John Langdon
Nicholas Gilman

Massachusetts
Nathaniel Gorham
Rufus King

Connecticut
William Samuel
Johnson
Roger Sherman

New York
Alexander Hamilton

New Jersey
William Livingston
David Brearley
William Paterson
Jonathan Dayton

Pennsylvania
Benjamin Franklin
Thomas Mifflin
Robert Morris
George Clymer
Thomas FitzSimons
Jared Ingersoll
James Wilson
Gouverneur Morris

Delaware
George Read
Gunning Bedford, Jr.
John Dickinson
Richard Bassett
Jacob Broom

Maryland
James McHenry
Daniel of St. Thomas Jenifer
Daniel Carroll

Virginia
John Blair
James Madison, Jr.

North Carolina
William Blount
Richard Dobbs Spaight
Hugh Williamson

South Carolina
John Rutledge
Charles Cotesworth
Pinckney
Charles Pinckney
Pierce Butler

Georgia
William Few
Abraham Baldwin

Amendments to the Constitution

(including six unratified amendments)

Amendment I   [Ratified 1791]

Congress shall make no law respecting an establishment of religion, or prohibiting the free exercise thereof; or abridging the freedom of speech, or of the press; or the right of the people peaceably to assemble, and to petition the government for a redress of grievances.

Amendment II   [Ratified 1791]

A well-regulated militia being necessary to the security of a free State, the right of the people to keep and bear arms shall not be infringed.

Amendment III   [Ratified 1791]

No soldier shall, in time of peace, be quartered in any house without the consent of the owner, nor in time of war, but in a manner to be prescribed by law.

Amendment IV   [Ratified 1791]

The right of the people to be secure in their persons, houses, papers, and effects, against unreasonable searches and seizures, shall not be violated, and no warrants shall issue but upon probable cause, supported by oath or affirmation, and particularly describing the place to be searched, and the persons or things to be seized.

Amendment V   [Ratified 1791]

No person shall be held to answer for a capital, or otherwise infamous crime, unless on a presentment or indictment of a grand jury, except in cases arising in the land or naval forces, or in the militia, when in actual service in time of war or public danger; nor shall any person be subject for the same offence to be twice put in jeopardy of life or limb; nor shall be compelled in any criminal case to be a witness against himself, nor be deprived of life, liberty, or property, without due process of law; nor shall private property be taken for public use without just compensation.

Amendment VI   [Ratified 1791]

In all criminal prosecutions, the accused shall enjoy the right to a speedy and public trial, by an impartial jury of the State and district wherein the crime shall have been committed, which district shall have been previously ascertained by law, and to be informed of the nature and cause of the accusation; to be confronted with the witnesses against him; to have compulsory process for obtaining witnesses in his favor, and to have the assistance of counsel for his defence.

Amendment VII   [Ratified 1791]

In suits at common law, where the value in controversy shall exceed twenty dollars, the right of trial by jury shall be preserved, and no fact tried by a jury shall be otherwise reexamined in any court of the United States, than according to the rules of the common law.

Amendment VIII   [Ratified 1791]

Excessive bail shall not be required, nor excessive fines imposed, nor cruel and unusual punishments inflicted.

Amendment IX   [Ratified 1791]

The enumeration in the Constitution, of certain rights, shall not be construed to deny or disparage others retained by the people.

Amendment X   [Ratified 1791]

The powers not delegated to the United States by the Constitution, nor prohibited by it to the States, are reserved to the States respectively, or to the people.

Unratified Amendment

[Reapportionment Amendment (proposed by Congress September 25, 1789, along with the Bill of Rights)]

After the first enumeration required by the first article of the Constitution, there shall be one Representative for every thirty thousand, until the number shall amount to one hundred, after which the proportion shall be so regulated by Congress, that there shall be not less than one hundred Representatives, nor less than one Representative for every forty thousand persons, until the number of Representatives shall amount to two hundred; after which the proportion shall be so regulated by Congress, that there shall not be less than two hundred Representatives, nor more than one Representative for every fifty thousand persons.

Amendment XI   [Ratified 1798]

The judicial power of the United States shall not be construed to extend to any suit in law or equity, commenced or prosecuted against one of the United States by citizens of another State, or by citizens or subjects of any foreign state.

Amendment XII   [Ratified 1804]

The electors shall meet in their respective States, and vote by ballot for President and Vice-President, one of whom, at least, shall not be an inhabitant of the same State with themselves; they shall name in their ballots the person voted for as President, and in distinct ballots the person voted for as Vice-President, and they shall make distinct lists of all persons voted for as President, and of all persons voted for as Vice-President, and of the number of votes for each, which lists they shall sign and certify, and transmit sealed to the seat of government of the United States, directed to the President of the Senate;—the President of the Senate shall, in the presence of the Senate and House of Representatives, open all the certificates and the votes shall then be counted;—the person having the greatest number of votes for President shall be the President, if such number be a majority of the whole number of electors appointed; and if no person have such majority, then from the persons having the highest numbers not exceeding three on the list of those voted for as President, the House of Representatives shall choose immediately, by ballot, the President. But in choosing the President, the votes shall be taken by States, the representation from each State having one vote; a quorum for this purpose shall consist of a member or members from two-thirds of the States, and a majority of all the States shall be necessary to a choice. And if the House of Representatives shall not choose a President whenever the right of choice shall devolve upon them, before *the fourth day of March* next following, then the Vice-President shall act as President, as in the case of the death or other constitutional disability of the President.

The person having the greatest number of votes as Vice-President shall be the Vice-President, if such number be a majority of the whole number of electors appointed; and if no person have a majority, then from the two highest numbers on the list the Senate shall choose the Vice-President; a quorum for the purpose shall consist of two-thirds of the whole number of Senators, and a majority of the whole number shall be necessary to a choice. But no person constitutionally ineligible to the office of President shall be eligible to that of Vice-President of the United States.

Unratified Amendment

[Titles of Nobility Amendment (proposed by Congress May 1, 1810)]

If any citizen of the United States shall accept, claim, receive or retain any title of nobility or honor or shall, without the consent of Congress, accept and retain any present, pension, office or emolument of any kind whatever, from any emperor, king, prince or foreign power, such person shall cease to be a citizen of the United States, and shall be incapable of holding any office of trust or profit under them or either of them.

Unratified Amendment

[Corwin Amendment (proposed by Congress March 2, 1861)]

No amendment shall be made to the Constitution which will authorize or give to Congress the power to abolish or interfere, within any State, with the domestic institutions thereof, including that of persons held to labor or service by the laws of said State.

Amendment XIII   [Ratified 1865]

Section 1.   Neither slavery nor involuntary servitude, except as a punishment for crime whereof the party shall have been duly convicted, shall exist within the United States, or any place subject to their jurisdiction.

Section 2.   Congress shall have power to enforce this article by appropriate legislation.

Amendment XIV   [Ratified 1868]

Section 1.   All persons born or naturalized in the United States, and subject to the jurisdiction thereof, are citizens of the United States and of the State wherein they reside. No State shall make or enforce any law which shall abridge the privileges or immunities of citizens of the United States; nor shall any State deprive any person of life, liberty, or property, without due process of law; nor deny to any person within its jurisdiction the equal protection of the laws.

Section 2.   Representatives shall be appointed among the several States according to their respective numbers, counting the whole number of persons in each State, excluding Indians not taxed. But when the right to vote at any election for the choice of Electors for President and Vice-President of the United States, Representatives in Congress, the executive and judicial officers of a State, or the members of the legislature thereof, is denied to any of the *male* inhabitants of such State, being *twenty-one* years of age and citizens of the United States, or in any way abridged, except for participation in rebellion, or other crime, the basis of representation therein shall be reduced in the proportion which the number of such male citizens shall bear to the whole number of *male* citizens *twenty-one* years of age in such State.

Section 3.   No person shall be a Senator or Representative in Congress, or Elector of President and Vice-President, or hold any office, civil or military, under the United States, or under any State, who, having previously taken an oath, as a member of Congress, or as an officer of the United States, or as a member of any State legislature, or as an executive or judicial officer of any State, to support the Constitution of the United States, shall have engaged in insurrection or rebellion against the same, or given aid or comfort to the enemies thereof. Congress may, by a vote of two-thirds of each house, remove such disability.

Section 4.   The validity of the public debt of the United States, authorized by law, including debts incurred for payment of pensions and bounties for services in suppressing insurrection or rebellion, shall not be questioned. But neither the United States nor any State shall assume or pay any debt or obligation incurred in aid of insurrection or rebellion against the United States, or any claim for the loss or emancipation of any slave; but all such debts, obligations, and claims shall be held illegal and void.

Section 5.   The Congress shall have power to enforce, by appropriate legislation, the provisions of this article.

Amendment XV   [Ratified 1870]

Section 1.   The right of citizens of the United States to vote shall not be denied or abridged by the United States or by any State on account of race, color, or previous condition of servitude.

Section 2.   The Congress shall have power to enforce this article by appropriate legislation.

Amendment XVI   [Ratified 1913]

The Congress shall have power to lay and collect taxes on incomes, from whatever source derived, without apportionment among the several States, and without regard to any census or enumeration.

Amendment XVII   [Ratified 1913]

Section 1.   The Senate of the United States shall be composed of two Senators from each State, elected by the people thereof, for six years; and each Senator shall have one vote. The electors in each State shall have the qualifications requisite for electors of [voters for] the most numerous branch of the State legislatures.

Section 2.   When vacancies happen in the representation of any State in the Senate, the executive authority of such State shall issue writs of election to fill such vacancies: Provided, that the Legislature of any State may empower the executive thereof to make temporary appointments until the people fill the vacancies by election as the Legislature may direct.

Section 3.   *This amendment shall not be so construed as to affect the election or term of any Senator chosen before it becomes valid as part of the Constitution.*

Amendment XVIII

[Ratified 1919; repealed 1933 by Amendment XXI]

Section 1.   *After one year from the ratification of this article the manufacture, sale, or transportation of intoxicating liquors within, the importation thereof into, or the exportation thereof from the United States and all territory subject to the jurisdiction thereof, for beverage purposes, is hereby prohibited.*

Section 2.   *The Congress and the several States shall have concurrent power to enforce this article by appropriate legislation.*

Section 3.   *This article shall be inoperative unless it shall have been ratified as an amendment to the Constitution by the legislatures of the several States, as provided by the Constitution, within seven years from the date of the submission thereof to the States by the Congress.*

Amendment XIX   [Ratified 1920]

Section 1.   The right of citizens of the United States to vote shall not be denied or abridged by the United States or by any State on account of sex.

Section 2.   Congress shall have the power to enforce this article by appropriate legislation.

Unratified Amendment

[Child Labor Amendment (proposed by Congress June 2, 1924)]

Section 1.   *The Congress shall have power to limit, regulate, and prohibit the labor of persons under eighteen years of age.*

Section 2.   *The power of the several States is unimpaired by this article except that the operation of State laws shall be suspended to the extent necessary to give effect to legislation enacted by Congress.*

Amendment XX   [Ratified 1933]

Section 1.   The terms of the President and Vice-President shall end at noon on the 20th day of January, and the terms of Senators and Representatives at noon on the 3rd day of January, of the years in which such terms would have ended if this article had not been ratified; and the terms of their successors shall then begin.

Section 2. The Congress shall assemble at least once in every year, and such meeting shall begin at noon on the 3rd day of January, unless they shall by law appoint a different day.

Section 3. If, at the time fixed for the beginning of the term of the President, the President-elect shall have died, the Vice-President-elect shall become President. If a President shall not have been chosen before the time fixed for the beginning of his term, or if the President-elect shall have failed to qualify, then the Vice-President-elect shall act as President until a President shall have qualified; and the Congress may by law provide for the case wherein neither a President-elect nor a Vice-President-elect shall have qualified, declaring who shall then act as President, or the manner in which one who is to act shall be selected, and such person shall act accordingly until a President or Vice-President shall have qualified.

Section 4. The Congress may by law provide for the case of the death of any of the persons from whom the House of Representatives may choose a President whenever the right of choice shall have devolved upon them, and for the case of the death of any of the persons from whom the Senate may choose a Vice-President whenever the right of choice shall have devolved upon them.

Section 5. Sections 1 and 2 shall take effect on the 15th day of October following the ratification of this article.

Section 6. This article shall be inoperative unless it shall have been ratified as an amendment to the Constitution by the Legislatures of three-fourths of the several States within seven years from the date of its submission.

Amendment XXI   [Ratified 1933]
Section 1. The eighteenth article of amendment to the Constitution of the United States is hereby repealed.

Section 2. The transportation or importation into any State, Territory, or Possession of the United States for delivery or use therein of intoxicating liquors, in violation of the laws thereof, is hereby prohibited.

Section 3. This article shall be inoperative unless it shall have been ratified as an amendment to the Constitution by conventions in the several States, as provided in the Constitution, within seven years from the date of the submission thereof to the States by the Congress.

Amendment XXII   [Ratified 1951]
Section 1. No person shall be elected to the office of the President more than twice, and no person who has held the office of President, or acted as President, for more than two years of a term to which some other person was elected President shall be elected to the office of President more than once. But this article shall not apply to any person holding the office of President when this Article was proposed by the Congress, and shall not prevent any person who may be holding the office of President, or acting as President, during the term within which this Article becomes operative from holding the office of President or acting as President during the remainder of such term.

Section 2. This article shall be inoperative unless it shall have been ratified as an amendment to the Constitution by the legislatures of three-fourths of the several States within seven years from the date of its submission to the States by the Congress.

Amendment XXIII   [Ratified 1961]

Section 1.   The District constituting the seat of Government of the United States shall appoint in such manner as the Congress may direct: A number of electors of President and Vice-President equal to the whole number of Senators and Representatives in Congress to which the District would be entitled if it were a State, but in no event more than the least populous State; they shall be in addition to those appointed by the States, but they shall be considered for the purposes of the election of President and Vice-President, to be electors appointed by a State; and they shall meet in the District and perform such duties as provided by the twelfth article of amendment.

Section 2.   The Congress shall have the power to enforce this article by appropriate legislation.

Amendment XXIV   [Ratified 1964]

Section 1.   The right of citizens of the United States to vote in any primary or other election for President or Vice-President, for electors for President or Vice-President, or for Senator or Representative in Congress, shall not be denied or abridged by the United States or any State by reason of failure to pay any poll tax or other tax.

Section 2.   The Congress shall have the power to enforce this article by appropriate legislation.

Amendment XXV   [Ratified 1967]

Section 1.   In case of the removal of the President from office or of his death or resignation, the Vice-President shall become President.

Section 2.   Whenever there is a vacancy in the office of the Vice-President, the President shall nominate a Vice-President who shall take office upon confirmation by a majority vote of both Houses of Congress.

Section 3.   Whenever the President transmits to the President pro tempore of the Senate and the Speaker of the House of Representatives his written declaration that he is unable to discharge the powers and duties of his office, and until he transmits to them a written declaration to the contrary, such powers and duties shall be discharged by the Vice-President as Acting President.

Section 4.   Whenever the Vice-President and a majority of either the principal officers of the executive departments or of such other body as Congress may by law provide, transmit to the President pro tempore of the Senate and the Speaker of the House of Representatives their written declaration that the President is unable to discharge the powers and duties of his office, the Vice-President shall immediately assume the powers and duties of the office as Acting President.

Thereafter, when the President transmits to the President pro tempore of the Senate and the Speaker of the House of Representatives his written declaration that no inability exists, he shall resume the powers and duties of his office unless the Vice-President and a majority of either the principal officers of the executive department[s] or of such other body as Congress may by law provide, transmit within four days to the President pro tempore of the Senate and the Speaker of the House of Representatives their written declaration that the President is unable to discharge the powers and duties of his office. Thereupon Congress shall decide the issue, assembling within forty-eight hours for that purpose if not in session. If the Congress, within twenty-one days after receipt of the latter written declaration, or, if Congress is not in session, within twenty-one days after Congress is required to assemble, determines by two-thirds vote of both Houses that the President is unable to discharge the powers and duties of his office, the Vice-President shall continue to discharge the same as Acting President; otherwise, the President shall resume the powers and duties of his office.

Amendment XXVI   [Ratified 1971]

Section 1.   The right of citizens of the United States, who are eighteen years of age or older, to vote shall not be denied or abridged by the United States or by any State on account of age.

Section 2.   The Congress shall have power to enforce this article by appropriate legislation.

Unratified Amendment

[Equal Rights Amendment (proposed by Congress March 22, 1972; seven-year deadline for ratification extended to June 30, 1982)]

Section 1.   *Equality of rights under the law shall not be denied or abridged by the United States or by any State on account of sex.*

Section 2.   *The Congress shall have the power to enforce, by appropriate legislation, the provisions of this article.*

Section 3.   *This amendment shall take effect two years after the date of ratification.*

Unratified Amendment

[D.C. Statehood Amendment (proposed by Congress August 22, 1978)]

Section 1.   *For purposes of representation in the Congress, election of the President and Vice-President, and article V of this Constitution, the District constituting the seat of government of the United States shall be treated as though it were a State.*

Section 2.   *The exercise of the rights and powers conferred under this article shall be by the people of the District constituting the seat of government, and as shall be provided by Congress.*

Section 3.   *The twenty-third article of amendment to the Constitution of the United States is hereby repealed.*

Section 4.   *This article shall be inoperative, unless it shall have been ratified as an amendment to the Constitution by the legislatures of three-fourths of the several states within seven years from the date of its submission.*

Amendment XXVII   [Ratified 1992]

No law, varying the compensation for the services of the Senators and Representatives, shall take effect, until an election of Representatives shall have intervened.

Admission of States to the Union

State	Year of Admission	State	Year of Admission
Delaware	1787	Michigan	1837
Pennsylvania	1787	Florida	1845
New Jersey	1787	Texas	1845
Georgia	1788	Iowa	1846
Connecticut	1788	Wisconsin	1848
Massachusetts	1788	California	1850
Maryland	1788	Minnesota	1858
South Carolina	1788	Oregon	1859
New Hampshire	1788	Kansas	1861
Virginia	1788	West Virginia	1863
New York	1788	Nevada	1864
North Carolina	1789	Nebraska	1867
Rhode Island	1790	Colorado	1876
Vermont	1791	North Dakota	1889
Kentucky	1792	South Dakota	1889
Tennessee	1796	Montana	1889
Ohio	1803	Washington	1889
Louisiana	1812	Idaho	1890
Indiana	1816	Wyoming	1890
Mississippi	1817	Utah	1896
Illinois	1818	Oklahoma	1907
Alabama	1819	New Mexico	1912
Maine	1820	Arizona	1912
Missouri	1821	Alaska	1959
Arkansas	1836	Hawaii	1959

Presidents of the United States

President	Term
George Washington	1789–1797
John Adams	1797–1801
Thomas Jefferson	1801–1809
James Madison	1809–1817
James Monroe	1817–1825
John Quincy Adams	1825–1829
Andrew Jackson	1829–1837
Martin Van Buren	1837–1841
William H. Harrison	1841
John Tyler	1841–1845
James K. Polk	1845–1849
Zachary Taylor	1849–1850
Millard Fillmore	1850–1853
Franklin Pierce	1853–1857
James Buchanan	1857–1861
Abraham Lincoln	1861–1865
Andrew Johnson	1865–1869
Ulysses S. Grant	1869–1877
Rutherford B. Hayes	1877–1881
James A. Garfield	1881
Chester A. Arthur	1881–1885
Grover Cleveland	1885–1889
Benjamin Harrison	1889–1893

President	Term
Grover Cleveland	1893–1897
William McKinley	1897–1901
Theodore Roosevelt	1901–1909
William H. Taft	1909–1913
Woodrow Wilson	1913–1921
Warren G. Harding	1921–1923
Calvin Coolidge	1923–1929
Herbert Hoover	1929–1933
Franklin D. Roosevelt	1933–1945
Harry S. Truman	1945–1953
Dwight D. Eisenhower	1953–1961
John F. Kennedy	1961–1963
Lyndon B. Johnson	1963–1969
Richard M. Nixon	1969–1974
Gerald R. Ford	1974–1977
Jimmy Carter	1977–1981
Ronald Reagan	1981–1989
George H. W. Bush	1989–1993
Bill Clinton	1993–2001
George W. Bush	2001–2009
Barack Obama	2009–2017
Donald J. Trump	2017–2021
Joseph R. Biden	2021–Present

Glossary of Key Terms

acquired immune deficiency syndrome (AIDS) Immune disorder that reached epidemic proportions in the United States in the 1980s. (p. 974)

affirmative action Programs meant to overcome historical patterns of discrimination against minorities and women in education and employment. By establishing guidelines for hiring and college admissions, the government sought to advance equal opportunities for minorities and women. (p. 939)

Agricultural Adjustment Act New Deal legislation that raised prices for farm produce by paying farmers subsidies to reduce production. Large farmers reaped most of the benefits from the act. The Supreme Court declared it unconstitutional in 1936. (p. 757)

America First Committee Isolationist organization founded by Senator Gerald Nye in 1940 to keep the United States out of World War II. (p. 786)

American Equal Rights Association Group of black and white women and men formed in 1866 to promote gender and racial equality. The organization split in 1869 over support for the Fifteenth Amendment. (p. 477)

American Expeditionary Forces (AEF) Established in 1917 after the United States entered World War I. These Army troops served in Europe under the command of General John J. Pershing. (p. 692)

American Federation of Labor (AFL) Trade union federation founded in 1886. Led by its first president, Samuel Gompers, the AFL sought to organize skilled workers into trade-specific unions. (p. 575)

American Indian Movement (AIM) An American Indian group, formed in 1968, that promoted "red power" and condemned the United States for its continued mistreatment of Native Americans. (p. 916)

American Plan Voluntary program initiated by businesses in the early twentieth century to protect worker welfare. The American Plan was meant to undermine the appeal of labor unions. (p. 714)

American Protective League (APL) An organization of private citizens that cooperated with the Justice Department and the Bureau of Investigation during World War I to spy on German residents suspected of disloyal behavior. (p. 695)

Anti-Imperialist League An organization founded in 1898 to oppose annexation of the Philippines. Some feared that annexation would bring competition from cheap labor; others considered Filipinos racially inferior and the Philippines unsuitable as an American territory. (p. 681)

appeasement The policy of England and France in 1938 that allowed the Nazis to annex Czechoslovak territory in exchange for Hitler promising not to take further land, a pledge he soon violated. (p. 784)

Atlantic Charter August 1941 agreement between Franklin Roosevelt and Winston Churchill that outlined potential war aims and cemented the relationship between the United States and Britain. (p. 787)

Bandung Conference A conference of twenty-nine Asian and African nations held in Indonesia in 1955; the countries declared their neutrality in the Cold War struggle between the United States and the Soviet Union and condemned colonialism. (p. 844)

Battle of the Little Big Horn 1876 battle in the Montana Territory in which Lieutenant Colonel George Armstrong Custer and his troops were massacred by Lakota Sioux. (p. 505)

Beats A small group of young poets, writers, intellectuals, musicians, and artists who attacked mainstream American politics and culture in the 1950s. (p. 868)

Berlin airlift During the Berlin blockade by the Soviets from 1948 to 1949, the U.S. and British governments dispatched their air forces to transport food and supplies to West Berlin. (p. 827)

Billion Dollar Congress The Republican-controlled Congress of 1890 that spent huge sums of money to promote business and other interests. (p. 555)

black codes Racial laws passed in the immediate aftermath of the Civil War by southern legislatures. The black codes were intended to reduce free African Americans to a condition as close to slavery as possible. (p. 471)

Black Lives Matter Social protest movement begun in the wake of the shooting death of Trayvon Martin by an armed civilian in 2013. Organized by protestors around the social media hashtag Black Lives Matter, the movement expanded throughout the nation after police killings of unarmed African Americans in Ferguson, Missouri; Staten Island, New York; Cleveland, Ohio; and Baltimore, Maryland in 2014 and 2015. (p. 1006)

Black Panther Party Organization founded in 1966 by Huey P. Newton and Bobby Seale to advance the black power movement in black communities. (p. 902)

Black Tuesday October 29, 1929, crash of the U.S. stock market. The 1929 stock market crash marked the beginning of the Great Depression. (p. 733)

Boland Amendment 1982 act of Congress prohibiting direct aid to the Nicaraguan Contra forces. (p. 977)

Bonus Army World War I veterans who marched on Washington, D.C., in 1932 to demand immediate payment of their service bonuses. President Hoover refused to negotiate and instructed the U.S. army to clear the capital of protesters, leading to a violent clash. (p. 755)

boss Leader of a political machine. Men like "Boss" George Washington Plunkitt of New York's Tammany Hall wielded enormous power over city life. (p. 622)

Brown v. Board of Education of Topeka, Kansas Landmark 1954 Supreme Court case that overturned the "separate but equal" principle established by *Plessy v. Ferguson* and applied to public schools. Few schools in the South were racially desegregated for more than a decade. (p. 871)

buffalo soldiers African American cavalrymen who fought in the West against the Indians in the 1870s and 1880s and served with distinction. (p. 506)

bully pulpit Term used by Theodore Roosevelt to describe the office of the presidency. Roosevelt believed that the president should use his office as a platform to promote his programs and rally public opinion. (p. 657)

Bush Doctrine President George W. Bush's proposal to engage in preemptive war against despotic governments, such as Iraq, deemed to threaten U.S. national security, even if the danger was not imminent. (p. 1017)

Californios Spanish and Mexican residents of California. Before the nineteenth century, Californios made up California's economic and political elite. Their position, however, deteriorated after the conclusion of the Mexican-American War in 1848. (p. 519)

Camp David accords 1978 peace accord between Israel and Egypt facilitated by the mediation of President Jimmy Carter. (p. 946)

carpetbaggers Derogatory term for white Northerners who moved to the South in the years following the Civil War. Many white Southerners believed that such migrants were intent on exploiting their suffering. (p. 479)

Chinese Exclusion Act 1882 act that banned Chinese immigration into the United States and prohibited those Chinese already in the country from becoming naturalized American citizens. (p. 605)

civic housekeeping Idea promoted by Jane Addams for urban reform by using women's traditional skills as domestic managers; caregivers for children, the elderly, and the needy; and community builders. (p. 640)

Civil Rights Act of 1964 Wide-ranging civil rights act that, among other things, prohibited discrimination in public accommodations and employment and increased federal enforcement of school desegregation. (p. 898)

Civilian Conservation Corps (CCC) New Deal work program that hired young, unmarried men to work on conservation projects. The CCC employed about 2.5 million men and lasted until 1942. (p. 759)

Cold War The political, economic, and military conflict, short of direct war on the battlefield, between the United States and the Soviet Union that lasted from 1945 to 1991. (p. 821)

collective bargaining The process of negotiation between labor unions and employers. (p. 574)

Commission on the Status of Women Commission appointed by President Kennedy in 1961. The commission's 1963 report, *American Women*, highlighted employment discrimination against women and recommended legislation requiring equal pay for equal work regardless of sex. (p. 912)

Committee on Public Information (CPI) Committee established in 1917 to create propaganda and promote censorship to generate enthusiasm for World War I and stifle antiwar dissent. (p. 694)

Compromise of 1877 Compromise between Republicans and southern Democrats that resulted in the election of Rutherford B. Hayes. Southern Democrats agreed to support Hayes in the disputed presidential election in exchange for his promise to end Reconstruction. (p. 487)

Comstock Lode Massive silver deposit discovered in the Sierra Nevada in the late 1850s. (p. 509)

conservative coalition Alliance of southern Democrats and conservative northern Republicans in Congress that thwarted passage of New Deal legislation after 1938. (p. 771)

Contract with America A document that called for reduced welfare spending, lower taxes, term limits for lawmakers, and a constitutional amendment for a balanced budget. In preparation for the 1994 midterm congressional elections, Republicans, led by Representative Newt Gingrich, drew up this proposal. (p. 1011)

convict lease The system used by southern governments to furnish mainly African American prison labor to plantation owners and industrialists and to raise revenue for the states. In practice, convict labor replaced slavery as the means of providing a forced labor supply. (p. 537)

corporation A form of business ownership in which the liability of shareholders in a company is limited to their individual investments. The formation of corporations in the late nineteenth century greatly stimulated investment in industry. (p. 540)

counterculture Young cultural rebels of the 1960s who rejected conventional moral and sexual values and used drugs to reach a higher consciousness. These so-called hippies bonded together in their style of clothes and taste in rock 'n' roll music. (p. 912)

court-packing plan Proposal by President Franklin Roosevelt in 1937 to increase the size of the Supreme Court and reduce its opposition to New Deal legislation. Congress failed to pass the measure, and the scheme increased resentment toward Roosevelt. (p. 770)

COVID-19 An infectious disease caused by a novel coronavirus that first appeared in China in 2019 and is responsible for the worldwide pandemic that followed. (p. 1035)

Coxey's army 1894 protest movement led by Jacob Coxey. Coxey and five hundred supporters marched from Ohio to Washington, D.C., to protest the lack of government response to the depression of 1893. (p. 588)

Cuba Libre Vision of Cuban independence developed by José Martí, who hoped that Cuban independence would bring with it greater social and racial equality. (p. 677)

D Day June 6, 1944, invasion of German-occupied France by Allied forces. The D Day landings opened up a second front in Europe and marked a major turning point in World War II. (p. 802)

Dawes Act 1887 act that ended federal recognition of tribal sovereignty and divided Indian land into 160-acre parcels to be distributed to Indian heads of household. The act dramatically reduced the amount of Indian-controlled land and undermined Indian social and cultural institutions. (p. 507)

decolonization The period after World War II through the 1960s when countries in Asia, Africa, and the Middle East gained independence from their European colonial rulers. In 1946 the United States gave the Philippines independence. (p. 843)

Deferred Action for Childhood Arrivals (DACA) This policy, initiated under the administration of Barack Obama in 2012, allows children who entered the country illegally to receive a two-year extension of their residency in the U.S. along with eligibility for work permits. (p. 1026)

depression of 1893 Severe economic downturn triggered by railroad and bank failures. The severity of the depression, combined with the failure of the federal government to offer an adequate response, led to the realignment of American politics. (p. 588)

détente An easing of tense relations with the Soviet Union during the Cold War. This process moved unevenly through the 1970s and early 1980s but accelerated when Soviet leader Mikhail Gorbachev came to power in the mid-1980s. (p. 937)

dollar diplomacy Term used by President Howard Taft to describe the economic focus of his foreign policy. Taft hoped to use economic policies and the control of foreign assets by American companies to influence Latin American nations. (p. 685)

Double V The slogan African Americans used during World War II to state their twin aims to fight for victory over Fascism abroad and victory over racism at home. (p. 794)

Economic Recovery Tax Act Act signed into law by President Ronald Reagan in 1981, that slashed income and estate taxes especially on those in the highest income brackets. (p. 972)

Eisenhower Doctrine A doctrine guiding intervention in the Middle East. In 1957 Congress granted President Dwight Eisenhower the power to send military forces into the Middle East to combat Communist aggression. Eisenhower sent U.S. marines into Lebanon in 1958 under this doctrine. (p. 845)

Environmental Protection Agency (EPA) Federal agency established by Richard Nixon in 1971 to regulate activities that resulted in pollution or other environmental degradation. (p. 949)

Equal Rights Amendment (ERA) A proposed amendment that prevented the abridgment of "equality of rights under law . . . by the United States or any State on the basis of sex." Not enough states had ratified the amendment by 1982, when the ratification period expired, so it was not adopted. (p. 948)

Espionage Act 1917 act that prohibited antiwar activities, including opposing the military draft. It punished speech critical of the war as well as deliberate actions of sabotage and spying. (p. 694)

ethnic cleansing Ridding an area of a particular ethnic minority to achieve ethnic homogeneity. In the civil war between Serbs and Croatians in Bosnia from 1992 to 1995, the Serbian military attempted to eliminate the Croatian population through murder, rape, and expulsion. (p. 1014)

eugenics The pseudoscience of producing genetic improvement in the human population through selective breeding. Proponents of eugenics often saw ethnic and racial minorities as genetically "undesirable" and inferior. (p. 611)

Exodusters Blacks who migrated from the South to Kansas in 1879 seeking land and a better way of life. (p. 481)

Fair Employment Practice Committee (FEPC) Committee established in 1941 to help African Americans gain a greater share of wartime industrial jobs. (p. 794)

Fair Labor Standards Act 1938 law that provided a minimum wage of 40 cents an hour and a forty-hour workweek for employees in businesses engaged in interstate commerce. (p. 767)

Farmers' Alliances Regional organizations formed in the late nineteenth century to advance the interests of farmers. The most prominent of these organizations were the Northwestern Farmers' Alliance, the Southern Farmers' Alliance, and the Colored Farmers' Alliance. (p. 584)

Federal Deposit Insurance Corporation (FDIC) Federal agency created in 1933 through New Deal legislation, that insured bank deposits up to $5,000, a figure that would substantially rise over the years. (p. 757)

Federal Employee Loyalty Program Program established by President Truman in 1947 to investigate federal employees suspected of disloyalty and Communist ties. (p. 835)

Fifteenth Amendment Amendment to the Constitution prohibiting the abridgment of a citizen's right to vote on the basis of "race, color, or previous condition of servitude." From the 1870s on, southern states devised numerous strategies for circumventing the Fifteenth Amendment. (p. 477)

Force Acts Three acts passed by the U.S. Congress in 1870 and 1871 in response to vigilante attacks on southern blacks. The acts were designed to protect black political rights and end violence by the Ku Klux Klan and similar organizations. (p. 484)

Fourteen Points The core principles President Woodrow Wilson saw as the basis for lasting peace, including freedom of the seas, open diplomacy, and self-determination for colonial peoples. (p. 697)

Fourteenth Amendment Amendment to the Constitution defining citizenship and protecting individual civil and political rights from abridgment by the states. Adopted during Reconstruction, the Fourteenth Amendment overturned the *Dred Scott* decision. (p. 472)

Free Speech Movement (FSM) Movement protesting policies instituted by the University of California at Berkeley that restricted free speech. In 1964 students at Berkeley conducted sit-ins and held rallies against these policies. (p. 910)

Freedmen's Bureau Federal agency created in 1865 to provide ex-slaves with economic and legal resources. The Freedmen's Bureau played an active role in shaping black life in the postwar South. (p. 464)

Freedom Rides Integrated bus rides through the South organized by CORE in 1961 to test compliance with Supreme Court rulings on segregation. (p. 897)

Freedom Summer 1964 civil rights project in Mississippi launched by SNCC, CORE, the SCLC, and the NAACP. Some eight hundred volunteers, mainly white college students, worked on voter registration drives and in freedom schools to improve education for rural black youngsters. (p. 899)

ghettos Neighborhoods dominated by a single ethnic, racial, or class group. (p. 606)

Ghost Dance Religious ritual performed by the Paiute Indians in the late nineteenth century. Following a vision he received in 1888, the prophet Wovoka believed that performing the Ghost Dance would cause whites to disappear and allow Indians to regain control of their lands. (p. 508)

Gilded Age Term coined by Mark Twain and Charles Dudley Warner to describe the late nineteenth century. The term referred to the opulent and often ostentatious lifestyles of the era's superrich. (p. 546)

glasnost Policy of political "openness" initiated by Soviet leader Mikhail Gorbachev in the 1980s. Under *glasnost*, the Soviet Union extended democratic elections, freedom of speech, and freedom of the press. (p. 984)

globalization The extension of economic, political, and cultural relationships among nations, through commerce, migration, and communication. Globalization expanded in the late twentieth century because of free trade agreements and the relaxation of immigration restrictions. (p. 988)

"The Gospel of Wealth" 1889 essay by Andrew Carnegie in which he argued that the rich should act as stewards of the wealth they earned, using their surplus income for the benefit of the community. (p. 544)

Grangers Members of an organization founded in 1867 to meet the social and cultural needs of farmers. Grangers took an active role in the promotion of the economic and political interests of farmers. (p. 582)

great migration Population shift of more than 400,000 African Americans who left the South beginning in 1917–1918 and headed north and west hoping to escape poverty and racial discrimination. During the 1920s another 800,000 blacks left the South. (p. 712)

Great Plains Semiarid territory in central North America. (p. 497)

Great Recession The severe economic decline in the United States and throughout the world that began in 2008, leading to bank failures, high unemployment, home foreclosures, and large federal deficits. (p. 1021)

Great Society President Lyndon Johnson's vision of social, economic, and cultural progress in the United States. (p. 903)

Gulf of Tonkin Resolution 1964 congressional resolution giving President Lyndon Johnson wide discretion in the use of U.S. forces in Vietnam. The resolution followed reported attacks by North Vietnamese gunboats on two American destroyers. (p. 907)

Harlem Renaissance The work of African American writers, artists, and musicians that flourished following World War I through the 1920s. (p. 722)

Haymarket Square Site of 1886 rally and violence in Chicago. In the aftermath of the events in Haymarket Square, the union movement in the United States went into temporary decline. (p. 574)

Hetch Hetchy valley Site of a controversial dam built to supply San Francisco with water and power in the aftermath of the 1906 earthquake. The dam was built over the objections of preservationists such as John Muir. (p. 656)

Holocaust The Nazi regime's genocidal effort to eradicate Europe's Jewish population during World War II, which resulted in the deaths of six million Jews. (p. 807)

Homestead Act 1862 act that established procedures for distributing 160-acre lots to western settlers, on condition that they develop and farm their land, as an incentive for western migration. (p. 512)

Homestead strike 1892 strike by steelworkers at Andrew Carnegie's Homestead steel factory. The strike collapsed after a failed assassination attempt on Carnegie's plant manager, Henry Clay Frick. (p. 578)

horizontal integration The ownership of as many firms as possible in a given industry by a single owner. John D. Rockefeller pursued a strategy of horizontal integration when he bought up rival oil refineries. (p. 539)

House Un-American Activities Committee (HUAC) U.S. House of Representatives committee established in 1938 to investigate domestic communism. After World War II, HUAC conducted highly publicized investigations of Communist influence in government and the entertainment industry. (p. 834)

Hull House This settlement house, based on Toynbee Hall in England, was established by Jane Addams and Ellen Starr in Chicago in 1889. It served as a center of social reform and provided educational and social opportunities for working-class poor and immigrant women and their children. (p. 640)

Hurricane Katrina Storm that hit the Gulf coast states of Louisiana, Mississippi, and Alabama in 2005. The hurricane caused massive flooding in New Orleans after levees broke. Federal, state, and local government responses to the storm were inadequate and highlighted racial and class inequities. (p. 1019)

Immigration Reform and Control Act Law signed by President Ronald Reagan in 1986, which extended amnesty to undocumented immigrants in the United States for a specified period and allowed them to obtain legal status. At the same time the law penalized employers who hired new illegal workers. (p. 975)

imperial presidency Term used to describe the growth of presidential powers during the Cold War, particularly with respect to war-making powers and the conduct of national security. (p. 826)

Indian Citizenship Act 1924 legislation that extended the right to vote and citizenship to all American Indians. (p. 727)

Indian Reorganization Act (IRA) 1934 act that ended the Dawes Act, authorized self-government for those living on reservations, extended tribal landholdings, and pledged to uphold native customs and language. (p. 769)

Industrial Workers of the World (IWW) Organization that grew out of the activities of the Western Federation of Miners in the 1890s and formed by Eugene V. Debs. Known as Wobblies, the IWW attempted to unite all skilled and unskilled workers in an effort to overthrow capitalism. (p. 579)

internment The relocation of persons seen as a threat to national security to isolated camps during World War II. Nearly all people of Japanese descent living on the West Coast were forced to sell or abandon their possessions and relocate to internment camps during the war. (p. 797)

Interstate Commerce Commission (ICC) Regulatory commission established by Congress in 1887. The commission investigated interstate shipping, required railroads to make their rates public, and could bring lawsuits to force shippers to reduce "unreasonable" fares. (p. 584)

Iran-Contra affair Ronald Reagan administration scandal involving the funneling of funds from an illegal arms-for-hostages deal with Iran to the Nicaraguan Contras in the mid-1980s. (p. 980)

Islamic State of Iraq and Syria (ISIS) Jihadist terrorist group originally founded in 1999, which gained strength from the sectarian violence that grew out of the 2003 U.S. invasion of Iraq. The group captured territory in Iraq and Syria and claimed responsibility for terrorist attacks in Paris, San Bernardino, California, and Lebanon. (p. 1028)

"island-hopping" This strategy, employed by the U.S. in World War II in the Pacific, directed American and Allied forces to avoid heavily fortified Japanese islands and concentrate on less heavily defended islands in preparation for a combined air, land, and sea invasion of Japan. (p. 803)

Jim Crow Late-nineteenth-century statutes that established legally defined racial segregation in the South. Jim Crow legislation helped ensure the social and economic inferiority of southern blacks. (p. 552)

jingoists Superpatriotic supporters of the expansion and use of military power. Jingoists such as Theodore Roosevelt longed for a war in which they could demonstrate America's strength and prove their own masculinity. (p. 675)

Knights of the Ku Klux Klan (KKK) Organization formed in 1865 by General Nathan Bedford Forrest to enforce prewar racial norms. Members of the KKK used threats and violence to intimidate blacks and white Republicans. (p. 484)

La Raza Unida (The United Race) A Chicano political party, formed in 1969, that advocated job opportunities for Chicanos, bilingual education, and Chicano cultural studies programs in universities. (p. 915)

laissez-faire French for "let things alone." Advocates of laissez-faire believed that the marketplace should be left to regulate itself, allowing individuals to pursue their own self-interest without any government restraint or interference. (p. 543)

League of Nations The international organization proposed by Woodrow Wilson after the end of World War I to ensure world peace and security in the future through mutual agreement. The United States failed to join the league because Wilson and his opponents in Congress could not work out a compromise. (p. 697)

Lend-Lease Act March 1941 law permitting the United States to lend or lease military equipment and other commodities to Great Britain and its allies. Its passage marked the end of American neutrality before the U.S. entered World War II. (p. 786)

Levittown Suburban subdivision built in Long Island, New York, in the 1950s in response to the postwar housing shortage. Subsequent Levittowns were built in Pennsylvania and New Jersey. (p. 862)

Little Rock Nine Nine African American students who, in 1957, became the first black students to attend Central High School in Little Rock, Arkansas. Federal troops were required to overcome the resistance of white officials and to protect the students. (p. 874)

Long Drive Cattle drive from the grazing lands of Texas to rail depots in Kansas. Once in Kansas, the cattle were shipped eastward to slaughterhouses in Chicago. (p. 511)

Lost Generation A term used by the writer Gertrude Stein to describe the writers and artists disillusioned with the consumer culture of the 1920s. (p. 721)

Manhattan Project Code name for the secret program to develop an atomic bomb. The project was launched in 1942 and directed by the United States with the assistance of Great Britain and Canada. (p. 805)

March on Washington for Jobs and Freedom August 28, 1963, rally by civil rights organizations in Washington, D.C., that brought increased national attention to the movement. (p. 898)

Marshall Plan Post–World War II European economic aid package developed by Secretary of State George Marshall. The plan helped rebuild Western Europe and served American political and economic interests in the process. (p. 825)

McCarthyism Term used to describe the harassment and persecution of suspected political radicals. Senator Joseph McCarthy was one of many prominent government figures who helped incite anti-Communist hysteria in the early 1950s. (p. 839)

#MeToo Movement The social movement of black and white women-spurred on by the election of Donald Trump as president-linked tens of millions of women through social media networks in opposition to sexual harassment and abuse in workplaces and educational institutions. In 2017, it conducted massive marches throughout the U. S. and the world. (p. 1034)

melting pot Popular metaphor for immigrant assimilation into American society. According to this ideal, all immigrants underwent a process of Americanization that produced a homogeneous society. (p. 614)

Mexican revolution 1911 revolution in Mexico, which led to nearly a decade of bloodshed and civil war. (p. 687)

military-industrial complex The government-business alliance related to the military and national defense that developed out of World War II and greatly influenced future development of the U.S. economy. (p. 789)

Mississippi Freedom Democratic Party (MFDP) Political party formed in 1964 to challenge the all-white state Democratic Party for seats at the 1964 Democratic presidential convention and run candidates for public office. Although unsuccessful in 1964, MFDP efforts led to subsequent reform of the Democratic Party and the seating of an interracial convention delegation from Mississippi in 1968. (p. 900)

Modern Republicanism The political approach of President Dwight Eisenhower that tried to fit traditional Republican Party ideals of individualism and fiscal restraint within the broad framework of the New Deal. (p. 880)

Montgomery Improvement Association Organization founded in Montgomery, Alabama, in 1955 to coordinate the boycott of city buses by African Americans. (p. 872)

Mormons Religious sect that migrated to Utah to escape religious persecution; also known as the Church of Jesus Christ of Latter-Day Saints. (p. 519)

muckrakers Investigative journalists who specialized in exposing corruption, scandal, and vice. Muckrakers helped build public support for progressive causes. (p. 639)

Mueller Report The report of Robert Mueller, special counsel for the Justice Department, into Russian interference in the 2016 presidential election. The report concluded that agents of the Russian government used social media and Internet hacking against the Democratic presidential candidate Hillary Clinton. The report concluded that Donald Trump cooperated with but did not conspire with the Russians. (p. 1035)

mujahideen Religiously inspired Afghan rebels who resisted the Soviet invasion of Afghanistan in 1979. (p. 945)

mutual aid societies Voluntary associations that provide a variety of economic and social benefits to their members. (p. 607)

mutually assured destruction (MAD) Defense strategy built around the threat of a massive nuclear retaliatory strike. Adoption of the doctrine of mutually assured destruction contributed to the escalation of the nuclear arms race during the Cold War. (p. 841)

National Association for the Advancement of Colored People (NAACP) Organization founded by W. E. B. Du Bois, Ida B. Wells, Jane Addams, and others in 1909 to fight for racial equality. The NAACP strategy focused on fighting discrimination through the courts. (p. 647)

National Energy Act Legislation signed into law by President Jimmy Carter in 1978, which set gas emissions standards for automobiles and provided incentives for installing alternative energy systems, such as wind and solar power. (p. 943)

National Interstate and Defense Highway Act 1956 act that provided funds for construction of 42,500 miles of roads throughout the United States. (p. 881)

National Labor Relations Act 1935 act (also known as the Wagner Act) that created the National Labor Relations

Board (NLRB). The NLRB protected workers' right to organize labor unions without owner interference. (p. 766)

National Organization for Women (NOW) Feminist organization formed in 1966 by Betty Friedan and like-minded activists. (p. 913)

National Origins Act 1924 act establishing immigration quotas by national origin. The act was intended to severely limit immigration from southern and eastern Europe as well as prohibit all immigration from East Asia. (p. 726)

National Recovery Administration (NRA) New Deal agency established in 1933 to create codes to regulate production, prices, wages, hours, and collective bargaining. The NRA failed to produce the intended results and was eventually ruled unconstitutional. (p. 758)

National Security Council (NSC) Council created by the 1947 National Security Act to advise the president on military and foreign affairs. The NSC consists of the national security adviser and the secretaries of state, defense, the army, the navy, and the air force. (p. 826)

National War Labor Board (NWLB) Government agency created in 1918 to settle labor disputes. The NWLB consisted of representatives from unions, corporations, and the public. (p. 693)

National War Labor Board Taking the same name of its World War I predecessor, this World War II board was established in 1942 to oversee labor-management relations. The board regulated wages, hours, and working conditions and authorized the government to take over plants that refused to abide by its decisions. (p. 792)

nativism The belief that foreigners pose a serious danger to a nation's society and culture. Nativist sentiment rose in the United States as the size and diversity of the immigrant population grew. (p. 611)

neoconservatives Disillusioned liberals who condemned the Great Society programs they had originally supported. Neoconservatives were particularly concerned about affirmative action programs, the domination of campus discourse by New Left radicals, and left-wing criticism of the use of American military and economic might to advance U.S. interests overseas. (p. 956)

Neutrality Acts Legislation passed between 1935 and 1937 to make it more difficult for the United States to become entangled in overseas conflicts. The Neutrality

Acts reflected the strength of isolationist sentiment in 1930s America. (p. 784)

New Deal The policies and programs that Franklin Roosevelt initiated to combat the Great Depression. The New Deal represented a dramatic expansion of the role of government in American society. (p. 756)

New Freedom Term used by Woodrow Wilson to describe his limited-government, progressive agenda. Wilson's New Freedom was offered as an alternative to Theodore Roosevelt's New Nationalism. (p. 660)

New Frontier President John F. Kennedy's domestic agenda. Kennedy promised to battle "tyranny, poverty, disease, and war," but, lacking strong majorities in Congress, he achieved relatively modest results. (p. 893)

New Look The foreign policy strategy implemented by President Dwight Eisenhower that emphasized the development and deployment of nuclear weapons in an effort to cut military spending. (p. 840)

New Nationalism Agenda articulated by Theodore Roosevelt in his 1912 presidential campaign. Roosevelt called for increased regulation of large corporations, a more active role for the president, and the extension of social justice using the power of the federal government. (p. 660)

New Negro 1920s term for the second generation of African Americans born after emancipation and who stood up for their rights. (p. 722)

New Right The conservative coalition of old and new conservatives, as well as disaffected Democrats. The New Right came to power with the election of Ronald Reagan in 1980. (p. 955)

New South Term popularized by newspaper editor Henry Grady in the 1880s, a proponent of the modernization of the southern economy. Grady believed that industrial development would lead to the emergence of a "New South." (p. 536)

new woman 1920s term for the modern, sexually liberated woman. The new woman, popularized in movies and magazines, flouted traditional morality. (p. 721)

Noble Order of the Knights of Labor Labor organization founded in 1869 by Uriah Stephens. The Knights sought to include all workers in one giant union. (p. 574)

North American Free Trade Agreement (NAFTA) Free trade agreement approved in 1993 by the United States, Canada, and Mexico. (p. 1013)

North Atlantic Treaty Organization (NATO) Cold War military alliance intended to enhance the collective security of the United States and Western Europe. (p. 828)

NSC-68 April 1950 National Security Council document that advocated the intensification of the policy of containment both at home and abroad. (p. 830)

nuclear freeze movement 1980s protests calling for a mutual freeze on the testing, production, and deployment of nuclear weapons and of missiles and aircraft designed primarily to deliver nuclear weapons. (p. 981)

Obergefell v. Hodges The 2015 U.S. Supreme Court decision legalizing same-sex marriage throughout the nation. (p. 1025)

Open Door 1899 policy in which Secretary of State John Hay informed the nations occupying China that the United States had the right of equal trade in China. (p. 683)

Operation Desert Storm Code name of the 1991 allied air and ground military offensive that pushed Iraqi forces out of Kuwait. (p. 994)

Organization of Petroleum Exporting Countries (OPEC) Organization formed by oil-producing countries to control the price and supply of oil on the global market. (p. 938)

Palmer raids Government roundup of some 6,000 suspected alien radicals in 1919–1920, ordered by Attorney General A. Mitchell Palmer and his assistant J. Edgar Hoover. The raids resulted in the deportation of 556 immigrants. (p. 710)

pandemic A disease prevalent in a country, continent, or the world. Examples include the Black Death, the 1918 influenza pandemic, and the 2020 coronavirus pandemic. (pp. 10, 696, 1035)

Patient Protection and Affordable Care Act (Obamacare) Passed in 2010, this law expanded health insurance to millions of Americans previously uncovered through a variety of measures including extension of Medicaid, setting up of health-insurance exchanges, allowing children to remain under their parents' coverage until the age of twenty-six, and preventing insurance companies from excluding coverage based on pre-existing conditions. (p. 1023)

Patriot Act   2001 law passed in response to the September 11 terror attacks. It eased restrictions on domestic and foreign intelligence gathering and expanded governmental power to deport immigrants. (p. 1017)

Pendleton Civil Service Reform Act   1883 act that required federal jobs to be awarded on the basis of merit through competitive exams rather than through political connections. (p. 626)

Pentagon Papers   Classified report on U.S. involvement in Vietnam leaked to the press in 1971. The report confirmed that the Kennedy and Johnson administrations had misled the public about the origins and nature of the Vietnam War. (p. 936)

perestroika   Policy of economic "restructuring" initiated by Soviet leader Mikhail Gorbachev. Gorbachev hoped that by reducing state control he could revive the Soviet economy. (p. 984)

Personal Responsibility and Work Opportunity Reconciliation Act   1996 act reforming the welfare system in the United States. The law required adults on the welfare rolls to find work within two years or lose their welfare benefits. (p. 1011)

Platt Amendment   1901 act of Congress limiting Cuban sovereignty. American officials pressured Cuban leaders to incorporate the amendment into the Cuban constitution. (p. 680)

Plessy v. Ferguson   1896 Supreme Court ruling that upheld the legality of Jim Crow legislation. The Court ruled that as long as states provided "equal but separate" facilities for whites and blacks, Jim Crow laws did not violate the equal protection clause of the Fourteenth Amendment. (p. 552)

political machine   Urban political organizations that dominated many late-nineteenth-century cities. Machines provided needed services to the urban poor, but they also fostered corruption, crime, and inefficiency. (p. 622)

Popular Front   A coalition formed in the mid-1930s of Communist Party members, New Deal liberals, unions, socialists, and civil rights advocates for social change rather than revolution. (p. 762)

Populists   The People's Party of America, formed in 1892. The Populists sought to appeal to both farmers and industrial workers. (p. 585)

Port Huron Statement   Students for a Democratic Society manifesto written in 1962 that condemned liberal politics, Cold War foreign policy, racism, and research-oriented universities. It called for the adoption of "participatory democracy." (p. 910)

pragmatism   Philosophy that holds that truth can be discovered only through experience and that the value of ideas should be measured by their practical consequences. Pragmatism had a significant influence on the progressives. (p. 638)

Proclamation of Amnesty and Reconstruction   1863 proclamation that established the basic parameters of President Abraham Lincoln's approach to Reconstruction. Lincoln's plan would have readmitted the South to the Union on relatively lenient terms. (p. 469)

Progressive Party   Third party formed by Theodore Roosevelt in 1912 to facilitate his candidacy for president. Nicknamed the "Bull Moose Party," the Progressive Party split the Republican vote, allowing Democrat Woodrow Wilson to win the election. (p. 660)

Pullman strike   1894 strike by workers against the Pullman railcar company. When the strike disrupted rail service nationwide, threatening the delivery of the mail, President Grover Cleveland ordered federal troops to get the railroads moving again. (p. 578)

Reaganomics   Ronald Reagan's economic policies based on the theories of supply-side economists and centered on tax cuts and cuts to domestic programs. (p. 971)

Red scare   The fear of Communist-inspired radicalism in the wake of the Russian Revolution. The Red scare following World War I culminated in the Palmer raids on suspected radicals. (p. 709)

Redeemers   White, conservative Democrats who challenged and overthrew Republican rule in the South during Reconstruction. (p. 484)

Roe v. Wade   The 1973 Supreme Court opinion that affirmed a woman's constitutional right to abortion. (p. 913)

Roosevelt Corollary   1904 addition to the Monroe Doctrine that affirmed the right of the United States to intervene in the internal affairs of Caribbean and

Latin American countries to preserve order and protect American interests. (p. 683)

Sacco and Vanzetti case 1920 case in which Nicola Sacco and Bartolomeo Vanzetti were convicted of robbery and murder. The trial centered on the defendants' foreign birth and political views, rather than the facts pertaining to their guilt or innocence. (p. 725)

Sanctuary Movement A network of religious groups that provided asylum for undocumented immigrants from Central America in the 1980s. (p. 968)

SALT II 1979 strategic arms limitation treaty agreed on by President Jimmy Carter and Soviet leader Leonid Brezhnev. After the Soviet Union invaded Afghanistan, Carter persuaded the Senate not to ratify the treaty. (p. 945)

scalawags Derisive term for white Southerners who supported Reconstruction. (p. 479)

Scottsboro Nine Nine African American youths convicted of raping two white women in Scottsboro, Alabama, in 1931. The Communist Party played a key role in defending the Scottsboro Nine and in bringing national and international attention to their case. (p. 749)

second front The invasion by U.S., British, and Canadian forces into German-occupied France to take pressure off the Soviet forces fighting the Germans on the eastern front. Josef Stalin had called for the invasion in 1942. The attack in western Europe did not begin until 1944, fostering resentment in Stalin. (p. 802)

second industrial revolution Revolution in technology and productivity that reshaped the American economy in the early twentieth century. (p. 716)

Sedition Act 1918 act appended to the Espionage Act. It punished individuals for expressing opinions deemed hostile to the U.S. government, flag, or military. (p. 695)

Servicemen's Readjustment Act (GI Bill) 1944 act that offered educational opportunities and financial aid to veterans as they readjusted to civilian life. Known as the GI Bill, the law helped millions of veterans build new lives after the war. (p. 858)

settlement houses Community centers established by urban reformers in the late nineteenth century. Settlement house organizers resided in the institutions they created and were often female, middle-class, and college educated. (p. 626)

sharecropping A system that emerged as the dominant mode of agricultural production in the South in the years after the Civil War. Under the sharecropping system, sharecroppers received tools and supplies from landowners in exchange for a share of the eventual harvest. (p. 480)

Sherman Antitrust Act 1890 act that outlawed monopolies that prevented free competition in interstate commerce. (p. 540)

sit-down strike A strike in which workers occupy their place of employment. In 1937 the United Auto Workers conducted sit-down strikes in Flint, Michigan, against General Motors to gain union recognition, higher wages, and better working conditions. The union won its demands. (p. 767)

skilled workers Workers with particular training and skills. Skilled workers were paid more and were more difficult for owners to replace than unskilled workers. (p. 570)

skyscrapers Buildings more than ten stories high that first appeared in U.S. cities in the late nineteenth century. Urban crowding and high prices for land stimulated the drive to construct taller buildings. (p. 618)

Social Darwinism The belief associated with the late nineteenth and early twentieth centuries and popularized by Herbert Spencer, that drew upon some of the ideas of Charles Darwin. Stressing individual competition and the survival of the fittest, Social Darwinism was used to justify economic inequality, racism, imperialism, and hostility to federal government regulation. (p. 543)

social gospel Religious movement that advocated the application of Christian teachings to social and economic problems. The ideals of the social gospel inspired many progressive reformers. (p. 638)

Social Security Act Landmark 1935 act that created retirement pensions for most Americans, as well as unemployment insurance. (p. 765)

Solidarity Polish trade union movement led by Lech Walesa. During the 1980s, Solidarity played a central role in ending Communist rule in Poland. (p. 986)

Southern Christian Leadership Conference (SCLC) Organization founded in 1957 by Martin Luther King Jr. and other black ministers to encourage nonviolent protests against racial segregation and disfranchisement in the South. (p. 874)

Stonewall riots The 1969 violence between gays and New York City police after the police raided the Stonewall Inn, a gay bar in Greenwich Village whose patrons fought the police in response to harassment. This encounter helped launch the gay liberation movement. (p. 917)

Strategic Arms Limitation Treaty (SALT I) 1972 agreement between the United States and Soviet Union to curtail nuclear arms production during the Cold War. The pact froze for five years the number of antiballistic missiles (ABMs), intercontinental ballistic missiles (ICBMs), and submarine-based missiles that each nation could deploy. (p. 937)

Student Nonviolent Coordinating Committee (SNCC) Civil rights organization that grew out of the sit-ins of 1960. The organization focused on taking direct action and political organizing to achieve its goals. (p. 875)

Students for a Democratic Society (SDS) Student activist organization formed in the early 1960s that advocated the formation of a "New Left" that would overturn the social and political status quo. (p. 910)

subtreasury system A proposal by the Farmers' Alliances in the 1880s for the federal government to extend loans to farmers and store their crops in warehouses until prices rose and they could buy back and sell their crops to repay their debts. (p. 584)

suffragists Supporters of voting rights for women. Campaigns for women's suffrage gained strength in the late nineteenth and early twentieth centuries and culminated in ratification of the Nineteenth Amendment in 1920. (p. 642)

Sun Belt The southern and western part of the United States. After World War II, millions of Americans moved to the Sun Belt, drawn by the region's climate and jobs in the defense, petroleum, and chemical industries. (p. 863)

sweatshops Small factories or shops in which workers toiled under adverse conditions. Business owners, particularly in the garment industry, turned tenement apartments into sweatshops. (p. 620)

systemic racism A form of racism that is embedded in U.S. legal, cultural, political, and economic institutions as a result of the history of enslavement and Jim Crow. It results in discrimination in criminal justice, employment, housing, health care, voting, and education. Also known as institutional racism. (p. 884)

Taft-Hartley Act 1947 law that curtailed unions' ability to organize. It prevented unions from barring employment to non-union members and authorized the federal government to halt a strike for eighty days if it interfered with the national interest. (p. 858)

Tea Party movement A loose coalition of conservative and libertarian forces that arose around 2008. Generally working within the Republican Party, the Tea Party advocates small government, low taxes, and reduced federal deficits. (p. 1023)

Teapot Dome scandal Oil and land scandal during the Warren Harding administration that highlighted the close ties between big business and the federal government in the early 1920s. (p. 715)

Teller Amendment Amendment to the 1898 declaration of war against Spain stipulating that Cuba should be free and independent. The amendment was largely ignored in the aftermath of America's victory. (p. 680)

tenements Multifamily apartment buildings that housed many poor urban dwellers at the turn of the twentieth century. Tenements were crowded, uncomfortable, and dangerous. (p. 619)

Tennessee Valley Authority (TVA) New Deal agency that brought low-cost electricity to rural Americans and redeveloped the Tennessee River valley through flood-control projects. The agency built, owned, and supervised a number of power plants and dams. (p. 757)

Tenure of Office Act Law passed by Congress in 1867 to prevent President Andrew Johnson from removing cabinet members sympathetic to the Republican Party's approach to congressional Reconstruction without Senate approval. Johnson was impeached, but not convicted, for violating the act. (p. 477)

Tet Offensive January 31, 1968, offensive mounted by Vietcong and North Vietnamese forces against population centers in South Vietnam. The offensive was turned back, but it shocked many Americans and increased public opposition to the war. (p. 908)

Thirteenth Amendment Amendment to the Constitution abolishing slavery. The Thirteenth Amendment was passed in January 1865 and sent to the states for ratification. (pp. 452, 469)

To Secure These Rights Report issued by President Harry Truman's Committee on Civil Rights in 1947 that advocated extending racial equality. Among its recommendations was the desegregation of the military, which Truman instituted by executive order in 1948. (p. 870)

transcontinental railroad A railroad linking the East and West Coasts of North America. Completed in 1869, the transcontinental railroad facilitated the flow of migrants and the development of economic connections between the West and the East. (p. 499)

Treaty of Fort Laramie 1851 treaty that sought to confine tribes on the northern plains to designated areas in an attempt to keep white settlers from encroaching on their land. In 1868, the second Treaty of Fort Laramie gave northern tribes control over the "Great Reservation" in parts of present-day Montana, Wyoming, North Dakota, and South Dakota. (p. 503)

Treaty of Medicine Lodge 1867 treaty that provided reservation lands for the Comanche, Kiowa-Apache, and Southern Arapaho to settle. Despite this agreement, white hunters soon invaded this territory and decimated the buffalo herd. (p. 503)

Treaty of Versailles Signed in 1919, this treaty officially ended World War I. President Woodrow Wilson went to France and played a major role in drafting the treaty, which established a League of Nations to prevent future wars. However, the U.S. Senate refused to ratify the treaty. (p. 698)

Triangle Shirtwaist Company Site of an infamous industrial fire in New York City in 1911. Inadequate fire safety provisions in the factory led to the deaths of 146 workers. (p. 620)

Truman Doctrine U.S. pledge to contain the expansion of communism around the world. Based on the idea of containment, the Truman Doctrine was the cornerstone of American foreign policy throughout the Cold War. (p. 825)

trust Business monopolies formed in the late nineteenth and early twentieth centuries through mergers and consolidation that inhibited competition and controlled the market. (p. 540)

Tulsa Massacre The invasion in 1921 by a mob of over 2,000 armed white supremacists into the African American Greenwood neighborhood of Tulsa, Oklahoma. The mob killed twenty-six blacks and burned down businesses and homes. (p. 712)

Tuskegee Institute African American educational institute founded in 1881 by Booker T. Washington. Following Washington's philosophy, the Tuskegee Institute focused on teaching industrious habits and practical job skills. (p. 645)

U.S. Immigration and Customs Enforcement (ICE) Federal agency created in 2003 under the Department of Homeland Security. It is used to keep undocumented immigrants from entering the United States and deporting those who do enter illegally. (p. 1034)

unions Groups of workers seeking rights and benefits from their employers through their collective efforts. (p. 573)

Universal Negro Improvement Association (UNIA) Organization founded by Marcus Garvey in 1914 to promote black self-help, pan-Africanism, and racial separatism. (p. 723)

unskilled workers Workers with little or no specific expertise. Unskilled workers, many of whom were immigrants, made up the vast majority of the late-nineteenth-century industrial workforce. (p. 570)

vertical integration The control of all elements in a supply chain by a single firm. For example, Andrew Carnegie, a vertically integrated steel producer, sought to own suppliers of all the raw materials used in steel production. (p. 539)

Vietcong The popular name for the National Liberation Front (NLF) in South Vietnam, which was formed in 1959. The Vietcong waged a military insurgency against the U.S.-backed president, Ngo Dinh Diem, and received support from Ho Chi Minh, the leader of North Vietnam. (p. 846)

Vietnamization President Richard Nixon's strategy of turning over greater responsibility for the fighting of the Vietnam War to the South Vietnamese army. (p. 934)

Voting Rights Act 1965 act that eliminated many of the obstacles to African American voting in the South and resulted in dramatic increases in black participation in the electoral process. (p. 900)

War Industries Board (WIB) Government commission created in 1917 to supervise the purchase of military supplies and oversee the conversion of the economy to meet wartime demands. The WIB embodied a government-business partnership that lasted beyond World War I. (p. 693)

War Powers Act 1973 act that required the president to consult with Congress within forty-eight hours of deploying military forces and to obtain a declaration of war from Congress if troops remained on foreign soil beyond sixty days. (p. 937)

War Production Board Board established in 1942 to oversee the economy during World War II. The War Production Board was part of a larger effort to convert American industry to the production of war materials. (p. 790)

Watergate Scandal and cover-up that forced the resignation of Richard Nixon in 1974. The scandal revolved around a break-in at Democratic Party headquarters in 1972 and subsequent efforts to conceal the administration's involvement in the break-in. (p. 940)

Woman's Christian Temperance Union (WCTU) Organization founded in 1874 to campaign for a ban on the sale and consumption of alcohol. In the late nineteenth century, under Frances Willard's leadership, the WCTU supported a broad social reform agenda. (p. 649)

Works Progress Administration (WPA) New Deal agency established in 1935 to put unemployed Americans to work on public projects ranging from construction to the arts. (p. 763)

Yalta Agreement Agreement negotiated at the 1945 Yalta Conference by Roosevelt, Churchill, and Stalin about the fate of postwar eastern Europe. The Yalta Agreement did little to ease growing tensions between the Soviet Union and its Western allies. (p. 804)

yellow journalism Sensationalist news accounts meant to provoke an emotional response in readers. Yellow journalism contributed to the growth of public support for American intervention in Cuba in 1898. (p. 678)

Young Americans for Freedom (YAF) A group of young conservatives from college campuses formed in 1960 in Sharon, Connecticut. The group favored free market principles, states' rights, and anticommunism. (p. 920)

Zimmermann telegram 1917 telegram in which Germany offered Mexico an alliance in the event that the United States entered World War I. The telegram's publication in American newspapers helped build public support for war. (p. 691)

zoot suit riots Series of riots in 1943 in Los Angeles, California, sparked by white hostility toward Mexican Americans. White sailors attacked Mexican American teenagers who dressed in zoot suits — suits with long jackets with padded shoulders and baggy pants tapered at the bottom. (p. 796)

Chapter 17

Excerpt(s) from *Age of Reform*, by Richard Hofstadter, copyright © 1955 by Richard Hofstadter. Used by permission of Alfred A. Knopf, an imprint of the Knopf Doubleday Publishing Group, a division of Penguin Random House LLC. All rights reserved.

Chapter 18

Anzia Yezierska, excerpts from *Bread Givers*, pp. 21–22. Copyright 1925 by Doubleday & Co., Inc., renewed 1952 by Anzia Yezierska. Reprinted with the permission of Persea Books, Inc (New York), www.perseabooks.com. All rights reserved.

Chapter 22

"Protest Against Maltreatment of Mexican Laborers in California. General Secretary Martin Torres of Mexican Regional Confederation of Labor to United States Ambassador Josephus Daniels," April 20, 1934. From *Decade of Betrayal: Mexican Repatriation in the 1930s* by Francisco E. Balderrama and Raymond Rodriguez. Copyright © 1995 University of New Mexico Press, 1995.

Excerpt(s) from *Towards a New Past*, by Barton J. Bernstein, Lloyd C. Gardner, and Eugene D. Genovese, copyright © 1968 by Penguin Random House LLC. Copyright © renewed 1996 by Barton J. Bernstein, Lloyd C. Gardner, and Eugene D. Genovese. Used by permission of Pantheon Books, an imprint of the Knopf Doubleday Publishing Group, a division of Penguin Random House LLC. All rights reserved.

John P. Davis, "A Black Inventory of the New Deal," *Crisis*, May 1935, 141–42. Copyright © 1935 by Crisis Publishing. The publisher wishes to thank The Crisis Publishing Co., Inc., the publisher of the magazine of the National Association for the Advancement of Colored People, for the use of this material first published in the May 1935 issue of *Crisis*.

Reproduced from *Dust Bowl Diary* by Ann Marie Low by permission of the University of Nebraska Press. Copyright 1984 by the University of Nebraska Press.

Chapter 23

Monica Sone, *Memories of Pearl Harbor*. From *Nisei Daughter*, by Monica Sone, copyright © 1953. Reprinted by permission of Little, Brown and Company, an imprint of Hachette Book Group, Inc., and the author.

Chapter 24

Henry Wallace, "The Way to Peace," in *The Annals of America* (Chicago: Encyclopedia Britannica, 1968), 16, 372–73. Reprinted from Annals of America © 1968, 1976 Encyclopedia Britannica, Inc.

Chapter 25

Jacquelyn Dowd Hall, "The Long Civil Rights Movement and the Political Uses of the Past," *Journal of American History*, 91 (March 2005): 1245–46. © 2005 by Oxford University Press-Journals. Republished with permission Oxford University Press-Journals; Permission conveyed through Copyright Clearance Center, Inc.

Steven F. Lawson, "Long Origins of the Short Civil Rights Movement, 1954–1968," in *Freedom Rights: New Perspectives on the Civil Rights Movement,* Daniel McGuire and John Dittmer, eds. (Lexington, Kentucky: University Press of Kentucky, 2011), 14–15, 19, 22–23. Copyright © 2011 by University Press of Kentucky. Used with permission.

From *A Place in El Paso: A Mexican-American Childhood* by Gloria Lopez-Stafford. Copyright © 1966 by University of New Mexico Press, 1996.

"Why No Chinese American Delinquents? Maybe It's Traditional Respect for Parents," *Saturday Evening Post,* April 30, 1955, 12. © SEPS licensed by Curtis Licensing Indianapolis, IN. All rights reserved. Used with permission.

Chapter 26

" 'Freedom' to the Delta," *Charleston Post,* June 24, 1964. Copyright © 1964 by The Post and Courier. Used with permission.

Letter from Joseph and Nancy Ellin to Dr. and Mrs. Ellin, Joseph and Nancy Ellin, Freedom Summer Collection, McCain Library and Archives, University of Southern Mississippi.

Michael J. Miller, Prospectus for the Mississippi Freedom Summer, Civil Rights Collection, McCain Library and Archives, University of Southern Mississippi. Used with permission.

Chapter 27

Zillah R. Eisenstein, ed., *Capitalist Patriarchy and the Case for Socialist Feminism* (New York: Monthly Review Press, 1978), 367–69, 371–72. Copyright © 1978 by Monthly Review Foundation. Used with permission.

A. Bartlett Giamatti, "A Liberal Education and the New Coercion." From *A Free and Ordered Space: The Real World of the University* by A. Bartlett Giamatti. Copyright © 1988, 1987, 1986, 1985, 1984, 1983, 1982, 1981, 1980, 1979. 1976, by A. Bartlett Giamatti. Used by permission of W. W. Norton & Company, Inc.

The Phyllis Schlafly Report 5, no. 7 (February 1972):1–4. Used with permission.

Mirta Vidal, Chicanas Speak Out, *Women: New Voice of La Raza* (New York: Pathfinder Press, 1971), 13–16. Copyright © 1971 by Pathfinder Press. Reprinted by permission.

Paul Weyrich, "Building the Moral Majority," *Conservative Digest*, August 1979, 18–19. Used with permission from the author.

Chapter 29

Khaled Abou El Fadl, "Face to Face: Stories from the Aftermath of Infamy," *ITVS Interactive*, accessed October 15, 2015, http://archive.itvs.org/facetoface/stories/khaled.html. Used with permission from the author.

Farnaz Fassihi, "Report from Baghdad, 2004." From *Women's Letters: America from the Revolutionary War to the Present*, Lisa Grunwald and Stephen J. Adler, eds. (New York: Dial Press, 2005), 758–60. Copyright © 2005 by Farnaz Fassihi. Used with permission.

Alice M. Greenwald, "Message from the Museum Director," 2014, 9/11 Memorial, https://www.911memorial.org. Copyright © 9/11 Memorial & Museum. Used with permission.

Diana Hoffman, "The Power of Freedom." Copyright © Diana Hoffman. Used with permission.

Alan Rusbridger and Ewen MacAskill, "Edward Snowden Interview," *Guardian*, July 18, 2014. Copyright © Guardian News & Media Ltd 2020. Used with permission.

Index

Letters in parentheses following page numbers refer to figures *(f)*, illustrations *(i)*, maps *(m)*, sources *(s)*, and tables *(t)*.

About the Authors

Authors Nancy A. Hewitt and Steven F. Lawson

Nancy A. Hewitt (PhD, University of Pennsylvania) is Professor Emerita of History and of Women's and Gender Studies at Rutgers University. Her publications include *Radical Friend: Amy Kirby Post and Her Activist Worlds*, for which she won the SHEAR prize in biography; *Women's Activism and Social Change: Rochester, New York, 1822–1872*; *Southern Discomfort: Women's Activism in Tampa, Florida, 1880s–1920s*, and the second edition of *A Companion to American Women's History*, edited with Anne M. Valk.

Steven F. Lawson (PhD, Columbia University) is Professor Emeritus of History at Rutgers University. His research interests include U.S. politics since 1945 and the history of the civil rights movement, with a particular focus on black politics and the interplay between civil rights and political culture in the mid-twentieth century. He is the author of many works including *Running for Freedom: Civil Rights and Black Politics in America since 1941*; *Debating the Civil Rights Movement*; *Black Ballots: Voting Rights in the South, 1944–1969*; and *In Pursuit of Power: Southern Blacks and Electoral Politics, 1965–1982*.